ROBERT DUNCAN

— A —

DESCRIPTIVE BIBLIOGRAPHY

ROBERT J. BERTHOLF
Preface by Robert Creeley

Black Sparrow Press ◆ Santa Rosa ◆ 1986

Frontispiece by Jess.

LIBRARY OF CONGRESS CATALOGING IN PUBLICATION DATA

Bertholf, Robert J.
    Robert Duncan : a descriptive bibliography.

    Includes index.
    1. Duncan, Robert Edward, 1919–   –Bibliography.
I. Title.
Z8247.47.b48 1986 [PS3507.U629] 016.811'54   84-16740
ISBN 0-87685-620-2
ISBN 0-87685-621-0 (signed)

For
Jess

CONTENTS

Illustrations Follow Page 134

Preface

Insofar as the world of poetry is an insistently human one—or, better, one in which the human lives at the edges of its own perception, in the common event of all else—there can be that disparity of response and use which must often make us recognize with a bitter disappointment how meager our responsibility has proved. There is no leader of this world, in the political sense of authority. But if one can hear Blake's proposal, "The authors are in eternity...," then that which has been so given, having no content in possessional time, will find place in person, as agency or instrument, so that he or she becomes voice for and of many, however single in fact.

Poetry is primary community, primarily communal. It does nothing, so to speak, because it is issue of all, and cannot be constrained to any one facet or preferred disposition of circumstance, because it moves and is moved with all. That is why one cannot be by definition a "good" poet, unless one speaks of the limited factor of performance—which, though practiced with brilliant intent and consummate resourcefulness, is still a given, found only by chance, never bought, sold, or bargained for. In this world, both timeless and only this very moment, there is a seemingly endless polyphony of voices, of all ages, places, times, and situations—all pleasure, all despair. It is as vulnerable as an hallucination, because it and all the world that keeps it a very literal physical company have, paradoxically, no defense against thought, especially that which has lost its feeling for the human, the music specific to a body which the mind might still recognize.

I must therefore put as simple testament not only my own deep respect for Robert Duncan, my own dependence on him as a brother in this art and as a teacher, as that person of my own imagination who *is* what a poet might be—but also make clear in this manner of emphasis that Robert Duncan has been that poet of my generation who brought the communal world of this art forward again, who broke down the specious and often hostile habits of those uses of a poetry which would turn it to profit, to personal law and order, to investments of self-approval, while denying it any power of initiating wonder, and final value that might matter. The reader now considering by means of this immensely useful listing of publications, together with some clear history of their circumstance of printing, what has been the practical pattern of Robert Duncan's life as a poet will very soon discover it has only that of the *practice* of a poetry, but not simply his own—as might be said of something bought and paid for—nor another's, if that one were to be only its prior owner. He has long insisted that language and the poetry it sustains, of all human things, are common, demand a common ground. As he says in respect of Whitman:

> Speech itself, nowhere other than common,
> every where the source from which we derive
> our individuality.

> ("The Adventure of Whitman's Line,"
> *Convivio*, ed. John Thorpe, 1983.)

9

It is now, happily, a common information that his use as source, as primary connection, for the poets of his world makes a geography far more ample than any of their particular intents, habits, or even accomplishments might describe. For example, only in the world of his generative and abiding transcendence of mundane literary categories could Henry Miller, Charles Olson, Kenneth Rexroth, Jack Spicer, Anaïs Nin, Louis Zukofsky, Denise Levertov, William Everson, myself and many, *many* others even begin to find room. As Whitman, he is originally and definitively American, defines a continuing person so *here*. But just as a science will engage a universe from a single instance of its manifest presence, so this poet reads the particular sounding syllable, the suddenly discovered congruence or discord, as expanding of all relation:

> From the seed of first light the galaxies
> move out to the extremities of imagined time and
> space; Lucifer "falling" is the circumference or
> boundary of the need of Creation.

("Introduction," *Bending the Bow,* 1968.)

The characteristic release of such power is an extraordinary intellectual energy, which can make of the *seeing* of the world, or, more aptly, its apprehension by whatever means we humanly can recognize, a vast and yet particularizing place of our lives with all else relating, a factual living tissue of those bounds/bonds.

So one may speak of him, however ineptly. One wants to make clear the *size* he constitutes, both in thinking and in practice, the parallels, variously, with Whitman, Dante, to an imagination which can bear, in birth and death, such human scale and occasion, go with it to whatever end. Therefore I cannot believe that he has ever once turned from this art and its commitments, however difficult its demands have proved. Yet to emphasize such a Puritan measure is also beside the point. No delights could ever have been more, as any reader or hearer of his poems well knows. Because such work as his is all a life, a world, and in it, miraculously, all opens, is possible, is there, or not here, meets with limit, breaks apart—to live.

Robert Creeley
Buffalo, N. Y.
February 28, 1984

Introduction

The contemporary American poet has benefited by the new technology of the publishing industry. He has also stated his independence from that technology by printing books and pamphlets privately and with small, fine presses. In some cases he manufactures books himself. Robert Duncan has been part of all these activities. The publication history of his works tells the story of one poet's engagement with the creative necessity to produce new forms in writings, independently, as well as his involvement (often troublesome) with commercial publishing companies. His publications challenge the definitions of descriptive bibliography. In developing the terms for this bibliography, I have drawn on the example of Donald Gallup in his *A Bibliography of Ezra Pound*, and on the Pittsburgh Series of bibliographies, mainly J. M. Edelstein's *Wallace Stevens: A Descriptive Bibliography*. When indecision about a procedure arose, I relied on Fredson Bowers' generative work *The Principles of Bibliographical Description* for direction. At this point I must acknowledge the very carefully prepared and useful book by Joan St. C. Crane, *Robert Frost: A Descriptive Catalogue of Books and Manuscripts in the Clifton Waller Barrett Library*, which often supplied the fully implemented example of Bowers' descriptive principles that made possible the adaptations of terms fitting for a work by Robert Duncan.

Section A. Following the examples of Donald Gallup, J. M. Edelstein, and Emily Wallace, in her *A Bibliography of William Carlos Williams*, I have attempted to give full descriptions of each publication. While using the standard terms of "edition," "state," and "issue," I have in several instances combined them with expressions that were more closely related to a given work. For example, *Of the War |* is described as "first edition, hardbound copies, first issue." And in other cases where the poet's signature or another special feature has been added after printing of the books, I have indicated that by "signed copies," or, as in the case of *Medieval Scenes*, as "second edition, *hors de commerce* copies." Multiple descriptive terms were necessary to delineate the publications accurately. I have maintained the definition of "edition" as all copies printed from a single setting of type, but where, in the relatively new off-set printing process, the printing plates have been sold from one publisher to another, and the book reprinted, I have borrowed the term "sub-edition" from Fredson Bowers to signify that change. The descriptions of *The Opening of the Field* and *Roots and Branches*, for example, are clearer and more appropriate because of the terms. In addition, I have extended the argument that dust jackets be given a legitimate part in the description to include the covers of the paperback publications, for, as in the case of the Roman numerals on the rear covers of the Grove Press printings of *The Opening of the Field*, the covers contain valuable information about printings, states, and editions.

In line with current bibliographic practices, I have used the term "gathering" in place of "signature" when the printing signatures have not been signed, and the term "impression" in place of "printing." Color identifications have been made from the ISCC-NBS Centroid Color Chart and have been indicated, as, for example, "(C-48)." After a color has been identified in a particular description, only its name is repeated inside that description. Untitled poems have been identified by the first lines placed in quotation marks followed by "(fl)," while untitled drawings have not been identified. In the description of privately published works, I have described the author's or the compiler's copy as the ideal copy, and then indicated the location of similar copies. And finally, in order to account for broadsides that have been folded or given a cover, as "The Song of The Border-Guard," I have introduced the term "folio broadside."

Where fitting, a commentary follows each description. I have gathered the information for these from unpublished letters and documents in libraries, published comments by Duncan, letters from publishers and editors, and conversations with Robert Duncan, Jess Collins, and other people concerned with the publication of individual works. These commentaries are based on the premise that the descriptions of the books do not exist apart from the publishing history of the book. The publishing history is the immediate literary context for the texts of the books.

Section B. This section lists books neither authored nor edited by Duncan in which a poem, essay, drawing or other contribution by Duncan appears. Gallup, Edelstein, and others give collations and descriptions of the books which contain first appearances. I have dropped the collations and descriptions but have included *all* appearances in book form. These anthology appearances, even in textbooks, indicate which poems are most appreciated, and direct, in part, which aspects of the poet's work will be subject to critical inquiry. When a piece appears for the first time, I have noted that fact.

Section C. This section lists all publications by Duncan in magazines, newspapers, and journals. Interviews have been considered publications by Duncan, and are included here. When there are two genres of publication in the same issue of a magazine or journal, for example, drawings and poems, or poems and reviews, separate entries for each genre have been made.

Section D. This section lists miscellaneous publications, both private and public, of the poet. Duncan's notes for his own readings and other poets' readings are mostly ephemeral items. The book blurbs that appear on the covers of books map out a path of literary associations. The drawings, Christmas cards, and other scattered publications, public and private, are part of the literary life of the poet and are taken as seriously as trade publications. Each is available in at least one library's holdings.

Section E, Section F, and *Section G.* These sections list letters, manuscripts, and notebooks now available in libraries as of 1980. The listings are chronological, and I have indicated the location of each item. The description of each item is full enough to make identification possible even when the item is not dated. Recent manuscript acquisitions by libraries are not included.

Section H lists chronologically translations into foreign languages.

Section I. This section gives a chronological list of the tapes and records, both commercial and private, of poetry readings and lectures by Duncan. I have regarded the recorded texts as the equivalent of a manuscript, so collations and contents of each tape or record follow the title, place, and date. Recent acquisitions by libraries are not included.

Section J. This section lists reviews, organized chronologically under the title reviewed, articles, books and parts of books, theses, and dissertations about Duncan. Books, articles, reviews, and interviews with only a passing reference to Duncan have not been listed.

Section K. The listings in this section are based on the premise that the contemporary poet has a close connection with colleges and universities. I have listed reviews and articles about Duncan in college and university publications. Miscellaneous items, association items, and musical settings are also listed in this section.

RJB
The Poetry/Rare Book Collection
The University at Buffalo
SUNY Buffalo, June 1984

Acknowledgments

Literally thousands of pieces of correspondence contributed to the making of this bibliography. Even a full listing of all the names of the correspondents would not be enough to state my gratitude to all those who patiently answered my inquiries. A full listing is not possible here. More specifically, I want to acknowledge those who made large contributions to this bibliography. Without the assistance of Robert Duncan and Jess Collins this book would never have begun; and it is they who supplied so many of the small details in the commentaries. They made the resources and hospitality of their household available to me with unhesitant warmth.   Paul Mariah, out of his dedication to Robert Duncan as a man and a poet, compiled the first lists, with the later assistance of Ray Rice, with which this book began. Their work reduced the amount of time necessary to produce full descriptions.

At the beginning I name James R. Lowell, proprietor of The Asphodel Book Shop. James Lowell sold me my first volumes of Duncan's poetry, and over the years he has informed my sense of contemporary poetry with precise information and a guiding wit. The following persons and institutions have made invaluable contributions of information and time consuming searching after errant facts that went into this bibliography: the staff of The Harry Ransom Humanities Research Center, University of Texas; Leslie Clark, Peter Hanff, and the staff of the Bancroft Library, University of California, Berkeley; Karl Gay, former Curator of the Poetry Collection, State University of New York at Buffalo; Holly Hall, Chief, Rare Books and Special Collections, and Timothy Murray, Curator of Manuscripts, Washington University; Michael Davidson and the staff of The Archive for New Poetry, University of California, San Diego; George Butterick, Special Collections, University of Connecticut; Donald Gallup, former Curator, Collection of American Literature, Beinecke Library, Yale University; Else Albrecht-Carríe, permissions editor, New Directions; and John Martin of Black Sparrow Press. I also thank the office of Research and Sponsored Programs at Kent State University for travel funds and research leave, and The University Libraries, The University at Buffalo for generous support of various kinds. I also acknowledge the following libraries which have given permission to quote from letters and other unpublished documents: The Berg Collection, New York Public Library; The Bancroft Library, University of California at Berkeley; Special Collections, The University of Iowa; Special Collections, Washington University in St. Louis; the Estate of Charles Olson and The Special Collections, University of Connecticut; Special Collections, Kent State University; The George Arnets Research Library, Syracuse University; and The Poetry/Rare Books Collection, The University at Buffalo. The photographs of Duncan's publications were taken by James Ulrich of The University at Buffalo's Educational Communications Center.

Finally, three people have made special contributions to this bibliography. Dean Keller, Head of Special Collections, Kent State University, is the first. Without his patience and impeccable guidance in bibliographical matters this project would never have been completed. Diane Morris keyboarded the text for typesetting: her talents and accomplishments are everywhere apparent in the complexities of the text. And, lastly, it is pleasing to acknowledge the hidden assistance of Anne R. Bertholf, whose great care has eliminated many inconsistencies in this book, and whose support in the household in a direct way made completing this book feasible. Errors and omissions which remain are solely my responsibility.

List of Library of Congress Abbreviations

AzU   University of Arizona, Tucson
CaBViV   University of Victoria Library, Victoria
CaBVaS   Simon Fraser University, Vancouver
CaMWU   University of Manitoba, Winnipeg
CaOTU   University of Toronto, Toronto
CBC   Canadian Broadcast Corporation, Toronto
CLU   University of California, Los Angeles
CSCU   University of Santa Clara, Santa Clara
CSf-APA   San Francisco State University, American Poetry Archive, San
            Francisco
CSfU   University of San Francisco, San Francisco
CSt   Stanford University, Stanford
CtU   University of Connecticut, Storrs
CtY   Yale University [Beinecke Library], New Haven
CU-B   Bancroft Library, University of California, Berkeley
CU-S   University of California, San Diego
CU-SB   University of California, Santa Barbara
CVI   California Institute of Arts, Valencia
DeU   University of Delaware, Newark
DLC   Library of Congress, Washington, D.C.
IaU   University of Iowa, Iowa City
ICU   University of Chicago, Chicago
InU   Indiana University, Bloomington
IEN   Northwestern University, Evanston
IU   University of Illinois, Urbana
KU   University of Kansas [Spenser Library], Lawrence
MoSW   Washington University, St. Louis
KTMF   Menninger Foundation, Topeka
NbU   University of Nebraska, Lincoln
NBuU   The University at Buffalo, Buffalo
NBuAKG   Albright Knox Gallery, Buffalo
NjR   Rutgers University, New Brunswick
NN   New York Public Library, New York City
NNC   Columbia University, New York City
NNU   New York University, New York City
NmU   University of New Mexico, Albuquerque
NSyU   Syracuse University, Syracuse
OKentU   Kent State University, Kent
OTU   University of Toledo, Toledo
OU   Ohio State University, Columbus
RU   University of Rhode Island, Kingston
TxU   University of Texas [The Harry Ransom Humanities Research
            Center], Austin
WaEcC   Central Washington State College Ellensburg
WaU   University of Washington, Seattle

A.
Books
Pamphlets
Broadsides and
Separate Publications

a. *First edition, regular copies:*

[in hollowed capital letters] HEAVENLY CITY | EARTHLY
CITY | [at lower right in regular type] ROBERT | DUNCAN |
1947 | WITH DRAWINGS BY MARY FABILLI [Berkeley: Bern
Porter].

Collation: [1-6]⁴; pp. [i-x], 1-9, [10], 11-19, [20], 21-33, [34-38].

Contents: pp. [i-iii] blank; p. [iv] portrait of RD by Mary Fabilli; p. [v]
title-page; p. [vi] copyright-page, "Bern Porter | Designed by Ben Kennedy |
and printed at The Gillick Press | Copyright | Robert Duncan | 1947 |
Berkeley"; p. [vii] contents-page; p. [viii] blank; p. [ix] section-title "Treesbank
Poems | 1946"; p. [x] blank; pp. 1-9 text; p. [10] section-title "Berkeley Poems
| 1946"; pp. 11-19 text; p. [20] section-title "Heavenly City, Earthly City"; pp.
21-33 text; p. 33 medallion head of Apollo by Mary Fabilli; pp. [34-38]
blank.

Text contents: TREESBANK POEMS [sequence-title for following four
poems] "I LISTEN IN THE SHADE TO ONE I LOVE" (fl)—"THE
SILENT THROAT IN THE DARK PORTENDS" (fl)—"SHALL I
ALONE MAKE MY WAY TO MY GRAVE" (fl)—"SLEEP IS A DEEP
AND MANY VOICED FLOOD" (fl)—AN APOLLONIAN ELEGY—
BERKELEY POEMS [sequence-title for following five poems] "AMONG
MY FRIENDS LOVE IS A GREAT SORROW" (fl)—AN ELEGIAC
FRAGMENT—A WOMAN'S DRUNKEN LAMENT—PORTRAIT OF
TWO WOMEN—I AM A MOST FLESHLY MAN—HEAVENLY CITY,
EARTHLY CITY.

Description: The text is printed on yellowish white (C-92) laid paper, 23.5 x
15.3 cm., watermarked "Hamilton Andarra." The gatherings are sewn with
white thread so that units of two leaves with deckled edges follow units of
two leaves with trimmed edges. The endpapers are of the same paper. The
cover is also of the same paper pasted over boards, 24.2 x 15.8 cm., and
contains a printed Hellenistic frieze in black (C-267) which runs continuously from front, spine to rear cover. A male figure playing a lyre appears on
the front cover between a hyena on the right and a lion on the left, with
various vegetation behind. Lettering on the front cover in hollowed capital
letters above the frieze reads "HEAVENLY CITY, | EARTHLY CITY." Let-
tering on the spine in regular type at the top reads from tail to head
"ROBERT DUNCAN." A female figure appears on the rear cover petting a
leopard with an antelope watching at the left. There is various vegetation
behind.

Dust jacket: The dust jacket is made from medium blue (C-182) laid paper
printed in black with the same frieze and lettering as the cover. The front
flap contains a 21 line statement under the heading "About | Robert Dun-

can," lines 4-21 of which are a quoted statement by RD. The rear flap contains six titles under the heading "Books by | Subscription," and below: "Bern Porter | 2303 Durant Avenue | Berkeley, California."

Published: 250 copies published Nov. 1947 at $2.75.

b. *First edition, signed copies:*

Title, Collation, Contents and Text contents are the same as above.

Description: These copies are bound in dark yellowish green cloth (approximately C-137) over boards, 24.3 x 15.8 cm. Lettering stamped in gold (very yellow C-82) on the spine reads from head to tail "HEAVENLY CITY | EARTHLY CITY ROBERT DUNCAN." The front and back covers are blank. The endpapers are printed in the same Hellenistic frieze that appeared on the covers of the regular copies. A colophon in holograph has been added on page [34] and reads: "This is number [number inserted] of 100 copies | specially bound by Eda Kavin | signed by the author and | the artist" [then two signatures] "Robert Duncan | Mary Fabilli." In some copies the words "This is" at the beginning of the colophon are omitted. The line breaks are different in some copies. Two poems in RD's holograph have been added on page [35], "THE BLESSED HERBERT IN HIS LOVE, DOES SING" (fl) [nine lines] and "FAITHLESS AND MANY MINDED MUSES" (fl) [seventeen lines]. The first is from 1946 and the second from 1947.

Dust jacket: The dust jacket is made from the same white laid paper used for the endpapers and contains the same Hellenistic frieze. Only a small number of copies (three are known) were distributed with this dust jacket.

Published: 100 copies published November 1947 at $5.00.

c. *First sub-edition, photocopied copies:*

[in holograph] Heavenly City | Earthly City | by | Robert Duncan | a true facsimile | edition of the 1947 | release attested | by | the publisher | Bern Porter [slash] 1964 | signed copy # [number inserted]. [Belfast, Maine].

Collation: [i], 1-33, [34].

Contents: p. [i] title-page; pp. 1-9 text; p. [10] section-title, "Berkeley Poems | 1946"; pp. 11-19 text; p. [20] section-title, "Heavenly City, Earthly City", pp. 21-33 text; p. [34] blank.

Text contents: same as First edition.

Description: This sub-edition has been reproduced on photocopy paper, 21.5 x 12 cm. and covered with heavy yellowish white (C-92) paper and bound at the heel edge with tape. The copy in the Colby College Library is enclosed in a handmade cardboard and paper box. The title-page is in the holograph of Bern Porter and is signed by him.

Published: 20 copies published in 1964 at $7.50.

d. *Second sub-edition, photo offset copies:*

HEAVENLY CITY | EARTHLY CITY | [at lower right] Robert | Duncan [Philadelphia: The Walton Press, 1971].

Collation: pp. [i-vi], 1-13, [14].

Contents: p. [i] title-page; p. [ii] acknowledgments-page, "reprinted by special | arrangement | [at bottom] [logo] | THE WALTON PRESS | 626 South 62nd Street | Philadelphia, Pa. 19143 | Tel. (215) 748-7200"; p. [iii] blank; p. [iv] portrait of RD by Mary Fabilli; p. [v] blank; p. [vi] frontispiece by Bern Porter; pp. 1-13 text; p. [14] blank.

Text contents: the poem HEAVENLY CITY, EARTHLY CITY.

Description: This sub-edition of the title poem was produced from photoplates made from the text of the First edition on yellowish white (C-92) wove paper, 20.3 x 15 cm., and then bound in a standard library binding. The only known copy, the one in the library of the University of Idaho, is bound in stiff black (C-267) boards, 20.8 x 15.6 cm.

Published: 30 copies published August 1971 at $2.50.

Notes: The statement on the front flap of the dust jacket reads: "Robert Duncan was born in Oakland, California (1919). Of *Heavenly City, Earthly City,* composed during 1946, he says '*The Treesbank Poems* were written at the farm of Hamilton and Mary Tyler in Sonoma County, the remaining works in Berkeley. The volume is arranged chronologically; yet the arrangement is shaped toward an apotheosis in the poem written at the end of the year. I owe much in the development of my poetics to the work of Wyatt and Surrey, to *The Temple* of George Herbert, to the work of such moderns as Wallace Stevens, D. H. Lawrence, the Spender translation of Rilke's *Duino Elegies,* and Edith Sitwell's *Street Songs.* In my psychological concept I am indebted to Sigmund Freud, Karl Barth, and particularly to *Dark Night of the Soul* by the 16th century St. John of the Cross'."

In a letter to the compiler dated 20 Sept. 1975, Bern Porter made the following comments about the First edition and the Second sub-edition, which he refers to as "2nd edition": "1st Edition | Designed by Ben Kennedy and Bern Porter. Printed for Bern Porter at the Gillick Press, Berkeley, November 1947, 350 copies 33 pages Illustrated by Mary Fabilli, Berkeley, close friend of author with full length portrait of the author, jacket and cover and colophon in india revealing the nude male, amulets, rings, animal scenes symbolizing the poets personal way of life. His first published portrait. Text widely read throughout Berkeley and Bay Area prior to publication and divided into three parts I Treesbank Poems, II Berkeley Poems, III Heavenly City Earthly City. Edition a financial loss and remaindered 1947-1949. 2nd Edition Designed by Bern Porter. Printed by Walton Press, Philadelphia, affiliate of Bern Porter Books by special arrangements with Bern Porter. August 1971, 30 copies, 24 pages. The text is the third section only of the First edition and bears its title on stem and title-page: Heavenly City Earthly City. Only the Fabilli colophon drawing is used along with a photographic frontispiece by Bern Porter, hand-signed and dated by him on dates of actual sale over a period of a year and Porter's version of the title. Walton Press ceased operations in December so that original intent of producing a second, even third group of 30 each was never realized." In response to queries by the compiler, Bern Porter made the following clarifications in a letter dated 24 Oct. 1978: "In 1969 a feeler was put out in the form of an announcement in B[ooks] i[n] P[rint] that one copy [of the first sub-edition] existed and others could be made if anyone was interested—ie if orders came in copies would be made to fill orders. About 20 did come in and about 20 full text xerox copies were made of the entire book held together with soft cover and staples. Thus this would be a second edition, xerox, full text. On the basis of this interest 30 copies (this would be a 3rd edition) were delivered here in Belfast in August 1971 in print of *only* the section of the full text called H[eavenly] C[ity] E[arthly] C[ity] plus a frontispiece photo of mine called H[eavenly] C[ity] E[earthly] C[ity] & signed by me. Hardbound photocopy of original text type."

When one of the signed copies with a dust jacket was offered for sale, Jack Shoemaker, of the firm Sand Dollar Books, entered the following note in his advance catalogue for 1977: "Mr Duncan has explained this dust jacket as follows: at the binders there were a few extra sheets of endpapers, and as a test one was drawn about the book as a dust jacket. The idea was abandoned. Mr. Duncan said 'This must be a very early subscriber's copy and the only one to escape with the dust jacket'." Not all of the copies that should have had signatures and poems written in them were produced. The copy in the Colby Library is number 61, giving an indication that at least that many copies were produced, though it has not been determined if a regular numbering procedure was followed.

A2   **POEMS 1948-49**   1949

a. *First dition, first state:*

[top] ROBERT DUNCAN | [middle] POEMS 1948-49 | [bottom] Berkeley Miscellany Editions [Berkeley, 1949].

Collation: [1-11]⁴; pp. [i-iv], [1-2], 3-4, [5], 6-10, [11-12], 13-17, [18-20], 21-52, [53-54], 55-60, [61-62], 63-64, [65-66], 67-84.

Contents: p. [i] title-page; p. [ii] acknowledgments-page, "Libertarian Press | Glen Gardner, N.J."; p. [iii] contents-page; p. [iv] blank; p. [1] section-title, "3/THREE SONGS FOR JERRY"; p. [2] blank; pp. 3-10 text; p. [11] section-title, "I TELL OF LOVE* [below] (*variations upon Pound's essay on [in italics] Cavalcanti and | his translation of Cavalcanti's [in italics] Donna Mi Prega)"; p. [12] blank; pp. 13-17 text; p. [18] blank; p. [19] section-title, "THE VENICE POEM"; p. [20] blank; pp. 21-52 text; p. [53] section-title, "HOMAGE TO THE | BROTHERS GRIMM"; p. [54] blank; pp. 55-60 text; p. [61] section-title, "REVIVAL"; p. [62] blank; pp. 63-74 text; p. [65] section-title, "A POET'S MASQUE" [below in italics] "written for Erika Braun | Hallowe'en 1948"; p. [66] blank; pp. 67-84 text.

Text contents: THREE SONGS FOR JERRY [section-title for following three poems] THE INEXPLICABLE HISTORY OF MUSIC—A WEEK-END OF THE SAME EVENT—SLEEPING ALL NIGHT—I TELL OF LOVE—THE VENICE POEM—HOMAGE TO THE BROTHERS GRIMM [section-title for following three poems] THE ROBBER MOON—STRAWBERRIES UNDER THE SNOW—THE DINNER TABLE OF HARLEQUIN—REVIVAL—A POET'S MASQUE.

Description: The text is printed on yellowish white (dull C-92) paper, 22.7 x 15.2 cm. The gatherings have been stapled three times from the side and glued to the medium gray (approximately C-265) paper wrappers. There are no endpapers. Printing on the front cover reads, [top] "ROBERT DUNCAN | [middle] POEMS 1948-49 | [bottom] Berkeley Miscellany Editions," while the lettering on the spine reads from head to tail, "Poems 1948-49 [space] ROBERT DUNCAN." The complete text of "The Venice Poem" appears in this state.

Published: 100 copies published in 1949 at $1.50.

b. *First edition, second state:*

Title, Collation, Contents, Text contents, and Description the same as the first state except that on page 31, lines 9-13 and 21-22 and on page 32, lines 15-16 and 22 are expurgated and replaced by solid lines.

Published: 400 copies published in 1949 at $1.50.

Notes: In all copies examined the number 5 does not appear on its designated page, when it should in the design of the book. In a letter to Henry Wenning dated 7 Nov. 1972, RD wrote: "I had wanted 100 of the 500 copies censored (for sale to sensitive old ladies at poetry readings), and the printers (who were sensitive old lady anarchists) reversed the proportions so that 100 uncensored copies and 400 censored copies were printed. This means that in some copies of the censored printing I wrote in the missing lines, once the uncensored copies were gone." In another letter to Wenning, dated 21 Nov. 1962, RD wrote that "the censored lines (in imitation of the censored lines in Pound's 'Canto LII' [use] bars to replace lines on pages 31 & 32)" (MoSW).

A3   **MEDIEVAL SCENES**   1950

a. *First edition, regular copies:*

[within a block print of very red (C-11), very yellow (C-82), and black (C-267) of a medieval court and stage, and in script]

MEDIEVAL | SCENES | BY ROBERT DUNCAN | CENTAUR
PRESS SAN FRANCISCO [1950].

Collation: [1]¹⁶; pp. [1-32].

Contents: pp. [1-2] blank; p. [3] half-title-page, "Medieval Scenes"; p. [4]
blank; p. [5] title-page; p. [6] copyright-page, "Copyright 1950 by Robert
Duncan"; p. [7] epigraph-page, [in italics] "Upon the wall of her bed
chamber, so | the legend goes, the poetess Laura Riding | had inscribed in
letters of gold: | [in regular caps] GOD IS A WOMAN"; p. [8] blank; pp.
[9-29] text; p. [30] colophon-page, "Printed from Centaur and Deepdene |
Italic faces, set by hand. Block print | by Kermit Sheets. 250 signed copies. |
[signature] Robert Duncan."

Text contexts: THE DREAMERS—THE HELMET OF GOLIATH—
THE BANNERS—THE KINGDOM OF JERUSALEM—THE FES-
TIVALS—THE MIRROR—THE REAPER—THE ADORATION OF
THE VIRGIN—HUON OF BORDEAUX—THE ALBIGENSES.

Description: The text is printed on pale yellow (light C-89) paper, 22.8 x 15.5
cm., with deckled edges. Some of the edges have been trimmed. The titles of
the poems have been printed in red (C-11) and the text of the poems in
black. The gathering has been sewn to the wrapper with light gray
(C-264) thread. The wrapper is made from heavy, deep red (C-16) paper with
the front edge deckled. The lettering on the front cover, in italics, reads
"Medieval Scenes," while the rear cover is blank.

Published: 250 copies published in 1950 at $1.25.

b. *Second edition, regular copies:*

[in script] Medieval Scenes | 1950 and 1959 | [in regular type] by | Robert
Duncan | With a Preface by the Author | And an Afterword by Robert
Bertholf | Kent, Ohio | The Kent State University Libraries | 1978.

Collation: [1]²⁸; pp. [1-56].

Contents: p. [1] half-title, [in script] "Medieval Scenes"; pp. [2-4] blank; p.
[5] title-page; p. [6] copyright-page, "© Robert Duncan | Afterword © Robert
Bertholf | Published for | The Friends of the Kent State University
Libraries"; pp. [7-8] "Preface"; p. [9] [in script] "Medieval Scenes | [in
Roman type] 1950"; p. [10] blank; p. [11] epigraph-page, [in italics] "Upon
the wall of her bed chamber, so | the legend goes, the poetess Laura Riding |
had inscribed in letters of gold: | [in Roman type] GOD IS A WOMAN"; pp.
[13-33] text; p. [34] blank; p. [35] [in script] "from | Medieval Scenes | [in
Roman type] Selected Poems | 1959"; pp. [36-47] text; pp. 48-50 blank; pp.
[51-53] "An Afterword"; p. [54] colophon-page, "This edition is printed in
14 Garamond Bold with | Italic type on Ivory Teton paper. There are 624 |
regular copies, 100 copies numbered and signed | by the author, and 26
copies lettered and signed by the author with a color photograph of the |

author's illumination for the [in italics] Medieval Scenes | papers"; pp. [55-56] blank.

Text contents: PREFACE—THE DREAMERS—THE HELMET OF GOLIATH—THE BANNERS—THE KINGDOM OF JERUSALEM—THE FESTIVALS—THE MIRROR—THE REAPER—THE ADORATION OF THE VIRGIN—HUON OF BORDEAUX—THE ALBIGENSES—THE DREAMERS—THE HELMET OF GOLIATH—THE BANNERS—THE KINGDOM OF JERUSALEM—THE FESTIVALS—THE MIRROR—THE REAPER—THE ALBIGENSES—AN AFTERWORD.

Description: The text is printed on pale yellow (light C-89) textured paper, 22.9 x 15.5 cm., with alternating deckled and trimmed edges. The titles of the poems are printed in very deep red (C-14) and the text in black. The gathering is stapled twice to the wrapper. The wrappers are made from medium blue (C-182) textured paper, 24.2 x 15.8 cm. Lettering on the front cover in red script reads "Medieval Scenes." The rear cover is blank. An errata slip, 7.5 x 18 cm., has been laid-in inside the front wrapper and reads: "ERRATA | recto leaf 10: title should read [in red] THE KINGDOM OF JERUSALEM | verso leaf 26, line 22: word should read 'The Dreamers'."

Published: 624 copies published 19 April 1978 at $4.00.

c. *Second edition, signed and numbered copies:*

Title, Collation, Contents, Text contents, and Description the same as the regular copies except the numbers 1-100 appear along with the author's signature above the colophon on page [54], the colophon-page. The gathering has been sewn to the wrapper with blue thread.

Published: 100 copies published 19 April 1978 at $10.00.

d. *Second edition, signed and lettered copies:*

Title, Collation, Contents, Text contents, and Description the same as the regular copies except that a colored photograph of the author's illumination of the MEDIEVAL SCENES papers, 17.2 x 12.6 cm., is pasted on recto of the first blank leaf, p. [54], the colophon-page. Some of the copies have been specially signed "for," plus the name of the individual purchaser. The gathering has been sewn to the wrapper with red thread.

Published: 26 copies published 19 April 1978 at $20.00.

e. *Second edition, hors de commerce copies:*

Title, Collation, Contents, Text contents, and Description the same as the regular copies except that four copies have been sewn with red thread, inscribed and signed by the author in black ink and numbered i-iv on p. [54], the colophon-page, which contains a color photograph of the author signing copies of the edition pasted-in. The colored photograph of the author's illumination of the MEDIEVAL SCENES papers is pasted-in on p. [3]. These copies have a blood stain on the rear cover. In addition, there are four copies, sewn with blue thread, numbered 1-4, inscribed and signed by the author on p. [54], the colophon-page.

Published: 8 copies published 19 April 1978 and not for sale.

Proof papers for Second edition. OKentU.

a. First galley proofs
   Collation: 13*l* all recto 58.5 x 22.8 cm.
   Contents: The text plus proofreader's and printer's markings.
b. Page proofs
   Collation: 43*l* all recto 28 x 21.6 cm.
   Contents: The text plus numerous spacing notations and comments by RD and Jess.

Notes: The ten poems comprising *Medieval Scenes* were written on ten successive days in February 1947 at a round table in a house shared by a group of students, returning GIs and other types, located at 2029 Hearst Street, Berkeley, California. In the "Author's Notes to the Medieval Scenes Papers," RD writes: "Since I had never studied The Middle Ages, I would be—as men in the Middle Ages were—mistaken about history, having only the popular legend of what was 'Medieval' to go by. And as a test or ordeal I set about to write one poem each night of succeeding nights. It was my idea that I would write without revision—straight off, as if dictated. But, as the manuscript shows, I reverted to my earlier way of beginning over again when I would lose the tenor of the poem in order to revive the impulse (of sound and vision) that led forward. Each evening I would 'find' the epigraph and move out along the line it opend. . . . As I worked on *Medieval Scenes* I had the sense for the first time in poetry not just of 'having' a poem, being seized by this utterance that had to fulfill itself, but of having a work to do and knowing that work as I did it."

The ten poems are an example of what Jack Spicer called a "serial poem"; however, because of restrictions on the number of pages, when the series was reprinted in *Selected Poems,* as RD writes in the "Author's Notes," "The Adoration of the Virgin and Huon were eliminated from the *Selected*—a decision I regretted at the time and consider now a disaster—for garbled or make-shift as I might think them, the two scenes are essential to the whole." The poems in the 1950 edition were printed by James Broughton and Kermit Sheets from a typed reading version, while the eight scenes in *SP* were printed from the original pencil drafts. Both versions appear in the second edition, which was published as the first in a series of pamphlets from the Special Collections Department of the Libraries at Kent State University.

A4   **FRAGMENTS OF A DISORDERD DEVOTION**   1952

a. *First edition, privately published:*

[in deep blue (C-183) holograph] FRAGMENTS | of a | disorderd | Devotion | 1952 | Robert Duncan [San Francisco; Privately published, 1952].

Collation: [1]⁴, [2-4]²; pp. [1-20].

Contents: 2 blank leaves; p. [1] title-page; p. [2] blank; pp. [3-5] text; p. [7] line drawing in blue (C-179); p. [8] blank; pp. [9-10] text; p. [10] line drawing; pp. [11-18] text; p. [19] colophon-page, "[number] / 50 | [date] | Robert Duncan"; p. [20] blank; 2 blank leaves.

Text contents: "UNKINGD BY AFFECTION" (fl)—5 PIECES—HERO SONG—AN IMAGINARY WOMAN—ELUARD'S DEATH.

Description: This booklet has been multilithed on white (C-263) wove paper, 20.2 x 14.6 cm., and the text reproduced from the author's holograph. Two blank leaves are bound around the gatherings and have not been counted in the collation. The outside one has been used to have the decorated cover folded over it, and so serves as an endpaper. These two leaves and the gatherings have been sewn with white (C-263) thread. A strip of masking tape has been laid around the spine to support the sewing points. The title-page, page [7], and pages [17-19] have been printed in blue (C-179), the remaining pages in black. The wrap-around covers, 20.5 x 15.3 cm., of white paper have been decorated with a line drawing in black. Within the drawing on the front cover appears the following in holograph: "Fragments | of a | Disorderd | Devotion | [at lower right] Robert | Duncan | 1952." Within the line drawing on the rear cover appear two profiles facing one another. The front and rear covers have been decorated in yellow (C-86), pink (C-2), gray reddish orange (C-39), deep olive green (C-126), deep gray (C-266), very orange yellow (C-66), and brilliant violet (C-206) crayons.

Published: 50 copies published fall 1952 and not for sale.

b. *Second edition, first issue:*

[in black holograph] FRAGMENTS | OF A | DISORDERD | DEVOTION | ROBERT DUNCAN [with FRAG, A, ORDER, ION, and D contained in a line drawing] [San Francisco: gnomon press, and Toronto: Island Press, 1966].

Collation: [1]¹²; pp. [1-24].

Contents: p. [1] blank; p. [2] copyright-page, "copyright © 1966 | Robert Duncan [below] publisht by gnomon press | 1171 Alabama Street | San Francisco, California | and | in Canada by Island press | 259 Humberside Avenue | Toronto 9, Ontario"; p. [3] title-page; p. [4] blank; pp. [5-6] text; p. [6] line drawing; pp. [7-10] text; p. [10] line drawing; pp. [11-15] text; p. [15]

line drawing; pp. [16-22] text; p. [23] colophon-page, [to right of line drawing] "50 copies of these poems were multilithd and| sent to friends for| Christmas 1952 with| individual covers done| in ink and crayons.| The text has been| newly drawn for this| edition [enclosed in a circle] RD| 1965"; p. [24] blank.

Text contents: UNKINGD BY AFFECTION—5 PIECES—HERO SONG—AN IMAGINARY WOMAN—ELUARD'S DEATH.

Description: The text is printed on pale yellow (light C-89) textured, laid paper, 22.3 x 16.3 cm., from the author's holograph, and the gathering has been attached to the wrapper with two staples. The wrapper is made from heavy medium yellowish green (C-120) paper. On the front wrapper appears a drawing of two facing busts in dark bluish green (C-165): within the bust on the left, the eye forms the center of a five-petal flower spreading on the face, while the eye of the bust on the right is represented by the eye of a bird which is imposed on the face. Lettering at the top in black reads: "FRAGMENTS| of a| DISORDERD DEVOTION| [between the figures] ROBERT| DUNCAN| [below in line with the slant of the two shoulders of the bust] ISLAND| GNOMON." The rear cover is blank.

Published: approximately 70 copies distributed but withdrawn from sale.

c. *Second edition, second issue:*

Title, Collation, Contents, Text contents, and Description the same as the Second edition, first issue, except that the wrapper has been replaced with one of gray yellow green (C-122) and the title-page has been reproduced on the front cover. The lettering in holograph, "gnomon press and Island press," has been added at the bottom. The rear cover is blank.

Published: approximately 500 copies published in 1966 at $1.50.

Notes: In a letter to Henry Wenning, dated 7 Nov. 1962, RD wrote: "In 1952 we had a friend who worked for the Committee for Free Asia offices here [San Francisco] and we were able to run this book off on their machine after hours as a Xmas gift edition (but only 15 were so distributed; the rest over years as cautiously 'awarded')" (MoSW). The copy described is RD's copy. No two are exactly the same, as the copies as CSfU and CtU indicate. The copy at NBuU, Jonathan Williams's copy, has an ink and crayon drawing of a woman extending over the front and rear covers. There is an extra leaf, front and rear, acting as a flyleaf and attachment for the wrappers and covers, but no extra leaves are wrapped around the interior leaves. The compiler's copy (originally given to James Broughton and inscribed to him "to star-kites, one and all") has a cover decorated in a crayon design of orange yellow (C-66), greenish blue (C169), yellow green (C-117), light purplish blue (C-199), pale orange yellow (C-73), and very reddish orange (C-34). The title in black ink in RD's hand runs from the head to the tail, with "Robert Duncan" horizontal at the middle of the cover, and "1952" and the bottom. The rear cover is blank. At this writing, approximately 35 copies have been awarded, and their distribution has been reserved for poets.

The second edition of 1966 was to be the first of a series of publications jointly produced by Victor Coleman's Island Press and Jonathan Greene's gnomon press. The advertisement for the publication reads as follows: "Gnomon Press & Island Press wish to announce the commencement of a select number of joint publications. The first of which is to be Robert Duncan's *Fragments Of A Disorderd Devotion,* price $1.50." The second publication in the series was to be Theodore Enslin's *Forms, The First Dimensions.* In a letter to the compiler, dated 2 Nov. 1978, Victor Coleman wrote: "Jonathan Greene had received permission from Duncan to reprint *Fragments . . .* and had sent me the newly drawn edition. It was my understanding at that time that the eventual cover was meant to be a title page. I commissioned a cover from Anton Van Dalen, Dutch born Toronto resident currently residing and exhibiting in New York (where he incidently works very closely with Saul Steinberg). I somewhat overzealously put the book into production without getting Duncan's OK about the cover design, and was further remiss in not consulting Jonathan Greene on the matter. The topper came when Van Dalen was given no credit, causing certain confusion over whether Duncan had done the drawing. I figure about 40-50 copies of the book with Van Dalen's cover drawing were sent out before Duncan's objection got to me; after which the Van Dalen covers were removed and the Duncan calligraphy replaced it." James Lowell of The Asphodel Book Shop, the distributor of the book, told the compiler that approximately 70 copies were sent to him. In a note written out for the Special Collections Department of the Kent State University Libraries, RD comments: "This cover was substituted by Victor Coleman for the cover which I had designd and was used on the first shipment of the book. When I saw the substitution on the copy air maild to gnomon in San Francisco, I 'hit the roof' and the Victor Coleman designd cover was withdrawn. In the intervening six years I have come to see Victor Coleman as a poet in his own right of first importance, particularly with his *Light Verse,* and now I consider his cover to be a most interesting conjunction of another poet's work with my own."

A5   **THE SONG OF THE BORDER-GUARD**   1952

First edition:

[in very red (C-11)] THE SONG OF THE BORDER-GUARD | [text in forty-four lines, in black] | [at lower right in very red] poem by ROBERT DUNCAN | design by Cy Twombly | [across bottom] Nicola Cernovich, [space] Publisher [space] Black Mountain Graphics Workshop [space] Black Mountain College [space] Black Mountain, North Carolina [1952].

Folio broadside: The text is printed on pale yellow (light C-89) laid paper, 49.6 x 31.8 cm., and pasted at the center fold to a medium reddish orange

(C-37) cover which contains a design printed in black on the outside cover by Cy Twombly.

Published: approximately 200 copies published in 1952 at an unknown price.

Notes: Jess Collins designed the original cover, but it was rejected and the present cover substituted at the time of printing. Joel Oppenheimer, who participated in the printing of the broadside, wrote in a letter to the compiler, dated 31 July 1978, that approximately 200 copies were printed. The approximate date of publication is established by a comment in a letter from Charles Olson to Robert Creeley, dated 30 March 1952: "The Duncan is just getting done (will shoot one off to you)" (CtU). The broadside was the second in a projected series of broadsides which Nicola Cernovich wanted to print at Black Mountain College. Charles Olson's *This* was the first in the series.

A6   **BOOB**   1952

First edition, privately published:

Boob Number One [collage pasted up by Jess Collins, with images and lettering selected by RD].

Boob Number Two "WHOSE THIS LIDDL BOOK COMING?" (fl) [text] in twenty-nine lines] [image of a young bird] [San Francisco: Privately published, 1952].

Broadsides: The collage and the text of the poem are printed on yellowish white (C-92) glossy paper, two leaves 21 x 27.9 cm.

Published: 250 copies published in 1952 and distributed free.

Notes: Boob Number One and Number Two are two broadsides produced as a pair by RD and Jess. Though 250 copies were printed in 1952, not all of the pairs have been distributed.

A7   **FAUST FOUTU**   1953

a. *First edition, privately published:*

[title-page in holograph] Faust Foutu | [to right of design] act | one | [within design] CAST | master of ceremonies | THE POET'S VOICE | A MUSE | FAUST | a BOY | MARGUERITE | THE DEVIL NURSE | HELEN OF TROY | GRETA GARBO | FAUST'S MOTHER | [beneath design] PROLOG. | BEFORE the curtain. the muse's Room. | SCENES. 1. FAUST'S STUDIO. 2. MARGUERITE | and her Devil-Nurse. In A Garden. | 3. Dark. Faust's Bedroom. 4. Dawn. | 5. Sleepwalking. a Place of Trial. | 6. Faust's Bedroom. 7. The Place of Trial. | 8. The Old Homestead. [San Francisco: Privately published, 1953].

Collation: pp. [i], 1-15, [ii], 16-59, [iii], 60-70.

Contents: p. [i] title-page; p. 1 [in holograph] "FAUST FOUTU: A COMIC MASQUE"; pp. 2-15 text; p. [ii] [in holograph] "ACT TWO | [design]"; pp. 16-38 text; p. 39 "ACT THREE"; pp. 39-59 text; p. [iii] blank; p. 60 "ACT FOUR"; pp. 60-70 text.

Text contents: the play FAUST FOUTU.

Description: The text has been mimeographed on yellowish white (C-92) wove paper, 27.9 x 21.5 cm., on rectos of the leaves only. Some copies have been stapled with covers of various composition, and some copies have been stapled from the side without covers. The title of the play appears at the top left of each recto leaf.

Published: 100 copies published in 1953 and not for sale.

b. ***Second edition, abbreviated copies:***

[title-page in holograph within design] FAUST [design] | [design] FOUTU | ACT ONE OF FOUR ACTS | A COMIC MASK | [design] | BY ROBERT DUNCAN | 1952-1954 [dot] SF [beneath design] | with decorations by the author [White Rabbit Press, 1958].

Collation: [1]¹⁰; pp. [i-iii], 1-15, [16-17].

Contents: pp. [i-ii] blank; p. [iii] title-page; pp. 1-15 text; p. [16] blank; p. [17] colophon-page, [printer's logo] "FROM THE WHITE RABBIT PRESS | MARCH 1958 | Part One of Four Parts. This | edition is limited to three | hundred copies of which two | hundred and seventy-eight copies | are for public sale; twenty-two | copies to be reserved for a | limited edition of the complete | work bound and decorated by the | author."

Text contents: Act I of the play.

Description: The text has been multilithed on yellowish white (C-92) wove paper, 21.7 x 16.5 cm. The gathering has been attached to the cover with white thread. The cover is made from heavy textured white stock, 21.7 x 16.5 cm. Lettering on the front cover in large bold letters reads "FAUST | FOUTU | BY | ROBERT DUNCAN | ACT I," while the rear cover is blank.

Published: 300 copies published in 1958 at an unknown price.

c. ***Third edition, regular copies:***

[title-page in holograph within a drawing of a head] Faust | Foutu | an entertainment | By | ROBERT DUNCAN | in FOUR PARTS | with decorations by the author [Stinson Beach, California: Enkidu Surrogate, 1959].

Collation: [1]³⁸; pp. [i-iv], [1], 2-13, [14], 15-24, [25], 26-31, [32-33], 34-36, [37], 38-57, [58], 59-71, [72].

Contents: p. [i] blank; p. [ii] copyright-page, "Copyright, [in holograph]

1960 by Robert Duncan | For production rights | apply to the author | Stinson Beach | California"; p. [iii] title-page; p. [iv] [at the left of a line drawing of two faces pointing to the right and left] ACT ONE [and above within a line drawing] THE CAST* [the cast, their parts, and the scenes] *As produced in a dramatic reading at | THE SIX gallery, 3119 Fillmore, San Francisco | January 1955"; pp. [1]-13 text; p. [14] [within a line drawing at top] "ACT 2," [then below the cast, their parts and the scenes]; pp. 15-24 text; p. [25] line drawing signed "RD"; pp. 26-36 text; p. [36] line drawing on bottom half of p.; p. [37] [at top within line drawing] "ACT THREE," then the cast, their parts and the scenes; pp. 38-57 text; p. [58] [within a line drawing] "ACT FOUR [and actors for] A SOLILOQUY FOR FIVE VOICES"; pp. 59-71 text; p. [72] colophon-page, "November 1959. an edition of seven hundred and | fifty copies of which fifty copies are numberd | 1 thru 50 and signd, including a special color | drawing by the author. published by ENKIDU SUR | ROGATE, p. o. box 14, Stinson Beach, California. | [publisher's logo]."

Text contents: the play FAUST FOUTU.

Description: The text has been multilithed on yellowish white (C-92) wove paper, 21.7 x 17.7 cm. Pages 20, 22, 17, and 49 are printed in deep blue (C-179) ink. The gathering is stapled to the cover twice. The cover wrapper is of heavy, very yellow (brighter than C-86) paper. The front cover contains a line drawing by RD of two busts, face to face, in black and green (C-141). Lettering within black rules in green reads horizontally, "FAUST," and vertically using the same "F," "FOUTU." Lettering in RD's holograph in a box made with a thick green rule at the bottom reads, "a comic masque | by | ROBERT DUNCAN." The rear cover is blank.

Published: 700 copies published Nov. 1959 at $3.50.

d. ***Third edition, signed and illustrated copies:***

Title, Collation, Contents, Text contents, and Description all the same as Third edition, regular copies except that on p. [72], the colophon-page, a drawing and a signature have been added. The compiler's copy contains an ink drawing of a head of a bearded man in green (C-141), blue (C-183), yellow (C-82), and red (C-11) ink. "Robert Duncan" in green ink appears just below the colophon; the following in black ink appears beneath the logo, "No 26 of 50"; and at the bottom, "this copy distributed April 1972 RD."

Published: 50 copies published Nov. 1959, but not all distributed, at an unknown price.

Notes: In a letter to Henry Wenning, dated 7 Nov. 1962, RD wrote: "In 1953 when this play was completed, I rented a mimeograph machine and ran off, 100 copies I think it was—of 72 pp.. Which furnished acting copies for the cast and for some of the audience" (MoSW). Some copies were mailed to associates with only the text of Acts I-III. In two cases known to the compiler, the fourth act was mailed at a later date. Differences resulting from stapling and mailing do not represent different issues of the text. Copies were mailed to Black Mountain College where Act I was performed in 1954, with music composed by Stefan Wolpe. A reading performance of the complete play was given in San Francisco in 1954. The mimeograph sheets in some cases were bound, as the copy at KU, which has a maroon binder and contains the imprint "American Theatre for Poets, Inc | 35 Cooper Square | NY | NY." A copy at CtU has a decorated cover and contains the embossed name "Black Mountain College," while the copy at MoSw is bound in yellow cloth with strips of blue and white over boards, with gold endpapers. Jonathan Williams's copy at NUBu has a cover decorated in a black and white design with a large monogramed RD to the left of the title in black running from the top to the heel of the page. The spine is formed by medical adhesive tape, and contains the play's title in black running down the spine.

At the time when the first act was printed, Joe Dunn, the publisher of White Rabbit Press, worked at the Greyhound bus station in San Francisco and produced books on Greyhound's printing equipment after working hours. In discussing Act I, RD wrote to Henry Wenning, in a letter dated 25 Oct. 1962: "The songs in this Act were rewritten between this edition and the Enkidu Surrogate edition of *Faust Foutu* completely done a year later. Authors were paid in copies by Joe Dunn—and generously, for we received all the copies above the number necessary to cover the cost of production (which in the case of White Rabbit was cheap, for Dunn printed them after hours at the place where he workd as a multilith operator). 300 copies of this pamphlet were printed; but I destroyd some 150 copies of my lot because I didnt want the single act for sale once it was clear Dunn was not going to be able to go ahead with the whole play" (MoSW). In another letter to Henry Wenning, dated Nov. 1962, he commented further: "I had two things in mind in rewriting the first act. One was that I had always been dissatisfied with some of the songs (the concert in act two is also rewritten). But the other is that I had not copyrighted the play previously and I wanted a definitive text that would be under copyright" (MoSW). In two letters to Robin Blaser, the first dated 6 Aug. 1958 and the second 5 Oct. 1959, RD made other comments about the play. "The second act of Faust Foutu off to White Rabbit—and for all my resolve not to be tempted to rework, I'd never liked Maggie's songs and spent two days sweating it out to patch them up. And then, the lid off, I let myself alter lines where I wanted to, cut the Marguerite interlude from the storm section. . . . It's been then with a vengence a period of re-writing" (CU-B).

At this time RD and Jess Collins were living at Stinson Beach, California, and it was there that the idea of Enkidu Surrogate as RD's own imprint was conceived. The imprint was a surrogate for White Rabbit Press. So, in the second letter to Robin Blaser, RD writes: "This week I got back the second act of FAUST FOUTU and I am starting a series myself ENKIDU SURROGATE with FAUST FOUTU complete; and a book by Jack [Spicer] (he gave me BILLY THE KID to start); but I learn its more economical to put out a full book than a pamphlet" (CU-B). The third edition, the one by Enkidu Surrogate, was designed to have 50 copies decorated by RD, but not all those copies were decorated. The compiler's copy, dated 1972, is number 26. In a letter to Henry Wenning, dated 25 Oct. 1962, RD commented on them: "These 'limited' copies were to be made up as they were subscribed, but then as the expenses of the book did not come to much I lackd interest in pressing the point of the limited edition. 7 copies have been made up to date. And I have on hand only 28 copies. . . . That would mean making the full 28 up signed and with the color drawing in each, the actual limited edition would be 35 not 50 copies. (Wow! what a confusion for bibliographers). But that is just how unofficial these fugitive publications were" (MoSW).

In a letter to Cid Corman, dated 25 Jan. 1954, RD commented on his play: "Faust is an effort at the dramatic personae of American St. Germain des Présian, an effort—only partially successful—at precipitating the content and form of the persona. These Fausts Foutu are our Prufrocks" (TxU).

A8   CAESAR'S GATE   1955

a. *First edition, regular copies:*

[in black] Robert Duncan | [in large deep red (C-13)] CAESAR'S GATE | [in black] POEMS 1949-50 | with collages by | Jess Collins | [at bottom] The Divers Press [dot] 1955 [Palma de Mallorca, Spain].

Collation: [1-8]⁴, [9]²; pp. [1-68].

Contents: pp. [1-3] blank; p. [4] seven titles listed under the heading "by Robert Duncan" and one title listed under the heading "by Jess Collins"; p. [5] title-page; p. [6] copyright-page, "All Rights Reserved" [in middle] "'The Second Night in the Week' and | 'Processionals I' appeared in ORIGIN X" [at bottom] "Printed in Spain"; p. [7] contents-page; p. [8] blank; p. [9] collage; p. [10] blank; pp. [11-15] [in RD's holograph] "PREFACE for *CAESAR'S GATE*"; p. [16] collage; p. [17] section-title, "FOUR POEMS | AS | A NIGHT SONG"; p. [18] blank; pp. [19-22] text; p. [23] blank; p. [24] collage; p. [25] section-title, "EYE SIGHT"; p. [26] collage; p. [27] [in RD's holograph] text; p. [28] collage; p. [29] text; p. [30] collage; p. [31] text; p. [32] collage; p. [33] text; p. [34] collage; p. [35] [in RD's holograph] text; p. [36] collage; p. [37] text; p. [38] collage; p. [39] text; p. [40] collage; p. [41] [in RD's holograph] text; p. [42] collage; p. [43] text; p. [44] collage; p. [45] text; p. [46] collage; p. [47] [in RD's holograph] text; p. [48] blank; p. [49] section-title, "GOODBYE TO YOUTH"; p. [50] collage; pp. [51-55] text; p. [56] collage; p. [57] section-title, "H.M.S. BEARSKIN"; p. [58] blank; pp. [59-65] text; p. [66] blank; p. [67] colophon-page, "This book was handset in Mercedes | and Futura types and printed by | Mossén Alcover in Palma de Mallorca, | September 1955. Limited to thirteen | copies, marked A to C and 1 to 10, | each with an original collage and | poem, signed by the artists; and two | hundred copies for regular distribution"; p. [68] blank.

Text contents: PREFACE FOR *CAESAR'S GATE*—FOUR POEMS AS A NIGHT SONG [section-title for following four poems] THE CONSTRUCTION—THE WALK TO THE VACANT LOT—THE WASTE, THE ROOM, THE DISCARDED TIMBERS—UPON WAKING AT HALF-PAST SIX IN THE MORNING—EYE SIGHT [section-title for following eleven poems] AURORA ROSE (1955)—THE SECOND NIGHT IN THE WEEK—PROCESSIONALS I—PROCESSIONALS II—TEARS OF ST. FRANCIS (1955)—UPON ANOTHER SHORE OF HELL—AN INCUBUS—SUNDAY (1955)—EYESIGHT I—EYESIGHT II—BON VOYAGE! (1955)—GOODBYE TO YOUTH [section-title] H.M.S. BEAR-SKIN [section-title for following six poems] HE ENTERTAINS AT A DINNER PARTY—HE CONSULTS THE TIDES—TO RUN WITH THE HARE & HUNT WITH THE HOUND—"GREAT GRIEF, THEN, HERSELF!" (fl)—HE LISTS SUBJECTS FOR GREAT POETRY: 1950—HE HAS A GOOD TIME THERE.

Description: The text and the collages are printed on white (dull C-263) glossy paper, 22 x 16.7 cm. The gatherings have been sewn with white thread and then glued to the wrappers. The wrappers are made from the same paper as used for the text, and they are folded over heavy paper stock with folds of 4 cm. inside the wrappers. A collage by Jess appears on the front cover. Lettering on the spine in deep red reads from head to tail, "CAESAR'S GATE [space] JESS COLLINS [a black dot] ROBERT DUNCAN." The rear cover is blank.

Published: 200 copies published Sept. 1955 at $2.00.

b. *First edition, numbered copies:*

Title, Collation, Contents, Text contents, and Description the same as the regular copies except that an original holograph poem by RD and a colored collage by Jess Collins, each 21.5 x 16.3 cm., are pasted on p. [5] and p. [6]. The poems had been written on typing paper, while the collage is made from the paper stock of *Life* magazine. Each copy is inserted in a heavy slip-case, covered with paper marbled with medium yellow brown (C-77), pale yellow (C-89), brilliant yellow (C-83), brilliant green (C-140), and then yellow gray (light C-93). The collage from the flyer announcement for the book has been pasted on the front cover of the case, and a deep reddish orange (C-38) label has been pasted on the spine with the following printing from head to tail in black: "CAESAR'S GATE [space] JESS COLLINS [dot] ROBERT DUNCAN." The copies are numbered 1-10 and signed on p. [67], the colophon-page, "Robert Duncan | Jess Collins." The titles of the pasted-in poems and collages are as follows: No. 1 SHADOWS OF THE SMOKE—No. 2 THE FAITH—No. 3 WHERE—No. 4 IN THE DOLLS HOUSE—

No. 5 WATCHERS—No. 6 CONSOLATIONS OF PHILOSOPHY—No. 7 TRAVERSALS OF THE CHURCH—No. 8 SHOW—No. 9 TO THE STAIRWELL—No. 10 THE DESCENTS OF NIGHT.

Published: 10 copies published Sept. 1955 at $10.00.

c. *First edition, lettered copies:*

Title, Collation, Contents, Text contents, and Description the same as numbered copies except that three copies are lettered A-C on the colophon-page. The titles of the pasted-in poems and collages are as follows: A, CIRCULATING LIGHTS—B, SOURCE MAGIC—C, PRESENCES. These copies were reserved for the poet, the artist, and the publisher, Robert Creeley.

Published: 3 copies published Sept. 1955 and not for sale.

d. *Second edition, first hardbound impression:*

[in RD's holograph] CAESAR'S GATE | poems 1949-50 | ROBERT DUNCAN | with paste-ups | by JESS | SAND DOLLAR | 1972 [Berkeley].

Collation: [1-9]⁸; pp. [1-14], i-xli, [xlii-xliv], xlv-xlix, [xl], ²1-3, [4-6], 7, [8], 9, [10], 11, [12], 13, [14], 15, [16], 17, [18], 19, [20], 21, [22], 23, [24], 25, [26], 27, [28], 29-32, [33-34], 35-37, [38], 39, [40], 41-48, [49-50], 51-54, [55], 56-57, [58], 59-73, [74-80].

Contents: pp. [1-5] blank; p. [6] seven titles under the heading "Other books in print by Robert Duncan" plus the statement: "'I do not intend to issue another collection of my | work since *Bending the Bow* until 1983 at which time | fifteen years will have passed.' | Robert Duncan, 1972"; p. [7] half-title-page, CAESAR'S GATE; p. [8] collage; p. [9] title-page; p. [10] copyright-page, "Copyright © 1959, 1968, 1970, 1972 | by Robert Duncan | Library of Congress Catalog No. [blank] | ACKNOWLEDGMENT: Some of these poems were first | published in the magazine *Origin;* and in the | following books: | *Caesar's Gate* (Divers Press) and *Poetic* | *Disturbances* (Maya Quarto series) | All Rights Reserved. | Cover, title-page medallion, and the plates in | illustration by Jess. Poems which appear in | the author's script, 1955, were written to | illustrate the artist's paste-ups. | This edition prepared in type-script and composed | by the author for Sand Dollar"; pp. [11-12] contents-pages; p. [13] section-title, "In Preface"; p. [14] collage; pp. i-xli text of "Preface (1972)"; p. [xlii] blank; p. [xliii] collage; p. [xliv] blank; pp. xlv-xlix text [in RD's holograph] of "Preface for CAESAR'S GATE | July 1955"; p. [1] collage; pp. 1-3 text; p. [4] blank; p. [5] collage and [in RD's holograph] section-title, "EYE SIGHT"; p. [6] collage; p. 7 [in RD's holograph] text; p. [8] collage; p. 9 text; p. [10] collage; p. 11 text; p. [12] collage; p. 13 [in RD's holograph] text; p. [14] collage; p. 15 [in RD's holograph] text p. [16] collage; p. 17 text; p. [18] collage; p. 19 text; p. [20] collage; p. 21 [in RD's holograph] text; p. [22] collage; p. 23 text; p. [24] collage; p. 25 text; p. [26] collage; p. 27 [in RD's holograph] text; p. [28] collage; pp. 29-32 text; p. [33] collage; p.

[34] blank; pp. 35-37 text; p. [38] collage; p. 39 text; p. [40] collage and [in RD's holograph] section-title, "POETIC DISTURBANCES"; pp. 41-48 text; p. [49] collage and [in RD's holograph] section-title, "APPEARANCES"; p. [50] blank; pp. 51-54 text; p. [55] collage; pp. 56-57 text; p. [58] collage; pp. 59-71 text of "Epilogue"; pp. 72-73 text; p. [74] blank; p. [75] colophon-page, "SAND DOLLAR [slash] 8 | Published by Jack Shoemaker. | 2600 copies printed in the Winter of 1972- | 1973, of which 600 are bound in cloth."; pp. [76-80] blank.

Text contents: Plate 1 EMBLEM for the Title-page (1972)—Plate 2 FRONTISPIECE—PREFACE (1972)—SOMETHING IS MOVING [section-title] THE HINT OF AN INFINITE REGRESSION—RECOVERING THE KNOWLEDGE OF A PAINFUL TIME—THE GATE—PAIN—LORCA—WHAT IS IT YOU HAVE COME TO TELL ME?—DICTION CONTRA DICTION—SOMETHING IS MOVING—Plate 3 HELL—PREFACE (1955) [section-title] HELL—WHERE WE ARE—THE CROWNS—Plate 4 NIGHT SONG—FOUR POEMS AS A NIGHT SONG [section-title for following four poems] THE CONSTRUCTION—THE WALK TO THE VACANT LOT—THE WASTE, THE ROOM, THE DISCARDED TIMBERS—UPON WAKING AT HALF-PAST SIX IN THE MORNING—Plate 5 EYE SIGHT—EYE SIGHT [section-title]—Plate 6 A ROAR AROSE—AURORA ROSE (1955)—Plate 7 THE SECOND NIGHT OF THE WEEK—THE SECOND NIGHT IN THE WEEK—Plate 8 PROCESSIONALS I—PROCESSIONALS I—Plate 9 PROCESSIONALS II—PROCESSIONALS II—Plate 10 TEARS OF ST. FRANCIS—TEARS OF ST. FRANCIS—Plate 11 UPON ANOTHER SHORE OF HELL—UPON ANOTHER SHORE OF HELL—Plate 12 AN INCUBUS—AN INCUBUS—Plate 13 DADDY SUNDAY—SUNDAY (1955)—Plate 14 EYESIGHT I—EYESIGHT I—Plate 15 EYESIGHT II—EYESIGHT II—Plate 16 BON VOYAGE!—BON VOYAGE! (1955)—Plate 17 GOODBYE TO YOUTH—GOODBYE TO YOUTH—Plate 18 HARES & HOUNDS—H.M.S. BEARSKIN [sequence-title for the following seven poems] HE ENTERTAINS AT A DINNER PARTY IN THE BARDO STATE—HE CONSULTS THE TIDES—TO RUN WITH THE HARE & HUNT WITH THE HOUND—GREAT GRIEF, THEN, HERSELF!—HE LISTS SUBJECTS FOR GREAT POETRY: 1950—HE HAS A GOOD TIME THERE—CODA—Plate 19 RUMORS—Plate 20 POETIC DISTUR-BANCES—POETIC DISTURBANCES [section-title] FORMS WITHIN FORMS—WHAT HAVE YOU COME TO TELL ME, GARCIA LORCA?—THE VOYAGE OF THE POET INTO THE LAND OF THE DEAD—Plate 21 APPEARANCES—APPEARANCES [section-title] AT HOME IN EDEN—FROM A SEASON IN HELL—THE CONQUEROR'S SONG—Plate 22 MOVING IN YOUR SIGHTS—MOVING IN YOUR SIGHTS—WE HAVE LEFT OF COURSE—A GAME OF KINGS—THERE MUST BE A REASON—SEE THE STONE LIONS CRY—BEFORE THE BEAUTIFUL THINGS TURN EVIL—Plate 23 ALTERATIONS—EPILOGUE [section-title] DICHTUNG KONTRA DICHTUNG: A

HYPNAGOGIC PHANTASY—[title in brackets] [THE MATTER OF THE BEES]—DESPAIR IN BEING TEDIOUS (1972).

Description: The text is reproduced by the photo-offset process on glossy white (dull C-263) paper, 21.6 x 16.2 cm. The gatherings have been sewn with white thread and glued to the spine. The endpapers are of white wove paper. The cover is made from dark green (approximately C-146) cloth over heavy boards 22.2 x 16.9 cm. An emblem composed by the initials of RD and Jess is stamped on the front cover, bottom right, in very yellow (gold) (C-82). The spine and rear cover are blank.

Dust jacket: The dust jacket is made from glossy paper, 22.2 x 16.9 cm., and the front cover reproduces the collage by Jess from the cover of the first edition. Deep red (C-13) lettering on the spine in RD's holograph reads from head to tail: "ROBERT DUNCAN [hollow dot] JESS [hollow dot] [space] [hollow dot] CAESAR'S GATE [hollow dot] [space] SAND DOLLAR [slash] 8." The rear cover is blank.

Published: 600 copies published winter 1973 at $8.50.

Note: Seven copies of the edition were bound in very heavy boards, have headbands and no dust jackets. They are advance copies.

e. *Second edition, first paperbound impression:*

Collation: [1-9]⁸, pp. [1-14], i-xli, [xlii-xliv], xlv-xlix, [xl], ²1-3, [4-6], 7, [8], 9, [10], 11, [12], 13, [14], 15, [16], 17, [18], 19, [20], 21, [22], 23, [24], 25, [26], 27, [28], 29-32, [33-34], 35-37, [38], 39, [40], 41-48, [49-50], 51-54, [55], 56-57, [58], 59-73, [74-80].

Title, Contents, and Text contents the same as second edition, first hardbound impression. These copies are bound in heavy white glossy paper covers with the same collage on the front and the same lettering on the spine as the dust jacket of the first impression. In this impression the signatures have been trimmed to leaves of 21.3 x 16.5 cm. and perfect bound.

Published: 2000 copies were announced as published winter 1963, but only 278 were distributed at $3.75.

f. *Second edition, second paperbound impression:*

Title, Contents, and Text contents and Description the same as second edition, first paperbound impression. The Collation is the same as the second edition, first hardbound impression. The gatherings have been trimmed to leaves of 21.6 x 16.8 and perfect bound. The inking of this impression is darker than the first paperbound impression.

Published: 2000 copies published winter 1973 at $3.75.

Proof papers (NBuU): Since the second edition was produced from the author's typescript, the proof papers consist of the author's typescript as published.

Notes: Both the first and second editions were announced by a flyer, which contained a collage by Jess and the necessary publication information. The following statement by the author appears in the flyer for the second edition: "In the Sand Dollar edition, CAESAR'S GATE stands now as volume three of Robert Duncan's collected poems. Twelve previously uncollected poems have been added to make this definitive book of Poems 1949, together with the entire contents of The Divers Press edition of 1955 with its conglomerate of paste-ups by Jess (with five additional paste-ups from 1955, and one done especially for this edition 1972) and prose poems and preface by Duncan 1955 'illustrating' the earlier work (with a 41 p. Preface 1972, and a 15 p. Postscript including a poem from 1972)." The 12 added poems from 1955 are: FORMS WITHIN FORMS—WHAT HAVE YOU COME TO TELL ME, GARCIA LORCA?—THE VOYAGE OF THE POET INTO THE LAND OF THE DEAD—AT HOME IN EDEN— FROM A SEASON IN HELL—THE CONQUEROR'S SONG—MOVING IN YOUR SIGHTS—WE HAVE LEFT OF COURSE—A GAME OF KINGS—THERE MUST BE A REASON—SEE THE STONE LIONS CRY—BEFORE THE BEAUTIFUL THINGS TURN EVIL—and the poem from 1972 is DESPAIR IN BEING TEDIOUS (1972). The five collages by Jess are FRONTISPIECE—RUMORS—POETIC DISTURBANCES—APPEARANCES—ALTERATIONS—and the collage from 1972 is EMBLEM for the Title-page (1972). In the second edition "THE SECOND NIGHT IN THE WEEK" is mistitled "THE SECOND NIGHT OF THE WEEK" on the Contents-page.

In a letter to Helen Adam, dated 15 July 1955, while the first edition was in preparation, RD wrote: "In writing the poems for the limited edition I turned for the first time since the *Medieval Scenes* to a series of visions— growing from contemplation of the collages done for the book. There are twelve done to date. The special magic of it is that it is a series written to be dispersed—I shall keep no copies of the poems (tho since both Jess and I will have copies of the edition two of the poems will remain with us). Thus each reader of the limited edition will start out with one part of a mysterious map or design. I myself shall have forgotten the nature of the chain. And perhaps see some of the other links, but never all of them. I, myself, will from time to time come across these odd pieces of a riddle. Like a recipe of fourteen pages cut up and sold page by page. In *Medieval Scenes* I 'crossed my eyes' in order to focus upon a group of people sitting around a table. In the *Caesar's Gate* poems I am looking at the order of Jess's collages, them- selves a hidden order."

The publisher of the second edition of this book, Jack Shoemaker, was the owner and operator of Sand Dollar Book Shop. In his advance book cata- logue for 1977, Mr. Shoemaker made the following annotation for the book: "The publication of this book involved us in a dispute with the printer over two factors: the binding on the paperback edition (they promptly fell apart even prior to opening) and the quality of the reproduction of Jess's collages. Obviously, this dispute occurred after we had all 2600 copies in hand. The compromise involved the printer reprinting the entire paperback edition, but we agreed to accept the hardback edition as initially delivered. For this reason, the reproduction of Jess's collages in the paperback edition is, we believe, vastly superior to those in the cloth edition as issued."

A9 **LETTERS** 1958

a. *First edition, paperbound copies:*

Letters, by Robert Duncan | poems mcmliii—mcmlvi [Highlands, North Carolina: Jonathan Williams, 1958].

Collation: [1]¹⁰, [2-4]⁶, [5]⁸; pp. [1-8], i-iv, [9-10], v-vi, [11-66].

Contents: pp. [1-5] blank; p. [6] colophon-page, "This is copy [number written in soft orange (C-50)] of 'Letters' by Robert Duncan, | with five drawings by the author of the ideal reader; | set & printed by Claude Fredericks in Pawlet (Vermont); | published by Jonathan Williams in Highlands (N.C.) | as Jargon fourteen; copyright by the author mcmlviii. | Of dx copies ccccl are on Arches, & lx, signed by the author | & bound by Tony Landreau with the author's endpapers, | are on Shogun"; p. [7] drawing; p. [8] blank; pp. i-iv "preface"; p. [9] drawing; p. [10] blank; pp. v-vi "preface"; p. [11] drawing; p. [12] blank; p. [13] contents-page; p. [14] blank; p. [15] title-page; p. [16] blank; pp. [17-52] text; p. [53] drawing; p. [54] blank; pp. [55-56] text; p. [56] drawing; pp. [57-62] text; p. [62] acknowledgments-page, under the heading "Acknowledgements & Bibliography" four editors and the titles of the magazines, and under the heading "Other books by Robert Duncan" eight titles; p. [63] drawing; pp. [64-66] blank.

Text contents: PREFACE—I FOR A MUSE MEANT (LETTERS FOR DENISE LEVERTOV)—II DISTANT COUNSELS OF ARTAUD (FOR PHILIP LAMANTIA)—III UPON TAKING HOLD (FOR CHARLES OLSON)—IV FIRST INVENTION ON THE THEME OF THE ADAM— V SHORT INVENTION ON THE THEME OF THE ADAM—VI FIGURES OF SPEECH (FOR HELEN ADAM)—VII METAMORPHOSIS— VIII WITH BELLS SHAKING—IX LIGHT SONG (FOR CHARLES OLSON)—X IT'S SPRING. LOVE'S SPRING—XI AT THE END OF A PERIOD (FOR HELEN ADAM)—XII FRAGMENT—XIII TRUE TO LIFE (FOR CHARLES OLSON)—XIV UPON HIS SEEING A BABY HOLDING THE FOUR OF HEARTS FOR HIM AND ANOTHER CARD CONCEALD (FOR ROBERT CREELEY)—XV WORDS OPEN OUT UPON GRIEF—XVI RIDING—XVII AT HOME—XVIII THE HUMAN COMMUNION. TRACES.—XIX PASSAGES OF A SENTENCE—XX RE- (FOR MIKE AND JO ANN MCCLURE)—XXI BROUGHT TO LOVE—XXII TO VOW—XXIII SPELLING THE WORD—XXIV CORRESPONDENCES—XXV AUGUST SUN—XXVI SOURCE—XXVII AN OWL IS AN ONLY BIRD OF POETRY (A VALE

FOR JAMES BROUGHTON)—XXVIII NEW TIDINGS—XXIX CHANGING TRAINS—XXX THE LANGUAGE OF LOVE, SIREN SONG.

Description: The text is printed on yellowish white (C-92) wove paper watermarked "Arches," 28.7 x 18.3 cm., and the gatherings are sewn with white thread. The author's drawings, pages [7], [9], [11], and [53], are on light yellow brown (C-76) rice paper, in deep brown (C-56) ink. The drawing on page [40] is in deep reddish orange (C-36). The gatherings are held together with three sewing tapes of linen and then glued to paper covers of the same stock as the text, which serve as endpapers. The cover wrapper is made from white laid paper marbled in soft orange (C-50), nearly very orange (C-48), light yellow (C-86) and white. A white label, 5.9 x .8 cm., has been pasted on the spine with the lettering in black reading from head to tail at the top of the spine, "LETTERS, BY ROBERT DUNCAN." The front and rear covers are blank.

Published: 450 copies published Nov. 1958 at $8.00.

b. *First edition, hardbound copies, first state:*

Collation: [1]⁴, [2]¹⁰, [3-5]⁶, [6]⁸, [7]⁴; pp. [1-16], i-iv, [17-18], v-vi, [19-82].

Title, Contents, and Text contents the same as First edition, paperbound copies.

Description: The text has been printed on white wove Shogun paper watermarked "Japan," 29.3 x 19.3 cm. An additional gathering of two leaves has been added at the front and rear, with the first leaf of the front gathering and the last leaf of the rear gathering serving as endpapers; they have been included in the collation. The gatherings are held together with three sewing tapes of linen and then glued to the cover. The endpapers have been decorated with black ink drawings by the author, and initialed by him at the front and the rear. The cover is made with stiff boards covered with the same marbled design that formed the wrapper for the paperbound copies. The spine has been covered with brownish black (C-65) leather which extends 1.3 cm. onto the front and rear covers. Lettering stamped in gold (C-82) on the spine reads from head to tail, "LETTERS, BY ROBERT DUNCAN." The copies have been numbered 1-60 in the colophon and signed "Robert Duncan" in black ink below the colophon. All the paperbound copies and an undetermined number of the hardbound copies contain a printing error on page iv of the "preface," lines 2 and 3 from the bottom: "inca-able" for "incapable."

Published: 60 copies published Nov. 1958, but only 45 sold at $12.50.

c. *First edition, hardbound copies, second state:*

Title, Collation, Contents, Text contents, and Description the same as the first state of the hardbound copies except that the printing error on p. iv of the "preface" has been corrected. It cannot be determined how many copies exist in the first and second states.

d. *First edition, hardbound, decorated copies:*

Title, Collation, Contents, Text contents, and Description the same as the hardbound copies except that a drawing in various watercolors, approximately 12 x 15 cm., has been pasted-in on p. [10]. A title appears below the drawing and the initials RD. Both first state and second state copies contain watercolors.

Published: 15 copies published Nov. 1958 at $20.00.

Notes: Claude Fredericks, the printer, in a letter to RD dated 20 Dec. 1957, wrote that the error on page iv was "corrected before most of the special edition was printed." The copy at NBuU is number 26 and is corrected; the copy at MoSW is number 13 and is corrected; but the compiler's copy is number 49 and is not corrected. It cannot be determined if the copies were bound in the exact order they were printed, or numbered in the exact order they were bound or printed. In a letter to the compiler, dated 21 Aug. 1978, Claude Fredericks wrote: "The binding of the hardbound edition was, as you know, not done by Tony Landreau even if the colophon says that it was. Originally Jonathan Williams, who commissioned the book, had told me he wanted Mr. Landreau to do the binding. But this turned out to be one of several misunderstandings between us, and in the end I had the binder who has bound most of my books do it. That was Arno Werner, who has his shop in Pittsfield, Massachusetts. The binding of the small edition, the paperbound edition, was done by me here in Pawlet with the assistance of a friend, Harold Farmer. I have always sewn myself any of the single-signature pamphlets I have issued, but this was the first—and only—time I have ever done an actual binding. Mr. Farmer and I sewed the signatures on a sewing frame and glued them into paper wrappers."

In the advertising flyer for the book, Duncan wrote: "The composition of LETTERS begins with 'Letter to Denise Levertov' and moves out over almost three years' work to complete a book presided over by an alphabet primary to world creation. These angelic letters then those powers hidden or discovered are substances of our speech. A naming of my peers too, and an exclamation of joy: Denise Levertov, Charles Olson, Robert Creeley, James Broughton, Mike McClure, Helen Adam—it is the presence of companions, named and unnamed, that inspires LETTERS. A book of primaries, a book of companions. A book of praises. I have stored here, as best I know how, the song of all I live by. For I adhere to form as the bee obeys the geometry of the hive."

The regular copies were originally to cost $3.50, the signed copies $7.50, and the decorated copies $12.50. The printing of the book took over a year to complete, and in the course of that printing there was a genuine attunement arrived at between poet and printer, when at the beginning of the project there was a great misunderstanding. In a letter to Claude Fredericks, dated

17 Jan. 1958, at the time when the third gathering was being printed, RD wrote: "Your care wins me; as we work together on these proofs it seems more and more to meet the care I have had for the making of the book in the writing. Especially I appreciate certain right instincts you have in correction of the manuscript." By the time the book was distributed, Jonathan Williams had raised the prices to $8.00 for the regular copies, $12.50 for the signed copies, and $20.00 for the decorated copies. There is one curious copy of the book, as Jonathan Williams describes in a letter to RD dated 15 April 1959: "I hold #11 which was sent from the binder back in December. This copy, inadvertently, contains a drawing by Franz Kline. Irene, the Gorgon, grabbed it out of my hands while I was eating at the Cedar Bar one evening on the pretext that she wanted to show it to people who would want to buy several copies. When I walked past the bar on the way out I found Kline (drunk) drawing pictures of Irene the Fair in the book. She told him it was hers, in the great North Beach tradition of responsible citizenship. And when I grabbed it out of her hands, she began screaming that I had stolen her valuable book. That's New York." When this copy was sold by Serendipity Books of Berkeley, California, the drawing by Kline had been removed.

A10 **SELECTED POEMS** 1959

a. *First edition, first issue:*

robert | duncan | selected | poems | [below] THE POCKET POETS SERIES: Number Ten | CITY LIGHTS BOOKS | San Francisco [1959].

Collation: [1]⁴⁰; pp. [1-4], 5-80.

Contents: p. [1] title-page; p. [2] copyright-page, "Library of Congress Catalogue Number: 59-9263 | © 1959 | by | Robert Duncan | [below] The Pocket Poets Series is published by | City Lights Books, 261 Columbus Avenue, | San Francisco 11, and distributed nationally | to bookstores by the Paper Editions Corporation. | Overseas distributor: W. S. Hall & Co."; pp. [3-4] contents-pages; p. [4] nine titles under the heading "BOOKS by ROBERT DUNCAN" and five titles under the heading "Unpublished"; pp. 5-80 text.

Text contents: TOWARD AN AFRICAN ELEGY—KING HAYDN OF MIAMI BEACH—from HEAVENLY CITY, EARTHLY CITY [section-title for following three poems] AMONG MY FRIENDS—SLEEP IS A DEEP AND MANY VOICED FLOOD—IN MEMORY OF TWO WOMEN—from MEDIEVAL SCENES [sequence-title for following eight poems] THE DREAMERS—THE HELMET OF GOLIATH—THE BANNERS—THE KINGDOM OF JERUSALEM—THE FESTIVALS—THE MIRROR—THE REAPER—THE ALBIGENSES—from DOMESTIC SCENES [sequence-title for following six poems] BREAKFAST—BUS FARE—MATCHES—RADIO—ELECTRIC IRON—PIANO—THE HOME-COMING—THE TEMPLE OF THE ANIMALS—from HOMAGE TO

THE BROTHERS GRIMM [section-title for following two poems] THE ROBBER MOON—STRAWBERRIES UNDER THE SNOW—JERUSALEM—THE VENICE POEM [sequence-title for following six poems] DESCRIPTION OF VENICE—TESTIMONY—IMAGINARY INSTRUCTIONS—RECORSO—THE VENUS OF LESPUGES—CODA—from CAESAR'S GATE [section-title for following three poems] THE DRINKING FOUNTAIN—PROCESSIONALS II—THE SECOND NIGHT IN THE WEEK.

Description: The book is printed on pale yellow (ivory) (light C-89) wove stock, 16 x 12.5 cm., and the gathering is stapled three times, but only the ones at the head and the tail attach the signature to the cover. The cover is made of heavy ivory, wove paper. A border of dark brown (C-59), 1.8 cm. at the head, 1.5 cm. at the tail, and 1.4 cm. at each edge runs continuously from front to rear cover. The lettering on the front cover, in ivory, within the border reads "THE POCKET POETS SERIES," while the lettering in the middle white area in dark brown reads "robert | duncan | selected | poems," and below in border in ivory, "NUMBER TEN." Lettering on the spine reads from head to tail in dark brown within the white area, "robert duncan selected poems." "$1.00" in ivory appears in the border at the top on the rear cover, while in the ivory middle area in dark brown lettering appears a sixteen-line statement in two paragraphs about RD and this book. The following notation appears at the bottom of the inside of the rear cover: "Printed at the Press of Villiers Publications Ltd. Ingestre Road, N.W.5, England."

Published: 1500 copies published July 1959 at $1.00.

b. *First edition, second issue:*

Collation: [1-5]⁸; pp. [1-4], 5-79, [80].

Title, Collation, Contents, Text contents, and Description the same as the first issue except that the volume has been sewn with white thread and the gatherings glued to the cover.

Published: 1500 copies published Aug. 1959 at $1.00.

Notes: In a letter to Charles Olson, dated 7 Feb. 1959, RD talked about the formation of the book: "To be independent of publishers! I'm going thru the business now with Ferlinghetti: when he asked for a 'Selected Poems' he was all agreement with my proviso that I would set a minimum text in which contents there would be no change (of 72 pp.) and indicate a maximum text in case he could afford a larger book. Since the text has been finished (a month ago) he is enthusiastic but still writes: 'isn't there anything you could use since 1950? Think it over.' This after my most adamant[,] short of threatening resistance on behalf of the integrity of the contents. As stands *Selected Poems* (1942-1950)—but Ferlinghetti don't want to have them dates—is a solid necessary item, it brings into print poems that were not in volumes before, shows by selection in *Medieval Scenes* and by returning to primary manuscript for text my critical estimate here, and includes in its entirety *The Venice Poem*. I've to set my jaw and my temper until I see it done" (CtU). The book was printed in England by Villiers Publications Ltd., who wire-stitched 1500 copies which were shipped 19 June 1959. RD rejected this binding, and the books were reprinted and bound in signatures.

A single copy of the First edition, second issue, has been rebound in deep orange yellow (C-72) over boards, 17 x 13.5 cm. The front and rear covers are blank, while the following lettering stamped in gold appears on the spine from head to foot: "Robert Duncan Selected Poems." The headbands are deep red (C-13), and the head edges have been painted red. Medium greenish blue (C-173) endpapers and ivory wove flyleaves have been added. It is not known how many copies were rebound in this fashion. The copy described is the compiler's, and no other copy is now known. This binding is not part of the regular publication of the book and is presumed to have been done privately. This copy has been signed by RD on the copyright-page and dated "July 1965."

A11   **THE OPENING OF THE FIELD**   1960

a. *First edition, first impression:*

[in black drawn letters against a white background] The Opening| of the| Field| [in white lettering against a black drawing of a tree] BY | ROBERT | DUNCAN | [photograph of children dancing in a ring set against a line drawing of a playground] [in white letters on black] GROVE| PRESS| NEW| YORK [1960].

Collation: [1-3]¹⁶; pp. [1-6], 7-96.

Contents: p. [1] half-title-page, "The Opening of the Field"; p. [2] ten titles under the heading "Also by Robert Duncan," and at the bottom, "Title-page especially designed for the author by Jess Collins," followed by an arrow pointing right; p. [3] title-page; p. [4] copyright and acknowledgments-page, "Copyright © 1960 by Robert Duncan | Library of Congress Catalog Card Number: 60-12562 | First Printing | "Some of the poems included in this volume have | appeared in the following periodicals [eighteen titles] | Distributed in Canada by | McClelland & Stewart Ltd., 25 Hollinger Road, Toronto 16 | MANUFACTURED IN THE UNITED STATES OF AMERICA"; pp. [5-6] contents-pages; pp. 7-96 text.

Text contents: OFTEN I AM PERMITTED TO RETURN TO A MEADOW—THE DANCE—THE LAW I LOVE IS MAJOR MOVER—THE STRUCTURE OF RIME I—THE STRUCTURE OF RIME II—A POEM SLOW BEGINNING—THE STRUCTURE OF RIME III—THE STRUCTURE OF RIME IV—THE STRUCTURE OF RIME V—THE STRUCTURE OF RIME VI—THE STRUCTURE OF RIME VII—

THREE PAGES FROM A BIRTHDAY BOOK—THIS PLACE RUMORD TO HAVE BEEN SODOM—THE BALLAD OF THE ENAMORD MAGE—THE BALLAD OF MRS NOAH—THE MAIDEN—(THE PROPOSITIONS)—FOUR PICTURES OF THE REAL UNIVERSE—EVOCATION—OF BLASPHEMY—NOR IS THE PAST PURE—CROSSES OF HARMONY AND DISHARMONY—A POEM OF DESPONDENCIES—POETRY, A NATURAL THING—KEEPING THE RHYME—A SONG OF THE OLD ORDER—THE QUESTION—THE PERFORMANCE WE WAIT FOR—AT CHRISTMAS—PROOFS— YES, AS A LOOK SPRINGS TO ITS FACE—YES, AS A LOOK SPRINGS TO ITS FACE—A POEM BEGINNING WITH A LINE BY PINDAR—THE STRUCTURE OF RIME VIII—THE STRUCTURE OF RIME IX—THE STRUCTURE OF RIME X—THE STRUCTURE OF RIME XI—A STORM OF WHITE—ATLANTIS—OUT OF THE BLACK—BONE DANCE—UNDER GROUND—THE NATURAL DOCTRINE—THE STRUCTURE OF RIME XII—THE STRUCTURE OF RIME XIII—ANOTHER ANIMADVERSION—THE INBINDING—MIRRORS—A PROCESS—RETURNING TO ROOTS OF FIRST FEELING—AFTER READING *BARELY AND WIDELY*—INGMAR BERGMAN'S *SEVENTH SEAT*—FOOD FOR FIRE, FOOD FOR THOUGHT.

Description: The text is printed on pale yellow (ivory) (light C-89) wove paper, 20.3 x 13.7 cm., and the gatherings are sewn with white thread and then glued to the paper cover. The cover is made from yellowish white (C-92) stock, 20.3 x 13.7 cm. At the head of the front cover in black drawn letters appears "The Opening of the Field | by Robert Duncan." In the middle is a design with splashes of brilliant bluish green (C-159) and light bluish green (bluer than C-163), and below that is an enlarged version of the photograph of children dancing that appears on the title-page. Printed at the far right edge, reading from tail to head is the following: "EVERGREEN ORIGINAL E 275 $1.45 (U. K. 10/6d.) [publisher's logo]." The lettering down the spine reads from head to tail, "THE OPENING OF THE FIELD [in bluish green] BY ROBERT DUNCAN [publisher's logo] [in black] E-275 [in bluish green] GROVE PRESS." The rear cover is solidly bluish green with the printing in ivory and black: [top left] "EVERGREEN ORIGINAL [publisher's logo] [space] E-275 [dash] $1.45 | U.K. 10/6d | In Canada: 20¢ additional. [in ivory] THE OPENING OF THE FIELD | BY | ROBERT DUNCAN." Three paragraphs about RD and his work follow, the first of which contains a quotation from RD, the second of which is generally historical, and the third of which consists of a sixteen line statement by Kenneth Rexroth. Below the statements: "Cover design by Roy Kuhlman | [in white] GROVE PRESS, INC., 64 University Place, New York 3, N.Y. | Evergreen Books Ltd., 17 Sackville St., London, W.1. | [in black] Distributed in Canada by McClelland & Stewart Ltd., 25 Hollinger Road, Toronto 16."

Published: 3000 copies published Oct. 1960 at $1.45 and 10 | 6d.

b. *First edition, second impression:*

Title, Collation, Contents, and Text contents the same as the first impression, but the copyright-page has been changed to read, "First Evergreen Edition 1960 | Second Printing." The reference to Canadian distributor has been dropped. In this impression the design on the title-page has been moved .6 cm. to the right, leaving a margin of .5 cm. at the gutter and a margin of .5 cm. at the right edge. The design has also been raised, leaving a .8 cm. margin at the tail. The inking on the title-page is lighter than on the first impression. The rear cover has also been changed. There is now a rectangle, 16.2 x 10.2 cm., solidly bluish green which contains the same three paragraphs as on the rear cover of the first impression, but with the deletion of the inaccurate information "he later edited *Phoenix*" from lines 6-7 of the second paragraph. There is an ivory border around the central bluish green block. The lettering in bluish green in the top border reads: "EVERGREEN ORIGINAL [publisher's logo] [space] [in black] E-275 [dash] $1.45 | U.K.: 10/6d." On some copies examined, a paper label with the price "$1.75" has been pasted over "$1.45." Lettering at the bottom, inside the block reads: "GROVE PRESS, INC., 64 University Place, New York 3, N.Y. | EVERGREEN BOOKS LTD., 20 New Bond St., London, W.l." In the margin at the lower right, the notation "ii" is printed as an indication of the second impression.

Published: 1800 copies published Feb. 1961 at $1.45 and 10/6d.

c. *First edition, third impression:*

Title, Collation, Contents, Text contents, and Description the same as second impression except that the copyright-page now reads, "First Evergreen Edition 1960." The design on the title-page has been made flush with the gutter and the tail of the p., as in the first impression, but the .5 cm. margin at the right edge of the second impression has been maintained. The photograph of the children dancing in a ring on the title-page has been brought forward and its focus sharpened. The inking on the title-page is darker than on the second impression. The design of the rear cover is the same, except for the following changes: lettering in bluish green at the head in the margin reads, "EVERGREEN ORIGINAL [publisher's logo] [space] E-275 [dash] $1.75." Lettering at the tail inside the bluish green block reads, "GROVE PRESS, INC., 80 University Place, New York, N.Y. 10003." The notation "iii" appears in the margin at the lower right as an indication of the third impression.

Published: 2000 copies published June 1966 at $1.75.

d. *First edition, fourth impression:*

Title, Collation, Contents, Text contents, and Description the same as the third impression except that the copyright-page now reads, "First Evergreen Edition 1960 | Fourth printing." The rear cover is the same as the third impression except that the notation "iv" appears in the margin at the lower right.

Published: 3000 copies published Feb. 1968 at $1.75.

e. ***First edition, fifth impression:***

Title, Collation, Contents, Text contents, and Description the same as the fourth impression except that the copyright-page now reads, "First Evergreen Edition 1960 | Fifth printing." The following passage has been added to the copyright-page after the list of periodical titles: "No part of this book may be reproduced | for any reason, by any means including | any method of photographic reproduction, | without the permission of the publishers." There has been a change in the lettering on the front cover, to read, "EVERGREEN ORIGINAL E-574-T $1.95," and the title and author in RD's holograph have been changed to block letters. The same changes in number and price appear at the head of the rear cover, and the color of the printing at the top and in the solid block has been changed to brilliant greenish blue (C-168). The notation "v" appears at the lower right in the margin as an indication of the fifth impression. And there has been a change of address to "Grove Press, Inc., 53 East 11th Street, New York, New York 10003" at the bottom of the printed block.

Published: 2000 copies published March 1971 at $1.95.

f. ***First edition, sixth impression, first issue:***

Collation: pp. [1-6], 7-96.

Title, Contents, Text contents, and Description the same as the fifth impression except that the copyright-page now reads, "First Evergreen Edition 1960 | Sixth Printing." The following line has been added to the copyright page after the notice of restriction about reproduction: "DISTRIBUTED BY RANDOM HOUSE, INC., NEW YORK." The text has been printed on a lightweight paper stock, the gatherings trimmed to 20.2 x 13.1 cm., and a perfect binding used. A change in price from $1.95 to $2.45 appears on the front cover and at the head of the rear cover. The lettering and the solid block have been changed to brilliant bluish green (C-159). The notation "vi" does not appear in the margin at the lower right, but the numbers "394-17301-5" appear in the bottom margin at the right. Ms. Sarah Uman of Grove Press, in a letter to the compiler dated 20 May 1976, wrote: "Please note that the sixth printing was the First Random House Edition." Some of the copies examined contain the logo of Random House stamped in red (C-16) on the top edges of the leaves.

Published: 2655 copies published March 1973 at $2.45.

g. ***First edition, sixth impression, second issue:***

Title, Collation, Contents, Text contents, and Description the same as the sixth impression, first issue, except that a white label has been pasted over the bottom of the bluish green rectangle and reads: "NEW DIRECTIONS, 333 SIXTH AVENUE, NEW YORK, N. Y. 10014."

Published: 345 copies published Dec. 1976 at $2.45.

h. *First sub-edition, first impression:*

[in holograph] The Opening | of the | Field | [in white lettering against a black drawing of a tree] BY | ROBERT | DUNCAN | [photograph of children dancing in a ring set against a line drawing of a playground] [at bottom, in white lettering] A New Directions Book [New York 1973].

Contents: p. [1] half-title, "The Opening of the Field"; p. [2] seven titles under the heading "Other books by Robert Duncan" and at the bottom, "Title page especially designed for the author by Jess"; p. [3] title-page, same as First edition, first impression, except that there is a .3 cm. margin at the right edge and a .2 cm. margin at the gutter, and the lettering in white, "A New Directions Book," now appears at lower right; p. [4] copyright-page, "Copyright © 1960 by Robert Duncan | Library of Congress Catalog Card Number 72-93976 | (ISBN: 0-8112-0480-4) | All rights reserved. Except for brief passages quoted in a | newspaper, magazine, radio or television review, no part of this | book may be reproduced in any form or by any means, electronic | or mechanical, including photocopying and recording, or by any | information storage and retrieval system, without permission in | writing from the Publisher." | [eighteen titles under the heading] "Some of these poems first appeared in the following periodicals" | "First published by Grove Press in 1960 | First published as New Directions Paperbook 356 in 1973 | Published simultaneously in Canada by McClelland & Stewart, Ltd. | Manufactured in the United States of America | New Directions Books are published for James Laughlin | by New Directions Publishing Corporation | 333 Sixth Avenue, New York 10014"; pp. [5-6] contents-page; pp. 7-96 text.

Collation, Text contents, and Description (except as follows below) the same as First edition, first impression.

Cover: The cover is made from heavy yellowish white (C-92) wove stock, 20.2 x 13.2 cm. On the front cover a reproduction of a black-and-white photograph of a field with oak trees on a ridge in the distance, 12.9 x 13.1 cm., appears on the lower portion of the cover, while at the top in large lettering "ROBERT | DUNCAN | [and in smaller lettering] The Opening of the Field" appears. Lettering down the spine reads from head to tail "ROBERT DUNCAN [space] THE OPENING OF THE FIELD [space] NDP356." The lettering on the rear cover reads, beginning at top left, "POETRY [slash] (ISBN: 0-8112-0480-4) | [in large lettering] ROBERT | DUNCAN | [in smaller lettering] THE OPENING OF THE FIELD." There are two paragraphs about RD and this book, the first of which begins with the same sentence that composed the first paragraph on the rear of the First edition. The remaining nine lines (for a total of eleven) give information about the author and the book and cite "[The] Structure of

Rime I." The second paragraph of six lines is a revision of the second paragraph of the statement on the rear of the First edition. A five line quotation by Gilbert Sorrentino (cited from *Poetry*) then follows. The remaining lines are as follows: [in brackets] "Other ND Paperbooks By Robert Duncan: *Bending the Bow,* NDP255, | $2.25, and *Roots and Branches,* NDP275, $1.75.| Cover photograph by George A. Tice; design by Gertrude Huston| A NEW DIRECTIONS PAPERBOOK [space] NDP356 [space] $2.45."

Published: 3010 copies published 25 April 1973 at $2.45.

i. *First sub-edition, second impression:*

Title, Collation, Contents, Text contents, and Description the same as First edition, first impression except that the gatherings have been trimmed to 20.2 x 13. cm. and a lighter paper stock used. "SECOND PRINTING" has been added to the copyright-page and at the top right of the rear cover. The price at the lower right of the rear cover has been changed to $3.75.

Published: 1101 copies published 11 April 1977 at $3.75.

j. *First sub-edition, third impression:*

Title, Collation, Contents, Text contents, and Description the same as First edition, first impression except that "THIRD PRINTING" appears at the top right corner of the rear cover and on the copyright-page. The following information has been added to the rear cover after "Other ND Paper books by Robert Duncan:" "About Robert Duncan: Robert Duncan: SCALES OF THE MARVELOUS, NDP 487, $5.95." The price at the lower corner of the rear cover has been changed to $4.25. On the page facing the title-page, p. [2], eleven titles now appear under the heading "ALSO BY ROBERT DUNCAN," and *"Robert Duncan: Scales of the Marvelous* (Edited by Robert J. Bertholf and Ian W. Reid)" appears under the heading "ABOUT ROBERT DUNCAN." The word "maiden's," line 9, p. 28, has been corrected to "maidens." and "maidens," line 13, p. 28, has been corrected to "maiden's."

Published: 2000 copies published 5 Nov. 1980 at $4.95.

k. *First English edition:*

ROBERT DUNCAN | The Opening of | the Field | [below] [publisher's logo] JONATHAN CAPE | THIRTY BEDFORD SQUARE | LONDON [1969].

Collation: [A]⁸, B-F⁸; pp. [1-6], 7-96.

Contents: p. [1] half-title-page, "The Opening of | the Field"; p. [2] eleven titles listed under the heading "By the same author"; p. [3] title-page; p. [4] copyright and acknowledgments-page, "First published in Great Britain 1969 | © by Robert Duncan | Jonathan Cape Ltd, 30 Bedford Square,

London, WCI | SBN 224 61627 7" | [eighteen titles under the heading] "Some of the poems in the volume have appeared | in the following periodicals | Printed in Great Britain by | Lowe & Brydone (Printers) Ltd, London | on paper made by John Dickinson & Co. Ltd | bound by A. W. Bain & Co. Ltd, London"; pp. [5-6] contents-pages; pp. 7-96 text.

Text contents: the same as First edition, first impression.

Description: The text has been reproduced by offset lithography on yellowish white (C-92) Bedford Antique Woven paper, 21.6 x 14.5 cm., and the signatures sewn with white thread and glued to the spine. The covers are made from pale greenish yellow (C-104) paper dappled with medium yellow (C-87) over heavy boards, 22.2 x 14.8 cm. The spine binding, made of brown black (C-65) elephant hide, extends 1.5 cm. onto the front and rear covers. Both the front and rear covers are blank. Lettering on the spine in very yellow (C-82) reads from tail to head, "[publisher's logo] [space] THE OPENING OF THE FIELD [decorated rule] ROBERT DUNCAN."

Dust jacket: The dust jacket is made from white (C-263) paper printed on the front, spine, and rear covers in red (C-12) and black in one continuous scene. There is a sun at the rear which shines across a landscape, and there is a figure at the point where a rainbow hits the ground looking into the world on the other side of the rainbow. In white on front cover at top: "The Opening of the Field | Robert Duncan." Lettering on the spine reads from tail to head, "[publisher's logo] The Opening of the Field Robert Duncan." The front flap contains a three paragraph statement of 39 lines about this book, drafted by Nathaniel Tarn but not so stated, while the final three lines read: "25s net | [rule] | IN UK ONLY | [rule] £1.25 net." The rear flap contains the titles of four books under the heading "LOUIS ZUKOFSKY," and below the final three lines: "SBN 224 61627 7 | Jacket design by Leigh Taylor | © Jonathan Cape, Ltd, 1979."

Proof copy: Title, Collation, Contents, and Text contents the same as the trade copies. This copy is paperbound with a stiff wrapper in a deep pink (C-3) exterior design accented with the logo of the publisher in white. A paper label, 12.5 x 12.5 cm., has been pasted on the front cover which contains the same blurb which appears on the front inside flap of the dust jacket of the trade copies, plus the notation "25s October." The number of proof copies has not been determined.

Published: an unknown number of copies published 9 Oct. 1969 at £1.25. In a letter to the compiler, dated 11 Aug. 1978, the publisher declined to disclose the number of copies printed.

Notes: The First edition, first impression, contained the following printing errors which were corrected in the second impression, but returned in the third impression and remained in the text until the first Sub-edition, third impression as noted above: p. 28, line 9, "holds particular maiden's" should read "holds particular maidens"; and p. 28, line 13, "when in an elderly maidens face" should read "when in an elderly maiden's face." The second error was corrected in the English edition, but not the first.

In a statement dated 31 Jan. 1958 as part of an application for a grant from the Guggenheim Foundation, RD made the following comment about his book, then in progress: "Begun in January 1956, the book was originally conceived as consisting of about fifty poems radiating from the image and the idea of a field, and, where inspired, from the Field Itself— known intimately as the given field of my own life, intellectually as the field of the language (or spirit), and imaginatively as the field given to Man (of many languages). I had estimated that three years would be dedicated to adoration and study of the Field, with the book as Testimony as best as I could write such a record" (CU-B). As the typescripts indicate, the book was originally entitled *The Field*. The book was first submitted to Wesleyan University Press for publication, but was rejected, as RD says in a letter to Robert Creeley, dated 27 Aug. 1959: "And the typescripts of *The Field* have won some new friends. Norman Holmes Pearson who was on the board at Wesleyan Press that turned down the book has been most affirmative about the work, and after *Selected Poems* sent a check for twenty-five dollars to me 'I had a little wind-fall and would you accept the enclosed check' to buy a drink in celebration" (on deposit at MoSW).

In 1959, the manuscript was submitted to the Macmillan Company, where M. L. Rosenthal was a reader, and accepted, which RD reported in a letter to Robin Blaser, dated 15 Aug. 1959: "MacMillan has taken *The Field*, with an offer of $150 in advance on royalties when I sign the contract" (CU-B). The book was set in type, and proofs were sent to RD, who returned his corrections along with some "General Remarks" about spacing, margins, and long lines, dated 27 Aug. 1959. The following comment about internal margins was entered as point "ii": "Many poems have inner lines with established inner margins. Beginning from the left these will be referrd to as first, second, and—where it appears—third inner margin.
ex. in poem #2:

> our articulations, our
> ⎸　　⎸measures.
> It is⎸the joy⎸that exceeds pleasure.
> 　　⎸You have passd the count, she said
> first　　second
> inner　　inner
> margin　margin

The first and second margins should be standardized (in the typescript they vary) according to the taste of the typographer. The third inner margin where it occurs depends upon aligning certain elements in the poems that are related in measure and meaning so that their interrelation is evident to the eye" (NSyU).

Even with this sort of precise typesetting and proofreading, there was a change of plans, and the book was not brought into print. By 12 Nov. 1959, Barney Rosset of Grove Press had read the manuscript (at this point it was Denise Levertov's copy), and through Donald Allen had expressed an interest in printing the book. The correspondence between RD and Donald Allen was an informal one, and though both parties agreed to the publication of the book, no formal contract was signed; as late as 14 Jan. 1960, the original manuscript and the corrected proofs had not been delivered to Grove from Macmillan. In February 1960, a disagreement arose between Duncan and Grove (RD corresponded with Dick Seaver) over the cover of the book, originally designed by Jess Collins. In a letter dated 23 Feb. 1960, RD wrote the following to Dick Seaver: "For you the cover of a book—even when it is closely allied as the cover of a paperbook is (as distinguished from the jacket on a hardbound book) to be integral to the whole—is a question of attractive packaging of a commodity. I have had occasion before and shall always have to attack at its roots what art becomes when it becomes a commodity. Today painting has all but become slave to the designs of a market where Picassos[,] De Koonings or The New York School are analogous as conspicuous expenditures to Jaguars, and whatever fancy cars. Style must be like a signature on a check, unique but dependably recognizable = cash value. Now, while in the late forties and early fifties I had a direct relation to what is rightly calld "action" painting— it was not then the commodity action painting, but a living movement. And, more importantly, since 1952 I have in ... [my] own work developed affinities with a view of the world that is—to use Whitehead's word— 'illustrated' by what we see. The structure of correspondence and melody is not only poorly but falsely allied with the come-on derived from the action strokes of so-called nature expressionists. If you think over what as a poet I come in *The Opening of the Field* to show nature to be, you may reflect that there is an incompatibility between the content and the dominant taste in Madison Avenue art. I don't live in New York, I live in a little town on the pacific coast; my household is not modern; it thrives, as the imagination thrives, upon images. So I had designd a cover in a mode close to my own work, where words and scene, image and experience have something like the exchange I seek in my medium" (NSyU). In a letter to Charles Olson, dated 7 March 1960, RD wrote that Grove "wouldn't take Jess's design for the cover" and "the deal is kaputt" for publishing the book (CtU). Later that month, RD reported to Robert Creeley in a letter dated 19 March 1960: "Finally, after completely breaking off over Jess's cover, Grove offerd a compromise deal on publishing the book—where Jess's cover design will be used as frontispiece; and their own design however they want it as the cover of the paperback—and I accepted" (on deposit at MoSW). By 23 June 1960, the dispute had been fully resolved and RD wrote again to Dick Seaver, this time returning the proofread galleys and a "final summary of marked points" (NSyU).

The book was published in October 1960. In a letter to Marilyn Meeker, Associate Editor at Grove, dated 12 Oct. 1960, RD wrote: "Thank you for sending on directly the advance copy of *The Opening of the Field*. First, may I note that the outside cover design, which I was prepared not to like (from the sample you had sent me some time ago), pleases me. Are the strokes of texture and the colors somewhat different from the sample you sent? And it is most pleasing to think of the book being there at last. I am aware too of the work and attention it has taken on the part of the Grove Press staff" (NSyU). The photograph by Paul Popper of the children dancing in a ring which appears on the title-page, and which appears on the front cover, was first published in Lewis Spence's *Myth and Ritual in Dance, Game and Rhyme* (London: Watts & Co., 1947), facing p. 88.

The first and second issues of the sixth impression resulted from a complicated series of events. Before March 1973, the Grove Press fifth impression was declared out of print, at which time the publication rights reverted to RD; New Directions then prepared an offset impression, which appeared 25 April 1973. In the meantime, despite the arrangements made with New Directions, the book was reprinted as the "First Random House Edition" (letter to the compiler from Sarah Uman of Grove Press, 6 May 1976). One thousand copies of the impression were remaindered by Random House and 345 copies sold to New Directions, which added its own label on the rear cover (letter to the compiler from Frederick Martin of New Directions, 8 April 1977).

A single copy of the First edition, first impression, has been rebound in dark greenish blue (approximately C-174) cloth over boards, 20.8 x 14.1 cm. The front and rear covers are blank, while the following lettering stamped in very yellow appears on the spine from head to foot, "Robert Duncan The Opening of the Field." The headbands are deep red (C-13), and the head edges have been painted red. White textured endpapers and white wove flyleaves have been added. The copy described is the compiler's, and it is not known how many copies were rebound in this fashion. This binding is not part of the regular publication of the book and is presumed to have been done privately.

A12   **AS TESTIMONY**   1964

a. *First edition, first impression:*

[inside a rectangle, 15.3 x 10.1 cm., printed over in reddish brown (approximately C-40) with a thick black (C-267) border] [in black] AS TESTIMONY: | THE POEM & | THE SCENE | [short rule] Robert Duncan | [short rule] | [in reddish brown below rectangle] white rabbit press san francisco [1964].

Collation: [1]^{12}; pp. [i-iv], 1-20.

Contents: p. [i] blank; p. [ii] copyright-page, "copyright 1964 by Robert Duncan | [short rule] printed in u.s.a. | [short rule] | white rabbit press box 2836 san francisco"; p. [iii] title-page; p. [iv] blank; pp. 1-20 text.

Text contents: THE "DOOR" POEM, by Harold Dull—THE "MAZE" POEM, by Joanne Kyger—NOTE—AS TESTIMONY: THE POEM & THE SCENE [an essay].

Description: The text is printed on yellowish white (C-92) wove paper, 23.3 x 15.2 cm., and the gathering is stapled twice to a light yellow brown (approximately C-76) paper cover of the same dimensions. The front cover contains the lettering in black, "AS TESTIMONY [short rule] Robert Duncan," while the rear cover contains the logo of the White Rabbit Press.

Published: 350 copies published summer 1964 at $1.50.

b. *First edition, second impression:*

[inside a rectangle, 15.1 x 10.1 cm., printed over in brown orange (approximately C-54) with a thin black border in black] [in black] AS TESTIMONY: | [in italics] the poem & the scene | [short expanded rule] | Robert Duncan | [short expanded rule] [below the rectangle in brown orange] white rabbit press: san francisco [1966].

Collation: [1]¹⁴; pp. [i-ii], 1-10, [iii-vi], 11-20, [21-22].

Contents: p. [i] title; p. [ii] copyright-page, "COPYRIGHT 1964 & 1966 by ROBERT DUNCAN"; pp. 1-10 text; pp. [iii-vi] four photographs; pp. 11-20 text; p. [21] colophon-page, [logo of White Rabbit Press] | "First printed in Summer, 1964, in an edition of | 350 copies. Second printing in January, 1966, | in an edition of 500 copies. Designed & printed at | the White Rabbit Press by Graham Mackintosh | [dot] | 24 Allen Street [dash] San Francisco"; p. [22] blank.

Text contents: same as first impression.

Description: The text is printed on white (C-92) wove paper, 23.2 x 15 cm., and the gathering is stapled twice to a light yellow brown (approximately C-76) paper cover of the same dimensions. Lettering on the front cover reads, "AS TESTIMONY | [rule] | Robert Duncan," while the rear cover is blank. Between pages 10 and 11, two leaves of glossy paper have been inserted and four photographs reproduced as follows: (1) Dora Dull and Tom Field; (2) Harold Dull, Joanne Kyger, and George Stanley; (3) Robert Duncan; (4) Duncan, Ebbe Borregaard and Jack Spicer.

Published: 1000 copies published in 1971 at $2.00.

A13   **WRITING WRITING**   1964

a. *First edition, regular copies:*

[cover title] [line drawing in RD's holograph: circle at upper right, then in a half-circle] writing writing | [curved line below] a composition book | [as part of line drawing] Robert Duncan | [as

part of line drawing] FOR MADISON 1953 | STEIN IMITA-
TIONS [Albuquerque, New Mexico: Sumbooks, 1964].

Collation: [1]³⁰; pp. [1-60].

Contents: p. [1] blank; p. [2] copyright-page, "Copyright 1964 by Robert
Duncan. | First Printing. | Title-page and cover illustrations by | the author. |
[below] SUMBOOKS, Spring, 1964."; p. [3] dedication-page, [in RD's
holograph] "Dedication | For the love of Gertrude Stein | in which I labord
to write in | whose mode; | and for Lynn | Brockway and Jess who found |
pleasure in some of these pieces | of writing-like-Stein. | Robert Duncan |
April 1964"; p. [4] [as part of line drawing] section-title, "FIRST | A
PREFACE"; pp. [5-7] text; p. [8] blank; p. [9] [circle at right] [in holograph
in half-circle] section-title, "writing writing"; p. [10] blank; pp. 11-23 text; p.
[24] blank; p. [25] section-title, "appendix one | ESSAYS | AND | TRY-
OUTS | [line drawing] [signature-emblem] RD"; p. [26] blank; pp. [27-35]
text; p. [36] blank; p. [37] section-title, "appendix two | POETICS: | [line
drawing] | [signature-emblem] RD"; p. [38] blank; pp. [39-58] text; p. [59]
blank; p. [60] colophon-page, "May, 1964. An edition of 375 copies of which
| 25 copies are signed, with an original drawing | by the author. | Published
by SUMBOOKS in Albuquerque, New Mexico."

Text contents: TURNING INTO—COMING OUT OF—MAKING UP—
OUT—A SCENE—THE BEGINNING OF WRITING—IMAGINING IN
WRITING—WRITING AS WRITING—POSSIBLE POETRIES: A
PRELUDE—POSSIBLE POETRIES: A POSTSCRIPT—POSSIBLE
POETRIES: A POSTSCRIPT—AN IMAGINARY LETTER—IMAGI-
NARY LETTER—IMAGINARY LETTER—MOTTO—DIVISION—
WRITING AT HOME IN HISTORY—I AM NOT AFRAID—AN
INTERLUDE. OF RARE BEAUTY—HUNG-UP—THE CODE OF
JUSTINIAN. A DISCOURSE ON JUSTICE—THE DISCOURSE ON
SIN—A POEM IN STRETCHING—DESCRIPTIONS OF IMAGINARY
POETRIES—SMOKING THE CIGARETTE—RHYME MOUNTAIN
PARTICULAR—AN ADVERTISEMENT FOR A FAIR PLAY—PROGRES-
SING—THIS IS THE POEM THEY ARE PRAISING AS LOADED—
ORCHARDS—A TRAIN OF THOUGHT—THE FEELING OF
LANGUAGE IN POETRY—SENTENCES: CARRYING WEIGHTS
AND MEASURES—THERE COULD BE A BOOK WITHOUT NATIONS
IN ITS CHAPTERS—6/16/53—6/22/53—6/27—REWRITING BYRON—
A MORASS—CANVAS COMING INTO ITSELF. FOR JESS—HOW DO
YOU KNOW YOU ARE THRU?—INCREASING—ROAD PIECE—
ROTUND RELIGION—THREE—SEVERAL POEMS. IN PROSE—
RINGS—SYLLABLES—STUFF ARK MOWER BOTTLE—ANOTHER
I DO.

Description: The typewritten and holograph text has been reproduced by
mimeograph on pale yellow (ivory) (C-89) paper, 22.7 x 17.5 cm. The
gathering is stapled three times, but only the ones at the head and the tail

attach the gathering to the cover. The cover is made from heavy brilliant blue (C-177) stock, 22.7 x 17.5 cm., with a cover title as described above; the rear cover is blank. One additional sheet folded to produce two leaves, 22.7 x 17.5 cm., printed verso first leaf and recto second leaf with 14 errata, and one additional poem, "A Birthday Dirge for Lynne Brown," is laid-in inside the front cover.

Published: 350 copies published May 1964 at $1.00.

b. *First edition, signed and illustrated copies:*

Title, Collation, Contents, Text contents, and Description the same as regular copies, except that RD's signature appears on the colophon-page along with an original crayon drawing, in various colors in each copy. The copies are numbered 1-25.

Published: 25 copies published May 1964 at an undetermined price.

c. *First sub-edition:*

Title, Collation, Contents, Text contents, and Description the same as the First edition except that the copyright-page reads: "© Copyright 1964, 1971 by Robert Duncan | First Trask House Printing | Title page and cover illustrations by | the author. | Originally printed by SUMBOOKS | Spring, 1964 | [below] Publication of this volume is made possible | by a grant from the National Endowment | for the Arts | Portland, Oregon: TRASK HOUSE, Inc., 1971," and the following appears inside the rear cover: "Published in an edition of one thousand copies | by | Carlos Reyes | at TRASK [space] HOUSE." The text is reproduced from plates made from the first edition on light yellow brown (light C-76) wove paper, with a cover of light blue (C-181), both 22.7 x 17.5 cm. The gathering is stapled to the rear cover with two staples.

Published: 1000 copies published in 1971 at $2.00.

Notes: Initially, the book was called *A Copy Book*, as RD wrote in a letter to Robert Creeley, dated 11 Sept. 1955: "About a week ago or so I sent off the first installment of *writing writing*, now to be calld *A COPY BOOK*" (on deposit at MoSW). And after the first edition of the volume, RD wrote to Henry Wenning in a letter dated 28 July 1964: "I'd said I wanted it to look like a school bluebook or exercise book" (MoSW).

A14   **ROOTS AND BRANCHES**   1964

a. *First edition, hardbound copies:*

ROOTS AND | BRANCHES | Poems by ROBERT DUNCAN | [below] CHARLES SCRIBNER'S SONS [dot] NEW YORK [1964].

Collation: [1-6]¹⁶; pp. [i-viii], ix-xi, [xii], [1-2], 3-69, [70-72], 73-176, [177-180].

Contents: p. [i] half-title-page [three decorated short rules at top right], "ROOTS AND BRANCHES"; p. [ii] blank; p. [iii] ten titles under the heading *"ALSO BY ROBERT DUNCAN"*; p. [iv] blank; p. [v] title-page; p. [vi] copyright-page, "COPYRIGHT © 1964 ROBERT DUNCAN | This book published simultaneously in the | United States of America and in Canada [dash] | Copyright under the Berne Convention | [rights statement in italics] All rights reserved. No part of this book | may be reproduced in any form without the | permission of Charles Scribner's Sons. | A-8.64[C] | PRINTED IN THE UNITED STATES OF AMERICA | [in italics] Library of Congress Catalog Card Number 64-24233"; p. [vii] acknowledgments-page, eighteen editors and magazines listed under the heading, "The author would like to thank the following editors for their appreciation . . ."; p. [viii] blank; pp. ix-xi contents-pages; p. [xii] blank; p. [1] section-title, "ROOTS AND BRANCHES"; p. [2] blank; pp. 3-69 text; p. [70] blank; p. [71] section-title, "WINDINGS"; p. [72] blank; pp. 73-176 text; pp. [177-180] blank.

Text contents: ROOTS AND BRANCHES (1959-60) [section-title] ROOTS AND BRANCHES—WHAT DO I KNOW OF THE OLD LORE?—NIGHT SCENES—A SEQUENCE OF POEMS FOR H.D.'S 73RD BIRTHDAY [sequence-title for six numbered poems] 1. DREAM DATA—2. "I MUST WAKE UP INTO THE MORNING WORLD" (fl)—3. "FATHER ADOPTED AND FATHER OF MY SOUL" (fl)—4. "THE GIST OF THE STORY . . ." (fl)—5. "O BE A NURSE TO ME AND TELL ME ONCE AGAIN" (fl)—6. "LADY, I HAVE HEARD NEWS OF YOU ONCE MORE" (fl)—A LETTER—NEL MEZZO DEL CAMMIN DI NOSTRA VITA—A DANCING CONCERNING A FORM OF WOMEN—THE LAW—APPREHENSIONS [sequence-title for five numbered poems] 1. "TO OPEN NIGHT'S EYE . . ." (fl)—2. THE DIRECTIVE—"I FOUND A MONUMENT OF WHAT I AM" (fl)—3. "DREAM OR VISION . . ." (fl)—"THEY HAD TAKEN HIM OUT OF TIME" (fl)—4. (STRUCTURE OF RIME XIV): "CIRE PERDUE . . ." (fl)—5. FIRST POEM. "IT IS THE EARTH TURNING . . ." (fl)—SECOND POEM. "HANDLE THE CARDS . . ." (fl)—CLOSE. "MARCH 27TH . . ." (fl)—SONNERIES OF THE ROSE CROSS—NOW THE RECORD NOW RECORD—VARIATIONS ON TWO DICTA OF WILLIAM BLAKE [sequence-title for seven numbered poems] 1. "THE AUTHORS ARE IN ETERNITY" (fl)—2. "HOW LONG DARE I WITHHOLD MYSELF" (fl)—3. "I AM THE AUTHOR OF THE AUTHORS" (fl)—4. "COME, EYES, SEE MORE THAN YOU SEE" (fl)—5. "MENTAL THINGS ALONE ARE REAL" (fl)—6. "FOR THE HEART, MY SISTER" (fl)—7. "THERE WAS THE EVENT THERE WAS" (fl)—COVER IMAGES—COME, LET ME FREE MYSELF—RISK—FOUR SONGS THE NIGHT NURSE SANG [sequence-title for four numbered poems] 1. "HOW LOVELY ALL THAT GLITTERS" (fl)—2. "IT MUST BE THAT HARD TO BELIEVE . . ." (fl)—3. "MADRONE TREE THAT WAS MY MOTHER" (fl)—4. "LET SLEEP TAKE HER . . ." (fl)—STRUCTURE OF RIME XV: "O MASK OF THE MANDRILL!" (fl)—STRUCTURE OF RIME XVI: "BACK TO

THE FIGURE" (fl)—STRUCTURE OF RIME XVII: "THIS POTION IS LOVE'S PORTION" (fl)—STRUCTURE OF RIME XVIII: "KUNDRY WAS WAGNER'S CREATION . . ." (fl)—OSIRIS AND SET—WINDINGS (1961-63) [section-title]—TWO PRESENTATIONS [sequence-title for two numbered poems] 1. "WE SEND YOU WORD OF THE MOTHER" (fl)—2. "YOU ARE GONE AND I SEND" (fl)—AFTER A PASSAGE IN BAUDELAIRE—SHELLEY'S *ARETHUSA* SET TO NEW MEASURES— AFTER READING H.D.'S *HERMETIC DEFINITIONS*—STRAINS OF SIGHT [sequence-title for two numbered poems] 1. "HE BROUGHT A LIGHT SO SHE COULD SEE" (fl)—2. "IN THE QUESTIONING PHRASE THE VOICE" (fl)—DOVES—RETURNING TO THE RHETORIC OF AN EARLY MODE—TWO ENTERTAINMENTS [sequence-title for following two poems] THE BALLAD OF THE FORFAR WITCHES' SING—A COUNTRY WIFE'S SONG—WHAT HAPPENED: PRELUDE [sequence-title for following two poems] ARGUMENT—"PUSS-IN-BOOTS, GUARDIAN, GENIUS" (fl)—A SET OF ROMANTIC HYMNS [sequence-title for five numbered poems] 1. "SWEET TONE! VIBRANT WING!" (fl)—2. "FOUNTAIN OF FORMS! LIFE SPRINGS . . ." (fl)—3. "THE LYRE'S A-BLAZE!" (fl)—4. "IN PRAISE OF ORPHEUS" (fl)—5. "THE DANCERS CROSS OVER TO THE OTHER SIDE" (fl)—THANK YOU FOR LOVE—FROM *THE MABINOGION*—FORCED LINES—A NEW POEM (FOR JACK SPICER)—SONNET 1: "NOW THERE IS A LOVE OF WHICH DANTE . . ." (fl)—SONNET 2: "FOR IT IS AS IF THE THREAD OF MY LIFE" (fl)—SONNET 3: FROM DANTE'S SIXTH SONNET—ANSWERING— ADAM'S WAY, a play upon theosophical themes: Scene 1—The Astral Garden—Scene 2—The Garden of Yahweh—CYPARISSUS—A PART-SEQUENCE FOR CHANGE [sequence-title for three numbered poems] 1. "IF THEY HAD CURSED THE MAN" (fl)—2. "I SHALL DRAW BACK" (fl)—3. "ESTRANGED. DEEPLY ESTRANGED" (fl)—STRUCTURE OF RIME XIX: "THE ARTISTS OF THE SURVIVAL . . ." (fl)—STRUCTURE OF RIME XX: "THE MASTER OF RIME TOLD ME . . ." (fl)— STRUCTURE OF RIME XXI: "LOST IN THE HOUR-MAZE . . ." (fl)— THE CONTINENT [sequence- title for six numbered poems] 1. "UNDER-EARTH CURRENTS . . ." (fl)—2. "A DIARY POEM TO DAY, GAIA . . ." (fl)—3. "THE HEAD CRUSHT SIDEWAYS . . ." (fl)—4. "THESE FIGURES: A SNAKE-OIL OF WATER" (fl)—5. "I AM SO FAR FROM YOU" (fl)—6. "THERE IS ONLY THE ONE TIME" (fl).

Description: The text is printed on yellowish white (C-92) wove paper, 20.3 x 14.2 cm. A single decorated rule, like the ones used on the first half-title page, appears to the left of the numbers on the left-hand pages and to the right of the numbers on the right-hand pages in the directional line. The gatherings have been sewn with white thread and glued; the center stitch is made with deep pink thread (C-3). The endpapers are of the same stock as the text. The cover is made from black (C-267) cloth over boards, 21.1 x 14.6

cm. The front and rear covers are blank, but the lettering on the spine in silver (no C-no.) reads from head to tail, "Duncan [space] [device] ROOTS AND BRANCHES [device] [space] SCRIBNERS."

Dust jacket: The dust jacket is made from white wove stock, enameled on the exterior side. The front and spine are overprinted with black and blue (C-178) to produce the sense of a textured image of a branch. Lettering on the front cover reads: "[in white] ROOTS | AND | BRANCHES | poems by | [in light blue (C-181)] ROBERT | DUNCAN." Lettering on the spine reads from head to tail, "[in light blue] DUNCAN [in white] ROOTS AND BRANCHES [in light blue] SCRIBNERS." The rear cover contains a reproduction of a photograph of the author by Patty Topalian, 12.3 x 11.6 cm., whose name appears at bottom right of the photograph. Directly below the photograph: "[in black] ROBERT DUNCAN [below] [in blue] Published by Charles Scribner's Sons [dot] New York." The front flap contains a two line quotation (in blue) by M. L. Rosenthal, which is followed by a twenty-three line statement about RD and the contents of this book. Below a rule, to the left of the publisher's logo: "ALSO AVAILABLE IN | PAPER-BACK AS A | SCRIBNER | FIRST EDITION." The rear flap contains a nine line biographical statement about RD under the heading, in blue, "about the author" and below, "JACKET FRONT· PHOTOGRAPH BY F. H. BURRELL."

Published: 1500 copies published Aug. 1964 at $4.50.

b. *First edition, paperbound copies:*

Title, Collation, Contents, and Text contents the same as the hardbound copies. The same paper has been used, but the gatherings have been trimmed to 20.3 x 13.6 cm., and the leaves perfect bound to the cover. The design and the lettering of the front cover are the same as the front cover of the dust jacket, except that the price "$1.95" has been added in white at the top right, and the logo, "SCRIBNER | FIRST | EDITIONS" has been added at the lower right. Lettering on the spine is the same as on the dust jacket. The rear cover at the top contains a blue rectangle, 2.1 x 13.4 cm., flush with the top edge, printed with the following lettering: "[in black] SCRIBNER FIRST EDITIONS | [in white] SUPERIOR NEW WRITING IN QUALITY PAPERBOUND FORM." Directly below is a white area, 13.2 x 9.5 cm., in which are printed in black authors and titles of books published by the house. A reduced reproduction of the photograph by Patty Topalian (the same one that appeared on the rear of the dust jacket) appears in the lower left corner, 8.7 x 6.4 cm. Beside it on the right is an area overprinted in blue, 8.7 x 7 cm., which contains a fourteen line statement (in black) under the heading "ROBERT DUNCAN," which is a combination of the statement from the rear flap of the dust jacket and the quotation by M. L. Rosenthal from the front flap of the dust jacket.

Published: 3500 copies published Aug. 1964 at $1.95.

c. *First English edition:*

ROOTS AND | BRANCHES | Poems by ROBERT DUNCAN | [below] [publisher's logo] | Jonathan Cape Thirty Bedford Square London [1970].

Collation: [A-L]⁸; pp. [i-xiv], [1-2], 3-69, [70-72], 73-176, [177-178].

Contents: pp. [i-ii] blank; p. [iii] half-title-page, "ROOTS AND BRANCHES"; p. [iv] blank; p. [v] ten titles under the heading "ALSO BY ROBERT DUNCAN"; p. [vi] blank; p. [vii] title-page; p. [viii] copyright-page, "First published in Great Britain 1970 | © by Robert Duncan | Jonathan Cape Ltd, 30 Bedford Square, London WC1 | SBN 224 61842 3 | [below] Printed in Great Britain | by Compton Printing Ltd, Aylesbury and London | bound by G. and J. Kitcat Ltd, London"; p. [ix] acknowledgments-page, eighteen editors and magazines listed under the heading, "The author would like to thank the following editors for their appreciation . . ."; p. [x] blank; pp. [xi-xiii] contents-pages; p. [xiv] blank; p. [1] section-title, "ROOTS AND BRANCHES"; p. [2] blank; pp. 3-69 text; p. [70] blank; p. [71] section-title, "WINDINGS"; p. [72] blank pp. 73-176 text; pp. [177-178] blank.

Text contents: same as First edition, hardbound copies. The leaves are bound in light gray (C-264) mottled paper over boards, 22.3 x 14 cm. The spine binding is of white (C-263) textured cloth which extends 2.3 cm. onto the front and rear covers. The front and rear covers are blank, while lettering on the spine in very yellow (C-82) reads horizontally, "ROOTS | AND | BRANCHES | [device] ROBERT | DUNCAN | [below] [publisher's logo]."

Dust jacket: The dust jacket is made from heavy white (approximately C-263) wove stock overprinted in very orange (C-48) and black. The cover reproduces an illustration by Gustave Doré of Dante and Virgil from the *Inferno:* Canto XIII, 34, "And straight the trunk exclaimed, 'Why pluckst thou me,'" in the translation of Rev. Henry Francis Cary. The illustration runs continuously from the front to the spine to the rear cover. Lettering on the front cover at the top reads in white, "ROOTS & BRANCHES | Poems | ROBERT DUNCAN." Lettering on the spine reads from head to tail in white, "ROOTS & BRANCHES Poems ROBERT DUNCAN [below] [publisher's logo]." The front flap, which is all white, contains a twenty-five line statement about RD and this book, most of which is reproduced from the front flap of the dust jacket of the first hardbound edition. At the bottom right: "35s net | [short rule] IN UK ONLY | [short rule] | £1.75 net." The rear flap, which is also white, contains the following at the bottom: "SBN 224 61842 3 | Jacket design by Leigh Taylor | © Jonathan Cape Ltd, 1970."

Published: An unknown number of copies published in 1970 at £1.75 ($4.50). In a letter to the compiler, dated 11 Aug. 1978, the publisher declined to disclose the number of copies printed.

d. *First sub-edition, first impression:*

ROOTS AND | BRANCHES | Poems by ROBERT DUNCAN | [below] A NEW DIRECTIONS PAPERBOOK [New York, 1969].

Collation: [1-6]¹⁶; pp. [iii-viii], ix-xi, [xii], [1-2], 3-69, [70-72], 73-176, [177-182].

Contents: p. [iii] half-title-page [three decorated short rules at top right], "ROOTS AND BRANCHES"; p. [iv] | eleven titles under the heading "ALSO BY ROBERT DUNCAN"; p. [v] title-page; p. [vi] copyright-page, "Copyright © 1964 by Robert Duncan | Library of Congress Catalog Card Number: 64-24233 | All rights reserved. Except for brief passages quoted in newspaper, | magazine, radio or television review, no part of this book may be | reproduced in any form or by any means, electronic or mechanical, | including photocopying and recording, or by any information storage | and retrieval system, without permission in writing from the Publisher. | First published by Charles Scribner's Sons, 1964. | First published as ND Paperbook 275, 1969. | Manufactured in the United States of America. | New Directions Books are published for James Laughlin by New Directions Publishing Corporation, | 333 Sixth Avenue, New York 10014"; p. [vii] acknowledgments-page, eighteen authors and magazines listed under the heading, "The author would like to thank the following editors for their appreciation . . ."; p. [viii] blank; pp. ix-xi contents-pages; p. [xii] blank; p. [1] section-title, "ROOTS AND BRANCHES"; p. [2] blank; pp. 3-69 text; p. [70] blank; p. [71] section-title, "WINDINGS"; p. [72] blank; pp. 73-176 text; pp. [177-178] blank; pp. [179-180] a list of "NEW DIRECTIONS PAPERBOOKS"; pp. [181-182] blank.

Text contents: The same as First edition, hardbound copies.

Description: The text is printed on yellowish white (C-92) wove paper, 20.3 x 13.7 cm., and the gatherings are sewn with white thread and glued to the cover. This sub-edition is reproduced from the First edition, and so a single decorated rule, like the one used on the first half-title-page, appears to the left of the numbers on the left-hand pages and to the right of the numbers on the right-hand pages in the directional line. The cover is made from heavy white stock enameled on the outside. The front cover contains a reproduction of a black-and-white photograph of trees with exposed roots and overhanging branches. Lettering below the photograph in black reads, "Roots and Branches | Poems by Robert Duncan." Lettering on the spine reads from head to tail, "Robert Duncan Roots and Branches [space] NDP275." At the top left of the rear cover the word "POETRY" appears, and below, "Roots and Branches | by Robert Duncan"; then follows a nine line statement about RD and the book, seven lines of which are quoted from RD. After quotations from reviews by Hayden Carruth and Carl Rakosi, the following appears: "Cover photograph by Wynn Bullock; design by David Ford | [in brackets] Also by Robert Duncan: *Bending the Bow* (poems), NDP255, $2.25 | A New Directions Paperbook [space] NDP275 $1.75."

Published: 3991 copies published Feb. 1969 at $1.75.

e. *First sub-edition, second impression:*

Title, Collation, Contents, Text contents, and Description the same as First sub-edition, first impression, except that "Second Printing" has been added on the copyright-page and at the top right of the rear cover. A paper label bearing the price "$3.25" has been pasted over the price "$1.75."

Published: 2546 copies published March 1969 at $3.25.

f. *First sub-edition, third impression:*

Title, Collation, Contents, Text contents, and Description the same as First sub-edition, first impression, except that "Third Printing" now appears on the copyright-page, and the price has changed to $3.25 in the last line on the rear cover. The headline on the rear cover now reads: "POETRY [slash] ISBN: 0-8112-0034-5 [space] THIRD PRINTING." The contents in brackets at the bottom of the page now read: "Also by Robert Duncan: *Bending the Bow* (poems), NDP255, $2.25; | *The Opening of the Field* (poems), NDP356, $2.45."

Published: 1076 copies published April 1974 at $3.25.

g. *First sub-edition, fourth impression:*

Title, Collation, Contents, Text contents, and Description the same as First sub-edition, first impression, except that "FOURTH PRINTING" now appears on the copyright-page and at the top right of the rear cover. The price has been changed to "$4.95."

Published: 1000 copies published April 1978 at $4.95.

Proof papers. CU-B.
a.   Galley proofs
    Collation: 36*l* all recto 61 x 17.8 cm.
    Contents: The text contents of the volume plus some markings in Robin Blaser's hand.

Notes: RD's difficulties with printers continued when the manuscript of this book was submitted to Scribner's. The editors of that house wanted RD to exclude "Night Scenes" from the book because its detailed exposition of homosexual lovemaking would possibly offend librarians. In response, RD wrote in a letter to Robert Creeley, dated 2 Jan. 1964: "After two drafts, I managed on the third to write a reply that recognized the above paragraph [in which "Night Scenes" was discussed] is not necessarily a mandate. But that was Dec 20 and I haven't got any answer yet. Even allowing for Xmas parties and New Year's binges, it looks like the insistence on the poem remaining in the works raised a problem—I told Hutter my business was with the truth of the whole, and that he would have to decide about the librarians himself—a pure publisher's worry. God! if we wrote with librarians in mind! I think of all the sneaky librarians and if I had them in mind would write dirty books for guilty readers, with calculated passages to make

peeping-tom and jenny book marms squirm with inDIGnition or even—
ation" (on deposit at MoSW). The poems were published as RD intended.

<table>
<tr><td>A15</td><td style="text-align:center">WINE</td><td style="text-align:right">1964</td></tr>
</table>

First edition:

WINE | [text in 51 lines] | Robert Duncan | Note: *Passages* 11, drawn from Baudelaire, "Du Vin et du Haschisch". The closing quote is from Rimbaud. | OYEZ 4. Copyright 1964 by Robert Duncan. Printed for Oyez by The Auerhahn Press in San Francisco.

Broadside: The text is printed on bluish white (C-189) laid paper with all but the left edge deckled, 42 x 30.3 cm.

Published: 350 copies published in 1964 at $1.50; 27 copies in a set with nine other broadsides, but only 25 sets sold at $45.00.

Proof papers. CtU.

a.   First proofs
     Collation: 1*l* recto 43.1 x 27.8 cm.
     Contents: The text with slight holograph changes in the spacing

b.   Galley proofs
     Collation: 1*l* recto 40.6 x 21.4 cm.
     Contents: The text with some space and line adjustments.

c.   Final proofs
     Collation: 1*l* recto 42.5 x 30.2 cm.
     Contents: The text as published.

d.   Drawing proofs
     Collation: 1*l* recto 42.5 x 30.2 cm.

Notes: In his book, *A Bibliography of the Auerhahn Press & its successor Dave Haselwood Books* (Berkeley: Poltroon Press, 1976), p. 86, Dave Haselwood writes about the first series of Oyez Broadsides, of which "Wine" is one: "Commissioned by Bob Hawley in 1964; published in editions of 350 at $1.50 each, 27 complete sets were signed of which 25 sold at $45.00 in portfolios made by Mrs. Hawley with a label in Centaur printed by Von Stromm (then of Cody's)." The portfolios are 45 x 33 cm. and contain a label 9.5 x 12.2 cm. with the following lettering: "Poems in Broadside | [in red (C-11)] Michael McClure : Brother Antoninus | [in black] Josephine Miles : Robert Duncan : Robert Creeley | [in red] OYEZ | [in black] David Meltzer : Denise Levertov : Charles Olson : Gary Snyder : William Bronk | [in red] First Series." "The publisher's set, in a gold tapestry portfolio [45.8 x 33 cm.] box with ties & printed label on front. Unique format made for the publisher by his wife Dorothy Hawley" [publisher's note] (CtU). The unique copy referred to is made from a portfolio with overlapping sides and covered with a brocade cloth with an intricate design in deep orange yellow (C-72), very orange yellow (C-66), and brilliant orange yellow (C-67) (CtU).

a. *First edition, paperbound copies, first impression:*

[the title-page contains an embossed, uncolored drawing of a female bust with a design above and below the bust and the title included in the drawing] MEDEA AT KOLCHIS | THE MAIDEN HEAD | ROBERT DUNCAN | [below] oyez [dot] berkeley [dot] 1965.

Collation: [1]⁶, [2-4]⁸; pp. [i-xii], 1-44, [45-48].

Contents: pp. [i-iv] blank; p. [v] title-page; p. [vi] copyright-page, "Copyright Robert Duncan | 1965 | Printed & designed by | GRAHAM MACKINTOSH | in an edition of 500 [dash] | 28 of which are hard-bound, | numbered & signed | by the author | [below] All applications for performance rights should be addressed to the author, | 3735 20th Street, San Francisco 10, California."; p. [vii] "A NOTE BY THE AUTHOR"; pp. [vii-x] "ANOTHER PREFACE. 1963/1965"; p. [xi] half-title-page, "MEDEA AT KOLCHIS | THE MAIDEN HEAD | [device]"; p. [xii] THE CAST & SCENES; pp. 1-44 text; pp. [45-48] blank.

Text contents: A NOTE BY THE AUTHOR—ANOTHER PREFACE. 1963/1965—MEDEA AT KOLCHIS THE MAIDEN HEAD.

Description: The text is printed on white (C-263) wove paper, 21.3 x 13.9 cm., the gatherings are sewn with white thread and then glued to the cover. The first and final leaves are folded under the front and rear flap of the cover and serve as endpapers. The cover is made from dark yellowish pink (C-30) textured stock, 21.5 x 14.1 cm. The front cover contains a drawing of a female bust, with a design above and below the bust and the poet's initials "RD" enclosed in the drawing. In an arch above the female head appears in black, "MEDEA AT KOLCHIS," and below horizontally, "THE MAIDEN HEAD." The lettering down the spine reads from head to tail, "MEDEA AT KOLCHIS [space] ROBERT DUNCAN [space] OYEZ." The rear cover is blank. The lettering "OYEZ [colon] Box 3014 [colon] Berkeley" appears at the bottom of the front flap; the rear flap is blank.

Published: 472 copies published in 1965 at $1.50.

b. *First edition, hardbound copies:*

Title, Collation, Contents, Text contents, and Description the same as the First edition, paperbound copies. These copies are bound in light yellowish brown (C-76) and pale yellow (ivory) (C-92) linen over boards 22.3 x 14.2 cm. The first and last leaves have been used to make the endpapers. The copies are numbered 1-28 and signed "Robert Duncan."

Dust jacket: The dust jacket is the same as the paper cover for the trade copies. There is also a second dust jacket with the same design, but printed on white enameled stock, with the design of the first dust jacket embossed on the front cover.

Published: 28 copies published in 1965 at $15.00.

c. *First edition, paperbound copies, second impression:*

[without embossed drawing] MEDEA AT KOLCHIS | THE MAIDEN HEAD | ROBERT DUNCAN | [below] oyez [dot] berkeley [dot] 1965.

Collation: [1]²⁸; pp. [i-viii], 1-44, [45-48].

Contents, Text contents, and Description the same as First edition, paperbound copies, first impression, except that the copyright-page replaces the statement of limitation with the following: "Second printing, July 1966 | OYEZ box 3014 Berkeley, California." The gathering has been stapled twice to the cover and trimmed to 21.5 x 13.8 cm., with the cover of the same color and design as the First edition, first impression, but lacking front and rear flaps.

Published: 1000 copies published July 1966 at $1.50

Proof papers. MoSW.

a. Galley proofs
    Date: [1965]
    Collation: 27*l* all recto 30.3 x 22.8 cm.
    Contents: The proofs contain the text contents plus some corrections in red pencil that are not in RD's hand.
b. Galley proofs for second impression. CtU.
    Date: [1966]
    Collation: 28*l* all recto 30.6 x 22.8 cm.
    Contents: The proofs contain the text contents plus some corrections but not in RD's hand.

Notes: In one copy, Graham Mackintosh made the following inscription: "The hardbound copies had dustjackets—we printed on the cover stock of the edition copies and also on white stock to see which would look best— they both looked fine so both were used" (copy in possession of Bradford Morrow).

The play was performed at Black Mountain College, 29 and 30 Aug. 1956. In the program notes for the performance, RD wrote: "We would like to account for the profound anxiety. But it is a weather—a saturation air of summer—that obstructs all account. Fear, desire, accusation, tenderness, joy, despair are caught up, unreleased, in the storm ahead. Tomorrow, the sky will be blue—yet all is unrelieved. The sun too is of the obstruction. A violent electricity charges such weather; even the flashes of lightning in the heat do not release the rain but portend greater devastation of agony. Where the rain will not come, sorcery flourishes. O, sure it rains, but sorcery flourishes. The swamp land, more terrible than the waste land. No innocent rain.

Uninformed, we must use the stage as it is. Without knowledge, dance our damnd rain dance as we can."

A17   THE SWEETNESS AND GREATNESS OF   1965
DANTE'S DIVINE COMEDY

a. *First edition, first impression:*

[within a rectangle marked in heavy black lines, 17.3 x 13.4 cm., there is a central crossing of reddish brown (C-40) lines. The horizontal line extends from the gutter nearly to the right edge, and the vertical line extends to within 3.8 cm. of the top and to within 1.8 cm. of the bottom edge. Just above the central intersection is a flower emblem drawn in reddish brown by the author. All the lettering is in the author's holograph.] The SWEETNESS and | GREATNESS of | DANTE'S DIVINE | COMEDY [flower emblem] [horizontal line, then below it in reddish brown] 1265 [reddish brown vertical line] 1965 | Lecture given October 27th, 1965 at | the Dominican College of San Rafael | ROBERT [reddish brown vertical line] DUNCAN | [below rectangle] open space [reddish brown vertical line] san francisco [1965].

Collation: [1]¹⁴; pp. [1-28].

Contents: p. [1] title-page; p. [2] copyright-page, "Copyright 1965 by Robert Duncan"; pp. [3-25] text; p. [26] Postscript; p. [27] colophon-page, "Edition of 500 copies published December, 1965. | Cover and title-page designs by the author. | Open Space [space] 24 Allen Street [space] San Francisco"; p. [28] blank.

Text contents: THE SWEETNESS AND GREATNESS OF DANTE'S DIVINE COMEDY—POSTSCRIPT.

Description: The text is reproduced from a typescript on yellowish white (ivory) (C-92) wove paper, 23.4 x 17.2 cm., and the gathering is attached to the cover with two staples. The cover is made from heavy white textured stock. The front cover contains a line drawing which is the author's version of "Strength," No. VIII of the Trumps Major in The Waite Tarot Deck. Within the drawing appears the following lettering: "[top left] 1265 | 1965 [top right] Robert | Duncan [woven into the drawing] The SWEETNESS | and | GREATNESS | of DANTE'S DIVINE | COMEDY | [bottom left] OPEN SPACE." The rear cover is blank.

Published: 500 copies published Dec. 1965 at $1.00.

b. *First edition, second impression:*

Title, Collation, Contents, Text contents, and Description the same as first impression, except for the following. The horizontal reddish brown line on the title-page stops at the right side of the rectangle; it no longer extends almost to the right edge. The colophon on p. [20] has been deleted. The booklet has been trimmed to 23.2 x 17.1 cm.

Published: 500 copies published 30 Jan. 1967 at $1.00.

A18   **UP RISING**   1965

First edition:

UP RISING | [text in 74 lines] | [at lower right] ROBERT DUNCAN | Passages 25 | [at tail, left middle] OYEZ [dot] BERKELEY | COPYRIGHT [dash] 1965 [dash] Robert Duncan | PRINTED BY GRAHAM MACKINTOSH.

Broadside: The text is printed on stiff yellowish white (approximately C-92) wove stock, 43.3 x 28 cm.

Published: approximately 2000 copies published and distributed free in 1965.

Note: All copies contain the printing error "milllions" in line 38. Approximately ten copies were printed on orange (C-50) stock, and were dividers to keep the count of the impression.

A19   **OF THE WAR**   1966

a. *First edition, paperbound copies, first issue (of text):*

PASSAGES | 22-27 | OF THE WAR | ROBERT DUNCAN | [below] OYEZ [Berkeley, 1966].

Collation: [1]⁸; pp. [1-16].

Contents: p. [1] title-page; p. [2] copyright and acknowledgments-page, "Copyright 1966 Robert Duncan | Passages 22, 23, and 24 appeard in *Poetry*, May, 1966. | Passages 25 appeard in *The Nation*."; pp. [3-13] text; pp. [14-16] blank.

Text contents: IN THE PLACE OF A PASSAGE 22—PASSAGES 23 BENEFICE—ORDERS PASSAGES 24—UP RISING PASSAGES 25—PASSAGES 26: THE SOLDIERS—TRANSGRESSING THE REAL PASSAGES 27.

Description: The text is printed on yellowish white (ivory) (C-92) wove paper, 23.1 x 15.2 cm., and the gathering is attached to the cover with two staples. The cover is made from heavy deep red (approximately C-13) wove stock,

23.1 x 15.2 cm. The front cover is overprinted in black with a photograph of a tank dragging a body, 12 x 15.2 cm. Lettering in red above the photograph reads, "ROBERT DUNCAN," and below the photograph, "OF THE WAR." The rear cover is blank.

Publication: 1000 copies published Oct. 1966 at $1.00.

b. *First edition, hardbound copies, first issue:*

Title, Collation, Contents, and Text contents are the same as paperbound copies. The text is on the same paper as the paperbound copies. Each copy contains a collage, front and rear, made from newspaper clippings and photographs on red paper, which serves as endpapers. A leaf of light yellow brown (lighter than C-76) paper containing splashes of red ink has been placed over the collages. One leaf of black paper has been laid-in before the cover of the paperbound edition, the recto of which contains part of the collage, and the verso of which is blank. These additions appear before and after a copy, including the cover, of the paperbound impression. On p. [15], a colophon has been added in RD's holograph which reads: "[number] of 6 | bound by Dorothy Hawley | and signed by the author | Robert Duncan." The copies have been bound in deep red cloth over boards 24 x 16 cm. The front and rear covers are blank, while the lettering on the spine reads from head to tail in black, "Of The War Robert Duncan [space] OYEZ."

Published: 6 copies published Oct. 1966 and not for sale.

c. *First edition, folio copies, second issue (of text):*

[cover-title, in black] PASSAGES 22-27 | [in deep reddish orange (C-36)] OF THE WAR | [in black] ROBERT DUNCAN | [below, in black] OYEZ [Berkeley, 1966].

Collation: [1-4]², pp. [1-16].

Contents: p. [1] cover-title; p. [2] colophon, acknowledgments-copyright-page, "This edition of 100 copies | signed by the author | [RD's signature] Robert Duncan | [below] Passages 22, 23, and 24 appeard in *Poetry*, May, 1966. | Passages 25 appeard in *The Nation*. | Copyright 1966 Robert Duncan"; pp. [3-13] text; pp. [14-16] blank.

Text contents: IN THE PLACE OF A PASSAGE 22—PASSAGES 23 BENEFICE—ORDERS PASSAGES 24—UP RISING PASSAGES 25— PASSAGES 26: THE SOLDIERS—TRANSGRESSING THE REAL PASSAGES 27.

Description: The text is printed on yellowish white (ivory) (C-92) wove paper with the watermark "Wash & Co | British Hand Made." The sheets, all with deckled edges, have been folded to form leaves 33.8 x 23.3 cm. Leaves two to four have been inserted inside the first leaf which serves as the cover, the front of which is the title-page. The four leaves have then been inserted inside a stiff wrapper of medium red (approximately C-15) stock, 35.7 x 24.5

cm. The wrapped leaves have then been placed in a folio made from heavy, light gray (C-264) stock with overlapping top, bottom, and side flaps to form a folio 36.3 x 25.2 cm. A label of white wove paper, 6 x 12.3 cm., has been pasted on the front with the lettering in reddish brown "OF THE WAR."

Published: despite the colophon, only 80 copies published Oct. 1966 at $20.00.

Proof papers. CtU.

a. First page proofs
   Date: [1966]
   Collation: 2*l* recto-verso, recto-verso, 31.7 x 22.8 cm.; 7*l* all recto 31.7 x 22.8 cm.; 1*l* recto 31.7 x 21 cm.; 1*l* recto 31.7 x 18 cm.

Notes: The paperbound copies were printed from plates made from proof copies of the folio issue; and between the time of the printing of the paperbound copies and the printing of the folio copies, RD revised five lines and added six lines to PASSAGES 26 : THE SOLDIERS and added the date of revision at the end of the poem, "October 1966." The advertising flyer for the limited edition of the book contains the following information: "In the autumn of 1966 we begin publication of a limited, fine edition of Robert Duncan's *OF THE WAR* (Passages 22-27). The poems were monotyped in nineteen point Van Dijck with Deepdene hand-set titles. When page proofs were pulled it was decided to issue a popular edition in reduced offset; subsequent to this publication several minor changes were made by the author. The corrected text was hand-printed in two colors on British handmade paper by the designer, Steven Van Strum. The books consist of four signatures measuring 9 x 12 inches laid loose in a two color stiff paper folder."

A20   **THE YEARS AS CATCHES**   1966

a. *First edition, paperbound copies, first impression:*

[reproduction of a photograph of RD, 13.9 x 11.4 cm.] [in deep reddish orange (C-36)] The Years As Catches | [in black] First poems (1939-1946) by Robert Duncan | Oyez Berkeley 1966.

Collation: [1-6]⁸, [7]⁶, [8]⁸; pp. [1-10], i-xi, [xii], ²[1-2], 3-93, [94-102].

Contents: pp. [1-2] blank; p. [3] half-title-page, "THE YEARS AS CATCHES"; p. 4 [blank]; p. [5] title-page; p. [6] copyright and acknowledgments-page, "Copyright © 1966 by ROBERT DUNCAN | HEAVENLY CITY, EARTHLY CITY | COPYRIGHT © 1947 | [ten titles under the heading] Certain of these poems appeared in the following magazines:"; pp. [7-8] contents-pages; p. [9] section-title, in reddish orange, "Introduction"; p. [10] blank; pp. i-xi text; p. [xii] blank; p. [1] section-title, in reddish orange, "The Years As Catches"; p. [2] blank; pp. 3-93 text; p. [94] blank; p. [95] section-title, "Bibliography"; p. [96] blank; pp. [97-99] "WORKS

WRITTEN 1937-1946 BY ROBERT DUNCAN"; p. [100] blank; p. [101] colophon-page, "Designed and printed by Graham Mackintosh | in an edition of 2,000 copies. | [short expanded rule] | 1,800 are bound in paper wrappers and 200 | in boards. 30 copies have been signed, num- | bered, and decorated by the author and are *hors de commerce*"; p. [102] blank.

Text contents: INTRODUCTION—PERSEPHONE—PASSAGE OVER WATER—from TOWARD THE SHAMAN—AN ARK FOR LAWRENCE DURRELL—THE AWAKENING INTO DREAM, LOVE THERE: OUT OF THE DREAM, AND OUR BEAUTIFUL CHILD—A HISTORY OF MY FAMILY—FRAGMENT—A SPRING MEMORANDUM: FORT KNOX—A LETTER TO JACK JOHNSON—AN ENCOUNTER—FROM RICHARD BURTON'S *ANATOMY OF MELANCHOLY*—VARIATIONS UPON PHRASES FROM MILTON'S *THE REASON OF CHURCH GOVERNMENT*—VARIATIONS IN PRAISE OF JESUS CHRIST OUR LORD—WITNESSES—THE UNRESTING—SNOW ON BUG HILL—MOTHER TO WHOM I HAVE COME HOME—AN AFRICAN ELEGY—THE YEARS AS CATCHES—KING HAYDN OF MIAMI BEACH—LOVEWISE—MOTHER BROTHER DOOR AND BED—7 QUESTIONS, 7 ANSWERS—MARRIAGE—RANDOM LINES: A DISCOURSE ON LOVE—HOMAGE AND LAMENT FOR EZRA POUND IN CAPTIVITY MAY 12, 1944—CHRISTMAS LETTER 1944—UPON WATCHING A STORM—THE END OF A YEAR—SONG—A CONGREGATION—TREESBANK POEMS [sequence-title for following four poems] "I LISTEN IN THE SHADE TO ONE I LOVE" (fl)—"THE SILENT THROAT IN THE DARK PORTENDS" (fl)—"SHALL I ALONE MAKE MY WAY TO MY GRAVE" (fl)—"SLEEP IS A DEEP AND MANY VOICED FLOOD" (fl)—AN APOLLONIAN ELEGY—BERKELEY POEMS [sequence-title for following five poems] "AMONG MY FRIENDS LOVE IS A GREAT SORROW" (fl)—AN ELEGIAC FRAGMENT—A WOMAN'S DRUNKEN LAMENT—PORTRAIT OF TWO WOMEN—I AM A MOST FLESHLY MAN—HEAVENLY CITY, EARTHLY CITY—BIBLIOGRAPHY.

Description: The text is printed on yellowish white (ivory) (C-92) wove paper, 22.7 x 15.2 cm.; the gatherings are sewn with white thread and glued to the paper cover. The cover is made from dark gray yellowish brown (C-81) textured stock, 22.7 x 15.2 cm. The front cover contains a reproduction of a photograph of RD imposed in black, and contains the following lettering below the photograph in very light greenish blue (C-171): "Robert Duncan | The Years As Catches." Lettering on the spine from head to tail in black reads, "The Years As Catches Robert Duncan [space] oyez." The rear cover is blank. The cover stock has a tendency to turn brownish with sun fading.

Published: 1800 copies published in 1966 at $2.50.

b. *First edition, hardbound copies:*

Title, Collation, Contents, Text contents, and Description the same as paperbound copies except that for these copies the paper cover has been pasted over boards, 23.3 x 15.3 cm. The endpapers are of the same stock as the text stock, and the headbands are very red (C-11) and brilliant yellow (C-83). Laid in all hardbound copies is a folio flyer, 23.4 x 14 cm., which contains a statement by Denise Levertov entitled "On Reading the Early Poetry of Robert Duncan," a poem by Charles Olson whose first line is "Yes, it was The Years as Catches which," publisher's information, and a reproduction of the same photograph of RD that appears on the title-page of the paperbound copies.

Dust jacket: The dust jacket is made from heavy, glossy yellowish white (C-92) stock, and contains on the front the same reproduction of the photograph of RD that appears on the front cover of the First edition, paperbound copies. The lettering at the bottom in very red (C-11) reads, "Robert Duncan | The Years as Catches." Lettering on the spine in red reads from head to tail, "The Years as Catches Robert Duncan [space] oyez." The rear cover is blank, as are the front and rear flaps.

Published: 170 copies published in 1966 at $9.00.

c. *First edition, special copies:*

Title, Collation, Contents, Text contents, and Description the same as hardbound copies except that in these copies the endpapers have been decorated with pencil drawings and signed by RD.

Published: 30 copies published in 1966 *hors de commerce*, but some offered for sale at $20.00.

d. *First edition, paperbound copies, second impression:*

Title, Collation, Contents, Text contents, and Description the same as the first impression except that the half-title now appears on p. [4] and not on p. [3] (as in the first impression) and the copyright-page adds "Second Printing (1977)." The copies were produced by the offset process from the first impression, so the reddish orange lettering on the title-page and for the section-titles now appears in black. The cover is made from light gray (C-264) wove stock, and the cover photograph of RD from the first impression has been reduced to 17.8 x 12.8 cm. Lettering below the photograph in white (C-263) reads, "Robert Duncan | The Years As Catches." Lettering on the spine in black reads from head to tail, "THE YEARS AS CATCHES [space] Robert Duncan [space] OYEZ." The rear cover is blank.

Published: 1117 copies published 20 April 1977 at $3.00.

Proof papers. CaBV
a.   Cover wrapper

b.	Advance half-title-page.
	Collation: 1*l* recto-verso 23.2 x 15.3 cm.
	Contents: The page contains RD's changes and notes recto and verso.
c.	Advance title-page
	Collation: 1*l* recto 23.2 x 15.3 cm.
	Contents: The title-page contains RD's changes and his inscription.
d.	Copyright-page
	Collation: 1*l* recto 23.2 x 15.3 cm.
	Contents: The copyright-page.
e.i.	Contents-pages
	Collation: 2*l* recto, recto 23.2 x 15.3 cm.
	Contents: The contents-pages contain RD's corrections and alterations.
e.ii.	Contents-pages
	Collation: 2*l* recto, recto 23.2 x 15.3 cm.
	Contents: Corrected contents-pages.
f.	Introduction
	Collation: 1*l* recto 23.2 x 15.3 cm.
	Contents: This is p. 18 with corrections.
g.	The text of the poems
	Collation: 90*l* all recto 23.2 x 15.3 cm.
	Contents: These are the proof pages with corrections and notes in RD's hand throughout, pages 3-93.
h.	Bibliography
	Collation: 6*l* all recto 23.2 x 15.3 cm.
	Contents: This is the text of the bibliography with RD's corrections, pp. 95-100.

Notes: At one point, RD wanted to call his collected early poems *The Looking Glass*. In the preparation of the manuscript for YAC, RD revised some pieces: for example, he cut out sections of TOWARD THE SHAMAN so that it appears here as "from TOWARD THE SHAMAN." He made other smaller changes: for example, A SPRING MEMORANDUM now appears as A SPRING MEMORANDUM: FORT KNOX. In a letter to Henry Wenning, dated 9 March 1966, RD commented: "The ms of my *The Years as Catches: First Poems 1939-1946*, with *Preface* is already with Oyez, a sizable volume finally. And planned to be uniform with Everson's First Poems volume (where, at Bill's insistence, an essay I did on the book has been added as an introduction)" (MoSW). In his own introduction to YAC, RD makes the following summary comment about the volume: "One of the factors in my returning now to these poems of it seems so long ago—other lives and other worlds ago—is that I would admit them as part of my life work. Certain of them have always been clearly realized as parts of what I have to do in the art: *Toward An African Elegy* or *King Haydn of Miami Beach*. And now, after some years of reaction against the poems of my first publisht book, as if they were mistaken in their poetics, I have seen them anew in making this collection and would bring that very disturbing poetics into the works. *The Berkeley Poems, The Apollonian Elegy* and *Heavenly*

City, Earthly City I mean to stand now as established measures in my art and keys of my intention. As once I moved away from them, putting them away as immature things, now I move back or out in an expanding structure to take them up again as conditions of my maturity."

The advertising flyer for the book contains the same statements by Charles Olson and Denise Levertov which appeared on the folio flyer laid-in the hardbound copies. The second has been reprinted as "For Robert Duncan's Early Poems," in Denise Levertov, *The Poet In The World* (New York: New Directions, 1973), p. 243, while the first has not been reprinted:

Yes, it was The Years as Catches which
having read in 1946-7—(Circle magazine, from
Telegraph Avenue, George Leite, Editor) I, arriving in San Francisco, 1947
    said
to Kenneth Rexroth who as always generously met me at the
station who's
Robert Duncan? And thereby
flew off
to meet him (Berkeley. Wow! Since then, Etc.)
Right, from the start. A **beautiful** Poet. The Wings of
poetry. And since, each gathering light, illumines
more. Ancient, permanent wings of
Eros - & of Orphism. Hail his
being ("Being"), and being
now! All our
    luck
                Charles Olson.

A21   **SIX PROSE PIECES**   1966

a. *First edition, regular copies:*

SIX PROSE PIECES | ROBERT | DUNCAN | [double rule] THE PERISHABLE PRESS LIMITED | M. CM. LXVI [Madison, Wisconsin, 1966].

Collation: [1-5]⁴; pp. [1-40].

Contents: pp. [1-4] blank; p. [5] title-page; pp. [6-7] blank; p. [8] copyright-page, [rule] "copyright, a.d. nineteen hundred and sixty six by robert duncan" [rule]; p. [9] acknowledgments-page, [rule] "ensuing illustration cut by print after a drawing by the author" [rule]; pp. [10-12] blank; p. [13] text; pp. [14-15] blank; pp. [16-17] text; pp. [18-19] blank; pp. [20] printer's illustration; p. [21] text; pp. [22-23] blank; pp. [24-25] text; pp. [26-27] blank; pp. [28-29] text; pp. [30-32] blank; p. [33] colophon, [rule] "this first printing of SIX PROSE PIECES | by Robert Duncan, is limited to seventy | copies. ten copies are for the author and | fifty for sale. the printing has been done | on the Washington at Robert Runser's | private ROB RUN PRESS near

Rochester, | Michigan. the type throughout is Goudy | Old Style & the paper is hand-made from | linen and cotton rags by the printer, W. S. | Hamady, from the *perishable press limited*, | whose work is known by the mark below: | [publisher's logo]"; pp. [34-40] blank.

Text contents: STRUCTURE OF RIME XXII—STRUCTURE OF RIME XXIII—STRUCTURE OF RIME XXIV—STRUCTURE OF RIME XXV—REFLECTIONS—STRUCTURE OF RIME XXVI : PASSAGES 20 AN ILLUSTRATION.

Description: The text is printed on pale green (C-149) textured paper, 22.8 x 18.2 cm. The side and lower edges are deckled, while the top is folded and uncut. The first and last sheets, however, have been cut so that the first and last leaves, though included in the collation, become the endpapers and are pasted to the cover. The gatherings have been sewn with yellowish white (C-92) thread, held with two sewing strips, and bound in boards, 23.5 x 18.9 cm., covered with green (darker than C-149) cloth. The author's holograph signature is stamped in very yellow (C-82) on the front cover, while the spine and the rear cover are blank.

Published: 70 copies published April 1966 but only 50 copies for sale at $30.00.

b. ***First edition, boxed copies:***

Title, Collation, Contents, and Text contents the same as the regular copies. The unsewn and unbound gatherings have been collected in a binder with overlapping flaps, bound with pale yellow (approximately C-89) cloth. The binder fits into a slipcase, 24 x 19.3 cm., covered with the same cloth. It has not been determined whether these special copies are part of the fifty copies for sale, or whether they were published in addition to the fifty copies. Copies are located at NNU and MoSW.

Published: 15 copies published April 1966 at $65.00.

Proof papers. MoSW.
a.   Structure of Rime XXIV.
     Collation: 1*l* recto 22.1 x 28.9 cm.
     Contents: This is the first partial proof, with notes and corrections in
     RD's hand and the initials of the printer WH.
b.   Structure of Rime XXV.
     Collation: 1*l* recto 22.1 x 28.9 cm.
     Contents: This is the first partial proof, with notes and corrections in
     RD's hand and the initials of the printer WH.
c.   Structure of Rime XXV.
     Collation: 1*l* recto 22.1 x 28.9 cm.
     Contents: This is the second proof, dated "29 xii 65" and initialed "OK
     RD."
d.   Structure of Rime XXV[1].

Collation: 1*l* recto 22.1 x 46 cm.

Contents: This is the second proof, dated "26 xii 65" and initialed "RD" with some notes and changes in his hand.

e. Structure of Rime XXII.

Collation: 1*l* recto 19.2 x 26 cm.

Contents: This is the first proof, with additions in RD's hand and signed "OK."

f. Structure of Rime XXIII.

Collation: 1*l* recto 15.2 x 22.1 cm.

Contents: This is the first proof, dated "8/1/66" and signed "OK RD."

g. Reflections.

Collation: 1*l* recto 22.1 x 46 cm.

Contents: This is the second proof, dated "26 XII 65," and it contains notes in the printer's and RD's hand.

h. [Author's Drawing].

Collation: 1*l* recto 22.8 x 18.3 cm.

Contents: This is the first proof of the author's drawing.

i. Structure of Rime XXIV.

Collation: 1*l* recto 27.8 x 17.8 cm.

Contents: This is the final proof, dated "2/16/66" and signed "OK RD."

Notes: Copies of one gathering which contains STRUCTURE OF RIME XXIV, STRUCTURE OF RIME XXV, and the first page of REFLECTIONS and the printer's illustration were given away by the printer. Some were marked "Proof," and though not a broadside they have that appearance. An unknown number were offered for sale at $25.00.

In the letter accompanying the manuscript of the volume, dated 11 Nov. 1965, RD wrote to Walter Hamady: "I am enclosing a ms of *Six Prose Pieces* which I hope may suit your purpose. 'Pieces' I prefer to 'Poems' here for the musical terms over the literary. The examples of your work you sent me are beautiful and I am excited at whatever possibility we can work out" (MoSW). When RD returned a first proof copy, he also sent the drawing which was reproduced by a woodcut and made the following comment in a letter dated 9 Dec. 1965: "I am enclosing a drawing done for the book. I realize that you are in your own art most concernd with illustrational arts; but at the same time I wld like to extend the inspiration of the *Structures of Rime* in the terms of my own drawing, wherein I have workt certain figures relating to the spirit, the eye and the ear, and conveyd the hypnogogic rigidity in-coiled of the line I want" (MoSW).

RD was in Vancouver, at the University of British Columbia, for the production of his play "Adam's Way" from 5 Jan. to 10 Feb. 1966, so there was a delay in reading and approving the proofs of the book. Finally, in a letter dated 23 April 1966, RD acknowledges the receipt of ten copies of the book and comments on its appearance: "Except for the lack of a title on the spine, I like the binding of six prose pieces much better than the dark brown paper on boards of the Creeley book. . . . At this point the handsomeness of the whole overcomes any eye, even if I had one, for fine points in printing. But your idea of a small edition on handmade paper, and a larger one on a good book paper is an improvement I think'' (MoSW). The larger edition was never produced.

A BOOK OF RESEMBLANCES

a. *First edition, regular copies:*

[double title-page with an underdrawing in yellowish pink (C-26) and the printing in hollowed black letters] RoBeRT DuNCaN | A BOOK OF RESEMBLANCES | Poems : 1950-1953 | Reproduced in Holograph of the | Author, & | Ornamented with Drawings | by Jess. | [below] [ornament] Henry Wenning [ornament] New Haven [ornament] 1966 [ornament].

Collation: [1]⁶, [2-7]⁸; pp. [i-vi], vii-ix, [x-xiv], 1-14, [15], 16, [17], 18-19, [20], 21, [22], 23-28, [29], 30-45, [46], 47-49, [50-51], 52, [53], 54-58, [59], 60-61, [62], 63-64, [65], 66-69, [70-71], 72, [73-74], 75-80, [81-82], 83-87, [88-90], 91, [92-94].

Contents: p. [i] half-title-page in yellowish pink, "A BOOK OF RESEMBLANCES"; pp. [ii-iii] title-pages; p. [iv] copyright-page, "© Text by Robert Duncan, drawings by Jess 1966"; p. [v] contents-page; p. [vi] blank; pp. vii-[x] [Introduction]; pp. [xi-xii] blank; p. [xiii] within an emblem in yellowish pink, half-title, "A BOOK OF | RESEMBLANCES"; p. [xiv] blank; p. 1 drawing; pp. 1-[15] text; pp. 3-13 underdrawings in yellowish pink; p. [15] drawing; p. 16 text; p. [17] drawing; pp. 18-19 text; p. [20] drawing; pp. [20-22] text; p. [22] drawing; pp. 23-28 text; p. [29] drawing; pp. 30-41 text; pp. 40-41 drawing; pp. 42-49 text; pp. 44-47 underdrawings in yellowish pink; pp. 48 and 49 drawings; pp. [50-51] drawing; pp. [50]-52 text; p. [53] drawing; pp. 54-61 text; pp. 55, 56, 57, 58, 59 drawings; pp. 60-61 underdrawings in yellowish pink; p. [62] drawing; pp. 63-64 text; p. [65] drawing; pp. 66-72 text; 69, [70], [71], [73], [74] drawings; pp. 75-80 text; pp. 78-79 in yellowish pink; pp. 77, [81-83] drawings; pp. 83-89 text; pp. 84, 85, 87, [88], [89], [90]-91 drawings; p. [91] text; p. [92] blank; p. [93] acknowledgments and colophon-page, "Certain of these poems previously appeared in the | following magazines: [nine titles] | Six of the illustrations have previously appeared in | *12 Poets and 1 Painter, Writing 3.* | This first edition of *A Book of Resemblances* has been | printed in fine-line offset lithography by The Meriden | Gravure Company. The edition has been limited to | 203 copies, signed by the author and the artist, after | which the plates were destroyed. | Copies A, B and C have been reserved for the poet, | the artist and the publisher; copies 1 to 200 are for | sale. | This is copy [number written in] | [in holograph] Robert Duncan | Jess."

Text contents: [INTRODUCTION]—THE HORNS OF ARTEMIS—AFRICA REVISITED—ADAM'S SONG—WORKING TOO LONG AT

IT—AN IMAGINARY WAR ELEGY—THE SONG OF THE BORDER-GUARD—AN ESSAY AT WAR—OF THE ART—FIVE PIECES—HERO SONG—AN IMAGINARY WOMAN—ELUARD'S DEATH—CATS (1)—CATS (2)—UNKINGD BY AFFECTION—DANCE, EARLY SPRING WEATHER MAGIC—FORCED LINES—A POEM IN STRETCHING—POETRY DISARRANGED—A BOOK OF RESEMBLANCES—A DREAM OF THE END OF THE WORLD—LORD MASTER MOUSE—SURREALIST SHELLS—THESE MIRACLES ARE MIRRORS IN THE OPEN SKY FOR PHILIP LAMANTIA—CONVERSION—SALVAGES: AN EVENING PIECE—REFLECTIONS—SALVAGES: LASSITUDE—FRIEDL—TWO POEMS FOR THE JEWS FROM THEIR BOOK OF THE SPLENDOR—THE SCATTERING—IMAGE OF HECTOR—THE LOVER.

Description: The text is printed on yellowish white (C-92) wove paper, 28 x 21.5 cm. The gatherings are sewn with white thread and glued. The endpapers are decorated in an intricate design centering on a bee. The book is bound in black (C-267) cloth over boards 28.5 x 22.2 cm. An emblem of a lion (which also appears on p. [22]) is stamped in very yellow (C-82) on the front cover. Lettering in gold on the spine reads from head to tail, "A BOOK OF RESEMBLANCES [space] ROBERT DUNCAN."

Published: 210 copies published 28 Nov. 1966 at $27.50.

b. *First edition, lettered copies:*

Title, Collation, Contents, Text contents, and Description the same as the regular copies except that three copies have been lettered A, B, C.

Published: Three copies were published 28 Nov. 1966 and reserved for RD, Jess Collins, and Henry Wenning.

Proof papers. MoSW.
Date: [1966]
a. Publisher's announcement: "Announcing | Robert Duncan's | A Book of Resemblances | Designed & Illustrated by | Jess."
    Collation: 2l recto-verso, recto-verso 27.9 x 21.4 cm.
    Contents: The announcement was printed on the same paper with the same design as the endpapers of the book. Recto, first leaf, lettering as above; verso, drawing and seven lines of "The Horns of Artemis." Recto second leaf contains a description of the book; verso second leaf contains the terms of sale.
b. "The Horns of Artemis" and "Of The War," pp. 1 and 45.
    Collation: 2l recto-verso, recto-verso 28 x 21.5 cm.
    Contents: Same as published text.
c. Endpapers.
    Collation: 3l all recto 28 x 42.9 cm.
    Contents: Same as published text.
d. A Book of Resemblances.

Collation: [1]⁶, [2-7]⁸; pp. [i-xiv], 1-94.

Contents: The same as published text, plus some markings and corrections in the hands of RD and Jess throughout.

Notes: The manuscript, with text and drawings, was completed by the end of 1953. The book was submitted for publication to Grove Press. In a letter to Robin Blaser, dated 19 Dec. 1957, RD lamented the time it had been under consideration: "Certainly I feel sad about the fate of my *Book of Resemblances* that languishes at Grove. The tease of even remote possibility of publication is another disease I've to turn out of house: and to regain some joy of reality" (CU-B). After another period of remaining unpublished, the book was set for publication by Andrew Hoyem and Dave Haselwood of The Auerhahn Press in 1962. Because of its length, it was decided to print it in two volumes. The first volume, which was announced, and an announcement mailed out, was to contain the following poems: THE HORNS OF ARTEMIS—AFRICA REVISITED— WORKING TOO LONG AT IT—ADAM'S SONG—AN IMAGINARY WAR ELEGY—THE SONG OF THE BORDERGUARD—AN ESSAY AT WAR—OF THE ART—FIVE PIECES—HERO SONG—AN IMAGINARY WOMAN— ELUARD'S DEATH—CATS (i)—CATS (ii)—HOME—DANCE : EARLY SPRING WEATHER MAGIC—A POEM IN STRETCHING—A BOOK OF RESEMBLANCES—POETRY DIS-ARRANGED—A DREAM OF THE END OF THE WORLD—LORD MASTER MOUSE—SURREALIST SHELLS—THESE MIRACLES ARE MIRRORS IN THE OPEN SKY FOR PHILIP LAMANTIA—CONVERSION—SALVAGES : AN EVENING PIECE—LOVE POEM—SALVAGES : LASSITUDE—FRIEDL— TWO POEMS FOR THE JEWS—THE SCATTERING—IMAGE OF HECTOR—THE LOVER.

In addition to the flyer announcing the book, an advertisement was planned, for which RD wrote the following statement: "The poems in this volume belong to 1950 and 1951, a period of transition, of falling and failing in love, and also of America's falling and failing in war. The Korean War and obsessive homosexual love presented for me corresponding references of lies and defeats, waste and loss. Graves's *The White Goddess* had appeared in 1948, and I had drawn from his argument coordinates of Moon, Muse, and Mother, that began to give a new locus for feeling in which homosexual lovers too had their Nature 'under the Moon's rule'.

"It is the period at the same time of falling and failing in poetry—'An Essay at War', deriving its impulse from Williams's *Paterson*, strives to contain as beauty flaws and inadequacies in the feeling of things— appropriate to the 'police action' in the Orient—a pathetic fallacy?

"Now at last, all this problematic stuff, is to be published, richly illumined by Jess in drawings that suggest the lasting quality of the poems—the evocations of an inner incurable Romance." By the fall of 1962, a dispute had arisen between the artists and the printers over the quality of the reproduction of the advertising flyer, and the quality of the paper to be used for the book. In a letter to Dave Haselwood, dated 16 Nov. 1962

(MoSW), RD withdrew the book from production, and a postcard was mailed by The Auerhahn Press on 19 Nov. 1962 declaring that the book had been "cancelled."

In 1966, negotiations began with Henry Wenning for the publication of the volume. The greatest of care was taken by the artists and publisher to insure a proper publication. In response to sample pages sent by Henry Wenning, RD wrote to him in a letter dated 19 Oct. 1966: "I don't know how we are going to bear up under the excitement of the WHOLE book. Jess was so wound up with seeing those pages and gloating over them he couldn't get to sleep. I think we should take a vacation with the book and just go ape over it" (MoSW).

One error occurred in the volume: in the poem "An Essay At War," p. 34, three lines from the bottom "than" appeared for "that," and the error was corrected when the poem was reprinted in *Derivations*, p. 17. In a memorandum on the letterhead of Henry Wenning, the publisher noted the distribution of all the copies of the edition: "3 copies, A, B, C, for R. D., J., & A and H. W.; 1 copy, Printer's copy, retained by Meriden Gravure; 2 copies, Defective. Double end papers, missing end papers. Destroyed, colophon and title-pages sent to R. D. and Jess. 1 extra copy sent to R. D. & Jess. Signed. Rendered un-defective thru skill & ingenuity of HWW; 200 copies sold or for sale; 2 copies to Library of Congress for copyright; 6 copies to R. D. and Jess and so marked by HWW 'for their friends'" (MoSW).

A23   **THE CAT AND THE BLACKBIRD**   1967

First edition:

[within a line drawing by Jess, and in calligraphy] THE CAT | AND | THE | BLACKBIRD | as | Told by Robert Duncan | & Pictured by Jess [San Francisco: White Rabbit Press, 1967].

Collation: pp. [i-iv], 1-7, [8], 9-17, [18], 19-21, [22], 23-32, [33], 34, [35], 36, [37], 38-46, [47], 48.

Contents: p. [i] half-title-page, "THE | CAT AND THE | BLACKBIRD"; p. [ii] copyright-page, "© 1967 by Robert Duncan & Jess"; p. [iii] title-page; p. [iv] half-title, "[drawing of a cat in top left corner] The cat | and | the | blackbird [drawing of a blackbird in bottom right corner]"; pp. 1-48 text and drawings.

Text contents: THE CAT AND THE BLACKBIRD [story].

Description: The book is printed on white (C-263) glossy paper, 30.4 x 23 cm. The covers are made from heavy white glossy stock and are attached to the text leaves with a very orange (C-48) spiral binder. The front cover has a drawn, irregular, wide black border 1.4 cm. from the four edges. Inside the border are drawings by Jess in orange with the following lettering in black: "[at top left] Robert Duncan | [at middle right] THE | CAT AND THE |

BLACKBIRD | [at bottom left] JESS | ILLUSTRATION | [at bottom right] WHITE RABBIT PRESS | SAN FRANCISCO." The rear cover contains the logo of the press. Inside the front cover a bookplate, 9.1 x 9.4 cm., which serves as a colophon, is pasted on. The plate has a border of decorated rule, and reads: "THIS BOOK BELONGS TO | [an empty line] | [below] Lithographed in an edition of 500 copies and | the plates then destroyed." The text is in holograph, and there is a drawing by Jess on every page except one.

Published: 500 copies published fall 1967 at $5.00.

Notes: The book was begun when RD and Jess discovered that there were very few suitable children's stories available for them to read to Brenda Tyler, the daughter of Mary and Hamilton Tyler, longtime friends of RD and Jess. Ten of the drawings were done in 1953-54, and the second round of drawings were done at Stinson Beach in 1958. The bookplate was not designed by Jess, so in several copies he has made drawings in crayon over and around it.

A24 **CHRISTMAS PRESENT,** 1967
CHRISTMAS PRESENCE!

a. *First edition, regular copies:*

[in deep reddish orange (C-36)] CHRISTMAS present, CHRISTMAS presence! | [text in 50 lines] | ROBERT DUNCAN [Los Angeles: Black Sparrow Press, 1967].

Broadside: The text is printed on yellowish white (C-92) wove paper, 34 x 17.5 cm., and attached to a backing made from green (C-141) stock. The colophon on the verso of the backing reads: "[publisher's logo] Printed December 1967 in an edition of 300 | by Graham Mackintosh as a Christmas Greeting to the | friends of the Black Sparrow Press."

Published: 212 copies published 6 Dec. 1967. Though intended not to be sold, some copies were sold at $10.00.

b. *First edition, signed copies:*

The same as regular copies, but signed by the author.

Published: 59 copies published 6 Dec. 1967, and not for sale.

Note: 25 of the regular copies were reserved for the author.

A25 **EPILOGOS** 1967

a. *First edition, regular copies:*

[cover title] EPILOGOS | ROBERT [within a very yellow (C-82) circular design, in holograph] RD [in type] DUNCAN [Los Angeles: Black Sparrow Press, 1967].

Collation: [1]⁸; pp. [i-ii], [1-2], 3-10, [11-14].

Contents: pp. [i-ii] blank; p. [1] drawing; p. [2] blank; pp. 3-10 text; p. [11] acknowledgments-page, "Written with the freedom made possible by a grant from | The National Endowment Fund for the Arts"; p. [12] colophon-page, "[name in holograph] Robert Duncan | [publisher's logo] | Printed June, 1967 in Los Angeles by Philip Klein for the Black | Sparrow Press. This edition is limited to one hundred and fifteen | copies: 15 copies handbound in boards and lettered A-O, which | are not for sale, and one hundred numbered copies in paper | wrappers, for sale, all signed and with an original drawing by | the poet. | This is copy No. [number in deep red (C-13) holograph]; | Copyright 1967 by Robert Duncan"; pp. [13-14] blank.

Text contents: the poem EPILOGOS.

Description: The text is printed on light yellow (C-86) textured paper, 15.8 x 15.5 cm.; the first two leaves have deckled edges and the remaining ones are trimmed. The gathering is sewn with deep pink (C-3) thread and attached to the cover. A drawing in black ink appears on page [1]. The cover is made from stiff deep red (approximately C-13) stock, 17 x 16.4 cm. A yellow circular design appears around the poet's hand-drawn initials, between "Robert" and "Duncan." "Epilogos" in large black letters appears above. The rear cover is blank.

Published: 100 copies published 17 July 1967 at $15.00.

b. *First edition, hardbound copies:*

Title, Collation, Contents, Text contents, and Description the same as the regular copies except that the gathering has been bound in black cloth over boards 17.2 x 16.7 cm. The front cover of the trade copies has been pasted onto the front cover, but the circular design does not appear. A crayon drawing appears on p. [1] in a variety of colors. The copies are signed and lettered A-O on the colophon-page.

Published: 15 copies published 20 Sept. 1967, but only 7 copies offered for sale at $35.00.

Notes: In two letters, RD commented on making the drawings for the volume; the first is to Adele and Henry Wenning, dated June 1967, and the second is to Ruth Witt-Diamant, dated 14 June 1967. "I am in the midst of a *tour de force* of drawing, so far the challenge is also all inspiration: the 115 drawings for my *Epilogos* that John Martin is publishing. I have done 32 to date (today, leaving off my sessions in order to get a letter or two at least out)" (MoSW). "[I've been] working from the image of an old man of the tree, the daimon Dianus or Virbius from a group of figures in Cook's *Zeus* and in another book *Deities and Dolphins*. Thru each of which operation I seek to draw out some face of the old man himself. Being 'sent' by books as others are sent by Marijuana or angelic interference, I've still to bring back some token of the things seen" (NN). Some of the drawings, like the one in the copy at CtY, are of Ezra Pound.

a. *First edition, numbered copies:*

THE | Truth & Life | of Myth | [in italics] An Essay in Essential Autobiography | [in Roman] ROBERT DUNCAN | [publisher's logo]| House of Books, Ltd. | NEW YORK| 1968.

Collation: [1-5]⁸; pp. [1-6], 7-78, [79-80].

Contents: p. [1] colophon-page, "THIS FIRST EDITION IS LIMITED | TO THREE HUNDRED NUMBERED COPIES | AND TWENTY-SIX LETTERED COPIES | SIGNED BY THE AUTHOR | THIS IS NO. [number in holograph]| [in RD's holograph] Robert Duncan"; p. [2] blank; p. [3] title-page; p. [4] copyright-page, "COPYRIGHT © 1968 BY ROBERT DUNCAN| ALL RIGHTS RESERVED [dot] PRINTED IN U.S.A."; p. [5] four quotations from various sources under the heading, "THE TRUTH & LIFE OF MYTH | [in italics] An Essay in Essential Autobiography"; p. [6] blank; pp. 7-78 text; p. [79] series colophon-page, "THIS IS NUMBER SIXTEEN OF | THE CROWN OCTAVOS| PUBLISHED BY HOUSE OF BOOKS, LTD. | 667 MADISON AVENUE, NEW YORK | THIS BOOK WAS SET IN CASLON OLD FACE| COMPOSITION AND PRESSWORK BY| THE ANTHOENSEN PRESS| PORTLAND, MAINE"; p. [80] blank.

Text contents: [essay] THE TRUTH AND LIFE OF MYTH—[poem] "YES, I CARE DEEPLY AND YET" (fl).

Description: The text is printed on yellowish white (C-92) wove paper, 19.1 x 12.6 cm., and the gatherings are sewn with white thread. The endpapers are white. The gatherings are bound in light blue (C-181) cloth over boards 19.5 x 13.1 cm. The front and rear covers are blank, while lettering on the spine in very yellow (C-82) reads from tail to head, "THE TRUTH & LIFE OF MYTH [device] DUNCAN." The book was published with a glassine wrapper.

Published: 300 copies published 9 Jan. 1969 at $15.00.

b. *First edition, lettered copies:*

Title, Collation, Contents, Text contents, and Description the same as the numbered copies except that these copies have been lettered A-Z and signed "Robert Duncan" on the colophon-page, p. [1].

Published: 26 copies published 9 Jan. 1969, for presentation only.

c. *First sub-edition, paperbound copies:*

THE | Truth & Life | of Myth | [in italics] An Essay in Essential Autobiography | ROBERT DUNCAN | [publisher's logo] | THE SUMAC PRESS| Freemont, Michigan | In cooperation with SOMA Books [1973].

Collation: [1-5]⁸; pp. [1-6], 7-78, [79-80].

Contents: pp. [1-2] blank; p. [3] title-page; p. [4] copyright-page, "COPYRIGHT © 1968 BY ROBERT DUNCAN | ALL RIGHTS RESERVED [dot] PRINTED IN U. S. A. | This book was first published in a limited edition by The House | of Books, Ltd. in 1968. | This volume is published in cooperation with SOMA Books. | (GEORGE QUASHA, EDITOR) | [below] Library of Congress Catalogue Card Number: 73-183486 | Standard Book Number: 912090-18-9"; p. [5] four quotations from various sources under the heading, "THE TRUTH & LIFE OF MYTH | [in italics] An Essay in Essential Autobiography"; p. [6] blank; pp. 7-78 text; pp. [79-80] blank.

Text contents: [essay] THE TRUTH AND LIFE OF MYTH—[poem] "YES, I CARE DEEPLY AND YET" (fl).

Description: The book is printed on white wove paper, 22.9 x 15 cm., and the gatherings glued to the cover. The cover is made from heavy white wove stock, enameled on the exterior surface. Lettering on the front cover reads: "the Truth & | Life of Myth | [reproduction of Blake's illumination, *Ezekiel's Vision,* 15 x 11.4 cm.] [to left of reproduction reading from tail to head] AN ESSAY IN ESSENTIAL AUTOBIOGRAPHY [dash] ROBERT DUNCAN." Lettering on the spine reads from head to tail, "THE TRUTH & LIFE OF MYTH [space] ROBERT DUNCAN [space] SUMAC PRESS." On the rear cover at the top left: "$2.45 | [in middle, a reproduction of a photograph of RD by Jane McClure, 7.1 x 6.7 cm.] [lettering vertically beside reproduction at right, reading from tail to head] PHOTO BY JANE MCCLURE." There is an eleven line statement about this book and about RD, followed by the publisher's logo and: "Cover illustration: *Ezekiel's Vision* by William Blake | Cover design: Ray Hoagland."

Published: 2500 copies published Jan. 1973 at $2.45.

Notes: This essay was first presented as a lecture at "A Meeting of Poets & Theologians to discuss Parable Myth and Language" held at The College of Preachers in Washington, D.C., 13-15 Oct. 1967. Before the text was printed in the First edition, there were two drafts (OKentU). The original cover for the First sub-edition was a collage by Jess; however, the collage was misplaced by a printer, and the present cover was selected by The Sumac Press.

A27   **NAMES OF PEOPLE**   1968

a. *First edition, regular copies:*

[within multiple light brown (C-57) rules 2.5 cm. from bottom, 1.8 cm. from the top, and 2.2 cm. from the right and left edges, with a single black rule as the interior border] Names of People | [short deep yellowish green (C-132) double rule] Robert Duncan | [a coat of arms with a sun, cats, and flowers in green] | Illustrated

by Jess | [short green double rule] BLACK SPARROW PRESS |
LOS ANGELES 1968.

Collation: [1-4]⁴, [5]⁶; pp. [1-4], 5-37, [38-44].

Contents: p. [1] title-page; p. [2] copyright-page, "Copyright © 1968 | by
Robert Duncan & Jess | [below within a box] BLACK SPARROW PRESS |
Post Office Box 25603 | Los Angeles, California | 90025"; p. [3] half-title,
[in holograph] "Stein imitations from 1952"; pp. [4]-37 illustrations and
text; p. [38] blank; p. [39] contents-page; p. [40] blank; p. [41] colophon-
page, [publisher's logo] "Printed August 1968 in Santa Barbara by | Noel
Young for the Black Sparrow | Press. This edition is limited to 250 |
numbered copies & 26 lettered | copies hors de commerce, | all signed by both
| author & artist. | This is copy No. | [number in holograph deep red (C-13)] |
[in holograph] Robert Duncan | Jess"; pp. [42-44] blank.

Text contents: [illustration] THE INSIDE INSIDE—FIRST—[illustration]
NAMES OF PEOPLE—NAMES OF PEOPLE—A LEAVE AS YOU
MAY—[illustration] U.S.—UPON HIS RETURN—[illustration] NICER—
TWO PAINTERS—[illustration] HASSEL SMITH—[illustration]
CORBETT—AN ARRANGEMENT—[illustration] WE SAW—[illustra-
tion] GRANNY'S—AN ABOUT FACE—[illustration] MAHL—A COAT
OF ARMS—[illustration] WE KNOW—REMEMBERING—[illustration]
NEAR—A MEXICAN STRAIGHT SUMMER—[illustration] DEMON
STRAIGHT—ROBERT BERG AT FLORENCE—[illustration] ALMOST—
AN EVENING AT HOME—[illustration] WATCH—A DESIGN FOR
FLACK—[illustration] SIR-10/FIN.

Description: The text is printed on yellowish white (C-92) wove paper, 28 x
21.6 cm., and the gatherings are sewn with white thread and glued to the
cover. The endpapers are white. The front and rear covers are made from
heavy, textured light yellowish brown (C-76) paper over boards 28.2 x 22.3
cm. The spine is bound in medium yellowish brown (C-77) leather stretching 3.3 cm. onto the front and rear covers. An enlarged version of the coat of
arms which appears on the title-page is stamped on the cover in very yellow
(C-82). Lettering stamped on the spine in very yellow reads from head to tail,
"NAMES OF PEOPLE [dot] Robert Duncan." The rear cover is blank. The
book was published with a clear plastic wrapper.

Published: 250 copies published 14 Oct. 1968 at $30.00.

b. *First edition, lettered copies:*

Title, Collation, Contents, Text contents, and Description the same as the
regular copies except that these copies have been lettered A-Z on the
colophon-page and signed by the poet and the artist.

Published: 26 copies published 14 Oct. 1968 and not for sale.

c. *First edition, special copies:*

Title, Collation, Contents, Text contents, and Description the same as the regular copies except that these copies have been bound in full leather, brown (C-77). All are signed by the poet and the artist. 3 are numbered and marked, "File Copy," 2 marked "Printer's Copy," and 1 each marked "Author's Copy," "Artist's Copy," "Pulbisher's Copy," and "Binder's Copy."

Published: 9 copies published 14 Oct. 1968 and not for sale.

Notes: This volume is the companion to *A Book of Resemblances*; the poems were written during the same period. The book went in and out of print in one day.

A28   **MY MOTHER WOULD BE A FALCONRESS**   1968

a. *First edition, restricted copies:*

MY MOTHER WOULD BE A FALCONRESS | [text in 72 lines] | ROBERT DUNCAN | [embossed and uncolored] oyez | Copyright 1968 by Robert Duncan [Berkeley, 1968].

Broadside: The text is printed on yellowish white (C-92) textured paper, 71.2 x 51 cm.

Published: approximately 100 copies published in 1968 and not intended for sale.

b. *First edition, signed copies:*

The same as the restricted copies except that these copies are numbered 1-75 and signed by RD. The compiler's copy is dated "Feb 7, 1968."

Published: 75 copies published in 1968 at $15.00.

c. *First edition, special copies:*

Same as the restricted copies except that these copies are lettered A-D, signed by RD, and contain a colored drawing of a falcon by RD.

Published: 4 copies published in 1968 and not intended for sale.

Note: This poem was written during the summer of 1964. It was originally part of A LAMMAS TIDING and only later made a separate poem.

A29   **BENDING THE BOW**   1968

a. *First edition, hardbound copies, first impression:*

BENDING | THE BOW | Robert | DUNCAN | New Directions | 1968 [New York].

Collation: [1-5]¹⁶; pp. [1-8], i-x, ²[1-2], 3-137, [138-142].

Contents: p. [1] half-title-page, "BENDING THE BOW"; p. [2] twenty-four titles under the heading, "Other Books by Robert Duncan"; p. [3] title-page; p. [4] copyright and acknowledgments-page, "Copyright © 1963, 1964, 1965, 1966, 1967, 1968 | by Robert Duncan | Library of Congress Catalogue Card No. 68-15879 | [seventeen titles listed after] ACKNOWLEDGMENT | All rights reserved. Except for brief passages quoted in a news- | paper, magazine, radio, or television review, no part of this | book may be reproduced in any form or by any means, elec- | tronic or mechanical, including photocopying and recording, | or by any information storage and retrieval system, without | permission in writing from the Publisher. | Book and jacket design by Graham Mackintosh. | Text set in Aldus type by J. S. Brooke. | Manufactured in the United States of America | New Directions Books are published for James Laughlin | by New Directions Publishing Corporation, | 333 Sixth Avenue, New York 10014"; pp. [5-7] contents-pages; p. [8] blank; pp. i-x "INTRODUCTION"; p. [1] half-title page "BENDING THE BOW"; p. [2] blank; pp. 3-137 text; p. [138] blank; pp. [139-140] "NOTES"; pp. [141-142] blank.

Text contents: PREFACE—SONNET 4—STRUCTURE OF RIME XXII—5TH SONNET—SUCH IS THE SICKNESS OF MANY A GOOD THING—BENDING THE BOW—TRIBAL MEMORIES, PASSAGES 1—AT THE LOOM, PASSAGES 2—WHAT I SAW, PASSAGES 3—WHERE IT APPPEARS, PASSAGES 4—THE MOON, PASSAGES 5—THE COLLAGE, PASSAGES 6—ENVOY, PASSAGES 7—STRUCTURE OF RIME XXIII—AS IN THE OLD DAYS, PASSSAGES 8—THE ARCHITECTURE, PASSAGES 9—THESE PAST YEARS, PASSAGES 10—SHADOWS, PASSAGES 11—WINE, PASSAGES 12—STRUCTURE OF RIME XXIV—STRUCTURE OF RIME XXV—REFLECTIONS—THE FIRE, PASSAGES 13—CHORDS, PASSAGES 14—SPELLING, PASSAGES 15—A LAMMAS TIDING—"MY MOTHER WOULD BE A FALCONRESS" (fl)—SAINT GRAAL (AFTER VERLAINE)—PARSIFAL (AFTER VERLAINE AND WAGNER)—THE CURRENTS, PASSAGES 16—MOVING THE MOVING IMAGE, PASSAGES 17—THE TORSO, PASSAGES 18—THE EARTH, PASSAGES 19—AN ILLUSTRATION, PASSAGES 20 (STRUCTURE OF RIME XXVI)—THE MULTIVERSITY, PASSAGES 21—IN THE PLACE OF A PASSAGE 22—BENEFICE, PASSAGES 23—ORDERS, PASSAGES 24—UP RISING, PASSAGES 25—THE CHIMERAS OF GÉRARD DE NERVAL [sequence-title for following eight poems] EL DESDICHADO—MYRTHO—HORUS—ANTEROS—DELPHICA—ARTEMIS—THE CHRIST IN THE OLIVE GROVE—GOLDEN LINES—EARTH'S WINTER SONG—MOIRA'S CATHEDRAL—A SHRINE TO AMEINIAS—NARRATION FOR ADAM'S WAY—THE SOLDIERS, PASSAGES 26—AN INTERLUDE—TRANSGRESSING THE REAL, PASSAGES 27—THE LIGHT, PASSAGES 28—EYE OF GOD, PASSAGES 29—STAGE DIRECTIONS, PASSAGES 30—GOD-SPELL—EPILOGOS—NOTES.

Description: The text is printed on yellowish white (C-92) wove paper, 20.2 x 13.5 cm., and the gatherings are sewn with white thread. The center thread is light pink (C-4). The gathering are glued to the binding. The endpapers are made from greenish yellow (C-105) paper, and the headbands are gray green (C-150). The covers are made from brilliant yellow (C-83) cloth over boards 20.8 x 14.3 cm. The front and rear covers are blank, but the lettering on the spine in very green (C-139) reads from head to tail, "Robert Duncan [slash] Bending the Bow [space] New Directions."

Dust jacket: The dust jacket is made from heavy yellowish white stock enameled on the exterior side. A reproduction of a photograph of RD in black and white by Nata Piaskowski forms the front cover with the following lettering in white at the bottom: "Robert Duncan [slash] Bending the Bow." Lettering on the spine is in white over black and reads from the head to the tail, "Robert Duncan [slash] Bending the Bow [space] New Directions." "Robert Duncan" in bold type appears at the top of the rear cover and under that a thirty-five line biographical and historical statement about the author printed in black on white. The following two lines appear at the bottom: "Please see the inside rear flap of this jacket for a list of Dun- | can's other books in print." The front flap contains "Robert Duncan [slash] Bending the Bow" in bold type, a forty-two line statement about this book, and the lines, "Jacket photo By Nata Piaskowski. | A New Directions Book [space] $5.00." The rear flap contains seven titles and names of publishers under the heading "OTHER BOOKS BY ROBERT DUNCAN," plus three lines referring to the special issue of *Audit/Poetry.*

Published: 1037 copies published 2 Feb. 1968 at $5.00.

b. *First edition, hardbound copies, second impression:*

Title, Collation, Contents, Text contents, Description, and Dust jacket the same as the first impression except that the twenty-four lines omitted from THE CHRIST IN THE OLIVE GROVE have been added to alter the pagination of the titles in the sequence THE CHIMERAS OF GÉRARD DE NERVAL. For the first impression: p. 84, THE CHIMERAS OF GÉRARD DE NERVAL, EL DESDICHADO; p. 85, MYRTHO; p. 86, HORUS; p. 87, ANTEROS; p. 88, DELPHICA; p. 89, ARTEMIS; pp. 90-91, THE CHRIST IN THE OLIVE GROVE; p. 92, GOLDEN LINES. For the second impression: p. 84, THE CHIMERAS OF GÉRARD DE NERVAL, EL DESDICHADO; pp. 84-85, MYRTHO; pp. 85-86, HORUS; pp. 86-87, ANTEROS; p. 87, DELPHICA; p. 88, ARTEMIS; pp. 89-91, THE CHRIST IN THE OLIVE GROVE; p. 92, GOLDEN LINES. The designation "Second Printing" appears at the bottom of the copyright-page.

Published: 1045 copies published Dec. 1969 at $5.00.

c. *First edition, paperbound copies, first issue:*

Title, Collation, Contents, and Text contents, and Description the same as the First edition, hardbound copies, first impression. The paper cover is made from heavy white stock enameled on one side. The contents of the front cover and the spine of the dust jacket of the hardbound edition are reproduced on the front cover and spine of this cover, but with "ND255" substituted for "New Directions" on the spine. The blurb from the inside front flap of the dust jacket has been reproduced on the rear cover with the addition of the word "Poetry" at the top left, and across the bottom, "A New Directions Paperbook [space] NDP255 $2.25."

Published: 5056 copies published 2 Feb. 1968 at $2.25.

d. *First edition, paperbound copies, second issue:*

Title, Collation, Contents, Text contents, and Description the same as the First edition, hardbound copies, first impression, except that the line in brackets, "Also by Robert Duncan: Roots and Branches (poetry), NDP 275, $1.75," has been added as the penultimate line on the rear cover.

Published: 1018 copies published 19 May 1969 at $2.25.

e. *First edition, paperbound copies, second impression:*

Title, Collation, Contents, and Text contents the same as the First edition, hardbound copies, second impression, with the alterations made in the sequence THE CHIMERAS OF GÉRARD DE NERVAL; and the Description is the same as the First edition paperbound copies, first issue, except that the designation "Second Printing" appears at the bottom of the copyright-page.

Published: 2917 copies published Dec. 1969 at $2.25.

f. *First edition, paperbound copies, third impression:*

Title, Collation, Contents, Text contents, and Description the same as the second impression except that the gatherings have been trimmed to 20.2 x 13. cm., and a perfect binding applied. Two changes have been made on the rear cover: the line at the top now reads, "Poetry [slash] ISBN: 0-8112-0033-7 [space] Third Printing," and the penultimate line added to the First impression, second issue, has been expanded into two lines to read, in brackets, "Also by Robert Duncan: The Opening of the Field (poetry), NDP356, | $2.45 Roots and Branches (poetry), NDP275, $1.75." The designation "Third Printing" has been added at the bottom of the copyright-page, and the following three lines added between lines 6 and 5 from the bottom: "First published clothbound (ISBN: 0-8112-0269-0) and as New Directions | Paperbook 255 (ISBN: 0-8112-0033-7) in 1968 | Published in Canada by McClelland & Stewart, Ltd."

Published: 2143 copies published Oct. 1973 at $2.25.

g. *First edition, paperbound copies, fourth impression:*

Title, Collation, Contents, Text contents, and Description the same as the third impression except for the following: the designation "FOURTH PRINTING" has been added at the bottom of the copyright-page and at the top right corner of the rear cover. At the bottom of the rear cover the prices of *The Opening of The Field* and *Roots and Branches* have been changed to "$3.75" and "$4.95," respectively, and a white paper label has been pasted over the price "$2.25," changing it to "$4.95." The new price is printed in purple (C-195).

Published: 1000 copies published 21 July 1978 at $4.95.

h. *First English edition, hardbound copies:*

BENDING | THE BOW | [rule] ROBERT DUNCAN | [at bottom] [publisher's logo]| Jonathan Cape Thirty Bedford Square London [1971].

Collation: [A]⁸, B-K⁸; pp. [1-8], i-x, ²[1-2], 3-137, [138-142].

Contents and Text contents the same as the First edition, hardbound copies, second impression.

Description: The text is printed on yellowish white (C-92) wove paper, 21.5 x 13.5 cm., from plates made from the First edition, second impression. The title "An Interlude" has been added in the proper place on the contents page. The endpapers are white, and the signatures are bound in medium gray (C-265) cloth over boards 22.4 x 14.4 cm. The front and rear covers are blank, while lettering on the spine in very yellow (C-82) reads from head to tail, "BENDING THE BOW Robert Duncan [space] [publisher's logo]." The copyright-page contains the following different information: "THIS COLLECTION FIRST PUBLISHED IN GREAT BRITAIN 1971" followed by copyright dates and "JONATHAN CAPE LIMITED | 30 BEDFORD SQUARE LONDON W. C. 1." The acknowledgments are the same, but the statement of the right of reprinting, the designer, and publisher statements are eliminated and replaced with: "PRINTED IN GREAT BRITAIN | BY LOWE AND BRYDONE (PRINTERS) LTD, LONDON | BOUND BY JAMES BURN AND CO. LTD, ESHER SURREY."

Dust jacket: The dust jacket is made from heavy yellowish white (C-92) wove stock overprinted with a brilliant greenish yellow (C-98) and black illustration of centaurs shooting arrows down at male figures in the water below them. The illustration runs continuously from the front cover, to the spine, to the rear cover. Printing in black at the top of the front cover reads, "Bending the Bow| Robert Duncan." Printing in white on the spine reads from head to tail, "Bending the Bow Robert Duncan [space] [publisher's logo in black]." The rear cover contains no lettering. The inside front flap contains a twenty-six line statement about RD's poetry and at bottom, "£1.95 net [short rule] | IN UK ONLY." The rear inside flap contains a thirty-two line biographical and historical statement about RD, which is a condensation of the statement on the rear cover of the dust jacket of the First edition, hardbound copies. There is also the following at the bottom: "ISBN 0 224 000536 7 | Jacket design by Leigh Taylor | © Jonathan Cape Ltd 1971."

Published: An unknown number of copies published in 1971 at £1.95 net. In a letter to the compiler dated 11 Aug. 1978, the publisher declined to disclose the number of copies printed.

Proof papers. MoSW.

Date: [1967]
a.   Galley proofs
     Collation: 4*l* all recto 55.7 x 21.7 cm.
     Contents: The text of GOD-SPELL—STAGE DIRECTIONS PASSAGES 30—EPILOGOS, plus corrections in RD's hand.
b.   Second galley proofs.
     Collation: 24*l* all recto 55.7 x 21.6 cm.
     Contents: The text of the poems from SONNET 4 through THE LIGHT, PASSAGES 28 plus notes and spacing adjustments and other markings throughout.
c.   Galley proofs.
     Collation: 3*l* all recto 55.7 x 22.1 cm.
     Contents: The text of SONNET [4]—5TH SONNET—SUCH IS THE SICKNESS OF MANY A GOOD THING—BENDING THE BOW—TRIBAL MEMORIES, PASSAGES 1. There are notes and corrections throughout, plus a long note, verso first leaf, in RD's holograph about his poetry.
d.   Galley proofs.
     Collation: 28*l* all recto 55.7 x 22.1 cm.
     Contents: The text of all the poems, with markings throughout, dated "10/10" and "10/11."
e.   Galley proofs for introduction and notes.
     Collation: 4*l* all recto 55.8 x 22.1 cm.
     Contents: The text plus notes throughout.
f.   Page proofs for *Bending The Bow.*
     Collation: 127*l* all recto 22 x 17.3 cm.
     Contents: The text of the title-page, then the poems from SONNET 4 through EYE OF GOD, PASSAGES 29. There are markings throughout.
g.   "Final" page proofs.
     Collation: 152*l* all recto 27.9 x 18.2 cm.
     Contents: The text of the entire book, except that the one page containing the final twenty-four lines of THE CHRIST IN THE OLIVE GROVE has been dropped and the pages following renumbered. There are a few notes and alterations.
h.   "Final" page proofs.
     Collation: 152*l* all recto 27.9 x 18.2 cm.

Contents: The same as "g" but without markings. This set was for the printer Graham Mackintosh.

Notes: The book was originally to be printed by Scribner's, as RD notes in a letter to George Starbuck dated 26 Dec. 1966: "Before I left for Thanksgiving I managed to get off to Scribner's the manuscript of a new book of poems *Bending the Bow*" (IU). By the spring of 1967, a complication had arisen with Scribner's. The editors at Scribner's wrote to RD asking that "Passages 13, 21, 25, and 26" be omitted from the volume: "This is not on the basis of the political sentiments expressed—which if anything are shared by the people here—but rather simply that these poems did not seem up to the rest of the work. They seemed rather didactic and shrill, without complexity or, broadly speaking, the fine quality of the other poems." This statement was quoted by RD in a letter to Robert Creeley, dated 23 Feb. 1967. RD continues in the same letter: "I wrote them that there were at least some who found THE FIRE and THE SOLDIERS to be among my best poems, and that these some included you, Denny [Denise Levertov], Rago [Henry Rago, editor of *Poetry*],...

"I didn't have time, what with being in the throws of moving and at the same time having work done on the new house, to hunt up specific commendations. Well, they (the Scribner's editors) do no more than ask *if* these poems could be omitted. To which I said NO, of course. And that if by April 10th I have not received the contract for the book, I will send the ms. to Oyez for publication" (on deposit at MoSW). Even though RD discussed the publication of the book with Robert Hawley, publisher of Oyez, in a note dated Spring 1967 (CtU), the book was not done by Oyez; instead, it was invited to New Directions. In a letter dated 4 Nov. 1967, RD wrote to Robert Creeley: "These days have waited on getting the New Directions book thru the printers—a job still not done. And I am all but finisht with the Preface for the same; have only a short concluding section to do." In the Preface, as RD says, he tried "to picture a scene in which something is happening as if in the poems I try to find out what is going on, rather than saying or telling something" (on deposit at MoSW). The direct reference here is the relationship of the poet to the Vietnam War.

The book was brought into print by New Directions in February 1968, and to assist in that publication RD prepared a statement about the placement of the lines on the page and the complicated spacing within the lines and within whole poems entitled "Kinds of Notation used in *Bending the Bow*" (MoSW), which includes the following statements: "In planning the typography of the book consider opening out the line as much as possible as opposed to closing it in. Often I want phrasings suspended in their own time within the poem and this must somehow be conveyd in the notation.... (As in the typed copy, I rather like typographical variety, I do not always keep the same indentation for an inner margin but allow the feel of the visual pattern of the poem to take over. Here, given that the notation is clear ... the typographer should decide in relation to his feelings of the appearance. . . . Whether an inner margin proceeds or returns in relation to other lines is notation; spacings or these inner margins, provided that they are distinctive, are a matter of typography. . . . Complexes of lines having individual margins: where lines on the typed page appear on a common vertical margin they are considered to be related as if starting from a common order: where lines do not line up in common with any other lines, what governs their placement is (i) their not aligning with other margins, and (ii) their preceding or following in relation to other lines. . . . In typography, what is important is that these three orders: lines within a stanza, stanzas, and section must be clearly differentiated."

After Paul Mariah discovered that three stanzas had been dropped from THE CHRIST IN THE OLIVE TREE, RD published a note [*Caterpillar*, 7 (1969), 89] explaining the omission: "After passing through galley proofs and page proofs on galley stock, the book was printed on special glossy stock for photolithographic reproduction in the East, and this final printing was checked by the author for the place of the figures in 'THE COLLAGE' 'SPELLING' and 'BENEFICE' (from drawings by Jess) which were entered in the text only at this final stage. . . . It did not occur to me that the printer could have 'lost' a page or have altered the numbering of the pages and the contents. . . . In the final copy sent to New Directions the printer Graham Mackintosh dropped what should have been page 92 and numbered to cover the error. In the second copy of the final printing, he dropped page 91, numbering what should have been page 92 in its place to cover." As stated above, the error was corrected in the second impression; however, the title AN INTERLUDE has remained off the title-page of all impressions except the one by Jonathan Cape.

A30   **THE FIRST DECADE**   1969

a. *First edition, regular copies:*

[double title-page] [in RD's holograph] Robert Duncan | [as an inverted mirror image of the first line, in light gray (C-264)] Robert Duncan | The First Decade | [in type at bottom right-hand page] selected poems 1940-1950 | Fulcrum Press [London, 1969].

Collation: [A-H]⁸, [I]⁴; pp. [1-8], 9-136.

Contents: p. [1] blank; pp. [2-3] title-pages; p. [4] acknowledgments and copyright-page, under the heading "Acknowledgements" ten titles of magazines and eight titles of his own books where the poems appeared previously, and the titles of five poems appearing for the first time in this book, "Copyright © Robert Duncan 1968. All rights reserved. | Printed in Great Britain for the Fulcrum Press 20 Fitzroy Square | London WI by Lavenham Press, Lavenham Suffolk. 150 copies | of this first edition separately printed on fawn glastonbury antique | laid paper are numbered and signed by the author. The book | design and typography is by Stuart Montgomery and the cover | is from the Whitley Bay series by Richard

Hamilton"; p. [5] twenty-three titles listed under the heading, "Other books by Robert Duncan"; pp. [6-7] contents-pages; p. [8] blank; pp. 9-136 text.

Text contents: A SPRING MEMORANDUM: FORT KNOX—AN AFRICAN ELEGY—THE YEARS AS CATCHES—KING HAYDN OF MIAMI BEACH—HOMAGE AND LAMENT FOR EZRA POUND IN CAPTIVITY MAY 12, 1944—A CONGREGATION—SLEEP IS A DEEP AND MANY VOICED FLOOD—AN APOLLONIAN ELEGY—BERKELEY POEMS [sequence-title for following four poems] "AMONG MY FRIENDS LOVE IS A GREAT SORROW" (fl)—AN ELEGIAC FRAGMENT—A WOMAN'S DRUNKEN LAMENT—PORTRAIT OF TWO WOMEN—HEAVENLY CITY, EARTHLY CITY—DOMESTIC SCENES [sequence-title for following ten poems] BREAKFAST—REAL ESTATE—BUS FARE—MAIL BOXES—MATCHES—BATH—RADIO—ELECTRIC IRON—LUNCH WITH BUNS—PIANO—MEDIEVAL SCENES [sequence-title for following ten poems] THE DREAMERS—THE HELMET OF GOLIATH—THE BANNERS—THE KINGDOM OF JERUSALEM—THE FESTIVALS—THE MIRROR—THE REAPER—THE ADORATION OF THE VIRGIN—HUON OF BORDEAUX—THE ALBIGENSES—THE HOMECOMING—THE TEMPLE OF THE ANIMALS—THE REVENANT—A WEEKEND OF THE SAME EVENT—SLEEPING ALL NIGHT—I TELL OF LOVE—THE VENICE POEM [sequence-title for following six poems] 1. A DESCRIPTION OF VENICE—TESTIMONY—2. IMAGINARY INSTRUCTIONS—RECORSO—3. THE VENUS OF LESPUGES—CODA—HOMAGE TO THE BROTHERS GRIMM [sequence-title for following three poems] THE ROBBER MOON—STRAWBERRIES UNDER THE SNOW—THE DINNER TABLE OF HARLEQUIN—JERUSALEM—REVIVAL—FOUR POEMS AS A NIGHT SONG [sequence-title for following four poems] THE CONSTRUCTION—THE WALK TO THE VACANT LOT—THE WASTE, THE ROOM, THE DISCARDED TIMBERS—BEFORE WAKING AT HALF-PAST SIX IN THE MORNING—THE SECOND NIGHT IN THE WEEK—PRO-CESSIONALS I—PROCESSIONALS II—GOODBYE TO YOUTH—THE HORNS OF ARTEMIS—AFRICA REVISITED—AN IMAGINARY WAR ELEGY—THE SONG OF THE BORDERGUARD.

Description: The text is printed on white (C-263) wove paper, 23.9 x 15 cm., and the gatherings are sewn with white thread and glued. The endpapers are of tan (approximately light yellowish brown C-76) laid paper watermarked with a crown and "Glastonbury." An enlarged signature of the author reproduced twice in dark brown (C-59) runs horizontally across the middle of both papers, at the front as well as at the rear. The gatherings have been bound in medium reddish brown (C-43) cloth over boards 24.4 x 15.3 cm. The front cover is blank. The lettering on the spine in very yellow (C-82) reads from head to tail, "Robert Duncan *The First Decade* Fulcrum." The rear cover is blank.

Dust jacket: The dust jacket is made from white wove stock enameled on the exterior surface. The front and back covers and the spine are decorated in a reproduction of a marbled design of medium reddish brown (C-43) and pink white (C-9). The lettering in black on the front cover reads, "Robert Duncan | The First Decade." Lettering on the spine from head to tail reads, "Robert Duncan The First Decade." The rear cover is blank. The front flap begins a three paragraph statement by RD about this book and its contents under the heading (in medium reddish brown) "Robert Duncan." Forty-three lines appear on the front flap (along with the price "35/-" at the bottom right), and twenty-one lines appear on the rear flap. The statement is signed in type, "Robert Duncan | San Francisco June 1968." Below the statement on the rear flap, under the heading "FULCRUM PRESS," appear the titles and authors of eighteen volumes published by the press.

Published: 3000 copies published Feb. 1969 at 35/-[$4.50].

b. *First edition, signed copies:*

Title, Collation, Contents, and Text contents the same as the regular copies. The text has been printed on light yellowish brown laid paper watermarked with a crown and "Glastonbury," and the endpapers are the same as those in the trade copies. The gatherings have been sewn with white thread, glued, and bound in textured medium yellowish brown (C-77) cloth over boards, with deep brown (C-75) and grayish yellow (C-90) headbands. Lettering on the spine is the same as on the regular copies. One additional line has been added on the acknowledgments-page: "Limited edition number [numbers in holograph] [number] / 150 [in RD's holograph] | Robert Duncan." The price has been clipped off the corner of the front flap, and the dust jacket has been covered with a clear plastic wrapper.

Published: Despite the colophon, only 135 copies were published Feb. 1969 at £ 6/6 [$17.50].

Notes: The poems that appear in book form for the first time are REAL ESTATE—MAIL BOXES—BATH—LUNCH WITH BUNS—THE REVENANT. An unknown number of the trade and signed copies were boxed together in pairs for distribution and sale.

A31   **DERIVATIONS**   1969

a. *First edition, regular copies:*

[all title-page in RD's holograph] Robert Duncan | [an inverted mirror image in light gray (C-264) of] Derivations | Derivations | [an inverted mirror image in light gray of] Derivations | Selected Poems | 1950-1956 | [in light gray] Fulcrum Press | London [1969].

Collation: [1-9]⁸; pp. [1-8], 9-24, [25-26], 27-38, [39-40], 41-54, [55-56], 57-64, [65-66], 67-70, [70-72], 73-86, [87-88], 89-138, [139-140], 141-144.

Contents: p. [1] [in holograph] half-title, "Robert Duncan | Derivations"; p. [2] blank; p. [3] title-page; p. [4] acknowledgments and copyright-page, under the heading [in holograph] acknowledgments twelve titles of magazines and seven titles of RD's own books where the poems appeared previously, and the titles of five poems appearing for the first time in this book, "Copyright © 1968 Robert Duncan First Edition. | All rights reserved. Printed in Great Britain by Villiers | Publications Ltd London NW5 for Fulcrum Press 20 Fitzroy | Square London W1. Book design and typography by Stuart | Montgomery. 150 copies of this edition separately printed on | fawn glastonbury antique laid paper and specially bound are | numbered and signed by the author"; pp. [5-7] [the heading "contents" in holograph] contents-pages; p. [8] blank; pp. 9-24 text; p. [5] [in holograph] section-title, "imitations of | Gertrude Stein | 1951-1952"; p. [26] blank; pp. 27-38 text; p. [39] [in holograph] section-title, "Writing Writing"; p. [40] blank; pp. 41-54 text; p. [55] [in holograph] section-title, "from Fragments | of a Disorderd | Devotion"; p. [56] blank; pp. 57-64 text; p. [65] [in holograph] section-title, "a little poetics"; p. [66] blank; pp. 67-70 text; p. [71] [in holograph] section-title, "imitations | of Gertrude Stein | 1953-1955"; p. [72] blank; pp. 73-86 text, p. [07] [in holograph] section-title, "Letters"; p. [88] blank; pp. 89-138 text; p. [139] [in holograph] section-title, "prose poems | from Caesar's Gate"; p. [140] blank; pp. 141-144 text.

Text contents: AN ESSAY AT WAR—IMITATIONS OF GERTRUDE STEIN 1951-1952 [section-title]—A LANGUAGE FOR POETRY—ARE CATS—NAMES OF PEOPLE—A LEAVE AS YOU MAY—POETRY PERMIT FOR VOLLEY—ALL THROUGH—POETRY MAY BE AS YOU PLEASE—A REPRIEVE AT DAWN—A SONG IS A GAME—AN ARRANGEMENT—WALKING ON KEARNEY STREET—DANCE EARLY SPRING WEATHER MAGIC—TURNING INTO—COMING OUT OF—MAKING UP—A SCENE—WRITING WRITING [section-title]—THE BEGINNING OF WRITING—IMAGINING IN WRITING—WRITING AS WRITING—POSSIBLE POETRIES: A PRELUDE—POSSIBLE POETRIES: A POSTSCRIPT—POSSIBLE POETRIES: A POSTCARD—AN IMAGINARY LETTER—IMAGINARY LETTER—IMAGINARY LETTER HIS INTENTION—MOTTO—DIVISION—WRITING AT HOME—I AM NOT AFRAID—AN INTERLUDE OF RARE BEAUTY—FROM FRAGMENTS OF A DISORDERD DEVOTION [section-title]—FIVE PIECES—HERO SONG—AN IMAGINARY WOMAN—ELUARD'S DEATH—UNKINGD BY AFFECTION—A LITTLE POETICS [section-title]—DESCRIPTIONS OF IMAGINARY POETRIES—A POEM IN STRETCHING—IMITATIONS OF GERTRUDE STEIN 1953-1955 [section-title]—RHYME MOUNTAIN PARTICULAR—THIS IS THE POEM THEY ARE PRAISING AS LOADED—ORCHARDS—SENTENCES—THERE COULD BE A BOOK WITHOUT NATIONS IN ITS CHAPTERS—6/16/53—6/22/53—6/27—A MORASS—HOW DO YOU KNOW YOU ARE THRU?—ROTUND

RELIGION—SEVERAL POEMS IN PROSE—RINGS—SYLLABLES—
STUFF ARK MOWER BOTTLE—ANOTHER IDO—SPANISH
LESSONS—LETTERS [section-title]—PREFACE—FOR A MUSE
MEANT—DISTANT COUNSELS OF ARTAUD—UPON TAKING
HOLD—FIRST INVENTION ON THE THEME OF THE ADAM—
SHORT INVENTION ON THE THEME OF THE ADAM—FIGURES
OF SPEECH—METAMORPHOSIS—WITH BELLS SHAKING—LIGHT
SONG—IT'S SPRING, LOVE'S SPRING—AT THE END OF A
PERIOD—FRAGMENT—TRUE TO LIFE—UPON HIS SEEING A
BABY HOLDING THE FOUR OF HEARTS—WORDS OPEN OUT
UPON GRIEF—RIDING—AT HOME—THE HUMAN COMMUNION
TRACES—PASSAGES OF A SENTENCE—RE—BROUGHT TO LOVE—
TO VOW—SPELLING THE WORD—CORRESPONDENCES—THE
GREEN LADY—AUGUST SUN—SOURCE—AN OWL IS AN ONLY
BIRD OF POETRY—NEW TIDINGS—CHANGING TRAINS—THE
LANGUAGE OF LOVE—THE SIREN SONG—PROSE POEMS FROM
CAESAR'S GATE 1955 [section-title]—AURORA ROSE—TEARS OF ST
FRANCIS—SOURCE MAGIC—CIRCULATING LIGHTS.

Description: The text is printed on white (C-263) wove paper, 23.8 x 15.1
cm., and the gatherings are sewn with white thread and glued. The
endpapers are of tan (approximately light yellowish brown C-76) laid
paper watermarked with a crown and "Glastonbury." The gatherings have
been bound in very red (C-11) cloth over boards 24.4 x 15.5 cm. The front
cover is blank. The lettering on the spine in very yellow (C-82) reads from
head to tail "Robert Duncan *Derivations* Fulcrum." The rear cover is blank.

Dust jacket: The dust jacket is made from white wove stock enameled on the
exterior surface. The front cover, the spine, and the rear cover are decorated
in a marbled design of very purplish red (C-254) and light pink (C-4).
Lettering on the front reads, "Robert Duncan | Derivations," and lettering
on the spine reads from head to tail, "Robert Duncan *Derivations*
Fulcrum." The rear cover is blank. The front flap reads (in purplish red),
"Robert Duncan | [photograph of RD, 7.6 x 6.2 cm., identified in the
compiler's copy by RD as 'Berkeley 1946'] Derivations." A three line blurb by
Charles Olson and a seven line blurb by Denise Levertov then follow; an
anonymous statement begins which runs over to the rear flap (six lines on
the front flap and ten lines on the rear flap). Under the heading
"FULCRUM PRESS" on the front flap appears the following: "20 Fitzroy
Square London W1 | distributed in the U.S.A. by Horizon Press Inc. | 156
Fifth Ave. New York N.Y. 10010 | Cover by Richard Hamilton." At bottom
right appears "35/-." After the blurb on the rear flap appears "Fulcrum
Press | 20 Fitzroy Square | London W1," and 22 authors and titles published
by the press.

Published: 3000 copies published Feb. 1959 at 35/- [$4.50].

b. *First edition, signed copies:*

Title, Collation, Contents, and Text contents all the same as the regular copies. The text has been printed on light yellowish brown laid paper watermarked with a crown and "Glastonbury," with endpapers the same as in the trade copies. The gatherings have been sewn with white thread, glued, and bound in textured medium yellowish brown (C-77) cloth over boards, with deep yellowish brown (C-75) and gray yellow (C-90) headbands. Lettering on the spine is the same as on the trade copies. One line has been added on the acknowledgements-page: "Limited edition number [numbers in holograph] [number]│ 150 [in RD's holograph] Robert Duncan." The price "35/-" does not appear at the bottom right of the front flap, and the dust jacket has been covered with a clear plastic wrapper.

Published: 150 copies published Feb. 1969 at £ 6/6 [$17.50].

c. *First edition, out-of-series copies:*

Title, Collation, Contents, and Text contents all the same as the regular copies, but twelve have been numbered and signed by the poet on the acknowledgements-page. A copy was listed in the catalogue of Black Sun Books, No. 23. A letter to the compiler, dated 28 Nov. 1977, from Mrs. Linda Tucker confirmed the existence of these copies: "However, we do recall that this book was especially numbered one through twelve, although it didn't change the physical description."

Notes: The poems that appear in book form for the first time are WALKING ON KEARNEY STREET—SPANISH LESSONS [wrongly called SPANISH LADY on the acknowledgments-page]—SOURCE MAGIC—CIRCULATING LIGHTS—A LANGUAGE FOR POETRY—ARE CATS—POETRY PERMIT FOR VOLLEY—ALL THROUGH—POETRY MAY BE AS YOU PLEASE—A REPRIEVE AT DAWN—A SONG IS A GAME. The second poem on page 47 has been misnamed on the contents-page POSSIBLE POETRIES: A POSTCARD, instead of POSSIBLE POETRIES: A POSTSCRIPT. In *Writing, WRITING* (A13) the second and third poems on page 47 were entitled "POSSIBLE POETRIES: A POSTSCRIPT". ELUARD'S DEATH has been mistitled ELUARDS DEATH on the contents-page. The poem THE GREEN LADY, written in the same period as the other poem in *Letters*, has been added to that sequence. A copy at TxU has a variant binding in very reddish orange cloth (approximately C-34). An unknown number of the regular and signed copies were boxed together in pairs for distribution and sale.

A32   **ACHILLES' SONG**   1969

a. *First edition, numbered copies:*

[in light olive (C-106)] ROBERT DUNCAN │ Achilles' Song │ The Phoenix Book Shop │ New York │ 1969.

Collation: [1]⁸; pp. [1-16].

Contents: pp. [1-2] blank; p. [3] title-page; p. [4] copyright-page, "©
copyright 1969 by Robert Duncan | Number 7 in the Oblong Octavo
Series"; pp. [5-12] text; p. [13] [Note]; p. [14] colophon-page, "This first
edition of Achilles' Song | is limited to twenty-six copies lettered A to Z, |
not for sale, and one hundred copies, | numbered and signed by the author. | The
lettered copies each contain | an original drawing by the author. | This is
copy No. [number inserted] | [in holograph] Robert Duncan"; pp. [15-16]
blank.

Text contents: ACHILLES' SONG—NOTE.

Description: The text is printed on pale yellow (light C-89) paper, 12.7 x 17.7
cm., with alternating trimmed and deckled edges. There is an additional
leaf, not included in the collation, 13.7 x 18.4 cm., of light olive stock, which
serves as endpapers, between the text leaves and the cover. The gathering,
including the extra leaf, is sewn to the cover with yellowish white (C-92)
thread. The cover is made from white (C-263) textured stock, and contains a
drawing of Achilles by RD on the right side of the front cover. To the left in
light olive, "Achilles' Song | Robert Duncan." The rear cover, and the front
and rear flaps are blank.

Published: 100 copies published 16 June 1969 at $15.00.

b. *First edition, lettered copies:*

Title, Collation, Contents, Text contents and Description the same as the
numbered copies except that each copy contains an original drawing on the
title-page, or on the blank page facing the title-page, in various designs and
various colored crayons; the copies are lettered A-Z in very red (C-11) and
signed by RD on the colophon-page. The drawing in the compiler's copy is
an ink drawing of a male face (presumably Achilles, though it is different
than the cover drawing) on the blank page facing the title-page. The
drawing has been colored-in with bluish green (approximately C-163),
purplish blue (C-199), very yellow green (C-115), brilliant orange yellow
(C-67), and brilliant yellow (C-83). There is a decorative border drawn in
purplish blue which runs across the bottom on the blank page to the
title-page. A heavy line of bluish green extends onto the title-page and then
is extended to represent the ocean surrounding the printed author and title.
A ship, with a sail and oars, outlined in black ink, and then colored in very
orange (C-48) and deep orange (C-51) rests in the sea of bluish green.
Sections of light orange (C-52) and bluish green appear in the decorative
border at the bottom of the page.

Published: 26 copies published 16 June 1969 and not for sale.

Notes: Twenty-four unsigned copies were retained by the publisher, Robert
Wilson, and were not for sale. The poem was originally entitled ACHILLES
and is dated "December 10th, 1968." The note on p. [13] reads: "The name

Leuke, the White Island, came to me in the voice of H. D. reading from her *Helen in Egypt*, and in her pronunciation giving not a Greek *eu* or the Anglicized *eu* as in *euphony*, but the Germanic *eu*. So, *Leuke* was *Loy-ke* and rimed with *Troy*." At least 4 copies have been marked "hors commerce" and distributed by the author.

A33   **PLAY TIME PSEUDO STEIN**   1969

a. *First edition:*

[cover title in author's holograph] [inside a hand-drawn border around the four sides of the cover a line drawing of a flower with the poet's initials at its center] from the LABORATORY RECORDS | Notebook of 1953 | [at left curving upward around drawing] 1942 A STORY | [in the middle] Play Time | [design] | Pseudo Stein | RD | [at right] | [dot] 5 [dot] 53 | [below drawing] A FAIRY PLAY [at left] The Poet's Press | 1969 | [curving up to right] HOW EXCITED WE GET [along bottom] a tribute to Mother Carey's chickens. [New York, 1969].

Collation: [1]⁶; pp. [1-12].

Contents: p. [1] drawing and text; p. [2] text; p. [3] drawing and text, pp. [4-5] drawings and text; p. [6] text; p. [7] drawing and text; p. [8] drawing; p. [9] text; p. [10] drawing and text; p. [11] copyright-page, "Copyright © 1969 | Robert Duncan"; p. [12] colophon-page, "This book, which was originally intended | as part of the series of signed holograph | limited editions published by Poets Press, | was shelved, due to a disagreement | between author & publisher on the | subject of numerology. | It has been produced in this numbered, | unsigned edition of 35 copies in order | to provide those who have subscribed | to the holograph with an item which | we feel would be of special interest | to them. It is not for sale. | Diane di Prima | Copy no. [number inserted]"

Text contents: 1942, A STORY—A FAIRY PLAY—HOW EXCITED WE GET.

Description: The text, in the author's holograph, is printed on pale yellow (C-89) laid paper watermarked "Arches," 17.7 x 13.9 cm., and the gathering is attached to the cover with two staples. The cover is made from medium bluish green (C-164) textured stock, 17.7 x 13.9 cm. The cover title is as described above, and the rear cover is blank.

Published: Officially, 35 copies were distributed in 1969 and were not for sale, but more copies have subsequently appeared for sale. The exact number is unknown.

b. *Second edition:*

[title-page in the author's holograph] [drawing of a flower with the poet's initials at its center] from the LABORATORY RECORDS | Notebook 1953 |

[at left curving upward around drawing] 1942 A STORY | [in the middle] Play Time | [two hollow dots] | Pseudo Stein [seven hollow dots] [at upper right curving down inside drawing] SMOKING THE CIGARETTE [below central title] RD | A FAIRY PLAY | [curving up inside drawing] HOW EXCITED WE GET | [below curving up] A BUTTER MACHINE [below at left] THE | TENTH | MUSE [drawing at the heel of the page] [San Francisco, 1969].

Collation: [1]¹²; pp. [1-24].

Contents: p. [1-2] blank; p. [3] title-page; p. [4] copyright-page, "© Robert Duncan, 1969"; pp. [5-8] Preface; p. [9] drawing; p. [10] blank; p. [11] drawing and text; p. [12] text; p. [13] drawing and text; p. [14-15] drawings and text; p. [16] text; p. [17] drawing and text; p. [18] drawing; p. [19] text; p. [20] drawing and text; p. [21] text; p. [22] drawing and text; pp. [23-24] blank.

Text contents: PREFACE—1942, A STORY—A FAIRY PLAY—HOW EXCITED WE GET—A BUTTER MACHINE—S.M.O.K.I.N.G. T.H.E. C.I.G.A.R.E.T.T.E.

Description: The text, in the author's holograph, is printed on yellowish white (C-92) wove paper, 17.9 x 14 cm., and the gathering is attached to the cover with two staples. The cover is made from gray greenish yellow (C-105) textured stock. The lettering and contents of the title-page appear on the front cover, and the rear cover is blank.

Published: an unknown number of copies published Dec. 1969 at $1.00.

Notes: The number of copies of the First edition in circulation is in doubt. If there were thirty-five numbered copies as the original colophon specifies, and additional copies were offered to book dealers, then there could be as many as fifty copies in distribution. Diane Di Prima informed the compiler that as many as 100 copies in addition to the announced 35 copies were probably printed. The compiler's copy is lettered "M," which supports the view in the Serendipity Book Shop's Catalogue #36, item #408: "Correct first edition. One of 35 copies signed by the publisher Diane Di Prima (of an entire edition of 50)." The line at the bottom of the cover title, "a tribute to Mother Carey's chickens," refers to Diane Di Prima and Alan Marlowe who produced the booklet.

Note: In his PREFACE to the Second editon, RD explains that he honored the request from Diane Di Prima and Alan Marlowe for a manuscript that would be fitting for the Poets Press series, mainly because the publication would be part of the community of poets and poetry: "In drawing up the manuscript I wrote in the colophon the provision that the author's edition of 26 copies lettered A thru Z and decorated specially by me would go 'as payment' to the author. I heard immediately from the Poet's Press: no 'author edition' went to the author. It was part of their agreement with [Robert] Wilson. We stood at that impasse. And I was informed by Diane and Alan that the deal was off; they would not publish the book." As the colophon of the First edition indicates, the book was printed to meet the obligations of subscriptions. For the Second edition, RD writes, "I have been able to include all five entries for 1/5/53, two more than the earlier format provided. No longer limited to the purposes of the limited editions game, I am able to issue the book for the regular trade."

A34   **POETIC DISTURBANCES**   1970

a. *First edition, regular copies:*

Poetic Disturbances [design in deep red (C-16)] | by Robert Duncan | Maya Quarto Eight [Berkeley, 1970].

Collation: [1]⁶; pp. [1-12].

Contents: p. [1] half-title-page, "Poetic Disturbances"; p. [2] blank; p. [3] title-page; p. [4] copyright-page, "Copyright © 1970 by Robert Duncan"; pp. [5-10] text; p. [11] blank; p. [12] colophon-page, "Maya Quarto Eight | was set in Bembo & Arrighi types | and printed by Clifford Burke | in an edition of 300 copies. | Fifty copies are on Tovil paper and are | numbered & signed by | the poet."

Text contents: POETIC DISTURBANCES—WHAT IS IT YOU HAVE COME TO TELL ME, GARCIA LORCA?—THE VOYAGE OF THE POET INTO THE LAND OF THE DEAD—I SAW THE RABBIT LEAP.

Description: The text is printed on pale yellow (C-89) laid paper, 25.5 x 19.2 cm., watermarked "CURTIS RAG." The gathering is sewn with white thread and attached to the cover, which is made from heavy, textured, dark greenish yellow (C-103) stock, 25.5 x 19.2 cm., the same size as the leaves. There is a label pasted on the front cover, 3.2 x 9.5 cm., containing in deep red (C-16), "Poetic Disturbances [design] Robert Duncan." The rear cover is blank.

Published: 250 copies published in 1970 at $1.75.

b. *First edition, numbered copies:*

Title, Collation, Contents, and Text contents the same as the regular copies. These copies are printed on Tovil, pale yellow laid paper, 25 x 20 cm., with a decorated watermark of the initials "FJH" on the first leaf, a watermark of the head of Christ with "1399" below on the second and sixth leaf, and the watermark of a hand on the fourth leaf. The gathering is sewn with white thread and attached to the cover, which is made from heavy medium yellow green (C-120) stock, 25.7 x 20.4 cm., the same size as the leaves. The edges of the cover and the leaves are deckled.

Published: 50 copies published in 1970 at $7.50.

Proof papers. NBuU.

a. Galley Proofs
Collation: 2*l* recto, recto 62.5 x 24.1 cm.
Contents: These leaves contain the text of the volume, uncorrected.

b. Page Proofs
Collation: 4*l*; 3*l* all recto-verso, 1*l* recto 25.4 x 19 cm.
Contents: These leaves contain the text of the volume, uncorrected.

c. Page Proofs
Collation: 4*l*; 3*l* all recto-verso, 1*l* recto 25.4 x 19 cm.
Contents: These leaves contain the text of the volume, with three corrections.

A35   **BRING IT UP FROM THE DARK**   1970

First edition:

[within a single dark yellowish brown (C-78) rule 3.6 cm. from the foot, 1.5 cm. from the head, and 2.6 cm. from the right and left edges] BRING IT UP FROM THE DARK | [text in twenty-four lines] | Robert Duncan | ©1970 by Robert Duncan [slash] Printed for Cody's Books at Cranium Press [Berkeley, 1970].

Broadside: The text is printed on pale yellow (light C-89) wove paper, 37.4 x 25.3 cm., watermarked at the bottom "CURTIS RAG."

Published: An unknown number of copies published in 1970 at an unknown price.

A36   **65 DRAWINGS**   1970

a. *First edition, regular copies:*

[title-page in RD's holograph, in black] a selection of | [in brown (C-55)] 65 | DRAWINGS | [in black] from one drawing-book | 1952-1956 | [in brown] RD | [in black] Black Sparrow Press | Los Angeles 1970.

Collation: pp. [i-xvi], 1-67.

Contents: pp. [i-ii] [very reddish orange (approximately C-34)] blank; p. [iii] title-page; p. [iv] copyright-page, [in RD's holograph] "Copyright © 1970 | by ROBERT DUNCAN | BLACK SPARROW PRESS | P. O. BOX 26503 | Los Angeles, California | 90025"; p. [v] dedication-page, "for JESS who was | always there"; p. [vi] blank; p. [vii] contents-page; p. [viii] blank; p. [ix] contents-page; p. [x] blank; p. [xi] half-title-page, "a selection of 65 drawings"; p. [xii] blank; p. [xiii] illustrated half-title-page in reddish orange and black, "65 | drawings | [in reddish orange] RD"; p. [xiv] blank; pp. [xv-xvi] [in reddish orange] blank; pp. 1-65 drawings; p. [66] colophon-page, "[in holograph] Robert Duncan | [publisher's logo] [number in red (C-110)] | Printed July 1970 in Santa Barbara by | Noel Young for the Black Sparrow Press. | Design by Barbara Martin. Cover & slipcase | by Earle Gray. This edition is limited | to 300 numbered copies, and 26 lettered | presentation copies each with an original | drawing by Robert Duncan, all copies | signed by the author"; p. [67] blank.

Text contents: [See Notes for explanations of abbreviations] 1. [r] THE KING—2. [d/r] HERO—3. [r] MASKED—4. THE IDEAL READER I—5. THE IDEAL READER II—6. THE IDEAL READER III—7. THE IDEAL READER IV—8. THE IDEAL READER V—9. THE IDEAL READER VI—10. THE IDEAL READER VII—11. FLOWERS AND THE MOON—12. [r] HERO—13. [r] CATS—14. [r] CATS—15. HOUSEHOLD TABLE WARE—16. THE BENIGN MAGE I—17. [d] THE BENIGN MAGE LISTENS TO A LITTLE SPIRIT OF THE DARK II—18. [d] THE BENIGN MAGE HIDES A POOR MAN IN THE FLOOD III—19. HE HEARS THE REQUEST OF A LITTLE CAT THAT WANTED TO RUN AWAY FOR AN AFTERNOON IV—20. HOW LIKE A LION THE BENIGN MAGE FEELS ON HIS CLOUD V—21. HE DID NOT MEAN TO TERRIFY THE DAISY VI—22. [d] IN DISGUISE OF A BEAR HE WAITS FOR THE DAISY TO RETURN VII—23. [d] HIDDEN IN THE SUN HE WAKES THE DAISY VIII—24. RETURNING FROM BETHLEHEM HE ENTERS A CAVE IX—25. [r] THINKING—26. COBRAS—27. ASPIRATION—28. HANDS—29. HERO—30. [d] THE AGED FAIRY LADY—31. [d] SHE STRIVES AGAINST A HEAVY WIND—32. [d] COMPANY—33. [d] RIDERS ON A CITY BUS—34. [r] FAR AWAY THOUGHT—35. ART NOUVEAU—36. FLIGHT OF THE GRECIAN BABES—37. GIRL FAIRY—38. [d] READING AT HOME—39. BIRDS—40. IN THE MOUNTAINS—41. [r] HERO—42. MOON LADY—43. [d/r] CONSOLATION—44. CAT—45. [d/r] STUDY—46. DAY DREAM—47. DESIGN FOR A TIFFANY VASE—48. READING—49. FAR AWAY—50. MALE HEAD—51. MALE NUDE—52. AN OLD BELDAME OF THE FAIRIE HEARS IT FROM A LITTLE BIRD—53. YAHVEH NOTICING THAT HELEN ADAM DON'T BELIEVE IN HIM—54. AN EARLY GOD MAKING A LITTLE IMAGE OF HIMSELF—55. A LOVELY EARLY GOD—56. [r] CATS—57. ALPHA AND OMEGA—58. SEEKING SHADE—59. HOUSEHOLD TABLE WARE—60. HER SMILE—61. ME TOO—62. AN ELABORATE HAIR-DO—63. THE EARNEST BEGONIA—64. [d/r] GRAND DECORATION—65. [r] READING.

Description: The drawings are printed on yellowish white (C-92) wove paper, 21.6 x 14 cm., and 21.6 x 28 cm. The leaves are unbound and laid into a double folding box. The box, 22.4 x 14.6 cm., has two folding flaps at the head and two at the tail; there is one each at the right and the left. A reddish brown slip, 7.7 x 10 cm., with the number in red is laid-in on top of the first blank leaf. The box is lined with the same reddish brown textured paper, and the exterior of the box is covered in cloth with a design in yellowish white, black (C-267), and brown (C-55). The folded box fits into a slipcase, 23.2 x 15.1 x 4.5 cm., covered in the same cloth. A brown leather label, 2.3 x 16.2 cm., has been glued to the spine of the folded box and reads, in very yellow (C-82) and in RD's holograph, from head to tail, "ROBERT DUNCAN [rule] BLACK SPARROW [rule] 65 DRAWINGS [rule]." The lettering is framed by a single very yellow rule.

Published: 300 copies published 26 Aug. 1970 at $20.00.

b. *First edition, lettered copies:*

Title, Collation, Contents, and Text contents the same as the regular copies. Each of these copies contains an original pencil drawing by RD, 21.6 x 14 cm., which is laid into a folder made from light blue (approximately C-18) textured paper of the same size. The folding box is of the same design as the trade copies, but the interior is now covered with blue paper; the exterior of the box and the slipcase are covered in brocade cloth with intricate designs in blue, dark blue (C-183), black (C-267), dark gray reddish brown (C-47), very yellow (C-82), and yellowish white. The label on the spine is dark blue leather and is stamped in very yellow the same as on the trade copies. These copies are lettered A-Z in very red (C-11) and signed on the colophon-page, "Robert Duncan."

Published: 26 copies published 26 Aug. 1970 at $60.00, plus 6 copies out of series.

Notes: The individual drawings in this collection are numbered, for the most part, on the verso of the leaves; but where they are numbered on the recto, this is indicated in the Text contents by [r]. Most of the drawings are on single leaves, but where they are on double leaves, this is indicated by [d]. It is also to be understood that the drawings appear only on the recto of the leaves and that no attempt has been made to account for the blank versos in the pagination.

c. *First edition, special copies:*

The same as the regular copies, except copies bear the following markings: 2 marked "For Copyright," 1 marked "Printer's Copy" and 1 marked "Binder's Copy."

Published: 4 copies published 26 Aug. 1970 and not for sale.

A37   **TRIBUNALS PASSAGES 31-35**   1970

a. *First edition, paperbound copies, first issue:*

[in black] ROBERT DUNCAN | [in large deep reddish orange (C-36) letters] TRIBUNALS | [in black] Passages 31-35 [below] [expanded decorated rule] | Los Angeles BLACK SPARROW PRESS 1970.

Collation: [1]¹⁶; pp. [i-vi], 1-24, [25-26].

Contents: pp. [i-ii] blank; p. [iii] title-page; p. [iv] copyright-page, "COPYRIGHT © 1970 BY ROBERT DUNCAN | ISBN 87685-083-2 (paper) | ISBN 87685-031-X (signed cloth) | BLACK SPARROW PRESS | P. O. BOX 25603, LOS ANGELES, CALIFORNIA | 90025"; p. [v] half-title-page, "TRIBUNALS: PASSAGES 31-35"; p. [vi] blank; pp. 1-24 text; p. [25] blank; p. [26] colophon-page, [publisher's logo] | "Designed and printed November 1970 for the | Black Sparrow Press by Saul & Lillian Marks at | the Plantin Press, Los Angeles. This edition is limited | to 1000 copies in paper wrappers; 250 hardcover | copies numbered & signed by the poet; and | 26 lettered presentation copies handbound in full | leather by Earle Gray & signed by the poet. | All hardbound copies include a supplementary | pamphlet containing facsimiles of 'Passages 34' | from the author's holograph notebook | and final typescript."

Text contents: PASSAGES 31 THE CONCERT—PASSAGES 32—PASSAGES 33—THE FEAST PASSAGES 34—BEFORE THE JUDGMENT PASSAGES 35.

Description: The text is printed on yellowish white (C-92) wove paper, 26 x 18.7 cm., and the gathering is attached to the endpapers and the cover with two staples. The endpapers, one leaf folded around the gathering, are made from yellowish brown (C-75) wove paper the same size as the text leaves, and the paper cover is made from light gray (C-264) wove stock of the same size. The lettering on the front cover reads: "[expanded decorated rule] | Tribunals | PASSAGES 31-35 | [design in yellowish brown, 6.7 x 10.2 cm.] | ROBERT DUNCAN." The rear cover is blank.

Published: 957 copies published Dec. 1970 at $2.00.

b. *First edition, paperbound copies, second issue:*

Title, Collation, Contents, and Text contents the same as the First edition, paperbound copies, first issue, except that 50 copies have been sewn with white thread and distributed to friends of the publisher and friends of the poet. There is some uncertainty over the number of copies actually produced. The publisher, John Martin, claims that only 25 copies were actually distributed.

Published: either 50 or 25 copies published Dec. 1970 and not for sale.

c. *First edition, hardbound copies, first issue:*

Title, Collation, Contents, and Text contents the same as the First edition, paperbound copies, first issue except that in these copies the numbers 1-250 in reddish orange appear below the colophon on p. [26], with the signature of the author below the number; and in these copies the extra leaf of yellowish brown is the actual endpaper, pasted to boards 26.9 x 19 cm. The boards are covered with paper containing a design in yellowish brown with a yellow gray (light C-93) background. An area 5 x 6.2 cm. surrounded by a decorated rule is not printed with the design and contains the following in black: "Robert Duncan | Tribunals | Passages 31-35." The spine is bound in medium yellow (C-87) cloth extending 1.7 cm. onto the front and rear covers and contains a light gray paper label (10.8 cm.) with the following lettering running from head to tail "[decoration] Robert Duncan TRIBUNALS Passages 31-35 [decoration]." The rear cover is blank. There is a clear plastic wrapper. A pocket made from the yellowish brown paper has been pasted onto the rear endpaper against the boards and contains the following pamphlet:

Robert Duncan | The Feast: Passages 34 | [expanded rule] | Facsimile of the Holograph notebook and of final typescript | [rule].

Collation: [1]⁸; pp. [1-16].

Contents: p. [1] title-page and [Introductory Note]; pp. [2-15] text; p. [16] blank.

Text contents: THE FEAST: PASSAGES 34.

Description: The text is printed on yellowish white wove paper, 20.3 x 15.2 cm., and the gathering is stapled twice. Both the author's notebook version and the typed version of the poem are reproduced. The introductory note is dated "San Francisco, November 1970."

Published: 250 copies published Dec. 1970 at $20.00.

d. *First edition, hardbound copies, second issue:*

Title, Collation, Contents, and Text contents the same as the first edition, paperbound copies, first issue, but these copies have been bound in full leather, deep brown (C-56), over boards 27.3 x 19.2 cm. The same lettering on the front cover and spine as on the hardbound copies, first issue appears on these copies stamped in very yellow (C-82). The letters A-Z in reddish orange appear below the colophon on p. [26], followed by RD's signature. The pamphlet is at the rear in a pocket as in the hardbound copies, first issue.

Published: twenty-six copies published 1 Dec. 1970 for presentation, but some offered for sale at $30.00.

e. *First edition, special copies:*

Title, Collation, Contents, Text contents, and Description the same as First edition, hardbound copies, second issue. The copies bear the following markings: 3 copies marked "Presentation Copy," 1 copy marked "Author's Copy," 1 copy marked "Publisher's Copy," and 1 copy marked "File Copy."

Published: 6 copies published 1 Dec. 1970 and not for sale.

Notes: In the note for the facsimile of the notebook and the typescript of THE FEAST: PASSAGES 34, RD wrote: "The facsimiles of the pages from my notebook where the original version of 'Passages 34' appears and of associated material, along with the typescript from which the book was printed, are added here to bring the reader closer to stages of my own work on the poem. The printer's work, where the poet himself is not the printer, is an extension of the author's intention; the typed copy, where the poet works in typing, is the realized statement of those intentions. With 'Passages,' I have come more and more to feel my original writing of the poem in my notebooks as a sketch, often completely realized there it is true, but also often a preliminary version subject to new developments when I come to work with the typewriter and its own special spacing and relationships on the page. This typed copy is for me the primary 'score' of the poem, and the printed version (though not this printed version) subject to close-space conventions of modern printing, in striving for a homogenized density of type on the page against open spaces, rides over decisions that appear in the typed version as notations of the music of the poem, minute silences in the space after a comma or a period." The question of providing spaces after punctuation and other spaces to notate the score of the poems involved RD in a struggle with the publisher and the printer, Saul Marks.

A38 **GROUND WORK** 1971

First edition, privately published:

GROUND WORK [San Francisco: Privately published, 1971]

Collation: pp. [i-ii], 1-12.

Contents: p. [i] A PROSPECTUS; p. [ii] blank; pp. 1-12 text.

Text contents: A PROSPECTUS | for the prepublication issue of GROUND WORK | to certain friends of the poet | Jan. 31, 1971—Dec. 20 ON GLEANINGS—Dec. 22—Dec. 28—Dec. 29—Jan. 22 [on] SANTA CRUZ PROPOSITIONS—SANTA CRUZ PROPOSITIONS [poem].

Description: This publication consists of a prospectus for and then multilithed copies of the author's typed entries from his notes and reflections about his writing and typed versions of the poems he was then writing. The reproductions have been made on 27.9 x 21.7 cm. standard bond typing paper, printed recto-verso so there are six leaves of text and one leaf, recto for the prospectus.

Published: 400 copies published by the author but not all distributed, 31 Jan. 1971, for a donation to defray printing costs.

Notes: In "A Prospectus," RD wrote: "Enclosed are the first twelve pages of what will be, when the project is completed, a volume of passages from notebooks current and old, poems in progress and previously unedited poems, starts and fits, drawings and propositions—GROUND WORK, relating to my work following BENDING THE BOW. I want a time and a space to work in that will be, as time and space were only in the years before others were interested in publishing me, the time and space of a life of the work itself. Once something like a hundred pages has been done and given that the feel of such a unit will be there, I propose to issue the volume as such for publication with a subscription limited to two hundred and fifty copies under copyright with the title PREPARING THE GROUND WORK. . . . GROUND WORK is to be unfinisht copy, *immediate* copy—having no middle men between the reader and the writer—the errors will be the writers, not the printers, the departures from printing conventions will be in for free, and there will be no publisher hounding the writer for copy to meet his schedule. I need at least a year of that."

A39 **NOTES ON JESS'S TRANSLATION SERIES** 1971

First edition, privately published:

NOTES ON JESS'S TRANSLATION SERIES | PREFACE FOR THE CATALOGUE [San Francisco: Privately published 1971]

Collation: pp. 13-18.

Contents: NOTES ON JESS'S TRANSLATION SERIES / PREFACE FOR THE CATALOGUE.

Text contents: [The preface has three sections:] ICONOGRAPHIC EXTENSIONS—PUNS, RHYMES, AND MULTIPHASIC ORGANIZA-TIONS—EXPLORING AND EXPOUNDING.

Description: The text is a multilithed reproduction of the author's typescript of the preface on three 27.9 x 21.7 cm. leaves printed recto-verso on standard bond typing paper. The text ends in the middle of a sentence.

Published: 400 [?] copies published by the author but not all distributed, spring 1971.

Note: This preface was printed as part of GROUND WORK, A38. It continues the pagination of the first installment, which was distributed in Jan. 1971. With some revisions, this preface appeared in TRANSLATIONS BY JESS. See B44.

A40 **ROBERT DUNCAN: AN INTERVIEW** 1971

First edition:

[in dark yellowish green (C-137)] ROBERT DUNCAN | an interview by | George Bowering & Robert Hogg | April 19, 1969 | [below] A Beaver Kosmos Folio [Toronto: The Coach House Press, 1971].

Collation: [1]¹⁶; pp. [1-32].

Contents: p. [1] title-page; p. [2] two photographs in dark yellowish green of RD; p. [3] "NOTE: This interview took place in Duncan's room at the Ritz-Carleton | Hotel in Montreal, the morning after his reading at Sir George Williams | University on April 19, 1969. In the transcription we have tried to find | some realizable ground between the language the poet might write & the | cellular way he makes phrases when he talks. The interviewers were Robert | Hogg & George Bowering"; p. [4] blank; pp. [5-31] text; p. [32] copyright-page, "Copyright 1971 by Robert Duncan | Copyright 1971 by George Bowering & Robert Hogg | Printed in Canada | at The Coach House Press, Toronto | [publisher's logo]."

Text contents: The text of the interview.

Description: The text is printed with yellowish green ink on greenish white (C-153) textured paper, 21 x 13.5 cm. The gathering is attached to the cover with two staples. The cover is made from heavy greenish white stock. Lettering on the front cover in deep purple (C-219) reads, "ROBERT DUNCAN | AN INTERVIEW," and below appears a reproduction of a photograph of RD in yellowish green and yellow (C-84). A smaller version of the photograph of RD in yellowish green printed in reverse appears at the bottom right of the rear cover, but this time RD is holding a beaver in his out-stretched hand.

Published: 1000 copies published in 1971 at $2.00.

A41   **THE MUSEUM**   1972

a. *First edition, first issue:*

the museum [Beyond Poetry: Brooklyn, NSW, Australia, 1972].

Collation: pp. [1-6].

Contents: p. [1] series-title, "BEYOND POETRY | ROBERT DUNCAN"; pp. [2-4] text; p. [5] acknowledgments-page; p. [6] blank.

Text contents: THE MUSEUM.

Description: The text is printed on light yellowish brown (approximately C-76) and also on white (approximately C-263) laid paper. A single leaf, 25.4 x 40.6 cm., has been folded twice to make the three leaves 25.5 x 13.3 cm. Page [5] contains a three line statement by RD: "In my commitment, there was a Reality behind the reality I knew | in making it up, a Reality to which everything I knew referred. The | world was a text, the code of many languages, yet to be broken." Artwork and layout by Robert Adamson.

Published: An unknown number of copies published in 1972 and distributed free.

b. *First edition, second issue:*

Title, Collation, Contents, Text contents, Description, and Publication the same except that an unknown number of copies were printed on white (approximately C-263) laid paper. No known priority.

Note: BEYOND POETRY was a series of publications edited by Cheryl Adamson and Chris Edwards.

A42   **IN MEMORIAM WALLACE STEVENS**   1972

a. *First edition, regular copies:*

[cover title] IN MEMORIAM | Wallace Stevens | [design in swirls]| ROBERT DUNCAN | [below] THE UNIVERSITY OF CONNECTICUT | STORRS | April 25, 1972.

Collation: [1]²; pp. [1-4].

Contents: p. [1] cover-title; p. [2] blank; p. [3] text; p. [4] colophon-page, "Issued by the Special Collections Department of the Wilbur | Cross Library, The University of Connecticut, in an editon | of 500 copies, to commemorate Robert Duncan's reading at | the Wallace Stevens Memorial Program, April 25, 1972. The | first 12 copies are signed by the poet."

Text contents: STRUCTURE OF RIME XXVII | IN MEMORIAM WALLACE STEVENS.

Description: This pamphlet is printed on heavy yellowish white (C-92) wove paper. One leaf has been folded to form two leaves, 25.4 x 17.3 cm.

Published: 488 copies published 25 April 1972 and not intended for sale.

b. *First edition, signed copies:*

Title, Collation, Contents, Text contents, and Description the same as First edition, regular copies except RD has signed the copies.

Published: 12 copies published 25 April 1972 and not intended for sale.

Note: In a letter dated 27 March 1972 to Professor Moynihan, then Chairman of the Department of English at the University of Connecticut, RD wrote: "I am pleased indeed to be able to accept your invitation to participate in the annual Wallace Stevens poetry evening at Storrs. The honor is the greater in that Stevens is for me one of the Master generation whose work is foundation of my own in poetry. I have sent to George Butterick the text of my Structure of Rime: In Memoriam Wallace Stevens inspired by the occasion, and I plan to present my reading to include the reading of at least one Wallace Stevens poem entire, and ten sentences from Wallace Stevens—and punctuated by passages from his poems. A construct upon rather than a comment upon his work" (CtU).

First edition, privately published:

[cover-title in RD's holograph] poems from | the margins | of Thom Gunn's | MOLY | [in brackets] [April 1971, New Haven | to Portland, Maine | and | October 1971, San Francisco] [end of brackets] | [hollow dot] for Thom who inspired them, | and Margie Cohn who gave me | the gift of the book *Moly* [hollow dot] | The Author's Typescript Edition | Robert Duncan San Francisco [1972].

Collation: [1]⁶; pp. [1-12].

Contents: p. [1] cover-title-page; p. [2] copyright-page, "Copyright © 1972 | [below] *GROUND WORK. Supplement 1* | The Author's Typescript Edition | Robert Duncan | 3267 Twentieth Street | San Francisco 94110"; pp. [3-11] text; p. [12] blank.

Text contents: INTERRUPTED FORMS—*THE ODYSSEY OF HOMER. BOOK X* [translated by Alexander Pope]—PREFACE TO THE SUITE TRANSLATED | FROM THOM GUNN'S *MOLY* 1 & 2—POEMS FROM THE MARGINS OF THOM GUNN'S *MOLY*—RITES OF PASSAGE— MOLY—SECOND TAKE ON *RITES OF PASSAGE*.

Description: The text has been multilithed from the typescript on white (C-263) wove paper, 21.5 x 17.8 cm. The gathering has been stapled twice.

Published: 250 copies published, Jan. 1972, for private distribution, but not all distributed.

Notes: © in author's hand does not appear in all copies. Some copies have been numbered and inscribed. The compiler's copy reads in RD's holograph on page [12]: "prepublication edition | This copy for Robert Bertholf | No. 21 of 250 copies | issued for private distribution | January 1972 RD." The inscription varies from copy to copy.

a. *First edition, regular copies, privately published:*

A SEVENTEENTH CENTURY SUITE | in homage to the Metaphysical | Genius in English Poetry [space]. | .[space] (1590-1690) | : being Imitations, Derivations | & Variations upon Certain Con- | ceits and Findings Made among | Strong lines [space]. | c. Nov. 5, 1971-Decm. 16, 1971 | . Aug. 5-18 and Oct. 22, 1973 [San Francisco: Privately published, 1973].

Collation: [1]¹⁶; pp. [1-32].

Contents: pp. [1-2] blank; p. [3] title-page; p. [4] copyright-page, "Copyright © 1973 by Robert Duncan"; pp. [5-29] text; p. [30] colophon-page [in author's holograph], "This copy for [in very red (C-11)] public sale | No. [number in red] of 250 copies | printed from the author's typescript | as part of the GROUND WORK | December 1973 | Robert Duncan | [in very red] RD"; pp. [31-32] blank.

Text contents: 1. "LOVE'S A GREAT COURTESY TO BE DECLARED" (fl)—2. SIR WALTER RALEGH, WHAT IS OUR LIFE?—FROM SIR WALTER RALEGH'S WHAT IS OUR LIFE?—3. "GO AS IN A DREAM" (fl)—4. ROBERT SOUTHWELL, THE BURNING BABE— FROM ROBERT SOUTHWELL'S THE BURNING BABE—5. "'A PRETTY BABE,' THAT BURNING BABE" (fl)—6. GEORGE HERBERT, JORDAN (I)—FROM GEORGE HERBERT'S JORDAN (I)—7. GEORGE HERBERT, JORDAN (II)—FROM GEORGE HERBERT'S JORDAN (II)—8. PASSAGES 36 [THESE LINES | COMPOSING THEMSELVES IN MY HEAD AS I AWOKE | EARLY THIS MORNING, IT BEING STILL DARK | DECEMBER 16, 1971]—9. BEN JONSON, HYMENAEI: OR THE SOLEMNITIES OF MASQUE, AND BARRIERS—[August 1973] "YES, THERE IS A TEACHING THAT I KNOW" (fl)—10. JOHN NORRIS OF BREMERTON, HYMN TO DARKNESS—CODA—A NOTE.

Description: The text is reproduced from the author's typescript on white (C-263) laid paper, 21.9 x 17.5 cm. The gathering is bound to the cover with two staples. The cover is made from heavy white textured stock. On the front cover two vertical rules run from head to tail, one 1.3 cm. from the right edge, the other the same distance from the gutter; two horizontal rules run from front to rear cover, one 1.3 cm. from the head and the other the same distance from the tail. The rear cover also has a rule 1.3 cm. from the gutter and another rule 1.3 cm. from the left edge running from the head to the tail. Inside the resulting rectangle on the front cover appears: "[in black holograph] A Seventeenth Century Suite | in homage to the Metaphysical | Genius in English Poetry 1590 | 1690 | [a drawing in three panels; the middle one has a drawing of a heart set into it] | :being Imitations, Derivations | & Variations upon Certain | Conceits and Findings Made | among Strong Lines | by Robert Duncan | c. Nov. 5, 1971—Dec. 16, 1971. | Aug 5-18 and Oct. 22, 1973." The edges of the heart on the copies for sale are colored in red.

Published: 125 copies published Dec. 1973 at $10.00.

b. *First edition, presentation copies, privately published:*

Title, Collation, Contents, Text contents, and Description the same as the regular copies except that the name of the person presented with the copy appears in black in place of "public sale" in the colophon; the number and "RD" also are in black.

Published: 125 copies published Dec. 1973 and not for sale.

Note: Some presentation copies have the name, number, and initials in red; the heart on the front cover is then in red. In like manner, some of the regular copies have the heart not colored in red, and the for "public sale," number, and initials are in black. Not all presentation copies have been distributed.

A45   **FEB. 22, 1973**   1973

First edition:

Feb. 22, 1973 [text in four lines] ROBERT DUNCAN | Set by the author at the Ārif Press | Feb. 24, 1973 [San Francisco].

Broadside: The text is printed on pale yellow (C-89) heavy textured paper, 28.4 x 21.6 cm.

Description: The copies approved have been decorated with crayon drawings in various colors, numbered 1-5 and signed by the author. Copies at MoSW, CaBVaS.

Published: 5 approved copies and 3 proof copies published 24 Feb. 1973 and not for sale.

A46   **MEMOIRS OF OUR TIME AND PLACE**   1974

First edition:

The Poetry Center presents . . . | VOICES OF THE '40S | a recreation of the "Festival of Modern Poetry—April 1947" | [short double rule] MEMOIRS OF OUR TIME AND PLACE | [text in 47 lines] | Robert Duncan | May 15, 1974 [San Francisco].

Broadside: The text is printed on light yellow (approximately C-86) wove paper, 28 x 21.5 cm.

Published: An unknown number of copies published 15 May 1964 and distributed free.

Note: The reading was held at the San Francisco Museum of Art. In the text of the prose broadside, RD wrote: "In the first event, the two evenings of the 1947 Festival of Modern Poetry, presented at the Labaudt Gallery, we found ourselves and began to hear our poems as belonging to a world of poets working with us, yes, but also we found that there was an audience. We had been told that modern poetry had no readers. That was the decisive message writ large in the 1930s. Yet in San Francisco hearers were ready. In time it appears that Madeline Gleason's Festivals were the first such Readings presented in the contemporary world; the first established public series, that is. Certainly, it was in San Francisco that the first audiences began. And it was in the context of that audience and of the powerful recognition of a community of poets beyond the groups and movements within that community—in a context, that is, instituted by that first venture in April 1947, that an all important change took place in the relation of the poem to its audience."

A47   **AN ODE AND ARCADIA**   1974

First edition:

[within double ornamental frames, 2 cm. from the top, 2.8 cm. from the bottom, and 1.6 cm. from each side] Robert Duncan | [in deep green (C-142)] An Ode and | Arcadia | [in black] Jack Spicer | [design in deep green] | [in black] Ark Press: Berkeley | 1974.

Collation: pp. [1-40].

Contents: pp. [1-2] blank; p. [3] half-title-page, "An Ode and Arcadia"; p. [4] blank; p. [5] title-page; p. [6] copyright-page, "Copyright © 1974 by Robert Duncan | Copyright © 1974 by F. J. Cebulski | Copyright © 1974 by Robin Blaser for the Estate of Jack Spicer | Drawing by Ariel c 1947"; pp. [7-12] "Introduction"; p. [13] section-title, "Jack Spicer"; p. [14] drawing; pp. [15-24] text; p. [25] section-title, "Robert Duncan"; p. [26] drawing; pp. [27-35] text; pp. [36-38] blank; p. [39] colophon-page, "One thousand copies printed by Wesley Tanner of Berkeley"; p. [40] blank.

Text contents: INTRODUCTION, by F. J. Cebulski—[LETTER FROM JACK SPICER TO KENNETH REXROTH]—AN ARCADIA FOR DICK BROWN—MR. J. JOSEPHSON, ON A FRIDAY AFTERNOON—"ARACHNE WAS STRUCK WITH HER SHUTTLE" (fl)—"AMONG THE COFFEE CUPS AND SOUP TOUREENS WALKED BEAUTY" (fl)—A LECTURE IN PRACTICAL AESTHETICS—"COME WATCH THE LOVE-BALLOON, THAT GREAT" (fl)—[LETTER FROM ROBERT DUNCAN TO KENNETH REXROTH]—ODE FOR DICK BROWN.

Description: This text is printed on yellowish white (C-92) wove paper, 20.3 x 12.6 cm., with the individual leaves perfect bound to the cover. The cover is made from heavy pale yellow (approximately C-89) paper. Lettering in green on the front cover reads: "An Ode | and Arcadia | [double square designs in deep reddish orange (C-38)] | [in deep green] Jack Spicer | Robert Duncan." Lettering on the spine in deep green reads from head to heel, "An Ode and Arcadia [space] Spicer and Duncan." The rear cover is blank. Drawings by Ariel [Parkinson] appear on p. [14] (of Jack Spicer) and p. [26] (of Robert Duncan).

Published: 1000 copies published in 1974 at $4.00.

First edition:

DANTE | [dot]| Robert Duncan | [below] THE INSTITUTE OF
FURTHER STUDIES [Canton, New York, 1974].

Collation: [1]²⁴; pp. [1-48].

Contents: p. [1] half-title-page, "8 | [dot] DANTE [dot] | [below] It is in the
social definition of freedom | that we most sense | the presence of the Law: |
pluralistic, multiphasic."; p. [2] blank; p. [3] title-page; p. [4] copyright-
page, "© Copyright 1974 by Robert Duncan | Cover by Guy Berard"; p. [5]
[preface]; p. [6] blank; pp. [7-25] text; p. [26] blank; pp. [27-45] text; pp.
[46-48] blank.

Text contents: DANTE ÉTUDES [PREFACE]—BOOK ONE [section-
title] I—II—III(1)—III(2)—IV(1)—IV(2)—V—VI—VII—VIII(1)—VIII(2)—
IX—X—XI—XII—XIII—XIV—XV—BOOK TWO [section-title] I—II—
III—IV—V VI VII—VIII—IX—X—BOOK THREE [section-title]
ETUDE FROM THE THIRD EPISTLE—ETUDE FROM THE FIFTH
EPISTLE (1)—ETUDE UPON THE FIFTH EPISTLE (II) FIRST
ETUDE FROM THE SEVENTH EPISTLE—SECOND ETUDE FROM
THE SEVENTH EPISTLE—THIRD ETUDE FROM THE SEVENTH
EPISTLE—ETUDE FROM THE FOURTH TREATISE OF THE
CONVIVIO CHAPTER XXVII—ETUDE FROM THE FOURTH
TREATISE OF THE *CONVIVIO* CHAPTERS XXVII and XXI.

Description: The text has been reproduced from the author's typescript on
yellowish white (C-92) wove stock, 21.5 x 14 cm. The title of the preface,
DANTE ÉTUDES, and the poet's signature appear in his holograph p. [5].
The gathering is attached to the cover with three staples. The cover is made
from heavy wove very pale violet (C-213) stock, 22.7 x 15.1 cm. The front
cover contains four rectangles drawn with a thin black rule, each one
smaller than the one outside it: 20.2 x 12.5 cm., 14 x 10.1 cm., 10.5 x 8.8 cm.,
and 9.9 x 8.2 cm. Lettering at the top across the second rectangle reads: "a
curriculum of the soul" | [between the second and third top lines of the
rectangles] "DANTE" | [the central rectangle contains an emblem of a
knight in armor in the foreground, and in the background a drawing of the
earth set against other bodies in space] | [between the lines of the first and
second rectangles at the bottom] "8 | ROBERT DUNCAN." The rear cover
contains a single rectangle drawn with a thin rule, 20.1 x 12.5 cm., with
three vertical rules in the center. Lettering on the rules reads from the tail to
the head, "the institute of further studies [two rules] box 482 canton, new
york 13617." Charles Olson's "Plan for a Curriculum of the Soul" is
reproduced on the inside of the covers.

Published: 450 copies published Nov. 1974 at $2.00.

First edition:

THE VENICE | POEM | ROBERT DUNCAN | PRISM [Sydney, Australia, 1975].

Collation: [1]²⁰; pp. [i-viii], 1-27, [28-32].

Contents: pp. [i-ii] blank; p. [iii] half-title-page, "THE VENICE POEM"; p. [iv] blank; p. [v] title-page; p. [vi] copyright-page, "First printed and published in Australia | 1975 | This book is copyright. | Apart from any fair dealing for the purposes of private study, research, | criticism or review as permitted under the Copyright Act, no part of this | publication may be reproduced, stored in a retrieval system or transmitted | in any form or by any means, electronic, mechanical, photocopying, | recording or otherwise without prior permission of the copyright owner. | © Robert Duncan 1975 | Published by *New Poetry* for the Poetry Society of Australia | Box N110 Grosvenor Street Post Office | Sydney, NSW, 2000 Australia | Photography by Jane McClure | Printed offset by Tonecraft Pty. Ltd., 24b Stanley Street, Peakhurst 2210 | Designed by Robert Adamson | ISBN 0 85689 010 1"; p. [vii] contents-page; p. [viii] blank; pp. 1-27 text; pp. [28-29] blank; p. [30] colophon-page, "This first Australian edition is limited to 500 copies. | [design] | Printed by Tonecraft Pty. Ltd., 24B Stanley Street, Peakhurst, 2210"; pp. [31-32] blank.

Text contents: THE VENICE POEM—1. A DESCRIPTION OF VENICE— TESTIMONY—2. IMAGINARY INSTRUCTIONS—RECORSO—3. THE VENUS OF LESPUGES—CODA.

Description: The book is printed on light yellowish brown (lighter than C-76) laid paper, 23.8 x 15.2 cm., watermarked "Beckett." The leaves are bound to the cover, made from stiff white (C-263) stock enameled on the exterior surface, with two staples. Lettering on the front cover reads at the top: "THE VENICE | POEM [photograph by Jane McClure of the poet sitting at the front window of his home, 12.3 x 15.1 cm.] | ROBERT DUNCAN." The rear cover at the top contains a photograph of the poet by Jane McClure at the rear window of his home, 12.1 x 15.1 cm. And under the photograph: "Photograph by Jane McClure, June 1975." There is a two paragraph, twelve line statement about RD, a three line quotation by Charles Olson, a three line anonymous statement from *The Times* (which also appears at the start of the statement on the front flap of the dust jacket of the English edition of *Bending The Bow*), and a one line quotation, anonymous, but by Robert Adamson, from *The Australian*.

Published: 500 copies published fall 1975 at $3.95 [$4.50 American].

A SONG FROM THE STRUCTURES OF RIME RINGING

a. *First edition, regular copies:*

[in black] Robert Duncan | [in reddish orange (C-35)] A SONG FROM THE STRUCTURES OF RIME RINGING | AS THE POET PAUL CELAN SINGS: | [in black] Chutes | Orange Export Ltd | 1977 [Malakoff, France].

Collation: [1-2]², [3]⁴; pp. [1-16].

Contents: p. [1] half-title-page, "A SONG FROM THE STRUCTURES OF RIME RINGING | AS THE POET PAUL CELAN SINGS:"; p. [2] blank; p. [3] title-page; pp. [4-6] blank; pp. [7-11] text; p. [12] blank; p. [13] colophon-page, "Composé et imprimé à la main | par Emmanuel Hocquard | le 5 juin 1977, à la S. M. I., | à 9 exemplaires numérotés | et signés par l'auteur. | [in pencil in RD's holograph] no [number inserted] | Robert Duncan"; pp. [14-16] blank.

Text contents: A SONG FROM THE STRUCTURES OF RIME RINGING AS THE POET PAUL CELAN SINGS.

Description: The text is printed on heavy yellowish white (C-92) textured paper, 12.1 x 16.5 cm., with alternating deckled and trimmed edges. The copies are numbered 1-9 and signed by RD on the colophon-page. The leaves have not been sewn, but are laid into a folder of the same paper, 12.8 x 17.1 cm., which serves as the cover. The title-page is repeated on the front cover; the rear cover and front and rear flaps are blank. The cover is enclosed in a glassine wrapper.

Published: 9 copies published 5 June 1977 at 60 fr.

b. *First edition, hors de commerce copies:*

Title, Collation, Contents, Text contents and Description the same as the regular copies except that these copies are numbered i-v, signed by RD on the colophon-page, with "hors commerce" added.

Published: 5 copies published 5 June 1977 and not for sale.

THE VENICE POEM

First edition:

[in deep yellowish brown (C-75)] The Venice Poem | [in holograph] ROBERT DUNCAN [Burlington, Vermont: Poets' Mimeo, 1978].

Collation: [1]²⁰; pp. [1-40].

Contents: p. [1] title-page; p. [2] "not for sale"; pp. [3-39] text; p. [40]

acknowledgments-page, [in holograph] "reprinted from *Selected Poems* (City | Lights 1959) o. p. | collected in *The First Decade: selected | poems: 1940-1950* (Fulcrum)."

Text contents: THE VENICE POEM.

Description: The text is printed on pale yellow (C-89) mimeograph paper, 14.1 x 10.8 cm., in deep yellowish brown ink, and the gathering is attached to the cover with two staples. The cover is made from medium purple (C-223) construction paper, 15.2 x 10.9 cm. The front cover contains the lettering "The Venice Poem | [geometric design]." The rear cover is blank. Another copy has a cover made from medium red (C-15) construction paper with the same front cover, but with an illustration of an old bicycle on the rear cover (OKentU).

Published: 48 copies published April 1978 and not for sale.

A52   **THE SENTINELS**   1979

a. *First edition:*

THE SENTINELS | [text in thirty-one lines] | [signature in pencil] Robert Duncan [line drawing of owls with] RD [within it]. [Kent, Ohio: The Costmary Press, 1979].

Broadside: The text is printed on very pale blue (paler than C-184) laid paper, 44.6 x 29.2 cm.

Description: The author has made a drawing of two owls with an enlarged "E," for the first word of the poem EARTH, which is a complementary drawing for the one at the bottom bearing the initials "RD." The colophon on the bottom verso reads: "Robert Duncan's 'The Sentinels' | Published by The Costmary Press, Kent, Ohio | in June 1979 in a lettered, signed edition | of 26 copies as a farewell tribute to | Robert Bertholf upon his departure from | Kent State University. This is copy | [letter in very red (C-11)] | [in black pen] Robert Duncan." The publisher's logo appears to the left of the colophon.

Published: 26 copies published 16 June 1969 for presentation, but 5 copies offered for sale at $35.00.

Proof papers.
One copy is marked in black ink under the colophon, "Proof Copy."

b. *Second edition, regular copies:*

The | Sentinels [line drawing of an owl in reddish brown (C-40)] | [text in 31 lines] | [in reddish brown] | Robert Duncan | Published by [in italics] Square Zero Editions. Limited to 126 copies, 26 of which are lettered and signed by |

the poet-illustrator. Designed and printed by Black Stone Press. Copyright 1979 by Robert Duncan. [San Francisco].

Broadside: The text is printed on grayish yellow (lighter than C-90) laid paper, 46.9 x 31.7 cm.

Description: The author has made a drawing of an owl which appears in reddish brown ink above the poem, and the author's name appears in the same ink below the poem at the lower right. Some of the sheets are watermarked with a crossed P over a Z.

Published: 100 copies published 9 Nov. 1979 at $12.50.

Note: Approximately 30 of these copies were given to the poet and may appear with his inscriptions and/or his designation of "hors de commerce."

c. *Second edition, signed copies:*

Same as regular copies except that 26 have been signed in pencil and lettered by the poet between the end of the poem and the colophon.

Published: 26 copies published 9 Nov. 1979 at $40.00.

A53   **VEIL, TURBINE, CORD, & BIRD**   1979

a. *First edition, numbered copies:*

[in black] ROBERT DUNCAN | SETS OF SYLLABLES, SETS OF WORDS, | SETS OF LINES, SETS OF POEMS | ADDRESSING: | [in darker than dark pink (C-6)] VEIL, TURBINE, CORD, & BIRD [Brooklyn, New York: Jordon Davies, 1979].

Collation: [1]^{10}; pp. [1-20].

Contents: pp. [1-2] blank; p. [3] title-page; p. [4] copyright-page, "Copyright © Robert Duncan 1979 | Published by Jordon Davies | 651 Carroll Street, Brooklyn, NY 11215"; p. [5] half-title-page, "VEIL, TURBINE, CORD, & BIRD"; p. [6] blank; pp. [7-17] text; p. [18] colophon-page, "This edition, limited to 200 signed and numbered copies, | was printed by Ronald Gordon at the Oliphant Press, | from Garamond type on Fabriano papers. | [in holograph] [a number] | Robert Duncan"; pp. [19-20] blank.

Text contents: PRELIMINARY EXERCISE:—NOTES DURING A LECTURE ON MATHEMATICS:—THE RECALL OF THE STAR MIRAFLOR—THE NAMING OF THE TIME EVER—I POUR FORTH MY LIFE FROM THIS BOUGH—THE TURBINE.

Description: The text is printed on pale yellow (C-89) laid paper, 15.5 x 15.5 cm., watermarked "PERVSIA" below a griffin. Some edges are deckled, and some are trimmed. The gathering is sewn with pale yellow thread and attached to the cover, which is made from heavy textured deep pink (C-6) stock, watermarked "ROMA" below an emblem of a wolf. The cover measures 16 x 16 cm., and there are front and rear flaps of 14.3 cm. A label, made from the same paper that the text is printed on, 4.1 x 7.4 cm., has been pasted on the front cover and contains the following "[rule] | VEIL, TURBINE, CORD, & BIRD | ROBERT DUNCAN | [rule]." The rear cover is blank. An erratum slip, made from the same paper that the text was printed on, 5.4 x 9.9 cm., contains the following information and has been laid-in before the title-page: "ERRATUM | page [in brackets] [14], line 4, for [in italics] may read [in italics] my."

Published: Despite the colophon, 221 copies published Dec. 1979, but only 200 copies offered for sale at $35.00.

b. *First edition, hors de commerce copies:*

Title, Collation, Contents, Text contents, and Description the same as numbered and signed copies, except these copies have been marked "hors commerce" on the colophon-page.

Published: 11 copies published Dec. 1979, but reserved for the poet's use. One copy marked "hors commerce" was given to James Merrill.

c. *First edition, out of series copies:*

Title, Collation, Contents, Text contents, and Description the same as numbered and signed copies.

Published: 10 copies published in Dec. 1979, but not for sale.

Notes: There was an announcement for the pamphlet printed on the same deep pink stock as the cover, and some were printed on pink white (C-9) stock, 9.5 x 15 cm. The announcement is made from a single sheet folded to form two leaves. Page [1] is the title-page: "VEIL, TURBINE, CORD, & BIRD | A poem by Robert Duncan." Page [2] is blank. Page [3] contains the following: "VEIL, TURBINE, CORD, & BIRD | Jordan Davies announces the publication of a | new book by Robert Duncan limited to 200 signed | and numbered copies, printed from Garamond type on | Fabriano papers and sewn in wrappers. | $35.00 | Dealers: 1-2 copies less 20%, 3 or more less 30% | Jordan Davies 651 Carroll Street Brooklyn, NY 11215." Page [4] is blank. In a letter to the compiler, the publisher explained the existence of extra copies of the pamphlet: "I sent Robert 10 copies which I marked 'hors commerce' and these are not numbered. I also sent a copy which I marked 'hors commerce' to James Merrill. That also was not numbered. So there are 11 copies marked 'hors commerce' and approximately 10 copies signed but not numbered which I supose should be considered 'out-of-series.'"

First edition, privately published:

AN EPITHALAMIUM by Robert Duncan | [text of the poem in ten lines] [San Francisco: Privately published, 1980].

Collation: [1]²; pp. [1-4].

Contents: p. [1] title and text of the poem, plus the signature of the poet in pencil; p. [2] colophon-page, in the poet's pencil holograph "No [number inserted] of 70 copies presented to the poet"; p. [3] announcement-page, "Mr. & Mrs. William Roth | announce the marriage of their daughter | Margaret Lamond Roth | to | DAVID JOHNSON BEST | on the afternoon of Tuesday, May 27th | nineteen hundred and eighty"; p. [4] blank.

Text contents: AN EPITHALAMIUM

Description: The poem and the invitation are printed on yellowish white (C-92) wove stock, watermarked "TH SAU" [only letters visible], 12.7 x 17.8 cm. The first letter of the first word "Now" has been enlarged: it appears to the left of the text of the poem and has been printed in greenish blue (C-169) ink. An additional invitation, on the same stock, 12.3 x 17.2 cm., has been inserted and reads: "Joan and Bill Roth | invite you to a gala feast and celebration of | the marriage of | Maggie and David Best | at the Pacific Union Club | 100 California Street, San Francisco | 7:00 pm, Tuesday, May 27, 1980 | RSVP 443-0944." Both invitations have been inserted in a matching envelope with the address "1275 Greenwich Street San Francisco 94107" printed on the rear flap.

Published: An unknown number of copies were mailed to guests, while 70 copies were presented to the poet. None was for sale.

a. *First edition, regular copies:*

[within single horizontal rules, in the author's holograph] ROBERT | DUNCAN | [circular ink drawings] | [vertically] THE FIVE SONGS | [within horizontal rules] Keepsake for The Friends of the UCSD Library | La Jolla, California | 1981.

Collation: [1]⁸; pp. [1-16], plus one leaf laid-in at the rear.

Contents: p. [1] title-page; p. [2] copyright-page, "[in holograph] Copyright © 1981 by Robert Duncan"; p. [3] half-title-page, "THE FIVE SONGS"; pp. [4-15] text; p. [16] colophon-page, " [in type] *The Five Songs* by Robert Duncan | was commissioned by The Friends of the UCSD Library | and the Archive for New Poetry | for publication 21 October 1981 in La Jolla, California | as the Friends' eighth keepsake | being a contribution to the inauguration of | Richard C. Atkinson as Chancellor of the | University of California, San Diego | and printed letterpress from the author's holograph | by Patrick Reagh in Glendale, California | in a handsewn edition of 2126 copies | consisting of 2000 copies | on 80-lb. Mohawk Superfine | with covers of 80-lb. Artlaid II text | and reserved for members | and a signed numbered edition | of 100 copies, numbered 1-100 for sale | and 26 copies lettered A-Z reserved for the publishers | on 125-gram Ragston | with covers of 130-gram Fabriano Roma | and the design on the title-page hand colored."

Text contents: [STRUCTURE OF RIME] OF THE FIVE SONGS—THE FIVE SONGS—[laid-in leaf] "THE FIVE SONGS" by Michael Davidson.

Description: The text is printed on yellowish white (C-92) wove paper, 21.6 x 14. cm., and the gathering is sewn with yellowish white nylon thread. The cover is made from reddish orange (lighter than deep reddish orange, C-38) matt finished stock, 22.1 x 14.3 cm. A circular ink drawing appears on the front cover in black ink. The text has been reproduced from the poet's holographic rendition of the poems. Each page containing the text has a ruled and decorated border, also by the poet.

Published: 2000 copies published 21 Oct. 1981 at $5.00.

b. *First edition, numbered copies:*

Title, Collation, Contents, Text contents, and Description the same as the regular copies except that the circular ink drawing on the title-page has been colored in deep yellowish green (C-132) and orange brown (C-53). Two small triangles at the head and two at the foot of the title-page have been colored in red (C-11). The colophon-page contains a number from 1 to 100 and the poet's signature. The cover is made from light grayish brown (lighter than C-60) laid stock, with the circular design on the front cover printed in deep reddish orange (C-38).

Published: 100 copies published 21 Oct. 1981 at $25.00.

c. *First edition, lettered copies:*

Title, Collation, Contents, Text contents, and Description the same as the numbered copies except that the colophon-page contains upper case letters from A to Z and the poet's signature. The gathering is sewn with thick yellow white linen thread.

Published: 26 copies published 21 Oct. 1981 and not for sale.

d. *First edition, out of series copies:*

Title, Collation, Contents, Text contents, and Description the same as the First edition, numbered copies bound in gray covers with the drawing colored-in on the title-page.

Published: 6 copies published 21 Oct. 1981 and not for sale.

Notes: Twenty-four copies of the regular edition have been lettered in lower case letters to match the upper case letters of the lettered and signed copies. What should have been copies "l" and "m" were not lettered. All 26 copies have been signed. Some of the copies lettered A to Z have been inscribed to individual patrons. The laid-in leaf contains a statement by Michael Davidson about the circumstances of the publication of the pamphlet, and some background information about RD and about the five poems.

A56   **QUAND LE GRAND FOYER**   1981

First edition:

Quand le grand foyer | descend dans les eaux | [in brackets] [PASSAGES]. | [text in thirty-one lines] | Robert Duncan | Published by Intersection [San Francisco, California] in an edition of one hundred copies hand-colored | and signed by the poet-illustrator. Designed and printed on twinrocker | paper by Wesley B. Tanner In Berkeley Copyright 1981 by Robert Duncan[.]

Broadside: The text is printed on yellowish white (slightly more yellow than C-92) laid paper, watermarked with a crown, 67.7 x 50.5 cm.

Description: The text of the poem is printed on the left half of the sheet. RD's hand-colored illustration appears on the right half of the sheet, and on the bottom of the far left side. The illustration described is the compiler's; no other example has been seen. There is a horizontal black line between the title and the bracketed [Passages]. Below in black is an outline of a plant. At the top right there is a sun in black and which is colored in with water colors of very reddish orange (C-34), very yellow (C-82), bluish green (C-160), and deep purplish blue (C-197). The top half of the sun appears against a background of pink (C-2). The plant below has been colored in with very green (C-139), brown (C-55), light grayish brown (C-60), pale green (C-149), and light olive (C-106) water colors. The poet has signed his name "Robert Duncan" and numbered each copy "[number] / 100" in pencil at the lower right corner.

Published: Officially 100 copies published in March 1981 at $50.00.

Note: Due to some difficulties between the printer, the publisher, and the poet, not all 100 copies of the broadside were illustrated. It is not known how many copies have been illustrated and sold. The compiler's copy is number ten.

First edition:

[in black] Robert Duncan | [in deep blue (C-179)] passages | [in large very red (C-11) letters] IN BLOOD'S DOMAIN | [text in fifty-two lines] | [in black, in holograph] Robert Duncan | [in deep blue] copyright 1982 by Robert Duncan | Of 300 copies printed by Black Mesa Press in conjunction with Woodland Pattern Book Center, this is number [number in holograph]. [Madison, Wisconsin, 1982].

Broadside: The text is printed on white (duller than C-263) textured stock 50 cm. x 32.3 cm., watermarked "MONTGOLFIER VIDALON LES ANNONAY ANC *NP* MANUF *EE* CANSON."

Published: 300 copies published Oct. 1982. 150 copies were for free distribution by The Woodland Pattern Book Center, while 50 were given to the poet, and 100 were offered for sale at $5.00.

Note: One misprint appears in the text: "éspouse" should read "épouse." On all copies examined the following notation has been written in by RD in black ink after the colophon line: "Erratum—line 18, for "éspouse" read "épouse."

First edition:

TOWARDS AN OPEN UNIVERSE. | by Robert Duncan | [below] [publisher's logo of a bird in flight] [Portree, Isle of Skye, Scotland: Aquila Publishing, 1984].

Collation: [A]^{10}; pp. [1-20].

Contents: page [1] title-page; copyright-page: [first line underlined] "Copyright 1982 © Robert Duncan | ISBN 0-7275-0272-7 | All rights reserved: No part of this book may be | reproduced in any manner without the prior written | permission of the publisher, except for brief | quotations in articles and reviews. | [one line underlined] AQUILA ESSAYS — NUMBER 17 | Published by Aquila Publishing | a trading division of | JOHNSTON GREEN & Co. (PUBLISHERS) LTD | P.O. Box 1, Portree, Isle of Skye, Scotland IV51 9BT"; pages [3-17] text; pages [18-20] publisher's advertisements.

Text contents: the text of the essay.

Description: The contents are printed on very light greenish blue (C-171) paper, and the gathering stapled twice to a stiff paper cover of pink (C-2) stock. Printing on the front cover reads "TOWARDS AN OPEN UNIVERSE | By Robert Duncan." The rear cover contains the following information: [publisher's logo] | This is the seventeenth in the AQUILA ESSAY series. | The series presents writers exploring the literature | of various countries. Some write about their own work, | others about other writers and topics, and some | examine famous and infamous books. | We are always pleased to read suitable MSS and if you have anything you think may be suitable, or just an idea please get in touch with us. MSS must be accompanied | by return postage in BRITISH stamps or International Reply Coupons. | AQUILA publish a wide selection of books and pamphlets, | printed by various methods such as litho, letter press | and mimeo. For a full list send the ubiquitous SAE or | three IRC's. Poetry, fiction, criticism etc are the main | interest, but we publish many other categories such | as humour, cookery, philosophy, music, etc | [line of ***] | [one line underlined] First published in July 1982 | by Aquila Publishing | a trading division of | JOHNSTON GREEN & Co. (PUBLISHERS) LTD | P.O. Box 1, Portree, Isle of Sky, Scotland IV51 9BT | ISBN 0 7275 0272 7 | [line underlined] Price £0-60 net.

Published: an unknown number of copies published July 1982 at £0-60.

Notes: The essay first appeared in *Poets on Poetry*, B15, and then was pirated in *Prospice* 2, C246, which is published by Aquila Publishing. This appearance as a pamphlet is a pirated edition, printed with neither the author's permission nor his knowledge.

A59   **IN PASSAGE**   1983

a. *First edition, regular copies:*

[in black] Robert Duncan | [in deep purplish orange (C-36)] IN PASSAGE | [text in eight lines] | [in black, in holograph] Robert Duncan | [in type] Printed at The Toothpaste Press for Bookslinger Editions, on the occasion of the author's reading | at Walker Art Center, 3 May 1983. Copyright 1983 Robert Duncan. This is number [number in black ink] of 90.

Broadside: The text is printed on yellowish white (C-92) laid paper, 33.7 x 25.3 cm, with two deckled edges.

Published: 40 copies were published and offered for sale at the time of RD's reading, 3 May 1983, at $4.00.

b. *First edition, boxed copies:*

Title and Broadside description the same as First edition, regular copies except that these copies were boxed with 20 other broadsides.

Published: 50 copies published 3 May 1983, but offered for sale at a later date at $85.00.

Note: The broadside was distributed for sale as one of a boxed set. The box has the following wording on a label on its front: [decoration] "Twenty-One Broadsides: Poems &| Prose from the 1982-1983 Walker Art| Center Reading Series Published| by Bookslinger Editions, St. Paul." [decoration] The text was printed on Kochi paper, with Weiss type face. In addition to the copies above, nine were reserved for the poet and ten for the publisher. None of these is intended for sale.

a. *First edition, paperbound copies, first impression:*

Robert Duncan | [medium double rules] | GROUND WORK | [medium double rules] | Before the War | [below] A New Directions Book [New York, 1984].

Collation: [1-6]¹⁶; pp. [i-xii], [1-2], 3-175, [176-180].

Contents: p.[i] half-title-page, "GROUND WORK"; p. [ii] credits-page, twelve titles under the heading "ALSO BY ROBERT DUNCAN", and one title under the heading "ABOUT ROBERT DUNCAN"; p. [iii] title-page; p. [iv] acknowledgments and copyright-page, "Copyright © 1968, 1969, 1970, 1971, 1972, 1974, 1975, 1976, 1977, 1982, 1984 by Robert Duncan | All rights reserved. Except for brief passages quoted in a newspaper, magazine, radio, or television review, no part of| this book may be reproduced in any form or by any means, electronic or mechanical, including photocopying and| recording, or by any information storage and retrieval system, without permission in writing from the Publisher." Fourteen titles appear under the heading "Some of the poems in this collection first appeared in the following books and magazines." Four titles appear under the heading "The following poems were originally published in pamphlets or as broadsides." "Manufactured in the United States of America | First published clothbound, in trade and limited editions, and as New Directions Paperbook 571 in 1984 | Published simultaneously in Canada by George J. McLeod, Ltd., Toronto| Library of Congress Cataloging in Publication Data| Duncan, Robert Edward 1919— | Ground work. | (A New Directions Book) | I. Title. | PS3507.U629G7 1984 [space] 811'.54 [space] 84-4889 | ISBN 0-8112-0895-8 | ISBN 0-8112-0896-6 (pbk.) | ISBN 0-8112-0915-6 (ltd. ed.) | New Directions Books are published for James Laughlin | by New Directions Publishing Corporation, | 80 Eighth Avenue, New York 10011"; pp. [v-vii] contents-pages; p. [viii] blank; pp. [ix-xi] [Preface], "SOME NOTES ON NOTATION"; p.[xii] blank; p. [1] second half-title-page, "GROUND WORK"; [2] blank; pp. 3-175 text; pp. [176-180] blank.

HEARTS—FOR THE SEA IS GOD'S— WHERE THE FOX OF THIS STENCH SULKS—IN TRUTH DOTH SHE BREATHE OUT POISON-OUS FUMES—THEN MANY A ONE SANG— IN MY YOUTH NOT UNSTAIND—AND A WISDOM AS SUCH—FOUR SUPPLEMENTARY ÉTUDES [section-title for following four poems] OF MEMORY—HERS—I TOO TREMBLING—BUT WE, TO WHOM THE WORLD IS—THE MISSIONARIES *(PASSAGES)*—THE TORN CLOTH—SONGS OF AN OTHER—EMPEDOKLEAN REVERIES *(PASSAGES)*—JAMAIS *(PAS-SAGES)*—AN INTERLUDE OF WINTER LIGHT—"EIDOLON OF THE AION"—THE PRESENCE OF THE DANCE / THE RESOLUTION OF THE MUSIC—CIRCULATIONS OF THE SONG.

Description: The text has been offset from the author's typescript on yellow-ish white (C-92) wove paper, 21.5 x 20 cm. The front matter on pp. [i-xi] and [1] has been set in type by the publisher. The gatherings have been sewn with yellowish white thread and bound and glued to a cover made of heavy, white (C-263) stock enameled on the outside. The front cover contains a border of two rules around its edge. A collage by Jess is in the middle. Above the collage, with double rules to the right and to the left appears the lettering in italics "Robert Duncan." Just below the author's name and above two double rules appears "GROUND WORK." Below the collage with double rules to the right and to the left appears in italics "Before the War." Lettering on the spine reads from head to heel: "[in italics] Robert Duncan [in Roman] GROUND WORK [in italics] Before the War." "NDP571" has been printed horizontally at the heel. At the top left of the rear cover appears "POETRY" and then in italics "Robert Duncan | [double rules] | [in Roman] GROUND WORK | [double rules] [in italics] Before the War." A fourteen line statement about RD and his work follows, and then statements by Gilbert Sorrentino and Hayden Carruth. Bracketed information gives the titles of three other books by RD and one about him published by New Directions. The follow-ing completes the rear cover: "Cover collage by Jess; design by Denise Breslin | A NEW DIRECTIONS PAPERBOOK [space] NDP571 | [at right] FPT ISBN 0-8112-0896-6 $10.95."

Published: 2275 copies published 31 July 1984 at $10.95.

b. *First edition, paperbound copies, second impression:*

Title, Collation, Contents, Text contents, and Description same as the First impression except that the paper used is ivory, and not yellowish white. "SECOND PRINTING" has been added as the final line on the acknowl-edgments and copyright-page. "SECOND PRINTING" also appears at the top right of the rear cover, on the same line as "POETRY."

Published: 1562 copies published 2 October 1984 at $10.95.

c. *First edition, hardbound copies:*

Title, Collation, Text, Text contents same as First edition, paperbound copies, First impression. Yellowish white paper has been used. The gatherings have been sewn with white thread and bound in brown (lighter than medium brown C-58) cloth over boards. The front cover of the binding is blank. The following appears on the spine in very yellow, reading from the head to the heel: "[in italics] Robert Duncan [in Roman] GROUND WORK [in italics] Before the War." "New | Directions" is printed horizontally at the heel of the spine. The rear cover is blank.

Dust jacket: The dust jacket is made from heavy white stock enameled on the outside. The front of the jacket is the same as the front cover of the paperbound copies. Lettering on the spine reads from head to heel: "[in italics] Robert Duncan [in Roman] GROUND WORK [in italics] Before the War." "New Directions" is printed horizontally at the heel of the spine. The rear of the jacket contains horizontal double rules one third of the way down, which are interrupted by the following: "Also available from New Directions." The double rules then continue to the right. Seven authors and thirty-one titles published by New Directions then are listed, followed by horizontal double rules. At the heel of the rear jacket appears the line, "NEW DIRECTIONS [space] 80 Eighth Avenue [space] New York 10011." The front flap contains the following: "FPT ISBN 0-8112-0895-8 $19.50 | Robert Duncan | [double rules] GROUND | WORK [double rules] | Before the War | [twenty-three line statement about the author and this book, which continues onto the rear flap] | [in italics] (continued on back flap) | A NEW DIRECTIONS BOOK." The rear flap contains the following: "[in italics] (continued from front flap) [ten lines about the author and this book, a statement by Gilbert Sorrentino, and a statement by Hayden Carruth]. Three titles appear under the heading "Also by Robert Duncan [and one under the heading] About the author." | Jacket collage by Jess; | design by Denise Breslin | [below] NEW DIRECTIONS | 80 Eighth Avenue [space] New York 10011."

Published: 733 copies published 31 July 1984 at $19.50.

d. *First edition, hardbound, signed copies:*

Title, Collation, Text, Text contents, and Description the same as First edition, hardbound copies. The signed copies have a colophon on page [177] which reads: "150 copies of this book | have been printed and bound by Murray Printing Company | and signed by the author. | This is number [number in holograph] | [in author's holograph] Robert Duncan." These copies do not have dust jackets. They have been bound in medium reddish orange (C-37) cloth over boards and enclosed in a slipcase bound in brown (approximately dark brown C-59) cloth.

Published: 150 copies published 31 July 1984 at $50.00.

Notes: Two errors appear on page [4] of the front matter: in line 6 "The Diverse Press" should read "The Divers Press," and in line 12 "In Memoriam Wallace Stevens, *Structure of Rime XXVIII*" should be listed as the poem published by The University of Connecticut and not "Over There."

The following errors appear in the text: page 60, line 25, Cocoon of What is, should read, Cocoon of that Is; page 111, line 4, of the whole harmony, should read, of the whole harmony''; page 136, line 18, but what does 'eenie deenie' mean?, should read but what does 'eenie deenie' mean?''; page 140, line 28, has it own solitude the speech, should read, has its own solitude the speech; page 152, line 12, Pleiade, should read Pléiade; page 172, line 30, He has climbed over the horizon like the sun,'' should read, "He has climbed over the horizon like the sun." In CODA to A SEVENTEENTH CENTURY SUITE six lines have been dropped between "persistent love" (line 10), and "deep as the darkness that in eyes" (line 11).

Poems published separately as broadsides, in pamphlets or books, listed below, show numerous differences in *Ground Work* from their previous publication. Spacing changes, adjustments to internal and external margins, line breaks and stanza breaks, as well as punctuation changes, additions and deletions of lines all appear. *Achilles Song*, A32; *A Song from The Structures of Rime Ringing as the Poet Paul Celan Sings*, A50; *Tribunals*, A37; *Bring It up from the Dark*, A35; *In Memoriam Wallace Stevens, Structure of Rime XXVIII*, A 42; *Poems from the Margins of Thoma Gunn's Moly*, A43; *A Seventeenth Century Suite in Homage to the Metaphysical Genius in English Poetry*, A44; *Dante*, A48.

The Sixth poem of Book One of *Dante*, [DE VULGARI ELOQUENTIA, I VI] now appears with the title BUT WE, TO WHOM THE WORLD IS as the fourth poem under the heading FOUR SUPPLEMENTARY ETUDES.

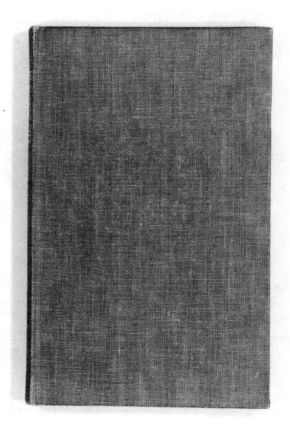

A1a (left), A1b (right). *Heavenly City, Earthly City.*

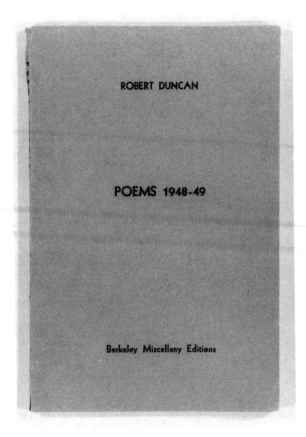

ROBERT DUNCAN

POEMS 1948-49

Berkeley Miscellany Editions

A2a. *Poems 1948–49.*

A2a (left), A2b (right). *Poems 1948-49*, unexpurgated and expurgated texts.

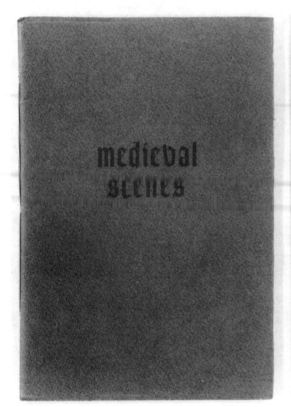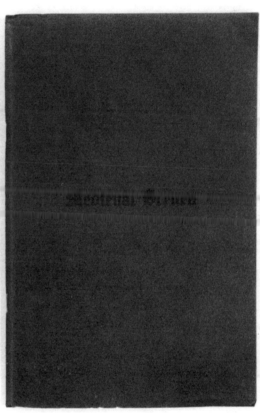

A3a (left), A3b (right). *Medieval Scenes.*

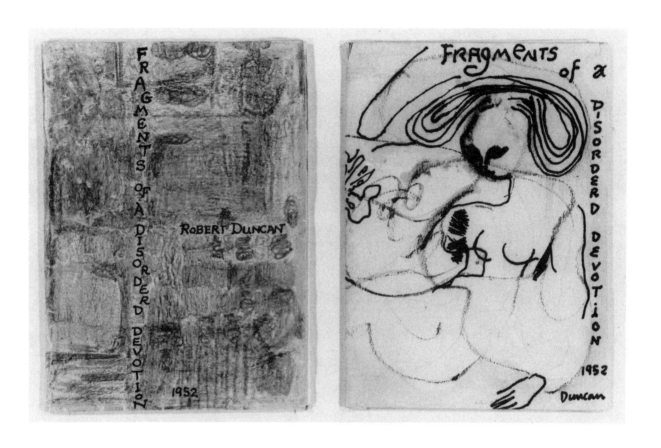

A4a. *Fragments of a Disorderd Devotion.* Left, James Broughton's copy.
Right, Jonathan Williams' copy.

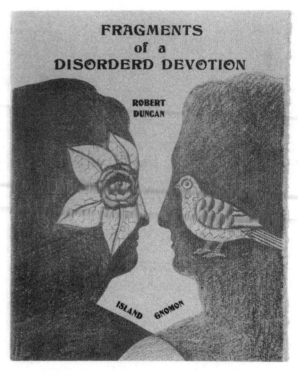

A4c (left), A4b (right). *Fragments of a Distorderd Devotion.*

THE SONG OF THE BORDER-GUARD

The man with his lion under the shed of wars
sheds his belief as if he shed tears.
The sound of words waits—
a barbarian host at the border-line of sense.

The enamourd guards desert their posts
harkening to the lion-smell of a poem
that rings in their ears.

—Dreams, a certain guard said,
    were never designd so
    to re-arrange an empire.

    Along about six o'clock I take out my guitar
    and sing to a lion
    who sleeps like a line of poetry
    in the shed of wars.

The man shedding his belief
knows that the lion is not asleep,
does not dream, is never asleep,
is a wide-awake poem
waiting like a lover for the disrobing of the guard;
the beautiful boundaries of the empire
naked, rapt round in the smell of a lion.

(The barbarians have passd over the significant phrase)

—When I was asleep,
    a certain guard says,
    a man shed his clothes as if he shed tears
        and appeard as a lonely lion
        waiting for a song under the shed-roof of wars.

I sang the song that he waited to hear,
I, the Prize-Winner, the Poet-Acclaimd.

Dear, dear, dear, dear, I sang.
believe, believe, believe, believe.
The shed of wars is splendid as the sky,
houses our waiting like a pure song
housing in its words the lion-smell
        of the beloved disrobed.

I sang: believe, believe, believe.

        I the guard because of my guitar
believe. I am the certain guard,
certain of the Beloved, certain of the Lion,
certain of the Empire. I with my guitar.
Dear, dear, dear, dear, I sing.
I, the Prize-Winner, the Poet on Guard.

The border-lines of sense in the morning light
are naked as a line of poetry in a war.

printed by ROBERT DUNCAN
designd by WORKSHOP
Robert Duncan
at Buffalo   1968

Nicola Cernovich, Publisher   Black Mountain Graphics Workshop   Black Mountain College   Black Mountain, North Carolina

A5. *The Song of the Border-Guard.*

A5. *The Song of the Border-Guard.* Cover design by Cy Twombly.

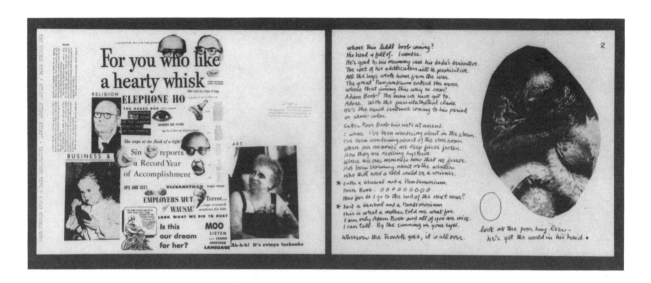

A6. *Boob 1 & 2.*

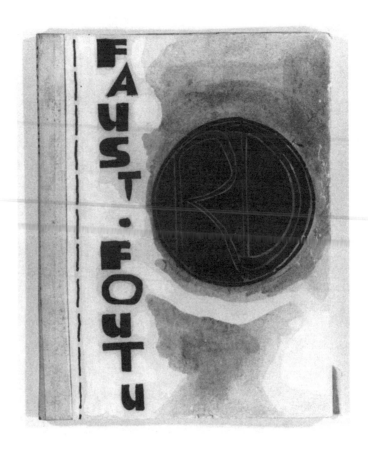

A7a. *Faust Foutu.*

A7b (right), A7c (left), A7d (middle). *Faust Foutu.*

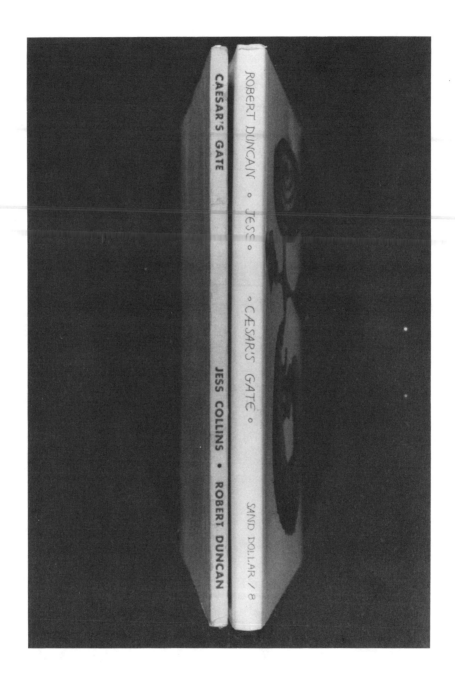

A8a (left), A8d (right). *Caesar's Gate.*

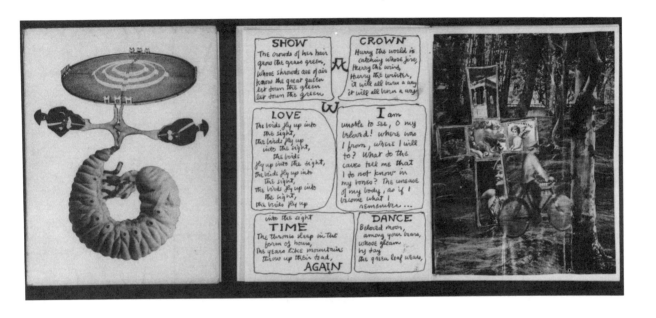

A8b. *Caesar's Gate.* With holograph poem by Duncan and collage by Jess Collins.

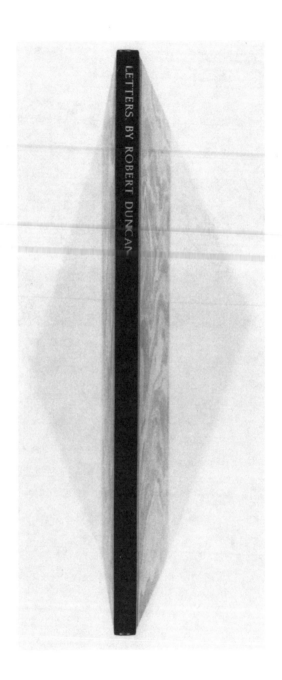

A9b. *Letters.*

A9a (middle), A9b (right), A9d (left). *Letters.*

THE POCKET POETS SERIES

robert
duncan
selected
poems

NUMBER TEN

A10b. *Selected Poems.*

A11a (left), A11k (middle), A11h (right). *The Opening of the Field.*

A12a. *As Testimony.*

A13a. *Writing Writing.*

A14a (bottom), A14d (middle), A14c (top). *Roots and Branches.*

A14a (left), A14d (middle), A14c (right). *Roots and Branches.*

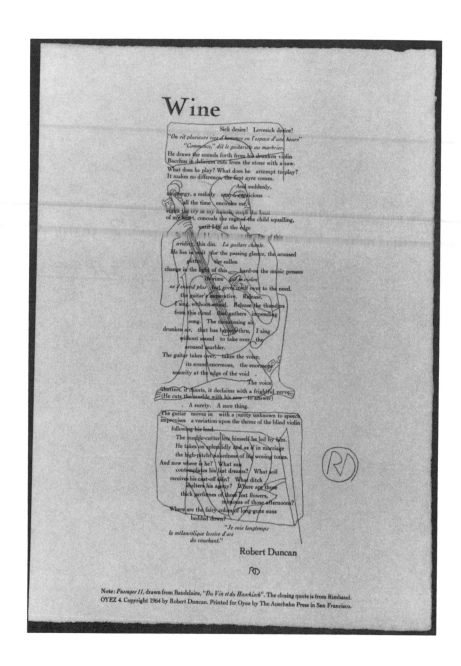

Wine

Sick desire! Lovesick desire!

"On vit plusieurs vies d'hommes en l'espace d'une heure"

"Commence," dit le guitariste au marbrier.

He draws the sounds forth from his drunken violin
Bacchus in delirium cuts from the stone with a saw.

What does he play? What does he   attempt to play?
It makes no difference, the first ayre comes.

          And suddenly,
An energy, a melody   sways capricious .

    all the time   encircles me,

stirs the cry in my hands, stops the beat
of my heart, conceals the rage of the child squalling,

    until I die at the edge

    avidity, this din. *La guitare chante.*

He lies in wait   for the passing glance, the aroused
glitter   the sullen
change in the light of this ____ hard-on the music presses
    its rime   *dit le violon*
ne s'entend plus   but gives itself over to the need,
the guitar's imperative.   Release,
I sing, without sound.   Release the thunders
from this cloud   that gathers   impending
    song.   The threatening air,
drunken air,   that has his way thru,   I sing
    without sound   to take over   the
    aroused marbler.

The guitar takes over,   takes the voice,
    its sound enormous,   the enormous
    sonority at the edge of the void .
          The voice
shatters, it chants, it declaims with a frightful verve.
(He cuts the marble with his saw   to answer)
    A surety.   A sure thing.

The guitar   moves in   with a purity unknown to speech
improvises   a variation upon the theme of the blind violin
    following his lead.

The marble-cutter lets himself be led by him.
He takes on splendidly and as if in marriage
the high-pitcht nakedness of his wooing tones.

And now where is he?   What sun
    contemplates his last dreams?   What soil
receives his cast-off skin?   What ditch
    shelters his agony?   Where are those
    thick perfumes of those lost flowers,
        memoirs of those afternoons?
Where are the fairy colors of long-gone suns
    bedded down?

        "Je vois longtemps
la mélancolique lessive d'ors
    du couchant."

          Robert Duncan

Note: *Passages 11*, drawn from Baudelaire, *"Du Vin et du Haschisch"*. The closing quote is from Rimbaud.
OYEZ 4. Copyright 1964 by Robert Duncan. Printed for Oyez by The Auerhahn Press in San Francisco.

A15. *Wine.*

A16a. *Medea at Kolchis – The Maiden Head.*

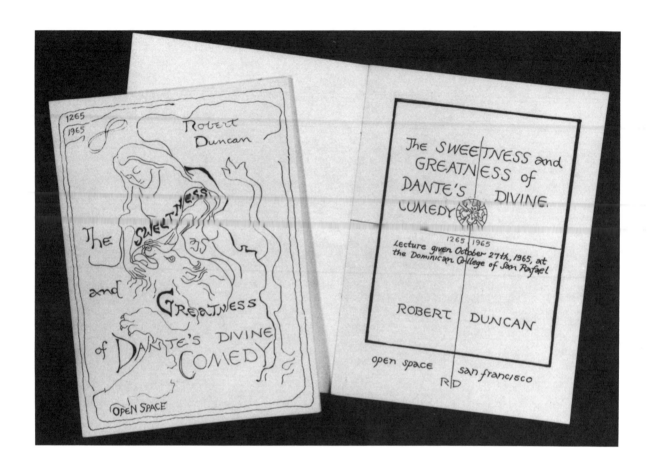

A17a. *The Sweetness and Greatness of Dante's Divine Comedy.* Title page at right.

UP RISING

NOW JOHNSON WOULD GO UP TO JOIN THE GREAT SIMULACRA OF MEN,
HITLER AND STALIN, TO WORK HIS FAME
WITH PLANES ROARING OUT FROM GUAM OVER ASIA,
ALL AMERICA BECOME A SEA OF TOILING MEN
STIRRD AT HIS WILL, WHICH WOULD BE A BLOATED THING,
DRAWING FROM THE UNDERBELLY OF THE NATION
SUCH BLOOD AND DREAMS AS SWELL THE IDIOT PSYCHE
OUT OF ITS COURSES INTO AN ELEMENTAL THING
UNTIL HIS NAME STINKS WITH BURNING MEAT AND HEAPT HONORS.

AND MEN AWAKE TO SEE THAT THEY ARE USED LIKE THINGS
SPENT IN A GREAT HECATOMB OF YOUTHS, THIS TEXAS BARBEQUE
OF ASIA, AFRICA AND ALL THE AMERICAS,
AND THE PROFESSIONAL MILITARY BEHIND HIM, THINKING
TO USE HIM AS THEY THOUGHT TO USE HITLER
WITHOUT LOSING CONTROL OF THEIR BUSINESS OF WAR,

BUT THE MANIA, THE RAVENING EAGLE OF AMERICA
AS LAWRENCE SAW HIM "BIRD OF MEN THAT ARE MASTERS,
LIFTING THE RABBIT-BLOOD OF THE MYRIADS UP INTO —"
SOMETHING TERRIBLE, GONE BEYOND BOUNDS, OR
AS BLAKE SAW FIGURES OF FIRE AND BLOOD RAGING,
— IN WHAT IMAGE? THE OMINOUS ROAR IN THE AIR,
THE OMNIPOTENT WINGS, THE ALL-AMERICAN BOY IN THE COCKPIT
LOOSING HIS FLOW OF NAPALM, BELOW IN THE JUNGLES
"ANY LIFE AT ALL OR SIGN OF LIFE" HIS TARGET, DRAWING NOW
NOT WITH CRAYONS IN HIS SECRET ROOM
THE BURNING OF HOMES AND THE TORTURE OF MOTHERS AND FATHERS
AND CHILDREN,
THEIR HAIR A-FLAME, SCREAMING IN AGONY, BUT
IN THE LINE OF DUTY, FOR THE MIGHT AND ENDURING FAME
OF JOHNSON, FOR THE VICTORY OF AMERICAN WILL OVER ITS
VICTIMS,
RELEASING HIS STORE OF DESTRUCTION OVER THE ENEMY,
IN TERROR AND HATRED OF ALL COMMUNAL THINGS, OF COMMUNION, OF
COMMUNISM:

HAS RAISED FROM THE PRIVATE ROOMS OF SMALL-TOWN BOSSES AND
BUSINESS MEN,
FROM THE COUNCIL CHAMBERS OF THE GANGS THAT RUN THE GREAT
CITIES,
SWOLLEN WITH THE VOTES OF MILLIONS,
FROM THE FEARFUL HEARTS OF GOOD PEOPLE IN THE SUBURBS TURNING
THE SAVORY MEAT OVER THE CHARCOAL BURNERS AND HEAPING THEIR
BARBEQUE PLATES WITH MORE THAN THEY CAN EAT,
FROM THE CLOSED MEETING-ROOMS OF REGENTS OF UNIVERSITIES AND
SESSIONS OF PROFITEERS —

BACK OF THE SCENE: THE ATOMIC STOCKPILE; THE VIALS OF SYNTHESIZED
DISEASES EAGER BIOLOGISTS HAVE DEVELOPED OVER HALF A CENTURY
DREAMING OF THE BODIES OF MOTHERS AND FATHERS AND CHILDREN AND
HATED RIVALS SWOLLEN WITH NEW PLAGUES, MEASLES GROWN ENORMOUS,
INFLUENZAS PERFECTED; AND THE GASSES OF DESPAIR, CONFUSION OF
THE SENSES, MANIA, INDUCING TERROR OF THE UNIVERSE, COMA,
EXISTENTIAL WOUNDS, THAT CHEMISTS WE HAVE MET AT COCKTAIL
PARTIES, PASSED DAILY AND WITH A HAPPY "GOOD DAY" OR "HELLO"
ON THE WAY TO CLASSES OR WORK HAVE WORKT
"TO MAKE WARS TOO TERRIBLE FOR MEN TO WAGE";

RAISED THIS SECRET ENTITY OF AMERICA'S HATRED OF EUROPE, OF
AFRICA, OF ASIA,
THE DEEP HATRED FOR THE OLD WORLD THAT HAD DRIVEN HIM OUT,
AND FOR THE ALIEN WORLD, THE NEW WORLD ABOUT HIM, THAT MIGHT
HAVE BEEN PARADISE
BUT WAS BEFORE HIS EYES ALREADY CLEARD BACK IN A HOLOCAUST OF
BURNING INDIANS, TREES AND GRASSLANDS,
REDUCED TO HIS REAL ESTATE, HIS PROJECTS OF EXPLOITATION AND
PROFITABLE WASTES,

THIS SPECTER THAT IN THE BEGINNING ADAMS AND JEFFERSON FEARD
AND KNEW
WOULD CORRUPT THE VERY BODY OF THE NATION
AND ALL SENSE OF OUR COMMON HUMANITY,
THIS BLACK BILE OF OLD EVILS ARISEN ANEW,
TAKES OVER THE VANITY OF JOHNSON;
AND THE VERY GLINT OF SATAN'S EYES FROM THE PIT OF HELL OF
AMERICA'S UNACKNOWLEDGED, UNREPENTED CRIMES THAT I SAW IN
GOLDWATER'S EYES
NOW SHINES FROM THE EYES OF THE PRESIDENT
IN THE SWOLLEN HEAD OF THE NATION.

ROBERT DUNCAN

Passages 25

OYEZ · BERKELEY
COPYRIGHT—1965—ROBERT DUNCAN
PRINTED BY GRAHAM MACKINTOSH

A18. *Up Rising.*

A19a. *Of the War.*

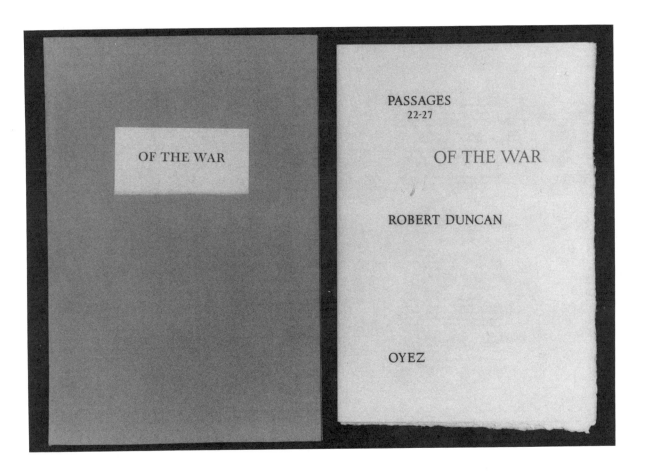

A19c. *Of the War.*

A20a (left), A20c(middle), A20b (right). *The Years As Catches.*

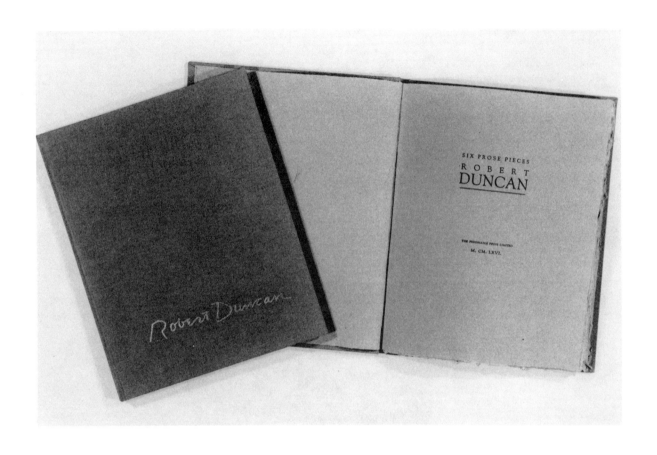

A21a. *Six Prose Pieces.*

A22a. *A Book of Resemblances.*

A23. *The Cat and the Blackbird.*

CHRISTMAS present,   Christmas presence!

In the story the three kings, Kaspar,
Balthasar and Melchior bring gifts,
regalia to the Child who in their recognition is

the King, incarnate spirit of the Star
they follow.   With these things
we must tell the secret of who we are.
                    Now, that Light
and Sol Invictus of the Empire have been
confounded.   The Mother

no more than a girl, virgin
color of the dawn sky,
holds the Infant Sun in her arms.

Star of Christmas eve,
Sun of Christmas day,

Your name, Jesus, has begun in my heart
again an allegiance to that Kingdom
"not of this world" the Child knows His.
            — I, Simon Peter,
who will yet three times, as the story requires,

deny my Lord, the Child in me, and hear
Chanticleer reply and crow to acclaim the Light,
three times cry out: *My fiery Lord arrives,*
and breaks upon the shores of Night
infant announcements of New Life!

"Behold the Man!" says Pilate.   Behold the Child!
For the whole play of Christmas day is there
in the Announcement: the *"For this was I born"* the
        "why hast thou forsaken me?"

(They shall look on Him Whom they pierced)

And we, redeemd in a Child's play, a Child's
suffering, light again
all the candles, stars in Night's tree, our
lives and gods in His name.   Most present He,
here, in the Place of the Skull, Time's
crucifix, in the flames where soldiers once again
slaughter the Innocents and priests proclaim
"He's dead!   We have no King but Caesar!"

Christmas presence, Christmas present!
As if we were no more than Kings, we men
bring our selves and signs as gifts, rejoicing,
and yet come in the darkest of times to rehearse

the old story of the darkest of times,
the birth of the Child in God,
the Christ-design in the girl's arms.
Truth's empire we hold to, where all empire falls. . .

"*King is your word,*" He said.   And yet
in the depth of all harms we set up our Christmas tree
as if it were a kingdom, and keep alight
the everlasting crowns of stars and gods, their flames to delite

the Child in His name.

                        —Robert Duncan

A24b. *Christmas present, Christmas presence!*

A25a. *Epilogos*. With author's illustration.

A26a (right), A26c (left). *The Truth & Life of Myth.*

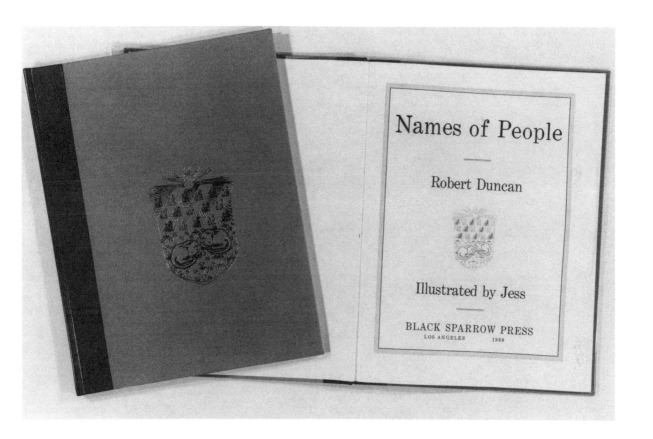

A27a. *Names of People.*

MY MOTHER WOULD BE A FALCONRESS

My mother would be a falconress,
And I, her gay falcon treading her wrist,
would fly to bring back
from the blue of the sky to her, bleeding, a prize,
where I dream in my little hood with many bells
jangling when I'd turn my head.

My mother would be a falconress,
and she sends me as far as her will goes.
She lets me ride to the end of her curb.
where I fall back in anguish.
I dread that she will cast me away.
for I fall, I mis-take, I fail in her mission.

She would bring down the little birds.
And I would bring down the little birds.
When will she let me bring down the little birds,
pierced from their flight with their necks broken,
their heads like flowers limp from the stem?

I tread my mother's wrist and would draw blood.
Behind the little hood my eyes are hooded.
I have gone back into my hooded silence,
talking to myself and dropping off to sleep.

For she has muffled my dreams in the hood she has made me,
sewn round with bells, jangling when I move.
She rides with her little falcon upon her wrist.
She uses a little wand like a whip
She sends me abroad to try my wings
and I come back to her. I would bring down
the little birds to her
I may not tear into, I must bring back perfectly.

I tear at her wrist with my beak to draw blood,
and her eye holds me, anguisht, terrifying.
She draws a limit to my flight.
Never beyond my sight, she says.

She trains me to fetch and to limit myself in fetching.
She rewards me with meat for my dinner.
But I must never eat what she sends me to bring her.

Yet it would have been beautiful, if she would have carried me,
always, in a little hood with the bells ringing,
at her wrist, and her riding
to the great falcon hunt, and me
flying up to the curb of my heart from her heart
to bring down the skylark from the blue to her feet,
straining, and then released for the flight.

My mother would be a falconress,
and I her gerfalcon, raised at her will,
from her wrist sent flying, as if I were her own
pride, as if her pride
knew no limits, as if her mind
sought in me flight beyond the horizon.

Ah, but high, high in the air I flew.
And far, far beyond the curb of her will,
were the blue hills where the falcons nest.
And then I saw west to the dying sun—
it seemd my human soul went down in flames.

I tore at her wrist, at the hold she had for me,
until the blood ran hot and I heard her cry out,
far, far beyond the curb of her will,

to horizons of stars beyond the ringing hills of the world where
   the falcons nest
I saw, and I tore at her wrist with my savage beak.
I flew, as if sight flew from the anguish in her eye beyond her sight,
sent from my striking loose, from the cruel strike at her wrist,
striking out from the blood to be free of her.

My mother would be a falconress,
and even now, years after this,
when the wounds I left her had surely heald,
and the woman is dead,
her fierce eyes closed, and if her heart
were broken, it is stilld,

I would be a falcon and go free.
I tread her wrist and wear the hood,
talking to myself, and would draw blood.

ROBERT DUNCAN

43/75
Robert Duncan
Feb 7, 1968

A28b. *My Mother Would Be A Falconress.*

A29a (left), A29h (right). *Bending the Bow.*

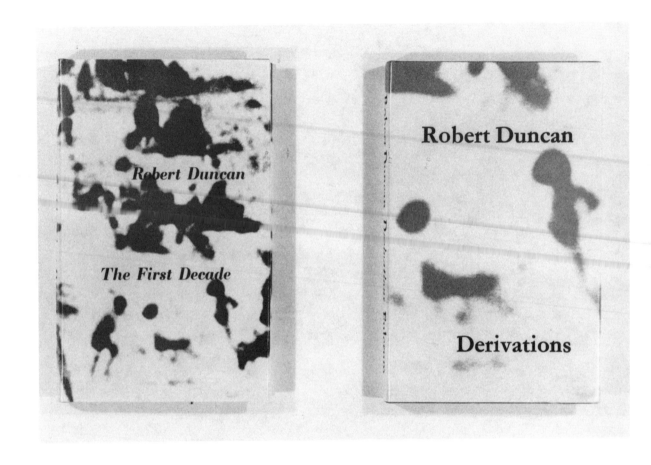

A30a (left), A31a (right). *The First Decade, Derivations.*

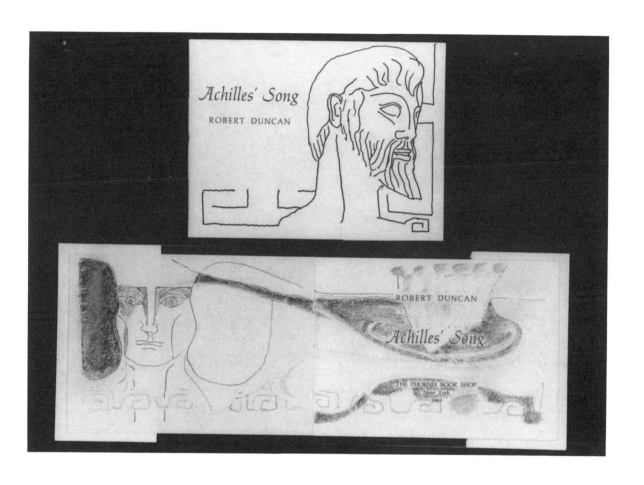

A32a (top), A32b (bottom). *Achilles' Song.*

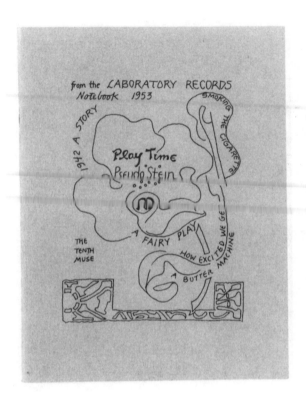
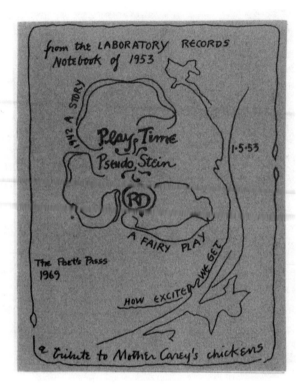

A33a (right), A33b (left). *Play Time Pseudo Stein.*

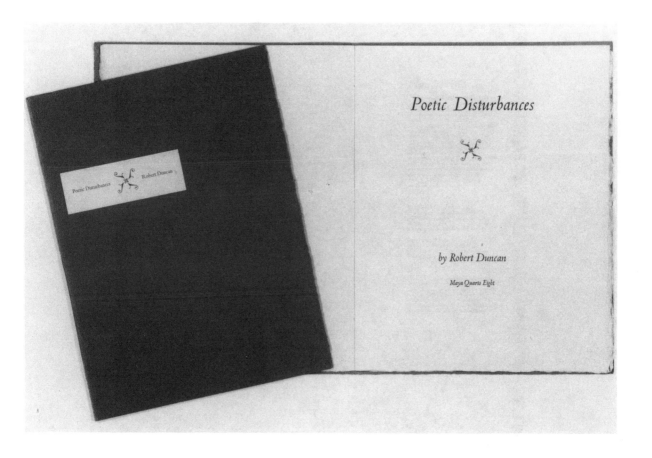

Poetic Disturbances

by Robert Duncan

Maya Quarto Eight

A34a (left), A34b (right). *Poetic Disturbances.*

BRING IT UP FROM THE DARK

Bring up from the dark water.
It will be news from behind the horizon.
Refugees, nameless people. Who are they?
What is happening? I do not know.
Out there. Where we can see nothing.
Where we can do nothing. Men of our own country
send deadly messengers we would not send
The cold wind of their desolation chills the first hint of morning,
Rumors of burnd houses, smoking fields, and now wraiths
of the dead men daily they kill rise
against us. It will go against us,

      pass, sweep on and beyond us.

The great house of our humanity
no longer stands. Men from our own country
stamp out, burn back, flush up from their refuge
with gasses, howling or silent, whatever
human or animal remains living there.

Bereft, the mothering sky
searches our faces, searches my heart.
What have I to do with these things
that now I am left destitute.
In the midst of my happiness, the worm
of man's misery coils in my heart.

Dream disclosed to me, I too am Ishmael.

Robert Duncan

Robert Duncan   April 1971

A35. *Bring It Up From The Dark.*

A36a (top), A36b (bottom). *65 Drawings.*

A37a (right), A37d (middle), A37c (left). *Tribunals.*

Dec. 20th ON GLEANINGS: To return to the studio work of writing
writing and learning my letters before the decade of publishing
1960-1970, of the three books, The Opening of the Field, Roots
and Branches, and Bending the Bow. The extension of the poem as
a field in process, the ramifications below and above the trunk
of vegetative life, and the vector force of the connection-spring
of the tension and the intent: these still appear "before" me;
all the poetry before me before me. With the Field, the Tree,
and the Bow, before me, I propose to return to the Ground-Work
(GROUND WORK, the title of the fourth book then! instead of
TRANSMISSIONS which I had taken for the title) GLEANINGS I had
proposed to be a record issued of work in progress for certain
friends as readers before publication, passages from notebooks,
drawings, inventions, the ground work of what I now see is to be
calld GROUND WORK--speculations and appreciations, associations,
rantings if need be, phantasies, lectures, nocturnes and mind
soul and spirit dances and inventions.

Dec. 21st Trying out the colors in a new box of crayons, too
late to set about making cards for the season, as a design of a
tree of lights arose to illuminate a card for Henry and Adele
Wenning (one of two cards I managed to make), I got a Christmas
poem:
      O tree of lights! tree of colors!
      How readily you arise to my
        designing hand, at hand
      to delite the eye, as ever
        night's branches, day's branches
      intermingling, moon and sun, stars
        and birds silver and gold
      or at the horizon transmuted
        crimson day's song . O tree
      of a million branches,
        tree of a million roots, tree
      of resources! Again,
      the treasury of fruits and presents,
        again the mosaic of many colors.

Dec. 22. Phantasies of the Ground. Jim Harrison singing his
Ghazals. I'd put my mind beside itself and sing, the fond remem-
berer proposes. In tune out of season. A season songster. The
sun goes down into my strings so that five o'clock is drowsily
aflame. The western sea goes blind with listening toward darker
blues. From whose music a girl's face comes forward not to be
recognized but to occupy the absence of the thought of her.

Dec. 28. From resources of mind that are all color, fountains
of Being akin to the world of vibrations, palaces of the Eye and
the Inner Ear, flow ideas of the Book of Formations, informations
of balance and movement that have their ground in what we see as
colors and hear as sounds, ratios and rhythms of what we know as
music. Attentive to the developments of melody that give birth
out of potentialities to glowing facts in the field of the actual,
the ground my being had taken in personality, in its own individ-
ualization, loses itself in the deeper ground, the ground of being alive in that deeper ground, the ground of music we are ever
reminded of in the depths of what man himself has created

A PROSPECTUS
for the prepublication issue of GROUND WORK
to certain friends of the poet
Jan. 31, 1971

   Enclosed are the first twelve pages of what will be, when
the project is completed, a volume of passages from notebooks
current and old, poems in progress and previously unedited
poems, starts and fits, drawings and propositions--GROUND WORK,
relating to my work following BENDING THE BOW. I want a time
and a space to work in that will be, as time and space were only
in the years before others were interested in publishing me,
the time and space of a life of the work itself. Once something
like a hundred pages has been done and given that the feel of
such a unit will be there, I propose to issue the volume as such
for publication with a subscription limited to two hundred and
fifty copies under copyright with the title PREPARING THE GROUND
WORK.

COSTS It is my hope that the company of friends of my work will
aid me in the project. To that end, with each installment of
pages I will send a statement of expenses to date, as below:

multilithography, 6 sheets, 12 pages (400 copies)	$67.10
envelopes (500)	10.77
transportation	3.00
postage for 50 copies maild (.12 each)	6.00
	$86.87

My labor, based on $20 for an eight hour day = $40.00
not taking into any account the original writing. $126.87

SOME ERRATA

   page 7 #1, line 8, for "elese" read "else"
   page 8 #2, line 16, for "Mouthe" read "Mouth"
   page 9 #2, line 16, comma after "persona"
           line 19, comma after "are"

  GROUND WORK is to be unfinisht copy, immediate copy--having
no middle men between the reader and the writer--the errors will
be the writers, not the printers, the departures from printing
conventions will be in for free, and there will be no publisher
hounding the writer for copy to meet his schedule. I need at
least a year of that.

A38. *Ground Work.*

NOTES ON JESS'S TRANSLATION SERIES

PREFACE FOR THE CATALOGUE

ICONOGRAPHIC EXTENSIONS

The whole sequence is a picture book, belonging then to the great primary tradition that extends from the illustrated walls of the Cro-magnon man's galleries to the emblematic and magical art of the Renaissance and the revival of enigma and visionary painting in the Romantic Movement. Its original may have been a child's coloring book, for each painting is a picture translated from a drawing, an engraving, a lithograph, or a photograph, in sepia or in black and white, into the density and color of oils. Still again, its original may have been a child's scrapbook or paste-up book, for the variety and readiness of its recognitions of what belongs. Paste-up or coloring book, the original the painter presents to us is just now coming into being in our mind out of whatever was--it is the primer of a new need in vision aroused in him by the demand of a missing beginning hidden in the disclosures of what he comes to see as his tradition.

His series of copies presented here belong to a larger constellation again of works in progress--romantic paintings, paste-ups, drawings and illustrations, constructions [ ] [ ] play with playthings rescued from throwaways of the world about him--in which he works to [ ] household our way of living, and, beyond, to illustrate, with all the glow and depth of color, the interplay of possible forms and boundaries, and the mysteries of Translation [ ] in turn, he sees his Translations as-- in Translation [ ] even as he has come to see the paintings of his beloved Renaissance [ ] Seed [ ] --"grown for seed", scattered abroad in the imaginations of men to give rise to new visionary generations. Our *being*, here, is ultimately generative in picturing, in continual imaginative reproduction.

It is important that they are copies, redundancies or visible ideas (where we must remember that the word *idea* comes from the Greek verb ἰδεῖν, meaning *to see*), making visible what the painter comes to see in the process of making it visible. His relation to the visible is as immediate as he draws from what he sees in the 1895 engraving from a painting by Dvořák as Cézanne's is as he draws from the mountain Sainte-Victoire. Each is painstakingly faithful in translating what he sees into his own world of paint and color. It is important that their work is fictional--what their eyes see they translate out of sight into factors of the painting they are creating which returns to sight. The painting by Cézanne becomes a primer to the eye seeing the mountain. The painting by Jess becomes primary to our view of the painting by Dvořák.

Translation 3, *Ex. 2 - Crito's Socrates*, rightly brings to mind Plato and his theory of the work of art as a copy of a copy of the original; and we might recall Ben Jonson's "It was excellently said of Plutarch, poetry was a speaking picture, and picture a mute poesy" and from his *De pictura*: "Picture is the invention of Heaven, the most ancient, and most akin to Nature. It is itself a silent work, and always of one and the same habit." Like the surrealists, Jess surrounds his pictures with texts and undermines our taking them for granted with titles that disturb any easy sense of what we see as apparent. The Translations in the visible world have their "originals", and

A39. *Notes on Jess's Translation Series.*

A40. *Robert Duncan: An Interview.*

BEYOND POETRY

the museum

ROBERT DUNCAN

Robert Duncan

A41a. *The Museum.*

IN MEMORIAM

Wallace Stevens

ROBERT DUNCAN

THE UNIVERSITY OF CONNECTICUT
STORRS
April 25, 1972

A42a. *In Memoriam Wallace Stevens.*

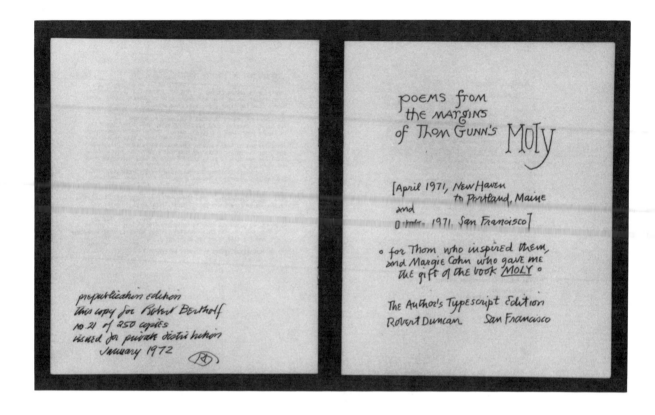

poems from
the margins
of Thom Gunn's MOLY

[April 1971, New Haven
            to Portland, Maine
and
O   1971, San Francisco]

○ for Thom who inspired them,
and Margie Cohn who gave me
the gift of the book MOLY ○

The Author's Typescript Edition
Robert Duncan   San Francisco

prepublication edition
this copy for Robert Bertholf
no. 21 of 250 copies
issued for private distribution
        January 1972

A43. *Poems from the Margins of Thom Gunn's Moly.*

A44a (right), A44b (left). *A Seventeenth Century Suite.*

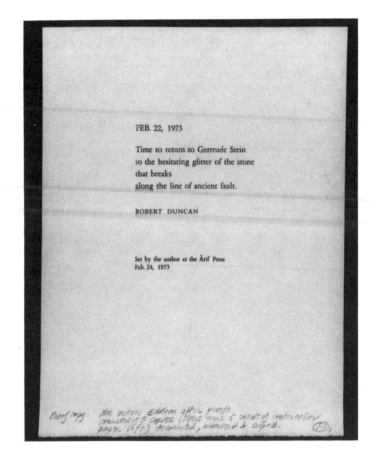

FEB. 22, 1973

Time to return to Gertrude Stein
to the hesitating glitter of the stone
that breaks
along the line of ancient fault.

ROBERT DUNCAN

Set by the author at the Ārif Press
Feb. 24, 1973

Proof copy. The actual Edition after proofs consisted of 5 copies (there were 5 sheets of watercolor paper. (8/r) decorated, numbered & signd.

A45. *Feb. 22, 1973.*

VOICES OF THE '40S
a recreation of the "Festival of Modern Poetry—April 1947"

MEMOIRS OF OUR TIME AND PLACE

The VOICES OF THE '40s program this evening presents a partial representation of the poets who were active in the Bay Area before the movements that were to define new directives in the '50s—the "New York School," the "Black Mountain" group, the Beat movement, and the "San Francisco Scene," as presented in Donald Allen's now classical anthology of the new poetry 1960. Allen Ginsberg's HOWL in 1955 is still for me the watershed. After HOWL, San Francisco would be famous throughout the world as a "center," a place where history is made in poetry, for poets to be compared only with New York, London, or Paris. Young men and women would come here from all over to seek recognition, to be part of what was happening.

But Allen Ginsberg had himself been drawn to San Francisco in 1954 because of its beginning fame. Kenneth Rexroth was its Prophet. CIRCLE magazine was its vehicle. Patchen and others would be drawn to the new Mecca. But back of Rexroth's picture of what the city promised was not only his hopes for the little group of poets who gathered around his own teaching—Philip Lamantia and myself at first, then Thomas Parkinson, Richard Moore, and William Everson—but, more important, I think, the community of poets at large that first began to know itself with the Poetry Festival readings initiated by Madeline Gleason in 1947.

In the years of the Poetry Festival, 1947-1952, I came to work in an entente with Madeline Gleason and James Broughton in which my own poetry reflected their work. After participating as a poet with the composer John Edmunds in the organization of a Festival of the poet-composer Campion's songs, Madeline began to think of a Festival of Contemporary Poetry to be presented after the model of music festivals. The time and place was ripe. In the aftermath of the Second World War, a number of poets were beginning to be active and coming to know of each others' work. Returning to San Francisco in 1945, I sought out Madeline Gleason after friends had given me her first book, POEMS, which had just been printed by the Grabhorn Press. When William Everson emerged from C.O. camp, I took him to meet her. It is not unfitting that I should present a perspective here drawn from my own life view, for I was active in a series of circles that were back of the gathering community. And, even where I was not myself a member, my concerns had often extended. In the late 1930s I had begun to read the work of the enduringly remarkable poets—Robert Horan, Jeanne McGahey, and Rosalie Moore Brown—who had begun to work with Lawrence Hart in what they called "Activist" poetry. Janet Lewis' work, for me, belonged to another world, but even here, through Rexroth's appreciations—he held the work of Janet Lewis and also of Yvor Winters in a particular regard—I had a personal sense of respect.

In the first event, the two evenings of the 1947 Festival of Modern Poetry, presented at the Labaudt Gallery, we found ourselves and began to hear our poems as belonging to a world of poets working with us, yes, but also we found that there was an audience. We had been told that modern poetry had no readers. That was the decisive message writ large in the 1930s. Yet in San Francisco hearers were ready. In time it appears that Madeline Gleason's Festivals were the first such Readings presented in the contemporary world; the first established public series, that is. Certainly, it was in San Francisco that the first audience began. And it was in the context of that audience and of the powerful growing recognition of a community of poets beyond the groups and movements within that community—in a context, that is, instituted by that first venture in April 1947, that an all important change took place in the relation of the poem to its audience.

There are major forces of the poetry of the period missing from the program—the picture is incomplete. Jack Spicer has died. Philip Lamantia and Kenneth Rexroth both would be needed for the essential hearing. Only a Series could present the period just preceding HOWL. Rosalie Moore Brown is a major representative of the "Activists," but only a solid program—certainly, the three, Robert Horan, Jeanne McGahey, and Rosalie Moore Brown, who won national recognition and were each selected as Yale Younger Poets in the tenure of W.H. Auden as judge—would supply a much needed part of the picture.

The VOICES OF THE '40s program might be then, hopefully, not an evening of nostalgia but an initial step toward a new vista—no backward look but a forward look that can only come from a gain in knowledge of the roots and foundations of the present practice of the art.

ROBERT DUNCAN
May 15, 1974

A46. *Memoirs of Our Time and Place.*

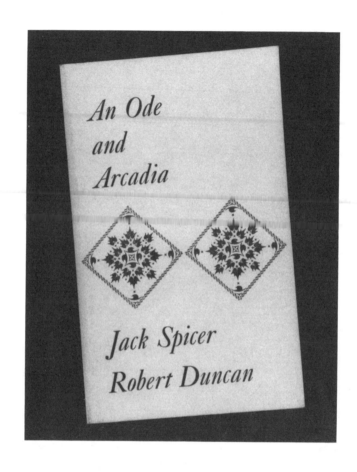

A47. *An Ode and Arcadia.*

A48. *Dante.*

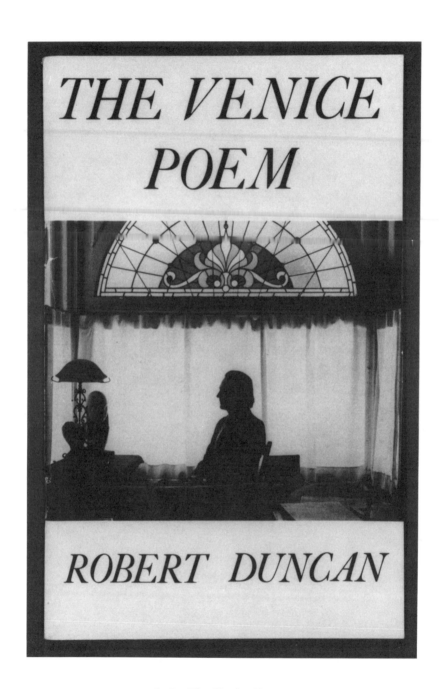

A49. *The Venice Poem.*

Robert Duncan

A SONG FROM THE STRUCTURES OF RIME RINGING
AS THE POET PAUL CELAN SINGS:

CHUTES

Orange Export Ltd
1977

A50a. *A Song From the Structures of Rime Ringing.*

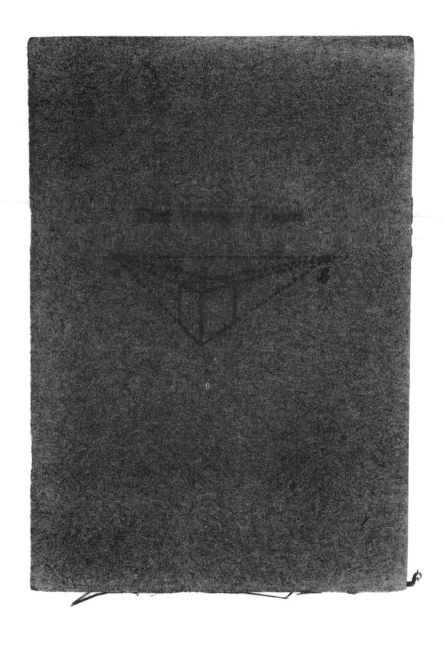

A51. *The Venice Poem.*

THE SENTINELS

Earth owls in ancient burrows clumpt
          the dream presents. I could return to look.
No other fragment remains. I wanted owls
and brought them back. The grey-brown earth-
haunted grass and bush and bushy birds
so near to death, silent as a family photograph,
still as if the sound of a rattle were missing,
the owls shifting into the stillness, thicket and hole
alive, impassive witnesses, thrive there
as ever — I've but to close my eyes and go.

The rest of that field and the company
I was among in that place are lost — ghost folk,
passing among whom I was a wraith,
awake, studious, writing, the blur
marrd and almost erased, unmarkt events.

It was night and cold and the light there
was an after-light. I wrapt my naked body
in my comforter against that wind. I
do not — I can not — I will not, trying,
recite the rest. It was grey day in an absence of the sun.
It was a place without a rattling sound,
a deaf waiting-room this place is close upon.

The scratching of my pen and my bending thought
move from this margin and return. Morning shrinks.
The owls shiver down into the secrets of an earth
I began to see when I lookt into the hole I feard
and then saw others in the clump of grass.
I was dreaming and where I dreamt a light had gone out
and in that light they blind their sight and sit
sentinel upon the brooding of owl-thought, counselings
I remember ever mute and alive, hidden in all things.

Robert Duncan

A52a. *The Sentinels.*

The
Sentinels

Earth owls in ancient burrows clampt
the dream presents. I could return to look.
No other fragment remains. I wanted owls
and brought them back. The grey-brown earth-
haunted grass and bush and bushy birds
so near to death, silent as a family photograph,
still as if the sound of a rattle were missing,
the owls shifting into the stillness, thicket and hole
alive, impassive witnesses thrive there
as ever—I've but to close my eyes and go.
The rest of that field and the company
I was among in that place are lost—ghost folk,
passing among whom I was a wraith,
awake, studious, writing, the blur
martd and almost erased, unmarkt events.
It was night and cold and the light there
was an after-light. I wrapt my naked body
in my comforter against that wind. I
do not—I can not—I will not, trying,
recite the rest. It was grey day in an absence of the sun.
It was a place without a rattling sound,
a deaf waiting room this place is close upon.
The scratching of my pen and my bending thought
move from this margin and return. Morning shrinks.
The owls shiver down into the secrets of an earth
I began to see when I lookt into the hole I feard
and then saw others in the clump of grass.
I was dreaming and where I dreamt a light had gone out
and in that light they blind their sight and sit
sentinel upon the brooding of owl-thought, counselings
I remember ever mute and alive, hidden in all things.

                                        Robert Duncan

Robert Duncan

Published by Jesuit Press Edition. Limited to 136 copies, 36 of which are lettered and signed by the poet-illustrator. Designed and printed by Black Stone Press. Copyright 1979 by Robert Duncan.

A52c. *The Sentinels.*

A53a. *Veil, Turbine, Cord, & Bird.*

AN EPITHALAMIUM by Robert Duncan

NOW for each the ring of day after day and before
sounds in each morning noon and evening hours
that art, the care and governing intent, heart/beat
in its wildness and errant mind declare a home
and come in partnership to share, twain in that
secret daily allegiance to enduring time and keep
of earth's good orders the spirit of marriage enjoins—
we gather to celebrate how in a young woman and a young man
our joys in their joys would be rememberd and alight
witness even in our fearful human shadowing stand.

Robert Duncan

A54. *An Epithalamium.*

A55a (left), A55b (right). *The Five Songs.*

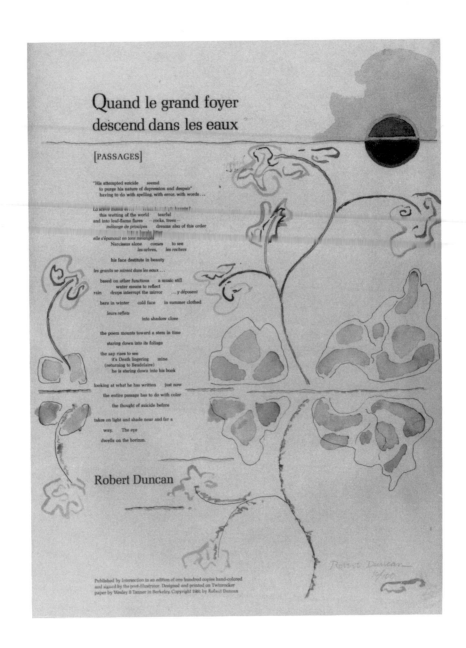

A56. *Quand le grand foyer descend dans les eaux.*

ROBERT DUNCAN

passages

IN BLOOD'S DOMAIN

The Angel Syphilis in the circle of Signators   looses its hosts   to swarm
  mounting the stem of being   to the head
                                            Baudelaire, Nietzsche, Swift
are not eased into Death
                          the undoing of Mind's rule in the brain.

"Yet it is in spirit that nature is timelessly enveloped."   And,   as above,   so below   there are
  spirochete invasions that eat at the sublime envelope,   nor alien,   but familiar
  Life in the dis-ease radiates   invisibilities devour my star

and Time restless crawls in center upon center   cells of lives within life conspire

Hel shines in the very word *Health*   as *Ill* in the Divine Will shines.

The Angel Cancer crawls across the signs of the Zodiac to reach its

appointed time   and   bringing down the carnal pride   bursts into flower—

Swift,   Baudelaire,   Nietzsche   into the heart Eternal of what Poetry is

answer to the genius and science of the Abyss.   The first sign of this advancing power

shows in Fear that goes   clear to the bone   to gnaw at the marrow.

The seeress Lou Andreas-Salomé   sees long before the hour arrives—

  [mais]   *"Tantôt sonnera l'heure   où le divin Hasard,*

  où l'auguste Vertu,   ton épouse encor vierge"   —where black the infected blood

  gushes forth from Rilke's mouth,   from his nose,   from his rectal canal

  news his whole body bears as its truth   of the septic rose

  Où le Repentir même   (ah!   la dernière auberge!)

                          Lovely then

that Death come to carry you away from the moment of this splendor
  that bursts the cells of your body   like a million larvae triumphant

    comes to life in the fruit   All the spreading seeds,   the viral array
    taking over flesh as the earth it is

                          scarlet eruptions

And the pneumatics torn in the secret workings of the Angel Tuberculosis

  (No,   I do not speak of Evils or of Agents of Death   but these Angels
    are attendants of lives raging within life,   under these Wings we dread

  viruses,   bacilli   come home to thrive in us   *où tout is dew*

    "Meurs,   vieux lâche!   il est trop tard!"   Die,   you old coward,
    it is too late.

                I feel the ringing of tomorrow's bell.

But what are at Pound's immortal Mind?   for the Cantos,   for *Les Fleurs du Mal*,
        so eat at Mind's conscience
    what malady?   what undoing-of-all-Good   workt behind speech?
    —are the matter I come from—these poisons I must know the hidden intentions of
    where "this coil of Geryon" (Djerjon)   said Mr Carlyle,   who now becomes

      Thomas Carlyle,   not the member of Congress,   but
                          the genius of "Hero Worship"   hin (our) congress

And if I know not my wound   it does not appear to suppurate?   In this intercourse
    "Adolf furious from perception"   —does this thought refer to Hitler?

Link by link I can disown no link of this chain from my conscience.

  Would you forget the furnaces of burning meat   purity demands?
  There is no ecstasy of Beauty in which I will not remember Man's misery.

Jesus   in this passage   —He is like a man coming forward in a hospital theater—
  cries out: I come not to heal but to tear the scab from the wound you wanted to forget.
  May the grass no longer spread out to cover the works of man in the ruin of earth.

What Angel,   what Gift of the Poison,   has brought into my body

  this sickness of living?   Into the very Gloria of Life's theme and variations
  my own counterpart of Baudelaire's terrible Ennuie?

                                            Robert Duncan

copyright 1980 by Robert Duncan

Of 100 copies printed by Black Mesa Press in conjunction with Woodland Pattern Book Center, this is number 203

Erratum— line 13, for "éspouse" read "épouse".

A57. *In Blood's Domain.*

A58. *Towards an Open Universe.*

Robert Duncan

IN PASSAGE

The guide is telling his story of these things

    a ring   a cup   an open book   a sword

I'd come to see. "Witness," he instructs "the tomb

    is ancient in which tomorrow is to lie

in state." In time you must terrify. Yet

    the testament is written in passing things—

the figures upon the wall shift, glow in the mind,

    go out: what I divine I come into and change.

Robert Duncan

Printed at The Toothpaste Press for Bookslinger Editions, on the occasion of the author's reading at Walker Art Center, May 3, 1983. Copyright 1983 Robert Duncan. This is number 70 of 90.

A59. *In Passage.*

A60c (right), A60d (left). *Ground Work.*

B.
Contributions to Books

NEW DIRECTIONS 10

New Directions | 10 | [in holograph] in prose and poetry | [below] AN ANNUAL EXHIBITION GALLERY OF NEW | AND DIVERGENT TRENDS IN LITERATURE | [New York: New Directions, 1948].

Contribution: HEAVENLY CITY, EARTHLY CITY, pp. 103-112.

B2 **THE FABER BOOK OF** 1956
MODERN AMERICAN VERSE

The Faber Book | of | Modern American Verse | edited by | W. H. Auden | Faber and Faber Limited | 24 Russell Square | London [1956].

Contribution: THE REAPER—HERO SONG, pp. 299-301.

B3 **NOONDAY 2** 1959

NOONDAY 2 | [down right edge] stories | articles | poetry | [publisher's logo] | The | Noonday | Press | New York [1959].

Contribution: THE MEADOW, pp. [49]-50.

B4 **O!** 1960

[cover-title] O! | [at left slanting up from left to right] Hawk's Well Press [space] JESS [New York, 1960].

Contribution: PRE-FACE, inside front cover. First appearance.

B5 **THE NEW AMERICAN POETRY** 1960

[repeated fleuron in a pattern 10.9 x 8.4 cm.] | THE NEW AMERICAN | POETRY: 1945-1960 | Edited by Donald M. Allen | [rule] | Grove Press, Inc. [dot] New York | Evergreen Books Ltd. [dot] London [1960].

Contribution: THE SONG OF THE BORDERGUARD—AN OWL IS AN ONLY BIRD OF POETRY—THIS PLACE RUMORD TO HAVE BEEN SODOM—THE DANCE—THE QUESTION—A POEM BEGINNING WITH A LINE BY PINDAR—FOOD FOR FIRE, FOOD FOR THOUGHT—DREAM DATA, pp. 40-59—PAGES FROM A NOTEBOOK, pp. 400-407.

Notes: The First edition was published in hardbound with a dust jacket and in paperback. George F. Butterick reports (*A Bibliography of Works by Charles Olson*, compiled by George F. Butterick & Albert Glover [New York: The Phoenix Book Shop, 1967, p. 29]): "By a special arrangement with Grove Press, copies of the paperbound edition were rebound in red cloth over boards by Peter Smith, with editor's name, title and 'Peter Smith' stamped in black on the spine. This special binding commenced in 1963, in lots of 200 copies each; approximately 750 bound to date at $5.00 a copy." In the seventh impression the title was shortened to THE NEW AMERICAN POETRY, and the design of the cover changed. The book has gone through twenty impressions for a total of approximately 137,300 copies. The seventeenth impression was the First Random House Printing, and all subsequent impressions are by Random House.

B6   **THE CRYSTAL CABINET**   1962

[double title-page] [left side] [engraving] | Horace Gregory | and Marya Zaturenska | Holt, Rinehart and Winston [slash] New York [right side] The Crystal Cabinet | An Invitation to Poetry | Wood engravings by Diane Bloomfield [1962].

Contribution: THE REAPER, pp. 68-69.

B7   **JONATHAN WILLIAMS, ELEGIES AND**   1962
             CELEBRATIONS

[double title-page with reproduction of a photograph by David Siskind extending across both pages] [printed in gold from left to right across both pages] elegies and celebrations [space] jonathan williams highlands [North Carolina] 1962.

Contribution: PREFACE, initialed "R. D.," p. [5]. First appearance.

Note: The book was printed by Verlagsdruckerie Gebr. Tron KG Karlsruhe-Durlach Germany, and published as Jargon 13(a) in an edition of 750 copies.

B8   **CONTEMPORARY AMERICAN POETRY**   1962

a. *First English edition:*
CONTEMPORARY | AMERICAN POETRY | [rule] | SELECTED AND INTRODUCED BY | DONALD HALL | [below] PENGUIN BOOKS [Harmondsworth, Middlesex, England, 1962].

Contribution: A POEM BEGINNING WITH A LINE BY PINDAR, pp. 41-49.

b. *First American edition:*
CONTEMPORARY | AMERICAN POETRY | [rule] | SELECTED AND INTRODUCED BY | DONALD HALL | [below] [publisher's logo] | PENGUIN BOOKS | Baltimore [dot] Maryland [1962].

Contribution: A POEM BEGINNING WITH A LINE BY PINDAR, pp. 41-49.

c. Second edition:

CONTEMPORARY | AMERICAN POETRY | [rule] | SELECTED AND INTRODUCED BY | DONALD HALL | Second Edition | (Revised and Expanded) | [below] [publisher's logo] | Penguin Books [Harmondsworth, Middlesex, England; and Baltimore, Maryland, 1972].

Contribution: A POEM BEGINNING WITH A LINE BY PINDAR, pp. 60-68.

B9   **A POETRY FOLIO**   1963

[cover title] SAN FRANCISCO ARTS FESTIVAL | A POETRY FOLIO | 1963.

Contribution: Broadside, UNKINGD BY AFFECTION?

Notes: This folio, made from heavy white stock, 53 x 35.5cm, with a cover label, 10.3 x 17.7 cm., and a cover title, contains eight unnumbered broadsides by various poets. RD's broadside is printed on heavy stock 43.2 x 32.5 cm, with a deckled right edge. The design consists of a drawing by Jess contained in four window panes. The two panes to the right contain the nineteen lines of the poem in RD's holograph. "Jess" appears at the lower left and "Robert Duncan" at the lower right. The verso indicates that the broadside was printed by George Lithograph, but the 300 copies of the Folio were assembled and distributed by the Auerhahn Press.

B10   **THE HAPPY MEADOW**   1964

WILFRED MELLERS | The Happy Meadow | CANTATA FOR | SPEAKER, CHILDREN'S VOICES | RECORDER CONSORT, GLOCK-ENSPIEL | XYLOPHONE & PERCUSSION | To Poems by | Robert Duncan and Yvor Winters | 8s 6d | NOVELLO | AND COMPANY LIMITED | 160 WARDOUR STREET | LONDON W1 [1964].

Contribution: OFTEN I AM PERMITTED TO RETURN TO A MEADOW, pp. [1]-5.

B11   **12 POETS & 1 PAINTER**   1964

WRITING 3 | [expanded rule] | 12 POETS AND 1 PAINTER | [expanded rule] | [San Francisco; Four Seasons Foundation, 1964].

Contribution: STRUCTURE OF RIME XIX, XX, XXI, pp. 16-18. First appearance.

BALLADS

BALLADS | by | Helen | Adam | Illustrated by | Jess | Acadia Press | New York [1964].

Contribution: PREFACE, pp. [5-7]. First appearance.

Note: In addition to the 1000 trade copies, 50 copies have decorated covers and additional drawings by Jess inside the front and rear covers.

B13 **SINGLE SOURCE** 1966

[in red-orange] SINGLE SOURCE | The Early Poems of William Everson | [in brackets] 1934-1940 | Introduction by Robert Duncan | [below] OYEZ [dot] BERKELEY [1966].

Contribution: INTRODUCTION, pp. ix-xiii. First appearance.

B14 **POEMS FOR YOUNG READERS** 1966

[at left margin a drawing of a tree trunk with a branch extending to the top right corner] POEMS FOR | YOUNG READERS | poets: | REED WHITMORE | ROBERT CREELEY | ROBERT BLY | JOSEPHINE MILES | GARY SNYDER | WILLIAM STAFFORD | DONALD HALL | MAY SWENSON | ROBERT DUNCAN | GALWAY KINNELL | CAROLYN KIZER | RICHARD EBERHART | W. S. MERWIN | 56th ANNUAL NCTE CONVENTION | NOVEMBER 24-26, 1966 [Houston, Texas: National Council of Teachers of English].

Contribution: THE LAW—A Statement about THE LAW—Robert Duncan [bibliographical statement], pp. 43-49.

Note: A reproduction of a photograph of RD by Nata Piaskowski appears on p. 42.

B15 **POETS ON POETRY** 1966

POETS | ON | POETRY | Edited by Howard Nemerov | [below] BASIC BOOKS, INC., PUBLISHERS | New York [space] London [1966].

Contribution: TOWARDS AN OPEN UNIVERSE, pp. 133-146. First appearance.

B16 **OUT OF THE WAR SHADOW** 1967

1968 PEACE CALENDAR | & | APPOINTMENT BOOK | OUT OF THE WAR SHADOW | An Anthology of Current Poetry | Compiled & Edited by Denise Levertov | WAR RESISTERS LEAGUE OF NEW YORK [1967].

Contribution: GOD-SPELL, p. [67].

A POETRY READING 1967
AGAINST THE VIETNAM WAR

Second impression, March 1967:
A | POETRY READING | AGAINST THE | VIETNAM WAR | collection
gathered by | ROBERT BLY and DAVID RAY | published by | THE
AMERICAN WRITERS | AGAINST THE VIETNAM WAR | 1967 |
Distributed by the Sixties Press [Madison, Minnesota].

Contribution: UP RISING, PASSAGES 25, pp. 24-25.

B18 **POETRY** 1967

POETRY | The Golden Anniversary Issue | Edited by | HENRY RAGO |
The University of Chicago Press | Chicago and London [1967].

Contribution: AFTER A PASSAGE IN BAUDELAIRE, pp. 32-33.

Note: This volume is a reprinting of the contents of the Oct.-Nov. 1962
double issue of *Poetry.*

B19 **THE NEW MODERN POETRY** 1967

The New Modern Poetry | British and American Poetry | Since World War II
| Edited by M. L. Rosenthal | The Macmillan Company, New York [1967].

Contribution: OFTEN I AM PERMITTED TO RETURN TO A
MEADOW—from A POEM BEGINNING WITH A LINE BY PINDAR (I,
II)—INGMAR BERGMAN'S *SEVENTH SEAL*—STRAINS OF SIGHT
(1, 2), pp. 48-54.

B20 **ARTISTS AND WRITERS PROTEST** 1967

ARTISTS AND WRITERS PROTEST | AGAINST THE WAR IN VIET-
NAM | [red rule] | [in middle] POEMS | [red rule, at bottom] | [New York:
Artists and Writers Protest Inc., 1967].

Contribution: PASSAGES 30, STAGE DIRECTIONS, pp. [13-15]. First
appearance.

Contribution: Five hundred copies of this oversized booklet, 45.7 x 30.7 cm.,
edited by Jack Sonenberg, were printed at the Profile Press in New York
City. One hundred copies numbered 1-100 were signed by the poets.

B21 **ROLLING RENAISSANCE** 1968

[printed diagonally from lower left to middle right] ROLLING
RENAISSANCE: SAN FRANCISCO UNDERGROUND ART IN CELE-
BRATION: 1945-1968 [San Francisco: Intersection and The Glide Urban
Center, 1968].

Contribution: JESS: PASTEUPS, p. 30. First appearance.

STONY BROOK HOLOGRAPHS

STONY BROOK HOLOGRAPHS [Stony Brook, New York: Stony Brook Poetics Foundation, 1968].

Contribution: Broadside, fragment of PASSAGES 33. First appearance.

Notes: This is a holograph version of a section of the poem, written by RD on one leaf of yellow white paper, 35.6 x 28 cm. Seven poets made ten holograph copies of their poems, which were then bound in a black portfolio, 40.5 x 31.3 cm., and tied with black strings on the sides. Ten sets were offered for sale.

B23 **PASTE UPS** 1968

PASTE UPS| BY| JESS| SAN FRANCISCO MUSEUM| OF| ART| MAY 31 - JUNE 30 [San Francisco, 1968].

Contribution: STRUCTURE OF RIME XXVI, p. [1]. First appearance.

Notes: This is a catalog for a show of Jess's collages in a folio, 24.1 x 21.6 cm, with a collage running continuously from front to rear. The rear flap serves as a title-page. The folio contains four leaves, 23.6 x 21.1 cm. The poem is dated "London, May 1968."

B24 **LANGUAGE AND WORLD ORDER** 1968

[design] LANGUAGE & WORLD ORDER| [design]| PROSPECTUS 1963 SYMPOSIUM [Ellensburg, Washington: Central Washington State College, 1968].

Contribution: MAN'S FULFILLMENT IN ORDER AND STRIFE, pp. 7-8. First appearance.

Note: This is an excerpt from the lecture delivered by RD at the conference 20 April 1968. The completed essay was published in *Caterpillar, 8/9* (1969), 229-249.

B25 **EVERGREEN REVIEW READER** 1968

[at upper right, ornament] Barney Rosset, editor| EVERGREEN| REVIEW | READER| 1957-1967| [ornament] A ten year anthology| [ornament] Grove Press, Inc., [slash] New York [1968].

Contribution: THIS PLACE, RUMORD TO HAVE BEEN SODOM, pp. 64-65.

B26 **WAR POEMS** 1968

WAR| POEMS| EDITED BY| DIANE DI PRIMA| THE POETS PRESS, INC.| NEW YORK CITY [1968].

Contribution: EARTH'S WINTER SONG—UP RISING, PASSAGES 25, pp. 10-15.

B27   **100 POSTWAR POEMS**   1968

100 POSTWAR | POEMS | British and American | Edited by | M. L. Rosenthal | The Macmillan Company, New York [1968].

Contribution: AFTER A PASSAGE IN BAUDELAIRE—STRAINS OF SIGHT 1 & 2—SHELLEY'S *ARETHUSA* SET TO NEW MEASURES, pp. 113-118.

B28   **PARABLE MYTH & LANGUAGE**   1968

[cover title, in green] A MEETING OF POETS | & THEOLOGIANS | to discuss | PARABLE | MYTH | & | LANGUAGE | Held | At the College of Preachers | Washington, D. C. | Sponsored by | The Advance Program, Washington Cathedral | & The Church Society for College Work [Cambridge, Massachusetts, 1968].

Contribution: THE TRUTH AND LIFE OF MYTH IN POETRY, pp. 37-44—poem of sixty-one lines beginning "YES, I CARE DEEPLY AND YET," rear cover—various comments in transcriptions of the discussions, pp. 14-18, 31-36, 53-56. Photographs appear on pp. 6, 31, and [74]. All First appearance.

Note: The proceedings of the conference were edited for publication by Tony Stoneburner.

B29   **THE AMERICAN LITERARY ANTHOLOGY 1**   1968

[across double title-pages, from left] the American Literary Anthology [slash] 1 | [at bottom] Selected by John Hawkes, Walker Percy, William | Styron (fiction); John Ashbery, Robert Creeley, | James Dickey (poetry); and William Alfred, | Robert Brustein, Benjamin DeMott, F. W. Dupee, | Susan Sontag, John Thompson (essays and criticism) | [on right page] The First Annual Collection of the | Best from the Literary Magazines | [publisher's device] | Farrar, | Straus & | Giroux | NEW YORK [1968].

Contribution: ORDERS, PASSAGES 24, pp. 46-49.

B30   **53 AMERICAN POETS**   1968

53 AMERICAN POETS | OF TODAY | Edited with Introduction & Notes by | RUTH WITT-DIAMANT | RIKUTARO FUKUDA | KENKYUSHA | TOKYO [1968].

Contribution: ROOTS AND BRANCHES—COME, LET ME FREE MYSELF, pp. 86-88.

B31 **A FIRST READER OF** 1969
CONTEMPORARY POETRY

A First Reader | of Contemporary | American Poetry | [at middle left] Edited by | Patrick Gleeson | San Francisco State College | [at lower right] Charles E. Merrill Publishing Company | A Bell & Howell Company | Columbus, Ohio [1969].

Contribution: STRUCTURE OF RIME XXIII—THE MULTIVERSITY— IN THE PLACE OF A PASSAGE 22—EARTH'S WINTER SONG, pp. 41-47.

B32 **CAUSAL MYTHOLOGY** 1969

CHARLES OLSON | CAUSAL MYTHOLOGY | Four Seasons Foundation | San Francisco: 1969.

Contribution: [INTRODUCTION], p. [1]. First appearance.

Note: This is a transcription of RD's introduction to Charles Olson's lecture delivered at the University of California Poetry Conference, Berkeley, 20 July 1965.

B33 **THE VOICE THAT IS GREAT WITHIN US** 1970

THE VOICE | THAT IS GREAT | WITHIN US | AMERICAN POETRY OF THE | TWENTIETH CENTURY | Edited by | Hayden Carruth | [device] | Bantam Books | [thin rule] | TORONTO [SLASH] NEW YORK [slash] LONDON | [thin rule] | A NATIONAL GENERAL COMPANY [1970].

Contribution: ROOTS AND BRANCHES—NIGHT SCENES—FOURTH SONG THE NIGHT NURSE SANG—A PART-SEQUENCE FOR CHANGE—AT THE LOOM, PASSAGES 2—ENVOY, PASSAGES 7— THE FIRE, PASSAGES 13, pp. 458-473.

B34 **THE SPECIAL VIEW OF HISTORY** 1970

Charles Olson: | The Special View | of History | Edited with an Introduction by | Ann Charters | Oyez Berkeley 1970.

Contribution: [TRANSCRIPTION OF INTERVIEW WITH RD BY ANN CHARTERS DEALING WITH BLACK MOUNTAIN COLLEGE], pp. 7-11. First appearance.

B35 **THE ARTISTIC LEGACY OF WALT WHITMAN** 1970

THE ARTISTIC LEGACY | OF WALT WHITMAN | A TRIBUTE to | Gay Wilson Allen | Edited by Edwin Haviland Miller | 1970 New York University Press [New York].

Contribution: CHANGING PERSPECTIVES IN READING WHITMAN, pp. 73-102. First appearance.

Note: This essay is the final version of a lecture first given at NYU, 18 April 1969, on the occasion of a Walt Whitman Celebration, and later at Kansas University, 8 May 1969, under the title "Walt Whitman: A Poet's View."

B36 **FORTY POEMS TOUCHING ON RECENT AMERICAN HISTORY** 1970

FORTY POEMS| TOUCHING ON| RECENT AMERICAN| HISTORY| edited by| ROBERT BLY| [publisher's device]| BEACON PRESS BOSTON | [expanded rule]| [1970].

Contribution: from A POEM BEGINNING WITH A LINE BY PINDAR, pp. 74-75.

Note: The selection consists of thirty-two lines from Section II of the poem. The book was published "simultaneously [in] casebound and [in] paperback editions."

B37 **THE NORTON ANTHOLOGY OF POETRY** 1970

THE| Norton Anthology| of Poetry| [decorated rule]| ARTHUR M. EASTMAN, Coordinating Editor| CARNEGIE-MELLON UNIVERSITY| ALEXANDER W. ALLISON| UNIVERSITY OF MICHIGAN| HERBERT BARROWS| UNIVERSITY OF MICHIGAN| CAESAR R. BLAKE| UNIVERSITY OF TORONTO| ARTHUR J. CARR| WILLIAMS COLLEGE| HUBERT M. ENGLISH, JR.| UNIVERSITY OF MICHIGAN| [publisher's logo inserted in decorated rule]| W [dot] W [dot] NORTON & COMPANY [dot] INC [dot] | NEW YORK [1970].

Contribution: SUCH IS THE SICKNESS OF MANY A GOOD THING—MY MOTHER WOULD BE A FALCONRESS—PARSIFAL—AN INTERLUDE, pp. 1127-1132.

Note: Published in hardbound, with dust jacket, and in paperback.

B38 **THE NORTON ANTHOLOGY OF POETRY** 1970

THE | Norton Anthology | of Poetry | SHORTER EDITION | [decorated rule] | ARTHUR M. EASTMAN, Coordinating Editor | CARNEGIE-MELLON UNIVERSITY| ALEXANDER W. ALLISON| UNIVERSITY OF MICHIGAN| HERBERT BARROWS| UNIVERSITY OF MICHIGAN | CAESAR R. BLAKE | UNIVERSITY OF TORONTO | ARTHUR J. CARR | WILLIAMS COLLEGE | HUBERT M. ENGLISH JR. | UNIVERSITY OF MICHIGAN | [publisher's logo inserted in decorated rule] | W [dot] W [dot] NORTON & COMPANY [dot] INC [dot] | NEW YORK [1970].

Contribution: MY MOTHER WOULD BE A FALCONRESS, pp. 565-566.

Note: Published in hardbound, with a dust jacket, and in paperback.

B39   **TRANSLATIONS BY AMERICAN POETS**   1970

Translations by | American Poets | EDITED BY JEAN GARRIGUE | OHIO UNIVERSITY PRESS [dot] ATHENS [Ohio, 1970].

Contribution: DREAMS—DU RÊVE—WINDWARD—AU VENT, pp. 90-95.

Note: The translations are from the French poems by André Breton.

B40   **NEW DIRECTIONS IN PROSE AND POETRY 23**   1971

[in large block letters in the center of the page] N D | [over large letters] New Directions in Prose and Poetry 23 | Edited by J. Laughlin | [publisher's logo] | A New Directions Book [New York, 1971].

Contribution: ACHILLES—A GLIMPSE—ANCIENT QUESTIONS, pp. 161-165. First appearance.

B41   **LIVE POETRY**   1971

LIVE | POETRY | edited by | Kathleen Sunshine Koppell | Holt, Rinehart and Winston, Inc. | New York Chicago San Francisco | Atlanta Dallas Montreal Toronto [1971].

Contribution: THE MULTIVERSITY, pp. 49-50.

B42   **A CATERPILLAR ANTHOLOGY**   1971

[double title-page, left side] A CATERPILLAR [right side] ANTHOLOGY [left side] A Selection of Poetry and [right side] Prose from CATERPILLAR Magazine | Edited by CLAYTON ESHLEMAN | Anchor Books | Doubleday & Company, Inc. | Garden City, New York | 1971.

Contribution: RITES OF PARTICIPATION, PARTS I & II, pp. 23-69.

B43   **C'MON EVERYBODY**   1971

C'MON EVERYBODY | Poetry of the Dance | Edited with an introduction | by | Peter Morgan | [below] [publisher's device] | CORGIBOOKS | TRANSWORLD PUBLISHERS LTD | A National General Company [London, 1971].

Contribution: KING HAYDN OF MIAMI BEACH—THE DANCE, pp. [60]-64.

[in reddish orange inside a reproduction of a seventeenth century Hermetic emblem which is printed in reddish orange and gray on a white background] TRANSLATIONS | [below the emblem] Introduction by Robert Duncan [space] [in reddish orange] Jess | 1971 [dash] Odyssia Gallery [dash] New York.

Contribution: ICONOGRAPHICAL EXTENSIONS, pp. i-ix. First appearance in a book.

Note: 1000 copies of this book are bound in paper wrappers, and 100 copies, bound in orange cloth over boards, are signed by both Jess and RD. These copies were printed by Black Sparrow Press for Odyssia Gallery. There was a second issue by Black Sparrow of 250 copies, bound in yellow cloth over boards, numbered 1-250, and signed by Jess and RD. There are five reserved copies bound in maroon velvet.

B45 **EARTH AIR FIRE & WATER** 1971

EARTH | AIR | FIRE | & | WATER | a collection of over 125 poems | selected and edited by | Frances Monson McCullough | Coward, McCann & Geoghegan New York [1971].

Contribution: ENVOY, PASSAGES 7, p. 159.

B46 **AN INTRODUCTION TO POETRY** 1972

Second edition:
LOUIS SIMPSON | State University of New York, | Stony Brook | An Introduction to Poetry | SECOND EDITION | ST. MARTIN'S PRESS NEW YORK [1972].

Contribution: TWO PRESENTATIONS, pp. 344-346.

B47 **THE NEW POCKET ANTHOLOGY OF** 1972
AMERICAN VERSE

THE NEW POCKET ANTHOLOGY OF | AMERICAN VERSE | From Colonial Days to the Present | Edited by OSCAR WILLIAMS | Newly Revised by | Hyman J. Sobiloff | [below] WASHINGTON SQUARE PRESS | POCKET BOOKS [dot] NEW YORK [1972].

Contribution: THE ROBBER MOON—SONNET 1, pp. 135-136.

B48 **THE WAYS OF THE POEM** 1972

The Ways of the Poem | Edited by Josephine Miles | University of California | Prentice-Hall, Inc., Englewood Cliffs, New Jersey [1972].

Contribution: MY MOTHER WOULD BE A FALCONRESS, pp. 354-356.

JESS: | PASTE-UPS | December 16, 1972 | TO | JANUARY 28, 1973 | Museum | of | Contemporary Art | Chicago, Illinois [1972].

Contribution: STRUCTURE OF RIME XXVII, p. [1].

Note: This is a catalog for a show of Jess's collages in folio, 24.5 x 21.6 cm., with a collage running continuously front and rear. The rear flap serves as the title-page. The cover is made from heavy white stock enameled on the exterior side, while the six interior leaves, 24 x 21.3 cm., are enameled on both sides, as is the one sheet folded to two leaves, 12 x 18.2 cm., containing additional collages.

B50 **SHAKE THE KALEIDOSCOPE** 1973

Shake the | Kaleidoscope | A New Anthology of Modern Poetry | Edited by | Milton Klonsky | PUBLISHED BY POCKET [publisher's logo] BOOKS NEW YORK [1973].

Contribution: SONNET 1—SONNET 2, pp. 219-221.

Second impression:
The Best of | Modern Poetry | (Original Title: Shake the Kaleidoscope) | Edited by | Milton Klonsky | PUBLISHED BY POCKET [publisher's logo] BOOKS NEW YORK [1975].

Contribution: SONNET 1—SONNET 2, pp. 219-221.

B51 **MYTHS AND MOTIFS IN LITERATURE** 1973

MYTHS | and | MOTIFS | in | LITERATURE | edited by | DAVID J. BURROWS | Douglas College | FREDERICK R. LAPIDES | University of Bridgeport | JOHN T. SHAWCROSS | City University of New York | [within design] F [with the following P slightly lower] P The Free Press, New York [1973].

Contribution: PARSIFAL (AFTER WAGNER AND VERLAINE), pp. 310-311.

B52 **THE NORTON ANTHOLOGY OF MODERN POETRY** 1973

THE | Norton Anthology | of Modern Poetry | EDITED BY | RICHARD ELLMANN | Goldsmiths' Professor of English Literature, Oxford University | AND | ROBERT O'CLAIR | Professor of English, Manhattanville College | [below] [rule] | W [dot] W [dot] NORTON & COMPANY [dot] INC [dot] New York [1973].

Contribution: AN AFRICAN ELEGY—THE BALLAD OF MRS NOAH—
POETRY, A NATURAL THING—AT CHRISTMAS—PERSEPHONE—
PASSAGE OVER WATER—WHAT I SAW, pp. 964-971.

B53   **AMERICA A PROPHECY**   1973

[in large block letters] AMERICA | A PROPHECY | A New Reading of
American Poetry | from Pre-Columbian Times to the Present | Edited by
GEORGE QUASHA and JEROME ROTHENBERG | Random House
[publisher's logo] New York [1973].

Contribution: TRIBAL MEMORIES, PASSAGES 1, pp. 27-28—PASSAGES
24, ORDERS, pp. 211-214—quotation from RD's article, THE LASTING
CONTRIBUTION OF EZRA POUND, p. 214—THE STRUCTURE OF
RIME I, pp. 355-374—quotation from "The H.D. Book," Part II, Chap. 4,
pp. 373-374—BENEFICE, PASSAGES 23, p. 445—quotation from RD's
essay RITES OF PARTICIPATION, p. 454—quotation from "The H.D.
Book" [1961], p. 543.

B54   **MODERN POEMS**   1973

Edited by RICHARD ELLMANN, Oxford University | and ROBERT
O'CLAIR, Manhattanville College | MODERN POEMS | An Introduction
to Poetry | W [dot] W [dot] NORTON & COMPANY [dot] INC [dot] NEW
YORK [1973].

Contribution: THE BALLAD OF MRS NOAH, pp. 358-360.

B55   **THE MALE MUSE**   1973

THE MALE MUSE | A Gay Anthology | [reproduction of a medallion with
the head of a man] | Edited by Ian Young | The Crossing Press
Trumansburg, New York [1973].

Contribution: SONNET 1—SUCH IS THE SICKNESS OF A MANY A
GOOD THING—5 PIECES—UNKINGD BY AFFECTION, pp. 23-27.

Note: Published in hardbound, with no dust jacket, and in paperback.

B56   **THE POETICS OF THE**   1973
          NEW AMERICAN POETRY

POETICS | OF THE NEW | AMERICAN POETRY | [rule] | Edited by |
Donald Allen & Warren Tallman | [rule] | Grove Press, Inc., New York
[1973].

Contribution: FROM A NOTEBOOK—NOTES ON POETICS REGARD-
ING OLSON'S *MAXIMUS*—IDEAS OF THE MEANING OF FORM—
TOWARDS AN OPEN UNIVERSE, pp. 185-225.

Note: This book was not distributed until 1974; it appeared in hardbound, with a dust jacket, and in paperback. The cover title is The Poetics of The New American Poetry.

B57 **MODERN AMERICAN POETRY CONFERENCE** 1973

Modern American Poetry Conference | featuring four American poets | May 25-27 | at the Polytechnic of Central London. [London: The Polytechnic of Central London, 1973].

Contribution: THE FEAST, PASSAGES 34—ACHILLES—ANCIENT QUESTIONS, pp. 41-47.

B58 **THE PRISONER** 1973

[double title-page containing a continuous line drawing in red] [at top is a quotation of the first three lines of OFTEN I AM PERMITTTED TO RETURN TO A MEADOW] [middle right] THE PRISONER | Carlos Reyes | [far right] NUMBER EIGHT. YES! CAPRA CHAPBOOK SERIES [right] CAPRA PRESS 1973 SANTA BARBARA.

Contribution: Title-page designed and drawn by RD, pp. [2-3].

B59 **THE FLOATING BEAR** 1973

THE FLOATING BEAR | a newsletter | Numbers 1-37, 1961-1969 | Edited by Diane di Prima & LeRoi Jones | Introduction and Notes | Adapted from Interviews with | Diane di Prima | [below] Laurence McGilvery, La Jolla, California | 1973.

Contribution: NIGHT SCENES, pp. 205-207—NOTES FROM A READING AT THE POETRY CENTER, SAN FRANCISCO, MARCH 1, 1959.

Note: This reprint edition was published in both a library binding and in paper wrappers. An undetermined number of copies have been signed by Diane di Prima.

B60 **MAKING IT NEW** 1973

Making It New | EDITED BY | JoAn E. Chace | William M. Chace [dash] Stanford University | CANFIELD PRESS [device] | SAN FRANCISCO, CALIFORNIA | A DEPARTMENT OF HARPER & ROW, PUBLISHERS, INC. | NEW YORK [dot] EVANSTON [dot] LONDON [1973].

Contribution: NEL MEZZO DEL CAMMIN DI NOSTRA VITA—THE MULTIVERSITY, pp. 75-80.

Note: A brief biographical note precedes each poem, and notes follow each poem.

[in large letters] LOVES, | ETC. [in regular caps] EDITED WITH AN INTRODUCTION BY | MARGUERITE HARRIS | [below] ANCHOR BOOKS | ANCHOR PRESS [slash] DOUBLEDAY | GARDEN CITY, NEW YORK | 1973.

Contribution: TO VOW, p. 12.

B62   **NEW DIRECTIONS IN PROSE AND POETRY 26**   1973

[in large block letters in the center of the page] N D | [over large letters] New Directions in Prose and Poetry 26 | Edited by J. Laughlin | with Peter Glassgold and Frederick R. Martin | [publisher's logo] A New Directions Book [New York, 1973].

Contribution: THE MUSEUM, pp. 35-38.

Note: Published in hardbound, with a dust jacket, and in paperback.

B63   **PROBES**   1973

[within a design, in red] PROBES [in black] An Introduction to Poetry | William K. Harlan | Diablo Valley College | The Macmillan Company, New York [1973].

Contribution: STRUCTURE OF RIME XXV, p. 33.

B64   **EXPLORING POETRY**   1973
Second edition:
EXPLORING | POETRY Second Edition | M. L. Rosenthal New York University | A. J. M. Smith Michigan State University | The Macmillan Company, New York [1973].

Contribution: AFTER A PASSAGE IN BAUDELAIRE, pp. 60-61— STRAINS OF SIGHT, pp. 134-135.

B65   **THE POET IN AMERICA**   1973

THE POET | IN AMERICA | 1650 TO THE PRESENT | Edited with an introduction by | Albert Gelpi | Stanford University | D. C. Heath and Company | Lexington, Massachusetts Toronto London [1973].

Contribution: THE LAW I LOVE IS MAJOR MOVER—ANSWERING— OFTEN I AM PERMITTED TO RETURN TO A MEADOW—TRIBAL MEMORIES, PASSAGES 1—AT THE LOOM, PASSSAGES 2—WHERE IT APPEARS, PASSAGES 4—THE MOON, PASSAGES 5, pp. 702-714.

GEORGE HERMS | Selected Works 1960-1973 | An exhibition presented by the Memorial Union Art Gallery | University of California [double dash] Davis | January 10 - February 16, 1973.

Contribution: OF GEORGE HERMS, HIS HERMES, AND HIS HERMETIC ART, p. 3. First appearance.

B67 **QUARTERLY REVIEW OF LITERATURE** 1974

Quarterly Review | of Literature | [rule] | 30TH ANNIVERSARY POETRY RETROSPECTIVE | Edited by T. Weiss and Renée Weiss | [below] QRL: Volume XIX, 1-2. 26 Haslet Avenue, Princeton, New Jersey 08540 | © Quarterly Review of Literature, 1974.

Contribution: FROM *THE MABINOGION*—A NEW POEM—TWO MESSAGES, pp. 232-238.

Note: Published in hardbound, with a dust jacket, and in paperback.

Second issue:
Contemporary Poetry | [rule] | A Retrospective from the *Quarterly Review of Literature* | Edited by T. Weiss and Renée Weiss | Princeton New Jersey | Princeton University Press [1975].

Contribution: FROM *THE MABINOGION*—A NEW POEM—TWO MESSAGES, pp. 232-238.

B68 **ALLEN VERBATIM** 1974

[in large bold type] ALLEN | LECTURES ON | [in large bold type] VERBATIM | POETRY, | POLITICS, | CONSCIOUSNESS | by Allen Ginsberg | edited by Gordon Ball | [below] McGRAW-HILL BOOK COMPANY | New York St. Louis San Francisco | Düsseldorf | London Mexico | Sydney Toronto [1974].

Contribution: ADVICE TO YOUTH (with Allen Ginsberg), pp. 103-130—EARLY POETIC COMMUNITY (with Allen Ginsberg), pp. 131-150. First appearance.

Note: Both contributions are transcriptions of tapes made at The Creative Arts festival at Kent State University, 5 and 7 April 1971. Published in hardbound, with a dust jacket, and later in paperback.

B69 **REVOLUTION OF THE WORD** 1974

[double title-page] [at left] JEROME | [running down vertically] ROTHENBERG [running horizontally] Tching prayed on the mountain and | wrote MAKE IT NEW [Chinese character, hsin] | on his bath tub | Day by day make it new | cut undergrowth | pile the logs | keep it going. —Ezra Pound *Canto* 53 [Chinese character, jih] [in bold letters] REVOLUTION | OF THE | [on the right side slanting down from left to right] WORD | A New Gathering of American | Avant Garde Poetry 1914-1945 | A CONTINUUM BOOK | THE SEABURY PRESS [dot] NEW YORK [1974].

Contribution: AN AFRICAN ELEGY, pp. 133-135.

Note: Published in hardbound, with a dust jacket, and in paperback.

B70   POETRY PAST AND PRESENT   1974

Poetry | past and present | Frank Brady | City University of New York | Martin Price | Yale University | [publisher's logo] Harcourt Brace Jovanovich Inc. | New York Chicago San Francisco Atlanta [1974].

Contribution: THIS PLACE RUMORD TO HAVE BEEN SODOM, pp. 412-413.

B71   FIFTEEN POEMS   1974

Fifteen | Poems | Bobbie | Louise | Hawkins | [at bottom in blue] Arif Press | Berkeley [slash] 1974.

Contribution: IN PREFACE, pp. [5-6]. First appearance.

Note: Twenty-six copies of this book have been bound in boards and signed by the poet, and 400 have been bound in paper wrappers.

B72   WORLDS   1974

WORLDS | SEVEN MODERN POETS | CHALRES CAUSLEY | THOM GUNN | SEAMUS HEANEY | TED HUGHES | NORMAN MACCAIG | ADRIAN MITCHELL | EDWIN MORGAN | [below] Photographs by | Fay Godwin, Larry Herman and Peter Abramowitsch | [rule] | Edited by Geoffrey Summerfield | Penguin Education [Harmondsworth, Middlesex, 1974].

Contribution: SECOND TAKE ON *RITES OF PASSAGE* p. 87.

Note: The poem was written as a variation on Thom Gunn's "Rites of Passage," which precedes it in the collection.

B73   ANGELS OF THE LYRE   1975

ANGELS OF THE LYRE | A GAY ANTHOLOGY | Edited by Winston Leyland | [below] Panjandrum Press [dot] Gay Sunshine Press | San Francisco 1975.

Contribution: THE TORSO, PASSAGES 18—THIS PLACE RUMORD TO HAVE BEEN SODOM

Note: Published in hardbound, without a dust jacket, and in paperback.

THE GIST OF ORIGIN

The Gist of [in bold type] Origin| 1951-1971 [slash]| an anthology| edited by Cid Corman [thin rule forming an empty rectangle, 10.8 x 12.8 cm.] | Grossman Publishers| A Division of The Viking Press [slash] New York [slash] 1975.

Contribution: THE SECOND NIGHT IN THE WEEK, pp. 45-46—LOVE POEM—FRIEDL—SONGS FOR THE JEWS FROM THEIR BOOK OF SPLENDOURS—A DREAM OF THE END OF THE WORLD, pp. 99-103—FROM THE DAY BOOK —excerpts from an extended study of H.D.'s poetry, pp. 263-273.

THE HEATH INTRODUCTION TO POETRY

The Heath| Introduction to| Poetry| [following seven lines printed in white inside a black triangle] with| a Preface| on Poetry and| a Brief History| by| Joseph de Roche | Northeastern University | [below] D. C. Heath and Company| Lexington, Massachusetts Toronto London [1975].

Contribution: OFTEN I AM PERMITTED TO RETURN TO A MEADOW, pp. 385-386.

TISH

TISH| No. 1-19| Frank Davey,| Editor| Vancouver, Talonbooks, 1975.

Contribution: FOR THE NOVICES OF VANCOUVER AUGUST 25-28 1962, pp. 253-257.

THE COLLECTED BOOKS OF JACK SPICER

[within a framing red rule] THE | COLLECTED | BOOKS OF | JACK SPICER | [drawing in green] EDITED & WITH A| COMMENTARY BY | ROBIN BLASER | [rule]| BLACK SPARROW PRESS| LOS ANGELES| 1975.

Contribution: QUESTIONNAIRE FOR "WORKSHOP IN BASIC TECHNIQUES" ROBERT DUNCAN, SEPTEMBER 24, 1958, pp. 357-358—LETTER TO JACK SPICER, pp. 362-363—LETTER TO JACK SPICER, pp. 365-366.

Note: Both letters are undated but were written in 1951. "This edition is published in paper wrappers [2968 copies]; there are 1000 hardcover copies; & 100 handbound in boards by Earle Gray which are numbered & signed by Robin Blaser."

A TEXT

A TEXT| for those how| ever here| choreography:| J. D. Whitney [Wausau, Wisconsin: Privately published, 1975].

Note: This collection, seventy-six leaves all recto, 21.7 x 14.2 cm., is mimeographed and bound with heavy paper wrappers by a two-prong metal clip. The collection contains 459 quotations from a large number of writers, eighteen of which are by RD. Seventy copies were published, but none was for sale.

B79   **I CAME TO THE CITY**   1975

I CAME TO THE CITY ESSAYS AND COMMENTS ON THE URBAN SCENE | MICHAEL E. ELIOT HURST Simon Fraser University | [below] Houghton Mifflin Company Boston | Atlanta Dallas Geneva, Illinois Hopewell, New Jersey Palo Alto London [1975].

Contribution: THIS PLACE RUMORD TO HAVE BEEN SODOM, p. 294

B80   **CONTEMPORARY AMERICAN POETRY**   1975

Second edition:

Contemporary | American | Poetry | Second Edition | Edited by | A. Poulin, Jr. | State University College at Brockport | State University of New York | HOUGHTON MIFFLIN COMPANY BOSTON | Atlanta Dallas Geneva, Illinois Hopewell, New Jersey Palo Alto London [1975].

Contribution: POETRY, A NATURAL THING—THE STRUCTURE OF RIME II—OFTEN I AM PERMITTED TO RETURN TO A MEADOW— INGMAR BERGMAN'S *SEVENTH SEAL*—BENDING THE BOW— THE TORSO, PASSAGES 18—SUCH IS THE SICKNESS OF MANY A GOOD THING—TRIBAL MEMORIES, PASSAGES 1—STRUCTURE OF RIME XXIII, pp. 105-115.
Note: A photograph of RD by Gerard Malanga appears on p. [104]; a biographical and critical statement appears on pp. 428-429.

Third edition: 1980

CONTEMPORARY | AMERICAN POETRY | THIRD EDITION | Edited by A. Poulin, Jr. | State University College at Brockport | State University of New York | HOUGHTON MIFFLIN COMPANY BOSTON | Dallas Geneva, Illinois Hopewell, New Jersey | Palo Alto London

Contribution: OFTEN I AM PERMITTED TO RETURN TO A MEADOW—THE STRUCTURE OF RIME II—INGMAR BERGMAN'S *SEVENTH SEAL*—SUCH IS THE SICKNESS OF MANY A GOOD THING—BENDING THE BOW—TRIBAL MEMORIES, PASSAGES 1— STRUCTURE OF RIME XXIII— MY MOTHER WOULD BE A FALCONRESS—THE TORSO, PASSAGES 18, pp. 119-131.

Note: A photograph of RD by Gerard Malanga appears on p. [118]; biographical and critical statement appears on pp. 531-532.

[cover-title] ROOF: [space] an | anthology of | poetry from | the Naropa I | nstitute, Bou | lder, Colorad | o, summer | of 1976. $2.00 [edited by Tom Savage and James Sherry, New York: Segue Press, 1976].

Contribution: A FANTASY PIECE FOR HELEN ADAM, p. 8. First appearance.

B82   **THE NEW OXFORD BOOK**   1976
           OF AMERICAN VERSE

The | New Oxford Book of American Verse | Chosen and Edited by | Richard Ellmann | New York | OXFORD UNIVERSITY PRESS | 1976.

Contribution: THE TEMPLE OF THE ANIMALS—OFTEN I AM PERMITTED TO RETURN TO A MEADOW—THIS PLACE RUMORD TO HAVE BEEN SODOM—THE BALLAD OF MRS NOAH—POETRY, A NATURAL THING—PERSEPHONE—PASSAGE OVER WATER—HOMAGE AND LAMENT FOR EZRA POUND IN CAPTIVITY, MAY 12, 1944—TRIBAL MEMORIES, PASSAGES 1—WHAT I SAW, PASSAGES 3, pp. 828-839.

B83   **CONTEMPORARY AMERICAN AND**   1976
           AUSTRALIAN POETRY

Contemporary | American | & | Australian | Poetry | Edited by | Thomas | Shapcott | [below] University of Queensland Press [St. Lucia, Queensland, Australia, 1976].

Contribution: MY MOTHER WOULD BE A FALCONRESS—ORDERS, PASSAGES 24—from *Dante Études, Book Three,* ÉTUDE FROM THE THIRD EPISTLE—TEARS OF ST FRANCIS, pp. 27-33.

Note: Published in hardbound, with dust jacket, and in paperback.

B84   **THE NEW NAKED POETRY**   1976

The New | Naked Poetry | Recent American poetry | in | open forms | edited by | Stephen Berg and Robert Mezey | The Bobbs-Merrill Company, Inc. | Indianapolis [1976].

Contribution: A POEM BEGINNING WITH A LINE BY PINDAR—A NEW POEM—UP RISING, PASSAGES 25—ARTICULATIONS, pp. 34-47.

Note: A photograph of RD by Thomas Victor appears on p. 34.

THE | [in red] DIVINE MYSTERY | A READING OF THE HISTORY OF
CHRISTIANITY DOWN TO | THE TIME OF CHRIST | BY | ALLEN
UPWARD | WITH AN INTRODUCTION BY | ROBERT DUNCAN |
[emblem in red] | Santa Barbara | ROSS-ERIKSON, INC., PUBLISHERS |
1976.

Contribution: INTRODUCTION, pp. ix-xxviii. First appearance.

Note: Published in hardbound, with a dust jacket, and in paperback.

B86 **TRANSLATIONS SALVAGES PASTE-UPS** 1977

[maroon rule] | TRANSLATIONS | [maroon rule] | SALVAGES | [maroon
rule] | PASTE-UPS | [maroon rule] | BY JESS | An exhibition organized by
the | Dallas Museum of Fine Arts | April 6 through May 15, 1977 | with the
participation of | University Art Museum, Berkeley | October 26 through
December 4, 1977 | Des Moines Art Center | October 26 through December 4,
1977 [Dallas: Dallas Museum of Fine Arts, 1977].

Contribution: AN ART OF WONDERING [introductory statement], pp.
[7-10]. First appearance.

B87 **NEW DIRECTIONS IN PROSE AND POETRY 34** 1977

[in large block letters in the center of the page] N D | [over large letters] New
Directions in Prose and Poetry 34 | Edited by J. Laughlin | with Peter
Glassgold and Frederick R. Martin | [publisher's logo] A New Directions
Book [New York, 1977].

Contribution: TWO PASSAGES: EMPEDOKLEAN REVERIES—JAMAIS,
pp. 1-8. First appearance of JAMAIS.

Note: Published in hardbound, with dust jacket, and in paperback.

B88 **IN CASABLANCA FOR THE WATERS** 1977

[in holograph, in large letters] IN CASABLANCA | for the waters | Nigel
Roberts | [below, in type] Wild & Woolley [publisher's logo] Sydney,
[Australia, 1977].

Contribution: A PREPUCAL FACE FOR NIGEL ROBERTS, p. [7].

B89 **TALKING POETICS FROM** 1978
NAROPA INSTITUTE

ANNALS OF THE | JACK KEROUAC SCHOOL | OF DISEMBODIED
POETICS | Talking Poetics from | Naropa Institute | Edited by Anne
Waldman and Marilyn Webb | Introduction by Allen Ginsberg | [publisher's
logo] | SHAMBHALA | Boulder & London | 1978.

Contribution: WARP AND WOOF: NOTES FROM A TALK, pp. 1-10.

Note: A photograph of RD by Andrea Craig appears on p. [xiv].

B90   **THE POETRY ANTHOLOGY**   1978

THE | POETRY | ANTHOLOGY | 1912-1977 | [rule] Sixty-five Years of America's Most | Distinguished Verse Magazine | [magazine's logo] | Edited by | Daryl Hine & Joseph Parisi | Houghton Mifflin Company | Boston 1978.

Contribution: A SPRING MEMORANDUM, pp. 229-231—A MORNING LETTER, pp. 344-345—AFTER A PASSAGE IN BAUDELAIRE, pp. 387-388.

Note: Published in hardbound and in paperback.

B91   **LE RÉCIT ET SA REPRÉSENTATION**   1978

LE RÉCIT | ET SA | REPRÉSENTATION | Colloque de Saint-Hubert 5-8 mai 1077 | Prélude de Jacques Sojcher et de Maurice Olender | [publisher's logo] | Payot, Paris | 106, Boulevard Saint-Germain | [short rule] | 1978 | [short rule].

Contribution: SON ÉCRIT D'UN TEXTE PARLÉ, pp. [65]-69.

B92   **WALLACE BERMAN RETROSPECTIVE**   1978

Wallace Berman | Retrospective | [rule] | October 24 to November 26, 1978 | An exhibition initiated and sponsored by | Fellows | of Contemporary Art | in cooperation with the Otis Art Institute Gallery | Otis Art Institute Gallery | Hal Glickman, Curator of the Exhibition, | Director of the Art Gallery | The Fort Worth Art Museum | University of California, Berkeley | September, October, November 1979 | Seattle Art Museum | January, February 1980 | This exhibition is supported by a grant from the National Endowment | for the Arts in Washington, D.C., a Federal Agency [Los Angeles, 1978].

Contribution: WALLACE BERMAN: THE FASHIONING SPIRIT, pp. 19-21, 23-24. First appearance.

B93   **TOWARDS A NEW AMERICAN POETICS**   1978

[within a box of orange and black rules, in red] TOWARDS A NEW | AMERICAN POETICS: | [in orange] ESSAYS & INTERVIEWS | Charles Olson | Robert Duncan | Gary Snyder | Robert Creeley | Robert Bly | Allen Ginsberg | [rule] | Edited by Ekbert Faas | Black Sparrow Press: Santa Barbara: 1978.

Contribution: ROBERT DUNCAN: INTERVIEW, pp. [53]-85. First appearance.

Note: "This edition is published in paper wrappers [3500 copies]; there are 1000 hardcover trade copies; & 125 copies have been handbound in boards by Earle Gray & are numbered & signed by the authors."

B94   **SURREALIST POETRY**   1978

English and American | SURREALIST POETRY | EDITED AND | WITH AN INTRODUCTION BY | Edward B. Germain | [below] [publisher's logo] | Penguin Books [Harmondsworth, Middlesex, 1978].

Contribution: EYESIGHT II—TURNING INTO—COMING OUT OF, pp. 211-212.

B95   **A GEOGRAPHY OF POETS**   1979

A Geography | of Poets | [rule] | AN ANTHOLOGY OF | THE NEW POETRY | [rule] Edited by Edward Field | [around publisher's logo] BANTAM BOOKS [dot] LONDON NEW YORK TORONTO [dot] [1979].

Contribution: THE TORSO, PASSAGES 18—SONNET 1, pp. 63-65.

B96   **DODEKA**   1979

[in brown] DODEKA | by John Taggart | with an introduction | by Robert Duncan | Membrane Press | 1979 [Milwaukee, Wisconsin].

Contribution: IN INTRODUCTION, pp. iii-xi. First appearance.

B97   **THE POET'S WORK**   1979

The Poet's Work: | [rule] | 29 Masters of 20th Century Poetry | on the Origins and Practice | of Their Art | Edited by Reginald Gibbons | Houghton Mifflin Company Boston 1979.

Contribution: NOTES ON POETIC FORM, pp. 260-262.

B98   **BENCHMARK & BLAZE**   1979

BENCHMARK & BLAZE: | [in italics] The Emergence of William Everson | edited by Lee Barlettt | [publisher's logo] The Scarecrow Press, Inc. | Metuchen, N.J. & London | 1979.

Contribution: SINGLE SOURCE: AN INTRODUCTION, pp. 69-73.

B99   **CALAFIA**   1979

CALAFIA | The California Poetry | [The Great Seal of the State of California] | PROJECT DIRECTOR: ISHMAEL REED | Y'BIRD BOOKS: BERKELEY [California], 1979.

Contribution: NEL MEZZO DEL CAMMIN DI NOSTRA VITA, pp. 111-113.

B100   **GIVING UP THE GHOST**   1980

GIVING UP THE GHOST | Aaron Shurin | Rose Deeprose Press | [San Francisco, California, 1980].

Contribution: PREFACE, pp. 7-8. First appearance.

B101   **ONE NIGHT STAND**   1980

JACK SPICER | ONE NIGHT STAND | & | OTHER POEMS | With a Preface by Robert Duncan | Edited by Donald Allen | Grey Fox Press | San Francisco [California, 1980].

Contribution: PREFACE, pp. [ix-xxvii]. First appearance.

B102   **HOMAGE TO FRANK O'HARA**   1980

HOMAGE | TO FRANK O'HARA | Edited by Bill Berkson & Joe Le Sueur | [publisher's device] | Creative Arts Book Company | Berkeley [dot] [California], 1980.

Contribution: ROBERT DUNCAN / ALLEN GINSBERG: DISCUSSION, p. 63.

Note: This piece is reprinted from *Big Sky, 11 / 12* (1978). See C271.

B103   **NEW DIRECTIONS IN PROSE AND POETRY 40**   1980

[in large block letters in the center of the page] ND | [over large letters] New Directions in Prose and Poetry 40 | Edited by J. Laughlin | with Peter Glassgold and Frederick R. Martin | [Publisher's logo] A New Directions Book [New York, 1980]

Contribution: AN ALTERNATE LIFE, pp. 33-48.

B104   **NEW COLLEGE**   1980

New College of California | San Francisco | B.A., B.A. [slash] M.A. | IN POETICS | 1980-1981 | Faculty [eight names including RD's] | Visiting Faculty [five names] [San Francisco: New College, 1980].

Contribution: WHY "POETICS?," pp. [iii]-iv. First appearance.

B105   **POETRY AN INTRODUCTION**   1981

Poetry | An Introduction | RUTH MILLER | State University of New York at Stony Brook | ROBERT A. GREENBERG | Queens College of the City University of New York | St. Martin's Press [space] New York [1981].

Contribution: MY MOTHER WOULD BE A FALCONRESS, pp. 353-355.

A CENTURY IN TWO DECADES

[title in red] A Century in Two Decades | A Burning Deck Anthology | 1961-1981 | [in italics] edited by Keith & Rosemarie Waldrop | [publisher's logo] | BURNING DECK | Providence [Rhode Island, 1982].

Contribution: SONNERIES OF THE ROSE CROSS ERIC SATIE WHOSE THOUGHT RETURNS TO HIS MASTER SAR PELADAN, pp. 20-22.

B107 **GAY SUNSHINE INTERVIEWS** 1982

Gay | Sunshine | Interviews | Volume 2 | EDITED BY WINSTON LEYLAND | Gay Sunshine Press | San Francisco [California, 1982].

Contribution: AARON SHURIN AND STEVE ABBOTT INTERVIEW ROBERT DUNCAN, pp. [77]-94.

Note: A photograph of RD reading in Australia, 1976, appears on p. [74], and a biographical note appears on p. [75].

B108 **CLAIMS FOR POETRY** 1982

Claims | for | Poetry | Donald Hall, Editor | Ann Arbor [space] The University of Michigan Press [1982].

Contribution: IDEAS OF THE MEANING OF FORM, pp. 78-94.

B109 **SYMPOSIUM OF THE WHOLE** 1983

SYMPOSIUM | OF THE | WHOLE | [rule] | A Range of Discourse Toward an Ethnopoetics | Edited with Commentaries | by | Jerome Rothenberg | Diane Rothenberg | UNIVERSITY OF CALIFORNIA PRESS | Berkeley [space] Los Angeles [space] London [1983].

Contribution: FROM "RITES OF PARTICIPATION," pp. 327-336.

B110 **THE PENGUIN BOOK OF** 1983
HOMOSEXUAL VERSE

THE PENGUIN BOOK OF | Homosexual | Verse | EDITED BY STEPHEN COOTE | [below] ALLEN LANE [London: Penguin Books Ltd, 1983].

Contribution: THE LOVER, p. 330.

B111 **HARRY JACOBUS** 1983

[in large black letters] HARRY JACOBUS | [below] SELECTED WORKS: 1968-1983 | MEMORIAL UNION ART GALLERY | UNIVERSITY OF CALIFORNIA, DAVIS | SEPTEMBER 30 THROUGH | NOVEMBER 4, 1983.

Contribution: [statement beginning] "ON THE SURFACE.....," p. [3]. First appearance.

Note: This exhibition checklist consists of one sheet of paper folded once to form two leaves 14.5 cm x 19 cm.

B112   **THE WORLD OF MARY BUTTS**   1984

[in red letters] THE WRITINGS AND THE | WORLD OF MARY BUTTS [reproduction of a photograph of Mary Butts] A Conference | The University of California, Davis | February 23rd and 24th, 1984.

Contribution: RE MARY BUTTS, p. [3].

Note: This program for the conference is made from a single sheet of paper folded twice to form three leaves 18.7 x 14.7cm. Other statements are contributed by Barbara Wagstaff and Robin Blaser. A poem by Mary Butts, "The Peace of God" appears on p. [2]. Other participants in the conference were Robert H. Byington and Kenneth Irby.

C.
Contributions to Periodicals

C1 A MOMENT OF ECSTASY. *The Target: Self Expression, The Aim of Kern, County Union High School Students of English*, II, 1 (May 1933), [2].

C2 AN INTERPRETATION. *The Target: Self Expression, The Aim of Kern, County Union High School Students of English*, III (May 1934), [4].

C3 EGO INVULNERATUS. *The Occident*, XXX, 1 (March 1937), 28.

C4 PEOPLE. *The Occident*, XXX, 2 (April 1937), 30-31.

C5 PAX VOBISCUM. *The Occident*, XXXI, 1 (Oct. 1937), 17-18.
Contents: CAPITALIST—FARMER—PROSTITUTE—MOTHER—COMMUNIST-PACIFIST—FASCIST MILITARIST.

C6 A CAMPUS POET SPROUTS SOCIAL CONSCIOUSNESS. *Campus Review*, [IV, 3] (15 Nov. 1937), 2.

C7 [TWO POEMS]. *Epitaph*, I, 1 (Spring 1938), [3-10, 25].
Contents: RITUAL—SELF-PORTRAIT AT 90.

C8 RELATIVITY, A LOVE LETTER AND RELATIVE TO WHAT: A LOVE LETTER. *Epitaph*, I, 1 (Spring 1938), [21-25].

C9 [TWO POEMS]. *The Phoenix*, II, 2 (Sept. 1939), 86-91.
Contents: THE GESTATION—THE PROTESTANTS (CANTO ONE).

C10 [LETTER, TO *THE PHOENIX*]. *The Phoenix*, II, 2 (Sept. 1939), 106-108.

C11 LES QUESTIONS SURRÉALISTES. *The California Grizzley* (March 1940), 21.

C12 [TWO POEMS]. *The Phoenix*, II, 3 (Easter 1940), 108-111.
Contents: WE HAVE FORGOTTEN VENUS—PERSEPHONE.

C13 ANNOUNCING RITUAL. *The Phoenix*, II, 3 (Easter 1940), [157].

C14 PASSAGE OVER WATER. *Ritual*, I, 1 (April 1940), [10].

C15 HAMLET: A DRAFT OF THE PROLOGUE. *Ritual*, I, 1 (April 1940), [19-23].

C16 A SONG FOR MICHAEL COONEY. *The Phoenix*, II, 4 (Autumn 1940), 80-81.

C17 [LETTER]. *The Phoenix*, II, 4 (Autumn 1940), 119-120.

C18 [EDITORIAL STATEMENT]. *Experimental Review*, 2 (Nov. 1940), [6].
Note: Written in collaboration with Sanders Russell.

C19 TOWARD THE SHAMAN. *Experimental Review*, 2 (Nov. 1940), [6].

C20 [FOUR REVIEWS]. *Experimental Review*, 2 (Nov. 1940), 78-[82].
Contents: AN EMBRYO FOR GOD: THE TROPIC OF CAPRI-CORN—A SEASON IN HELL BY ARTHUR RIMBAUD—AMERIKA, BY FRANZ KAFKA—PORTRAIT OF THE ARTIST AS A YOUNG DOG BY DYLAN THOMAS.

C21 [THREE POEMS]. *Experimental Review*, Supplement (Jan. 1941), [2-3]. (Ed. Robert Symmes, Virginia Admiral, Sanders Russell, and Jack Johnson).
Contents: POEM—AN ARK FOR LAWRENCE DURRELL—THE AWAKENING INTO DREAM, LOVE THERE: OUT OF THE DREAM, AND OUR BEAUTIFUL CHILD.

C22 [TWO PROSE PIECES]. *Experimental Review*, 3 (Sept. 1941), [31-33, 42].
Contents: CONCERNING THE MAZE—FRAGMENT FROM A JOURNAL.

C23 A HISTORY OF MY FAMILY. *Experimental Review*, 3 (Sept. 1941), [34-35].

C24 [REVIEW OF] NEW DIRECTIONS 1940. *Experimental Review*, 3 (Sept. 1941), [107-108].

C25 A LETTER FOR JACK JOHNSON. *View*, I (Feb.-March 1942), 6.

C26 [TWO POEMS]. *Poetry*, LX, 2 (May 1942), 76-80.
Contents: A SPRING MEMORANDUM—A PAIR OF URANIAN GARTERS FOR AURORA BLIGH.

C27 KENNETH PATCHEN: THE DARK KINGDOM. *Accent*, III, 1 (Autumn 1942), 64.

C28 THE HOMOSEXUAL IN SOCIETY. *Politics*, I, 7 (Aug. 1944), 209-211.

C29 THE POLITICS OF THE UNREJECTED. *Politics*, II, 1 (Jan. 1945), 30-31. [Letter].
Note: This letter was written in response to an article: George P. Elliot, "'Where are you Going?' said Reader to Writer," *Politics*, I, 8 (Sept. 1944), 245-247.

C30 NOTES ON SOME PAINTERS AND POETS. *Retort*, II, 3 (Winter 1945), 31-34.

C31 WHAT TO DO NOW, with a reply by William Kuenning. *Direct Action*, (Summer 1945), 35-42.

C32 WITNESSES. *Death*, I, 1 (Summer 1946), 38.

C33 THE YEARS AS CATCHES. *Circle* 7/8 (Fall 1946), 1-4.

C34 KING HAYDEN [*sic*] OF MIAMI BEACH. *The Occident* (Winter 1946), 42-44.

C35 [FOUR POEMS]. *The Ark*, I (Spring 1947), 24-31.
Contents: SLEEP IS A DEEP AND MANY-VOICED FLOOD—AN ENCOUNTER—AT AN ANARCHIST MEETING—HOMAGE AND LAMENT FOR EZRA POUND: May 12, 1944.

C36 REVIEWING *VIEW*, AN ATTACK. *The Ark*, I (Spring 1947), 62-67.

C37 VARIATIONS UPON PHRASES FROM MILTON'S *THE REASON OF CHURCH GOVERNMENT*. *Contour Quarterly*, I, 1 (April 1947), 3-6.

C38 [REVIEW OF GERTRUDE] STEIN: FOUR IN AMERICA. *The Occident* (Fall 1947), 38.

C39 [LETTER]. *Four Pages*, 1 (Jan. 1948), 2, 3.
Note: This is a note on a list of authors and works which "form a critical basis for a 'new poetry' given the past decade."

C40 THE HOMECOMING. *The Pacific Spectator*, II, 1 (Winter 1948), 48-49.
Note: The poem appears as part of a small anthology with an introduction by its editor Muriel Rukeyser entitled "A Group of Region Poets."

C41 NOTES ON THE PSYCHOLOGY OF ART. *The Occident* (Spring 1948), 26-30.

C42 [REVIEW OF] THE POETICS OF MUSIC: STRAVINSKY. *The Occident* (Spring 1948), 53-54.

C43 [LETTER]. *Four Pages*, 4 (April 1948), 4.

C44 THE HELMET OF GOLIATH. *The Tiger's Eye*, I, 4 (June 1948), 50-51.

C45 TOWARD AN AFRICAN ELEGY. *Circle*, 10 (Summer 1948), 94-96.

C46 A DESCRIPTION OF VENICE. *Berkeley Miscellany*, 1 (Summer 1948), 1-10. (Ed. Robert Duncan).

C47 [NOTE]. *Four Pages*, 8 (Aug. 1948), 2.

C48 A NOTE ON TONE IN POETRY. *Literary Behavior* (Fall 1948/49), 13-14.
Note: This is a publication of the Writer's Conference entitled "Writer's Conference Report."

C49 [THREE POEMS]. *Berkeley Miscellany*, 2 (Spring 1949), 25-29.
Contents: 3 POEMS IN HOMAGE TO THE BROTHERS GRIMM:

THE ROBBER MOON—THE STRAWBERRIES UNDER THE
SNOW—THE DINNER TABLE OF HARLEQUIN.

C50 LOVE - A STORY. *The Occident* (Fall 1949), 5-15.

C51 [ESSAY] AS PART OF A SYMPOSIUM THE POET AND POETRY.
The Occident (Fall 1949), 39-40.
Note: Other poets in the Symposium were William Everson, Rosalie
Moore, Jack Spicer, and Leonard Wolf.

C52 DOMESTIC SCENES. *Quarterly Review of Literature*, VI, 4 (Spring
1952), 351-357.
Contents: BREAKFAST—REAL ESTATE—BUS FARE—MAIL
BOXES—MATCHES—BATH—RADIO—ELECTRIC IRON—
LUNCH WITH BUNS—PIANO.

C53 A LITTLE FREEDOM FOR POETS PLEASE. *The Artist's View*, 0
(May 1952), [4].

C54 WALKING ON KEARNEY STREET. *The Artist's View*, 0 (May
1952), [4].

C55 POEMS. *Origin*, first series, 6 (Summer 1952), 76-87, 122-126.
Contents: EARLY HISTORY: THE FIRST DAY—THE CITIES OF
THE PLAIN—THE GOLDEN AGE—THE SECOND NIGHT IN
THE WEEK—PROCESSIONAL OF THE DEAD—AFRICA
REVISITED—THE HORNS OF ARTEMIS.

C56 AN OPEN LETTER TO *CITY LIGHTS*. *City Lights*, I, 1 (July
1952), 1.

C57 ELUARD'S DEATH. *Origin*, first series, 9 (Spring 1953), [2-4].

C58 PAGES FROM A NOTEBOOK. *The Artist's View*, 5 (July 1953), [2-4].
Contents: 1. [UNTITLED].—2. NOTES MIDWAY ON MY
FAUST.—3. IN COMPLETE AGREEMENT ON WRITING.—4.
DESCRIPTION OF IMAGINARY POETRIES.

C59 SALVAGES AN EVENING PIECE. *City Lights*, 4 (Fall 1953), 31.
Note: The poem was reprinted in *The Nation*, CXCIII, 22 (23 Dec.
1961), 519, as part of an essay by Denise Levertov entitled "What is a
Prose Poem?"

C60 [LETTER TO] NEAR-FAR MISTER OLSON. *Origin*, first series,
12 (Spring 1954), 210-211.

C61 LETTERS TO OLSON: LIGHT SONG. *The Occident* (Spring
1954), 19-20.

C62 AN A MUSE MENT. *The Black Mountain Review*, I, 3 (Autumn
1954), 19-22.

C63 [SIX POEMS]. *Origin*, first series, 14 (Autumn 1954), 123-128.
Contents: LOVE POEM—SALVAGES. LASSITUDE.—FRIEDL—A CONVERSION—SONGS FOR THE JEWS FROM THEIR BOOK OF SPLENDOURS—DREAM OF THE END OF THE WORLD.

C64 FRAGMENT. *Poems and Pictures*, 2 (1954), [4].

C65 [TWO POEMS]. *The Black Mountain Review*, 5 (Summer 1955), [36-39].
Contents: SEVERAL POEMS. IN PROSE—SHELLS.

C66 FROM A NOTEBOOK. *The Black Mountain Review*, 5 (Summer 1955), 209-212.
Note: The entry is dated "11/1/54."

C67 NOTES. *The Black Mountain Review*, 6 (Spring 1956), 5-14.

C68 AN OWL IS AN ONLY BIRD OF POETRY (ANOTHER VALE FOR JAMES BROUGHTON). *The Black Mountain Review*, 6 (Spring 1956), 165-169.

C69 NOTES ON POETICS REGARDING OLSON'S "MAXIMUS." *The Black Mountain Review*, 6 (Spring 1956), 201-211.

C70 THE REAPER. *Truth: A Magazine*, CLVI, 4153 (27 April 1956), 479.

C71 OF THE ART. *The Needle*, I, 1 (April 1956), [5].

C72 [TWO POEMS]. *Ark II/Moby I* (1956/1957), 10-12.
Contents: Untitled poem beginning, "OFTEN I AM PERMITTED TO RETURN TO A MEADOW"(fl)—THE LAW I LOVE IS MAJOR MOVER.

C73 [THREE POEMS]. *Evergreen Review*, I, 2 (Feb. 1957), 21-29.
Contents: THIS PLACE, RUMORD TO HAVE BEEN SODOM—THE FEAR THAT PRECEDES—THE STRUCTURE OF RIME I, II, III, IV, V, VI, VII.

C74 [FOUR POEMS]. *Botteghe Oscure*, XIX (Spring 1957), 339-345.
Contents: HERO SONG—OF THE ART—ADAM'S SONG—THE GREEN LADY.

C75 (THE PROPOSITIONS). *Measure*, 1 (Summer 1957), 40-48.

C76 THE BALLAD OF MRS NOAH. *Botteghe Oscure*, XX (Autumn 1957), 282-284.
Note: At this printing the ballad is dedicated to Madeline Gleason.

C77 [FIVE POEMS]. *Poetry*, XC, 6 (Sept 1957), 350-355.
Contents: A MORNING LETTER—THE TEMPLE OF THE ANIMALS—THERE'S TOO MUCH SEA ON THE BIG SUR—POEM—A RIDE TO THE SEA.
Note: RD was awarded the Union League Prize for this contribution to *Poetry*.

C78 [TWO POEMS]. *Measure*, 2 (Winter 1958), 24-26, 32-33.
    Contents: THE MAIDEN—THE DANCE.

C79 [LETTER]. *Measure*, 2 (Winter 1958), 62-63.

C80 IN THE SIGHT OF A LYRE, LITTLE SPEAR, A CHAIR. *Poetry*,
    XCI, 4 (Jan. 1958), 256-260.
    Note: This is a review of *Selected Poems*, by H.D.

C81 A RISK OF SYMPATHIES. *Poetry*, XCI, 5 (Feb. 1958), 328-332.
    Note: This is a review of *True and False Unicorns*, by James
    Broughton.

C82 [SIX POEMS]. *Poetry*, XCI, 6 (March 1958), 377-384.
    Contents: BROUGHT TO LOVE—TO VOW—METAMORPHOSIS—
    RE—WORDS OPEN OUT UPON GRIEF—AUGUST SUN.

C83 UPON TAKING HOLD. *Chicago Review*, XII, 1 (Spring 1958), 7-8.

C84 [LETTER] TO THE EDITOR OF *POETRY*. *Poetry*, XCII, 3 (June
    1958), 196-197.

C85 A STORM OF WHITE. *Poetry*, XCIII, 6 (March 1959), 305-370.

C86 AGAINST NATURE. *Poetry*, XCIV, 1 (April 1959), 54-59.
    Note: This is a review of *The Sorrows of Priapus*, by Edward
    Dahlberg.

C87 OUT OF THE BLACK. *The Nation*, CLXXXVIII, 17 (25 April 1959),
    365.

C88 DREAM DATA. *J*, 1 (Aug./Sept. 1959), [15].

C89 [TWO POEMS]. *Foot*, [1] ([Sept. 1959]), [18], [39-47].
    Contents: LORD MASTER MOUSE—POEM BEGINNING WITH
    A LINE BY PINDAR.

C90 A NOTE AND A POEM. *Migrant*, 2 (Sept. 1959), 22-23.
    Contents: A NOTE—SOLITUDE.

C91 EVOCATION. *Big Table*, I, 3 (1959), 40-41.

C92 DEAR CARPENTER. *J*, 2 ([Oct. 1959]), [10-12].

C93 FOUR POEMS. *Poetry*, XCV, 1 (Oct. 1959), 29-35.
    Contents: FOOD FOR FIRE, FOOD FOR THOUGHT—UNDER
    GROUND—BONE DANCE—RETURNING TO ROOTS OF
    FIRST FEELING.

C94 YES, AS A LOOK SPRINGS TO ITS FACE. *The Nation*,
    CLXXXIX, 11 (Oct. 1959), 200.

C95 A SEQUENCE OF POEMS FOR H.D.'S BIRTHDAY, SEPTEMBER
    10, 1959/ FINISHED OCTOBER 24, 1959. *J*, 4 ([Nov. 1959]), [2-6].

C96 THE SONG OF THE RIVER TO ITS SHORES. *J*, 5 ([Dec. 1959]), [10-11].

C97 THE NATURAL DOCTRINE. *Chicago Review*, XIII, 4 (Winter 1959), 76.

C98 A POEM BEGINNING WITH A LINE BY PINDAR. *Evergreen Review*, IV, 11 (Jan.-Feb. 1960), 134-142.

C99 FOUR PICTURES OF THE REAL UNIVERSE. *Trobar*, 1 (1960), 4-5.

C100 [TWO POEMS]. *Folio*, XXV, 3 (Summer 1960), 2-3.
Contents: POETRY, A NATURAL THING—THREE PAGES FROM A BIRTHDAY BOOK.

C101 FOUR PICTURES OF THE REAL UNIVERSE. *Big Table*, I, 4 (1960), 83-84.

C102 FROM NOTES ON *THRONES*: RHETORIC. A CONTRASTING VIEW OF CREATION. *Migrant*, 8 (Sept. 1960), 25-26.

C103 A POEM. *Migrant*, 8 (Sept. 1960), 33-34.
Note: An explanatory note precedes this untitled poem, which begins with the line, "Come, let me free myself from all that I love."

C104 INGMAR BERGMAN'S *SEVENTH SEAL*. *Chelsea*, 8 (Oct. 1960), 53-54.
Note: This issue of *Chelsea* was devoted to plays and political poetry and was edited by David Ignatow.

C105 A POEM OF DESPONDENCIES. *The Nation*, CXCI, 17 (19 Nov. 1960), 399.

C106 FROM APPREHENSIONS. *Big Table*, II, 5 (1960), 38-39.

C107 NEL MEZZO DEL CAMMIN DI NOSTRA VITA. *National Review*, X, 1 (14 Jan. 1961), 20.

C108 APPREHENSIONS. *Evergreen Review*, V, 16 (Jan./Feb. 1961), 56-67.

C109 PROPERTIES AND OUR REAL ESTATE. *Journal for the Protection of All Beings*, 1 (1961), 84-94.

C110 A POEM SLOW BEGINNING. *Trobar*, 2 ([1961]), 9-10.

C111 [FOUR POEMS]. *Trobar*, 3 (June 1961), 14-18.
Contents: STRUCTURE OF RIME XV—STRUCTURE OF RIME XVI—STRUCTURE OF RIME XVII—STRUCTURE OF RIME XVIII.

C112 IDEAS OF THE THE MEANING OF FORM. *Kulchur*, 4 (1961), 60-74.

C113 THE POETIC VOCATION: ST. JOHN PERSE. *Jubilee: a magazine of the church and her people*, IX, 7 (Nov. 1961), [36-41].

C114 FIRE DYING, FROM AN ESSAY AT WAR. *The Nation*, CXCIII, 18 (25 Nov. 1961), 434.

C115 [TWO POEMS]. *Poetry*, XCIX, 3 (Dec. 1961), 168-177.
Contents: THE LAW—TWO DICTA OF WILLIAM BLAKE.

C116 OSIRIS AND SET. *Set*, 1 (Winter 1961-62), 2-3.

C117 SHELLEY'S *ARETHUSA* SET TO A NEW MEASURE. *Origin*, second series, 4 (Jan. 1962), 50-52.

C118 OFTEN I AM PERMITTED TO RETURN TO A MEADOW. *Side II*, I, 6 (18 April 1962), 1.

C119 WHAT DO I KNOW OF THE OLD LORE? *Measure*, 3 (Summer 1962), 11-12.

C120 NIGHT SCENES I, II, III. *The Floating Bear*, 19 (1962), [1-3].

C121 AFTER READING H.D.'S *HERMETIC DEFINITIONS*. *Trobar*, 4 (1962), 1-3.

C122 FOR THE NOVICES OF VANCOUVER. *Tish*, 13 (14 Sept. 1962), 3-5.
Note: This is a review of the first twelve issues of *Tish*.

C123 AFTER A PASSAGE IN BAUDELAIRE. *Poetry*, CI, 1/2 (Oct.-Nov. 1962), 32-33.

C124 *FOR LOVE*, BY ROBERT CREELEY. *New Mexico Quarterly*, XXXII, 3/4 (Autumn/Winter 1962-63), 219-224.
Note: This is a review of *For Love*, by Robert Creeley.

C125 [SEVEN POEMS]. *Burning Deck*, 1 (Fall 1962), 26-34.
Contents: AN ARRANGEMENT—LOVE POEM—LORD MASTER MOUSE—THE SCATTERING—IMAGES OF HECTOR—THE LOVER—STRAINS OF SIGHT.

C126 [THREE POEMS]. *Foot*, 2 (1962), 19-20, 54-57.
Contents: A DANCING CONCERNING A FORM OF WOMEN— NOW THE RECORD NOW RECORD—SONNERIES OF THE ROSE CROSS ERIK SATIE WHOSE THOUGHT RETURNS TO HIS MASTER SAR PELADAN.

C127 SONNERIES OF THE ROSE CROSS ERIK SATIE WHOSE THOUGHT RETURNS TO HIS MASTER SAR PELADAN. *Burning Deck*, 2 (Spring 1963), 74-77.

C128 RISK. *Poetry*, CI, 6 (March 1963), 383-386.

C129 WEAVING THE DESIGN. *The Rivoli Review*, 0, 1 (1963), 6.

C130 [THREE SONNETS]. *Yale Literary Magazine*, CXXXI (April 1963), 29-30
Contents: SONNET I—SONNET II—SONNET III.

C131 [LETTER TO EDITOR]. *Genesis West*, I, 4 (Summer 1963), 319.

C132 FROM THE DAY BOOK (EXCERPTS FROM AN EXTENDED STUDY OF H.D.'S POETRY). *Origin*, second series, 10 (July 1963), 1-47.

C133 [LETTER, TO CID CORMAN, 10 AUG. 1962]. *Origin*, second series, 10 (July 1963), 49.

C134 SONNET 4. *The Nation*, CXCVII, 5 (24 Aug. 1963), 97.

C135 FOUR SONGS THE NIGHT-NURSE SANG. *Poems From The Floating World*, 5 (1963), 2-5.

C136 LOVE. *Kulchur*, 11 (Autumn 1963), 20-32.

C137 5TH SONNET. *The Nation*, CXCVII, 13 (26 Oct. 1963), 262.

C138 THE CONTINENT. *Poetry*, CIII, 1/2 (Oct.-Nov. 1963), 28-32.
Note: RD won the Levinson Prize for this poem.

C139 A PART-SEQUENCE FOR *CHANGE*. *Change*, 1 (1963), 13-14.

C140 [FIVE POEMS]. *Quarterly Review of Literature*, XII, 3 (1963), 184-195.
Contents: FROM *THE MABINOGION*—DOVE— A NEW POEM (FOR JACK SPICER)—TWO MESSAGES—RETURNING TO THE RHETORIC OF AN EARLY MODE.

C141 [TWO POEMS, UNTITLED]. *Open Space*, 2 (Feb. 1964), [13-17].
Note: The poems were reprinted as TRIBAL MEMORIES, PASSAGES 1, and AT THE LOOM, PASSAGES 2.

C142 [THREE POEMS]. *The Review*, 10 (Jan. 1964), [11]-13.
Contents: YES, AS A LOOK SPRINGS TO ITS FACE—KEEPING THE RHYME—from A POEM BEGINNING WITH A LINE BY PINDAR.

C143 WHAT HAPPEND: PRELUDE. *Open Space*, valentine issue (Feb. 1964), [14-21].
Contents: ARGUMENT—PUSS-IN-BOOTS, GUARDIAN, GENIUS.

C144 POSTSCRIPT FOR *OPEN SPACE, JANUARY 1964*. *Open Space*, valentine issue (Feb. 1964), [22-23].

C145 [CORRECTIONS]. *Open Space*, 2 (Feb. 1964), [34].
Note: RD gives corrections for WHAT HAPPEND: PRELUDE.

C146 INCREASING. *Semina*, 8 (1963), n.pag.
  Note: The poem appears on an unbound and unnumbered leaf, along with a photograph of RD.

C147 [EXCERPTS FROM A LETTER TO KENNETH IRBY]. *Sum*, 2 (Feb.1964), 28.

C148 OSIRIS AND SET. *Granta*, LXVIII, 1234 (7 March 1964), 8.
  Note: This issue contains a special section entitled "American Supplement," including work by Zukofsky, Creeley, Dawson, Dorn, Duncan, Eigner, Kelly, Levertov, Loewinsohn, Olson, Wieners, and Woolf.

C149 THESE PAST YEARS (PASSAGES 9). *Imago*, 2 (1964), [22-23].

C150 [THREE POEMS]. *The Rivoli Review*, 0, 2 (1964), 15-17.
  Contents: PASSAGES III—PASSAGES 3—[PASSAGES] 4.

C151 PROPOSITIONS I CAN USE IN KOLLER'S NOTES. *Sum*, 3 (May 1964), 8

C152 A NEW POEM (FOR JACK SPICER). *Open Space*, 5 (May 1964), [12-14].

C153 [FIVE POEMS]. *Open Space*, 6 (June 1964), [20-27].
  Contents: PASSAGES 5—PASSAGES 6—PASSAGES 7—PASSAGES 8—PASSAGES 9.
  Note: The poems were reprinted as THE COLLAGE PASSAGES 6—ENVOY PASSAGES 7—AS IN THE OLD DAYS PASSAGES 8—THE ARCHITECTURE PASSAGES 9—THESE PAST YEARS PASSAGES 10.

C154 [NOTE AND TWO POEMS]. *Open Space*, 7 (July 1964), [6-10].
  Contents: A NOTE FOR *OPEN SPACE* 7—THE STRUCTURE OF RIME XIII—SHADOWS.
  Note: The Note gives the first account in print of the forms of "The Passages" sequence. Duncan gives corrections for the numbering, and some corrections for lines in previously published poems of the sequence.

C155 A NOTE FOR *OPEN SPACE 8*. *Open Space*, 8 (Aug. 1964), [6].

C156 [FIVE POEMS]. *Open Space*, 8 (Aug. 1964), 7-13.
  Contents STRUCTURE OF RIME XXIV—CHORDS—SPELL-ING—AT LAMMAS TIDE—SAINT GRAAL (AFTER VERLAINE).
  Note: The poem MY MOTHER WOULD BE A FALCONRESS, as yet untitled, appears here as part of AT LAMMAS TIDE.

C157 PARISFAL: THE EASTER MAGIC (AFTER WAGNER AND VERLAINE). *Open Space*, 9 (Sept. 1964), [41-42].

C158 [TWO POEMS]. *Trobar*, 5 (1964), 33-35.
   Contents: SUCH IS THE SICKNESS OF MANY A GOOD
   THING—BENDING THE BOW.

C159 [TWO POEMS]. *Fuck You, A Magazine of the Arts*, VII, 5 (Sept. 1964),
   [18-20].
   Contents: OLD TESTAMENT—NEW TESTAMENT.

C160 NOTES ON POETICS: REGARDING OLSON'S "MAXIMUS."
   The Review 10 (Jan. 1964), 36-42.

C161 ORIENTED BY INSTINCTS BY STARS. *Poetry*, CV, 2 (Nov. 1964),
   131-133.
   Note: This is a review of *The Poems of the Air*, by James Dickey.

C162 MOVING THE MOVING IMAGE [PASSAGES 17]. *Open Space*, 11
   (Nov. 1964), 13-14.

C163 NOVICES: OCTOBER 17, 3-4 AM, 1963. *Matter*, 3 ([Dec. 1964]), [1-3].

C164 THE H.D. BOOK: CHAPTER 5. *Aion; A Journal of Traditionary
   Science* (Dec. 1964), [5-29].

C165 FOURTH SONG (from FOUR SONGS THE NIGHT-NURSE
   SANG). *The Nation*, CXCIX, 18 (7 Dec. 1964), 443.

C166 [THREE POEMS]. *Open Space*, 12 (Dec. 1964), [2-6].
   Contents: THE TORSO, PASSAGES 18—THE EARTH, PASSAGES
   19—STRUCTURE OF RIME 20, AN ILLUSTRATION.
   Note: This issue also contains two photographs of RD, one by Patty
   Topalian and one by Go Go Nesbitt.

C167 NOTES FROM A READING AT THE POETRY CENTER, SAN
   FRANCISCO, MARCH 1, 1959. *The Floating Bear*, 31 (1965), [12-13].

C168 THE FIRE. *Poetry*, CVI, 1-2 (April-May 1965), 32-36.

C169 THE MULTIVERSITY. *Synapse*, 4 (May 1965), [1-3].
   Note: This issue, devoted to San Francisco Poets, carried an
   announcement of The Berkeley Poetry Conference, 12-24 July 1965, at
   the University of California.

C170 TAKING AWAY FROM GOD HIS SOUND. *The Nation*, CC, 22 (31
   May 1965), 595-598.
   Note: This is a review of *Ace of Pentacles* and *The Hotel Wentley
   Poems*, by John Wieners.

C171 TWO POEMS. *Niagara Frontier Review*, [2] (Spring-Summer 1965),
   14-17.
   Contents: CHORDS—SAINT GRAAL (AFTER VERLAINE).

C172 THE GIFT OF TONGUES OR THE IMAGINATION. *Wild Dog*,
   18 (17 July 1965), 25-27.

C173 UP RISING. *The Nation*, CCI, 7 (13 Sept. 1965), 146-147.
Note: A letter to the editor, by Hayden Carruth, as a response to UP RISING, appeared in *The Nation*, CCI, 9 (27 Sept. 1965), 148; a second response to the poem from J. C. Fisccalini appeared in *The Nation*, CCI, 11 (11 Oct. 1965), 204.

C174 THE LASTING CONTRIBUTION OF EZRA POUND. *Agenda*, IV, 2 (Oct.-Nov. 1965), 23-26.
Note: This is a special issue in honor of Ezra Pound's eightieth birthday.

C175 [STATEMENT]. *Matter*, 3 ([Dec. 1965]), [1-3].

C176 MELVILLE AFTER *PIERRE. Wild Dog*, 19/20 (8 Dec. 1965), 16.

C177 [THREE POEMS]. *Poetry*, CVIII, 1 (April 1966), 1-8.
Contents: IN THE PLACE OF PASSAGE 22—BENEFICE PASSAGES 23—ORDERS PASSAGES 24.

C178 ROOTS AND BRANCHES. *The National Observer*, 11 (11 July 1966), 24.

C179 BEGINNINGS: CHAPTER 1 OF THE H.D. BOOK PART I *Coyote's Journal*, 5/6 (July 1966), 8-31.

C180 LAMMAS DREAM POEM. *The Paris Review*, 36 (Winter 1966), 74-76.

C181 EARTH'S WINTER SONG. *Some/thing*, 3 (Winter 1966), [71-72].

C182 [A LETTER AND PHOTOGRAPH]. *San Francisco Oracle*, I, 4 (16 Dec. 1966), 14.
Note: A letter concerning Lenore Kandel's *The Love Book* appears with a photograph of RD by Hap Stewart.

C183 A SHRINE TO AMEINIAS: PARMENIDES' DREAM. *The Journal of Creative Behavior*, I, 2 (Spring 1967), 129-132.

C184 MASTURBATION: FOR THE INNOCENCE OF THE ACT. *R*C* Lion*, 3 (Spring 1967), 46-55.

C185 MOIRA'S CATHEDRAL. *Haravec*, 2 (March 1967), 50-51.

C186 [TWO POEMS]. *Poetry*, CX, 3 (June 1967), 141-147.
Contents: PASSAGES 28: THE LIGHT—EYE OF GOD: PASSAGES 29.

C187 AT THE POETRY CONFERENCE: BERKELEY/AFTER THE NEW YORK STYLE. *Angel Hair*, 3 (Summer 1967), [33-34].

C188 THE H.D. BOOK, PART I: CHAPTER 2. *Coyote's Journal*, 8 (1967), 27-35.

C189 A PLAY WITH MASKS. *Audit/Poetry*, IV, 3 (1967), 2-24.
Note: This issue is devoted completely to the work of RD.

C190 NARRATION FOR CONCERT READING VERSION OF ADAM'S WAY. *Audit/Poetry*, IV, 3 (1967), 24-30.

C191 MISCELLANEOUS UNCOLLECTED PIECES. *Audit/Poetry*, IV, 3 (1967), 30-33.
Contents: A DERIVATION FROM RIMBAUD (1948)—A GAME OF KINGS (1950)—A VILLANELLE (1950)—ALTERATION (1950).

C192 UNCOLLECTED STEIN IMITATIONS FROM THE PERIOD OF WRITING WRITING (1953). *Audit/Poetry*, IV, 3 (1967), 33-34.
Contents: THE KING: A REGRET—CLOUDY.

C193 [SEVEN PIECES]. *Audit/Poetry*, IV, 3 (1967), 34-37.
Contents: A NEW VERSION OF HEAVENLY CITY, EARTHLY CITY—IMAGINARY LETTER—YOUNG MEN—SENSATIONAL NEWS—HEADLINES—RESERVE MOON HANDLE MAKER AND WING—AT THE BAKERY—THE CANNIBALISTIC COOKIE-PEOPLE.

C194 THE CHIMERAS OF GERARD DE NERVAL. *Audit/Poetry*, IV, 3 (1967), 38-42.
Contents: EL DESDICHADO (THE DISINHERTED)—MYRTHO—HORUS—ANTEROS—DELPHICA—ARTEMIS—THE CHRIST IN THE OLIVE GROVE— GOLDEN LINES.

C195 RETURNING TO LES CHIMÈRES OF GÉRARD DE NERVAL. *Audit/Poetry*. IV, 3 (1967), 42-64.
Note: This is an essay, which includes letters, about Robin Blaser's translation of Nerval's poems. Duncan gives his own notes and states his position about the process of translation.

C196 SOME VERSIONS OF PASSAGES 26. *Audit/Poetry*, IV, 3 (1967), 62-64.

C197 RITES OF PARTICIPATION. *Caterpillar*, 1 (Oct. 1967), 6-29.
Note: This is Chap. 6 of Part I of "The H.D. Book."

C198 PASSAGES 30, STAGE DIRECTIONS. *Caterpillar*, 1 (Oct. 1967), 30-34.

C199 "HOW MANY MILES TO LOVE AND BACK"(fl). *The Tenth Muse: Poetry and Literary Ephemera Catalogue 21*. San Francisco: The Tenth Muse (1968), cover poem.

C200 AN INTERLUDE. *The Atlantic*, CCXI, 1 (Jan. 1968), 52-53.

C201 RITES OF PARTICIPATION (Part II, continued from Caterpillar 1). *Caterpillar*, 2 (Jan. 1968), 125-154.
Note: This is the second section of Chap. 6 of Part I of "The H.D. Book."

C202 A COMMENTARY. *Vector*, IV , 3 (Feb. 1968), 9.

C203 ELEGY WRITTEN 4. 7. 53 FOR JACK SPICER. *San Francisco Earthquake*, I, 3 (Spring 1968), 75-78.
Note: A photograph of Jack Spicer appears on page 74.

C204 TWO CHAPTERS FROM H.D. *TriQuarterly*, 12 (Spring 1968), 67-98.
Note: These are Chaps. 3 and 4 of Part I of "The H.D. Book."

C205 THE ZINZENDORF PASSAGES. *The Wivenhoe Park Revue*, 2 ([1968]), 21-27.
Contents: THE COLLAGE, PASSAGES 6— ENVOY, PASSAGES 7—AS IN THE OLD DAYS, PASSAGES 8—THE ARCHITECTURE, PASSAGES 9—THESE PAST YEARS, PASSAGES [10].

C206 H.D. BOOK: (PART I: BEGINNINGS. CHAPTER 5 . OCCULT MATTERS). *Stony Brook*, 1/2 (Fall 1968), 4-19.

C207 NIGHTS AND DAYS. *Sumac*, I, 1 (Fall 1968), 101-146.
Note: This is Chap. 1 of Part II of "The H.D. Book."

C208 [TWO POEMS]. *Poetry*, CXIII, 3 (Dec. 1968), 170-187
Contents: PASSAGES 31, THE CONCERT—PASSAGES 32 (ANCIENT REVERIES AND DECLARATIONS).

C209 THE H.D. BOOK. PART II NIGHTS AND DAYS: CHAPTER 2. *Caterpillar*, 6 (Jan. 1969), 16-38.

C210 FROM A POEM BY JOHN ASHBERY. *The Lampeter Muse*, III, 4 (Spring 1969), 3.

C211 IF I HAD KIN. *Vector*, V, 4 (March 1969), 24.

C212 THE H.D. BOOK: PART II. NIGHTS AND DAYS. CHAPTER 4. *Caterpillar*, 7 (April 1969), 27-60.

C213 [NOTE AND POEM]. *Caterpillar*, 7 (April 1969), 89-91.
Note: This is a note concerning the omission of three stanzas of part IV and all of part V of the poem THE CHRIST IN THE OLIVE GROVE as it was printed in *BB*, followed by the missing sections.

C214 [NOTE]. *The Occident*, new series, III (Spring/Summer 1969), 108-111.
Note: This note appears as part of an Occident Symposium on the question: "Is there anything to like in contemporary literature?" Other contributors include Howard Nemerov, Richard Eberhart, Louis Untermeyer, and Frederick Crews.

C215 KEEPING THE WAR INSIDE. *Journal for the Protection of All Beings, (Green Flag)*, 3 (July 1969), [36].

C216 THE H.D. BOOK, PART 2, CHAPTER 3. *Io*, 6 (Summer 1969), 117-140.

C217 [UNTITLED ESSAY]. *Magazine of Further Studies*, 6 ([1969]), [39-40].

C218 FROM THE H.D. BOOK, PART II CHAPTER 5. *Stony Brook*, 3/4 (Fall 1969), 336-347.

C219 A CRITICAL DIFFERENCE OF VIEW. *Stony Brook*, 3/4 (Fall 1969), 360-363.

C220 MAN'S FULFILLMENT IN ORDER AND STRIFE. *Caterpillar*, 8/9 (Oct. 1969), 229-249.

C221 JACK SPICER, POET; 1925-1965. *California Librarian*, XXXI, 4 (Oct. 1970), 250.

C222 PROPOSITIONS I CAN USE IN KOLLER'S NOTES. *Scree* (March 1971), [4]].

C223 INTERPRETATIONS JUNE 11, 1971. OVER THERE. *Georgia Straight, Writing Supplement*, 8 (27 July 1971), 6.

C224 GLIMPSES OF THE LAST DAY (FROM CHAPTER 11 OF THE H.D. BOOK). *Io*, 10 (1971), 212-215.

C225 [TWO POEMS]. *Poetry Review*, LXII, 3 (Autumn 1971), 237-241.
Contents: SANTA CRUZ PROPOSITIONS (FOR N. O. BROWN EXPOUNDING THE TEXTS OF VICO AND JOYCE IN THE COPULATION OF A THIRD UNREVEALED TEXT: REVEALING ITSELF)—INTERRUPTED FORMS. ONE.

C226 EXTRACTS FROM A DISCUSSION AMONG DAVID ANTIN, ROBERT DUNCAN FOLLOWING ANTIN'S READING ON OCTOBER 27. *November*, [1] (Nov. 1971), 9-11.
Note: This discussion was transcribed by David Bromige.

C227 A GLOOMING PEACE. *Writing—Grape Writing Supplement*, 11 (15 March 1972), 1-3.
Note: This introduction to an essay on Shakespeare's *Romeo and Juliet* was given as a talk, 29 Feb. 1972, and transcribed by Cynthia Kellog.

C228 FROM: A SUITE OF METAPHYSICAL POEMS / CONCEITS IN HOMAGE TO THE SEVENTEENTH CENTURY / GENIUS IN POETRY. *Open Reading*, 1 (March 1972), 18-19.

C229 [TWO POEMS]. *Fathar*, 4 (June 1972), [3].
Contents: AFTER SHAKESPEARE'S SONNET 76—SECOND TAKE ON SHAKESPEARE'S SONNET SEVENTY-SIX.

C230 SHAKESPEARE'S *ROMEO AND JULIET* AS IT APPEARS IN THE MYSTERIES OF A LATE TWENTIETH CENTURY POETICS. *Fathar*, 4 (June 1972), [54-58].

C231 STRUCTURE OF RIME XXVIII: IN MEMORIAM WALLACE STEVENS. *The Grape Writing Supplement*, 12 (21-27 June 1972), [32].

C232 POEMS FROM THE MARGINS OF THOM GUNN'S *MOLY*. *Poetry Review*, LXIII, 3 (Autumn 1972), 195-203.
Contents: THE ODYSSEY OF HOMER – BOOK X—PREFACE TO THE SUITE TRANSLATED FROM THOM GUNN'S 'MOLY'— POEMS FROM THE MARGINS OF THOM GUNN'S 'MOLY'— RITES OF PASSAGE—MOLY—SECOND TAKE ON 'RITES OF PASSAGE.'

C233 SHE. *Open Reading*, 2 (Fall 1972), 12-13.

C234 THE DANCE. *Dance Perspectives*, 52 (Winter 1972), 10-11.
Note: This special issue is an anthology of twentieth century dance poems, edited by Jack Anderson, with drawings by Howard Hussey.

C235 THE MUSEUM. *New Poetry*, XX, 4 and 5 (Oct.-Dec. 1972), 8-10.

C236 [NOTE]. *New Poetry*, XXI, 4 (1973), 65.
Note: Duncan's comment on Sappho is quoted as part of an advertisement for a special issue of *New Poetry*, "In Homage to Orpheus."

C237 THE HOMOSEXUAL IN SOCIETY. *Fag Rag*, 5 (Summer 1973), 3, 20.

C238 IN MEMORIAM: FRANCIS WEBB 1925-73. *New Poetry*, XXI, 4 (1973), 2.
Note: After the head note, STRUCTURE OF RIME XXIII is quoted in full. Following the poem appears the notation "Structure of Rime XXIII / Robert Duncan." The head note and the final note are in the holograph of Robert Adamson.

C239 POEMS FROM THE MARGINS OF THOM GUNN'S *MOLY*. *Manroot*, 9 (Fall 1973), 32-38.
Contents: INTERRUPTED FORMS—THE ODYSSEY OF HOMER. BOOK X—PREFACE TO THE SUITE TRANSLATED FROM THOM GUNN'S *Moly*—POEMS FROM THE MARGINS OF THOM GUNN'S *Moly*—RITES OF PASSAGE—MOLY—SECOND TAKE ON *RITES OF PASSAGE*.

C240 EXTRACTS FROM A DISCUSSION AMONG DAVID ANTIN, ROBERT DUNCAN AND OTHERS FOLLOWING ANTIN'S READING OF OCTOBER 27, 1971, AT CALIFORNIA STATE AT SONOMA. *Open Reading*, second series, 4/5 (Winter-Spring 1974), 43-47.
Note: An additional paragraph of comment by David Antin is added to this reprinting of the discussion as transcribed by David Bromige. See C226.

C241 LETTER TO JESS AFTER HIS VISIT TO OLSON IN NEW YORK HOSPITAL, 1970. *Olson: The Journal of the Charles Olson Archives*, 1 (Spring 1974), 4-6.

C242 A PREFACE PREPARED FOR MAPS #6: THE ISSUE. *Maps*, 6 (1974), 1-16.
Note: Maps #6 is a special issue devoted to the work of RD. Primary and secondary materials appear as well as photographs.

C243 A SEVENTEENTH CENTURY SUITE (COMPLETE). *Maps*, 6 (1974), 17-41.

C244 FROM NOTES ON THE STRUCTURE OF RIME DONE FOR WARREN TALLMAN SPRING 1961. *Maps*, 6 (1974), 42-52.

C245 PREFACE TO A READING OF PASSAGES 1-22. MARCH 6, 1970. *Maps*, 6 (1974), 53-67.

C246 TOWARDS AN OPEN UNIVERSE. *Prospice*, 2 (1974), 11-12.
Note: This is an unauthorized reprinting of RD's essay.

C247 EARLY POETIC COMMUNITY. *The American Poetry Review*, III, 3 (Fall 1974), 54-58.
Note: This is a transcription of a tape of a panel discussion with Robert Duncan and Allen Ginsberg made at the Kent State University Creative Arts Festival, 7 April 1971. The selection was transcribed and edited by Gordon Ball.

C248 A STRAY POEM. NOTES READING RENE FULOP-MILLER'S *THE POWER AND SECRET OF THE JESUITS*. (c. 1959). *Fathar*, [6] (Sept. 1974), 46-47.

C249 SEVEN POEMS WITH NOTE. *Manroot*, 10 (Late Fall 1974 / Winter 1975), 26-43.
Contents: IN THE STREET—THE NEW HESPERIDES: AT MARLOWE'S TOMB—ELEGY WRITTEN 4. 7. 53 FOR JACK SPICER—NOTE [ON SOLITUDE]—SOLITUDE—I SAW THE RABBIT LEAP—A DISCOURSE ON LOVE—AND NOW I HAVE RETURND.
Note: The last two poems are from the 1947 period and should be first to keep the chronology accurate.

C250 NOTE. *Manroot*, 10 (Late Fall 1974 / Winter 1975), 146.
Note: The note concerns the contents of Stan Persky's magazine *Open Space*.

C251 [TWO PIECES]. *Io*, 19 (1974), 29-31.
Contents: READING RICH BLEVINS' ESSAY "THE MOMENT OF VISION" AND THINKING OF POUND'S *CANTOS*—NOTES OCT. 31, 1973 ON THE STRUCTURE OF A POETIC TEMPERAMENT.

C252 KOPÓLTUŠ: NOTES ON ROLAND BARTHES, *ELEMENTS OF SEMIOLOGY*. *Credences*, I, 1 [Feb. 1975], 2-6.

C253 [RE JEROME ROTHENBERG]. *Vort*, III, 1, (1957), 127.
Note: This note was originally intended as a blurb for Jerome Rothenberg's book *Poland*, but did not arrive at the publisher's in time to be used.

C254 FROM THE H.D. BOOK. *Credences*, I, 2 (July 1975), 50-94.
Contents: PART II, CHAPTER 5—PART II, CHAPTER 7.—PART II, CHAPTER 8.

C255 (PASSAGES) EMPEDOKLEAN REVERIES. *The Capilano Review*, 8/9 (Fall 1975/ Spring 1976), 300-304.

C256 PASSAGES [HOMAGE TO THE YOUTHFUL POET ZUKOF-SKY, LEADING TOWARD HIS 'A' 23]. *New Poetry*, XXIV, 1 (1976), 32-33.

C257 [TWO POEMS]. *Credences*, I, 3 (May 1976), 56-63.
Contents: AN INTERLUDE OF WINTER LIGHT   PASSAGES 37 O!

C258 "I HAVE / NOTHING TO GO ON" (fl). *Wind Bell*, XV, 1 (Summer 1976), 3.

C259 ROBERT DUNCAN'S INTERVIEW. *Unmuzzled Ox*, IV, 2 (1976), 79-96.
Note: A drawing by RD appears as part of the interview, page 87. The interview was conducted by Howard Mesch.

C260 "THE BLESSED HERBERT IN HIS LOVE DOES SING"(fl). *Unmuzzled Ox*, IV, 2 (1976), 91.
Note: This is a facsimile reproduction of the RD holograph version of the poem written in the limited edition of *Heavenly City, Earthly City*.

C261 FROM DANTE ETUDES: III(1)—III(2)—IV(1)—IX. *New Poetry*, XXIV, 3 (1976), 11-17.

C262 A PARTISAN VIEW. *Meanjin Quarterly*, XXV, 4 (Dec. 1976), 368-369.
Note: This is a review of *Contemporary American & Australian Poetry*, ed. Thomas Shapcott.

C263 IN THE SOUTH. *New Poetry*, XXIV, 4 (Nov. 1976-Feb. 1977), 31-34.

C264 CIRCULATIONS OF THE SONG AFTER JALAL AL-DIN RUMI. *Partisan Review*, XLIV, 1 (1977), [87-98].

C265 TO MASTER BAUDELAIRE. *Credences*, II, 1 (March 1977), 36-40.
Contents: TOWARD HIS MALAISE—AMONG HIS WORDS—THE FACE.

C266 AN ALTERNATE LIFE. *New Poetry*, XXV, 2 (June 1977), 5-20.

C267 ENTRETIEN AVEC ROBERT DUNCAN. *Le Bulletin Centre national d'art et culture Georges Pompidou*, 3 (June / Sept, 1977), 16-18.
Note: The interview was conducted by Laurence Louppe.

C268 [THREE PIECES]. *Firehouse*, 21 (19 Feb. 1978), [1], [3-4].
Contents: THE STRUCTURE OF RIME VIII—FROM *THE H.D. BOOK*; CHAPTER 5—FROM "PREFACE" TO *CAESAR'S GATE* (1972).

C269 LE SONNET OÙ SONNE LA SONNETTE DÈS LES DERNIÈRS [*sic*] JOURS TOUJOURS FAIT SON RETOUR. *Credences*, II, 2/3 (March 1978), 60-63.

C270 POETRY BEFORE LANGUAGE. *The Journal of Biological Experience: Studies in the Life of the Body*, I, 1 (Summer 1978), 46-50.

C271 ROBERT DUNCAN / ALLEN GINSBERG: DISCUSSION. *Big Sky*, 11/12 (1978), 46-50.
Note: This piece is reprinted from *Allen Verbatim*, ed. Gordon Ball.

C272 [TWO ESSAYS]. *Boundary 2*, VI, 1 (Spring / Fall 1978), 233-239, 293-199.
Contents: AFTER *FOR LOVE*—A READING OF *THIRTY THINGS*.

C273 AS TESTIMONY: READING ZUKOFSKY THESE FORTY YEARS. *Paideuma*, VII, 3 (Winter 1978), 421-427.

C274 AN ENTRY. *Foot*, 6 (1978), [25-26].
Note: This poem is dated 1957.

C275 FOR THE ASSIGNATION OF THE SPIRIT. *Wind Bell*, XVI, 1 (Winter 1978-79), 41.

C276 THE H.D. BOOK, PART TWO: NIGHTS AND DAYS, CHAPTER 9. *Chicago Review*, XXX, 3 (Winter 1979), 37-88.

C277 JOHNNY'S THING. *Truck*, 21 ([Spring 1979]), [42].

C278 AT CAMBRIDGE AN ADDRESS TO YOUNG POETS NATIVE TO THE LAND OF MY MOTHERTONGUE. *Periodics: A Magazine Devoted to Prose*, 5 (Spring 1979), 35-36.

C279 VEIL TURBINE CORD BIRD. *Bombay Gin*, 6 (Summer 1978-Spring 1979), 50-53.

C280 THE WORLD OF JAIME DE ANGULO [A CONVERSATION BETWEEN BOB CALLAHAN AND ROBERT DUNCAN]. *The Netahualcoyotl News*, I, 1 (Summer 1979), [1], 5, 14-16.

C281 ROBERT DUNCAN: INTERVIEW [BY AARON SHURIN AND STEVE ABBOTT]. *Gay Sunshine*, 40/41 (1979), [1]-8.
Note: Three photographs of RD appear with the interview: (1) RD reading in Australia; (2) RD Summer 1942, Berkeley; (3) photo by Harry Redl of RD with Jess, and portrait, San Francsico, 1957.

C282 INTERVIEW / WORKSHOP WITH ROBERT DUNCAN [BY AARON SHURIN AND STEVE ABBOTT]. *Soup*, [1] (1980), 30-57, 79.
Note: This interview contains additional material from the interview published in *Gay Sunshine*. See C281.

C283 AN INTERVIEW WITH ROBERT DUNCAN [BY EKBERT FAAS]. *Boundary 2*, VII, 2 (Winter 1980), 1-19.

C284 AN INTERVIEW WITH ROBERT DUNCAN [BY JACK R. COHN AND THOMAS J. O'DONNELL]. *Contemporary Literature*, XXI, 4 (Autumn 1980), 513-548.

C285 FROM THE H.D. BOOK PART II· NIGHTS AND DAYS CHAPTER 11, *Montemora*, 8 (1981), 79-113.

C286 THE CLOSENESS OF MAN: AN INTERVIEW WITH ROBERT DUNCAN, BY GERALD NICOSIA. *The Unspeakable Vision of the Individual*, 12 (1981), 13-27.
Note: This issue of the magazine has a separate title, *Beat Angels*.

C287 [TWO POEMS]. *Temenos*, 1 (1981), 107-109.
Contents: THE CHERUBIM (1)—THE CHERUBIM (2).

C288 REFLECTOR INTERVIEW: ROBERT DUNCAN. *Reflector* (1982), 49-59.

C289 CRISIS OF SPIRIT IN THE WORD. *Credences*, new series II, 1 (Summer 1982), 63-68.

C290 [NOTE AND POEM]. *WCH WAY*, 4 (Summer 1982), 5-16.
Contents: STATEMENT BY THE AUTHOR ON THE FOLLOW-ING POEM—SANTA CRUZ PROPOSITIONS.

C291 [THREE POEMS]. *Hambone*, 2 (Fall 1982), 115-120.
Contents: QUAND LE GRAND FOYER DESCEND DANS LES EAUX [PASSAGES]—ENTHRALLD—*PASSAGES* AFTER PASSAGES.

C292 CIRCULATIONS OF THE SONG AFTER JALĀL AL-DĪN RŪMĪ. *Temenos*, 4 (1983), 77-86.

C293 [EIGHT POEMS]. *Ironwood*, XI, 2 (Fall 1983), 28-32D, 136-139.
Contents: WHOSE—CLOSE—AT THE DOOR—THE DIG-NITIES—FOR ME TOO, I, LONG AGO SHIPPING OUT WITH

THE CANTOS—CHILDHOOD'S RETREAT—AND IF HE HAD
BEEN WRONG FOR ME—CHILDLESS.

C294 [TWO PROSE SELECTIONS]. *Ironwood*, XI, 2 (Fall 1983), 47-64,
95-133.
Contents: THE H.D. BOOK: BOOK II CHAPTER 10—LETTERS
TO ROBIN BLASER & JACK SPICER.
Note: The letters to Blaser and Spicer were edited by Gary Burnett.

C295 [TWO ESSAYS]. *Convivio*, 1 (1983), 15-29, 129-145.
Contents: THE ADVENTURE OF WHITMAN'S LINE—THE
SELF IN POSTMODERN POETRY.

C296 LET ME JOIN YOU AGAIN. *Convivio*, 1 (1983), 30-35.

C297 THE ACTIVE MODE OF COMPOSITION. *Convivio*, 1 (1983),
72-94.
Note: A subtitle for this title is "STUDENT NOTES FROM
LECTURES BY ROBERT DUNCAN IN 1980-81." The selection was
edited by John Thorpe from notes taken by himself, Carl Grundberg,
and Louis Patler at RD lectures at the New College.

D.
Program Notes for Readings
Book Blurbs
Drawings
Christmas Cards
Notes Distributed to Classes
   and Readings
Other

D1   Program Notes for Poetry Readings at The Poetry Center, San Francisco State College.

a. Randall Jarrell
Date: 3 Oct. 1956
Collation: 2*l* recto, recto 27.9 x 21.6 cm.
Contents: The notes include a list of books, "Biographical Particulars," "Descriptive Criticism," and are signed (with a typewriter) "Robert Duncan | Assistant Director | The Poetry Center."

b. Robert Duncan
Date: 10 Oct. 1956
Collation: 1*l* recto 27.9 x 21.6 cm.
Contents: The notes include a list of books, "Biographical Particulars," and a fifteen line statement under the heading, "Of His Work Robert Duncan Writes."

c. Allen Ginsberg and Gregory Corso
Date: 21 Oct. 1956
Collation: 2*l* recto, recto 27.9 x 21.6 cm.
Contents: The notes include a list of books, "Program Notes," and a twenty-six line statement under the heading, "'Two People Who Are Not Afraid': A Critical Note."

d. Madeline Gleason and Brother Antoninus, O. P. (William Everson)
Date: 2 Dec. 1956
Collation: 3*l* all recto 27.9 x 21.6 cm.
Contents: The notes include a partial listing of books and a two page, single spaced statement under the heading, "Memoirs of Our Time and Place."

e. Richard Wilbur
Date: 12 Dec. 1956
Collation: 2*l* recto, recto 27.9 x 21.6 cm.
Contents: The notes include a list of books, "Biographical Particulars," and a "Descriptive History."

f. Charles Olson
Date: 21 Feb. 1957
Collation: 3*l* all recto 27.9 x 21.6 cm.
Contents: The notes consist of a list of books, a list of articles on literary theory, "Biographical Particulars," and long single spaced statements under the headings, "Notes," "Background," and "Poetics."

g. A Group Reading of "The Will," a work in progress by Robert Duncan
Date: March 1957

Collation: 1*l* recto 27.9 x 21.6 cm.

Contents: The notes consist of a list of the cast and a three paragraph statement under the heading, "Notes on the Writing of the Play."

h. Robert Lowell

Date: 27 March 1957

Collation: 2*l* recto, recto 27.9 x 21.6 cm.

Contents: The notes consist of a list of books, "Biographical Particulars," and a four paragraph statement under the heading, "Notes."

i. Helen Adam and Jess Collins

Date: 7 April 1957

Collation: 1*l* recto 27.9 x 21.6 cm.

Contents: The notes consist of a two paragraph statement under the heading, "Memoirs of Our Time and Place."

j. William Everson

Date: 11 April 1957

Collation: 1*l* recto 27.9 x 21.6 cm.

Contents: The notes consist of a partial listing of books and a two paragraph statement under the heading, "Memoirs of Our Time and Place," which is the same text that appeared in the notes for the reading of 2 Dec. 1956.

k. Helen Adam and Jack Spicer

Date: 11 April 1957

Collation: 1*l* recto 27.9 x 21.6 cm.

Contents: The notes consist of a one page statement about the two poets under the heading, "Notes."

l. A Workshop Reading "Poetry As Magic"

Date: 9 June 1957

Collation: 1*l* recto 27.9 x 21.6 cm.

Contents: The notes consist of a three paragraph statement under the heading, "Notes," and a list of the poets who will read.

m. Jack Spicer and Conrad Pendleton

Date: [Fall 1957]

Collation: 2*l* recto, recto 27.9 x 21.6 cm.

Contents: A three paragraph statement appears under the heading, "Notes on Jack Spicer: Memoirs of Our Time and Place." There is also a ten line statement about Conrad Pendleton.

n. Marianne Moore

Date: 11 Oct. 1957

Collation: 2*l* recto, recto 27.9 x 21.6 cm.

Contents: The notes consist of a short list of books and then a two page, single spaced statement under the heading, "Notes on the Poetics of Marianne Moore."

o. Denise Levertov
Date: 19 Jan. 1958
Collation: 2*l* recto, recto 27.9 x 21.6 cm.
Contents: The notes consist of a list of books, "Biographical Notes," and a page-and-a-half, single spaced statement under the heading, "Introductory Notes."

p. A Group Reading of Plays by James Keilty
Date: 25 Jan. 1959
Collation: 1*l* recto 27.9 x 21.6 cm.
Contents: The notes consist of a list of the readers for the plays. RD contributed a seven line statement.

q. Robert Duncan
Date: 1 March 1959
Collation: 4*l* all recto 27.9 x 21.6 cm.
Contents: The notes consist of a list of the books RD will read from and then a list of the poems. A two paragraph statement under the heading, "A Disclosure," and a three paragraph statement under the heading, "Memoirs of My Time and Place" follow the list.

r. Robert Duncan
Date: 2 March 1959
Collation: 3*l* all recto 27.9 x 21.6 cm.
Contents: The notes consist of a bibliography, a list of the poems RD will read, a two paragraph statement under the heading, "A Disclosure," and a three paragraph statement under the heading, "Memoirs of My Time and Place."

s. Robert Creeley
Date: 16 July 1959
Collation: 3*l* all recto 27.7 x 21.6 cm.
Contents: The notes consist of a short bibliography, a two paragraph statement under the heading, "Notes from the Poet," and a seven paragraph statement by RD under the heading, "Introductory Notes."

t. Robert Duncan
Date: 10 Dec. 1963
Collation: 2*l* recto, recto 27.9 x 21.6 cm.
Contents: The notes consist of a list of the poems RD will read, a "Biographical Summary," a list of "Principal Works," and a one page, single-spaced statement under the heading, "Concerning the Art. This December 1963."

u. Robert Duncan
Date: 11 Dec. 1963
Collation: 2*l* recto, recto 27.9 x 21.6 cm.
Contents: The notes consist of a list of the poems RD will read, a one

paragraph statement under the heading, "Summary of Life and Words, Scenes and Times," and a one page statement under the heading, "Concerning the Art. This December 1963."

Note: All these notes have been duplicated in purple ink.

Book Blurbs

D2   Broughton, James. *Musical Chairs.* San Francisco: The Centaur Press, 1950.
Note: Statement on rear flap of dust jacket.

D3   Broughton, James. *True & False Unicorns.* New York: Grove Press, 1957.
Note: Statement on rear cover.

D4   Levertov, Denise. *Overland to the Island.* Highlands, N.C.: Jonathan Williams Publisher, 1958.
Note: Statement on front flap of dust jacket.

D5   Eigner, Larry, *Another Time In Fragments.* London: Fulcrum Press, 1967.
Note: Statement on front flap of dust jacket.

D6   Voelcker, Hunce. *The Hart Crane Voyages.* New York: The Brownstone Press, 1967.
Note: Statement on rear cover. The same statement was reprinted on two separate advertisements for the book by The Brownstone Press and on one advertisement by Tompkin Square Press Ltd.

D7   Dorn, Edward. *Gunslinger 1 & 2.* London: Fulcrum Press, 1970.
Note: Statement on dust jacket of hardbound copies and rear cover of paperbound copies.

D8   Grossinger, Richard. *Solar Journal: Oecological Sections.* Los Angeles: Black Sparrow Press, 1970.
Note: The introduction by RD, on white paper, consists of a single leaf folded twice and is laid in; the same introduction on light blue paper served as the advance announcement for the book.

D9   Broughton, James. *A Long Undressing.* Highlands, N.C.: The Jargon Society, 1971.
Note: Statement on rear of dust jacket.

D10   D[oolittle], H[ilda]. *Hermetic Definition.* New York: New Directions, 1972.
Note: Statement on rear of dust jacket of hardbound copies and rear cover of paperbound copies.

D11   Fredman, Stephen. *Seaslug.* San Francisco: Panjandrum Press, 1973.
Note: Statement on rear cover.

D12 Adam, Helen. *Selected Poems & Ballads*. New York: Helikon Press, 1974. Second Printing.
Note: Statement on rear flap of dust jacket.

D13 Matthias, John. *Turns*. Chicago: The Swallow Press Inc., 1975.
Note: RD quoted in statement on front flap of dust jacket.

D14 Gleason, Madeline. *Here Comes Everybody: New & Selected Poems*. San Francisco: Panjandrum Press, 1975.
Note: Statement on rear cover.

D15 Davidson, Michael. *The Mutabilities & The Foul Papers*. Berkeley: Sand Dollar Books, 1976.
Note: Statement on front flap of dust jacket.

D16 Hogg, Robert. *Of Light*. Toronto: The Coach House Press, 1978.
Note: Statement on rear flap of dust jacket.

D17 D[oolittle], H[ilda]. *End To Torment: A Memoir of Ezra Pound*, ed. Norman Holmes Pearson and Michael King, with poems from "Hilda's Book" by Ezra Pound. New York: New Directions, 1979.
Note: Statement on rear of dust jacket of hardbound copies.

Drawings

D18 [TWO ILLUSTRATIONS]. *The Occident*, XXX, 2 (April 1937), 30, 31.

D19 THE TROTSKYITE MENACE ON CAMPUS. *Campus Review*, [IV, 3] (15 Nov. 1937), 2.

D20 [THREE DRAWINGS, UNTITLED]. *Epitaph*, I, 1 (Spring 1938), [front cover verso, 10, 20].

D21 IMPROVISION ON THE METHOD OF MIRO. *Experimental Review*, 2 (Nov. 1940), [cover design].

D22 [COVER DRAWING]. *The Artist's View*, 5 (July 1953), [1].

D23 [COVER DRAWING]. *George Stanley's The Love Root*. San Francisco: White Rabbit Press, 1958.

D24 [COVER DRAWING]. *Foot*, [1] ([Sept. 1959]).
Note: Reproduced for *Foot*, 3 (1979), as the cover drawing.

D25 [UNTITLED DRAWING]. *Open Space*, 12 (Dec. 1964), [17-18].

D26 SNAKE DRAWING. *Open Space*, 12 (Dec. 1964), [43].

D27 [COVER DRAWING]. *Kenkyusha* (Feb. 1974). Tokyo, Japan.
Note: Drawing of a man leaning over to pet a cat. In RD's holograph: "He hears the request | of a little cat that wanted to run away for an afternoon."

D28 [COVER DRAWING]. *Catalogue of The Tenth Muse #10*, n.d.

D29 [COVER DRAWING]. *Catalogue of The Tenth Muse #17*, n.d.

D30 [COVER DRAWING]. *Catalogue of The Tenth Muse #25*, n.d.

D31 [COVER DRAWING]. *Catalogue of The Tenth Muse #31*, n.d.

D32 [MAP OF POETIC TERRITORY]. Ms. CU-B.
Date: [1951-52]
Collation: 2*l*, 1*l* recto 28 x 21.9 cm., 1*l* recto 21.9 x 14 cm.
Contents: This is a "map" of the poetic position of Duncan and Spicer.

D33 DRAWING. Ms. On deposit at MoSW.
Date: 2 April 1955
Contents: This is a drawing in black ink, with the following lines written over it: "The commentator adds profundities. | The reader | hears | outside the very | nightingale piping."
Note: This drawing accompanied a letter to Robert Creeley, dated 2 April 1955.

D34 THE WORLD OF BLAKE. Ms. NBuU.
Date: 23 April [19]56
Collation: 1*l* recto 30.1 x 21.6 cm.
Contents: This is a drawing done with dark brown ink on tan paper of a squatting figure, with the title at the left and the inscription, "It is | by some Poet's | lightning | immediate | magic," at the right, and at the bottom, "The Cry of the Kicked Beast." At the lower right: "For Helen Adam this 23rd of | April 56." The initials "RD" appear above the final line.

D35 "THE POET'S LOFTY BROW." Ms. CU-SB.
Date: c. 1957
Collation: 1*l* recto 21.5 x 16 cm.
Contents: This is an ink drawing signed and dated by the poet.
Note: This drawing was enclosed in a letter to John Martin, dated 7 July 1966. E759.

D36 [UNTITLED DRAWING]. Ms. CU-SB.
Date: 1959
Collation: 1*l* recto 28 x 21.5 cm.
Contents: There are four ink-and-crayon drawings on this leaf, one of which is an early version of the logo for Enkidu Surrogate press.
Note: The drawings were enclosed in a letter to John Martin, dated 7 July 1966. E759.

D37 [INK DRAWING]. Ms. CtU.
Date: 18 Dec. 1961
Collation: 1*l* recto 23.9 x 8 cm.

Contents: This is a drawing in black ink over a pencil sketch. There are also four lines of unpublished verse on this leaf.

Note: The drawing and verse were enclosed in a letter to Charles Olson, dated 18 Dec. 1961. E571.

D38 [UNTITLED DRAWING]. Ms. CtU.
Date: 1964
Collation: 1l recto 34.2 x 24 cm.
Contents: This is the underdrawing for the broadside "Wine."

D39 "UPON A PROFESSOR READING YEATS" Ms. OKentU.
Date: n. d.
Collation: 1l recto 21.7 x 20.1 cm.
Contents: The drawing is on yellow paper, which has been mounted on a leaf of gray paper, 30.3 x 22.9 cm.

D40 [FOUR DRAWINGS ENTITLED] DIVERTISEMENT. Ms. MoSW.
Date: n. d.
Collation: 2l recto-verso, recto-verso 27.8 x 20.2 cm.
Contents: These are four pen and ink drawings by RD.

D41 [COVER DRAWING]. *Bombay Gin*, 6 (Summer 1978-Spring 1979).

Christmas Cards

Note: In the descriptions of the Christmas Cards, indications of colors follow the letters or words that are colored.

D42 Christmas-New Year's Card. WaU.
Date: [19 Dec. 1956]
Collation: 2l recto-verso, recto 12.8 x 14.5 cm.
Contents: This card is made from a single leaf of white paper folded. Recto of the first leaf contains decorations in black pen around the edge with the two designations "AIRC" and "ROIX" at the top middle of the leaf. Below the greeting, "[in RD's holograph] Greetings from | Robert Duncan | and | [in Jess's holograph] Jess," appears. Verso of the first leaf contains a section 1.5 cm. on each side of the center fold running from top to bottom in salmon, green, gold, blue, brown, orange, ochre, and purple crayons. There is the following inscription running across the central colored section onto recto of the second leaf: "To Eve Triem that in song [black pencil] | JOYOUS ACCLAMATI | [brown crayon] ON Dwells Most True | [black pencil] [ornament] | [green crayon] We send | [orange crayon] [ornament] [green crayon] DECLARATIONS OF JOY FOR | [black pencil] [ornament] | [blue crayon] THE NEW YEAR | [purple crayon] [ornament]." Recto of the second leaf contains the following poem in RD's holograph (black ink): "Our arts | we devote to | acclamation | of the Word | with salmon | with blue | with gold | in the green | acclaim | O ye souls | that begrudge | the Lord! | with orange | with ochre | with purple | in the green | acclaim | Joy in the year."

D43 Christmas Card. TxU.

Date: 1958

Collation: 2*l* recto, recto 13.9 x 9.6 cm.

Contents: Recto of the first leaf contains a pencil drawing by the author and is initialed "RD." The edges of the white paper are colored with green crayon. Recto of the second leaf contains a thirteen line poem in the author's holograph beginning, "With winter roses let there be bronze." The same page contains pencil drawings by the author, and "Robert Duncan | Jess Collins | 1958-1959" in holograph.

D44 Christmas Card. CU-B.

Date: [1959]

Collation: 2*l* recto-verso, recto 13.5 x 8.8 cm.

Contents: This card is made from a single sheet folded. On recto of the first leaf appears a drawing in red, yellow, green, and brown crayon, while on the verso in typescript the following: "Christmas | Greetings | from | Robert Duncan." Recto of the second leaf contains a fifteen line typescript (black ribbon) of a poem beginning, "O Christmas Eve."

D45 Christmas Card. CtY.

Date: 25 Dec. [1959]

Collation: 2*l* recto-verso, recto 16.3 x 7.1 cm.

Contents: This card is made from a single leaf of white paper folded. Recto of the first leaf contains a pencil drawing of a rose and the initials "RD." Verso of the first leaf contains the following inscription in the poet's holograph at the bottom: "Robert Duncan 1959-1960." Recto of the second leaf contains a twenty line poem beginning, "seed that in March | died in the earth," in the poet's holograph.

D46 Christmas Card. CtU (2 copies), CaBVaS, CtY, OKentU.

Date: 1959-60.

Collation: 1*l* recto-verso 12.3 x 7.8 cm., 1*l* recto 14.9 x 12 cm.

Contents: The second leaf consists of one sheet of stiff paper to which has been pasted a border of red and gold design, 1.3 cm. wide, which comes to the edge at top, bottom, and left, but which leaves a 1.5 cm. strip running from top to bottom at right, in which is written in RD's holograph, from top to bottom, "1959/60." In the center of the second leaf have been pasted two leaves, 12.3 x 7.8 cm., so that verso of the second leaf of that insert becomes part of the original backing and the recto becomes the recto of the original first leaf. The recto of the first leaf, then, is decorated with green, blue, red, and yellow colored pencils and inscribed, in RD's holograph at the top, "Greetings" in black pen and likewise at bottom left, "Robert," and at bottom right, "and Jess." Across the verso of the first leaf and the recto of the second leaf, in RD's holograph (black pen), is the translation of Rilke's poem, "The Child." The following inscription also appears: "The Child [black ink] from [purple pencil] Rilke [black ink] 's [brown pencil] Neuen Gedichte | anderer Teil [blue pencil] 31 July-1 August 1907 [black ink]." Below the text of the poem appears a footnote for the word "trage" used in the poem. Signed "RD" at the bottom, with a purple line running across between the poem and the footnote.

Note: The copy described was mailed to Charles Olson. It is missing the date "1959/60," but another copy (CtU) does contain it. Also to Michael McClure. CaBVaS. Also to Norman Holmes Pearson. CtY. The card at OKentU has been numbered "1969-70" and an a. n. s. by Jess appears on the verso of the principal leaf.

D47 Christmas Card. CtY, CU-B.
      Date: [14 Dec. 1961]
      Collation: 1*l* recto 9.6 x 14.5 cm.
      Contents: This card consists of one leaf of white paper with an ink drawing colored in with brown, yellow, and orange crayons. The inscription "RD Christmas 1961" appears at the bottom of the leaf in the poet's holograph (pencil). A more elaborately decorated card is at CU-B. E568.

D48 Christmas Card. CtU, TxU.
      Date: [1961]
      Collation: 2*l* recto, recto 13.1 x 10.2 cm.
      Contents: Two leaves are formed from a single leaf of tan rice-like paper. Recto of the first leaf contains a picture of "The Pine Tree Fairy," 11.2 x 8 cm., pasted on. Recto of the second leaf is inscribed in RD's holograph, "YULE | TIDE | TIDE | Robert and Jess [black ink]."
      Note: A similar card was mailed to Louis Zukofsky (TxU).

D49 Christmas Card. CU-B.
      Date: [1962?]
      Collation: 1*l* recto-verso 9.5 x 12 cm.
      Contents: The verso is a colored reproduction of a bird. Lettering on the verso in red pen with white inside the block letters reads: "Christmas Joys, | ROBIN | From Robert and Jess, O!"

D50 Christmas Card. CtY.
      Date: 1962
      Collation: 2*l* recto, recto 19.6 x 7.3 cm.
      Contents: This card consists of two leaves of gold paper. Recto of leaf one contains a color illustration of an angel pasted on, while the recto of leaf two contains an inscription, date, and the poet's signature.

D51 Christmas Card. CtU, TxU, CU-B.
      Date: 1962
      Collation: 2*l* recto-verso, recto 15.3 x 11.4 cm.

Contents: The two leaves are formed from a single leaf of light brown, folded construction paper. A picture of Orpheus playing a lyre and surrounded by animals has been pasted on the recto of the first leaf. Verso of the first leaf contains the inscription in RD's holograph, "from Robert | and | Jess." Recto of the second leaf contains the inscription in RD's holograph, "for Betty & Charles | this Christmas tide | and year's turn | 1962-1963." Six lines of unidentified but printed poetry have been pasted on, lower right of recto two.

Note: A similar card was mailed to Louis Zukofsky (TxU) and a more elaborate one to Robin Blaser (CU-B).

D52 FROM *THE MABINOGION*.

Date: [1963]

Collation: 8*l* all recto-verso, plus one leaf as cover, with cover title 23 x 15.4 cm.

Contents: This is an offprint, with a cover stapled to the leaves twice, of the poems RD published in *Quarterly Review of Literature*. The poems are: FROM *THE MABINOGION*—DOVES—A NEW POEM—TWO MESSAGES—RETURNING TO THE RHETORIC OF AN EARLY MODE. Some copies were used as a Christmas Card for 1963. These copies have an illustration in RD's hand on the inside front cover.

D53 Christmas Card. CU-B.

Date: 1963

Collation: 1*l* recto-verso 12.7 x 14.5 cm.

Contents: The card is made from white paper and has on the recto a colored reproduction of a woman with four children before her. A rose has been pasted on so that it sits in her hand. Lettering in black at lower left reads, "from | Robert | and Jess," and at lower right in red on gold tape pasted on, "Season's Greetings." The verso contains a colored reproduction of a humming bird at a flower. Two red-and-yellow flowers (reproductions) have been pasted on. Lettering down the right edge reads, "1963 [dot] 4."

D54 Christmas Card. CU-B.

Date: [Dec. 1964]

Collation: 2*l* recto, recto 11.2 x 11.5 cm.

Contents: The card is made from a single piece of orange construction paper. The first leaf has been folded over from the bottom right to upper left, forming a triangle, and so exposing the bottom triangular section of the second leaf. Lettering on the first leaf in black ink reads, "Xmas," and lettering on the second leaf following down the line of the fold, "Robins," and then to the right, "64." A second card at CU-B follows a similar construction.

D55 Christmas Card. CaBVaS.

Date: [16 Dec. 1964]

Collation: 2*l* recto-verso; 1*l* 23.5 x 15.9 cm., 1*l* 23.8 x 16.1 cm.

Contents: Recto of the first leaf is a color reproduction entitled "Tiny Tim." Verso of the first leaf has at the left margin, running from top to bottom, the inscription in RD's holograph, "Christmas [ornament] | [ornament] Greetings" [black pen], and has running along the bottom margin, "1964-65 [space] Robert Duncan & Jess Collins [black pen]." Recto of the second leaf is made of red construction paper. There is a band of gold tape running across the top and bottom of the verso of the first leaf and the recto of the second leaf; the tape runs vertically at the joint of the two leaves and forms a binding. In the middle of the recto of the second leaf is a black and white reproduction of carolers and, below, the text of the carol "Chrystmasse of Olde," 15.4 x 10.6 cm., is pasted onto the red paper.

D56 Christmas Card. CtU, CaBVaS.

Date: [1964]

Collation: 2*l* recto, recto 16.4 x 11.5 cm.

Contents: The two leaves are formed from a single leaf of red, folded construction paper. A piece of bright blue paper has been pasted on the recto of the first leaf, and then a picture of a crèche scene is pasted on leaving a 1 cm. border of blue paper around the picture. The greeting "A Peaceful Christmas" appears in RD's holograph at the top recto of the first leaf. Recto of the second leaf contains a passage in RD's holograph from Boehme's *Aurora*, and is signed "Robert and Jess" in the lower left corner.

Note: It seems that all the cards for 1964 were made from red construction paper. A card in the personal collection of Jonathan Williams confirms this, as does the card to Michael McClure now at CaBVaS.

D57 Christmas Card. CtU (2 copies), InU.

Date: 1965

Collation: 6*l*; 1*l* recto-verso, 4*l* all recto, 1*l* blank, 13.4 x 17.1 cm.

Contents: Recto of the first leaf contains a decoration in RD's hand in white, blue, and black crayons and the holograph inscription, "Earth's Winter Song." Verso of the first leaf contains the holograph inscription, "our fond wishes and | salutations | to my fellow | child of mid-winter | Christling-Beast | Robert." Rectos of leaves two to five contain the poem EARTH'S WINTER SONG in RD's holograph as published in *BB*, pp. 93-95. Signed "RD/1965" on the recto of leaf 5.

Note: Similar cards are in the possession of Jonathan Williams and in the collection at CtU, as sent to John Martin. Another card mailed to Henry Rago is also similar and contains the following inscription on the verso of the first leaf: "with our fond wishes | and

remembrance | Christmas 1965 | Robert Duncan | and | Jess Collins"
(InU).

D58   Christmas Card. CU-B.
Date: 1965
Collation: 1*l* recto 14.4 x 15.4 cm.
Contents: The card is made from green construction paper. A colored reproduction of a girl floating in a green shell, 10.2 x 12.1 cm., has been pasted on. Lettering at the top in black ink reads, "Christmas [space] 1965," and the lines below the reproduction read: "When each day is opened may all its hours sing | and all your wishes be as gifts | to set before the King | for Robin and Stan from Jess and Robert."

D59   Christmas Card. CtY.
Date: 1965
Collation: 3*l*; 2*l* recto-verso, recto-verso 8.4 x 14.1 cm.; 1*l* recto-verso 8.4 x 7 cm.
Contents: The card is made from a single piece of white paper folded once. The third leaf, which is surrounded with gold tape, is attached to the top of the second leaf and folds over it. Recto of the first leaf contains a circular design in pink, orange, yellow, and blue crayons, and over it in gold lettering, "B O R N | AI." Verso of the first leaf and recto of the second leaf contain a color illustration of a fairy talking to a fish, with the lettering in gold, "F & | SING." Recto of the attached piece contains another illustration and the word "NOEL," while its verso contains the following lettering in black ink: "FOR A HAPPY | NEW YEAR | Design 1965 | from Robert and Jess." Verso of the second leaf contains a colored illustration of a grasshopper with the letter "g" in gold.

D60   Christmas Card. CtY, InU, NBuU, CU-B.
Date: 1966
Collation: 1*l* recto 24 x 18.6 cm.
Contents: This card is composed of a single leaf of stiff light green paper, 24 x 18.6 cm., onto which has been pasted another leaf, 22.4 x 18.1 cm., which is the trimmed-down p. [88] of *BR*. The center section which in other cards contains the poem THE SCATTERING has been covered over with a leaf of light green paper, 8.2 x 13.2 cm., on which has been inscribed the following message with colored pens: "W [orange] e heard it as a cry. [blue] I [orange] t was the [blue] W [orange] ord [blue]. | Today [red] is [green] Bethlehem [red] ! [green] I [red] n each the [green] B [red] abe again [green] | heralded, denied a place, given all gifts [blue] | the human store of [green] K [orange] ingship [green], M [orange] agic and [green] | W [orange] isdom may bring [green]. T [red] hen, at last, the [blue] | Crucifixion [red], everlasting T [red] estament and [blue] | F [orange] iction of [green] T [orange] ruth upon the [green] C [orange] ross faced and | redeemd [green]. W [orange] e heard it as a cry [blue]. Today [red] | is [green]

Jerusalem [red] ! [green] Today Today Today [orange] the [green] |
Why hast Thou forsaken me [blue]. Today [red] | the apostasy [green] !
Today [orange], faith lost, given away [green] | We rise again to life in
[blue] Thee [red] | —RD [brown]." At bottom left, "1966-7" [brown],
and at bottom right, "JS" (black).

D61 Christmas Card. CtY.
Date: 1967 (?)
Collation: 2*l* recto, recto 15.9 x 10.8 cm.
Contents: An oval has been cut out of the first leaf, and an old
commercial Christmas card has been pasted on the verso of the first
leaf so that a scene of a rural winter and the inscription "A Merry
Christmas" shows through the oval. The card is made out of white
paper, but the pasted on paper is bright blue. Recto of the second leaf
contains an inscription and the signatures, "Robert Duncan | Jess
Collins."

D62 Christmas Card. CaBVaS.
Date: [10 Dec. 1968]
Collation: 2*l* recto-verso, recto 14.5 x 18.5 cm.
Contents: Recto of the first leaf is made of tan paper with green tape
at the top edge forming a binding. Verso of the first leaf contains a
color reproduction of a lion and the following inscription: "Dear
Michael & Jo Ann | & Jane—we wish | you the happiest of holidays |
[in green crayon in Jess's holograph] and a lion's lordly share | of the
year's good things | [in red crayon in RD's holograph] R [in green
crayon] obert | [in red crayon] Love | Jess [in green crayon]." Recto of
the second leaf contains a color reproduction of a lion.

D63 Christmas Card. OKentU, MoSW.
Date: 11 Dec. [1968]
Collation: 2*l* recto-verso, recto 28.2 x 21.5 cm.
Contents: This card is made from two leaves from Jess's book
Gallowsongs, with the printed matter appearing on the verso of the
first leaf and the recto of the second leaf. On the recto of the first leaf
is the note in RD's hand, "A Calendar page for your New Year from
Jess's Morgenstern translations & illustrations, the whole happily
may find its publication in 1969." Then follow fourteen lines of a
poem entitled, A GLIMPSE. Initialed "RD."

D64 Christmas Card. NBuU.
Date: [Dec. 1970]
Collation: 3*l*; 2*l* recto-verso, recto-verso 15 x 18.1 cm.; 1*l* recto 14.5 x
18.1 cm.
Contents: This card is made from two leaves of a children's book. The
front cover has gold and orange paper pasted on it, and then a black
and white cutout figure of a winged lion, with one paw holding up a
book, has been pasted on the paper. The inscription below in Jess's

hand reads, "Dear Helen and Pat—I hope your holidays are grand!" Verso of the first leaf contains a colored reproduction of a tiger, while recto of the second leaf contains a colored reproduction of a jaguar. There are further inscriptions on these leaves and an a. n. s. by Jess on the verso of the second leaf. A strip of green tape binds the leaves together. Recto of the third leaf, which is laid in, contains an a. n. s. by RD.

D65 Christmas Card. CaBVaS, CtY.
Date: [8 Dec. 1971]
Collation: 2*l* recto-verso, recto; 1*l* 8.4 x 10.5 cm., 1*l* 17.1 x 10.6 cm.
Contents: The card is made from the cover stock from *The Cat and the Blackbird*. Recto of the first leaf contains an address and stamp. Verso of the first leaf contains designs from *The Cat and the Blackbird*. Recto of the second leaf contains the following inscription: "Happy [green pen] | [pink rule] | Turn of the Year [green pen] | [gold rule] | with love to | Michael & Joanne & Jane | from Jess | [blue pen] and Robert [black pen] | [gold rule]." All but RD's signature is in Jess's holograph.
Note. A similar card was sent to Norman Holmes Pearson as the holiday greeting for 1972 CtY.

D66 Christmas Card. CtY, OKentU.
Date: 1971
Collation: 2*l* recto-verso, recto-verso; 1*l* 21.5 x 18.2 cm., 1*l* 21.5 x 17.4 cm.
Contents: This card is made from a single leaf folded. Recto of the first leaf contains an ink drawing by Jess illustrating the text of RD's poem THE BURNING BABE, which appears in the poet's holograph on the verso of the first leaf, recto-verso of the second leaf. An illustration by the poet and the inscription "November RD 1971" appear on the verso of the second leaf. This card was reproduced by the photo-offset process.

D67 Christmas Card. CtU.
Date: n. d.
Collation: 2*l* recto, recto 15.2 x 12 cm.
Contents: The two leaves are formed out of a single leaf of purple construction paper with a top fold. Recto of the first leaf is in RD's holograph: "To | Charles and Betty [black pen] | Seasons Greetings [pasted-on gold decal with red lettering and small green Christmas trees at either end of a 0.7 x 7.3 cm. strip] | from | Robert and Jess [black pen]." Recto of the second leaf contains a pasted on picture of a woman surrounded by five children.

D68 Christmas Card. OKentU.
Date: n. d.
Collation: 2*l* recto-verso, recto 13.4 x 9 cm.
Contents: Recto of the first leaf contains a colored drawing of a

woman holding a lamb. Verso of the first leaf contains the following in typescript (black ribbon): "Christmas | Greetings | from | ROBERT and JESS." Recto of the second leaf contains a fifteen line poem beginning, "O Christmas Eve." Verso of the second leaf is blank.

Notes For Classes and Readings

D69 WORKSHOP IN BASIC TECHNIQUES.
Date: 24 Sept. 1958
Collation: 2l recto, recto 27.9 x 21.6 cm.
Contents: This is a questionnaire (duplicated) for RD's class.

D70 From NOTES ON THE STRUCTURE OF RIME DONE FOR WARREN TALLMAN SPRING 1961.
Collation: 2l recto, recto 35.7 x 21.6 cm.
Contents: This is a typescript (mimeographed) of the text of the notes as printed in *Maps*, 6 (1974), 42-45, with some additions and revisions.

D71 NOTES ON POETICS REGARDING OLSON'S *MAXIMUS*.
[Vancouver, B.C.: Privately published, 1961].
Collation: 5l all recto 35.5 x 21.8 cm.
Note: The essay was mimeographed in an unknown number of copies and distributed to the members of Warren Tallman's classes at the University of British Columbia.

D72 IDEAS OF THE MEANING OF FORM. [Vancouver: Privately published, 1961]. UC.
Collation: 10l all recto 21.5 x 35.5 cm.
Note: This mimeographed version of the essay was printed for Warren Tallman's classes at the University of British Columbia. The essay was published in an altered version in *Kulchur* 4 (1961), 60-74. This copy is inscribed affectionately to Charles Olson on the top and bottom of the front page and signed by RD. The inscription reads, in part: "This copy for the man who most demands of me the effort that awakens radiance in life. Whose *Projective Verse* essay still challenges and cannot be taken for granted in my thought. Each time I understand it anew."

D73 [ONE POEM AND A NOTE]. CU-S.
Titles: PASSAGES 26: THE SOLDIERS—FROM A NOTEBOOK.
Date: [1966?]
Collation: 3l all recto, 35.5 x 21.5 cm.
Contents: This is a typescript (mimeographed) of the text of the poem as it appeared in *Of the War*, pp. [10-13], and a selection from FROM A NOTEBOOK as it appeared in *The New American Poetry*, pp. 401-402.

Note: The place and date of the printing of this item are unknown. Also, it is not known how many copies were printed, or for what occasion.

D74 [STATEMENT FOR SOCIETY FOR INDIVIDUAL RIGHTS].
a. WELCOME TO S. I. R.
Date: [1968]
Contents: RD contributed one paragraph of seventeen lines for this announcement for a reading.
b. WELCOME TO THE SECOND ANNUAL S. I. R. POETRY READING
Date: [1969]
Contents: RD contributed the same statement as in item "a."

D75 PREFACE TO A READING OF PASSAGES 1-22.
Date: 6 March 1970.
Collation: 2*l* recto, recto 27.9 x 21.6 cm.
Contents: This is the text (mimeographed) of the statement as published in *Maps*, 6 (1974), 53-55.
Note: This statement was handed out at a reading of the poems in Berkeley sponsored by Cody's Books.

D76 PROSPECTUS FOR "STUDIES IN IDEAS OF THE POETIC IMAGINATION." OKentU.
Date: 1972
Collation: 1*l* recto 27.9 x 21.6 cm.
Contents: This is a prospectus (photocopied) for a three-week course taught at Kent State University in the fall of 1972.

Other Publications

D77 Advertisement for the Capricorn Press. *Experimental Review*, II (Nov. 1940), [83-84].

D78 Advertisement for *Experimental Review* No. 4. NBuB.
Date: Sept. 1941
Collation: 1*l* recto 27.9 x 21.6 cm.
Contents: This is the advertisement for the fourth issue of the magazine laid into the third issue.

D79 Letter. CU-B.
Date: April 1953
Collation: 1*l* recto 27.9 x 21.6 cm.
Contents: This is a letter written to raise money for the Kingubu Gallery.

D80 [Statement]. San Francisco: Poetry Center, San Francisco State College, 1956.

Note: RD is quoted on p. [4] of this four page announcement for the readings during the fall season of 1956.

D81 [Statement for] Poetry Center Calendar. San Francisco: Poetry Center, San Francisco State College, 1957.
Note: RD is quoted on p. [2] of this eight leaf announcement for the Spring 1957 calendar of readings.

D82 Easter Card. A. ms. NBuU.
Date: Easter 1957
Collation: 2*l* recto-verso, recto 16.2 x 15.5 cm., as folded.
Contents: The recto of the first leaf contains an ink drawing of lilies initialed by RD, and the verso of the first leaf contains the inscription: "for Helen, Pat and Mother Adam| Easter 1957." Recto of the second leaf contains a nine line unpublished poem beginning, "I sing praise of song that is not mine." Second verso is blank.
Note: The card is made from heavy white wove paper folded once.

D83 Duncan, Robert. [On *Letters*]. [Flyer]. Highlands, N. C. : Jonathan Williams, [1958].
Note: RD contributes an 18 line statement about his book *Letters*. The flyer also includes information about the cost of the book.

D84 [Contributor's Note]. *Jubilee: a magazine of the church and her people*, IX, 7 (Nov. 1961), 1.

D85 Program Notes for *Adam's Way*.
a. Notes for production of Act One, 1 Oct. 1962, at San Francisco Tape Music Center.
Collation: 1*l* recto, but folded to make two leaves, 21.5 x 21.9 cm.
Note: The printed matter (in blue ink) verso first leaf and recto second leaf.
Contents: The cast of players, drawings, and a statement about the writing of the play.
b. Notes for production of the whole play, 17 and 22 June 1976, at the San Francisco Museum of Art.
Collation: 2*l* recto-verso, recto 10.9 x 14 cm.
Contents: Recto of the first leaf contains a drawing by RD, verso of the first leaf contains a statement about the play; recto of the second leaf contains the cast of players, verso of the second leaf is blank.

**E.
Letters**

E1   Dillon, George. t. l. s., 1*l* recto 27.8 x 21.6 cm. Provincetown, Mass., [17 July 1941]. ICU.

E2   Sirs [Dillon, George]. t. l. s., 2*l* recto, recto 27.9 x 21.6 cm. Berkeley, [April 1942]. ICU.

E3   Sirs [Quinn, Kerker]. a. l. s., 1*l* recto 28 x 21.6 cm. New York City, [1944]. IU.

E4   Ransom, [John Crowe]. t. l., 2*l* recto, recto 28 x 21.6 cm. [New York City], [Oct. 1944]. MoSW.

E5   Quinn, [Kerker]. a. l. s., 1*l* recto 27.9 x 21.5 cm. Guerneville, Calif., [Dec. 1945]. IU.

E6   Sirs [Quinn, Kerker]. a. p. c. s., 1*l* verso 14 x 8.2 cm. Guerneville, Calif., [31 Jan. 1946]. IU.

E7   [Spicer, Jack]. a. l. s., 1*l* recto-verso 28 x 21.7 cm. Treesbank [Sebastopol, Calif., 1947]. CU-B.
Note: A typescript of FOUR PIECES accompanied this letter. F16.

E8   [Spicer], Jack. a. l. s., 2*l* recto-verso, recto-verso 28 x 21.7 cm. Treesbank [Sebastopol, Calif., 1947]. CU-B.
Note: A typescript of the poem A THIRD DISCOURSE ON LOVE appears on the verso, and the typescript of FRAGMENT OF A DRAMA accompanied this letter. F15.

E9   Stephan, Ruth. a. l. s., 1*l* recto 27.9 x 21.6 cm. Berkeley, 1947. CtY.

E10   Stephan, Ruth. a. l. s., 1*l* recto 21.6 x 14.2 cm. [Berkeley, 1947]. CtY.

E11   Stephan, [Ruth]. t. l., 1*l* recto 27.8 x 21.5 cm. Berkeley, [1947]. CtY.

E12   [Spicer], Jack. a. l. s., 1*l* recto-verso 27.9 x 21.6 cm. Berkeley, [26 Feb. 1947]. CU-B.

E13   [Spicer], Jack. a. l. s., 2*l* recto-verso, recto 26.3 x 18.4 cm. [Berkeley], 20 March 1947. CU-B.

E14   [Spicer], Jack. t. l. s., 2*l* recto-verso, recto 21.7 x 21.6 cm. New York City, [Spring 1947]. CU-B.

E15   Zukofsky, [Louis]. t. l. s., 1*l* recto 27.8 x 21.5 cm. New York City, [June 1947]. TxU.

E16   Zukofksy, [Louis]. a. l. s., 1*l* recto-verso 27.8 x 21.5 cm. Berkeley, [July 1947]. TxU.

E17   [Spicer], Jack. a. l., 8*l* all recto 10.9 x 9.2 cm. [Berkeley], [1947/48?]. CU-B.

E18   [Spicer], Jack. a. l. s., 3*l* all recto-verso 21 x 16.5 cm. [Berkeley], [1948]. CU-B.

Note: An early holograph version of RD's poem JERUSALEM appears on the verso of the third leaf.

E.19 [Olson, Charles]. a. l. s., 2*l*, recto-verso, recto-verso 21.5 x 14 cm. Berkeley, [1948]. CtU.
Note: This letter was written and signed by RD, Robin Blaser, and Donald Allen as a joint effort.

E.20 Stephan, [Ruth]. a. l. s., 1*l* recto 21.5 x 13.6 cm. Berkeley, [Winter 1948]. CtY.

E.21 Sirs [Quinn, Kerker]. t. & a. n. s., 1*l* recto 21.6 x 14 cm. Berkeley, [Feb. 1948]. IU.

E.22 [Olson, Charles]. t. p. c., 1*l* verso 8.2 x 13.9 cm. Berkeley, [24 Nov.] 1948. CtU.

E.23 Keough, Edna. a. l., 1*l* recto-verso 27.9 x 21.6 cm. San Francisco, [1949]. CU-B.
Note: This letter was not mailed.

E.24 Russell, Peter. a. l. s., 1*l* recto 21.5 x 15.1 cm. Berkeley, [1949]. NBuU.

E.25 D[oolittle], H[ilda]. t. l. s., 2*l* recto, recto 28 x 21.8 cm. Berkeley, [Jan.-March 1949]. CtY.

E.26 The Editors/Tiger's Eye. t. l. s., 1*l* recto 21.5 x 16.3 cm. Berkeley, [Oct. 1949]. CtY.
Note: The letter is stamped as received by the editors on 17 Oct. 1949.

E.27 Editors—/The Tiger's Eye. a. l. s., 1*l* recto 27.9 x 21.7 cm. Berkeley, [Oct. 1949]. CtY.
Note: The letter is stamped as received by the editors on 26 Oct. 1949.

E.28 P[arkinson], T[homas]. t. l., 1*l* recto 27.9 x 21.6 cm. San Francisco, 8 May 1950. CU-B.

E.29 [Spicer], Jack. a. l. s., 4*l* recto-verso, recto-verso, recto-verso, recto 21.5 x 13.8 cm. San Francisco, [1950-1951]. CU-B.
Note: The text of this letter appears in *The Collected Books of Jack Spicer*, pp. 365-66. B77.

E.30 [Broughton], Jimmy, & Kermit [Sheets]. t. l., 1*l* recto-verso 28 x 21.7 cm. [San Francisco, 1951]. OKentU.

E.31 [Broughton], Jimmy, & [Kermit] Sheets. t. l. s., 1*l* recto 28 x 21.6 cm. [San Francisco, 1951]. OKentU.
Note: 1*l* recto of typed comments from a letter to RD from Cid Corman accompanied this letter.

E.32 Corman, [Cid]. t. l. s., 1*l* recto-verso 27.8 x 21.5 cm. San Francisco, [1951]. TxU.

E33   Corman, [Cid]. t. l. s., 1*l* recto-verso 21.5 x 20.2 cm. San Francisco, [24 Oct. 1951]. TxU.

E34   [Spicer], Jack. a. l., 1*l* recto-verso 28 x 21.9 cm. San Francisco, [1952?]. CU-B.

E35   [Broughton], Jaimy. t. & a. l. s., 1*l* recto-verso 27.8 x 21.5 cm. [San Francisco], [1952]. OKentU.

E36   Corman, [Cid]. a. l. s., 1*l* recto 21.6 x 16.1 cm. San Francisco, [1952]. TxU.

E37   P[ound], E[zra]. t. l. s., 1*l* recto-verso 21.5 x 17.6 cm. [San Francisco, 1952?]. NBuU.

E38   P[ound], E[zra]. a. l. s., 1*l* recto-verso 21.6 x 21.4 cm. [San Francisco, 1952?]. NBuU.

E39   Americans Abroad. [Broughton, James & Kermit Sheets]. t. l. s., 2*l* recto-verso, recto 21.5 x 17.6 cm. San Francisco, [Spring 1952]. OKentU.

E40   [Broughton], Jaime, & Kermutt [Sheets]. t. l. s., 1*l* 27.9 x 21.5 cm. [San Francisco, Spring 1952]. OKentU.

E41   Corman, [Cid]. t. l. s., 1*l* recto-verso 21.5 x 13.8 cm. San Francisco, [8 April 1952]. TxU.

E42   Olson, [Charles]. t. l., 1*l* recto 27.9 x 21.5 cm. San Francisco, [8 April] 1952. CtU.
       Note: A typescript of AN ABOUT FACE/FOR CLAIRE MAHL accompanied this letter. F62.

E43   [Spicer, Jack]. a. p. c. s., 1*l* verso 8.2 x 14. cm. San Francisco, [9 May 1952]. CU-B.

E44   [Broughton, James]. a. & t. l. s., 2*l* recto-verso, recto-verso 28 x 21.6 cm. [San Francisco], 23 May 1952. OKentU.
       Note: This letter contains typed lines from AN ESSAY AT WAR—BARTH CARPENTER. MADELINE GLEASON—MADELINE GLEASON—BARTH, BARTH. A LOVELY FLAG—MADELINE GLEASON IN SPANISH DISGUISE—MADELINE GLEASON AND BARTH CARPENTER—AT INTERVALS. The first entry appeared in BR and the remaining pieces in NP, under the title AN EVENING AT HOME.

E45   [Broughton], Jimmy. t. l. s., 2*l* recto, recto 28 x 21.7 cm. San Francisco, [Fall 1952]. OKentU.
       Note: A typescript of A DIVERTISEMENT OR TWO accompanied this letter. F63.

E46 Boys of Boytown [Broughton, James, and Kermit Sheets]. t. l. s., 1*l* recto-verso 28 x 21.5 cm. San Francisco, [Fall 1952]. OKentU.
Note: The typescript of the following items appears inside this letter: [two scenes proposed for FAUST FOUTU]: A POET'S FROM KIPPEL—A POET—DANCE: EARLY SPRING WEATHER MAGIC—A MEXICAN STRAIGHT SUMMER OR PARTIAL PORTRAIT OF BROCK. The final two items appeared in BR and NP.

E47 Americans Abroad [Broughton, James, and Kermit Sheets]. a. l., 2*l* recto-verso, recto-verso 28 x 27.7 cm. San Francisco, [Fall 1952]. OKentU.

E48 [Broughton], Jimmy. a. l. s., 1*l* recto-verso 21.6 x 16.4 cm. San Francisco, [Fall 1952]. OKentU.

E49 [Broughton], Jaime. t. l. s., 1*l* recto-verso 28 x 21.5 cm. San Francisco, [Fall 1952]. OKentU.
Note: An additional holograph note appears at bottom verso.

E50 [Sheets], Kermit [and James Broughton]. t. l., 2*l* recto, recto, 28 x 21.7 cm. San Francisco, [Sept. 1952] OKentU

E51 Angel-Pie [Broughton, James]. t. l., 1*l* recto 27.7 x 21.5 cm. San Francisco, [Sept.-Oct. 1952]. OKentU.

E52 Corman, [Cid]. t. l. s., 1*l* recto 21.6 x 17 cm. San Francisco, [23 Oct. 1952]. TxU.

E53 Corman, [Cid]. a. l. s., 1*l* recto 21.6 x 17.6 cm. San Francisco, [26 Nov. 1952]. TxU.

E54 Real Bearoughton [Broughton, James]. t. l. s., 1*l* recto-verso 27.7 x 21.4 cm. San Francisco, [1952/1953]. OKentU.
Note: Accompanying this letter is a letter from Curtis Whittington addressed to The Centaur Press, 1*l* recto-verso 27.8 x 21.5 cm., which contains a holograph unsigned note from RD.

E55 [Broughton], Jimmy, and Kermit [Sheets]. t. l. s., 1*l* recto-verso 27.9 x 21.6 cm. San Francisco, [1953]. OKentU.
Note: An additional note in the poet's holograph appears at the bottom verso.

E56 [Broughton, James]. t. l. s., 1*l* recto 28 x 21.6 cm. [San Francisco, 1953]. OKentU.

E57 Corman, [Cid]. a. l. s., 1*l* recto 27.8 x 21.5 cm. San Francisco, [1953]. TxU.

E58 [Broughton], Jimmy. a. l. s., 2*l*; 1*l* recto-verso 21.5 x 16.3 cm., 1*l* recto-verso 21.5 x 20.3 cm. San Francisco, [Spring 1953]: OKentU.
Note: Verso of the second leaf contains the holograph poem LORD MOUSE, which appears in BR as LORD MASTER MOUSE.

E59 [Broughton], James. a. l., 1*l* recto-verso 30.5 x 21.2 cm. [San Francisco, Spring 1953] and 10 May 1953. OKentU.

E60 [Broughton, James]. a. & t. l., 1*l* recto 28 x 21.6 cm. [San Francisco, Fall 1953]. OKentU.

E61 [Broughton], Jaimy. t. l. s., 1*l* recto-verso 27.9 x 21.7 cm. San Francisco, [1954?]. OKentU.

E62 Olson, Charles. t. l. s., 1*l* recto 27.8 x 21.5 cm. San Francisco, [1954?]. CtU.

E63 Corman, [Cid]. a. l. s., 1*l* recto 27.8 x 21.5 cm. San Francisco, 25 Jan. 1954. TxU.

E64 Olson, [Charles]. a. l., 3*l* recto-verso, recto, recto: 2*l* 21.3 x 21.5 cm., 1*l* 21.5 x 19.7 cm. San Francisco, [March-April 1954]. CtU.
Note: An additional holograph note appears on the verso of the third leaf.

E65 Roethke, [Theodore]. t. l. s., 1*l* recto 27.5 x 21.7 cm. San Francisco, [Spring/Summer 1954]. WaU.

E66 Olson, [Charles]. a. l. s., 2*l* recto-verso, recto-verso 27.5 x 21.5 cm. San Francisco, 17 June [1954]. CtU.

E67 Olson, [Charles]. a. l. s., 2*l* recto-verso, recto 21.4 x 21.5 cm. San Francisco, 29 June 1954. CtU.
Note: A typescript of TRUE TO LIFE accompanied this letter. F71.

E68 Creeley, [Robert]. t. l. s., 1*l* recto 13.52 x 21.5 cm. San Francisco, [July 1954]. On deposit at MoSW.

E69 Olson, [Charles]. a. l. s., 4*l* all recto-verso 21 x 21.5 cm. San Francisco, [8 Aug. 1954]. CtU.

E70 Sirs [unidentified]. t. l. s., 1*l* recto 28 x 21.8 cm. San Francisco, 14 Aug. 1954. CU-B.

E71 Olson, [Charles]. a. l. s., 1*l* recto-verso 27.8 x 21.5 cm. San Francisco, [19 Aug. 1954]. CtU.

E72 [Creeley, Robert]. a. n. s., 1*l* recto 27.5 x 21.6 cm. San Francisco, [Fall 1954]. On deposit at MoSW.

E73 [Witt-Diamant], Ruth. t. l. s., 2*l* recto, recto 27.8 x 21.5 cm. San Francisco, 2 Sept. 1954. NN.

E74 Olson, [Charles]. a. & t. l. s., 2*l* recto-verso, recto 27.8 x 21.5 cm. San Francisco, 2 Sept. 1954. CtU.

E75 [Pound, Ezra]. a. p. c. s., 1*l* verso 14 x 8.2 cm. San Francisco, [16 Sept. 1954]. CtY.
Note: The holograph message is in the form of a poem.

E.76   [Blaser], Robin. a. l. s., 1*l* recto 30.4 x 18.3 cm. San Francisco, 21 Sept. 1954. CU-B.

E.77   [Witt-Diamant], Ruth. t. l. s., 1*l* recto 27.8 x 21.5 cm. San Francisco, 15 Oct. 1954. CU-B.

E.78   [Witt-Diamant], Ruth. t. l. s., 1*l* recto 27.8 x 21.5 cm. San Francisco, 1 Nov. [1954]. CU-B.

E.79   Olson, [Charles]. a. l. s., 2*l* recto-verso, recto 27.8 x 21.5 cm. San Francisco, 11 Nov. 1954. CtU.

E.80   Creeley, [Robert]. a. l. s., 1*l* recto 30.2 x 18.5 cm. San Francisco, 15 Jan. [1955]. On deposit at MoSW.

E.81   Olson, [Charles]. a. n. s., 1*l* recto 25.3 x 15.8 cm. Fort Smith, Ark., [11 Feb. 1955]. CtU.

E.82   Olson, [Charles]. a. l. s., 2*l* recto, recto 27.6 x 21.5 cm. New York City, [Feb. 1955]. CtU.

E.83   Creeley, [Robert]. a. l. s., 1*l* recto-verso 28.7 x 20 cm. Lisbon, Portugal, 18 March [1955]. On deposit at MoSW

E.84   Creeley, Robert. a. p. c. s., 1*l* recto 8.8 x 13.6 cm. [Palma de Mallorca], [Spring 1955]. On deposit at MoSW.

E.85   Creeley, [Robert]. t. l. s., 2*l* recto, recto 27.5 x 21.6 cm. Bañalbufar, Mallorca, [Spring 1955]. On deposit at MoSW.

E.86   [Creeley], Bob. a. l. s., 2*l* recto-verso, recto-verso 21.6 x 15.7 cm. Bañalbufar, Mallorca, [Spring 1955]. On deposit at MoSW.

E.87   [Creeley], Bob. a. l., 1*l* recto-verso 21.5 x 15 cm. Bañalbufar, Mallorca, [Spring 1955]. On deposit at MoSW.

E.88   [Creeley], Bob. a. l. s., 1*l* recto 27.5 x 21.6 cm. Bañalbufar, Mallorca, [Spring 1955]. On deposit at MoSW.

E.89   Olson, Charles. t. n., 1*l* recto 9.7 x 21.5 cm. Bañalbufar, Mallorca, [Spring 1955]. CtU.
        Note: Note is entitled "Postscript."

E.90   Creeley, [Robert]. t. & a. l. s., 1*l* recto 21.5 x 14 cm. Bañalbufar, Mallorca, [Spring 1955]. On deposit at MoSW.

E.91   Dear Creeleys. a. l. s., 2*l* recto, recto 21.6 x 16.8 cm. Bañalbufar, Mallorca, 2 April [1955]. On deposit at MoSW.
        Note: A signed, black-ink drawing accompanied this letter. D33

E.92   [Witt-Diamant], Ruth. a. l. s., 2*l* recto, recto 27.5 x 21.2 cm. Bañalbufar, Mallorca, 3 April [19]55. CU-B.

E.93   [Zukofsky], Louis. a. l. s., 1*l* recto 27.5 x 21.5 cm. Bañalbufar, Mallorca, 3 April 1955. TxU.

E94 [Creeley], Robert & Ann. a. l. s., 1*l* recto 21.6 x 15.7 cm. Bañalbufar, Mallorca, 7 April 1955. On deposit at MoSW.

E95 [Adam], Helen. a. l. s., 2*l*; 1*l* recto 22 x 21.2 cm., 1*l* recto 27.5 x 21.2 cm. Bañalbufar, Mallorca, 8 April 1955. NBuU.
Note: a. n. s., 1*l* recto from Jess Collins to Helen Adam, accompanied this letter.

E96 [Creeley], Bob. a. l. s., 4*l*; 3*l* recto-verso, 1*l* recto, all 21.6 x 15.8 cm. Bañalbufar, Mallorca, 9 April 1955. On deposit at MoSW.

E97 [Spicer], Jack. a. l. s., 2*l* recto, recto 28.1 x 21 cm., Bañalbufar, Mallorca, 16 April 1955. CU-B.
Note: A typescript of the two poems A BALLAD FOR HELEN ADAM and A SONG AFTER THE MANNER OF BLAKE was enclosed with this letter. F85.

E98 Corman, [Cid]. a. l. s., 4*l* all recto 27.5 x 21.2 cm. Bañalbufar, Mallorca, 18 April 1955. TxU.

E99 [Creeley], Robert. a. l. s., 1*l* recto 27.5 x 21.6 cm. Bañalbufar, Mallorca, 20 April [1955]. On deposit at MoSW.

E100 [Zukofsky], Louis. t. l. s., 2*l* recto, recto 27.5 x 21.4 cm. Bañalbufar, Mallorca, 16 May 1955. TxU.

E101 Olson, [Charles]. t. l. s., 2*l* recto, recto 27.8 x 21.5 cm. Bañalbufar, Mallorca, 17 May 1955. CtU.
Note: Part III of NOTES ON POETICS REGARDING *MAXIMUS* accompanied this letter. F86.

E102 [Creeley], Bob. t. l. s., 1*l* recto-verso 27.9 x 21.6 cm. Bañalbufar, Mallorca, 20 May 1955. On deposit at MoSW.

E103 [Broughton], Jimmy. t. & a. l. s., 2*l* recto, recto 27.5 x 21.3 cm. [Bañalbufar, Mallorca, June 1955]. OKentU.

E104 [Broughton], Jimmy. a. l. s., 2*l* recto, recto, 27.8 x 21.4 cm. [Bañalbufar, Mallorca], 4 June 1955. OKentU.

E105 Olson, Charles. a. l. s., 1*l* recto 27.8 x 21.5 cm. Bañalbufar, Mallorca, 19 June [1955]. CtU.
Note: A typescript of NOTES ON THE POETICS OF CHARLES OLSON IN *MAXIMUS* accompanied this letter. F87.

E106 Olson, [Charles]. a. & t. l. s., 3*l* all recto 27.4 x 21.2 cm. Bañalbufar, Mallorca, 20 and 21 June [1955]. CtU.

E107 Creeley, [Robert]. a. l. s., 1*l* recto 27.5 x 21.6 cm. Bañalbufar, Mallorca, [Summer 1955]. On deposit at MoSW.

E108 [Broughton], Jimmy. t. & a. l. s., 1*l* recto-verso 31.5 x 21.5 cm. [Bañalbufar, Mallorca], 11 July 1955. OKentU.

E109 [Creeley], Robert. t. l. s., 1*l* recto 31.5 x 20.5 cm. Bañalbufar, Mallorca, 13 July [19]55. On deposit at MoSW.

E110 [Adam], Helen. a. l. s., 1*l* recto-verso 31.6 x 21.5 cm. Bañalbufar, Mallorca 15 July [19]55. NBuU.

E111 [Witt-Diamant], Ruth. t. & a. l. s., 1*l* recto-verso 31.5 x 21.4 cm. Bañalbufar, Mallorca, 16 July [19]55. CU-B.

E112 [Adam], Helen. a. l. s., 1*l* recto-verso 27.8 x 21.4 cm. Bañalbufar, Mallorca, [17 July 1955]. NBuU.
Note: The holograph text of a twelve line poem beginning "WHAT DID LEARNED COLERIDGE KNOW"(fl) appears on the verso. A typescript of THE GREEN LADY accompanied this letter. F88.

E113 Eigner, [Larry]. a. l. s., 1*l* recto 27.8 x 21.5 cm. Bañalbufar, Mallorca, 22 July [1955]. CtU.

E114 [Creeley], Bob. t. l. s., 1*l* recto 31.5 x 21.5 cm. Bañalbufar, Mallorca, 28 July 1955. On deposit at MoSW.

E115 [Zukofsky], Louis. a. l. s., 1*l* recto-verso 31.5 x 21.5 cm. Bañalbufar, Mallorca, 14 Aug. 1955. TxU.

E116 [Creeley], Bob. a. l. s., 1*l* recto-verso 31.5 x 21.5 cm. Bañalbufar, Mallorca, 14 Aug. 1955. On deposit at MoSW.

E117 Olson, [Charles]. t. & a. l. s., 1*l* recto-verso 31.5 x 21.4 cm. Bañalbufar, Mallorca, 15 Aug. 1955. CU-B.

E118 [Blaser], Robin. a. l. s., 1*l* recto-verso 31.5 x 21.4 cm., Bañalbufar, Mallorca, 15 Aug. 1955. CU.

E119 [Creeley], Bob. a. & t. l. s., 1*l* recto-verso 31.5 x 21.5 cm. Bañalbufar, Mallorca, 15 and 17 Aug. [19]55. On deposit at MoSW.

E120 [Adam], Helen. a. l. s., 1*l* recto-verso 31.6 x 21.5 cm. Bañalbufar, Mallorca, 20 Aug. [19]55. NBuU.

E121 [Creeley], Bob. t. l., 1*l* recto 15 x 21.2 cm. Bañalbufar, Mallorca, 24 Aug. [19]55. On deposit at MoSW.

E122 [Creeley], Bob. t. & a. l. s., 1*l* recto-verso 15.5 x 21.4 cm. Bañalbufar, Mallorca, 25 Aug. 1955. On deposit at MoSW.

E123 [Adam], Helen. a. l. s., 1*l* recto-verso 31.6 x 21.5 cm. Bañalbufar, Mallorca, 26 Aug. [19]55. NBuU.

E124 [Olson, Charles]. t. & A. l. s., 1*l* recto-verso 31.5 x 21.5 cm. Bañalbufar, Mallorca, 28 Aug. 1955. CtU.

E125 [Creeley], Bob. t. l. s., 1*l* recto-verso 31.5 x 21.5 cm. Bañalbufar, Mallorca, 30 Aug. [19]55. On deposit at MoSW.

E126 [Creeley], Robert. t. l. s., 1*l* recto-verso 27.2 x 21.2 cm. Bañalbufar, Mallorca, [Fall 1955]. On deposit at MoSW.

E127 [Olson], Charles. a. p. c. s., 1*l* verso 10.5 x 14.8 cm. [Europe], [Fall 1955]. CtU.

E128 [Creeley], Bob. t. & a. l. s., 1*l* recto 31.5 x 21.5 cm. Bañalbufar, Mallorca, 1 Sept. [19]55. On deposit at MoSW.

E129 [Broughton], Jimmy. a. l. s., 1*l* recto 31.5 x 21.5 cm. [Bañalbufar, Mallorca], 4 Sept. 1955. OKentU.

E130 [Zukofsky], Louis. a. l. s., 1*l* recto-verso 31.5 x 21.5 cm. Bañalbufar, Mallorca, 8 Sept. 1955. TxU.

E131 [Creeley], Bob. t. l. s., 1*l* recto-verso 31.5 x 21.5 cm. Bañalbufar, Mallorca, 11 Sept. [19]55. On deposit at MoSW.

E132 [Corman], Cid. a. l. s., 1*l* recto 31.5 x 21.5 cm. Bañalbufar, Mallorca, 12 Sept. 1955 TxU.

E133 [Witt-Diamant], Ruth. a. l. s., 1*l* recto-verso 31.6 x 21.5 cm. Bañalbufar, Mallorca, 15 Sept. 1955. CU-B.

E134 [Adam], Helen. a. & t. l. s., 2*l* recto-verso, recto-verso 31.6 x 21.5 cm. Bañalbufar, Mallorca, 17 Sept. 1955. NBuU.

E135 [Broughton], Jimmy. a. l. s., 1*l* recto-verso 31.5 x 21.5 cm. [Bañalbufar, Mallorca], 26 Sept. 1955. OKentU.

E136 [Creeley], Bob. a. l. s., 1*l* recto-verso 27.8 x 21.6 cm. Bañalbufar, Mallorca, 26 Sept. 1955. On deposit at MoSW.

E137 [Adam], Helen. a. l. s., 1*l* recto-verso 31.6 x 21.5 cm. Bañalbufar, Mallorca, 1 Oct. [19]55. NBuU.

E138 [Creeley], Bob. a. l. s., 2*l* recto-verso, recto-verso 31.5 x 21.5 cm. Bañalbufar, Mallorca, 2 Oct. [19]55. On deposit at MoSW.

E139 [Olson], Charles & Bob [Creeley]. t. l. s., 1*l* recto-verso 31.5 x 20.5 cm. Bañalbufar, Mallorca, 6 and 7 Oct. [19]55. On deposit at MoSW.

E140 [Corman], Cid. a. l. s., 1*l* recto-verso 24.3 x 21.3 cm. Bañalbufar, Mallorca, 7 Oct. 1955. TxU.

E141 [Creeley], Bob. a. l. s., 1*l* recto-verso 31.5 x 21.5 cm. Bañalbufar, Mallorca, 8 Oct. [19]55. On deposit at MoSW.
Note: The letter contains twenty-four lines of the poem UPON HIS SEEING A BABY HOLDING THE FOUR OF HEARTS FOR HIM AND ANOTHER CARD CONCEALD.

E142 [Blaser], Robin. a. l. s., 1*l* recto 27.8 x 21.4 cm. [Bañalbufar, Mallorca], 10 Oct. 1955. CU-B.

E143 [Creeley], Bob. t. & a. l. s., 1*l* recto-verso 31.5 x 21.5 cm. Bañalbufar, Mallorca, 20 Oct. 1955. On deposit at MoSW.
Note: A typescript of FROM A NOTEBOOK accompanied this letter. F91.

E144 [Creeley], Bob. t. & a. l. s., 1*l* recto-verso 27.9 x 21.9 cm. Bañalbufar, Mallorca, 25 Oct. 1955. On deposit at MoSW.

E145 [Creeley], Bob. t. & a. l. s., 1*l* recto-verso 27.9 x 21.9 cm. Bañalbufar, Mallorca, 31 Oct. [19]55. On deposit at MoSW.

E146 [Blaser], Robin. a. l., 1*l* recto-verso 27.9 x 21.8 cm. [Bañalbufar, Mallorca], 14 Nov. 1955. CU-B.

E147 [Creeley], Bob. a. l. s., 2*l* recto, recto 26.8 x 21 cm. Paris, 24 Nov. 1955. On deposit at MoSW.

E148 [Adam] Helen. a. l. s., 2*l* recto, recto 26.9 x 21 cm. Paris, 30 Nov. 1955. NBuU.

E149 [Creeley], Bob. a. l. s., 1*l* recto 26.8 x 21 cm. Paris, [Dec. 1955]. On deposit at MoSW.

E150 [Blaser], Robin. t. & a. l. s., 1*l* recto 26.8 x 21 cm. Paris, 1 Dec. 1955. CU-B.

E151 [Creeley], Bob. a. l. s., 1*l* recto-verso 27.2 x 21.2 cm. [Paris], 2 Dec. 1955. On deposit at MoSW.

E152 [Witt-Diamant], Ruth. a. l. s., 1*l* recto-verso 27.2 x 21.1 cm. [Paris], 16 Dec. [1955]. CU-B.

E153 [Witt-Diamant], Ruth. a. l. s. (photocopy), 2*l* recto, recto 27.9 x 21.6 cm. [Paris, 18 Dec. 1955]. CSf-APA.

E154 [Corman], Cid. a. p. c. s., 1*l* verso 9 x 13.9 cm. [England, Jan. 1956]. TxU.

E155 [Broughton], James. t. l. s., 1*l* recto-verso 20 x 24.7 cm. London, [5 Jan. 1956]. OKentU.

E156 [Witt-Diamant], Ruth. a. l. s., 1*l* recto-verso 27.9 x 21.6 cm. London, 8 Jan. 1956. CU-B.

E157 [Witt-Diamant], Ruth. t. l. s., 1*l* recto-verso 19.9 x 24.6 cm. London, 17 Jan. 1956. CU-B.

E158 [Blaser], Robin. a. l. s., 1*l* recto-verso 19.9 x 24.5 cm. London, 24 Jan. 1956. CU-B.

E159 [Creeley], Robert. t. l. s., 1*l* recto-verso 26 x 20.5 cm. Bañalbufar, Mallorca, [Feb. 1956]. On deposit at MoSW.

E160 [Creeley], Bob. a. l. s., 1*l* recto-verso 20 x 24.4 cm. Lodsworth, England, 1 Feb. [1956]. On deposit at MoSW.

E161 [Adam], Helen. a. & t. l. s., 1*l* recto-verso 24.5 x 20 cm. London, 1 Feb. [19]56. NBuU.
    Note: A pen-and-ink drawing appears at bottom recto.

E.162 [Broughton], James. t. & a. l. s., 1*l* recto-verso 20 x 24.7 cm. Paris, 5 Feb. 1956. OKentU.
Note: This letter contains an early version of the poem OFTEN I AM PERMITTED TO RETURN TO A MEADOW.

E.163 [Witt-Diamant], Ruth. a. l. s., 1*l* recto-verso 19.9 x 24.6 cm. Bañalbufar, Mallorca, 10 Feb. [19]56. CU-B.

E.164 [Olson], Charles. t. l. s., 2*l* recto, recto 25.2 x 21.3 cm. Bañalbufar, Mallorca, 20 Feb. 1956. CtU.
Note: There is a short holograph note by RD at bottom recto of the second leaf.

E.165 [Witt-Diamant], Ruth. t. l. s., 1*l* recto-verso 20.3 x 24.2 cm. Bañalbufar, Mallorca, 23 Feb. 1956. CU-B.

E.166 [Corman], Cid. t. l. s., 1*l* recto 20.4 x 25.1 cm. Bañalbufar, Mallorca, [23 Feb. 1956]. TxU.
Note: A typescript of Ezra Pound's CANTO PROCEEDING (72 Circa), which appeared in *Vice Versa*, I, 3/4/5 (Jan. 1942), 1-2, accompanied this letter.

E.167 [Adam], Helen. a. l. s., 2*l* recto, recto 25.3 x 20.3 cm. Bañalbufar, Mallorca, 24 Feb. [19]56. NBuU.
Note: A typescript A BALLAD FOR HELEN ADAM accompanied this letter. F101.

E.168 [Broughton], James. a. l. s., 1*l* recto-verso 27 x 21 cm. [Bañalbufar, Mallorca], 24 Feb. 1956. OKentU.

E.169 [Witt-Diamant], Ruth. t. l. s., 1*l* recto-verso 24 x 21 cm.Bañalbufar, Mallorca, 25 Feb. 1956. CU-B.

E.170 [Blaser], Robin. t. l. s., 1*l* recto 25.7 x 20.4 cm. [Bañalbufar, Mallorca], 26 Feb. 1956. CU-B.

E.171 [Zukofsky], Louis. t. & a. l. s., 1*l* recto-verso 24 x 20.3 cm. Bañalbufar, Mallorca, 28 Feb. 1956. TxU.

E.172 Creeley, [Robert]. a. l. s., 2*l* recto-verso, recto-verso 27.5 x 21.2 cm. Bañalbufar, Mallorca, [Spring 1956]. On deposit at MoSW.

E.173 [Blaser], Robin. a. l. s., 3*l* all recto 27.5 x 21.2 cm. Palrua, Portugal, [March 1956]. CU-B.

E.174 [Blaser], Robin. a. n. s., 1*l* recto 25.1 x 20.3 cm. Lisbon, Portugal, 12 March 1956. CU-B.

E.175 [Blaser], Robin. a. l. s., 1*l* recto-verso 27.8 x 21.6 cm. [Lisbon, Portugal], 15 March 1956. CU-B.

E.176 [Olson], Charles. a. n., 1*l* recto 21 x 14 cm. [Black Mountain, N. C.], [March-June 1956]. CtU.

E177 [Witt-Diamant], Ruth. a. l. s., 3*l* all recto 25.7 x 20.4 cm. Black Mountain, N. C., 27 March 1956. CU-B.

E178 [Creeley], Bob. t. & a. l. s., 2*l* recto, recto 21.2 x 20.4 cm. Black Mountain, N. C., 27 March 1956. On deposit at MoSW.

E179 [Zukofsky], Louis. a. l. s., 3*l* all recto 25.2 x 20.4 cm. Black Mountain, N. C., 27 March 1956. TxU.
Note: There is a short holograph note from Charles Olson to Louis Zukofsky included in this letter.

E180 [Rumaker], Mike. a. l. s., 1*l* recto 25.2 x 20.3 cm. Black Mountain, N. C., 28 March 1956. CtU.

E181 [Creeley], Bob. t. l. s., 1*l* recto 25.7 x 20.4 cm. Black Mountain, N. C., 28 March 1956. On deposit at MoSW.

E182 [Rumaker], Mike. t. l. s., 1*l* recto 28.1 x 21.7 cm. Black Mountain, N. C., 30 March 1956. CtU.

E183 [Blaser], Robin. t. l. s., 2*l* recto, recto 25.2 x 20.4 cm. [Black Mountain, N. C.], 30 March 1956. CU-B.

E184 [Witt-Diamant], Ruth. t. l. s., 3*l* all recto 25.7 x 20.4 cm. Black Mountain, N. C., 4, 10, and 11 April 1956. CU-B.

E185 [Broughton], James. a. l. s., 4*l* all recto 25.1 x 20.5 cm. [Black Mountain, N. C.], 11 April 1956.
Note: An untitled early version of THE DANCE, accompanied this letter. F103.

E186 [Creeley], Bob. t. & a. l. s., 1*l* recto 21.2 x 20.4 cm. Black Mountain, N. C., 18 April 1956. On deposit at MoSW.

E187 [Creeley], Bob. t. l. s., 1*l* recto 21.2 x 20.4 cm. Black Mountain, N. C., 21 April 1956. On deposit at MoSW.

E188 [Adam], Helen. t. & a. l. s., 1*l* recto-verso 31.5 x 20.3 cm. Black Mountain, N. C., 23 April 1956. OKentU.
Note: An early version of THE STRUCTURE OF RIME I appears in typescript on the verso.

E189 [Blaser, Robin]. t. l. s., 1*l* recto 21.4 x 21.6 cm. [Black Mountain, N. C.], 26 April 1956. CU-B.

E190 [Rexroth], Martha. t. l. s. (carbon), 2*l* recto, recto 27.6 x 20.5 cm. Black Mountain, N. C., [May 1956]. On deposit at MoSW.

E191 [Creeley], Bob. t. l. s., 1*l* recto 21.2 x 20.4 cm. [Black Mountain, N. C.], 27 July 1956. On deposit at MoSW.

E192 [Spicer], Jack. t. l. s., 1*l* recto-verso 27.8 x 21.6 cm. Black Mountain, N. C., [May 1956]. CU-B.

E193 [Witt-Diamant], Ruth. t. & a. l. s., 1*l* recto 27.7 x 21.6 cm. Black Mountain, N. C., 5 May 1956. CU-B.

E194 [Gleason], Maddie. a. l. s., 1*l* recto 23.2 x 21.5 cm. Black Mountain, N. C., 5 May 1956. CSfU.

E195 [Creeley], Bob. a. l. s., 2*l* recto-verso, recto-verso 27.7 x 21.5 cm. Black Mountain, N. C., 10 May 1956. On deposit at MoSW.

E196 [Witt-Diamant], Ruth. t. l. s., 1*l* recto 27.8 x 21.5 cm. Black Mountain, N. C., 11 May 1956. CU-B.

E197 [Rumaker], Mike. t. l. s., 1*l* recto 25.1 x 20.4 cm. Black Mountain, N. C., 12 May 1956. CtU.

E198 [Witt-Diamant], Ruth. a. l. s., 2*l* recto-verso, recto 26.6 x 20.1 cm. Black Mountain, N. C., 15 May 1956. CU-B.

E199 [Creeley], Bob. a. l. s., 3*l* all recto 27.6 x 20.5 cm. Black Mountain, N. C., 18 May 1956. On deposit at MoSW.

E200 [Creeley], Bob. a. l. s., 2*l* recto-verso, recto 27.7 x 20.2 cm. Black Mountain, N. C., 22 May [19]56. On deposit at MosW.

E201 [Broughton], Jamie. t. & a. l. s., 1*l* recto-verso 27.7 x 21.6 cm. [Black Mountain, N. C., June 1956]. OKentU.

E202 [Broughton], Jaimie. t. l. s., 1*l* recto-verso 28 x 21.5 cm. [Black Mountain, N. C.], 3 June 1956. OKentU.

E203 [Spicer], Jack. t. l. s., 1*l* recto-verso 27.8 x 21.7 cm. New York City, [7 June 1956]. CU-B.

E204 [Corman], Cid. a. l. s., 1*l* verso 27.8 x 21.5 cm. Black Mountain, N. C., 7 June 1956. TxU.
Note: This letter is written on the verso of the first announcement of the Jargon Society's publication of RD's book, *Letters*.

E205 "Zuks/large & small." [Zukofsky, Louis, Celia, & Paul]. a. l. s., 1*l* recto-verso 27.9 x 21.6 cm. Black Mountain, N. C., 7 June 1956. TxU.

E206 [Rumaker], Mike. a. l. s., 1*l* recto 27.8 x 21.5 cm. Black Mountain, N. C., 13 June 1956. CtU.
Note: The advertisement for RD's book, *Letters* accompanied this letter.

E207 [Creeley], Bob. a. l. s., 1*l* recto 27.9 x 21.6 cm. Black Mountain, N. C., [July 1956]. On deposit at MoSW.

E208 [Witt-Diamant], Ruth. t. l. s., 1*l* recto-verso 27.9 x 21.7 cm. Black Mountain, N. C., 15 July 1956. CU-B.

E209 [Broughton], Jaime. a. & t. l. s., 1*l* recto-verso 21.3 x 20.2 cm. [Black Mountain, N. C.], 16 July 1956. OKentU.

E210 [Blaser], Robin. a. l. s., 1*l* recto-verso 27.9 x 21.7 cm. New York City, 25 July 1956. CU-B.

E211 [Spicer], Jack. t. l. (carbon), 2*l* recto, recto 27.8 x 21.6 cm. [San Francisco, Fall 1956]. CU-B.
Note: This letter was printed in *The Collected Books of Jack Spicer.* B77.

E212 Olson, Charles. a. n., 1*l* recto 8.3 x 13.8 cm. San Francisco, [Fall 1956]. CtU.

E213 [Blaser], Robin. t. l. s., 1*l* recto 20.7 x 21.7 cm. San Francisco, [Fall 1956]. CU-B.

E214 Peyton, [   ]. t. l. s., 1*l* recto 28 x 21.6 cm. San Francisco, 11 Sept. 1956. ICU.

E215 [Olson], Charles. t. l. s., 1*l* recto-verso 28 x 21.5 cm. San Francisco, [Sept./Oct. 1956]. CtU.

E216 [Rumaker], Mike. a. l. s., 1*l* recto 27.8 x 21.6 cm. San Francisco, 5 Oct. 1956. CtU.

E217 [Rumaker], Mike. a. p. c. s., 1*l* verso 13.9 x 8.2 cm. San Francisco, 8 Oct. 1956. CtU.

E218 Noonday Press. t. l. (carbon), 1*l* recto 27.9 x 21.6 cm. San Francisco, 25 Oct. 1956. CU-B.

E219 Kizer, [Benjamin]. t. l. (carbon), 1*l* recto 28.1 x 21.6 cm. San Francisco, [Oct./Nov. 1956]. CSf-APA.

E220 Trumball, Marjorie. t. l. (carbon), 1*l* recto 27.9 x 21.6 cm. San Francisco, 1 Nov. 1956. CU-B.

E221 Kizer, [Benjamin]. t. l. (carbon), 1*l* recto 27.9 x 21.8 cm. San Francisco, 2 Nov. 1956. CSF-APA.

E222 [Triem], Eve. a. l. s., 1*l* recto 27.9 x 21.5 cm. San Francisco, 5 Nov. 1956. WaU.

E223 Kizer, Benjamin. t. l. (carbon), 1*l* recto 27.9 x 21.8 cm. San Francisco, 21 Nov. 1956. CSf-APA.

E224 [Blaser], Robin. a. l. s., 2*l* recto-verso, recto-verso 27.8 x 21.7 cm. San Francisco, 28 Nov. 1956. CU-B.

E225 [Creeley], Bob. a. l. s., 1*l* recto-verso 27.9 x 21.7 cm. San Francisco, [Dec. 1956]. On deposit at MoSW.

E226 Olson, Charles. a. l. s., 1*l* recto-verso 28 x 18.5 cm. San Francisco, [Dec. 1956]. CtU.

E227 Carmody, Francis James. t. l. (carbon), 1*l* recto 27.9 x 21.8 cm. San Francisco, 6 Dec. 1956. CSf-APA.

E228 [Creeley], Bob. a. l. s., 1*l* recto-verso 27.9 x 21.6 cm. San Francisco, [11 Dec. 1956]. On deposit at MoSW.

E229 [Creeley], Bob. a. l. s., 1*l* recto 27.9 x 21.7 cm. San Francisco, 12 Dec. [1956]. On deposit at MoSW.

E230 Brakebill, Harry. t. l. (carbon), 1*l* recto 27.9 x 21.5 cm. San Francisco, 13 Dec. 1956. CU-B.

E231 [Creeley], Bob. t. l. s., 1*l* recto-verso 27.8 x 21.6 cm. San Francisco, 17 Dec. 1956. On deposit at MoSW.

E232 [Olson], Charles. t. l. s., 1*l* recto 26.4 x 18.1 cm. San Francisco, 20 Dec. 1956. CtU.

E233 [Triem], Eve. a. l. s., 1*l* recto 27.9 x 21.6 cm. San Francisco, 26 Dec. 1956. WaU.

E234 [Olson, Charles]. a. p. c., 1*l* verso 14 x 8.2 cm. San Francisco, [1956/1957]. CtU.

E235 [Hodes], Ida. t. l. s., 1*l* recto-verso 27.9 x 21.5 cm. San Francisco, 1 Jan. 1957. CU-B.

E236 [Blaser], Robin. a. l. s., 1*l* recto-verso 32.9 x 21.5 cm. San Francisco, 6 Jan. 1957. CU-B.

E237 Kenner, Hugh. t. l. (carbon), 1*l* recto 27.9 x 21.8 cm. San Francisco, 14 Jan. 1957. CSf-APA.

E238 Chapman, Roger E. t. l. (carbon), 1*l* recto 27.9 x 21.8 cm. San Francisco, 14 Jan. 1957. CSf-APA.

E239 Melville, Mrs. Charles J. t. l. (carbon), 1*l* recto 27.9 x 21.7 cm. San Francisco, 17 Jan. 1957. CSf-APA.

E240 [Olson], Charles. a. l. s., 1*l* recto 27.8 x 21.6 cm. San Francisco, 21 Jan. 1957. CtU.

E241 Gidlow, Elsa. t. l. (carbon), 1*l* recto 27.9 x 21.6 cm. San Francisco, 22 Jan. [19]57. CU-B.

E242 [Triem], Eve. a. l. s., 1*l* recto 27.9 x 21.6 cm. San Francisco, 22 Jan. 1957. WaU.

E243 Powell, Lawrence Clark. t. l. (carbon), 1*l* recto 27.9 x 21.6 cm. San Francisco, 25 Jan. 1957. CSf-APA.

E244 [Olson], Charles. a. l. s., 1*l* recto 27.8 x 21.6 cm. San Francisco, 25 Jan. 1957. CtU.

E245 Rago, [Henry]. t. l. s., 1*l* recto 27.8 x 21.7 cm. San Francisco, 12 Feb. 1957. ICU.

E246 [Blaser], Robin. a. l. s., 1*l* recto-verso 27.7 x 21.7 cm. San Francisco, [13 Feb. 1957]. CU-B.

E247 Piper, Henry. t. l. (carbon), 1*l* recto 27.9 x 21.6 cm. San Francisco, 14 Feb. 1957. CU-B.

E248 [Zukofsky], Louis. a. l. s., 2*l* recto-verso, recto 27.8 x 21.7 cm. San Francisco, 16 Feb. [1957]. TxU.

E249 Patchell, Robert. t. l. (carbon), 1*l* recto 27.9 x 21.6 cm. San Francisco, 26 Feb. 1957. CU-B.

E250 Von Valkenburg, Emma. t. l. (carbon), 1*l* recto 28.1 x 21.6 cm. San Francisco, 5 March 1957. CSf-APA.

E251 [Blaser], Robin. a. l. s., 1*l* recto-verso 27.7 x 21.7 cm. San Francisco, 10 March 1957. CU-B.

E252 [Creeley], Bob. a. l. s., 1*l* recto 27.9 x 21.5 cm. San Francisco, 11 March [19]57. On deposit at MoSW.
Note: A typescript of part 5 of THE PROPOSITIONS accompanied this letter. F124.

E253 Sirs [Harcourt Brace]. t. l. (carbon), 1*l* recto 27.9 x 21.6 cm. San Francisco, 12 March 1957. CU-B.

E254 Peterson, Mr. t. l. (carbon) 1*l* recto 27.9 x 21.6 cm. San Francisco, 15 March [19]57. CU-B.

E255 [Blaser], Robin. a. l. s., 1*l* recto-verso 27.7 x 21.7 cm. San Francisco, 18 March 1957. CU-B.
Note: Ditto sheets from Jack Spicer's Poetry Workshop containing the texts of FOUR PICTURES OF THE REAL UNIVERSE, OF BLASPHEMY, AND THRESHING SONG accompanied this letter. F125.

E256 [Triem], Eve. a. n. s., 1*l* recto 27.9 x 21.6 cm. San Francisco, [20 March 1957]. WaU.
Note: This note is in the center of a leaf which is an invitation to a celebration of the rising of Kore, and it is surrounded by a drawing in green, orange, and olive crayon. The following line in RD's holograph appears at the bottom of the leaf: "She has all ready risen. Her terrible green is on all earth side."

E257 [Blaser], Robin. a. l. s., 2*l* recto, recto 27.8 x 21.6 cm. Stinson Beach, 24 March 1958. CU-B.

E258 [Blaser], Robin. a. l. s., 1*l* recto 27.8 x 21.7 cm. San Francisco, 3 April 1957. CU-B.

E259 [Olson], Charles. a. l. s., 2*l* recto-verso, recto-verso 27.8 x 21.6 cm. San Francisco, 13 April 1957. CtU.

E260 [Blaser], Robin. a. l. s., 3*l* all recto-verso 27.8 x 21.7 cm. San Francisco, 30 April 1957. CU-B.

E261 [Olson], Charles. t. l. s., 1*l* recto 27.8 x 21.5 cm. San Francisco, 30 April 1957. CtU.
Note: Accompanying this letter is a typescript of a poem by Peggy Pond Church entitled THE POET AS BIG AS A BEAR, which is about Charles Olson.

E262 [Blaser], Robin. t. l. s., 1*l* recto 27.8 x 21.7 cm. San Francisco, [May 1957]. CU-B.

E263 Anderson, Lee. t. l. s., 1*l* recto 27.9 x 21.6 cm. San Francisco, 2 May 1957. MoSW.

E264 [Olson], Charles. a. l. s., 1*l* recto 27.8 x 21.6 cm. San Francisco, 13 May [1957]. CtU.

E265 [Blaser], Robin. a. l. s., 1*l* recto-verso 27.7 x 21.7 cm. San Francisco, 13 May 1957. CU-B.
Note: A typescript of (THE PROPOSITIONS) 4 & 5, SONG, AND THREE PAGES FROM A BIRTHDAY BOOK accompanied this letter. F129.

E266 [Zukofsky], Louis. a. l. s., 1*l* recto 27.8 x 21.5 cm. San Francisco, 22 May 1957. TxU.

E267 [Blaser], Robin. a. l. s., 2*l* recto-verso, recto 27.9 x 21.6 cm. San Francisco, 26 and 28 May 1957. CU-B.
Note: A typescript of EVOCATION accompanied this letter. F130.

E268 Olson, [Charles]. a. l. s., 2*l* recto-verso, recto 27.8 x 21.5 cm. San Francisco, 4 June 1957. CtU.

E269 [Rumaker], Mike. a. l. s., 3*l* all recto 27.8 x 21.5 cm. San Francisco, 5 June 1957. CtU.

E270 [Blaser], Robin. a. l. s., 1*l* recto 27.8 x 21.7 cm. San Francisco, 7 June 1957. CU-B.

E271 [Blaser], Robin. a. l. s., 2*l* recto-verso, recto-verso 27.8 x 21.6 cm. San Francisco, 9 June 1957. CU-B.

E272 [Blaser], Robin. a. l. s., 1*l* recto-verso 27.7 x 21.7 cm. San Francisco, 10 June 1957. CU-B.
Note: A typescript list of the contents of a proposed volume of poems covering the years 1942-1952 accompanied this letter along with the typescript of YAC. F132.

E273 Gidlow, Elsa. t. l. (carbon), 1*l* recto 27.9 x 21.6 cm. San Francisco, 11 June 1957. CU-B.

E274 [Blaser], Robin. a. l. s., 2*l* recto-verso, recto-verso 27.9 x 21.5 cm. San Francisco, 15 June 1957. CU-B.
Note: A typescript of CROSSES OF HARMONY AND DIS-HARMONY accompanied this letter. F133.

E275 Rago, Henry. a. n. s., 1*l* recto 20.3 x 12.7 cm. San Francisco, 16 June 1957. ICU.

E276 Moore, Marianne. t. l. s., 1*l* recto 27.9 x 21.6 cm. San Francisco, 17 June 1975. CSf-APA.

E277 [Blaser], Robin. a. l. s., 2*l* recto-verso, recto-verso 27.8 x 21.6 cm. San Francisco, 18 and 22 June 1957. CU-B.

E278 Olson, Charles. t. l. s., 1*l* recto 26.6 x 18.2 cm. San Francisco, 20 June 1957. CtU.

E279 Gidlow, Elsa. t. l. (carbon), 1*l* recto 27.9 x 21.6 cm. San Francisco, 27 June 1957. CU-B.

E280 [Blaser], Robin. a. l. s., 1*l* recto-verso 27.9 x 21.0 cm. San Francisco, [July 1957]. CU-B.

E281 Rahv, Philip. t. l. s., 1*l* recto 21.5 x 14 cm. San Francisco, 5 July 1957. NjR.

E282 Rago, Henry. a. l. s., 1*l* recto-verso 28 x 21.7 cm. San Francisco, 6 July 1957. ICU.
Note: This letter accompanied RD's review of James Broughton's *True & False Unicorn*, A RISK OF SYMPATHIES. F135.

E283 [Blaser], Robin. a. l. s., 1*l* recto-verso 21.5 x 19.5 cm. San Francisco, 12 July 1957. CU-B.

E284 [Blaser], Robin. a. n. s., 1*l* recto 22.7 x 21.6 cm. San Francisco, 15 July 1957. CU-B.

E285 Rago, Henry. a. l. s., 1*l* recto 21.5 x 21.5 cm. San Francisco, 17 July 1957. ICU.

E286 [Creeley], Bob. a. l. s., 1*l* recto-verso 28 x 21.6 cm. San Francisco, 24 July [19]57. On deposit at MoSW.

E287 Zukofskys, large and small [Louis, Celia & Paul]. a. l. s., 1*l* recto 30.5 x 18.3 cm. San Francisco, 25 July 1957. TxU.

E288 [Creeley], Bob. a. l. s., 1*l* recto-verso 28 x 21.6 cm. San Francisco, 30 July [19]57. On deposit at MoSW.
Note: A typescript of A POEM OF DESPONDENCIES accompanied this letter. F134.

E289 [Eigner], Larry. a. p. c. s., 1*l* verso 13.9 x 8.2 cm. San Francisco, 6 Aug. [1957]. CtU.

E290 [Blaser], Robin. t. l. s., 1*l* recto-verso 28 x 21.7 cm. San Francisco, 18 Aug. [1957]. CU-B.
Note: A short holograph note appears at bottom verso.

E291 Rago, Henry. t. l. s., 1*l* recto 28 x 21.6 cm. San Francisco, 18 Aug. 1957. ICU.
Note: RD's review of H.D.'s *Selected Poems*, IN THE SIGHT OF A LYRE, A LITTLE SPEAR, A CHAIR, accompanied this letter. F136.

E292 [Blaser], Robin. t. l. s., 2*l* recto-verso, recto 28 x 21.7 cm. San Francisco, 22 Aug. 1957. CU-B.
Note: A typescript of POETRY, A NATURAL THING and THREE POEMS IN MEASURE ONE: AN OPEN LETTER accompanied this letter. F137.

E293 [Olson], Charles. a. & t. l. s., 3*l* all recto-verso 27.8 x 21.5 cm. San Francisco, 24 Aug. 1957. CtU.
Note: This letter cites, in typescript, a portion of a letter to RD from John Wieners, 1*l* recto, and includes a typescript of Marianne Moore's poem ROSEMARY, 2*l* recto. There are also typescripts of the poems DESPONDENCIES and POETRY, A NATURAL THING, 3*l* recto-verso, which appeared in OF, the first as A POEM OF DESPONDENCIES and the second with the same title but with deletions and changes.

E294 Marshall, [Edward]. a. l. s., 1*l* recto 28 x 21.7 cm. San Francisco, 29 Aug. 1957. INU

E295 [Blaser], Robin. a. & t. l. s., 1*l* recto-verso 27.9 x 21.6 cm. San Francisco, 31 Aug. 1957. CU-B.

E296 [Triem], Eve. a. l. s., 2*l* recto-verso, recto 28 x 21.6 cm. San Francisco, 2 Sept. 1957. WaU.

E297 [Blaser], Robin. a. & t. l. s., 2*l* recto-verso, recto 28 x 21.7 cm. San Francisco, 11 Sept. 1957. CU-B.

E298 [Blaser], Robin. a. & t. l. s., 2*l* recto-verso, recto-verso 27.9 x 21.7 cm. San Francisco, 13 Sept. 1957. CU-B.

E299 Rago, [Henry]. t. l. s., 1*l* recto 28 x 21.7 cm. San Francisco, 17 Sept. 1957. ICU.

E300 [Blaser], Robin. a. l. s., 2*l* recto-verso, recto-verso 27.9 x 21.7 cm. San Francisco, 27 and 28 Sept. 1957. CU-B.

E301 [Olson], Charles. a. l. s., 1*l* recto-verso 27.8 x 21.5 cm. San Francisco, 1 and 29 Sept. 1957. CtU.
Note: An untitled song beginning "SING FAIR THE LADY"(fl) was enclosed in this letter and was published with revisions in OF. F145.

E302 [Zukofsky], Louis. a. l. s., 1*l* recto-verso 27.8 x 21.7 cm. San Francisco, 24 Sept. and 1 Oct. 1957. TxU.

E303 Moore, [Marianne]. a. l. s., 1*l* recto 27.9 x 21.6 cm. San Francisco, 1 Oct. 1957. CSf-APA.

E304 Rago, Henry. a. & t. l. s., 1*l* recto-verso 28 x 21.7 cm. San Francisco, 1 Oct. 1957. ICU.

E305 [Olson], Charles. a. l. s., 1*l* recto-verso 27.8 x 21.5 cm. San Francisco, 5 Oct. 1957. CtU.
Note: This letter contains seven lines of an unpublished poem by RD typed in. A typescript of THREE POEMS IN MEASURE ONE: AN OPEN LETTER accompanied this letter. F138.

E306 Rago, [Henry]. t. l. s., 1*l* recto 28 x 21.7 cm. San Francisco, 7 Oct. 1957. ICU.
Note: A two line holograph note appears at bottom recto of this letter.

E307 [Creeley], Bob. a. & t. l. s., 2*l* recto-verso, recto-verso 27.9 x 21.6 cm. San Francisco, 25 Oct. [1957]. On deposit at MoSW.
Note: A typescript of SONG OF FAIR THINGS, published as A SONG OF THE OLD ORDER, appears in this letter. The program notes for Marianne Moore's reading at The Poetry Center, San Francisco State College, 11 Oct. 1957, accompanied this letter.

E308 Rago, Henry. t. l. s., 1*l* recto-verso 28 x 21.7 cm. San Francisco, 25 Nov. 1957. ICU.
Note: RD's typescript of [SIX POEMS]—BROUGHT TO LOVE—TO VOW—METAMORPHOSIS—RE—WORDS OPEN UPON GRIEF—AUGUST SUN accompanied this letter. F150.

E309 [Creeley], Bob. a. l. s., 2*l* recto-verso, recto 23.5 x 21.6 cm. San Francisco, 26 Nov. 1957. On deposit at MoSW.

E310 [Witt-Diamant], Ruth. t. l. s., 1*l* recto 27.9 x 21.7 cm. San Francisco, 27 Nov. 1957. CU-B.

E311 Rago, Henry. t. l. s., 1*l* recto 28 x 21.7 cm. San Francisco, 27 Nov. 1957. ICU.

E312 [Zukofsky], Louis. a. l. s., 1*l* recto 27.8 x 21.7 cm. San Francisco, 30 Nov. 1957. TxU.

E313 [Witt-Diamant], Ruth. a. l. s., 1*l* recto-verso 27.9 x 21.7 cm. San Francisco, 3 Dec. 1957. CU-B.

E314 [Witt-Diamant], Ruth. t. l. s., 1*l* recto 27.9 x 21.6 cm. San Francisco, 3 Dec. 1957. CU-B.

E315 Rago, Henry. a. p. c. s., 1*l* verso 14 x 8.2 cm. San Francisco, 9 Dec. 1957. ICU.

E316 Rago, Henry. a. l. s., 1*l* recto 21.6 x 14 cm. San Francisco, 11 Dec. 1957. ICU.

E317 Rago, [Henry]. a. p. c. s., 1*l* verso 14 x 8.2 cm. San Francisco, [13 Dec. 1957]. ICU.

E318 [Blaser], Robin. a. l. s., 2*l* recto-verso, recto-verso 27.9 x 21.7 cm. San Francisco, 19 Dec. 1957. CU-B.

E319 [Rago, Henry]. a. n. s., 1*l* recto 21.6 x 13.9 cm. San Francisco, 27 Dec. 1957. ICU.

E320 [Witt-Diamant], Ruth. a. l. s., 1*l* recto 27.9 x 21.6 cm. San Francisco, 28 Dec. 1957. CU-B.

E321 [Olson], Charles. a. l. s., 1*l* recto-verso 32.9 x 21.6 cm. San Francisco, 8 Jan. 1958. CtU.
Note: A typescript of THE PERFORMANCE WE WAIT FOR—AT CHRISTMAS—A POEM BEGINNING WITH A LINE BY PINDAR—PROOFS, and YES, AS A LOOK SPRINGS FROM ITS FACE accompanied this letter. F161.

E322 [Blaser], Robin. a. l. s., 2*l*, 1*l* recto-verso 33 x 21.6 cm., 1*l* 14.3 x 21.6 cm. San Francisco, 14 Jan. 1958. CU-B.

E323 [Blaser], Robin. a. l. s., 1*l* recto 20 x 21.6 cm. San Francisco, 27 Jan. 1958. CU-B.

E324 [Creeley], Bob. t. l. s., 2*l* recto-verso, recto-verso 21.7 x 16.5 cm. San Francisco, 28 Jan. 1958. On deposit at MoSW.
Note: A typescript of THE PERFORMANCE WE WAIT FOR and PROOFS accompanied this letter. F162, F163.

E325 Rago, [Henry]. t. p. c. s., 1*l* verso 8.2 x 14 cm. San Francisco, 1 Feb. 1958. ICU.

E326 [Blaser], Robin. a. l. s., 1*l* recto 27.9 x 21.6 cm. San Francisco, 4 Feb. 1958. CU-B.
Note: Enclosed in this letter is the holograph version of the poem A PRIVATELY, VILLANELLE OF POEMS DANCING for Robin Blaser. F165.

E327 [Olson], Charles. a. l. s., 1*l* recto 14 x 21.5 cm. San Francisco, 5 Feb. 1958. CtU.

E328 [Blaser], Robin. a. l. s., 1*l* recto-verso 27.9 x 21.7 cm. San Francisco, 15 Feb. 1958. CU-B.

E329 Rago, Henry. a. l. s., 1*l* recto-verso 28 x 21.7 cm. San Francisco, 17 Feb. 1958. ICU.

E330 [Blaser], Robin. a. l. s., 3*l* all recto-verso 27.8 x 21.7 cm. San Francisco, 20 Feb. 1958. CU-B.

E331 [Blaser], Robin. a. l. s., 1*l* recto-verso 27.9 x 21.6 cm. Stinson Beach, 26 Feb. 1958. CU-B.

Note: A typescript of RD's poem PASSAGE OVER WATER as it appeared in *Ritual*, I, 1 (April 1940), [10], is contained in this letter. There is a short holograph note at bottom verso.

E332 Z[ukofsky, Louis]. a. l. s., 1*l* recto 22.9 x 21.7 cm. San Francisco, 1 March 1958. TxU.

E333 [Blaser], Robin. a. l. s., 1*l* recto-verso 27.9 x 21.6 cm. San Francisco, 4 March 1958. CU-B.

E334 [Olson], Charles. a. l. s., 1*l* recto-verso 27.8 x 21.5 cm. San Francisco, 10 March 1958. CtU.
Note: The musical score of "Song no Six" (from *Maximus*) set to music by Pauline Oliveros accompanied this letter, also the typescript of THE STRUCTURE OF RIME VIII-XI. F167.

E335 Guest, Barbara. a. l. s., 1*l* recto 21.5 x 19 cm. Stinson Beach, 25 March 1958. NjR.

E336 Guest, Barbara. t. l. s., 1*l* recto 21.5 x 14 cm. Stinson Beach, 28 March 1958. NjR.

E337 Eigner, [Larry]. a. l. s., 1*l* recto-verso 27.8 x 21.5 cm. Stinson Beach, 28 March 1958. CtU.

E338 [Blaser], Robin. a. p. c. s., 1*l* verso 15.1 x 10.1 cm. Stinson Beach, [Spring 1958]. CU-B.

E339 [Spicer], Jack. a. l. s., 1*l* recto-verso 27.9 x 21.7 cm. [Stinson Beach], 3 April 1958. CU-B.
Note: A typescript of A STORM OF WHITE accompanied this letter. F168.

E340 [Blaser], Robin. a. l. s., 1*l* recto-verso 27.9 x 21.7 cm. Stinson Beach, 3 April 1958. CU-B.
Note: A typescript of A STORM OF WHITE and a typescript of Robert Creeley's poem THE THREE LADIES accompanied this letter. F187.

E341 Zuk[ofsky, Louis]. a. l. s., 1*l* recto-verso 21.5 x 16.3 cm. Stinson Beach, 17 April 1958. TxU.

E342 [Witt-Diamant], Ruth. t. l. s., 1*l* recto 27.9 x 21.5 cm. Stinson Beach, 22 April 1958. CU-B.

E343 [Zukofsky], Louis. a. l. s., 2*l* recto-verso, recto-verso 27.8 x 21.7 cm. Stinson Beach, 26 April 1958. TxU.

E344 Zuks [Zukofsky, Louis, Celia, & Paul]. a. l. s., 2*l*; 1*l* recto-verso 27.8 x 21.5 cm., 1*l* recto-verso, 21.5 x 19.2 cm. Stinson Beach, 12 May 1958. TxU.

E345 [Kyger], Joanne. a. l. s., 1*l* recto-verso 27.9 x 21.5 cm. Stinson Beach, 22 May 1958. CU-B.

E346 Zuks/large and small [Louis, Celia, & Paul]. a. l. s., 1*l* recto 21.4 x 19.2 cm. Stinson Beach, 5 June 1958. TxU.

E347 [Blaser], Robin. a. l. s., 1*l* recto-verso 27.9 x 21.6 cm. Stinson Beach, 3 and 6 June 1958. CU-B.
Note: A typescript of A STORM OF WHITE, ATLANTIS, and BONE DANCE accompanied this letter. F169.

E348 [Blaser], Robin. a. l. s., 1*l* recto-verso 27.9 x 21.5 cm. Stinson Beach, 27 June 1958. CU-B.

E349 [Blaser], Robin. a. l. s., 2*l* recto-verso, recto-verso 27.9 x 21.6 cm. Stinson Beach, 29 June 1958. CU-B.

E350 [Blaser], Robin. a. l. s., 2*l* recto, recto 27.8 x 21.5 cm. Stinson Beach, 4 July 1958. CU-B.
Note: This letter contains a holograph poem entitled A LITTLE POEM FOR ROBIN. Accompanying this letter are typescripts of the final lines of DANSE MACABRE and the full text of UNDER GROUND. Also enclosed is a typescript of Ebbe Borregaard's poem beginning "Each found himself at the end of. . . ." F171.

E351 [Blaser], Robin. a. l. s., 1*l* recto-verso 27.8 x 21.7 cm. Stinson Beach, 22 July 1958. CU-B.

E352 [Blaser], Robin. a. l. s., 1*l* recto-verso 32.9 x 21.6 cm. Stinson Beach, 28 July 1958. CU-B.

E353 [Blaser], Robin. a. l. s., 2*l* recto-verso, recto 27.9 x 21.4 cm. Stinson Beach, 6 and 11 Aug. 1958. CU-B.

E354 [Blaser], Robin. a. l. s., 1*l* recto-verso 27.7 x 21.6 cm. Stinson Beach, 21 Aug. 1958. CU-B.

E355 [Blaser], Robin. a. l. s., 2*l* recto-verso, recto-verso 27.7 x 21.6 cm. Stinson Beach, 27 Aug. 1958. CU-B.

E356 [Blaser], Robin. a. l. s., 1*l* recto-verso 27.7 x 21.6 cm. Stinson Beach, 28 Aug. 1958. CU-B.

E357 [Blaser], Robin. a. l. s., 3*l* all recto-verso 21.6 x 16.4 cm. Stinson Beach, 2 Sept. 1958. CU-B.

E358 Blaser, [Robin]. a. l. s., 2*l* recto-verso, recto-verso 27.9 x 21.7 cm. Stinson Beach, 29 Oct. 1958. CU-B.
Note: The texts of the poems ANIMADVERSION I and ANIMADVERSION II are contained in this letter.

E359 [Olson], Charles. a. l. s., 2*l* recto-verso, recto-verso 27.8 x 21.5 cm. San Francisco, 3 Nov. 1958. CtU.

E360 [Blaser], Robin. a. l. s., 1*l* recto-verso 27.9 x 21.7 cm. Stinson Beach, 5 Nov. 1958. CU-B.

E361 [Blaser], Robin. a. l. s., 1*l* recto-verso 27.9 x 21.6 cm. Stinson Beach, 29 Nov. 1958. CU-B.

E362 [Olson], Charles. a. l. s., 3*l* all recto-verso 16.4 x 21.5 cm. Stinson Beach, 1 Dec. 1958. CtU.
Note: A portion of a letter from Bobbie Creeley to RD is typed in recto of the first leaf.

E363 [Blaser], Robin. a. l. s., 2*l* recto-verso, recto 27.9 x 21.6 cm. Stinson Beach, 5 Dec. 1958. CU-B.

E364 [Olson, Charles]. a. n. s., 1*l* recto 21.5 x 16.3 cm. Stinson Beach, 11 Dec. 1958. CtU.

E365 Zuks [Louis, Celia, & Paul]. a. l. s., 1*l* recto-verso 27.8 x 21.7 cm. Stinson Beach, 19 Dec. 1958. TxU.

E366 [Broughton], James. t. l. s., 1*l* recto 27.8 x 21.6 cm. San Francisco, 28 Dec. 1958. OKentU.

E367 [Hodes], Ida. t. l. (photocopy), 1*l* recto 27.9 x 21.6 cm. [Stinson Beach, 1959?]. CSf APA.

E368 [Blaser], Robin. a. l. s., 1*l* recto-verso 27.8 x 21.5 cm. Stinson Beach, 9 Jan. 1959. CU-B.

E369 [Witt-Diamant], Ruth. t. l. s., 1*l* recto 27.9 x 21.5 cm. Stinson Beach, 11 Jan. 1959. CU-B.

E370 Rago, [Henry]. t. l. s., 1*l* recto 27.8 x 21.6 cm. Stinson Beach, 12 Jan. 1959. ICU.

E371 [Blaser], Robin. a. l. s., 1*l* recto-verso 27.8 x 21.6 cm. Stinson Beach, 20 Jan. 1959. CU-B.

E372 Rago, Henry. t. l. s., 1*l* recto 27.8 x 21.6 cm. Stinson Beach, 27 Jan. 1959. ICU.

E373 Zuk[ofsky, Louis]. a. l. s., 1*l* recto-verso 21.6 x 16.4 cm. Stinson Beach, 30 Jan. 1959. TxU.

E374 [Hodes], Ida. t. l., 1*l* recto-verso 21.6 x 18.7 cm. Stinson Beach, [Feb. 1959]. CU-B.

E375 Mrs. Publisher [Zukofsky, Celia]. a. l. s., 1*l* recto 27.8 x 21.7 cm. Stinson Beach, 4 Feb. 1959. TxU.

E376 [Olson], Charles. a. l. s., 3*l*; 1*l* recto-verso 21.5 x 19.2 cm., 1*l* recto-verso 22.7 x 21.5 cm., 1*l* recto-verso 21.5 x 15.5 cm. Stinson Beach, 7 Feb. 1959. CtU.

E377 [Witt-Diamant], Ruth. t. l. s., 1*l* recto 27.8 x 21.5 cm. Stinson Beach, 11 Feb. 1959. CU-B.

E378 [Blaser], Robin. a. l. s., 1*l* recto-verso 24 x 27.7 cm. Stinson Beach, 11 Feb. 1959. CU-B.
Note: A typescript of A DISCLOSURE and notes from RD's reading of Paracelsus accompanied this letter. F184, F185.

E379 [Broughton], James. a. l. s., 2*l* recto-verso, recto 21.5 x 21.5 cm. [Stinson Beach], 11 Feb. 1959. OKentU.
Note: Drawings by RD appear on recto and verso of the first leaf.

E380 [Blaser], Robin. a. l. s., 1*l* recto-verso 27.9 x 21.6 cm. Stinson Beach, 20 Feb. 1959. CU-B.

E381 [Blaser], Robin. a. l. s., 1*l* recto-verso 22.3 x 21.6 cm. Stinson Beach, 23 Feb. 1959. CU-B.
Note: A typescript of UNCOLLECTED PIECES, FEB 1959 accompanied this letter. F186.

E382 [Blaser], Robin. a. l. s., 1*l* recto-verso 27.9 x 21.6 cm. Stinson Beach, 28 Feb. 1959. CU-B.

E383 Rago, [Henry]. a. l. s., 1*l* recto 28 x 21.6 cm. Stinson Beach, 4 March 1959. ICU.

E384 [Kyger], Joanne. a. l. s., 2*l* recto-verso, recto 21.5 x 20.2 cm. Stinson Beach, 6 March 1959. CU-B.

E385 [Adam], Helen. a. l. s., 1*l* recto-verso 27.9 x 21.6 cm. Stinson Beach, 18 March 1959. OKentU.
Note: A holograph manuscript of the poem ROOTS AND BRANCHES accompanied this letter. F188.

E386 Guest, Barbara. t. l. s., 1*l* recto 28 x 21.5 cm. Stinson Beach, 20 March 1959. NjR.

E387 [Spicer], Jack. a. p. c. s., 1*l* verso 14 x 8.2 cm. Stinson Beach, [4 April 1959]. CU-B.

E388 [Blaser], Robin. a. l. s., 1*l* recto 33 x 21.6 cm. Stinson Beach, 15 April 1959. CU-B.

E389 [Olson], Charles. a. l. s., 1*l* recto-verso 21.5 x 19.4 cm. Stinson Beach, 2 May 1959. CtU.

E390 Rago, Henry. t. l. s., 1*l* recto 28 x 21.6 cm. Stinson Beach, 4 May 1959. ICU.

E391 [Blaser], Robin. t. l. s., 1*l* recto 27.9 x 21.6 cm. Stinson Beach, 8 May 1959. CU-B.

E392 [Blaser], Robin. a. l. s., 2*l* recto-verso, recto 21.6 x 13.8 cm. Stinson Beach, 22 May 1959. CU-B.

E393 [Weiners], John. a. l. s. (thermofax), 3*l* all recto 33 x 21.8 cm. San Francisco, 24 May 1959. CU-B.

E394 [Adam], Helen. a. p. c. s., 1*l* verso 13.9 x 8.3 cm. Stinson Beach, 26 May 1959. NBuU.

E395 Rago, Henry. a. & t. l. s., 2*l* recto-verso, recto-verso 21.7 x 16.2 cm. Stinson Beach, 3 June 1959. ICU.

E396 [Creeley], Bob. a. l. s., 1*l* recto 21.5 x 17.5 cm. Stinson Beach, 10 June 1959. On deposit at MoSW.

E397 To The Chronicle. t. l. s., 1*l* recto 33 x 27.7 cm. Stinson Beach, 23 June 1959. CU-B.

E398 [Witt-Diamant], Ruth. t. l. s., 1*l* recto 27.8 x 21.5 cm. Stinson Beach, 23 June 1959. CU-B.

E399 Hogan, William. t. l., 1*l* recto 27.9 x 21.5 cm. Stinson Beach, 23 June 1959. CU-B.

E400 Zuks—the small ones and the large one [Zukofsky, Louis, Celia, & Paul]. a. l. s., 2*l* recto-verso, recto-verso 21.7 x 16.5 cm. Stinson Beach, 23 June 1959. TxU.

E401 [Hodes], Ida. t. l. s., 1*l* recto 27.9 x 21.5 cm. San Francisco, 24 June 1959. CU-B.

E402 Sirs [Quinn, Kerker]. t. p. c. s., 1*l* verso 14 x 8.2 cm. Stinson Beach, 30 June 1959. IU.

E403 [Blaser], Robin. a. l. s., 3*l* all recto-verso 16.5 x 21.7 cm. Stinson Beach, 2 July 1959. CU-B.

E404 Rago, [Henry]. a. n. s., 1*l* recto 21.6 x 16.5 cm. Stinson Beach, 2 July 1959. ICU.

E405 Aldington, Mrs. t. l. s., 1*l* recto 30.3 x 18.4 cm. Stinson Beach, 5 July 1959. CtY.

E406 [Hodes], Ida. t. n., 1*l* recto 22.2 x 21.4 cm. Stinson Beach, 6 July 1959. CU-B.

E407 Rago, Henry. t. l. s., 1*l* recto 28 x 21.6 cm. Stinson Beach, 10 July 1959. ICU.

E408 [Creeley], Bob & Bobbie. t. p. c. s., 1*l* verso 14 x 8.2 cm. Stinson Beach, [14 July 1959]. On deposit at MoSW.

E409 D[oolittle], H[ilda]. a. l. s., 1*l* recto 30.3 x 18.4 cm. Stinson Beach, 20 July 1959. CtY.

E410 [Anderson, Lee]. t. l. s., 1*l* recto 27.8 x 21.6 cm. Stinson Beach, [Aug. 1959]. MoSW.

E411 Rago, Henry. a. l. s., 2*l* recto, recto-verso 21.5 x 13.8 cm. Stinson Beach, 10 Aug. 1959. ICU.

Note: A typescript of THE INBINDING MIRRORS A PROCESS and RETURNING TO ROOTS OF FIRST FEELING accompanied this letter. F189.

E412 Pearson, Norman Holmes. a. l. s., 2*l* recto-verso, recto-verso 27.9 x 21.5 cm. Stinson Beach, 10 Aug. 1959. CtY.

E413 D[oolittle], H[ilda]. a. l. s., 1*l* recto 27.9 x 21.5 cm. Stinson Beach, 14 Aug. 1959. CtY.

E414 D[oolitle], H[ilda]. a. l. s., 3*l* all recto 28 x 21.6 cm. Stinson Beach, 15 Aug. [1959]. CtY.

E415 Pearson, Norman Holmes. a. n. s., 1*l* recto 21.6 x 14.1 cm. Stinson Beach, 15 Aug. [1959]. CtY.

E416 [Blaser], Robin. t. l. s., 1*l* recto 30.3 x 18.5 cm. Stinson Beach, 15 Aug. 1959. CU-B.

E417 [Witt-Diamant], Ruth. t. l. s., 1*l* recto 27.8 x 21.5 cm. Stinson Beach, 19 Aug. 1959. CU-B.

E418 [Creeley], Bob. t. l. s., 2*l* recto-verso, recto-verso 27.9 x 21.6 cm. Stinson Beach, 26 Aug. 1959. On deposit at MoSW.

E419 [Witt-Diamant], Ruth. t. l. s., 1*l* recto 27.9 x 21.5 cm. San Francisco, 29 Aug. 1959. CU-B.

E420 D[oolittle], H[ilda]. a. l. s., 3*l* all recto 28 x 21.6 cm. Stinson Beach, 3 Sept. 1959. CtY.
Note: A typescript of A SEQUENCE OF POEMS FOR H.D.'S BIRTHDAY accompanied this letter. F191.

E421 [Blaser], Robin. a. l. s., 1*l* recto-verso 28 x 21.5 cm. Stinson Beach, 4 Sept. 1959. CU-B.

E422 [Weiners], John. a. l. s. (thermofax), 2*l* recto, recto 27.9 x 21.5 cm. [San Francisco], 9 Sept. 1959. CU-B.

E423 P[earson], N[orman] H[olmes]. a. l. s., 1*l* recto-verso 28 x 21.6 cm. Stinson Beach, 14 Sept. 1959. CtY.

E424 Anderson, Lee. t. l. s., 1*l* recto 28 x 21.6 cm. Stinson Beach, 18 Sept. 1959. MoSW.

E425 Sirs [Quinn, Kerker]. t. p. c. s., 1*l* verso 14 x 8.2 cm. Stinson Beach, 23 Sept. 1959. IU.

E426 Krim, [Seymour]. t. l. s., 1*l* recto 27.9 x 21.6 cm. Stinson Beach, 27 Sept. 1959. IaU.

E427 Ward, Tony. t. l. s., 1*l* recto 28 x 21.6 cm. Stinson Beach, 27 Sept. 1959. CLU.

E428 [Spicer], Jack. a. l. s., 2*l*, 1*l* recto 18.5 x 21.6 cm., 1*l* recto 17.3 x 21.6 cm. Stinson Beach, [27 Sept. 1959]. CU-B.
Note: This letter is written around RD's drawing for the logo for EN-KIDU SURROGATE.

E429 Anderson, Lee. a. n. s., 1*l* recto 21.5 x 14.1 cm. San Francisco, 30 Sept. [1959]. MoSW.

E430 [Blaser], Robin. a. l. s., 1*l* recto 30.4 x 18.3 cm. Stinson Beach, 3 Oct. 1959. CU-B.

E431 Krim, Seymour. t. l. s., 1*l* recto 21.6 x 16.6 cm. Stinson Beach, 12 Oct. [19]59. IaU.

E432 [Witt-Diamant], Ruth. t. l. s., 1*l* recto 27.9 x 21.7 cm. Stinson Beach, 16 Oct. 1959. CU-B.

E433 Krim, Seymour. a. l. s., 1*l* recto 27.7 x 21.6 cm. Stinson Beach, 19 Oct. [19]59. IaU.

E434 Krim, Seymour. a. l. s., 1*l* recto 27.9 x 21.6 cm. Stinson Beach, 23 Oct. 1959. IaU.

E435 [Creeley], Bob. a. l. s., 3*l* recto-verso, recto-verso, recto 27.9 x 21.6 cm. Stinson Beach, 28 Sept., and 3 and 26 Oct. [19]56. On deposit at MoSW.

E436 [Creeley], Bob. t. l. s., 1*l* recto-verso 21.5 x 15.8 cm. Stinson Beach, [Nov. 1959]. On deposit at MoSW.

E437 D[oolittle], H[ilda]. a. n. s., 1*l* recto 21.6 x 13.8 cm. Stinson Beach, 1 Nov. 1959. CtY.
Note: A typescript of the completed poem A SEQUENCE OF POEMS FOR H.D.'S BIRTHDAY, SEPTEMBER 10, 1959 FINISHED OCTOBER 24, 1959 accompanied this letter. F194.

E438 Krim, Seymour. t. n. s., 1*l* recto 21.6 x 18 cm. Stinson Beach, 2 Nov. [19]59. IaU.

E439 [Witt-Diamant], Ruth. t. & a. l. s., 1*l* recto 21.5 x 16.5 cm. Stinson Beach, 6 Nov. 1959. CU-B.

E440 [Olson], Charles. a. l. s., 1*l* recto-verso 33 x 21.5 cm. Stinson Beach, 10 Nov. 1959. CtU.

E441 Pearson, [Norman Holmes]. a. l. s., 1*l* recto-verso 28 x 21.6 cm. Stinson Beach, 11 Nov. 1959. CtY.

E442 Roethke, [Theodore]. a. l. s., 3*l* recto-verso, recto-verso, recto 28 x 21.6 cm. Stinson Beach, 11 Nov. 1959. WaU.

E443 Birney, Earle. t. l. s., 1*l* recto 27.8 x 21.5 cm. Stinson Beach, 13 Nov. 1959. CaOTU.

E444 [Creeley], Bob. t. l. s., 3*l* recto-verso, recto-verso, recto 27.9 x 21.6 cm. Stinson Beach, 20 Nov. [19]59. On deposit at MoSW.

E445 Birney, Earle. t. l. s., 1*l* recto 27.8 x 21.5 cm. Stinson Beach, 21 Nov. 1959. CaOTU.

E446 [Adam], Helen. a. p. c. s., 1*l* verso 13.9 x 8.3 cm. Stinson Beach, [3 Dec. 1959]. NBuU.

E447 [Blaser], Robin. a. l. s., 2*l* recto-verso, recto 28 x 21.6 cm. Stinson Beach, 5 Dec. 1959. CU-B.

E448 [Witt-Diamant], Ruth. t. l. s., 1*l* recto 27.9 x 21.7 cm. Stinson Beach, 23 Dec. 1959. CU-B.

E449 Pearson, [Norman Holmes]. a. l. s., 1*l* recto-verso 27.9 x 21.6 cm. Stinson Beach, 23 Dec. 1959. CtY.

E450 [Roethke], Ted & Beatrice. a. l. s., 1*l* recto 27.8 x 21.6 cm. Stinson Beach, 30 Dec. 1959. WaU.

E451 [Creeley], Bob. a. l. s., 1*l* recto-verso 27.9 x 21.6 cm. Stinson Beach, 2 Jan. 1960. On deposit at MoSW.
Note: A typescript of the poem THE LAW accompanied this letter. F197.

E452 D[oolittle], H[ilda]. a. & t. l. s., 1*l* recto 30.4 x 18.3 cm. Stinson Beach, 2 Jan. 1960. CtY.

E453 Olson, Charles. a. l. s., 1*l* recto-verso 27.8 x 21.5 cm. Stinson Beach, 4 Jan. 1960. CtU.
Note: A typescript of NEL MEZZO DEL CAMMIN DI NOSTRA VITA accompanied this letter. F198.

E454 Eigner, [Larry]. a. l. s., 1*l* recto-verso 19.7 x 21.5 cm. Stinson Beach, 6 Jan. 1960. CtU.

E455 Krim, Seymour. t. l. s., 2*l* recto, recto 27.9 x 21.7 cm. Stinson Beach, 12 Jan. 1960. IAU.

E456 [Olson, Charles]. a. n. s., 1*l* recto-verso 22.7 x 15.1 cm. Stinson Beach, 21 Jan. 1960. CtU.

E457 Pearson, [Norman Holmes]. t. l. s., 1*l* recto 27.9 x 21.7 cm. Stinson Beach, 21 Jan. 1960. CtY.

E458 [Brakhage], Stan. t. l. (carbon), 1*l* 27.9 x 21.5 cm. San Francisco, 2 Feb. 1960. CtU.

E459 Eigner, [Larry]. a. l. s., 1*l* recto 21 x 21.5 cm. Stinson Beach, 3 Feb. 1960. CtU.

E460 [Eigner], Larry. a. n. s., 1*l* recto 21.5 x 16.5 cm. Stinson Beach, 4 Feb. 1960. CtU.

E461 Posner, [David]. t. l. s., 2*l* recto, recto 27.9 x 21.7 cm. Stinson Beach, 4 Feb. 1960. NBuU.

E462 [Creeley], Bob. t. & a. l. s., 1*l* recto 30.5 x 18.2 cm. Stinson Beach, 4 and 5 Feb. [19]60. On deposit at MoSW.
Note: A typescript of part 1 of APPREHENSIONS (untitled) accompanied this letter. F201.

E463 Rago, [Henry]. t. l. s., 1*l* recto 28 x 21.6 cm. Stinson Beach, 5 Feb. 1960. ICU.

E464 [Olson], Charles. a. l. s., 2*l* recto-verso, recto-verso 34 x 21.5 cm. Stinson Beach, 6 Feb. 1960. CtU.
Note: Both leaves contain pencil holographs by Charles Olson. The following parts of the poem APPREHENSIONS accompanied this letter: 1, and 2 THE DIRECTIVE, SECOND VERSION. F202.

E465 Pearson, [Norman Holmes]. t. l. s., 1*l* recto 27.9 x 21.7 cm. Stinson Beach, 6 Feb. 1960. CtY.

E466 Seaver, Richard. t. l. s., 1*l* recto 27.8 x 21.5 cm. Stinson Beach, 12 Feb 1960. NSyU.

E467 [Creeley], Bob. a. l. s., 2*l* recto, recto 21.6 x 18.5 cm. Stinson Beach, 15 Feb. 1960. On deposit at MoSW.
Note: A typescript of the second section of APPREHENSIONS was enclosed with this letter. F203.

E468 Seaver, [Richard]. t. l. s., 1*l* recto 27.8 x 21.5 cm. Stinson Beach, 19 Feb. 1960. NSyU.

E469 Seaver, Dick. t. l. s., 1*l* recto 27.8 x 21.5 cm. Stinson Beach, 23 Feb. 1960. NSyU.

E470 [Brakhage], Stan. t. l. (carbon), 1*l* recto 27.9 x 21.5 cm. Stinson Beach, 24 Feb. 1960. CtU.

E471 Seaver, [Richard]. t. l. s., 1*l* recto 27.8 x 21.5 cm. Stinson Beach, 27 Feb. 1960. NSyU.

E472 [Blaser], Robin. t. & a. l. s., 1*l* recto-verso 21.5 x 14.2 cm. Stinson Beach, 3 March 1960. CU-B.

E473 Zuks [Zukofsky, Louis, Celia, & Paul]. a. l. s., 1*l* recto-verso 21.4 x 21.7 cm. Stinson Beach, 3 March 1960. TxU.

E474 [Olson], Charles. a. l. s., 1*l* recto-verso 21.5 x 15.7 cm. Stinson Beach, 7 March 1960. CtU.
Note: The poem APPREHENSIONS, THIRD MOVEMENT accompanied this letter. F204

E475 Seaver, Dick. t. l. s., 1*l* recto 27.8 x 21.5 cm. Stinson Beach, 15 March 1960. NSyU.

E476 Eshleman, [Clayton]. t. l., 1*l* recto 27.9 x 21.5 cm. Stinson Beach, 15 March 1960. CaBVaS.
Note: A typescript of POETRY, A NATURAL THING and a typescript of THREE PAGES FROM A BIRTHDAY BOOK accompanied this letter. F205, F206.

E477 Rago, Henry. t. l. s., 1*l* recto-verso 28 x 21.7 cm. Stinson Beach, 15 March 1960. ICU.

E478 [Creeley], Bob. t. l. s., 1*l* recto 30.2 x 18.2 cm. Stinson Beach, 19 March 1960. On deposit at MoSW.
Note: A sixteen line poem beginning "I SAW THE RABBIT LEAP," appears in the letter.

E479 Seaver, Richard. t. l. s., 1*l* recto 27.8 x 21.5 cm. Stinson Beach, 22 March 1960. NSyU.

E480 Eshleman, Clayton. a. l. s., 1*l* recto 27.9 x 21.5 cm. Stinson Beach, 25 March 1960. CaBVaS.

E481 [Pearson], Norman [Holmes]. t. l. s., 1*l* recto 28 x 21.6 cm. Stinson Beach, 27 March 1960. CtY.

E482 [Creeley], Bob. a. l. s., 1*l* recto-verso 27.9 x 21.6 cm. Stinson Beach, 28 March 1960. On deposit at MoSW.
Note: A typescript of the fourth and fifth movements of APPRE-HENSIONS accompanied this letter. F207.

E483 [Witt-Diamant], Ruth. t. l. s., 1*l* recto 27.9 x 21.7 cm. Stinson Beach, 30 March 1960. CU-B.

E484 [Doolittle, Hilda]. a. p. c. s., 1*l* verso 10.5 x 14.8 cm. New Haven, Conn., 21 April 1960. CtY.

E485 P[earson], N[orman] H[olmes]. t. l. s., 2*l* recto, recto 21.9 x 21.7 cm. New York City, 3 May 1960. CtY.

E486 [Olson], Charles. a. l. s., 2*l* recto-verso, blank 21.7 x 14 cm. [Boston], 4 May 1960. CtU.

E487 D[oolittle], H[ilda]. a. n. s., 1*l* recto 27.8 x 21.6 cm. New York City, 13 May 1960. CtY.

E488 D[oolittle], H[ilda]. a. l. s., 3*l* all recto 28 x 21.6 cm. Stinson Beach, 27 May 1960. CtY.

E489 [Creeley] Bob. a. l. s., 2*l* recto-verso, recto 27.9 x 21.6 cm. Stinson Beach, 1 June 1960. On deposit at MoSW.
Note: A typescript of TWO DICTA OF WILLIAM BLAKE accompanied this letter. F209.

E490 Rago, Henry. t. l. s., 1*l* recto 27.9 x 21.7 cm. Stinson Beach, 1 June 1960. ICU.

E491 Rago, Henry. t. l. s., 1*l* recto 27.9 x 21.6 cm. Stinson Beach, 7 June 1960. ICU.

E492 [Blaser], Robin. a. n. s., 1*l* recto 21.6 x 17.7 cm. Stinson Beach, 8 June 1960. CU-B.

E493 Seaver, [Dick]. t. l. s., 1*l* recto 27.8 x 21.5 cm. Stinson Beach, 11 June 1960. NSyU.

E494 Seaver, Dick. t. l. s., 2*l* recto, recto 27.8 x 21.5 cm. Stinson Beach, 13 June 1960. NSyU.

E495 [Pearson], Norman [Holmes]. t. l. s., 1*l* recto-verso 27.8 x 21.4 cm. Stinson Beach, 2 July 1960. CtY.
Note: A typescript of two leaves of "The H.D. Book" accompanied this letter. F210.

E496 [Eigner], Larry. t. n. s., 1*l* recto 21.4 x 13.1 cm. Stinson Beach, 6 July 1960. CtU.
Note: This note contains two lines in RD's holograph at the bottom of the leaf, and comments in Eigner's holograph appear on this note.

E497 Seaver, [Dick]. t. l. s., 1*l* recto 27.8 x 21.5 cm. Stinson Beach, 3 Aug. 1960. NSyU.
Note: There is a short note in RD's holograph at the bottom of this letter.

E498 D[oolittle], H[ilda]. a. l. s., 1*l* recto-verso 27.8 x 21.4 cm. Stinson Beach, 10 Aug. 1960. CtY.

E499 [Pearson], Norman [Holmes]. a. l. s., 2*l* recto-verso, recto 27.8 x 21.5 cm. Stinson Beach, 10 Aug. 1960. CtY.

E500 [Spicer], Jack. a. l. s., 4*l* recto-verso, recto-verso, recto, recto 21.6 x 16.4 cm. [Stinson Beach], 15 Aug. 1960. CU-B.

E501 Meeker, Marilyn. t. l. s., 1*l* recto 27.8 x 21.5 cm. Stinson Beach, 11 Sept. 1960. NSyU.

E502 [Creeley], Bob. a. l. s., 1*l* recto-verso 27.9 x 21.6 cm. Stinson Beach, 12 Sept. 1960. On deposit at MoSW.

E503 [Pearson], Norman [Holmes]. 1*l* recto-verso 27.7 x 21.4 cm. Stinson Beach, 12 Sept. 1960. CtY.
Note: A typescript of (TOWARD A STUDY OF H.D.) plus a typescript of FOUR SONGS THE NIGHT NURSE SANG accompanied this letter. F214, F215, F217.

E504 [Pearson], Norman [Holmes]. t. l. s., 1*l* recto 27.8 x 21.4 cm. Stinson Beach, 16 Sept. 1960. CtY.
Note: A typescript of (TOWARD A STUDY OF H.D.) accompanied this letter. F216.

E505 [Eigner], Larry. t. n. s., 1*l* recto 17.2 x 21.5 cm. Stinson Beach, 22 Sept. 1960. CtU.
Note: Two short pencil holograph comments by Eigner appear in the margins of this note.

E506 [Pearson], Norman [Holmes]. a. l. s., 1*l* recto 21.6 x 16.4 cm. Stinson Beach, 26 Sept. 1960. CtY.

E507 [Pearson], Norman [Holmes]. a. l. s., 3*l* all recto 24.2 x 21.5 cm. Stinson Beach, 26 Sept. 1960. CtY.

E508 D[oolittle], H[ilda]. a. l. s., 3*l* all recto-verso 28.5 x 21.5 cm. Stinson Beach, 1 and 12 Oct. 1960. CtY.
Note: A typescript of TOWARDS A STUDY OF H.D.: BEGINNINGS accompanied this letter. F218.

E509 [Pearson], Norman [Holmes]. a. n. s., 1*l* recto 20 x 21.5 cm. Stinson Beach, 2 Oct. 1960. CtY.

E510 [Creeley], Robert. a. l., 1*l* recto-verso 26 x 21.5 cm. Stinson Beach, 12 Oct. 1960. On deposit at MoSW.

E511 Meeker, Marilyn. t. l. s., 2*l* recto, recto 27.8 x 21.5 cm. Stinson Beach, 12 Oct. 1960. NSyU.

E512 [Spicer], Jack. a. l. s., 1*l* recto-verso 21.4 x 17.8 cm. [Stinson Beach], 17 Oct. 1960. CU-B.

E513 Adam, Helen, Pat & Mother. a. l. s., 2*l* recto, recto 27.8 x 21.4 cm. Stinson Beach, 20 Oct. 1960. NBuU.
Note: On the verso of these leaves appear a typescript of STRUCTURE OF RIME XVIII, STRUCTURE OF RIME XV, and STRUCTURE OF RIME XVI. The first poem was retitled STRUCTURE OF RIME XVII. F219.

E514 D[oolittle], H[ilda]. a. l. s., 1*l* recto 30.4 x 18.2 cm. Stinson Beach, 28 Oct. 1960. CtY.

E515 [Adam], Helen & Pat. a. l. s., 2*l* recto-verso, recto-verso 21.5 x 14.4 cm. Stinson Beach, 31 Oct. 1960. NBuU.

E516 D[oolitle], H[ilda]. a. l. s., 2*l* recto-verso, recto-verso 21.5 x 14.1 cm. Stinson Beach, 31 Oct. 1960. CtY.

E517 [Pearson], Norman [Holmes]. t. l. s., 1*l* recto-verso 28.3 x 21.5 cm. Stinson Beach, 12 Nov. 1960. CtY.

E518 [Creeley], Bob. a. l. s., 1*l* recto 30.5 x 18 cm. Stinson Beach, 23 Nov. 1960. On deposit at MoSW.
Note: A typescript of FOUR SONGS THE NIGHT-NURSE SANG and RISK accompanied this letter. F221.

E519 [Creeley], Bob. a. l. s., 1*l* recto-verso 33 x 20.3 cm. Stinson Beach, 14 Dec. 1960. On deposit at MoSW.

E520 Zuks [Zukofsky, Louis, Celia, & Paul]. a. l. s., 4*l* recto, recto, recto, blank 21.4 x 16.4 cm. Stinson Beach, 20 Dec. 1960. TxU.

E521 [Creeley], Bob. t. l. s., 1*l* recto 30.5 x 18.2 cm. Stinson Beach, 22 Dec. 1960. On deposit at MoSW.

E522 [Creeley], Bob. a. n. s., 1*l* recto 27.9 x 21.6 cm. Stinson Beach, [1961]. On deposit at MoSW.
Note: The note is written around the edges of an announcement for Gerrit Lansing's magazine, *Set.*

E523 Olson, Charles. a. l. s., 1*l* recto-verso 28 x 19.4 cm. San Francisco, [1961]. CtU.

E524 D[oolittle], H[ilda]. a. l. s., 1*l* recto 30.4 x 18.2 cm. Stinson Beach, 2 Jan. 1961. CtY.

E525 [Pearson], Norman [Holmes]. a. l. s., 1*l* recto-verso 27.8 x 21.4 cm. Stinson Beach, 2 Jan. 1961. CtY.

E526 Schmidt, [Judith]. t. n. s., 1*l* recto 27.8 x 21.5 cm. Stinson Beach, 18 Jan. 1961. NSyU.

E527 Seaver, Dick. t. l. s., 1*l* recto 27.8 x 21.5 cm. Stinson Beach, 28 Feb. 1961. NSyU.

E528 D[oolittle], H[ilda]. a. & t. l., 4*l* all recto-verso 21.5 x 13.9 cm. Stinson Beach, 8 March 1961. CtY.

E529 [Pearson], Norman [Holmes]. a. l. s., 1*l* recto-verso 27.9 x 21.5 cm. San Francisco, 13 March 1961. CtY.

E530 [Olson], Charles. a. l. s., 3*l* all recto-verso 21.5 x 14 cm. San Francisco, 15 March 1961. CtU.
Note: This letter contains annotations in pencil in Charles Olson's hand.

E531 [Adam], Helen & Pat. a. n. s., 2*l* recto, recto 19.7 x 10.8 cm. San Francisco, [April 1961]. NBuU.
Note: Recto of the second leaf contains a drawing by RD with the caption below: "Robert Duncan reciting Arethusa to Shelley's ghost."

E532 [Pearson], Norman [Holmes]. t. l. s., 1*l* recto 27.8 x 21.5 cm. San Francisco, 3 April 1961. CtY.
Note: A typescript of SHELLEY'S *ARETHUSA* PUT INTO A NEW MEASURE accompanied this letter. F236.

E533 [Pearson], Norman [Holmes]. t. l. s., 1*l* recto 27.8 x 21.5 cm. San Francisco, 5 April 1961. CtY.
Note: A typescript of A LITTLE DAY BOOK, pp. 31-43, accompanied this letter. F237.

E534 [Blaser], Robin. a. n. s., 1*l* recto 18.4 x 14.1 cm. San Francisco, 9 April 1961. CU-B.

E535 D[oolittle], H[ilda]. a. & t. l., 6*l*; 5*l* recto-verso, 1*l* recto 27.8 x 21.5 cm. San Francisco, 7 and 18 April 1961. CtY.

E536 [Spicer], Jack. a. l. s., 1*l* recto 27.9 x 21.6 cm. [San Francisco], 21 April 1961. CU-B.

E537 [Spicer], Jack. a. l. s., 2*l* recto-verso, recto-verso 27.9 x 21.5 cm. [San Francisco], 28 April 1961. CU-B.

E538 [Blackburn], Paul. a. l. s., 1*l* recto-verso 21.5 x 16.2 cm. San Francisco, 7 May 1961. CU-S.

E539 [Blaser], Robin & Jim [Felts]. a. p. c. s., 1*l* verso 14 x 8.2 cm. San Francisco, 9 May 1961. CU-B.

E540 [Blackburn], Paul. a. l. s., 1*l* recto-verso 21.5 x 16.2 cm. [San Francisco], 7 and 19 May 1961. CU-S.

E541 [Blackburn], Paul. t. l. s., 1*l* recto 21.5 x 21.5 cm. San Francisco, 25 May 1961. CU-S.

E542 [Pearson], Norman [Holmes]. t. l. s., 1*l* recto 28 x 21.6 cm. San Francisco, 5 June 1961. CtY.
Note: A typescript of RD's poem AFTER READING H.D.'S *HERMETIC DEFINITIONS* accompanied this letter. F240.

E543 [Pearson], Norman [Holmes]. t. l. s., 1*l* recto 27.9 x 21.6 cm. San Francisco, 13 June 1961. CtY.
Note: A typescript of A LITTLE DAY BOOK, pp. 44-52 and p. 32 as a substitution for p. 32, accompanied this letter. F237.

E544 [Blackburn], Paul. t. l. s., 1*l* recto 21.6 x 16.8 cm. [San Francisco], 16 June 1961. CU-S.

E545 D[oolittle], H[ilda]. a. l. s., 1*l* recto-verso 27.8 x 21.5 cm. San Francisco, 28 June 1961. CtY.

E546 [Creeley], Bob. a. & t. l. s., 3*l* all recto-verso 27.9 x 21.6 cm. San Francisco, 8 July 1961. On deposit at MoSW.

E547 [Pearson], Norman [Holmes]. a. l. s., 3*l* all recto-verso 21.5 x 16 cm. San Francisco, 31 July 1961. CtY.
Note: A typescript of A LITTLE DAY BOOK pp. 137-174, accompanied this letter. F237.

E548 [Olson], Charles. t. p. c. s., 1*l* verso 8.2 x 14 cm. San Francisco, 20 Aug. 1961. CtU.

E549 D[oolittle], H[ilda]. a. l. s., 1*l* recto 30.4 x 18.2 cm. San Francisco, 21 Aug. 1961. CtY.

E550 [Adam], Helen. a. n. s., 1*l* recto 21.6 x 17.5 cm. San Francisco, 22 Aug. [19]61. NBuU.
Note: A typescript of THE BALLAD OF THE FORFAR WITCHES' SING accompanied this letter. F241.

E551 [Creeley], Bob. a. l. s., 3*l* recto-verso, recto-verso, recto 21.5 x 20.5 cm. San Francisco, 27 Aug. 1961. On deposit at MoSW.

E552 [Spicer], Jack. a. l. s., 1*l* recto 27.9 x 21.7 cm. San Francisco, 31 Aug. 1961. CU-B.

E553 [Blaser], Robin. a. l. s., 1*l* recto 23.6 x 21.5 cm. San Francisco, [Fall 1961]. CU-B.

E554 [Blackburn], Paul. a. l. s., 2*l* recto-verso, recto-verso 20.4 x 21.6 cm. [San Francisco], 9 Sept. 1961. CU-S.

E555 [McClure], Mike. a. l. s., 1*l* recto-verso 24 x 21.5 cm. San Francisco, 12 Sept. 1961. CaBVaS.

E556 Sorrentino, [Gilbert]. a. l. s., 1*l* all recto-verso; 1*l* 21.5 x 19 cm., 2*l* 21.5 x 18 cm., 1*l* 24 x 21.5 cm. San Francisco, 12 Sept. 1961. DeU.

E557 Invisible World [Spicer, Jack]. a. l. s., 3*l* recto-verso, recto-verso, recto 27.9 x 21.7 cm. [San Francisco], 14 Sept. 1961. CU-B.

E558 [Adam], Helen. t. & a. p. c. s., 1*l* verso 8.2 x 14 cm. San Francisco, [4 Oct. 1961]. NBuU.
Note: This card contains eleven revised lines for THE BALLAD OF THE FORFAR WITCHES' SING, which RD had sent to Helen Adam in a letter dated 22 Aug. 1961.

E559 [Pearson], Norman [Holmes]. a. l. s., 2*l* recto-verso, recto-verso 21.6 x 13.8 cm. San Francisco, 10 Oct. 1961. CtY.

E560 [McClure], Mike. a. l. s., 2*l* recto-verso, recto-verso 24.5 x 21.6 cm. San Francisco, 16 Oct. 1961. CaBVaS.

E561 [Creeley], Bob. a. l. s., 1*l* recto-verso 27.9 x 21.6 cm. San Francisco, 17 Nov. 1961. On deposit at MoSW.

E562 Rago, Henry. t. l. s., 1*l* recto 27.9 x 21.6 cm. San Francisco, 18 Nov. 1961. ICU.

E563 [Creeley], Bob. a. l. s., 1*l* recto 21.5 x 20 cm. San Francisco, 29 Nov. [19]61. On deposit at MoSW.

E564 Hammond, Mac. t. l. s., 1*l* recto 27.9 x 21.6 cm. San Francisco, 30 Nov. 1961. NBuU.

E565 Zweig, [Kenneth C.]. t. l. (carbon), 1*l* recto 28 x 21.7 cm. San Francisco, 12 Dec. 1961. OKentU.

E566 [Broughton], James. t. l. s., 1*l* recto 28 x 21.7 cm. [San Francisco], 12 Dec. 1961. OKentU.

E567 [Broughton], James. a. l. s., 1*l* recto 27.9 x 21.6 cm. [San Francisco], 12 Dec. 1961. OKentU.

E568 [Pearson], Norman [Holmes]. a. l. s., 2*l* recto-verso, recto 27.9 x 21.6 cm. Stinson Beach, 14 Dec. 1961. CtY.
Note: RD's Christmas card for 1961 accompanied this letter. D47.

E569 [Creeley], Bob. a. l. s., 2*l* recto-verso, recto-verso 21.5 x 17.3 cm. San Francisco, 15 Dec. 1961. On deposit at MoSW.

E570 Zweig, [Kenneth C.]. t. l. (carbon), 1*l* recto 28 x 21.7 cm. San Francisco, 15 Dec. 1961. OKentU.

E571 [Olson], Charles. a. l. s., 3*l* recto, recto-verso, recto 21.5 x 19.2 cm. San Francisco, 18 Dec. 1961. CtU.
Note: An ink drawing accompanied this letter. D37.

E572 [Adam], Helen. a. l. s., 2*l* recto-verso, recto-verso 28 x 21.6 cm. San Francisco, 23 Jan. 1962. NBuU.
Note: This letter contains thirty lines which, with revisions, became the third section of WHAT HAPPENED: PRELUDE. F256.

E573 [Creeley], Bob. a. p. c. s., 1*l* recto 14 x 8.2 cm. San Francisco, 26 Jan. 1962. On deposit at MoSW.

E574 [Adam], Helen. a. l. s., 3*l* all recto-verso 28 x 21.6 cm. San Francisco, 31 Jan. 1962. NBuU.
Note: Seventy-five lines of what became the fourth section of WHAT HAPPEND: PRELUDE appeared in this letter. F257.

E575 [Adam], Helen. a. l. s., 2*l* recto-verso, recto 28 x 21.7 cm. San Francisco, 6 Feb. 1962. NBuU.

E576 Jones, LeRoi. a. l. s., 1*l* recto 27.8 x 21.5 cm. San Francisco, 6 Feb. 1962. NSbSU.

E577 [Adam], Helen & Pat. a. n. s., 1*l* recto 20.5 x 21.7 cm. San Francisco, 12 Feb. 1962. NBuU.

E578 [Creeley], Bob. a. l. s., 1*l* recto-verso 21.6 x 20.5 cm. San Francisco, 20 Feb. 1962. On deposit at MoSW.

E579 [Creeley], Bob. t. l. s., 1*l* recto-verso 27.9 x 21.6 cm. Stinson Beach, 21 Feb. 1962. On deposit at MoSW.

E580 [Pearson], Norman [Holmes]. a. l. s., 2*l* recto-verso, recto 27.9 x 21.7 cm. San Francisco, 26 Feb. 1962. CtY.

E581 Rago, Henry. t. l. s., 1*l* recto 27.8 x 21.5 cm. San Francisco, 9 March 1962. InU.

E582 [Pearson], Norman [Holmes]. a. l. s., 1*l* recto-verso 25.4 x 20.4 cm. New York City, 12 April 1962. CtY.

E583 [Creeley], Bob. a. l. s., 1*l* recto-verso 16.3 x 13.3 cm. San Francisco, 15 May [19]62. On deposit at MoSW.

E584 [Blaser], Robin. a. l. s., 2*l* recto-verso, recto-verso 19.7 x 14.8 cm. Washington, D. C., 30 May 1962. CU-B.

E585 [Spicer], Jack. a. l. s., 1*l* recto-verso 27.8 x 21.5 cm. [San Francisco], 5 June 1962. CU-B.

E586 [Spicer], Jack. a. & t. l. s., 1*l* recto-verso 21.7 x 18.5 cm. San Francisco, 12 June 1962. CU-B.
Note: A typescript of THANK YOU FOR LOVE—FROM *THE MABINOGION*—FORCED IMAGES accompanied this letter. F259.

E587 Rago, Henry. t. l. s., 1*l* recto 21.5 x 17.3 cm. San Francisco, 18 June 1962. InU.

E588 Rago, Henry. a. p. c. s., 1*l* verso 13.9 x 8.3 cm. San Francisco, [Summer 1962]. InU.

E589 [Creeley], Bob. a. l. s., 2*l* recto-verso, recto 23.5 x 20.5 cm. San Francisco, 20 July and 10 Aug. 1962. On deposit at MoSW.
Note: A typescript of a review of Creeley's *For Love,* entitled AND THERE EVER TO DISCOURSE OF LOVE accompanied this letter. F260.

E590 [Hoyem, Andrew]. a. n. s., 1*l* recto 27.9 x 21.6 cm. San Francisco, 13 Aug. 1962. MoSW.

E591 [Pearson], Norman [Holmes]. a. l. s., 2*l* recto-verso, recto 28 x 21.6 cm. San Francisco, 14 Aug. 1962. CtY.

E592 [Zukofsky], Celia & Louis. a. l. s., 1*l* recto-verso 21.6 x 18.5 cm. San Francisco, 20 Aug. 1962. TxU.
Note: A typescript of SONNET 1, SONNET 2, and SONNET 3 accompanied this letter. F261.

E593 [Blaser], Robin. a. l. s., 1*l* recto 28 x 21.6 cm. San Francisco, 29 Aug. 1962. CU-B.

E594 Wenning, Henry. t. l. s., 1*l* recto 27.8 x 21.5 cm. San Francisco, 1 Sept. 1962. MoSW.

E595 [Pearson], Norman [Holmes]. a. l. s., 1*l* recto-verso 27.9 x 21.5 cm. San Francisco, 5 Sept. 1962. CtY.
Note: A typescript of WINDINGS Part (I) accompanied this letter. F263.

E596 [Pearson], Norman [Holmes]. a. l. s., 2*l* recto-verso, recto-verso 21.5 x 19.5 cm. San Francisco, 12 Sept. 1962. CtY.
Note: A typescript of WINDINGS Parts II and III accompanied this letter. F263.

E597 Wenning, Henry. a. p. c. s., 1*l* verso 13.9 x 8.3 cm. San Francisco, 16 Sept. 1962. MoSW.

E598 [Pearson], Norman [Holmes]. a. l. s., 1*l* recto-verso 27.9 x 21.5 cm. San Francisco, 18 Sept. 1962. CtY.
Note: A typescript of WINDINGS Part IV accompanied this letter. F263.

E599 [Creeley], Bob. t. l. s., 2*l* recto-verso, recto 21.7 x 17.7 cm. San Francisco, 2 Oct. 1962. On deposit at MoSW.

E600 [Creeley], Bob. a. l. s., 1*l* recto-verso 21.5 x 18.4 cm. San Francisco, 8 and 10 Oct. 1962. On deposit at MoSW.

E601 [Blaser], Robin. a. l. s., 2*l* recto-verso, recto 23 x 21.6 cm. San Francisco, 11 Oct. 1962. CU-B.

E602 Wenning, Henry. t. l. s., 2*l* recto, recto 27.8 x 21.5 cm. San Francisco, 25 Oct. 1962. MoSW.

E603 [Pearson], Norman [Holmes]. a. l. s., 2*l* recto-verso, recto 28 x 21.6 cm. San Francisco, 27 Oct. 1962. CtY.

E604 Wenning, Henry. t. l. s., 1*l* recto 28 x 21.6 cm. San Francisco, 30 Oct. 1962. MoSW.

E605 Wenning, Henry. t. l. s., 2*l* recto, recto 27.8 x 21.5 cm. San Francisco, 7 Nov. 1962. MoSW.

E606 Wenning, Henry. t. l. s., 1*l* recto 28 x 21.6 cm. San Francisco, 13 Nov. 1962. MoSW.

E607 X.... t. l. (carbon), 1*l* recto 21.5 x 16.1 cm. San Francisco, 15 Nov. [1962]. MoSW.
Note: This is a carbon copy of a possible form letter to be used in returning subscriptions to The Auerhahm Press edition of BR after that edition was cancelled.

E608 [Haselwood], Dave. t. l. (carbon), 2*l* recto, recto 27.8 x 21.5 cm. San Francisco, 16 Nov. 1962. MoSW.

E609 [Haselwood], Dave, and Andrew [Hoyem]. t. l. (carbon), 1*l* 27.8 x 21.5 cm. San Francisco, 17 Nov. 1962. MoSW.

E610 Wenning, Henry. t. l. s., 2*l* recto, recto 27.8 x 21.5 cm. San Francisco, 19 Nov. 1962. MoSW.

E611 Wenning, Henry. t. l. s., 1*l* recto-verso 27.8 x 21.5 cm. San Francisco, 21 Nov. 1962. MoSW.

E612 Schaff, David. t. l. s., 1*l* recto 21.5 x 16.1 cm. San Francisco, 24 Nov. 1962. MoSW.

E613 [Jones], LeRoi. a. l. s., 1*l* recto 22.5 x 21.5 cm. San Francisco, 20 Dec. 1962. MoSW.

E614 [Creeley], Bob. a. l. s., 2*l* recto-verso, recto-verso 22.3 x 21 cm. San Francisco, 26 Dec. [19]62. On deposit at MoSW.

E615 [Creeley], Bob. a. l. s., 4*l*; 2*l* recto-verso 24.5 x 20.5 cm, 1*l* recto-verso 20.8 x 20.5 cm., 1*l* recto 21.5 x 20.5 cm. San Francisco, 3 Jan. [19]63. On deposit at MoSW.

E616 [Olson], Charles. a. l. s., 2*l* recto-verso, recto-verso 27.8 x 21.5 cm. San Francisco, 9 Jan. 1963. CtU.

E617 Wenning, [Henry]. t. l. s., 1*l* recto 21.5 x 17.2 cm. San Francisco, 10 Jan. 1963. MoSW.

E618 [Jones], LeRoi. a. l. s., 3*l* recto-verso, recto-verso, recto 22 x 21.5 cm. San Francisco, 14 Jan. 1963. MoSW.

E619 O[pen] Space. t. l. s., 1*l* recto 27.9 x 21.5 cm. San Francisco, 21 Jan. 1963. CU-B.

E620 [Gleason], Maddy. a. l. s., 1*l* recto-verso 21.7 x 21.5 cm. [San Francisco], 1 Feb. 1963. CSfU.

E621 [Adam], Helen. a. l. s., 1*l* recto-verso 20.3 x 12.6 cm. San Francisco, [5 Feb. 1963]. NBuU.
Note: The letter was written by Jess Collins, but a note from RD appears on the verso.

E622 [Creeley], Bob. a. & t. l. s., 1*l* recto-verso 27.9 x 21.7 cm. San Francisco, 12 Feb. [19]63. On deposit at MoSW.

E623 [Blaser], Robin. a. l. s., 1*l* recto-verso 27.9 x 21.6 cm. San Francisco, 12 Feb. 1963. CU-B.

E624 [Olson], Charles. a. l. s., 6*l* all recto; 4*l* 21.5 x 17.8 cm., 1*l* 21.5 x 19 cm., 1*l* 22.3 x 21.5 cm. San Francisco, 9 March 1963. CtU.

E625 [Blaser], Robin. a. l. s., 1*l* recto 21.7 x 15 cm. San Francisco, 11 March 1963. CU-B.

E626 Wenning, Henry. t. l. s., 4*l* all recto; 2*l* 21.7 x 21.5 cm., 1*l* 19.8 x 21.5 cm. San Francisco, 25 March 1963. MoSW.
Note: There is an addition to this letter in RD's holograph, bottom recto of the second leaf.

E627 [Pearson], Norman [Holmes]. a. l. s., 4*l* all recto; 3*l* 23.7 x 21.6 cm., 1*l* recto 20.7 x 21.6 cm. San Francisco, 28 March 1963. CtY.

E628 [Creeley], Bob. a. l. s., 4*l* all recto 20.3 x 20.5 cm. San Francisco, 30 March [19]63. On deposit at MoSW.

E629 [Jones], LeRoi. a. l. s., 2*l* recto, recto 21.4 x 20.4 cm. San Francisco, 1 April 1963. MoSW.

E630 [Jones], LeRoi. a. l. s., 2*l* recto-verso, recto 27.8 x 21.5 cm. San Francisco, 2 April 1963. MoSW.

E631 [Sorrentino], Gil[bert]. a. l. s., 2*l*; 1*l* recto-verso 22.2 x 21.5 cm., 1*l* 16.8 x 21.5 cm. San Francisco, 5 April 1963. DeU.

E632 [Pearson], Norman [Holmes]. a. l. s., 2*l* recto-verso, recto-verso 27.9 x 21.6 cm. San Francisco, 12 April 1963. CtY.

E633 Rago, Henry. t. l. s., 1*l* recto 21.6 x 21.5 cm. San Francisco, 17 April 1963. InU.

E634 Schaff, David. a. l. s., 4*l* all recto 22 x 21.5 cm. San Francisco, 25 April 1963. MoSW.

E635 [Olson], Charles. a. l. s., 4*l* all recto; 3*l* 21.2 x 21.5 cm., 1*l* 22.9 x 21.5 cm. San Francisco, 26 April 1963. CtU.
Note: A typescript of THE CONTINENT accompanied this letter. F271.

E636 Schevill, James. t. l. s., 1*l* recto 22.7 x 21.7 cm. [San Francisco], 15 May 1963. CSf-APA.

E637 [Olson], Charles. a. l. s., 1*l* recto-verso 27.8 x 21.5 cm. San Francisco, 28 May 1963. CtU.

E638 [Blaser], Robin. t. l. s., 1*l* recto 27.9 x 21.6 cm. San Francisco, 8 June 1963. CU-B.

E639 [Pearson], Norman [Holmes]. a. l. s., 3*l* recto, recto-verso, recto-verso 21.5 x 18 cm. San Francisco, 10 June 1963. CtY.
Note: A typescript of THE CONTINENT accompanied this letter. F273.

E640 [Wenning], Henry. a. l. s. 2*l*; 1*l* recto-verso 21.5 x 21.5 cm., 1*l* recto 23.6 x 21.5 cm. San Francisco, 11 June 1963. MoSW.

E641 [Creeley], Bob. a. l. s., 4*l* all recto 22.8 x 20.5 cm. San Francisco, 27 June [19]63. On deposit at MoSW.

E642 [Jones], LeRoi. a. l. s., 4*l* all recto 21.5 x 21.5 cm. San Francisco, 27 June 1963. MoSW.

E643 Schevill, James. t. l. s., 1*l* recto 28 x 21.6 cm. [San Francisco], 5 July 1963. CSf-APA.

E644 [Olson], Charles. a. n. s., 1*l* recto 21.5 x 16 cm. San Francisco, 8 July 1963. CtU.

E645 [Creeley], Bob. a. l. s., 1*l* recto-verso 28 x 18.2 cm. San Francisco, 15 July 1963. On deposit at MoSW.

E646 [Jones], LeRoi. a. l. s., 2*l* recto-verso, recto 10.7 x 13.7 cm. San Francisco, 18 July 1963. MoSW.

E647 [Jones], LeRoi. a. l. s., 2*l* recto-verso, recto-verso 10.7 x 16 cm. San Francisco, 21 Aug. 1963. MoSW.

E648 [Pearson], Norman [Holmes]. a. l. s., 4*l* all recto 23 x 21.7 cm. San Francisco, 4 Sept. 1963. CtY.

E649 [Blaser], Robin. a. l. s., 1*l* recto-verso 21.1 x 21.6 cm. San Francisco, 11 Sept. 1963. CU-B.

E650 [Wenning], Henry. a. l. s., 2*l* recto-verso, recto-verso 27.8 x 21.5 cm. San Francisco, 21 Oct. 1963. MoSW.

E651 [Sorrentino], Gil[bert]. t. l. s., 1*l* recto 28 x 21.5 cm. San Francisco, 30 Sept. 1963. DeU.

E652 [Wenning], Henry. a. l. s., 2*l* recto, recto 21.5 x 20 cm. San Francisco, 5 Nov. 1063. MoSW

E653 [Rago], Henry. a. l. s., 3*l* all recto 27.8 x 21.5 cm. San Francisco, 5 Nov. 1963. InU.

E654 [Creeley], Bob. a. l. s., 3*l* all recto-verso 21.7 x 18 cm. San Francisco, 20 and 21 Nov. 1963. On deposit at MoSW.
Note: A typescript of SUCH IS THE SICKNESS OF MANY A GOOD THING accompanied this letter. F272.

E655 [Olson], Charles. a. l. s., 5*l* all recto; 4*l* 21.5 x 18.2 cm., 1*l* 21.5 x 21.5 cm. San Francisco, 20 Dec. 1963. CtU.

E656 [Pearson], Norman [Holmes]. a. l. s., 1*l* recto-verso 31 x 18.3 cm. San Francisco, 28 Dec. 1963. CtY.

E657 [Rosset], Barney. a. n. s., 1*l* recto 35.5 x 21.5 cm. San Francisco, 30 Dec. 1963. NSyU.
Note: This note was written on the bottom of the letter to [Wilfrid] Mellers dated 30 Dec. 1963. E659

E658 [Blaser], Robin. a. l. s., 3*l* all recto 27.9 x 21.7 cm. San Francisco, 30 Dec. 1963. CU-B.

E659 Mellers, [Wilfred]. a. l. s., (phoptocopy), 1*l* recto 35.5 x 21.5 cm. San Francisco, 30 Dec. 1963. NSyU.

E660 [Hawley, Robert]. a. n. s., 1*l* recto 8.5 x 19.1 cm. San Francisco, [1964]. CtU.

E661 [Creeley], Bob. a. l. s., 2*l* recto-verso, recto-verso 21.7 x 20 cm. San Francisco, 2 Jan. 1964. On deposit at MoSW.

E662 O[pen] Space. t. n. s., 1*l* recto 20.2 x 21.6 cm. San Francisco, 18 Jan. 1964. CU-B.

E663 [Wenning], Henry. a. l. s., 1*l* recto-verso 21.5 x 20.5 cm. San Francisco, 11 Feb. 1964. MoSW.

E664 [Creeley], Bob. a. l. s., 2*l*; 1*l* recto-verso 21.7 x 20.5 cm., 1*l* recto-verso 23 x 21 cm. San Francisco, 19 Feb. 1964. On deposit at MoSW.

E665 [Blaser], Robin. t. l. s., 1*l* recto-verso 22.9 x 21.6 cm. San Francisco, 22 Feb. 1964. CU-B.

E666 Seaver, Dick. t. l. s., 1*l* recto 27.8 x 22.5 cm. San Francisco, 2 March 1964. NSyU.

E667 [Pearson], Norman [Holmes]. a. p. c. s., 1*l* verso 14 x 8.2 cm. San Francisco, [12 March 1964]. CtY.

E668 [Creeley], Bob. a. l. s., 1*l* recto-verso 21.7 x 16.5 cm. San Francisco, 15 March [19]64. On deposit at MoSW.

E669 [Rago], Henry. t. l. s., 1*l* recto 22.8 x 15.3 cm. San Francisco, 26 May 1964. InU.

E670 [Olson], Charles. a. l. s., 3*l* all recto-verso 22.9 x 15.3 cm. San Francisco, 29 May 1964. CtU.
Note: A seven leaf typescript (carbon copy) of six poems entitled: I, II, 4, PASSAGES 5, PASSAGES 6, and PASSAGES 7 accompanied this letter. F278.

E671 [Olson], Charles. a. l. s., 1*l* recto-verso 27.8 x 21.5 cm. San Francisco, 18 June 1964. CtU.
Note: The typescripts of PASSAGES 7, PASSAGES 8, and PASSAGES 9 accompanied this letter. F279.

E672 [Creeley], Bob & Bobbie. a. l. s., 3*l*; 2*l* recto-verso 21.6 x 20.2 cm., 1*l* recto 21.6 x 19.6 cm. San Francisco, 26 June [19]64. On deposit at MoSW.

E673 [Olson], Charles. a. l. s., 3*l* all recto-verso 27.8 x 21.6 cm. San Francisco, 29 June 1964. CtU.

E674 [Olson], Charles. a. l. s., 1*l* recto-verso 23.2 x 21.5 cm. San Francisco, 3 July 1964. CtU.
Note: PASSAGES 12 and PASSAGES 13 were written 3 July 1964 and accompanied this letter. F280.

E675 [Rago], Henry. t. l. s., 1*l* recto 21.6 x 18.8 cm. San Francisco, 14 July 1964. InU.

E676 [Wenning], Henry & Adele. a. l. s., 1*l* recto-verso 22.5 x 21.5 cm. San Francisco, 15 July 1964. MoSW.

E677 [Wenning], Henry & Adele. a. l. s., 1*l* recto 22.5 x 21.5 cm. San Francisco, 15 July 1964. MoSW.

E678 [Rago], Henry. t. l. s., 1*l* recto 21.6 x 21.6 cm. San Francisco, 15 July 1964. InU.

E679 [Schaff], David. a. l. s., 2*l* recto-verso, recto-verso 21.5 x 18.7 cm. San Francisco, 28 July 1964. MoSW.

E680 [Jones], LeRoi. a. l. s., 1*l* recto-verso 22.5 x 21.5 cm. San Francisco, 29 July 1964. MoSW.

E681 [Schmidt], Judith. a. n. s., 1*l* recto 27.8 x 21.5 cm. San Francisco, 30 July 1964. NSyU.
Note: This note appears on the top of the letter to James G. Taaffe dated 30 July 1964. E682.

E682 Taaffe, James G. t. l. (carbon), 1*l* recto 27.8 x 21.5 cm. San Francisco, 30 July 1964. NSyU.

E683 [Adam], Helen & Pat. a. l. s., 2*l* recto, recto 23 x 21.6 cm. San Francisco, 1 Aug. 1964. NBuU.

E684 [Schmidt], Judith. a. n. s., 1*l* recto 27.8 x 21.5 cm. San Francisco, 10 Aug. 1964. NSyU.
Note: This note appears on the bottom of the letter to William Koshland dated 10 Aug. 1964. E686.

E685 Koshland, [William]. t. l. s. (carbon), 1*l* recto 27.8 x 21.5 cm. San Francisco, 10 Aug. 1964. NSyU.

E686 [Schmidt, Judith]. t. l. s., 1*l* recto 27.8 x 21.5 cm. San Francisco, 14 Aug. 1964. NSyU.

E687 [Creeley], Bob & Bobbie. a. l. s., 4*l*; 3*l* all recto-verso 27.9 x 21.6 cm, 1*l* recto 21.6 x 16.5 cm. San Francisco, 24 and 26 Aug. [1964]. On deposit at MoSW.

E688 [Allen], Don. t. l. (carbon), 1*l* recto 27.9 x 21.6 cm. San Francisco, 26 Aug. 1964. On deposit at MoSW.

E689 [Creeley], Bob. a. l. s., 3*l*; 1*l* recto-verso 21.6 x 18.7 cm., 1*l* recto-verso 21.6 x 18.5 cm., 1*l* recto 21.6 x 16.5 cm. San Francisco, 30 Aug. [19]64. On deposit at MoSW.

E690 [Wenning], Henry. t. l. s., 1*l* recto 27.8 x 21.5 cm. San Francisco, 29 Sept. 1964. MoSW.
Note: Enclosed in this letter is a list of books about Surrealism and about art that RD wanted to purchase, 1*l* recto 27.8 x 21.5 cm. (carbon).

E691 [Saroyan], Aram. a. n. s., 1*l* recto 21.5 x 16.5 cm. San Francisco, 10 Oct. 1964. NNU.

E692 [Rago], Henry. t. l. s., 1*l* recto 27.8 x 21.5 cm. San Francisco, 20 Oct. 1964. InU.

E693 [Dickey], James. t. l. s., 1*l* recto-verso 27.9 x 21.6 cm. San Francisco, 21 Oct. 1964. MoSW.

E694 [Schaff], David. a. l. s., 1*l* recto 21.5 x 18.5 cm. San Francisco, 5 Nov. 1964. MoSW.
Note: A typescript of MOVING THE MOVING IMAGE [PASSAGES 17]—WINE—THE FIRE—THE EARTH PASSAGES 19 and STRUC-TURE OF RIME XXVI PASSAGES 20 accompanied this letter. F281, F282, F283.

E695 Hawley, [Robert]. a. l. s., 1*l* recto-verso 28 x 21.6 cm. San Francisco, 16 Nov. 1964. CtU.
Note: A list of names and addresses (a. n., 1*l* recto 20.2 x 21.7 cm.) accompanied this letter.

E696 [Creeley], Bob. a. l. s., 2*l* recto-verso, recto-verso 21.6 x 18.6 cm. San Francisco, 30 Nov. 1964. On deposit at MoSW.
Note: A typescript of THE CURRENTS, PASSAGES 16—MOVING THE MOVING IMAGE [PASSAGES 17]—THE TORSO, PASSAGES 18 and THE EARTH, PASSAGES 19 accompanied this letter. F284.

E697 [Pearson], Norman [Holmes]. a. l. s., 2*l* recto-verso, recto-verso 27.9 x 21.6 cm. San Francisco, 15 Dec. 1964. CtY.

E698 Rico [Quadarini, Federico]. a. l. s., 1*l* recto 22.9 x 14.8 cm. San Francisco, [1965?]. CaBVaS.

E699 [Hawley, Robert]. a. n. s., 1*l* recto 13.7 x 10.5 cm. San Francisco, [1965?]. CtU.

E700 [Hamady], Walter. a. p. c. s., 1*l* verso 14 x 8.2 cm. San Francisco, 1 Jan. 1965. MoSW.

E701 [Olson], Charles. a. l. s., 2*l*; recto-verso 21.5 x 21.5 cm., recto-verso 22.3 x 21.5 cm. San Francisco, 22 Jan. 1965. CtU.

E702 [Creeley], Bob. a. l. s., 1*l* recto 22.5 x 20.5 cm. San Francisco, 24 Jan. [19]65. On deposit at MoSW.

E703 [Creeley], Bob & Bobbie. a. l. s., 2*l* recto-verso, recto-verso 22.5 x 20.8 cm. San Francisco, 1 Feb. 1965. On deposit at MoSW.

E704 [Wenning], Henry. a. l. s., 1*l* recto-verso 21.6 x 21.3 cm. San Francisco, 4 Feb. 1965. MoSW.

E705 Olson, Charles. a. l. s., 1*l* recto-verso 21.5 x 18.5 cm. San Francisco, [11] Feb. 1965. CtU.

E706 [Schmidt], Judith. t. l. s., 1*l* recto 27.8 x 21.5 cm. San Francisco, 15 Feb. 1965. NSyU.

E707 [Eshleman], Clayton. t. l. s., 1*l* recto 20.7 x 21.5 cm. San Francisco, 18 Feb. 1965. NNU.

E708 [Broughton], James. a. l. s., 1*l* recto-verso 28 x 21.6 cm. [San Francisco], 24 Feb. 1965. OKentU.

E709 [Adam], Helen & Pat. a. l. s., 5*l* all recto-verso 23 x 14 cm. San Francisco, 28 March 1965. NBuU.
Note: The first and second leaf recto-verso were written by Jess Collins.

E710 [Hawley, Robert]. a. l. s., 1*l* recto 21.5 x 19.6 cm. San Francisco, 27 May 1965. CtU.
Note: This letter accompanied the corrected proof sheets for the second printing of MEDEA AT KOLCHIS THE MAIDEN HEAD.

E711 Clark, Thomas. t. l. s., 1*l* recto 27.8 x 21.5 cm. San Francisco, 9 June 1965. KU.
Note: A typescript of LAMMAS DREAM POEM accompanied this letter. F290.

E712 [Creeley], Bob. a. l. s., 2*l* recto-verso, recto-verso 27.9 x 21.6 cm. San Francisco, 14 June [19]65. On deposit at MoSW.

E713 [Persky], Stan. t. l. s., 1*l* recto 28 x 21.6 cm. San Francisco, 3 Aug. 1965. CU-B.

E714 [Wenning], Henry. t. l. s., 1*l* recto 21.5 x 15 cm. San Francisco, 3 Aug. 1965. MoSW.

E715 [Creeley], Bob. a. l. s., 4*l* all recto 21.7 x 15.5 cm. San Francisco, 14 Aug. [19]65. On deposit at MoSW.

E716 [Creeley], Bob. a. l. s., 1*l* recto-verso 27.9 x 21.6 cm. San Francisco, 19 Aug. [19]65. On deposit at MoSW.

E717 Hawley, Robert. t. l. s., 2*l* recto, recto-verso 27.9 x 21.6 cm. San Francisco, 24 Aug. 1965. CtU.
Note: Bottom recto and top verso of the second leaf contain a note in RD's hand.

E718 Hawley, [Robert]. t. l. s., 1*l* recto 27.9 x 21.6 cm. San Francisco, 3 Sept. 1965. CtU.

E719 [Blackburn], Paul and Sara. a. l. s., 2*l* recto-verso, recto 27.8 x 21.5 cm. San Francisco, 28 Sept. 1965. CU-S.

E720 [Marlowe], Alan & Diane. a. l. s., 2*l* recto-verso, recto-verso 27.8 x 21.5 cm. San Francisco, 29 Sept. 1965. NSbSU.

E721 Schmidt, Judith. t. n. s., 1*l* recto 21.5 x 19.8 cm. San Francisco, 5 Oct. 1965. NSyU.

E722 Rosset, Barney. t. l. s., 1*l* recto 21.5 x 19.8 cm. San Francisco, 5 Oct. 1965. NSyU.

E723 [Blaser], Robin. a. l. s., 4*l*; 3*l* recto-verso, 1*l* recto 27.9 x 21.7 cm. San Francisco, [Nov. 1965]. CU-B.

E724 [Creeley], Bob. a. l. s., 4*l* all recto-verso 21.6 x 16.8 cm. San Francisco, 11 Nov. [19]65. On deposit at MoSW.

E725 Hamady, Walter. a. l. s., 4*l* all recto 21.5 x 18.7 cm. San Francisco, 11 Nov. 1965. MoSW.

E726 Hawley, [Robert]. t. l. s., 1*l* recto 27.8 x 21.6 cm. San Francisco, 22 Nov. 1965. CtU.

E727 [Blaser], Robin. a. l. s., 1*l* recto-verso 27.9 x 21.7 cm. San Francisco, 24 Nov. 1965. CU-B.

E728 [Hamady], Walter. a. l. s., 1*l* recto 21.5 x 18.7 cm. San Francisco, 4 Dec. 1965. MoSW.

E729 Hamady, [Walter]. a. l. s., 1*l* recto-verso 21.5 x 16.5 cm. San Francisco, 9 Dec. 1965. MoSW.

E730 [Blackburn], Paul. t. l. s., 1*l* recto-verso 27.8 x 21.5 cm. San Francisco, 17 Dec. 1965. CU-S.

E731 [Adam], Pat and Helen. a. l. s., 3*l* recto-verso, recto-verso, recto 27.9 x 21.7 cm. San Francisco, 22 Dec. [19]65. NBuU.

E732 [Hamady], Walter. a. l. s., 1*l* recto-verso 17.9 x 21.6 cm. San Francisco, 31 Dec. 1965. MoSW.

E733 Zuk[ofsky, Louis]. a. l. s., 1*l* recto 27.8 x 21.5 cm. San Francisco, 13 Feb. 1966. TxU.

E734 [Creeley], Bob. a. l. s., 2*l* recto-verso, recto-verso 20.4 x 12.7 cm. San Francisco, 15 Feb. 1966. On deposit at MoSW.

E735 [Hawley], Bob & Steven [Van Strum]. t. l. s., 2*l* recto, recto 27.9 cm. x 21.7 cm. San Francisco, 4 Jan. [1966]. CtU.
Note: The letter is signed on the first leaf; also included is a signed carbon copy of that leaf.

E736 [Wenning], Henry. a. l. s., 5*l*; 4*l* all recto-verso, 1*l* recto 27.6 x 21.2 cm. Vancouver, British Columbia, 14 Jan. 1966. MoSW.

E737 Hamady, [Walter]. a. l. s., 1*l* recto-verso 27.8 x 21.5 cm. San Francisco, 18 Jan. 1966. MoSW.

E738 [Creeley], Bob. a. l. s., 2*l* recto-verso, recto 21.2 x 13.5 cm. Vancouver, British Columbia, 26 Jan. 1966. On deposit at MoSW.

E739 Zuk[ofsky], Louis. a. l. s., 1*l* recto 27.8 x 21.7 cm. San Francisco, 13 Feb. 1966. TxU.

E740 Hamady, [Walter]. a. l. s., 1*l* recto-verso 21.5 x 19.5 cm. San Francisco, 16 Feb. 1966. MoSW.

E741 [Olson], Charles. a. l. s., 1*l* recto 27.8 x 21.6 cm. San Francisco, 7 March 1966. CtU.

E742 [Wenning], Henry. a. & t. l. s., 3*l* recto, recto, recto 27.8 x 21.5 cm., San Francisco, 9 March 1966. MoSW.
Note: Two typed leaves, recto, recto 27.8 x 21.5 cm., entitled "Publication list for Jess" accompanied this letter.

E743 [Wenning], Henry. t. l. s., 2*l* recto, recto, 27.8 x 21.5 cm. San Francisco, 25 March 1966. MoSW.

E744 [Creeley], Bob. a. l. s., 2*l* recto-verso 27.9 x 21.6 cm. San Francisco, 4 April 1966. On deposit at MoSW.

E745 [Adam], Helen & Pat. a. l. s., 3*l*; 1*l* recto-verso 20.7 x 19.7 cm., 2*l* recto-verso 21.7 x 19.7 cm. San Francisco 10 April 1966. NBuU.
Note: The recto of the first leaf contains six lines of an unpublished "rune," and recto-verso of the second leaf contain twenty-two lines in typescript intended for a second part of the play *ADAM'S WAY*.

E746 [Schmidt], Judith. t. n. s., 1*l* recto 19.8 x 21.5 cm. San Francisco, 11 April 1966. NSyU.

E747 Terris, Virginia. t. l. (carbon), 1*l* recto 27.8 x 21.5 cm., San Francisco 11 April 1966. NSyU.

E748 Rosset, Barney. t. l. s., 1*l* recto 27.8 x 21.5 cm. San Francisco 11 April 1966. NSyU.

E749 Hawley, Robert. t. l. s., 1*l* recto 29.9 x 21.7 cm. San Francisco 14 April 1966. CtU.

E750 [Hamady], Walter. a. l. s., 1*l* recto-verso 21.5 x 18 cm. San Francisco 23, April 1966. MoSW.

E751 [Van Strum], Steve[n]. a. n., 1*l* recto 16.5 x 24.2 cm. San Francisco, [May?] 1966. CtU.
Note: This note is written on the outside of a manila envelope, and has to do with the publication of YAC.

E752 [Wenning], Henry. t. l. s., 1*l* recto-verso 24 x 21.5 cm. San Francisco, 6 May 1966. MoSW.
Note: There is a holograph note to Henry Wenning at the bottom verso of this typed letter.

E753 [Wenning, Henry]. a. l. s., 1*l* recto-verso 21.5 x 15 cm. San Francisco, 9 May 1966. MoSW.

Note: This letter accompanied a typescript of the introduction for BR. F301.

E754 Hawley, Bob. t. n. s., 1*l* recto 20.2 x 21.6 cm. San Francisco, 24 May 1966. CtU.

E755 [Wenning], Henry. a. l. s., 1*l* recto-verso 27.8 x 21.5 cm. San Francisco, 13 June 1966. MoSW.

E756 [Hawley], Robert. t. & a. l. s., 1*l* verso 8.3 x 14 cm. San Francisco [23 June 1966]. CtU.

E757 Martin, John. t. l. s., 1*l* recto 28 x 22.5 cm. San Francisco, 4 July 1966. CU-SB.

E758 [Blackburn], Paul. a. l. s., 1*l* recto-verso 21.5 x 19.3 cm. San Francisco, 4 July 1966. CU-S.

E759 Martin, John. a. l. s., 1*l* recto-verso 22 x 19 cm. San Francisco, 7 July 1966. CU-SB.
Note: Two drawings, "The Poet's Lofty Brow" and "Stinson Beach 1959" accompanied this letter. D35, D36.

E760 [Wenning], Henry. t. l. s., 2*l* recto-verso, recto 27.8 x 21.5 cm. San Francisco 24 July 1966. MoSW.
Note: There is a note in RD's hand at the bottom recto of the second leaf. A typescript entitled "Text for page 3 of Announcement for A Book of Resemblances" accompanied this letter. F303.

E761 [Blaser], Robin. a. n. s., 1*l* recto 27.9 x 21.7 cm. San Francisco, 28 July 1966. CU-B.
Note: Typescripts of the poems PASSAGES 26: THE SOLDIERS and TRANGRESSING THE REAL : PASSAGES 27 accompanied this note. F304, E305.

E762 [Adam], Helen & Pat. a. l. s., 1*l* recto-verso 24 x 21.6 cm. San Francisco 28 July [19]66. NBuU.
Note: A typescript of AN INTERLUDE accompanied this letter. F306.

E763 [Olson], Charles. a. p. c. s., 1*l* verso 10.2 x 14.8 cm. Annandale-on-Hudson, 25 Aug. 1966. CtU.
Note: The photograph on the recto is entitled "Bauernhof bei Jeuer in Ostfriesland."

E764 [Wenning], Henry. t. l. s., 1*l* recto-verso 27.8 x 21.5 cm. San Francisco, 25 Aug. 1966. MoSW.
Note: A list of people who wished to order BR, 1*l* typed, recto 27.8 x 21.5 cm., accompanied this letter.

E765 [Blaser], Robin. a. l. s., 4*l* all recto-verso; 1*l* 22.7 x 21.7 cm., 1*l* 23 x 21.7 cm., 1*l* 19.5 x 21.7 cm., 1*l* 19.8 x 21.7 cm. San Francisco, [Fall 1966]. CU-B.

E766 [Wenning], Henry. a. l. s., 1*l* recto-verso 22 x 21.5 cm. San Francisco, 1
Sept. 1966. MoSW.

E767 [Schmidt], Judith. t. l. s., 1*l* recto 21.5 x 27.8 cm. San Francisco, 1 Sept.
1966. NSyU.

E768 [Creeley], Bob. a. l. s., 2*l* recto-verso, recto 23 x 12.7 cm. San Francisco,
15 Sept. 1966. On deposit at MoSW.
Note: A typescript of EYE OF GOD, PASSAGES 29 accompanied this
letter. F308.

E769 [Olson], Charles. a. l. s., 1*l* recto-verso 21.8 x 21.5 cm. San Francisco,
15 Sept. 1966. CtU.
Note: A typescript of PASSAGES 28, THE LIGHT and EYE OF
GOD, PASSAGES 29 accompanied this letter. F307.

E770 [Schmidt], Judith. t. l. s., 1*l* recto 27.8 x 21.5 cm. San Francisco, 22
Sept. 1966. NSyU.

E771 Clark, [Thomas] & [Andrew] Crozier. t. l. s., 1*l* recto 27.8 x 21.5 cm.
San Francisco, 22 Sept. 1966. NNC.

E772 [Wenning], Henry. a. l. s., 1*l* recto-verso 21.5 x 17 cm. San Francisco,
24 Sept. 1966. MoSW.
Note: Accompanying this letter are 2*l* recto, recto 27.8 x 21.5 cm.,
typed, entitled "Notes on Proofs" and "Artist's notes on Proofs." RD
and Jess have both signed the notes. There is also an a. n. 1*l*, recto 16.2
x 5 cm., containing two corrections for the proof sheets of BR. F309
F310.

E773 [McClure], Mike. a. l. s., 1*l* recto 27.9 x 21.6 cm. San Francisco, 28
Sept. 1966. CaBVaS.

E774 [Wenning], Henry. t. l., 1*l* recto 27.9 x 21.6 cm. San Francisco, 7 Oct.
1966. MoSW.

E775 [Schmidt], Judith. t. l. s., 1*l* recto 19.8 x 21.5 cm. San Francisco, 7 Oct.
1966. NSyU.

E776 [Wenning], Henry. a. l. s., 1*l* recto-verso 27.8 x 21.5 cm. San Francisco,
19 Oct. 1966. MoSW.

E777 [Wenning], Henry. a. l. s., 1*l* recto 20.3 x 12.8 cm. San Francisco, 24
Oct. [1966]. MoSW.
Note: A typescript of CORRECTIONS FOR *A BOOK OF
RESEMBLANCES* accompanied this note. F310.

E778 [Wenning], Henry. a. l. s., 1*l* recto-verso 27.8 x 21.5 cm. San Francisco,
25 Oct. 1966. MoSW.

E779 [Creeley], Bob. a. l. s., 2*l* recto-verso, recto-verso 27.9 x 21.6 cm. San
Francisco, 29 Oct. 1966. On deposit at MoSW.

E780 [Wenning], Henry. a. l. s., 1*l* recto 27.9 x 21.6 cm. San Francisco, 5 Nov. 1966. MoSW.

E781 [Creeley], Bob. a. l. s., 1*l* recto-verso 27.9 x 21.6 cm. San Francisco, 13 Nov. 1966. On deposit at MoSW.

E782 [Hawley], Bob. t. l. s., 1*l* recto 29.9 x 21.6 cm. San Francisco, 2 Dec. 1966. CtU.

E783 [Adam], Helen & Pat. a. l. s., 2*l* recto-verso, recto-verso 28 x 21.6 cm. San Francisco, 4 Dec. 1966. NBuU.

E784 [Wenning], Henry. t. l. s., 1*l* recto 27.8 x 21.5 cm. San Francisco, 4 Dec. 1966. MoSW.

E785 [Pearson], Norman [Holmes]. a. l. s., 1*l* recto-verso 27.9 x 21.7 cm. San Francisco, 7 Dec. 1966. CtY.

E786 [Starbuck], George. t. l. s., 1*l* recto-verso 27.9 x 21.5 cm. San Francisco, 26 Dec. 1966. IaU.

E787 Eshleman, [Clayton]. t. l. s., 1*l* recto 21.5 x 16 cm. San Francisco, 29 Dec. 1966. NNU.

E788 Hawley, Robert. a. n. s., 1*l* recto 24 x 31.7 cm. San Francisco, [1967]. CtU.

E789 [Olson], Charles. a. l. s., 3*l* all recto 27.8 x 21.7 cm. San Francisco, [1967]. CtU.

E790 [Olson], Charles. a. l. s., 2*l* recto-verso, recto 27.8 x 21.5 cm. San Francisco, 7 Jan. 1967. CtU.

E791 [Wenning], Henry. a. l. s., 2*l* recto-verso, recto 27.8 x 21.5 cm. San Francisco, 7 Jan. 1967. MoSW.

E792 [Wenning], Henry. t. l. s., 1*l* recto-verso 27.8 x 21.5 cm. San Francisco, 10 Jan. 1967. MoSW.

E793 Warsh, Lewis. a. p. c. s., 1*l* verso 14 x 8.2 cm. San Francisco, [19 Jan. 1967]. NNU.

E794 [Adam], Helen & Pat. a. l. s., 2*l* recto-verso, recto 28 x 21.7 cm. San Francisco, 21 Jan. 1967. NBuU.

E795 [Wenning], Henry. a. l. s., 2*l* recto-verso, recto 27.8 x 21.5 cm. San Francisco, 3 Feb. 1967. MoSW.

E796 [Creeley], Bob. a. & t. l. s., 1*l* recto-verso 27.9 x 21.6 cm. San Francisco, 8 and 11 Feb. 1967. On deposit at MoSW.

E797 [Creeley], Bob. a. & t. l. s., 2*l* recto-verso, recto-verso 27.9 x 21.6 cm. San Francisco, 23 Feb. 1967. On deposit at MoSW.

E798 Stoneburner, [Tony]. a. l. s., 2*l* recto-verso, recto-verso 28 x 27.8 cm. San Francisco, 27 Feb. 1967. OKentU.

E799 [Eshleman], Clayton. a. l. s., 2*l* recto-verso, recto-verso 27.9 x 21.7 cm. San Francisco, 1 March 1967. NNU.

E800 Blackburn, Paul & Sara. a. p. c. s., 1*l* verso 8.2 x 14 cm. San Francisco, [1 March 1967]. CU-S.

E801 [Wenning], Henry & Adele. a. l. s., 1*l* recto-verso 25.4 x 19.5 cm. San Francisco, 2 March 1967. MoSW.

E802 [Creeley], Bob. t. l. s., 1*l* recto 27.9 x 21.6 cm. San Francisco, 6 April 1967. On deposit at MoSW.

E803 [Adam], Helen & Pat. a. l. s., 2*l* recto-verso, recto 18.3 x 13.8 cm. San Francisco, 12 April 1967. OKentU.

E804 [Eshleman], Clayton. a. l. s., 1*l* recto 22.7 x 21.7 cm. San Francisco, 18 April 1967. NNU.

E805 Van Strum, Steve[n]. a. n. s., 1*l* recto 28 x 21.6 cm. Buffalo, [1 May 1967]. CtU.

E806 [Wenning], Henry & Adele. a. l. s., 2*l* recto-verso, recto-verso 27.8 x 21.5 cm. San Francisco, [June 1967]. MoSW.

E807 [Wenning], Henry. a. l., 2*l* recto-verso, recto 27.8 x 21.5 cm. San Francisco, 13 June 1967. MoSW.

E808 [Witt-Diamant], Ruth. t. l. s., 2*l* recto, recto 27.8 x 21.5 cm. San Francisco, 14 June 1967. NN.

E809 Schmidt, Judith. t. l. s., 1*l* recto 27.8 x 21.5 cm. San Francisco, 14 June 1967. NSyU.

E810 [Wenning], Henry & Adele. a. l. s., 2*l* recto-verso, recto-verso 27.9 x 21.6 cm. San Francisco, [June-July 1967]. MoSW.

E811 [Creeley], Bob & Bobby. a. l. s., 3*l*; 2*l* recto-verso, recto-verso, 1*l* recto 27.9 x 21.6 cm. San Francisco, 19 June and 1 July 1967. On deposit at MoSW.

E812 [Eshleman], Clayton. a. l. s., 1*l* recto-verso 27.9 x 21.6 cm. San Francisco, 13 July 1967. NNU.

E813 [Creeley], Bob & Bobbie. a. l. s., 1*l* recto-verso 21.6 x 17.8 cm. San Francisco, 1 Aug. 1967. On deposit at MoSW.

E814 [Eigner], Larry. a. l. s., 2*l* recto-verso 21.6 x 21.6 cm., 21.5 x 21.5 cm. San Francisco, 11 and 18 Aug. 1967. CtU.

E815 Stoneburner, Tony. t. l. s., 1*l* recto 28 x 21.8 cm. San Francisco, 7 Sept. 1967. OKentU.

E816 Stoneburner, [Tony]. t. l. s., 1*l* recto 20.3 x 21.6 cm. San Francisco, 13 Sept. 1967. OKentU.

E817 Stoneburner, Tony. t. l. s., 1*l* recto 28 x 21.7 cm. San Francisco, 14 Sept. 1967. OKentU.

E818 [Wenning], Henry. a. l. s., 1*l* recto-verso 27.9 x 21.6 cm. San Francisco, 18 Sept. 1967. MoSW.

E819 [ ], Jim. a. n. s., 1*l* recto 17.2 x 15.1 cm. [Granville, Ohio, Oct. 1967]. MoSW.

E820 [Adam], Helen. a. l. s., 2*l* recto, recto 21.7 x 14 cm. San Francisco, 27 Oct. 1967. NBuU.

E821 [Stoneburner], Tony. t. l. s., 1*l* recto 28 x 21.7 cm. San Francisco, 27 Oct. 1967. OKentU.

E822 [Creeley], Bob. a. l., 2*l* recto-verso, recto-verso 27.9 x 21.6 cm. San Francisco, 30 Oct., 4 and 12 Nov. 1967. On deposit at MoSW.

E823 [Wenning], Henry. a. l. s., 1*l* recto-verso 28 x 21.6 cm. San Francisco, 9 Nov. 1967.

E824 [Creeley], Bob. a. l. s., 1*l* recto-verso 27.9 x 21.6 cm. San Francisco, 12 Nov. 1967. On deposit at MoSW.

E825 [Eshleman], Clayton. a. l. s., 1*l* recto-verso 27.9 x 21.7 cm. San Francisco, 27 Nov. 1967. NNU.

E826 [Wenning], Henry. a. l. s., 1*l* recto-verso 23.2 x 21.7 cm. San Francisco, 11 Dec. 1967. MoSW.

E827 [Wenning], Henry. t. l. (carbon), 2*l* recto, recto 27.8 x 21.5 cm. San Francisco, 12 Jan. [1968]. MoSW.

E828 [Wenning], Henry. t. l. s., 2*l* recto, recto 27.8 x 21.5 cm. San Francisco, 31 Jan. 1968. MoSW.

E829 [Adam], Helen & Pat. a. l. s., 1*l* recto-verso 28 x 21.7 cm. San Francisco, 26 Feb. 1968. NBuU.

E830 Schmidt, Judith. t. l. s., 1*l* recto 27.8 x 21.5 cm. Buffalo, 9 July 1968. NSyU.

E831 [Wenning], Henry. a. l. s., 2*l* recto-verso, recto-verso 27.8 x 21.5 cm. Buffalo, 15 July 1968. MoSW.

E832 [Schmidt], Judith. t. l. s., 1*l* recto 27.8 x 21.5 cm. Buffalo, 16 July 1968. NSyU.

E833 [Hawley], Robert. t. l. s., 1*l* recto 28 x 21.7 cm. San Francisco, 10 Aug. 1968. CtU.

E834 [Schmidt], Judith. t. l. s., 1*l* recto 27.8 x 21.5 cm. San Francisco, 21 Aug. 1968. NSyU.

E835 Randall, James. t. l. s., 2*l* recto, recto 27.7 x 20.4 cm. San Francisco, 24 Aug. 1968. RU.
Note: A short holograph note by RD appears at bottom recto of the second leaf.

E836 [Wenning], Henry. t. l. s., 1*l* recto-verso 27.8 x 21.5 cm. San Francisco, 26 Aug. 1968. MoSW.

E837 [Wenning], Henry. t. l. s., 1*l* recto 27.8 x 21.5 cm. San Francisco, 30 Aug. 1968. MoSW.

E838 [Creeley], Bob. t. l. s., 1*l* recto-verso 27.9 x 21.6 cm. San Francisco, 12 Oct. 1968. On deposit at MoSW.
Note: A typescript of WORK IN PROGRESS OCTOBER 12, 1968 accompanied this letter. F330.

E839 [Pearson], Norman [Holmes]. a. n. s., 1*l* recto 27.9 x 21.6 cm. San Francisco, 25 Oct. 1968. CtY.

E840 [Adam], Helen & Pat. a. l. s., 2*l* recto, recto 28.4 x 21.7 cm. San Francisco, 9 Dec. 1968. NBuU.
Note: This letter is written on the first leaf recto of two leaves, reproduced, from Jess's manuscript of his then unpublished *Gallowsongs*. The pages appear verso of the first leaf and recto of the second leaf and are identified as "how the Gallowschild Remembers The Names of the Months" and by drawings by Jess. The border of the first leaf recto at the gutter has been decorated with a single red rule running from head to heal and with the following lettering in green separated by red dots: "LOVING [dot] JOYING [dot] LIVING [dot] BEING [dot] DOING [dot] GOINGS [dot] ON." A matching red rule appears at the right margin and the word "jingle" is repeated in green eleven times. The design is in Jess's hand, and he signs the letter and the design at the right margin. This letter was the Christmas greeting to Helen and Pat Adam for that year. The typescript for ACHILLES was laid in between the leaves. F332.

E841 [Pearson], Norman [Holmes]. a. l. s., 2*l* recto, verso 28.4 x 21.6 cm. San Francisco, 9 Dec. 1968. CtY.
Note: The letter is written on recto, verso of a leaf from Jess Collins's book *Gallowsongs*.

E842 Schmidt, [Judith]. t. l. s., 1*l* recto 27.8 x 21.5 cm. San Francisco, 11 Dec. 1968. NSyU.

E843 [Pearson], Norman [Holmes]. a. l. s., 1*l* recto-verso 21.5 x 22.5 cm. San Francisco, 14 Dec. 1968. CtY.

E844 [Creeley], Bob. a. l. s., 1*l* recto-verso 27.9 x 21.6 cm. San Francisco, 18 Dec. 1968. On deposit at MoSW.

E845 [Olson, Charles]. a. l. s., 1*l* verso 28.4 x 21.5 cm. San Francisco, [Jan. 1969]. CtU.
Note: The letter is written on the verso of a leaf from Jess Collins's book *Gallowsongs.*

E846 [Olson], Charles. a. l. s., 3*l* all recto-verso 278 x 21.6 cm. San Francisco, 8 and 17 Jan. 1969. CtU.

E847 [Eigner], Larry. a. l. s., 3*l* all recto 21.5 x 18.8 cm. San Francisco, 4 Feb. 1969. CtU.

E848 [Creeley], Bob. a. l. s., 4*l*; 3*l* all recto-verso, 1*l* recto 22.9 x 21.6 cm. San Francisco, 9 March 1969. On deposit at MoSW.

E849 [Finlay], Sue & Ian [Hamilton]. a. l. s., 1*l* recto-verso 30.5 x 17.3 cm. San Francisco, 9 April 1969. InU.

E850 [Martin, John]. a. l. s., 1*l* recto-verso 27.3 x 15.5 cm. [San Francisco, May/June 1969]. NmU.

E851 [Wenning], Henry & Adele. a. l. s., 2*l* recto-verso, recto 27.8 x 21.5 cm. San Francisco, 10 June 1969. MoSW.

E852 [Creeley], Bob. a. l. s., 4*l* all recto-verso 23.4 x 21.6 cm. San Francisco, 3 Aug. [19]69. On deposit at MoSW.

E853 [Creeley], Bob. a. l. s., 2*l* recto-verso, recto-verso 21.8 x 17.9 cm. Ellensberg, Wash., 14 Oct. 1969. On deposit at MoSW.

E854 [Adam], Helen. a. l. s., 2*l* recto-verso, recto-verso 22.3 x 15.3 cm. San Francisco, 24 Oct. [19]69. NBuU.
Note: A note by Jess Collins appears on the verso of the second leaf. A manuscript of CALL HIM NIGHT'S LORD accompanied this letter. F337.

E855 [Creeley], Bob. a. l. s., 2*l* recto-verso, recto-verso 27.9 x 21.7 cm. San Francisco, 29 Oct. 1969. On deposit at MoSW.

E856 [Creeley], Bob & Bobby. a. n. s., 1*l* recto-verso 15.2 x 11.2 cm. San Francisco, 8 Dec. 1969. On deposit at MoSW.

E857 Olson, [Charles]. a. l. s., 3*l* all recto-verso 21.5 x 14 cm. San Francisco, 18 Dec. 1969. CtU.

E858 [Creeley], Bob. a. l., 2*l* recto-verso, recto 27.9 x 21.6 cm. San Francisco, 4, 6 and 16 Feb. 1970. On deposit at MoSW.

E859 [Schmidt], Judith. a. n. s., 1*l* recto 27.8 x 21.5 cm. San Francisco, [March 1970]. NSyU.
Note: RD's note is written on the bottom of a letter to him from Judith Schmidt dated 12 March 1970. (E860).

E860 [Schmidt], Judith. t. l. s. (photocopy), 1*l* recto 27.8 x 21.5 cm. San Francisco, 12 March 1970. NSyU.

E861 [Eshleman], Clayton. t. l. s., 1*l* recto 27.9 x 21.6 cm. San Francisco, 17 May 1970. NNU.

E862 [Creeley], Bob. a. l. s., 1*l* recto-verso 27.8 x 21.6 cm. San Francisco, 16 June 1970. On deposit at MoSW.
Note: This letter accompanied RD's notes and comments on Creeley's *A Day Book*. F338.

E863 [Pearson], Norman [Holmes]. a. l. s., 3*l* recto-verso, recto-verso, recto 22.7 x 15.2 cm. San Francisco, 6 Aug. 1970. CtY.

E864 [Pearson], Norman [Holmes]. a. n. s., 1*l* recto 22.7 x 15.2 cm. San Francisco, 21 Aug. 1970. CtY.

E865 [Creeley], Bob. a. l. s., 1*l* recto-verso 27.9 x 21.4 cm. San Francisco, 17 Oct. 1970. On deposit at MoSW.

E866 [Pearson], Norman [Holmes]. a. l. s., 1*l* recto-verso 27.9 x 21.5 cm. San Francisco, 9 Nov. 1970. CtY.

E867 [Pearson], Norman [Holmes]. a. l. s., 1*l* recto-verso 28 x 21.5 cm. San Francisco, 29 Jan. 1971. CtY.
Note: RD's privately published edition of his *Ground Work* accompanied this letter.

E868 [Lowell], Jim. a. n. s., 1*l* recto 23.4 x 16.3 cm. [Cleveland, Ohio, April 1971]. OKentU.

E869 Price, [Martin]. a. n. s., 1*l* recto 22.8 x 15.2 cm. San Francisco, 12 April 1971. CtY.

E870 [Pearson], Norman [Holmes]. a. l. s., 3*l* recto-verso, recto-verso, recto 27.9 x 21.5 cm. San Francisco, 13 April 1971. CtY.

E871 [Grossinger], Richard. a. l. s., 3*l* all recto 22.8 x 15.7 cm. San Francisco, 30 June 1971. CaBVaS.

E872 Lyon, Melvin. a. l. s., 2*l* recto-verso, recto 27.8 x 21.5 cm. San Francisco, 12 Nov. 1971. NbU.

E873 [Broughton], James. a. l. s., 2*l*; 1*l* recto 33.8 x 15.2 cm., 1*l* 22.8 x 15.2 cm. [San Francisco], 13 Nov. 1971. OKentU.

E874 [Pearson], Norman [Holmes]. a. l. s., 2*l* recto-verso, recto-verso 27.9 x 21.5 cm. San Francisco, 20 Nov. 1971. CtY.
Note: The author's offset typescript reproduction of his poems INTER-RUPTED FORMS. ONE—PREFACE TO THE SUITE TRANS-LATED FROM THOM GUNN'S *MOLY*—POEMS FROM THE MARGINS OF THOM GUNN'S *MOLY*—RITES OF PASSAGE—MOLY—SECOND TAKE ON *RITES OF PASSAGE* accompanied this letter.

E875 [Adam], Helen & Pat. a. l. s., 2*l* recto, recto 15.2 x 11.4 cm. San Francisco, 11 Dec. 1971. NBuU.

E876 Moynihan, [William]. a. l. s., 1*l* recto 27.8 x 21.5 cm. San Francisco, 27 March 1972. CtU.

E877 [Pearson], Norman [Holmes]. a. l. s., 6*l* all recto 22.8 x 15.2 cm. San Francisco, 5 April 1972.
Note: The author's edition of POEMS FROM THE MARGINS OF THOM GUNN'S *MOLY* accompanied this letter.

E878 [Pearson], Norman [Holmes]. a. l. s., 2*l* recto-verso, recto-verso 28 x 21.5 cm. San Francisco, 2 and 4 June 1972. CtY.

E879 [Pearson], Norman [Holmes]. a. l. s., 6*l* all recto 22.8 x 15.2 cm. San Francisco, 20 and 25 July 1972. CtY.

E880 [Creeley], Bob & Bobbie. a. l. s., 3*l* all recto-verso 27.8 x 21.6 cm. San Francisco, 27 July 1972. On deposit at MoSW.

E881 Linenthal, Mark. a. n. s., 1*l* recto 21.8 x 15.1 cm. [San Francisco], 6 Aug. 1972. CSf-APA.

E882 [Adam], Helen & Pat. a. l. s., 2*l* recto-verso, recto-verso 28.1 x 21.6 cm. San Francisco, 30 Aug. 1972. NBuU.

E883 [McConville], Mary. a. l. s., 2*l* recto-verso, recto-verso 27.9 x 21.6 cm. San Francisco, 6 Nov. 1972. OKentU.

E884 [Donley], Carol. a. l. s. (photocopy), 1*l* recto-verso 27.9 x 21.6 cm. San Francisco, 7 Nov. [19]72. OKentU.

E885 [Blevins], Rich. a. l. s., (photocopy), 2*l* recto-verso, recto-verso 27.9 x 21.6 cm. San Francisco, 7 Nov. [19]72. OKentU.

E886 [Adam], Helen. a. l. s., 2*l* recto-verso, recto-verso 27.9 x 21.6 cm. San Francisco, 21 Nov. 1972. NBuU.

E887 [Meanor], Pat. a. l. s., 4*l* all recto-verso 27.9 x 21.7 cm. San Francisco, 18 Dec. 1972. OKentU.

E888 [McConville], Mary. a. l. s. (photocopy), 4*l* all recto-verso 27.9 x 21.6 cm. San Francisco, 20 Dec. 1972. OKentU.

E889 [Nurmi], Ruth. a. l. s., 5*l* all recto-verso 27.9 x 21.6 cm. San Francisco, 2 Jan. 197[3]. OKentU.

E890 [Pearson], Norman [Holmes]. a. l. s., 1*l* recto-verso 27.9 x 21.7 cm. San Francisco, 25 Jan. 1973. CtY.

E891 [Creeley], Bob. a. l. s., 3*l* all recto-verso 27.9 x 21.7 cm. San Francisco, 21 Feb. 1973. On deposit at MoSW.

E892 [Creeley], Bob. a. l. s., 2*l* recto-verso, recto-verso 27.9 x 21.7 cm. San Francisco, 14 and 16 March 1973. On deposit at MoSW.

E893 Gay, Carl. t. l. s., 1*l* recto 27.9 x 21.7 cm. San Francisco, 19 March 1973. NBuU.

E894 [Blevins], Rich. a. l. s. (photocopy), 2*l* recto-verso, recto-verso 27.9 x 21.7 cm. San Francisco, 9 April 1973. OKentU.

E895 [Pearson], Norman [Holmes]. a. l. s., 2*l* recto-verso, recto-verso 27.9 x 21.5 cm. San Francisco, 1 May 1973. CtY.

E896 [Butterick], George. a. l. s., 1*l* recto-verso 27.9 x 21.5 cm. San Francisco, 4 Oct. 1973. CtU.
Note: Included in this letter is a photocopy of A CANTO FOR EZRA POUND, 6*l* all recto 27.8 x 21.5 cm. See letter to Charles Olson, [1948]. E19.

E897 [Grossinger], Richard & Lindy. a. n. s., 1*l* recto 21.6 x 17.8 cm. San Francisco, 28 Nov. 1973. CaBVaS.

E898 [Pearson], Norman [Holmes]. a. l. s., 3*l* recto-verso, recto-verso, recto 27.9 x 21.5 cm. San Francisco, 13 Dec. 1973. CtY.

E899 [Pearson], Norman [Holmes]. a. l. s., 1*l* recto-verso 27.9 x 21.5 cm. San Francisco, 1 Jan. 1974. CtY.

E900 [Creeley], Bob. a. l. s., 2*l* recto-verso, recto-verso 27.8 x 21.5 cm. San Francisco, 6, 9, and 13 March 1974. On deposit at MoSW.

E901 [Pearson], Norman [Holmes]. a. l. s., 3*l* all recto-verso 27.9 x 21.5 cm. San Francisco, 14 May 1974. CtY.

E902 [Pearson], Norman [Holmes]. a. l. s., 3*l* all recto 22.5 x 15.2 cm. San Francisco, 16 Oct. 1974. CtY.

E903 [Creeley], Bob. t. l. s., 3*l* all recto 28.8 x 21.5 cm. San Francisco, 4 and 11 Nov. 1974. On deposit at MoSW.

E904 [Adam], Helen & Pat. a. l. s., 4*l*; 2*l* recto-verso, recto 21.7 x 13.8 cm., 2*l* recto-verso, recto-verso 22.9 x 15.3 cm. Riverside and San Francisco, 9 and 17 Jan. 1975. NBuU.

E905 [Adam], Helen & Pat. a. l. s., 2*l* recto-verso, recto 33.8 x 21.6 cm. San Francisco, 3 April 1975. NBuU.

E906 [Pearson], Norman [Holmes]. a. l. s., 2*l* recto-verso, recto-verso 33.1 x 21.6 cm. San Francisco, 3 April 1975. CtY.

E907 [Adam], Helen. a. l. s., 2*l* recto-verso, recto-verso 33.8 x 21.6 cm. San Francisco, 8 April 1975. NBuU.

E908 Gay, [Karl]. a. l. s., 1*l* recto 27.9 x 21.6 cm. San Francisco, 8 May 1975. NBuU.

E909 [Pearson], Norman [Holmes]. a. l. s., 1*l* recto-verso 27.9 x 21.6 cm. San Francisco, 20 May 1975. CtY.

E910 Curator,/Charles Olson Archives. [George Butterick]. t. & a. l. s., 1*l* recto 27.9 x 21.6 cm. San Francisco, 20 May 1975. CtU.

E911 [ ]. a. n. s., 1*l* recto 22.8 x 15 cm. San Francisco, 9 June 1975. CU-S.

E912 [Adam], Helen & Pat. a. l. s., 3*l* all recto 28 x 21.4 cm. San Francisco, 19 and 23 June 1975. NBuU.

E913 Fagin, Larry. t. l. s., 1*l* recto 27.9 x 21.5 cm. San Francisco, 26 Jan. 1976. CtU.

E914 [Creeley], Bob. a. l. s., 2*l* recto-verso, recto 27.7 x 21.6 cm. San Francisco, 12, 13 and 16 July 1976. On deposit at MoSW.

E915 [Adam], Helen. a. l. s., 1*l* recto-verso 27.9 x 21.6 cm. San Francisco, 23 July 1976. NBuU.

E916 [Adam], Helen. a. l. s., 1*l* recto 35.6 x 21.6 cm. San Francisco, 15 and 19 Oct. 1976. NBuU.

E917 [Creeley], Bob. t. l. & ms. s., 2*l* recto-verso, recto-verso 27.7 x 21.6 cm. San Francisco, 11 Feb. 1977. On deposit at MoSW.
Note: The letter contains a typescript of A MAISTRE BAUDELAIRE: TOWARD HIS MALAISE and AMONG MY WORDS AND THE FACE.

E918 [Adam], Helen & Pat. a. l. s., 1*l* recto 33.6 x 21.6 cm. San Francisco, 21 March 1977. NBuU.

E919 [Creeley], Bob & Penny. t. l. s., 1*l* recto 27.7 x 21.6 cm. San Francisco, 8 Oct. 1977. On deposit at MoSW.

E920 Meanor, Pat. t. l. s., 1*l* recto 27.9 x 21.5 cm. San Francisco, 18 Jan. 1978. OKentU.

E921 Meanor, Pat. t. l. s., 1*l* recto 27.9 x 21.5 cm. San Francisco, 10 Feb. 1978. OKentU.
Note: A note in the poet's hand appears at the bottom and side of this letter.

E922 [Meanor], Pat. a. l. s., 1*l* recto-verso 27.9 x 21.6 cm. San Francisco, 2 Sept. 1978. OKentU.

E923 [Creeley], Bob. t. l. s., 1*l* recto 27.9 x 21.6 cm. San Francisco, 16 Oct. 1978. On deposit at MoSW.

E924 [Creeley], Bob. a. l. s., 1*l* recto-verso 27.9 x 21.6 cm. San Francisco, 15 Nov. 1978. On deposit at MoSW.

E925 Caraher, Brian. t. l. s., 1*l* recto 27.9 x 21.6 cm. San Francisco, 2 Feb. 1979. NBuU.

F.
Manuscripts

F1   [Two Poems]. T. ms. ICU.

Date: [June 1941].

Collation: 5*l* all recto 28 x 21.8 cm.

Contents: This is a typescript (black ribbon) of the poems A SPRING MEMORANDUM—A PAIR OF URANIAN GARTERS FOR AURORA BLIGH as they appeared in *Poetry.* C26.

Note: This typescript, which now contains some editorial markings, was first sent to *Poetry* with a cover letter by Anaïs Nin.

F2   SOME WORK DONE WHILE AT ASHFIELD, MASS | NOVEMBER 1942 [space] ROBERT DUNCAN | A SHEAF FOR DICK AND CLARA. A. ms. OKentU.

Date: Nov. 1942.

Collation: 6*l* all recto-verso 28 x 21.5 cm.

Contents: "Blood is part of that" [drawing]—I IMAGINE—"THE SNOW IS ON THE HEARTH" (fl)—VARIATIONS IN PRAISE OF JESUS CHRIST OUR LORD—VARIATIONS UPON PHRASES FROM MILTON'S *THE REASON OF CHURCH GOVERN-MENT*— VARIATIONS UPON WORDS: CONSCIENCE, CONTINUAL FEATS, NATURAL IMPEDIMENT, REMORSE, DISGRACE, REPROACH, IMPERFECTION, INFIRMITY, FEET, A COMPANY OF FINE CLASSES, CHANCE, OVERMUCH MOVED, MODERATE, RIDER, SELFISH, STOCK, COMMON, EVERY AIR, DOG, DARES, COURAGE (from Burton's *Anatomy of Melancholy*).

Note: The fourth poem, and the final three poems were collected in YAC with revisions. The remaining poems are unpublished.

F3   Translations from André Breton's *Poèmes* (NRF, Gallimard, 1948). T. ms. CU-B.

Date: Oct. 1943.

Collation: 7*l* all recto; 4*l* 27.9 x 21.6 cm., 1*l* 19.5 x 21.6 cm., 2*l* 22.9 x 21.6 cm.

Contents: This is the typescript (black ribbon) of the following translations done by RD: PLEINE MARGE (FULL MARGIN)—from LES ÉTATS GÉNÉRAUX: IL Y AURA (THERE WILL BE)—AU VENT (WINDWARD)—DANS LES SABLES (IN THE SANDS)— DU RÊVE (DREAMS)—notes on the translations.

Note: RD knew Breton's poems before their publication.

F4   [Untitled Prose Piece]. A. ms. MoSW.

Date: [Oct. 1944].

Collation: 1*l* recto 28 x 21.6 cm.

Contents: This is the first draft, with changes and deletions, of RD's letter to John Crowe Ransom, Oct. 1944. E4.

F5   HOW IN THE DARK. T. ms. CU-B.

Date: [1945].

Collation: 1*l* recto 27.8 x 21.4 cm.

Contents: This is a typescript (black ribbon) of a fifteen line unpublished poem.

F6 [Untitled Poem]. T. ms. CU-B.
Date: [1945/46].
Collation: 1*l* recto 27.7 x 21.4 cm.
Contents: This is a typescript (black ribbon) of an unpublished poem, "IF I LOVE BROKE" (fl).

F7 A RIDE TO THE SEA. T. ms. CU-B.
Date: [1945/46].
Collation: 1*l* recto 28 x 21.7 cm.
Contents: This is a typescript (black ribbon) of the text of the poem.

F8 "SLEEP IS A DEEP AND MANY VOICED FLOOD" (fl). T. ms. CU-B.
Date: 1946.
Collation: 1*l* recto 27.8 x 21.5 cm.
Contents: This is a typescript (black ribbon) of the text of the poem.

F9 A CANTO FOR EZRA POUND. T. ms. CU.
Date: Dec. 1946.
Collation: 6*l* all recto 27.5 x 21.2 cm.
Contents: This is a typescript (black ribbon) of an unpublished poem written to Ezra Pound.
Note: This poem was written by RD, Jack Spicer, Jo Frankel, and Hugh O'Neill. See the letter to George Butterick, 4 Oct. 1973, for RD's identification of his and some of the other parts of this poem. E896.

F10 THE WARRING KINGDOMS. T. ms. CU-B.
Date: [1946/47].
Collation: 7*l* all recto 27.9 x 21.6 cm.
Contents: This is a typescript (black carbon) of the unpublished poem.

F11 IDLE LIVING AT CLOSE QUARTERS. T. ms. CU-B.
Date: [1946/47].
Collation: 2*l* recto, recto 28 x 21.6 cm.
Contents: This is a typescript (black ribbon) of the unpublished poem.

F12 WORKING TOO LONG AT IT. T. ms. CU-B.
Date: [1946/47].
Collation: 1*l* recto 27.8 x 21.5 cm.
Contents: This is a typescript (black ribbon) of the text of the poem.

F13 UPON JACK'S RETURN: DOMESTIC SCENES. A. ms. CU-B.
Date: 1947.
Collation: 9*l* all recto 27.7 x 21.5 cm.

Contents: This is the pencil holograph version of the following poems: BREAKFAST—REAL ESTATE—BUS FARE—MAIL BOXES—MATCHES—BATH—RADIO—ELECTRIC IRON—LUNCH WITH BUNS—PIANO.

Note: The poems were revised for their first appearance in *Quarterly Review of Literature.* The poem MAIL BOXES is signed by RD and dated 1947. C52.

F14 A THIRD DISCOURSE ON LOVE. T. ms. CU-B.
Date: 1947.
Collation: 1 *l* recto 28 x 21.6 cm.
Contents: This is a typescript (black ribbon) of the text of the poem.
Note: This typescript accompanied a letter to Jack Spicer, dated 1947. E8.

F15 [FRAGMENT OF A DRAMA]. T. ms. CU-B.
Date: [1947].
Collation: 7 *l* all recto; 5 *l* 27.7 x 21.2 cm., 2 *l* 27.8 x 21.6 cm.
Contents: This typescript (black ribbon) consists of fragments of an unpublished play.
Note: This typescript accompanied a letter to Jack Spicer, dated 1947. E8.

F16 [Four Pieces]. T. ms. CU-B.
Date: [1947].
Collation: 2 *l* recto-verso, recto-verso 28 x 21.7 cm.
Contents: This is a typescript (black ribbon) of the following pieces: PROLETARIAN SONG—THE INTERNATIONAL HOUSE—SEX— FIVE EARLY STORIES.
Note: This typescript accompanied a letter to Jack Spicer, dated 1947. The second and third pieces are dated 1937. E7.

F17 A SECOND DISCOURSE ON LOVE: 1947. T. ms. CU-B.
Date: 1947.
Collation: 2 *l* recto, recto 28 x 21.7 cm.
Contents: This is a typescript (black ribbon) of the text of the poem.
Note: A note on the manuscript indicates that this poem is one of the "Treesbank Poems," but it was not published as such.

F18 UPON HEARING LEONARD WOLF'S POEM ON A MADHOUSE, JANUARY 13, 1947. T. ms. CU-B.
Date: Jan. 1947.
Collation: 3 *l* all recto 27.9 x 21.5 cm.
Contents: This is a typescript (black ribbon) of the text of the poem. Two stanzas of the poem appear as the holograph additions to the signed copies of HCEC.

F19 The MEDIEVAL SCENES Papers. A. & T. ms. OKentU.
Date: [Feb. 1947].

a. Untitled [THE DREAMERS] A. ms. (pencil).

Collation: 1*l* recto 27.9 x 21.6 cm.

Contents: The epigraph appears before the poem, which has thirty lines that were revised for publication.

b. THE HELMET OF GOLIATH. A. ms. (pencil).

Collation: 3*l* all recto 26.8 x 21.4 cm.

Contents: This is the text of the poem, forty-seven lines, with the epigraph, which differs slightly from the published version.

c.1. THE BANNERS. A. ms. (pencil).

Collation: 1*l* recto 27.9 x 21.6 cm.

Contents: This is a draft of twenty-two lines, later much revised for publication, with the epigraph.

c.2. THE BANNERS. A. ms. (pencil).

Collation: 2*l* recto, recto 27.9 x 21.6 cm.

Contents: This is a twenty-six line draft of the poem, with substantial differences from published version.

d.1. THE KINGDOM OF JERUSALEM. A. ms. (pencil)

Collation: 1*l* recto 27.9 x 21.6 cm.

Contents: This a nineteen line draft of the poem, with the epigraph.

d.2. THE KINGDOM OF JERUSALEM. A. ms. (pencil)

Collation: 2*l* recto, recto 27.9 x 21.6 cm.

Contents: This a thirty-five line draft of the poem.

e.1. THE FESTIVALS. A. ms. (pencil)

Collation: 1*l* recto 27.9 x 21.7 cm.

Contents: This is a twenty-two line draft of the poem.

e.2. THE FESTIVALS A. ms.

Collation: 2*l* recto, recto 279 x 21.7 cm.

Contents: With the epigraph, this a fifty line draft of the poem with three lines crossed out. Some revisions were later made for publication.

f.1. Untitled [THE MIRROR]. A. ms. (pencil)

Collation: 1*l* recto 27.9 x 21.5 cm.

Contents: This is a twenty-one line draft of the poem.

f.2. THE MIRROR. A. ms. (pencil).

Collation: 2*l* recto, recto 27.9 x 21.5 cm.

Contents: With the epigraph, this is a forty-six line version of the poem, with only slight differences from published version.

g.1. [THE ADORATION OF THE VIRGIN]. A. ms. (pencil)

Collation: 2*l* recto-verso, recto 27.9 x 21.6 cm.

Contents: The two recto pages contain a thirty-nine line draft of the poem, with some slight differences from published version. Verso of the first leaf contains a fourteen line draft of the poem with the epigraph.

g.2. [THE ADORATION OF THE VIRGIN]. A. ms. (pencil)

Collation: 1*l* recto 27.9 x 21.6 cm.

Contents: This is a draft of the final twelve lines of the poem.

h.1. HUON OF BORDEAUX. A. ms. (pencil).

Collation: 1*l* recto-verso 27.9 x 21.5 cm.

Contents: With the epigraph, this is a twenty line draft of the poem, with substantial differences from published version. Verso contains a seven line draft of THE ADORATION OF THE VIRGIN plus epigraph.

h.2. HUON OF BORDEAUX. A. ms. (pencil)

Collation: 1*l* recto-verso 27.9 x 21.5 cm.

Contents: Recto contains a twenty-eight line draft of the poem with the epigraph. Verso contains the epigraph of THE ADORATION OF THE VIRGIN.

i.1. THE ALBIGENSES. A. ms. (pencil).

Collation: 1*l* recto 28 x 21.7 cm.

Contents: This is a five line draft of the poem, plus the epigraph.

i.2. THE ALBIGENSES. A. ms. (pencil).

Collation: 1*l* recto 28 x 21.7 cm.

Contents: This is a twenty-one line draft of the poem.

i.3. THE ALBIGENSES. A. ms. (pencil).

Collation: 1*l* recto 28 x 21.7 cm.

Contents: This is a twenty-two line draft of the poem.

i.4. THE ALBIGENSES. A. ms. (pencil).

Collation: 2*l* recto, recto 28 x 21.7 cm.

Contents: This is a thirty-two line draft of the poem.

i.5 THE ALBIGENSES. A. ms. (pencil).

Collation: 2*l* recto, recto 28 x 21.7 cm.

Contents: This is a thirty-five line version of the poem, with only slight differences from published version.

j. A MEDIEVAL SLUMBERING. A. ms. (black ink).

Collation: 5*l* all recto 27.9 x 21.5 cm.

Contents: The text of the following poems as published in SP appears here: THE DREAMERS—THE HELMET OF GOLIATH— THE BANNERS.

k. A MEDIEVAL SLUMBERING. T. ms. (black ribbon).

Collation: 1*l* recto 27.9 x 21.6 cm.

Contents: This is a typed version of item "a" above.

l. MEDIEVAL SCENES. T. ms. (black ribbon).

Collation: 22*l* all recto 27.9 x 21.6 cm.

Contents: With the epigraphs, this is a typescript of the completed series: THE DREAMERS—THE HELMET OF GOLIATH—THE BANNERS—THE KINGDOM OF JERUSALEM—THE FESTI- VALS—THE MIRROR—THE REAPER—THE ADORATION OF THE VIRGIN—HUON OF BORDEAUX—THE ALBIGENSES.

m. NOTES TO *MEDIEVAL SCENES*. T. ms. (black ribbon)

Collation: 6*l* all recto 27.8 x 21.7 cm.

Contents: In these typescript notes RD has supplied the sources for the epigraphs and the poems.

n. [Two Poems]. T. ms. (black ribbon).

Collation: 3*l* all recto 27.9 x 21.5 cm.

Contents: This is a typescript of HUON OF BORDEAUX and THE ADORATION OF THE VIRGIN as prepared for SP with line numbers at the left edge.

o. AUTHOR'S NOTES SEPTEMBER 1962 | TO THE MEDIEVAL SCENES PAPERS. A. ms. (black ink).

Collation: 2*l* recto-verso, recto-verso 28.1 x 21.7 cm.

Contents: RD's comments (black ink) about the constitution of the papers prepared at the time of their first sale.

p. [Note]. A. ms. (black ink).

Collation: 1*l* recto 28 x 21.7 cm.

Contents: Dated 17 April 1972, this note by RD authorizes the scholarly use of the papers.

Note: The papers are contained in a standard file folder, 22.9 x 29.9 cm., the front cover of which is decorated with a crayon drawing of a medieval scene by RD.

F20 ODE FOR DICK BROWN UPON THE TERMINATION OF HIS PAROLE MARCH 17, 1947. T. ms. CU-B.

Date: March 1947.

Collation: 1*l* recto 27.9 x 21.7 cm.

Contents: This is a typescript (black ribbon) of the text of the poem as it was later published in *An Ode and Arcadia,* by Jack Spicer and Robert Duncan (Berkeley: Ark Press, 1974). A47.

Note: A holograph letter, signed, to Jack Spicer appears on the verso.

F21 THE HELMET OF GOLIATH. T. ms. CtY.

Date: [1947/48].

Collation: 2*l* recto, recto 27.8 x 21.5 cm.

Contents: This is a typescript (black ribbon) of the text of the poem which differs from both the version in SP and the version in *Medieval Scenes.*

F22 [UNMAILED LETTER TO WILLIAM CARLOS WILLIAMS]. A. ms. CU-B.

Date: [1948?]

Collation: 1*l* recto 28 x 21.6 cm.

Contents: The text of the letter.

F23 THE POET AS A MIRROR WRITES RUNES. A. ms. CU-S.

Date: 1948.

Collation: 1*l* recto 27.9 x 21.6 cm.

Contents: This is the text (black pen) of the unpublished poem.

Note: The date was added by RD to the manuscript at a later time. E895.

F24 A LOOKING GLASS. T. ms. CU-B.
    Date: [1948?].
    Collation: 28*l* all recto 28 x 21.7 cm., except 1*l* recto 11 x 21.7 cm.
    Contents: This is a typescript (black ribbon) of the text of the following
    poems: DOMESTIC SCENES [sequence-title for following ten
    poems] BREAKFAST—REAL ESTATE—BUS FARE—MAIL
    BOXES—MATCHES—BATH—RADIO—ELECTRIC IRON—
    LUNCH WITH BUNS—PIANO—IDEAS OF FLYING— MEDIE-
    VAL SCENES [sequence-title for following ten poems] THE DREA-
    MERS—THE HELMET OF GOLIATH—THE BANNERS— THE
    KINGDOM OF JERUSALEM—THE FESTIVALS—THE MIR-
    ROR—THE REAPER—THE ADORATION OF THE VIRGIN—
    HUON OF BORDEAUX—THE ALBIGENSES—AND NOW I
    HAVE RETURND—DIONYSIUS AT THE CROSSROADS— THE
    NEW HESPERIDES (INVOCATION—RHAPSODY).

F25 RHAPSODY. T. ms. CU-B.
    Date: [1948].
    Collation: 3*l* all recto 27.9 x 21.6 cm.
    Contents: This is a typescript (black ribbon) of the poem. It is desig-
    nated as the fourth part of THE NEW HESPERIDES from "A Look-
    ing Glass."

F26 THE VENICE POEM Papers. T. & A. ms. CU-B.
    Date: [1948].
    a. [I TELL OF LOVE]. T. ms. (black ribbon).
    Collation: 1*l* recto 28 x 21.7 cm.
    Contents: The text of the poem as published, but not part of THE
    VENICE POEM.
    b. THE VENICE POEM. A. ms. (pencil).
    Collation: 2*l* recto, recto 27.9 x 21.5 cm.
    Contents: This is an early draft of the poem's beginning lines.
    c. THE VENICE POEM A. ms. (black ink).
    Collation: 1*l* recto 24.2 x 15.3 cm.
    Contents: Lines deleted from the published poem.
    d. DESCRIPTION OF VENICE. A. ms. (pencil).
    Collation: 1*l* recto 27.9 x 21.6 cm.
    Contents: This is an early draft of the poem.
    e. IMAGINARY INSTRUCTIONS. A. ms. (pencil).
    Collation: 2*l* recto, recto 24.3 x 15.3 cm.
    Contents: This is an early draft of the poem.
    f. GREEN HOMAGE. T. ms. (black ribbon).
    Collation: 2*l* recto, recto 27.9 x 21.7 cm.
    Contents: The text of a deleted section of the poem.
    g. IMAGINARY INSTRUCTIONS. A. ms. (pencil).
    Collation: 1*l* recto-verso 27.9 x 21.6 cm.
    Contents: An expanded draft of "e" above.

h. IMAGINARY INSTRUCTIONS. T. ms. (black ribbon)

Collation: 7*l* all recto 28 x 21.6 cm.

Contents: This is the typescript of two different versions, both of which differ from the published poem.

i. [Untitled]. A. ms. (pencil).

Collation: 1*l* recto 27.9 x 21.6 cm.

Contents: The text of deleted and unpublished lines.

j. [THE VENICE POEM]. T. ms. (black ribbon).

Collation: 11*l*; 7*l* all recto-verso, 4*l* all recto 27.9 x 21.6 cm.

Contents: This is a typescript of A DESCRIPTION OF VENICE—TESTIMONY—IMAGINARY INSTRUCTIONS—RECORSO—LA VENUS DE LESPUGUE with some differences from the published version.

k. THE VENUS OF LESPUGUE. A. ms. (black ink).

Collation: 1*l* recto 21.6 x 14.1 cm.

Contents: This is a draft of seven lines of the poem.

l. THE VENUS OF LESPUGUE. A. ms. (pencil).

Collation: 1*l* recto-verso 21.5 x 12.9 cm.

Contents: This is an expanded draft of "k" above.

m. RECORSO. A. ms. (black ink)

Collation: 1*l* recto 27.9 x 21.6 cm.

Contents: This is an early draft of the poem.

n. THE VENUS OF LESPUGUE. A. ms. (black pen).

Collation: 3*l* recto, recto-verso, recto-verso 27.8 x 21.7 cm.

Contents: This is an expanded version of "l" above.

o. THE VENUS OF LESPUGUE. T. ms. (black ribbon).

Collation: 1*l* recto 27.8 x 21.7 cm.

Contents: This is a typescript of the first lines of the poem.

p. CODA. A. ms. (black ink).

Collation: 1*l* recto 27.9 x 21.6 cm.

Contents: This is an early version of the poem.

q. CODA. A. ms. (black pen).

Collation: 1*l* recto 27.9 x 21.6 cm.

Contents: This is an expanded version of "p" above with five stanzas of the poem.

r. THE VENICE POEM. T. ms. (black ribbon).

Collation: 7*l* recto-verso, recto-verso, recto, recto, recto, recto-verso, recto 27.9 x 21.6 cm.

Contents: This is a typescript of the whole poem, with small changes from the published version.

s. SOLO, DUO, TRIO. A. ms. (black ink).

Collation: 1*l* recto-verso 27.8 x 21.6 cm.

Contents: This is the text of lines deleted from the poem.

t. CODA. T. ms. (black ribbon).

Collation: 4*l* all recto 27.9 x 21.6 cm.

Contents: This is a typescript of the poem.

u. CODA. A. ms. (black ink).
Collation: 3*l* recto-verso, recto, recto 21.4 x 13.7 cm.
Contents: This is a version that with small changes became "t" above.

F27 [Untitled Poem]. A. ms. CU-B.
Date: [1948/49].
Collation: 2*l* recto-verso, recto-verso 24.2 x 15.3 cm.
Contents: This is a pencil holograph of the text of an unidentified and unpublished poem.

F28 THE ENIGMA OF LOVE. A. ms. CU-B.
Date: [1948/49].
Collation: 2*l* recto-verso, recto 25.8 x 20.2 cm.
Contents: This is a holograph draft of the poem.

F29 IDEAS OF FLYING. T. ms. CU-B.
Date: [1948/49?].
Collation: 5*l* all recto 27.8 x 21.5 cm.
Contents: IDEAS OF FLYING [essay on tightrope walking and fictions].

F30 [NOTES ON THE VENICE POEM]. A. ms. CU-B.
Date: [1948/49].
Collation: 1*l* recto-verso 21.8 x 13.5 cm.
Contents: These are RD's notes on the people who appear in the poem.

F31 INTRODUCTION. T. ms. CU-B.
Date: [May 1949].
Collation: 4*l* all recto 27.8 x 21.7 cm.
Contents: This is a typescript (black ribbon), single spaced, of the introduction for a collection of early poetry. Not published.

F32 THE HORNS OF ARTEMIS. A. & T. ms. MoSW.
a. [Untitled Poem]. A. ms.
Date: [1949].
Collation: 1*l* recto 21.5 x 17.5 cm.
Contents: This is an early holograph version in pencil of the poem.
b. THE HORNS OF ARTEMIS. T. ms.
Date: [1952?].
Collation: 1*l* recto 21.5 x 11.5 cm.
Contents: This is a typescript (black ribbon) of the poem with changes and corrections of the earlier untitled version.
c. THE HORNS OF ARTEMIS. T. ms.
Date: [1949].
Collation: 1*l,* recto 27.5 x 21.5 cm.
Contents: A note by RD specifies that this typescript (black ribbon) is a "transcription into Jaime de Angelo's typewriter phonemes sometime in 1949."

Note: The version of the poem published in *Origin*, 6 (Summer 1952), differs slightly from manuscript "b" and slightly from the version published in RB.

F33 H. M. S. BEARSKIN. T. ms. CU-B.
Date: [1949?].
Collation: 3*l* all recto 27.9 x 21.6 cm.
Contents: This is a typescript (black ribbon) of the sequence in eight parts, which was originally entitled "The Land of the Dead."

F34 FOUR POEMS AS A NIGHT SONG. T. ms. CU-B.
Date: 1949.
Collation: 2*l* recto, recto 27.8 x 21.5 cm.
Contents: This is a typescript of the text as it appeared in *Caesar's Gate.*

F35 AFRICA REVISITED. A. ms. MoSW.
Date: [1949].
Collation: 10*l* all recto; 6*l* 27.8 x 21.5 cm., 4*l* 27.5 x 21.5 cm.
Contents: This is an early holograph version of the poem which was revised substantially for later publication. The poem is written partly in ink and partly in pencil.

F36 [Untitled Notebook Prose]. A. ms. CU-B.
Date: 12 and 17 Feb. [1949].
Collation: 2*l* recto-verso, recto-verso 25.8 x 20.2 cm.
Contents: These are holograph notes on form and love.

F37 THE CONQUEROR'S SONG. A. ms. CU-S.
Date: 15 July 1949.
Collation: 1*l* recto 27.9 x 21.6 cm.
Contents: This is the text (black pen) of the poem.
Note: The date was added to the manuscript by RD at a later time. The poem appeared in the second edition of *Caesar's Gate.*

F38 [Two Poems]. A. ms. CU-S.
Date: [1949/50?].
Collation: 1*l* recto-verso 27.9 x 21.6 cm.
Contents: This is the text of the unpublished poems NOT I WLD NOT BE INTERESTED IN A DISINTERESTED SCIENCE OF POLITICS—THE YOUNG MAN WHO WROTE THIS MASQUE.

F39 [Three Pieces]. A. ms. CU-S.
Date: [1949/50?].
Collation: 14*l*; 2*l* recto-verso, recto-verso, 12*l* a recto 24 x 15 cm.
Contents: This is a manuscript of the text of the three unpublished pieces THE PLAY OF IDEAS—WATCHING THE CALVINIST—THE THUNDER HIDES THE GREEN.

F40 [Fragment] FOR A KING HAYDN TAPE SEQUENCE. A. ms. CU-S.

Date: [1949/50?].

Collation: 1*l* recto 15.4 x 21.5 cm.

Contents: This is the text of the fragment beginning "1st program."
The text is unpublished.

F41 I CANNOT SLEEP. T. ms. CU-B.

Date: [1949/50?].

Collation: 2*l* recto, recto 28 x 21.7 cm.

Contents: This is a typescript (black ribbon) of the unpublished
poem.

F42 [Two Poems]. T. ms. CU-B.

Date: [1950].

Collation: 2*l* recto, recto-verso 27.9 x 21.7 cm.

Contents: This is the typescript (black ribbon) of the text of the
unpublished poems A DREAM—PEBBLES.

Note: A holograph letter to Jack Spicer appears on the top verso of the
first leaf and bottom verso of the second leaf.

F43 [Untitled Poem]. A. ms. MoSW.

Date: [1950].

Collation: 3*l* all recto 21.6 x 20.2 cm.

Contents: This is an early holograph (black ink and pencil) version
of AN IMAGINARY WAR ELEGY.

F44 WE NEVER RECOVER. A. ms. CU-S.

Date: [1950].

Collation: 1*l* recto-verso 16 x 21.3 cm.

Contents: This is the text of the unpublished poem.

F45 "THE SINGLE HOWL OF WORDS THAT IS LIKE A HOLD" (fl).
A. ms. CU-S.

Date: [1950].

Collation: 1*l* recto 20.8 x 17 cm.

Contents: This is the text of the unpublished and untitled poem.

F46 AN ELEGY. T. ms. MoSW.

Date: [1950].

Collation: 2*l* recto, recto 27.8 x 21.5 cm.

Contents: This is a typescript (black ribbon) of the poem which was
later entitled AN IMAGINARY WAR ELEGY. This version contains
changes in RD's holograph. The following subtitle was deleted in
later printings: "Constructed upon two themes: A note by Robert
Payne upon two poems by Mao-Tze-tung and an evening glass of
Cutty Sark Blended Scots Whiskey."

F47 IMAGINARY WAR ELEGIES. T. ms. CU-B.

Date: [1950].

Collation: 2*l* recto, recto 27.8 x 21.6 cm.

Contents: This is a typescript (black ribbon) of the text of the poem, with the present title in the author's holograph, as it appeared with slight revisions in BR under the title AN IMAGINARY WAR ELEGY.

F48 IRREGULAR VILLANELLE. A. ms. OU.
Date: [1950].
Collation: 1*l* recto 21.6 x 16.1 cm.
Contents: This is a holograph version of the poem which later appeared as A VILLANELLE, with deletions, changes, and stanza length adjustments.

F49 [Three Poems]. T. ms. CU-B.
Date: [1950/51?].
Collation: 4*l* all recto 27.8 x 21.5 cm.
Contents: This is a typescript (black ribbon) of the texts of the poems FIVE PIECES—HERO SONG—ADAM'S SONG which differs slightly from the published versions.

F50 AFRICA REVISITED. A. ms. MoSW
Date: [1950/51].
Collation: 10*l* all recto; 6*l* 27.8 x 21.5 cm., 4*l* 27.5 x 21.5 cm.
Contents: This is an early holograph version of the poem which was later revised substantially.

F51 MINNEAPOLIS-OCTOBER 1950. T. ms. CU-B.
Date: [1950/51].
Collation: 1*l* recto 21.6 x 15.6 cm.
Contents: This is a typescript (black ribbon) of Spicer's poem and RD's "critical revision" of the poem. A note in RD's holograph appears at the top and bottom of the leaf.

F52 THE SONG OF THE BORDER-GUARD. A. ms. CU-B.
Date: [1951].
Collation: 1*l* recto-verso 21.5 x 17.6 cm.
Contents: This is a holograph (black ink) version of the poem as it was printed as a broadside at Black Mountain College and collected in RB, with slight revisions.

F53 [Eleven Poems]. T. ms. CU-B.
Date: [1951?].
Collation: 9*l* all recto 28 x 21.7 cm.
Contents: This is a typescript (black ribbon) of the texts of the following poems written in the period of RB: IMAGE OF HECTOR—IT WAS MY LION—THERE COULD BE A BOOK WITHOUT NATIONS IN ITS CHAPTERS—ORCHARDS: A TRAIN OF THOUGHT—THIS IS THE POEM THEY ARE PRAISING AS LOADED—FRIEDL—THEY TORE HIS BODY APART AT THE END OF THE SERVICES—SHORT INVENTION ON THE

THEME OF THE ADAM—METAMORPHOSIS—LORD MASTER
MOUSE—ELEGY.

F54 COLORED TIES, OR A GOODBYE BOOK FOR JIMMY
BROUGHTON. A. & T. ms. OKentU.
Date: [1951].
a. A. ms.
Collation: 3*l* all recto-verso 27.9 x 21.7 cm.
Contents: This is a holograph (black pen) version of the following
poems: 1. A PERIOD OF HISTORY—2. A JUNGLE OF MINOR
POETRY LINES FOR—3. A REAL RIGHT ACTIVIST HANDLE—
4. A LIST IS NOT REMEMBER—5. CRYING OUT LOUD—6. A
BUSINESS LETTER—6. A BUSINESS LETTER; PARAGRAPH
TWO—7. THE HISTORY IN A PERIOD LATER—8. EASY IS
DOING IT AGAIN—9. CODA—10. UNIVERSAL MILITARY
TRAINING FOR ALL. Verso of the third leaf contains twenty-nine
lines beginning "MOVES AS I WANT FOR PART OF" and twenty-
nine lines beginning "I WONDER IF I SHOULD GET MARRIED
TO LOVE."
b. T. ms.
Collation: 4*l* all recto 27.9 x 21.5 cm.
Contents: This is a typescript (black ribbon) of the same poems as in
item "a." The lines from the verso of the final leaf are not included.

F55 A LEAVE AS YOU MAY FOR JOHN RYAN. T. ms. OKentU.
Date: July 1951.
Collation: 1*l* recto-verso 21.6 x 17.6 cm.
Contents: This is a typescript (black ribbon) of the text of the follow-
ing: [untitled four lines]—POETRY PERMIT FOR VOLLEY [ten
lines]—ALL THROUGH [six lines]—POETRY MAY BE AS YOU
PLEASE [thirteen lines of prose]—A REPRIEVE AT DAWN [six
lines]—A SONG IS A GAME [nine lines]—[untitled eight lines].
There is an a. n. s. on the verso.

F56 NAMES OF PEOPLE. T. ms. OKentU.
Date: July 1951.
Collation: 1*l* recto-verso 27.9 x 21.6 cm.
Contents: This is a typescript (black ribbon) of the text of the poem
as published.
Note: The verso contains the following inscription in pencil in RD's
hand: "Names | OF | People | Robert Duncan | July 1951."

F57 FIRST INVENTION ON THE THEME OF THE ADAM. T. ms.
CU-B.
Date: [1951/52].
Collation: 1*l* recto 27.9 x 21.6 cm.
Contents: This is a typescript (black ribbon) of the first four sections
of the poem.

F58 The AN ESSAY AT WAR Papers. A. & T. ms. MoSW.
Date: [1951/52].
a. A. ms. (black ink).
Collation: 1*l* recto 21.8 x 17.4 cm.
Contents: Twenty-three lines plus an early version of the first twenty lines of the poem.
b. A. ms. (black ink).
Collation: 1*l* recto-verso 23.5 x 18.5 cm.
Contents: recto, thirty-four lines which become BR, p. 23, line twenty-one to bottom of p. 24, minus the final ten lines; verso, eight lines of an early version of the first twenty lines of the poem.
c. A. ms. (black ink).
Collation: 1*l* recto-verso 23.5 x 18.5 cm.
Contents: recto, thirty-four lines (from bottom, p. 23, to bottom p. 24, minus final seven lines), with five lines not published; verso, seventeen lines, with first six deleted, which become last eleven lines (bottom, p. 24) from "a window" to "the glow" (top, p. 25).
Note: With changes, this is an expansion of item "b."
d. A. ms. (blue ink).
Collation: 2*l* recto, recto 21.5 x 20.1 cm.
Contents: Fifty-two lines from bottom, p. 23, to top, p. 24.
Note: With changes, this is a version of item "c."
e. A. ms. (black ink).
Collation: 2*l* recto, recto 27.9 x 21.7 cm.
Contents: The text was slightly revised and published as from "What can I teach you" (middle, p. 27) to end of Part I (p. 30).
f. A. ms. (black ink).
Collation: 4*l* all recto 21.7 x 20.1 cm.
Contents: First leaf, fifteen lines which become the eight lines (on p. 33) from "Anew" to "in that"; second leaf, seven lines of the prose passage (p. 33) beginning "In a poem" (much revised) plus six lines of poetry (revised) which become the six lines following the prose; third leaf, same prose as second leaf plus seventeen lines of poetry which become (with revision) the seven lines following the prose (p. 33); fourth leaf, same prose as the second leaf plus ten lines of poetry (to bottom, p. 33), plus eight unpublished lines.
g. A. ms. (pencil)
Collation: 2*l* recto, recto 27.9 x 21.6 cm.
Contents: Forty-nine lines which become (with major revision) the first twenty-six lines of Part V (pp. 37-38).
h. T. ms. (black ribbon).
Collation: 1*l* recto 27.8 x 21.5cm.
Contents: Eleven lines of prose (p. 33), plus fifty-four lines unpublished.
i. T. ms. (carbon copy).
Date: [1967].

Collation: 12*l* all recto 27.8 x 21.5 cm.

Contents: This is the text of the poem as it was prepared for *Derivations;* there were slight changes in spelling; for example, "pushd" for "pusht" in line four.

j. T. ms. (black ribbon).

Collation: 15*l* all recto 27.9 x 21.6 cm.

Contents: First eighteen lines as published; two revised lines, then the text skips to prose (bottom, p. 25) "it is the first" and continues. Sixty-two lines (unpublished) appear after the line "creating the world" and before the prose "in a poem" (p. 33). Part VI does not appear.

k. T. ms. (black ribbon).

Collation: 15*l* all recto 27.9 x 21.6 cm.

Contents: The text begins with "so we calld" (p. 23) and runs to bottom of p. 24 with additional lines. Second leaf begins "and the genius of the moment." The lines (p. 25) beginning "Even the sub-human" to "we too are gatherd" do not appear. The prose section (p. 25) beginning "it is first" has been much revised. Three half lines have been deleted from the beginning of Part II (p. 30). Sixty lines have been deleted which appeared between "creating the world in its like-ness" and "in a poem" (p. 33), and eleven half lines that appeared between "what good will this do" and "in that" (p. 33) have been deleted. Three lines that appeared before "bombs, fragments of bodies" (p. 34) have been deleted, as have three lines that appeared after "in the silence and rubble thereafter" (p. 38). There is no separate Part VI.

l. "Part VI." T. ms. (black ribbon)

Collation: 1*l* recto 27.9 x 21.6 cm.

Contents: The text as published with some revisions.

m. A. ms. (black ink).

Collation: 1*l* recto 27.9 x 21.6 cm.

Contents: Twenty-four lines, beginning "There is only the cold hearth" (p. 42) which become the end of Part V.

n. A. ms. (black ink).

Collation: 1*l* recto 27.9 x 21.6 cm.

Contents: Twenty-three lines, beginning "But Victory, itself is the substitute Kermit said," which become the concluding lines of Part II (p. 34).

o. A. ms. (black ink).

Collation: 1*l* recto 21.6 x 18.9 cm.

Contents: Seventeen lines beginning "Even the subhuman" (p. 25).

p. A. ms. (black ink).

Collation: 2*l* recto-verso, recto 27.9 x 21.7 cm.

Contents: Fifty-four lines from "it is the first named" (p. 25) to "What can I teach you" (p. 27).

Note: These lines are written in a University of California examination booklet.

q. A. ms. (black ink).

Collation: 1*l* recto-verso 20.3 x 12.6 cm.

Contents: Thirty-two lines of deleted poetry.

Note: Page numbers refer to pages in BR.

F59 AN ESSAY AT WAR. T. ms. OKentU.
Date: [1952].
Collation: 14*l* all recto 27.9 x 21.6 cm.
Contents: This is a typescript (carbon) of the text of the poem as published, with slight changes. ⟋

F60 AN ABOUT FACE | FOR CLAIRE MAHL. T. ms. OKentU.
Date: [19]52.
Collation: 1*l* recto 27.9 x 21.6 cm.
Contents: This is a typescript (black ribbon) of the text of the poem as published, with a single stanza change. The poem is decorated in a design of various colored crayons.

F61 FAUST FOUTU: A COMIC MASK. T. ms. CU-B.
Date: April 1952.
Collation: 5*l*; 4*l* recto-verso 28 x 21.7 cm.; 1*l* recto 28 x 21.7 cm.
Contents: This is a typescript (carbon copy) of the first act of the play as it was later published by White Rabbit Press. A holograph note to Jack Spicer appears on the verso of the fifth leaf.

F62 AN ABOUT FACE | FOR CLAIRE MAHL. T. ms. CtU.
Date: [8 April] 1952.
Collation: 1*l* recto 27.9 x 21.5 cm.
Contents: The text of the poem as it appeared, with slight changes, in NP, pp. 21-22.
Note: The typescript (black ribbon) was enclosed in a letter to Charles Olson, dated 8 April 1952. E42.

F63 A DIVERTISEMENT [*sic*] OR TWO. T. ms. OKentU.
Date: [Fall 1952].
Collation: 1*l* recto 27.9 x 21.6 cm.
Contents: This is a typescript (black ribbon) of the following items under the title above: A SHORT STORY. IDLE LIVING AT CLOSE QUARTERS—AT THE BAKERY (a study of pronouns of reference).
Note: This typescript accompanied a letter to James Broughton, dated [Fall 1952]. E45.

F64 [Three Poems]. T. ms. OKentU.
Date: [Dec. 1952].
Collation: 1*l* recto-verso 27.8 x 21.5 cm.
Contents: This is a typescript (black ribbon) of the following poems: A BIRTHDAY DIRGE FOR LYNNE BROWN—FRIEDL— SALVAGES. AN EVENING PIECE.
Note: The last two appeared in BR with slight revisions. An a. n. s. appears on the recto.

F65   H. M. S. BEARSKIN. T. ms. OKentU.

Date: [1952/53?].

Collation: 3*l* all recto 27.9 x 21.7 cm.

Contents: 1. HE ENTERTAINS AT A DINNER PARTY—2. HE CON-
SULTS THE TIDES—3. TO RUN WITH THE HARE AND HUNT
WITH THE HOUND—4. "GREAT GRIEF, THEN, HERSELF"
(fl)—5. HE SINGS A SONNET—6. HE LISTS SUBJECTS FOR
GREAT POETRY—7. HE HAS A GOOD TIME— 8. "ALL THE
WAY OF FOREVER" (fl).

Note: This is a typescript (black ribbon) of the texts of the poems as
they appeared in *Caesar's Gate* with some revisions.

F66   A BOOK OF RESEMBLANCES. A. ms. MoSW.

Cover title: "Illustrator's Dummy with notes of explanation | and
expectation—to be taken in coordination | with the original manu-
script of Holograph Drawings | for | *A Book of Resemblances* | by
Robert Duncan."

Date: [1953].

Collation: This is a notebook with a brown cover, with 91*l* 27.9 x 21.6
cm. and 15*l* 27.5 x 21.6 cm. numbered leaves.

Contents: This is the original manuscript, including the illustrator's
drawings, of the book before it was engaged in the publication process.
The illustrator's note on p. 1 reads: "These drawings were begun in
1952 following the finishing of 'An Essay at War'—and the projected
form of the book I wanted to design was a play upon 'high style,' in
an homage to Beardsley, as he shows in *Morte d'Arthur*, and avoiding
his grotesque. This means that thruout *A Book of Resemblances*
platemaking and printing should aim at uniform dense black areas,
sharply defined, while yet maintaining those fine white lines and
pointed [cusps] embedded within these areas. Also critical is the simul-
taneous fine hair-line."

F67   LETTERS FOR DENISE LEVERTOV: AN A MUSE MENT. T. ms.
CU-B.

Date: [1954].

a. *Collation:* 3*l* all recto 27.8 x 21.7 cm.

Contents: This is a typescript (black ribbon) of the poem as published,
with some revisions and a title change, in *Letters*.

b. *Collation:* 3*l* all recto 28 x 21.6 cm.

Contents: This is an untitled typescript (black ribbon) of the text of
the poem, with notes added, as published in *Letters*.

F68   LETTERS TO OLSON: LIGHT SONG. T. ms. CtU.

Date: [1954].

Collation: 2*l* recto, recto 27.8 x 21.4 cm.

Contents: This is a typescript (black ribbon) of a poem which appeared
in *Letters*, with slight changes in spacing and capitalization, as
LIGHT SONG.

F69 LETTERS FOR CHARLES OLSON: ON TAKING HOLD. T. ms.
On deposit at MoSW.
Date: Feb. 1954.
Collation: 2*l* recto, recto 27.9 x 21.6 cm.
Contents: This is a typescript (black ribbon) of the text of the poem
as published as UPON TAKING HOLD in *Letters*.

F70 LIGHT SONG. T. ms. CU-B.
Date: March 1954.
Collation: 1*l* recto 28 x 21.5 cm.
Contents: This is a typescript (black ribbon) of the text of the poem
as it appeared in *Letters* with slight changes.

F71 TRUE TO LIFE. T. ms. CtU.
Date: 20, 24, and 27 June 1954.
Collation: 1*l* recto 27.8 x 21.5 cm.
Contents: This is a typescript (black ribbon) of the poem as it appeared
in *Letters* with slight changes.
Note: The poem accompanied a letter to Charles Olson, dated 29
June 1954. E67.

F72 [Unpublished Prose]. T. ms. OKentU.
Date: [Fall 1954].
Collation: 9*l* all recto 27.9 x 21.6 cm.
Contents: This is a typescript (black ribbon) of several pieces which
have the appearance of transcribed journal entries: TWO PIECES
FOR HELEN ADAM—OTHER NOTES FROM A NOTEBOOK,
10/17/54—10/18/54—11/1/54—10/29/54. A THIRD PIECE FOR
HELEN ADAM.
Note: The leaves have been bound in a yellow folder, 28.7 x 23 cm.

F73 LETTER FOR DENISE LEVERTOV: AN A MUSE MENT. T. ms.
CtU.
Date: [1954/55].
Collation: 1*l* recto-verso 27.9 x 21.7 cm.
Contents: This typescript (carbon copy) gives the text of the poem as
it appears in *Letters*, but with slight changes in spacing and line
arrangements.

F74 LETTER FOR OLSON: ON TAKING HOLD. T. ms. CtU.
Date: [1954/55].
Collation: 1*l* recto 21.5 x 27.9 cm.
Contents: This is a typescript (carbon copy) of the poem printed in
Letters, pp. [17-19], as UPON TAKING HOLD; however, fourteen
additional lines have been added to the end of the poem in *Letters*.
Note: The first part of the title (LETTER FOR OLSON) is a carbon
copy, while the second part (ON TAKING HOLD) is typed in black
ribbon.

F75 a. LETTERS TO PHILIP LAMANTIA: DISTANT COUNSELS
OF ARTAUD. T. ms. CU-B.
Date: [1954/55].
Collation: 1*l* recto 28 x 21.6 cm.
Contents: This is a typescript (black ribbon) of the text of the poem
as it appeared in *Letters,* with slight changes.
b. DISTANT COUNSELS OF ARTAUD—1—FOR PHILIP LAMAN-
TIA. CU-B.
Date: [1945/55].
Collation: 1*l* recto 28.1 x 21.6 cm.
Contents: This is a typescript (black ribbon) of the text of the poem,
with an altered title.

F76 METAMORPHOSES. T. ms. On deposit at MoSW.
Date: [1955].
Collation: 2*l* recto, recto 27.9 x 21.6 cm.
Contents: This is a typescript (black ribbon) of the text of the poem
as published in *Letters.* The final two lines, here crossed out, are
restored in the published version.

F77 THE STRUCTURE OF RIME. T. ms. CU-B.
Date: [1955].
Collation: 2*l* recto, recto 27.6 x 21.2 cm.
Contents: This is a typescript (blue ribbon) of early drafts of THE
STRUCTURE OF RIME I AND II, but here presented as one poem.

F78 POEMS FROM THE ZOHAR. T. ms. CU-B.
Date: [1955?].
Collation: 1*l* recto 28 x 21.6 cm.
Contents: This is a typescript (black ribbon) of two poems, numbered
1 and 2, and unpublished.

F79 LETTERS TO PHILIP LAMANTIA: DISTANT COUNSELS OF
ARTAUD. T. ms. MoSW.
Date: [1955].
Collation: 1*l* recto 27.5 x 21.6 cm.
Contents: This is a typescript (black ribbon) of the text of the poem.

F80 3 POEMS FROM A BIRTHDAY BOOK (FOR JAMES
BROUGHTON). T. ms. MoSW.
Date: [1955].
Collation: 1*l* recto 27.9 x 21.6 cm.
Contents: This is a typescript (black ribbon) of the text of the poems.

F81 [Untitled]. T. ms. OKentU.
Date: [1955].
Collation: 19*l* all recto; 1*l* 25.9 x 21.5 cm.; 18*l* 27.8 x 21.4 cm.
Contents: This is a typescript (black ribbon, except the first leaf
which is a carbon) of the texts of the following poems: THE HORNS

OF ARTEMIS—AN IMAGINARY WAR ELEGY—AFRICA REVIS-
ITED—ADAM'S SONG—THE SONG OF THE BORDER-
GUARD—FIVE PIECES—HERO SONG—AN IMAGINARY
WOMAN—UNKINGD BY AFFECTION—OF THE ART—
ELUARD'S DEATH.

Note: The first leaf contains the following note in RD's hand: "The
first 6 pages are now contained in and to be in *Caesar's Gate.* This is
installment one of manuscript."

F82   AN OWL IS AN ONLY BIRD OF POETRY. T. ms. s. OKentU.
Date: 1955.
Collation: 3*l* all recto 31.6 x 21.5 cm.
Contents: This is a typescript (black ribbon) of the text of the poem,
signed "RD" and dated.

F83   [Untitled]. T. ms. OKentU.
Date: [1955].
Collation: 14*l* all recto 31.8 x 21.4 cm.
Contents: This is a typescript (carbon copy) of the texts of the follow-
ing poems published in *Writing Writing:* TURNING INTO— COM-
ING OUT OF—MAKING UP—A SCENE—WRITING
WRITING—THE BEGINNING OF WRITING—IMAGINING IN
WRITING—WRITING AS WRITING—POSSIBLE POETRIES:
A PRELUDE—POSSIBLE POETRIES: A POSTSCRIPT—AN
IMAGINARY LETTER—IMAGINARY LETTER—IMAGINARY
LETTER—MOTTO DIVISION—WRITING AT HOME IN HIS-
TORY—I AM NOT AFRAID—AN INTERLUDE. OF RARE
BEAUTY—THE CODE OF JUSTINIAN. A DISCOURSE ON JUS-
TICE—THE DISCOURSE ON SIN—A POEM IN STRETCH-
ING—DESCRIPTIONS OF IMAGINARY POETRIES— SMOKING
THE CIGARETTE—RHYME MOUNTAIN PARTICULAR—AN
ADVERTISEMENT. FOR A FAIR PLAY— PROGRESSING—THIS
IS THE POEM THEY ARE PRAISING AS LOADED—
ORCHARDS—A TRAIN OF THOUGHT—THE FEELING OF
LANGUAGE IN POETRY—SENTENCES: CARRYING WEIGHTS
AND MEASURES—6/6/53—6/22/53— REWRITING BYRON—A
MORASS—A CANVAS COMING INTO ITSELF—HOW DO YOU
KNOW YOU ARE THERE— INCREASING—ROAD PIECE—
ROTUND RELIGION—THREE— SEVERAL POEMS. IN
PROSE—RINGS—SYLLABLES—STUFF ARK MOWER BOT-
TLE—ANOTHER I DO.

F84   FROM A NOTEBOOK 11/9/54. T. ms. CU-B.
Date: [1955].
Collation: 1*l* recto 27.5 x 21.2 cm.
Contents: This is a typescript (blue ribbon) of the prose piece.

F85 [Two Poems]. T. ms. CU-B.
Date: [16 April 1955].
Collation: 2*l* recto-verso, recto 27.6 x 21.4 cm.
Contents: This is a typescript (black ribbon) of the text of the two poems: A BALLAD FOR HELEN ADAM—A SONG AFTER THE MANNER OF BLAKE.
Note: This typescript accompanied a letter to Jack Spicer, dated 16 April 1955. E97.

F86 [Part III of Prose Essay]. T. ms. CtU.
Date: [17 May 1955].
Collation: 2*l*; 1*l* recto 27.8 x 21.5 cm., 1*l* recto, 12.9 x 21.5 cm.
Contents: This section (carbon copy) of an essay later became, with revisions, part of RD's essay NOTES ON POETICS REGARDING OLSON'S *MAXIMUS*, as published in *Black Mountain Review,* 6 (Spring 1956), 201-211. C69.
Note: This prose piece accompanied a letter to Charles Olson, dated 17 May 1955. E101.

F87 NOTES ON THE POETICS OF CHARLES OLSON IN *MAXIMUS*. T. ms. CtU.
Date: 19 June [1955].
Collation: 4*l* all recto 27.8 x 21.5 cm.
Contents: This is an early version of the essay NOTES ON POETICS REGARDING OLSON'S *MAXIMUS* published in *Black Mountain Review.* C69.
Note: This typescript (black ribbon) accompanied a letter to Charles Olson, dated 19 June 1955. E105.

F88 THE GREEN LADY. T. ms. NBuU.
Date: [July 1955].
Collation: 1*l* recto-verso 27.7 x 21.4 cm.
Contents: This is a typescript (black carbon) of the poem, but this version differs (there are deletions, additions, and revisions) from the publication in *Botteghe Oscure.* C74.
Note: The typescript accompanied a letter to Helen Adam, dated 17 July 1955. E112.

F89 A PUNCH & JUDY GARLAND. A. ms. On deposit at MoSW.
Date: [Aug. 1955].
Collation: 1*l* 31.5 x 21.5 cm., folded to form eight leaves.
Contents: This is a holograph (black ink) version of fifty lines of the poem beginning, "Never Mind in| trying this pleasure."

F90 [WRITING WRITING]. T. ms. On deposit at MoSW.
Date: [Sept. 1955].
Collation: 14*l* all recto-verso 30 x 21.7 cm.
Contents: This is a typescript (black ribbon) of the text of the volume as published, except that A POEM IN STRETCHING and "NO, I CAN'T REACH YOU" (fl) appear after THE DISCOURSE ON SIN.

F91   FROM A NOTEBOOK. T. ms. On deposit at MoSW.
Date: [20 Oct. 1955].
Collation: 16*l* all recto 32 x 20.5 cm.
Contents: This is a typescript (black ribbon) of RD's notes on his reading, mainly of Blake, Joyce, and the Zohar, during the spring of 1955.
Note: The typescript accompanied a letter to Robert Creeley, dated 20 Oct. 1955. E143.

F92   SONG FOR HELEN ADAM IN THE MANNER OF BLAKE. T. ms. On deposit at MoSW.
Date: [21 Oct. 1955].
Collation: 1*l* recto 27.6 x 21.3 cm.
Contents: This is a typescript (black ribbon) of twenty lines of the poem.

F93   (POEMS). A. ms. OKentU.
Date: [Dec. 1955].
Collation: 1*l* recto 21.9 x 17.5 cm.
Contents: This is a holograph (black ink) version of the text of the unpublished poem with a drawing.

F94   [Three Poems]. T. ms. CU-B.
Date: [1955/56].
Collation: 1*l* recto 27.9 x 21.6 cm.
Contents: This is a typescript (black ribbon) of the text of the poems A SHELL—ON LEAVING ULLSWATER—POEM.

F95   THE STRUCTURE OF RIME: V. A. ms. OU.
Date: [1956].
Collation: 1*l* recto 27.7 x 21.5 cm.
Contents: This is an early holograph version of the poem which appeared with major changes and additions in OF.

F96   AN INCUBUS. T. ms. CU-B.
Date: [1956?].
Collation: 1*l* recto 21.6 x 20.1 cm.
Contents: This is a typescript (black ribbon) of the text of the poem as it appeared in *Caesar's Gate.*

F97   *Letters.* T. ms. CU-B.
Date: [1956].
a. *Collation:* 31*l* all recto; 1*l* 27.9 x 21.4 cm., 16*l* 31.6 x 21.4 cm., 11*l* 27.9 x 21.4 cm., 3*l* 26.7 x 21.1 cm.
Contents: 1, LETTERS FOR DENISE LEVERTOV—2, FOR PHILIP LAMANTIA—3, FOR CHARLES OLSON—4, FIRST INVENTION ON THE THEME OF THE ADAM—5, SHORT INVENTION ON THE THEME OF THE ADAM—6, FOR HELEN ADAM—7, META-MORPHOSIS—8, FOR HELEN ADAM—9, FOR CHARLES

OLSON—10, IT'S SPRING. LOVE'S SPRING—11, FOR HELEN
ADAM—12, FRAGMENT—13, FOR CHARLES OLSON—14, FOR
ROBERT CREELEY—15, WORDS OPEN OUT UPON GRIEF—
16, FROM A NOTEBOOK—17, FROM A NOTEBOOK—18, THE
HUMAN COMMUNION. TRACES— 19, FROM A NOTEBOOK—
20, FOR MICHAEL MCCLURE— 21, BROUGHT TO LOVE—22,
TO VOW—23, FROM A NOTEBOOK—24, FROM A NOTEBOOK—
25, AUGUST SUN— 26, FROM A NOTEBOOK—27, A VALE FOR
JAMES BROUGHTON— 28, NEW TIDINGS—29, CHANGING
TRAINS—30, THE LANGUAGE OF LOVE-THE SIREN SONG.
Note: This is a typescript (blue ribbon) of the poems as they appeared
in *Letters*, with numerous title changes and slight revisions throughout.

b. *Collation:* 32*l* all recto 26.9 x 21 cm.

Contents: The same as "a."

Note: This is a typescript (black ribbon) of the poems as they appeared
in *Letters*, with title changes and revisions throughout. The changes
and revisions in this typescript differ from those in "a."

F98 [THE DANCE]. T. ms. CU-B.

Date: [1956].

a. *Collation:* 1*l* recto 25.2 x 20.4 cm.

Contents: This is a typescript (black ribbon) of a draft of the poem.
"This is the first version" appears across the top in RD's holograph.
There are holograph notes in the margin.

b. *Collation:* 1*l* recto 28 x 21.6 cm.

Contents: This is a typescript (black ribbon) of the second version of
the poem, revised for publication. There are notes in the margins.
The title "Into the Waltz, Dancer" has been added.

F99 MEDEA: PART ONE: THE MAIDENHEAD AS PLAYED AT
BLACK MOUNTAIN COLLEGE AUGUST 1956. T. ms. CU-B.

Date: 1956.

Collation: 27*l* all recto 27.9 x 21.7 cm.

Contents: This is a typescript (black ribbon) of the play, but revisions
were made for publication.

F100 [Untitled]. A. ms. OKentU.

Date: [Jan./March 1956].

Collation: 1*l* recto 27.9 x 21.5 cm.

Contents: This is a list of contents (black ink) for a proposed
magazine.

F101 A BALLAD FOR HELEN ADAM. T. ms. NBuU.

Date: [24 Feb. 1956].

Collation: 3*l* all recto 27.2 x 21.2 cm.

Contents: This is a typescript (blue ribbon) of the text of the poem in
ninety-eight lines. An a. n. s. from RD appears on the top recto of the

first leaf and bottom recto of the third leaf. Three small changes in the author's hand appear in the text.

Note: This typescript accompanied a letter to Helen Adam, dated 24 Feb. 1956. E167.

F102 MEMO: ROBERT E. SYMMES TO ROBERT CREELEY. T. ms. MoSW.

Date: 23 March 1956.

Collation: 1*l* recto 27.9 x 21.6 cm.

Contents: This is a typescript (black ribbon) of a note from RD to Creeley originating from Black Mountain College.

F103 THE DANCE. T. ms. OKentU.

Date: [11 April 1956].

Collation: 2*l* recto, recto 25.1 x 20.5 cm.

Contents: This is a typescript (black ribbon) of an early, untitled version of THE DANCE which was later published in *Measure* with revisions. C79.

Note: This typescript accompanied a letter to James Broughton, dated 11 April 1956. E185.

F104 THE DANCE. T. ms. CtU.

Date: Easter 1956.

Collation: 3*l* all recto 25.5 x 20.2 cm.

Contents: This is a typescript (black ribbon) of an early, untitled version of the poem THE DANCE, which omits the final lines of the poem as it first appeared in *Measure*. C79.

Note: The poem is signed and inscribed to Charles Olson on the third leaf. "This is the egg I laid for thee. | Easter 1956."

F105 THE ORIGINS OF OLD SON. T. ms. CtU.

Date: Summer 1956.

Collation: 12*l* all recto 27.8 x 21.5 cm.

Contents: This is a typescript of the text of the play.

Note: This play was written by RD at Black Mountain College. The play is initialed RD on leaf one and inscribed to Charles Olson: "Inscribed to Charles, who—as here—provides the | fulcrum for what ever practices out of a geometry | this imaginary one might move a real world by."

F106 [Seven Poems]. T. ms. CU-B.

Date: [Winter 1956/57].

Collation: 5*l* all recto 27.7 x 21.5 cm.

Contents: This is a typescript (black ribbon) of the first six poems as they appeared first in *Evergreen Review*. The final poem is unpublished. THE STRUCTURE OF RIME I—THE STRUCTURE OF RIME II—THE STRUCTURE OF RIME III—THE STRUCTURE OF RIME IV—THE STRUCTURE OF RIME V—THE STRUCTURE OF RIME VI—"O HAPPY HAPPY BARD" (fl).

F107 A RISK OF SYMPATHIES. T. ms. OKentU.
  Date: [1957].
  Collation: 5*l* all recto 27.9 x 21.7 cm.
  Contents: This is a typescript (carbon) of the text of RD's review of
  James Broughton's *True & False Unicorn.* D3.

F108 *A Book of Resemblances.* T.ms. CU-B.
  Date: [1957].
  Collation: 85*l* all recto 28 x 21.7 cm.
  Contents: This is a typescript (carbon copy) of the text of the following
  poems. There are many changes and variants from the texts as pub-
  lished in the book: THE HORNS OF ARTEMIS— AFRICA REVIS-
  ITED—ADAM'S SONG—WORKING TOO LONG AT IT—AN
  IMAGINARY WAR ELEGY—THE SONG OF THE BORDER-
  GUARD—AN ESSAY AT WAR—OF THE ART—FIVE PIECES—
  HERO SONG—AN IMAGINARY WOMAN—ELUARD'S
  DEATH—THREE PROSE POEMS—CATS (1)—CATS (2)—
  HOME— AN ARRANGEMENT—DANCE: EARLY SPRING
  WEATHER MAGIC—AUBADE—FORCED LINES—THE LAND-
  SCAPE REVISED TO PORTRAY A REALITY—AN INTERLUDE.
  OF RARE BEAUTY—A POEM IN STRETCHING—INCREAS-
  ING— SMOKING THE CIGARETTE—A TRAIN OF
  THOUGHT— THIS IS THE POEM THEY ARE PRAISING AS
  LOADED— ORCHARDS—SENTENCES: CARRYING WEIGHTS
  AND MEASURES—A BOOK OF RESEMBLANCES—HOW DO
  YOU KNOW YOU ARE THRU?—ROTUND RELIGION—
  THREE— RHYMING MOUNTAIN PARTICULAR—SEVERAL
  POEMS. IN PROSE—POETRY DISARRANGED—A BIRTHDAY
  DIRGE FOR LYNNE BROWN—A DREAM OF THE END OF THE
  WORLD— LORD MASTER MOUSE—SURREALIST SHELLS—
  THESE MIRACLES ARE MIRRORS IN THE OPEN SKY FOR
  PHILIP LAMANTIA—CONVERSION—SALVAGES: AN EVE-
  NING PIECE—LOVE POEM—SALVAGES: LASSITUDE—
  FRIEDL— TWO POEMS FOR THE JEWS—THE SCATTER-
  ING—IMAGE OF HECTOR—THE LOVER—THE FEAR THAT
  PRECEDES CHANGES OF HEAVEN.

F109 [A SONG OF THE OLD ORDER]. T. ms. CU-B.
  Date: [1957].
  Collation: 1*l* recto-verso 27.9 x 21.7 cm.
  Contents: This is a typescript (black ribbon) of the text of the poem
  as it appeared in OF with slight revisions.

F110 THE MAIDEN. T. ms. CU-B.
  Date: [1957].
  Collation: 1*l* recto 27.9 x 21.6 cm.
  Contents: This is a typescript (black ribbon) of the final four stanzas

of the poem, as it appeared in OF with some revisions. The first leaf of the manuscript is missing.

F111 SONG OF THE HARP AMONG THE STARS. A. ms. NBuU.
Date: [1957].
Collation: 1*l* recto 23.3 x 21.6 cm.
Contents: This is a holograph version of the twenty-three line, unpublished poem, which appears with a drawing of a woman's head. The designation "Song of Romance/for the Maidens/Bower/—3—for Helen" appears at the lower right.

F112 A POEM BEGINNING WITH A LINE BY PINDAR. T. ms. ICU.
Date: [1957].
Collation: 3*l* recto-verso, recto-verso, recto 32.7 x 21.6 cm.
Contents: This is a typescript (carbon) of the poem as it later appeared in *Foot.* C89.
Note: A short holograph note from the poet to Henry Rago appears at the top recto of the first leaf. The poem was rejected by *Poetry.*

F113 CORBETT. T. ms. CU-B.
Date: [1957]
Collation: 1*l* recto 27.9 x 21.6 cm.
Contents: This is a typescript (black ribbon) of the poem as it appeared in NP.

F114 SONG OF THE LIGHT-CHILD. A. ms. OKentU.
Date: [1957].
Collation: 1*l* recto 22.8 x 21.6 cm.
Contents: This is a holograph (black ink) version of the text of the poem. The following inscription appears at the bottom: "Songs of Romance/for the Maidens/Bower —2— for James." The leaf also contains a line drawing.

F115 [Eight Pieces]. T. ms. CU-B.
Date: [1957].
Collation: 5*l* all recto 27.8 x 21.4 cm.
Contents: THE BEGINNING OF WRITING—IMAGINING IN WRITING—WRITING AS WRITING—POSSIBLE POETRIES: A PRELUDE—POSSIBLE POETRIES: A POSTSCRIPT—POSSIBLE POETRIES: A POSTSCRIPT—AN IMAGINARY LETTER— IMAGINARY LETTER. This is a typescript (black ribbon) of the pieces as they are printed in *Writing Writing.*

F116 [Six Pieces]. T. ms. CU-B.
Date: [1957].
Collation: 1*l* recto-verso 27.9 x 21.7 cm.
Contents: This is a typescript (black ribbon) of the texts of the following pieces: A LEAVE AS YOU MAY: FOR JOHN RYAN— POETRY PERMIT FOR VOLLEY—ALL THROUGH—POETRY MAY BE

AS YOU PLEASE—A REPRIEVE AT DAWN—A SONG IS A
GAME.

F117 [Nine Poems]. T. ms. CU-B.
Date: [1957].
Collation: 12*l* all recto 28 x 21.6 cm.
Contents: This is a typescript (black ribbon) of the following poems:
THE REVENANT—DEAR JOSEPH, THESE ARE WEARY DAYS
[1942]—VARIATIONS IN PRAISE OF JESUS CHRIST OUR
LORD—SNOW ON BUG HILL—MOTHER TO WHOM I HAVE
COME HOME—CHRISTMAS LETTER 1944—AND NOW I HAVE
RETURND—INVOCATION—ELEGY.

F118 [Nine Poems]. T. ms. CU-B.
Date: [1957].
Collation: 13*l* all recto 27.8 x 21.5 cm.
Contents: This is a typescript (black ribbon) of the following poems:
HERO SONG—AN IMAGINARY WAR ELEGY—THE JERUSA-
LEM BECAME THE GOAL—NOTHING IS MORE PRECIOUS
THAN THE RED SAND OF THE SEA—AN IMAGINARY
WOMAN—THE WAR WITHIN WITHOUT THE WAR (FOR
ROBIN BLASER)—"THE MOON SHINING IN THE WINDOW"
(fl)—THE SECOND NIGHT IN THE WEEK—FOUR POEMS AS
A NIGHT SONG.

F119 THE USE OF THE UNCONSCIOUS IN UNITY. T. ms. CU-B.
Date: [1957].
Collation: 10*l* all recto 33.2 x 21.8 cm.
Contents: This is a thermofax copy of the text of the essay.

F120 (THE PROPOSITIONS). T. ms. CU-B.
Date: [1957].
Collation: 5*l* all recto 27.9 x 21.6 cm.
Contents: This is a typescript (carbon) of the first three sections of the
poem.

F121 (THE PROPOSITIONS). T. ms. OU.
Date: [1957].
Collation: 5*l* recto 27.9 x 21.6 cm.
Contents: This is a typescript (black ribbon) of the poem as it
appeared, with slight editorial changes, in *Measure* (C75), and with
larger changes in OF.

F122 [Application for Guggenheim Fellowship]. T. ms. CtU.
Date: 1957.
Collation: 1*l* recto 27.8 x 21.5 cm.
Contents: In this application (black ribbon) entitled "Statement of
Plans," RD proposes to finish the poems for OF and to finish the play
"The Will." He then wants to "undertake the study of the poetics of

Stein, Pound, Eliot, H.D., Marianne Moore, William Carlos Williams,
and Wallace Stevens."

F123 FROM THESE STRANDS BECOMING. T. ms. CtU.
Date: 1957.
Collation: 4*l* all recto 28 x 21.5 cm.
Contents: This essay (black ribbon typescript) consists of four parts:
INTRODUCTION—CALIFORNIA ORIGINS—TEACHERS—
THE DRAWING.
Note: The original essay was rejected by *Evergreen Review*, but some
of the material was taken over into the first two chapters of "The H.D.
Book": "Beginnings: Chapter 1 of the H.D. Book," *Coyote's Journal*,
5/6 (1966), and "The H.D. Book, Part I: Chapter 2," *Coyote's Journal*,
8 (1967). The essay is inscribed to Olson and signed by Duncan. There
are slight emendations in the author's hand.

F124 [THE PROPOSITIONS, 5]. T. ms. On deposit at MoSW.
Date: [11 March 1957].
Collation: 1*l* recto 28.4 x 20.6 cm.
Contents: This is a typescript (black ribbon) of the text of part five of
the poem as it appeared with revisions in OF.
Note: This typescript accompanied a letter to Robert Creeley, dated 11
March 1957. E252.

F125 [Three Poems]. T. ms. CU-B.
Date: [18 March 1957].
Collation: 2*l* recto, recto 27.8 x 21.5 cm.
Contents: These are ditto sheets which contain the texts of the follow-
ing poems: FOUR PICTURES OF THE REAL UNIVERSE— OF
BLASPHEMY—THRESHING SONG.
Note: The first two were printed in OF. These leaves accompanied a
letter to Robin Blaser, dated 18 March 1957. E255.

F126 [Five Poems]. T. ms. ICU.
Date: [Spring 1957].
Collation: 5*l* all recto 27.5 x 21.6 cm.
Contents: This is the typscript (black ribbon) of the following poems
as they appeared in *Poetry:* A MORNING LETTER—THE TEMPLE
OF THE ANIMALS—THERE'S TOO MUCH SEA ON THE BIG
SUR—POEM—A RIDE TO THE SEA. C77.
Note: The poem entitled POEM was given its title by the editor. The
proof sheets, 1*l* recto 60 x 20.3 cm., 1*l* recto 41.4 x 20.3 cm., contain
slight changes in RD's holograph. RD was awarded the Union League
for Poetry prize for this contribution.

F127 [Two Poems, One Prose Piece]. T. ms. CtU.
Date: [15 April 1957].
Collation: 4*l*; 3*l* recto, 1*l* recto-verso 27.8 x 21.5 cm.

Contents: This is a typescript (black ribbon) of the texts of the two poems and the prose piece OF BLASPHEMY as they appear, with revisions, in OF. FOUR PICTURES OF THE REAL UNIVERSE—EVOCATION—OF BLASPHEMY.

Note: Verso of the fourth leaf contains a letter to Charles [Olson], a. l. s., San Francisco, [15 April 1957].

F128 *Selected Poems: Derivations.* T. ms. CU-B.

Date: [May 1957].

Collation: 100*l* all recto 27.9 x 21.5 cm.

Contents: 3 PROSE POEMS FROM MY NOTEBOOK—CAT, HOUSEHOLD [which became CATS (1), CATS (2)], UNKINGD BY AFFECTION]—AN AFRICAN ELEGY—THE YEARS AS CATCHES—KING HAYDN OF MIAMI BEACH—EARLY HISTORY: THE FIRST DAY, THE CITIES OF THE PLAIN— THE GOLDEN AGE—MEDIEVAL SCENES [sequence-title for following ten poems] THE DREAMERS—THE HELMET OF GOLIATH—THE BANNERS—THE KINGDOM OF JERUSALEM—THE FESTIVALS—THE MIRROR—THE REAPER— THE ADORATION OF THE VIRGIN—HUON OF BORDEAUX— THE ALBIGENSES—JERUSALEM—THE HORNS OF ARTEMIS—THE IMAGINARY WAR ELEGY—WORKING TOO LONG AT IT [from *Writing Writing*]—THE SONG OF THE BORDER-GUARD—FIVE PIECES—HERO SONG—AN IMAGINARY WOMAN—ELUARD'S DEATH—VARIATIONS UPON PHRASES FROM MILTON'S *THE REASON OF CHURCH GOVERNMENT*—THERE'S TOO MUCH SEA ON THE BIG SUR—THE ENIGMA OF LOVE—EARLY HISTORY—AN IMAGINARY WAR ELEGY—JERUSALEM—WORKING TOO LONG AT IT—A DREAM OF THE END OF THE WORLD—THE MASTER OF MANDRAKE PARK—AT THE BAKERY—THE CANNIBALISTIC COOKIE—PEOPLE (A STUDY IN PRONOUNS IN REFERENCE)—SURREALIST SHELLS—CONVERSION— TWO POEMS FOR THE JEWS FROM THEIR BOOK OF SPLENDOR—SALVAGES—AN EVENING PIECE—LORD MASTER MOUSE—FRIEDL—THE SCATTERING—IMAGE OF HECTOR—ROMANTICS: SALVAGES III—CLOUDS AND SCINTILLATIONS—THE FEAR THAT PRECEDES CHANGES OF HEAVEN—SALVAGES: LASSITUDES—LOVE POEM—A BOOK OF RESEMBLANCES—AN AFRICAN ELEGY—KING HAYDN OF MIAMI BEACH—VARIATIONS UPON PHRASES FROM MILTON'S *THE REASON OF CHURCH GOVERNMENT*—DOMESTIC SCENES [sequence title for following ten poems] BREAKFAST—REAL ESTATE—BUS FARE—MAIL BOXES—MATCHES—BATH—RADIO—ELECTRIC IRON—LUNCH WITH BUNS—PIANO—THE NEW HESPERIDES: INVOCATION, RHAPSODY, ELEGY—RHAPSODY—THERE'S TOO MUCH SEA ON THE BIG SUR—THE HOMECOMING— THE

TEMPLE OF THE ANIMALS—THE ENIGMA OF LOVE— A
RIDE TO THE SEA—SOLO—DUO—TRIO—A MORNING LET-
TER—BETWEEN THE ACTS—OF THE CHARACTER— THE
HORNS OF ARTEMIS—AFRICA REVISITED—WORKING TOO
LONG AT IT—ADAM'S SONG.

F129 [Three Poems]. T. ms. CU-B.
Date: [13 May 1957].
Collation: 2l recto, recto 27.9 x 21.6 cm.
Contents: This is a typescript (black ribbon) of the following poems
as they appeared in OF: (THE PROPOSITIONS) #4 #5—SONG—
THREE PAGES FROM A BIRTHDAY BOOK.
Note: SONG was retitled THIS PLACE RUMORD TO HAVE BEEN
SODOM. This typescript accompanied a letter to Robin Blaser, dated
13 May 1957. E265.

F130 EVOCATION. T. ms. CU-B.
Date: [28 May 1957].
Collation: 1l recto 27.7 x 21.7 cm.
Contents: This is a typescript (black ribbon) of the poem as it appeared
in OF.
Note: This typescript accompanied a letter to Robin Blaser, dated 28
May 1957. E267.

F131 THE YEARS AS CATCHES. T. ms. CU-B.
Date: [10 June 1957].
Collation: 3l all recto 27.7 x 21.7 cm.
Contents: This is a typescript (black carbon) of the poem as it appeared
in *Circle.* C33.
Note: This typescript accompanied a letter to Robin Blaser, dated 10
June 1957. E272.

F132 PLAN "A" FOR *DERIVATIONS*, BEING A SELECTION OF
POEMS 1942-1952. T. ms. CU-B.
Date: [10 June 1957].
Collation: 1l recto 27.8 x 21.5 cm.
Contents: This typescript (black ribbon) gives the titles of the poems
to be included in the proposed volume.
Note: This typescript accompanied a letter to Robin Blaser, dated 10
June 1957. E272.

F133 CROSSES OF HARMONY AND DISHARMONY. T. ms. CU-B.
Date: [15 June 1957].
Collation: 2l recto, recto 27.8 x 21.6 cm.
Contents: This is a typescript (black ribbon) of the text of the poem
with an accompanying carbon copy.
Note: This typescript accompanied a letter to Robin Blaser, dated 15
June 1957. E274.

F134 A POEM OF DESPONDENCIES. T. ms. On deposit at MoSW.
Date: July 1957.
Collation: 1*l* recto 28 x 21.6 cm.
Contents: This is a typescript (black ribbon) of the text of the poem.
Note: This typescript accompanied a letter to Robert Creeley, dated 30 July 1957. E288.

F135 A RISK OF SYMPATHIES. T. ms. ICU.
Date: [6 July 1957].
Collation: 5*l* all recto 28 x 21.6 cm.
Contents: This is a typescript (black ribbon) of the review of James Broughton's *True & False Unicorn* as it appeared in *Poetry.* C81.
Note: This typescript accompanied a letter to Henry Rago, dated 6 July 1957. The proof sheets, filed with the typescript, 1*l* recto 20.5 x 20.2 cm., 1*l* recto 50 x 20.2 cm., 1*l* recto 13.7 x 20.2 cm., contain slight changes in RD's holograph. E282.

F136 IN THE SIGHT OF A LYRE, A LITTLE SPEAR, A CHAIR. T. ms. ICU.
Date: 18 Aug. 1957.
Collation: 5*l* all recto 27.9 x 21.7 cm.
Contents: This is a typescript (black ribbon) of RD's review of H.D.'s *Selected Poems* as it appeared in *Poetry.* C80.
Note: This typescript accompanied a letter to Henry Rago, dated 17 Aug. 1957. The proof sheets, filed with the typescript, 1*l* recto 44.3 x 20.2 cm., 1*l* recto 34.3 x 20.2 cm., contain slight changes in RD's hand and are initialed and dated by RD "Nov. 27 [19]57." E291.

F137 [Two Pieces]. T. ms. CU-B.
Date: [22 Aug. 1957].
Collation: 2*l*; 1*l* recto 28 x 21.7 cm., 1*l* recto-verso 27.9 x 21.7 cm.
Contents: These are typescripts (black ribbon) of the first poem, as it appears in OF, and the prose piece: POETRY, A NATURAL THING—THREE POEMS IN MEASURE ONE: AN OPEN LETTER.
Note: These typescripts accompanied a letter to Robin Blaser, dated 22 Aug. 1957. E292.

F138 THREE POEMS IN MEASURE ONE: AN OPEN LETTER. T. ms. CtU.
a. *Date:* 5 Oct. 1957.
Collation: 2*l* recto-verso, recto-verso 27.9 x 21.7 cm.
Contents: This is a typescript (black carbon) of an essay which discusses the poems ONE by Edward Marshall, THE RICK OF GREEN WOOD by Edward Dorn, and BRINK by Larry Eigner.
Note: This copy was mailed to Larry Eigner, and contains Eigner's comments throughout in his typescript (black ribbon) in the margins.

301

b. *Date:* 24 Aug. 1957.

Collation: 4*l* all recto; 1*l* 25.5 x 21.5 cm., 3*l* 28 x 21.5 cm.

Contents: This is a photocopy of the same essay stated in F138a, but without Larry Eigner's comments. E305.

F139 THREE POEMS IN MEASURE ONE: AN OPEN LETTER. T. ms. (carbon) OKentU.

Date: 24 Aug. 1957.

Collation: 2*l* recto-verso, recto-verso 27.9 x 21.7 cm.

Contents: This is a commentary on poems by Edward Marshall, Larry Eigner, and Edward Dorn.

F140 [NOTES ON] HELEN ADAM AND JESS COLLINS. T. ms. OKentU.

Date: [Sept. 1957].

Collation: 1*l* recto 27.9 x 21.6 cm.

Contents: This is a typescript (carbon) of RD's notes for a poetry reading by Helen Adam and Jess Collins sponsored by The Poetry Center, and held at the Telegraph Hill Neighborhood Association.

F141 [Two Poems]. T. ms. CU-B.

Date: [Fall 1957].

Collation: 4*l* all recto 28 x 21.7 cm.

Contents: This is a typescript (black ribbon) of the poems as they appear in OF with some revisions: THE QUESTION—THE PERFORMANCE WE WAIT FOR.

Note: There is a short holograph note by RD at the bottom recto of the second leaf.

F142 EXEMPLA. T. ms. CU-B.

Date: [Fall 1957].

Collation: 2*l* recto, recto 27.7 x 21.6 cm.

Contents: This is a typescript (blue ribbon) of the poem.

F143 THREE POEMS IN MEASURE ONE: AN OPEN LETTER. T. ms. CU-B.

Date: Sept. 1957.

Collation: 2*l* recto-verso, recto-verso 27.9 x 21.7 cm.

Contents: This is a typescript (carbon copy) of the prose commentary on poems by Edward Marshall, Larry Eigner and Edward Dorn. See F138, F139.

F144 [Untitled Song]. T. ms. s. TxU.

Date: Sept. 1957.

Collation: 1*l* recto-verso 27.8 x 21.7 cm.

Contents: This is a typescript (black ribbon) of the text of the song.

Note: The song begins "Sing fair the Lady" and appeared in OF— with slight changes and with the repetition of the first stanza as the final stanza—as A SONG OF THE OLD ORDER. This typescript is signed and dated Sept. 1957 in RD's holograph on the bottom verso.

F145 [Untitled Song]. T. ms. CtU.

> *Date:* [29 Sept. 1957].
>
> *Collation:* 2*l* recto, recto 27.8 x 21.5 cm.
>
> *Contents:* This is a typescript (black ribbon) of the text of the song.
>
> *Note:* The song begins "Sing fair the Lady" and appeared in OF—with slight changes and with the restatement of the first stanza as the final stanza—as A SONG OF THE OLD ORDER. The typescript accompanied a letter to Charles Olson, dated 1 and 29 Sept. 1957. E301.

F146 THE QUESTION. T. ms. On deposit at MoSW.

> *Date:* [Oct. 1957].
>
> *Collation:* 1*l* recto 27.9 x 21.6 cm.
>
> *Contents:* This is a typescript (black ribbon) of the text of the poem as published in OF.

F147 THE QUESTION. T. ms. TxU.

> *Date:* [Oct. 1957].
>
> *Collation:* 1*l* recto 27.8 x 21.7 cm.
>
> *Contents:* This is a typescript (black ribbon) of the text of the poem as it appeared in OF.

F148 THE QUESTION. T. ms. CtU.

> *Date:* [Oct. 1957].
>
> *Collation:* 2*l* recto-verso, recto 28 x 21.5 cm.
>
> *Contents:* The typescript (black ribbon) and the text of the poem as it appeared in OF is surrounded by an a. l. s. beginning on the first leaf, top recto, and continuing onto the second leaf, bottom recto, and the second leaf verso.

F149 THE QUESTION. T. ms. s. CtY.

> *Date:* 29 Oct. 1957.
>
> *Collation:* 2*l* recto, recto 27.8 x 21.5 cm.
>
> *Contents:* This is a typescript (black ribbon) of the text of the poem as it appeared in OF.
>
> *Note:* The typescript is inscribed at the top of the first leaf, "for Ezra Pound these verses workd | that will be included in 'The Opening of the Field.'" There is also a holograph note at the bottom of the second leaf which is signed and dated by RD. This typescript has two holes punched at the left margin. It is dated 29 Oct. 1957 by RD.

F150 [Six Poems]. T. ms. ICU.

> *Date:* [25 Nov. 1957].
>
> *Collation:* 5*l* all recto; 3*l* 27.8 x 21.5 cm., 1*l* 16.6 x 19.9 cm. pasted on 1*l* 27.9 x 21.7 cm., 1*l* 27.8 x 17.9 cm.
>
> *Contents:* This is a typescript (black ribbon) of the poems as they appeared in *Poetry*: BROUGHT TO LOVE—TO VOW—META-MORPHOSIS—RE—WORDS OPEN UPON GRIEF—AUGUST SUN. C82.

Note: The editorial markings adjust the spaces between stanzas and parts of the poem. There are three short notes in the poet's holograph indicating that three of the poems had previously been sent to other magazines. The proof sheets, filed with the typescript 1*l* recto 41.2 x 20.3 cm., 1*l* recto 52 x 20.4 cm., 1*l* recto 29.6 x 20.4 cm., contain changes in the editor's and the poet's hand. This typescript accompanied a letter to Henry Rago, dated 25 Nov. 1957. E308.

F151 LIST OF POETS SUGGESTED FOR READING AT THE POETRY CENTER. T. ms. CU-B.
Date: 27 Nov. 1957.
Collation: 3*l* all recto 27.9 x 21.7 cm.
Contents: This is a typescript (black ribbon) of the list of poets for readings.

F152 (FOR ROBIN) AT CHRISTMAS. A. ms. s. CU-B.
Date: 15 Dec. 1957.
Collation: 1*l* recto 27.9 x 20.2 cm.
Contents: This is RD's holograph (black ink) draft of the poem which appeared in OF with revisions.
Note: At the bottom of the page, the following appears in RD's hand: "original ms of| AT CHRISTMAS| RD Dec 15, 1957."

F153 [Three Prose Pieces]. T. ms. PH.
Date: [1958].
Collation: 3*l* all recto 27.9 x 21.9 cm.
Contents: This is a typescript (black ribbon) of the three pieces as they appeared in *Letters.* Each piece is initialed, and each contains holograph changes by the poet: CHANGING TRAINS—THE LANGUAGE OF LOVE—THE SIREN SONG.

F154 Notes [for *Selected Poems*]. T. ms. CU-B.
Date: [1958].
Collation: 3*l* all recto, 27.8 x 21.7 cm.
Contents: This is a typescript (black ribbon) of notes for THE HELMET OF GOLIATH—THE KINGDOM OF JERUSALEM— THE MIRROR—HUON OF BORDEAUX—THE ALBIGENSES— THE VENICE POEM. The notes were not used in SP.

F155 from HEAVENLY CITY, EARTHLY CITY. T. ms. CU-B.
Date: [1958].
Collation: 3*l* all recto 27.7 x 21.6 cm.
Contents: This is a typescript (black ribbon) of the final nine stanzas of the poem.

F156 *Selected Poems.* T. ms. CU-B.
Date: [1958].
Collation: 10*l* all recto 27.8 x 21.6 cm.
Contents: This is a typescript (black ribbon) of the texts of the follow-

ing poems as prepared for SP but not used: THE HORNS OF ARTE-
MIS—AFRICA REVISITED—WORKING TOO LONG AT IT—
ADAM'S SONG.

F157 [Nine Poems]. T. ms. CU-B.
Date: [1958].
Collation: 14*l* all recto 27 x 21.6 cm.
Contents: This is a typescript (black ribbon) of the following poems:
FOUR PICTURES OF THE REAL UNIVERSE—OF BLAS-
PHEMY—EVOCATION—FOR THE INNOCENCE OF THE ACT—
FROM THESE STRANDS BECOMING, INTRODUCTION— CAL-
IFORNIA ORIGINS—THE BALLAD OF MRS. NOAH— THE
MAIDEN—A BALLAD OF THE ENAMORD MAGE.
Note: FROM THESE STRANDS BECOMING, INTRODUCTION,
and CALIFORNIA ORIGINS were not published in OF, but the
remaining poems were, and with revisions.

F158 (Major Revisions, & New Poems from *The Opening of the Field*). T.
ms. CU-B.
Date: [1958].
Collation: 5*l* all recto 27.8 x 21.6 cm.
Contents: OFTEN I AM PERMITTED TO RETURN TO A
MEADOW [with slight revision, now as published in OF]—[revision
for] THE STRUCTURE OF RIME I—A POEM SLOW BEGIN-
NING—OF BLASPHEMY—[revision for] THE QUESTION— [revi-
sion for] AT CHRISTMAS—YES, AS A LOOK SPRINGS TO ITS
FACE—YES, AS A LOOK SPRINGS TO ITS FACE—THE NATU-
RAL DOCTRINE. There are holograph markings in the margins
indicating the name and number of the poems.
Note: These revisions were made for poems still unpublished, but
which would appear in OF.

F159 A SAMPLER. A. ms. s. CSfU.
[in holograph black pen] A| SAM| PLER| FOR| MADELINE [yellow,
purple, and green crayon-decorated squares].
Date: Jan. 1958.
Collation: [1]⁶; pp. [1-12].
Contents: p. [1] title; p. [2] blank; pp. [3-9] decorations and text; pp.
[10-12] blank.
Text Contents: "NO! THIS IS NOT GOOD" (fl)—EVOCATION—
KEEPING THE RHYME—YES, AS A LOOK SPRING FROM ITS
FACE—THE QUESTION.
Note: The covers are made from stiff white paper with the following
lettering on the front: "A [in red crayon]| SAMPLER [in pink crayon]
| [blue crayon rule]." The rear cover contains the following inscription:
"for Madeline Gleason| January 1958| RD." The text is in the author's
holograph, black pen, and the paper is white. The decorations on p.
[3] are done with green and yellow crayons; the decorations on p. [5]

are done in gold, green, salmon, blue, and light blue crayons; the decorations on pp. [6-7] are done in green, orange, and yellow crayons in squares; the decorations on p. [9] are done in circles of gold, blue, red and purple crayons.

F160 MONEYS RAISED FOR DENISE LEVERTOV READING TO DATE: JANUARY 8, 1958. T. n. CU-B.
Date: 8 Jan. 1958.
Collation: 1*l* recto 17.2 x 13.9 cm.
Contents: This is a typescript (black ribbon) of the report of the collection of $97.00.

F161 [Five Poems]. T. ms. CtU.
Date: [8 Jan. 1958].
Collation: 6*l*; 2*l* recto-verso, 4*l* recto; 4*l* 32 x 21.5 cm., 2*l* 27.6 x 21.6 cm.
Contents: This is a typescript (carbon copy) of the following poems: THE PERFORMANCE WE WAIT FOR—AT CHRISTMAS—A POEM BEGINNING WITH A LINE BY PINDAR—PROOFS—YES, AS A LOOK SPRINGS FROM ITS FACE. All poems contain spacing changes and revisions as they appear in OF.
Note. A typed note appears at the top of the first leaf: "Being pages 36, 37, 38, 39, 40, 41, 42 of *The Opening Of The Field*." The initial leaf contains the second half of section 11 of THE PINDAR POEM and appears as a extra leaf of this typescript. These poems accompanied a letter to Charles Olson, dated 8 Jan. 1958. E321.

F162 THE PERFORMANCE WE WAIT FOR. T. ms. On deposit at MoSW.
Date: [28 Jan. 1958].
Collation: 2*l* recto, recto 28 x 21.6 cm.
Contents: This is a typescript (carbon) of the text of the poem.
Note: This typescript accompanied a letter to Robert Creeley, dated 28 Jan. 1958. E324.

F163 PROOFS. T. ms. On deposit at MoSW.
Date: [28 Jan. 1958].
Collation: 1*l* recto 28 x 21.6 cm.
Contents: This is a typescript (black ribbon) of the text of the poem.
Note: This typescript accompanied a letter to Robert Creeley, dated 28 Jan. 1958. E324.

F164 *The Opening of the Field.* T. ms. CU-B.
Date: 31 Jan. 1958.
Collation: 48*l* all recto 27.9 x 21.7 cm., 1*l* (no. 40) 7.5 x 21.7 cm.
Contents: This is a typescript (carbon) of "Text to date of *The Opening of The Field* submitted as the primary Project to the Guggenheim Foundation for a fellowship in poetry": DESCRIPTION—OFTEN I AM PERMITTED TO RETURN TO A MEADOW—THE LAW I LOVE IS MAJOR MOVER—THE STRUCTURE OF RIME I—THE

STRUCTURE OF RIME II— THE STRUCTURE OF RIME III—
THE STRUCTURE OF RIME IV—THE STRUCTURE OF RIME
V—THE STRUCTURE OF RIME VI—THE STRUCTURE OF
RIME VII—A POEM SLOW BEGINNING—THIS PLACE,
RUMORD TO HAVE BEEN SODOM—3 PAGES FROM A BIRTH-
DAY BOOK—A BALLAD OF THE ENAMORD MAGE—THE
MAIDEN—(THE PROPOSITIONS)—FOUR PICTURES OF THE
REAL UNIVERSE— EVOCATION—OF BLASPHEMY—FOR
THE INNOCENCE OF THE ACT—CROSSES OF HARMONY
AND DISHARMONY—A POEM OF DESPONDENCIES—
POETRY, A NATURAL THING—KEEPING THE RHYME—A
SONG OF THE OLD ORDER—THE QUESTION—THE PER-
FORMANCE WE WAIT FOR—AT CHRISTMAS—PROOFS—YES,
AS A LOOK SPRINGS FROM ITS FACE—[first four stanzas of] A
POEM BEGINNING WITH A LINE BY PINDAR—SOLITUDE—
THE STRUCTURE OF RIME VIII—THE STRUCTURE OF RIME
IX—THE STRUCTURE OF RIME X—THE STRUCTURE OF
RIME XI. The pages are numbered. The texts show many variants
from those published in OF. Pages 40-45 are missing, and were sent to
Donald Allen.

F165 A PRIVATELY, VILLANELLE OF POEMS DANCING (for Robin
Blaser). A. ms. CU-B.
Date: [4 Feb. 1958].
Collation: 1l recto-verso 27.9 x 21.6 cm.
Contents: This is a holograph text of the unpublished poem.
Note: This manuscript accompanied a letter to Robin Blaser, dated 4
Feb. 1958. E326.

F166 [LETTER] TO THE EDITOR OF *POETRY*. T. ms. ICU.
Date: [March/April 1958].
Collation: 2l recto, recto 28 x 21.7 cm.
Contents: This is a typescript (black ribbon) of the letter as it appeared
in *Poetry*. C84.

F167 [Four Poems]. T. ms. CtU.
Date: [10 March 1958].
Collation: 3l all recto 27.8 x 21.5 cm.
Contents: This is a typescript (black carbon) of the texts of the follow-
ing poems as they appeared in OF, with some changes in the first
three poems and no changes in the fourth poem: STRUCTURE OF
RIME VIII—STRUCTURE OF RIME IX—STRUCTURE OF RIME
X—STRUCTURE OF RIME XI.
Note: The poems accompanied a letter to Charles Olson, dated 10
March 1958. E334.

F168 A STORM OF WHITE. T. ms. CU-B.
Date: [3 April 1958].

Collation: 1*l* recto 27.9 x 21.7 cm.

Contents: This is a typescript (black ribbon) of the text of the poem as published in OF.

Note: This typescript accompanied a letter to Jack Spicer, dated 3 April 1958. E339.

F169 [Three Poems]. T. ms. CU-B.

Date: [6 June 1958].

Collation: 2*l* recto, recto 27.9 x 21.7 cm.

Contents: This is a typescript (black ribbon) of the following poems as they appeared in OF, with some revisions. A STORM OF WHITE—ATLANTIS—BONE DANCE.

Note: The two leaves are numbered pp. 49-50. This typescript accompanied a letter to Robin Blaser dated 3 and 6 June 1958. E347.

F170 A STORM OF WHITE. T. ms. ICU

Date: [Summer 1958].

Collation: 1*l* recto 28 x 21.5 cm.

Contents: This is a typescript (black ribbon) of the poem as it appeared in *Poetry.* C85.

Note: The proof sheet, filed with this typescript, 1*l* recto 29.9 x 20.9 cm., is initialed and dated by the poet "1/27/59."

F171 [Two Poems]. T. ms. CU-B.

Date: [4 July 1958].

Collation: 2*l* recto, recto 27.9 x 21.7 cm.

Contents: This is a typescript (black ribbon) of the final lines of DANSE MACABRE and UNDER GROUND as they appeared in OF.

Note: This typescript accompanied a letter to Robin Blaser, dated 4 July 1958. E350.

F172 AGAINST NATURE. T. ms. ICU.

Date: [Fall 1958].

Collation: 6*l* all recto 27.8 x 21.6 cm.

Contents: This is a typescript (black ribbon) of the review of Edward Dahlberg's *The Sorrows of Priapus* as it appeared in *Poetry.* C86.

Note: The title has been added in RD's holograph. The proof sheets, filed with this typescript, 1*l* recto 46.3 x 20.2 cm., 1*l* recto 46.7 x 20.2 cm., 1*l* recto 11.6 x 20.2 cm., have been initialed and dated by RD "March 4, [19]59."

F173 AN OCCASIONAL BALLAD. A. ms. NBuU.

Date: [1959?].

Collation: 1*l* recto 27.8 x 21.6 cm.

Contents: This is the text, in thirty-four lines, of a ballad intended as a Christmas greeting.

Note: The text is in brown ink on yellow paper. A 3.2 cm. fold has been made at the left edge, and the inscription in holograph blue pen, "for/the/Adam/family," appears at the top of the folded section. RD has signed his name in blue ink at the top right corner.

F174 From *The Opening of the Field*. T. ms. CLU.
Date: 1959.
Collation: 4*l* all recto; 2*l* 27.8 x 21.6 cm., 1*l* 17.3 x 21.6 cm., 1*l* 27.8 x 21.6 cm.
Contents: This is a typescript (black ribbon) of the following poems: ATLANTIS—YES, AS A LOOK SPRINGS TO ITS FACE [incomplete]—THE INBINDING MIRRORS A PROCESS REFERRING TO ROOTS OF FIRST FEELING—INGMAR BERGMAN'S *SEVENTH SEAL*.

F175 [Two poems]. T. ms. CU-B.
Date: [1959].
Collation: 1*l* recto-verso 28 x 21.5 cm.
Contents: This is a typescript (black ribbon) of the texts of the following poems: A SONG OF FORTUNE—LESSON FOR THE LEARNED.

F176 RISK. T. ms. CU-B.
Date: [1959].
a. *Collation:* 2*l* recto, recto 28 x 21.5 cm.
Contents: This is a typescript (black ribbon) of an incomplete draft of the poem.
b. *Collation:* 2*l* recto, recto 27.8 x 21.4 cm.
Contents: This is a typescript (black ribbon) of the text of the poem.

F177 I KNOW MYSELF. T. ms. CU-B.
Date: [1959].
Collation: 1*l* recto 27.8 x 21.5 cm.
Contents: This is a typescript (black ribbon) of a short prose essay.

F178 THE SONG OF THE BORDER-GUARD. T. ms. CU-B.
Date: 1959.
Collation: 1*l* recto 27.8 x 21.6 cm.
Contents: This is a typescript of the text of the poem.
Note: The following appears at the top right: "Selected Poems| Black Mountain Broadside #2| Origin."

F179 A DANCING CONCERNING A FORM OF WOMEN. T. ms. MoSW.
Date: [1959].
Collation: 1*l* recto 27.8 x 21.5 cm.
Contents: This is a typescript (black ribbon) of the poem which appeared in RB with additions and revisions. The leaf is initialed "RD."

F180 a. THE FIELD. T. ms. CtY, OKentU.
Date: [1959].
Collation: One unnumbered leaf as contents-page followed by 62*l* all

numbered, all recto 27.8 x 21.5 cm.

Contents: OFTEN I AM PERMITTED TO RETURN TO A MEADOW—THE DANCE—THE LAW I LOVE IS MAJOR MOVER—THE STRUCTURE OF RIME I—THE STRUCTURE OF RIME II—A POEM SLOW BEGINNING—THE STRUCTURE OF RIME III—THE STRUCTURE OF RIME IV—THE STRUCTURE OF RIME V—THE STRUCTURE OF RIME VI—THE STRUCTURE OF RIME VII—THREE PAGES FROM A BIRTHDAY BOOK—THIS PLACE RUMORD TO HAVE BEEN SODOM—THE BALLAD OF THE ENAMORD MAGE—THE BALLAD OF MRS. NOAH—THE MAIDEN—(THE PROPOSITIONS)—FOUR PICTURES OF THE REAL UNIVERSE—EVOCATION—OF BLASPHEMY—NOR IS THE PAST PURE—CROSSES OF HARMONY AND DISHARMONY—A POEM OF DESPONDENCIES—POETRY, A NATURAL THING—KEEPING THE RHYME—A SONG OF THE OLD ORDER—THE QUESTION— THE PERFORMANCE WE WAIT FOR—AT CHRISTMAS— PROOFS—YES, AS A LOOK SPRINGS TO ITS FACE—YES, AS A LOOK SPRINGS TO ITS FACE—A POEM BEGINNING WITH A LINE BY PINDAR—THE STRUCTURE OF RIME VIII—THE STRUCTURE OF RIME IX—THE STRUCTURE OF RIME X— THE STRUCTURE OF RIME XI—A STORM OF WHITE— ATLANTIS—OUT OF THE BLACK—BONE DANCE—UNDER GROUND—THE NATURAL DOCTRINE—THE STRUCTURE OF RIME XII—THE STRUCTURE OF RIME XIII—ANOTHER ANIMADVERSION—THE INBINDING—AFTER READING *BARELY AND WIDELY*—INGMAR BERGMAN'S *SEVENTH SEAL*—FOOD FOR FIRE, FOOD FOR THOUGHT.

Note: This typescript (carbon) of THE FIELD contains fifty numbered poems. The poems are separated from one another by double rules. The poem THE INBINDNG has four parts: "The Inbinding," "Mirrors," "A Process," "Returning to Roots of First Feeling." In the published version, these are listed as individual poems. There are minor variations in lines, spacing, and punctuation as well as slight word and phrase variations throughout this typescript as compared with the published version.

b. Another copy of the above. OKentU.

This copy has a line drawing on the title-page and is contained in a folder with the following lettering in green crayon: "The Field, poems 1956-1959."

F181 a. THE OPENING OF THE FIELD: POEMS 1956-1959. T. ms. CU-B.

Date: 1959.

Collation: One unnumbered leaf with dedication on recto, 63*l*, all 27.8 x 21.5 cm., with rectos alternating as typed and as blank. The verso follows a reversed alternation so that the blank half-leaves and typed half-leaves face each other: first leaf, recto typed, verso blank: second leaf, recto blank, verso typed: third leaf, recto typed, verso blank and so on. The poems, not the leaves, are numbered 1-48; the typed leaves are numbered 1-63. There is one additional leaf numbered 64.

Contents: OFTEN I AM PERMITTED TO RETURN TO A MEADOW—THE DANCE—THE LAW I LOVE IS MAJOR MOVER—THE STRUCTURE OF RIME I—THE STRUCTURE OF RIME II—A POEM SLOW BEGINNING—THE STRUCTURE OF RIME IV—THE STRUCTURE OF RIME VI—THE STRUCTURE OF RIME V—THREE PAGES FROM A BIRTHDAY BOOK—THIS PLACE RUMORD TO HAVE BEEN SODOM—THE BALLAD OF THE ENAMORD MAGE—THE BALLAD OF MRS. NOAH—THE MAIDEN—(THE PROPOSITIONS)—FOUR PICTURES OF THE REAL UNIVERSE—EVOCATION—OF BLASPHEMY—NOR IS THE PAST PURE—CROSSES OF HARMONY AND DISHARMONY—A POEM OF DESPONDENCIES—POETRY, A NATURAL THING—KEEPING THE RHYME—A SONG OF THE OLD ORDER—THE QUESTION—THE PERFORMANCE WE WAIT FOR—AT CHRISTMAS—PROOFS—YES, AS A LOOK SPRING TO ITS FACE—YES, AS A LOOK SPRINGS TO ITS FACE—A POEM BEGINNING WITH A LINE BY PINDAR—THE STRUCTURE OF RIME VIII—THE STRUCTURE OF RIME IX— THE STRUCTURE OF RIME X—THE STRUCTURE OF RIME XI—A STORM OF WHITE—ATLANTIS—OUT OF THE BLACK—BONE DANCE—UNDER GROUND—THE NATURAL DOCTRINE—THE STRUCTURE OF RIME XII—"I REMEMBER IN SPAIN" (fl)—ANOTHER ANIMADVERSION—THE INBINDING—AFTER READING *BARELY AND WIDELY*—INGMAR BERMAN'S *SEVENTH SEAL.*

Note: This typescript (carbon) has a plain gray cardboard frontispiece with a drawing in brown, green, purple, gold, salmon crayon, and black pen. The words "THE | OPENING | OF THE FIELD" (black pen) appear in the middle of the leaf, and "POEMS 1956-1959 [space] ROBERT DUNCAN" (black pen) appears across the bottom. The frontispiece is 27.9 x 21.6 cm. The frontispiece and the texts are held in a plain black binder, and the pasted-on title label reads: "THE OPENING OF THE FIELD | POEMS 1956-1959 | ROBERT DUNCAN" (black pen). In this typescript THE STRUCTURE OF RIME VI appears before THE STRUCTURE OF RIME V, and THE STRUCTURE OF RIME VII does not appear. THE STRUCTURE OF RIME III also does not appear. In this typescript, the poem THE INBINDNG is not divided into the separate parts entitled "The Inbinding," "Mirrors," "A Process," and "Returning To Roots of First Feeling." The section called MIRRORS in the published version is entitled

"Images" in this typescript. The poem INGMAR BERGMAN'S *SEV-ENTH SEAL* is not numbered, and the poem FOOD FOR FIRE, FOOD FOR THOUGHT does not appear. There are minor variations in lines, spacing, and punctuation as well as slight word and phrase variations throughout this typescript as compared with the published version.

    b. Another copy of the above. CU-B.

F182 THE FIELD. T. ms. CtU.

Date: 1959.

Collation: One unnumbered leaf with the recto as title-page, one unnumbered leaf as contents-page, 63*l*, all 27.8 x 21.5 cm., with the rectos alternating as typed and as blank, thus numbered. The verso follows a reversed alternation so that blank half-leaves and typed half-leaves face each other: first leaf, recto typed, verso blank: second leaf, recto blank, verso typed: third leaf, recto typed, verso blank.

Contents: OFTEN I AM PERMITTTED TO RETURN TO A MEADOW—THE DANCE—THE LAW I LOVE IS MAJOR MOVER—THE STRUCTURE OF RIME I—THE STRUCTURE OF RIME II—A POEM SLOW BEGINNING—THE STRUCTURE OF RIME III—THE STRUCTURE OF RIME IV—THE STRUC-TURE OF RIME V—THE STRUCTURE OF RIME VI—THE STRUCTURE OF RIME VII—THREE PAGES FROM A BIRTH-DAY BOOK—THIS PLACE RUMORD TO HAVE BEEN SODOM—THE BALLAD OF THE ENAMORD MAGE—THE BALLAD OF MRS. NOAH—THE MAIDEN—(THE PROPOSITIONS)—FOUR PICTURES OF THE REAL UNIVERSE—EVOCATION—OF BLASPHEMY—NOR IS THE PAST PURE—CROSSES OF HAR-MONY AND DISHARMONY—A POEM OF DESPONDENCIES—POETRY, A NATURAL THING—KEEPING THE RHYME—A SONG OF THE OLD ORDER—THE QUESTION—THE PERFOR-MANCE WE WAIT FOR—AT CHRISTMAS—YES, AS A LOOK SPRINGS TO ITS FACE (1)—YES, AS A LOOK SPRINGS TO ITS FACE (2)—A POEM BEGINNING WITH A LINE BY PINDAR—THE STRUCTURE OF RIME VIII—THE STRUCTURE OF RIME IX—THE STRUCTURE OF RIME X—THE STRUCTURE OF RIME XI—A STORM OF WHITE—ATLANTIS—OUT OF THE BLACK—BONE DANCE—UNDER GROUND—THE NATURAL DOCTRINE—THE STRUCTURE OF RIME XII—THE STRUC-TURE OF RIME XIII—I REMEMBER IN SPAIN—ANOTHER ANIMADVERSION—THE INBINDING— RETURNING TO ROOTS OF FIRST FEELING—AFTER READING *BARELY AND WIDELY*—INGMAR BERGMAN'S *SEVENTH SEAL*—FOOD FOR FIRE, FOOD FOR THOUGHT.

Note: This typescript (black ribbon) is bound in an orange folder and held together with three fasteners through three holes at the left edge.

The title-page reads, "THE FIELD| POEMS 1956-1959| Robert Duncan," and is surrounded by a drawing (black ink) by the author. Inscribed in another author's drawing at bottom right, "This copy for| Charles Olson." In OF, the two poems entitled YES, AS A LOOK SPRINGS TO ITS FACE are no longer numbered 1 and 2. In OF, the poem INBINDING has been divided into four poems, THE INBINDING—MIRRORS—A PROCESS—RETURNING TO ROOTS OF FIRST FEELING. In THE FIELD, the poem THE INBINDING appeared with the subdivisions "Images," "A Process," and "Returning to Roots of First Feeling." In "THE FIELD," there are fifty numbered poems. All poems contain minor variations of several types: spelling changes, line and spacing adjustments, stanza length changes, punctuation changes, slight word and phrase revisions.

F183 [Four Poems]. T. ms. ICU.
Date: [Spring 1959].
Collation: 5*l* all recto 27.8 x 21.5 cm.
Contents: This is a typescript (black ribbon) of the poems as they appeared in *Poetry:* FOOD FOR FIRE, FOOD FOR THOUGHT—UNDER GROUND—BONE DANCE—RETURNING TO ROOTS OF FIRST FEELING. C93.
Note: The editor has deleted seven lines from the end of the poem BONE DANCE. The proof sheets, filed with the typescript, 1*l* recto 37 x 20.3 cm., 1*l* recto 61 x 20.3 cm., 1*l* recto 29.1 x 20.3 cm., contain some markings in RD's holograph.

F184 A DISCLOSURE. T. ms. s. CU-B.
Date: [11 Feb. 1959].
Collation: 1*l* recto 27.9 x 21.7 cm.
Contents: This is a typescript of the text of the notes that appeared in the program for RD's reading at the SF State poetry reading, 1 March 1959.
Note: This typescript accompanied a letter to Robin Blaser, dated 11 Feb. 1959. E378.

F185 GISTS FROM PHILIPPUS AUREOLUS THEOPHRASTUS BOMBASTUS VON HOHENHEIM, CALLED PARACELSUS. T. ms. CU-B.
Date: [11 Feb. 1959].
Collation: 1*l* recto 23.8 x 21.6 cm.
Contents: This is a typescript (black ribbon) of quotations from the author's reading in Paracelsus.
Note: The typescript accompanied a letter to Robin Blaser, dated 11 Feb. 1959. E378.

F186 UNCOLLECTED PIECES, FEB. 1959. T. ms. CU-B.
Date: 23 Feb. 1959.
Collation: 7*l* all recto 27.9 x 21.5 cm.
Contents: "LADIES AND GENTLEMEN, WELCOME TO MY

STAGE WHICH YOU SEE" (fl)—"WE FACE ALL IN EVERY
MOMENT" (fl)—HEAR THE LAUGHTER OF THE LIONS—
"SCENES FROM THE WAR" (fl)—I WONDER IF I SHOULD GET
MARRIED TO LOVE—HE DID NOT WEAR HIS SCARLET
COAT—A TRANSLATION FROM *A SEASON IN HELL*—A
GAME OF KINGS—"TO SING OF LOVE; AGAIN, GREAT LOVE
IS DEAD" (fl)—"A BOAT/-WITH THE INTERIM OF A LINE
ADRIFT FROM" (fl).

Note: These poems derive from the period 1947 to 1955, and are poems
which were not included in either HCEC or SP. In *Audit/Poetry*,
C191, the following poems appeared: A TRANSLATION FROM *A
SEASON IN HELL* as A DERIVATION FROM RIMBAUD—A
GAME OF KINGS—"TO SING OF LOVE; AGAIN, GREAT LOVE
IS DEAD" (fl) as A VILLANELLE—"A BOAT/-WITH THE
INTERIM OF A LINE ADRIFT FROM" (fl) as ALTERATION.

Note: This typescript accompanied a letter to Robin Blaser, dated 23
Feb. 1959. E381.

F187 A STORM OF WHITE. T. ms. CU-B
    Date: 3 April 1959.
    Collation: 1*l* recto 28 x 21.6 cm.
    Contents: This is a typescript (black ribbon) of the poem as it appeared
    in OF. The leaf is numbered as p. 49. E340.

F188 ROOTS AND BRANCHES. A. ms. NBuU.
    Date: [18 March 1959].
    Collation: 1*l* recto 27.9 x 21.6 cm.
    Contents: This is a version of the poem in the poet's hand as it
    appeared in RB, with small revisions. A pen-and-ink drawing appears
    on the same page, along with the poet's initials.
    Note: This manuscript accompanied a letter to Helen Adam, dated 18
    May 1959. E385.

F189 [Two Poems]. T. ms. ICU.
    Date: [10 Aug. 1959].
    Collation: 2*l* recto, recto 28 x 21.7 cm.
    Contents: This is a typescript (black ribbon) of the texts of the follow-
    ing poems: THE INBINDING MIRRORS A PROCESS— RETURN-
    ING TO ROOTS OF FIRST FEELING.
    Note: This typescript accompanied a letter to Henry Rago, dated 10
    Aug. 1959. E411.

F190 GENERAL REMARKS. T. ms. NSyU.
    Date: 27 Aug. 1959.
    Collation: 6*l* all recto 27.8 x 21.5 cm.
    Contents: In this typescript (black ribbon) RD gives general remarks
    on spacing, margins, and line lengths for the publisher of OF, at this
    point the Macmillan Co., and then gives the corrections and revisions
    of the proofs.

F191 A SEQUENCE OF POEMS FOR H.D.'S BIRTHDAY. T. ms. CtY.
Date: [3 Sept. 1959].
Collation: 2*l* recto, recto 28 x 21.6 cm.
Contents: This is a typescript (black ribbon) of the text of the poem consisting of parts 1-4. Parts 3 and 4 appeared as parts 5 and 6 when the poem was published in RB. A three line note in the poet's hand at bottom recto of the second leaf indicates that the poem is "in progress."
Note: This typescript accompanied a letter to H.D., dated 3 Sept. 1959. E420.

F192 A SEQUENCE OF POEMS FOR H.D.'S BIRTHDAY. T. ms. CU-B.
Date: [Sept.-Oct. 1959].
Collation: 2*l* recto, recto 28 x 21.5 cm.
Contents: This is a typescript (black ribbon) of parts 1-4 of the poem, with revisions, as it appeared in RB.

F193 A SEQUENCE OF POEMS FOR H.D.'S BIRTHDAY, SEPTEMBER 10, 1959 | FINISHED OCTOBER 24, 1959. T. ms. CtU.
Date: 24 Oct. 1959.
Collation: 4*l* all recto 27.8 x 21.5 cm.
Contents: This is a typescript of the poem as it appeared in RB.
Note: The typescript (black ribbon) is signed by RD on the recto of the fourth leaf.

F194 A SEQUENCE OF POEMS FOR H.D.'S BIRTHDAY, SEPTEMBER 10, 1959 FINISHED OCTOBER 24, 1959. T. ms. CtY.
Date: [1 Nov. 1959].
Collation: 4*l* all recto 28 x 21.6 cm.
Contents: This is the typescript (black ribbon) of the text of the poem as it appeared in RB.
Note: This typescript accompanied a letter to H.D., dated 1 Nov. 1959. E437.

F195 EXTRACTS FROM CORRESPONDENCE RE DUNCAN'S *The Opening of the Field.* T. ms. NSyU.
Date: 10 Nov. 1959-27 Jan. 1960.
Collation: 2*l* recto, recto 27.8 x 21.5 cm.
Contents: This is a short collection (photocopy) of extracts from letters between Donald Allen and RD concerning the publication of OF: DA to RD, Nov. 1959; RD to DA, 18 Nov. 1959; DA to RD, 2 Dec. 1959; RD to DA, 5 Dec. 1959; DA to RD, 8 Dec. 1959; DA to Barney Rosset, 8 Dec. 1959; DA to RD, 19 Dec. 1959; RD to DA, 11 Jan. 1960; DA to RD, 14 Jan. 1960; RD to DA, 27 Jan. 1960.

F196 THE HOMOSEXUAL IN SOCIETY. T. ms. MoSW.
Date: [Dec. 1959].
Collation: 10*l* all recto 28 x 27.7 cm.
Contents: This is a typescript (black ribbon) of the revised version of the essay of 1944.

F197 THE LAW. T. ms. On deposit at MoSW.
Date: Jan. 1960.
Collation: 2l recto, recto 27.9 x 21.6 cm.
Contents: This is a typescript (black ribbon) of the text of the poem as it was published, with revisions, in RB.
Note: This typescript accompanied a letter to Robert Creeley, dated 2 Jan. 1960. E451.

F198 NEL MEZZO DEL CAMMIN DI NOSTRA VITA. T. ms. CtU.
Date: [4 Jan. 1960].
Collation: 2l recto, recto 27.8 x 21.5 cm.
Contents: This is a typescript (black ribbon) of the poem as it appeared in *National Review*, C107, with some changes, and later in RB. This copy contains emendations in the author's hand.
Note: This typescript accompanied a letter to Charles Olson, dated 4 Jan. 1960. E453.

F199 [LETTER OF RECOMMENDATION]. T. ms. CtU.
Date: [Feb. 1960].
Collation: 2l recto-verso, recto 27.8 x 21.5 cm.
Contents: "Report to the John Simon Guggenheim Memorial Foundation concerning Charles Olson as a candidate for fellowship to continue work in Gloucester on Part II of THE MAXIMUS POEMS: the order and achievement of THE MAXIMUS POEMS." In addition to a typescript (black carbon) of the letter in support of Olson, the manuscript contains two holograph notes from RD to Charles Olson: the first begins top recto of the first leaf and concludes on the bottom verso of the first leaf; the second is contained on the verso of the second leaf.

F200 APPREHENSIONS. T. ms. CU-B.
Date: [Feb. 1960].
a. Collation: 5l all recto 27.9 x 21.8 cm.
Contents: This is a typescript (black ribbon) with pages numbered [1]-8, (pp. 4-6 are missing) of parts I and II of the poem, later published in RB with some changes.
b. Collation: 2l recto, recto 27.8 x 21.5 cm.
Contents: This is a typescript (black ribbon) of the third part of the poem, as published with some revisions in RB.

F201 [APPREHENSIONS, 1]. T. ms. On deposit at MoSW.
Date: [4 Feb. 1960].
Collation: 1l recto 30.5 x 18.2 cm.
Contents: This is an untitled typescript (black ribbon) of the text of the first section of the poem as published in RB, with some revisions.
Note: This typescript accompanied a letter to Robert Creeley, dated 4 Feb. 1960. E462.

F202 APPREHENSIONS. T. ms. CtU.
    Date: [6 Feb. 1960].
    Collation: 3*l*; 2*l* recto, recto 28 x 21.5 cm., 1*l* recto 22.7 x 21.5 cm.
    Contents: This is a typescript (black ribbon) of "1," "2 Directive," and
"second version" of the poem APPREHENSIONS. The first section
appeared, with slight revisions, in *Big Table* (C106), while the whole
poem, with additions and revisions, appeared in RB.
    Note: This typescript accompanied a letter to Charles Olson, dated 6
Feb. 1960. E464.

F203 APPREHENSIONS 2. T. ms. On deposit at MoSW.
    Date: [15 Feb. 1960].
    Collation: 2*l* recto, recto 28 x 21.6 cm.
    Contents: This is a typescript (black ribbon) of the text of the poem
as it was published in RB, with slight revisions.
    Note: This typescript accompanied a letter to Robert Creeley, dated 15
Feb. 1960. E467.

F204 APPREHENSIONS, THIRD MOVEMENT. T. ms. CtU.
    Date: 7 March 1960.
    Collation: 2*l* recto, recto 27.8 x 21.5 cm.
    Contents: This is a typescript (black ribbon) of the third section of the
poem as it appeared in RB. Part of the typescript is titled "[revision
to First Movement]" and contains major line and stanza revisions.
    Note: This typescript accompanied a letter to Charles Olson, dated 7
March 1960. E474.

F205 POETRY, A NATURAL THING. T. ms. CaBVaS.
    Date: [15 March 1960].
    Collation: 1*l* recto 27.9 x 21.5 cm.
    Contents: This is a typescript (carbon) of the text of the poem as it
appeared in *Folio* (C100), and OF.
    Note: The typescript also contains a short holograph note by RD and
editorial markings. It accompanied a letter to Clayton Eshleman,
dated 15 March 1960. E476.

F206 THREE PAGES FROM A BIRTHDAY BOOK. T. ms. CaBVaS.
    Date: [15 March 1960].
    Collation: 1*l* recto 27.9 x 21.5 cm.
    Contents: This is a typescript (carbon) of the text of the prose piece as
it appeared in *Folio*, C100.
    Note: The typescript also contains a short holograph note by RD and
editorial markings. It accompanied a letter to Clayton Eshleman,
dated 15 March 1960. E476.

F207 APPREHENSIONS, 4TH MOVEMENT, MOVEMENT. T. ms. On
deposit at MoSW.
    Date: [28 March 1960].
    Collation: 3*l* all recto 27.9 x 21.6 cm.

Contents: This is a typescript (black ribbon) of the text of the movements as they were published in RB, with slight revisions.
Note: This typescript accompanied a letter to Robert Creeley, dated 28 March 1960. E482.

F208 APPREHENSIONS. T. ms. CtY.
Date: May 1960.
Collation: 8*l* all recto 27.9 x 21.6 cm.
Contents: This typed version of the poem has been reproduced with ditto masters (purple ink) and is the text of the poem as published in RB, pp. 30-43.
Note: The notation "for H.D., May 1960, Robert Duncan" appears in the poet's hand, top recto of the first leaf, and an ink drawing of a human head appears on the recto of the eighth leaf.

F209 TWO DICTA OF WILLIAM BLAKE. T. ms. On deposit at MoSW.
Date: [1 June 1960].
Collation: 3*l* all recto 27.9 x 21.6 cm.
Contents: This is a typescript (black ribbon) of the text of the poem as published in RB, with slight revisions.
Note. This typescript accompanied a letter to Robert Creeley, dated 1 June 1960. E489.

F210 [THE H.D. BOOK]. T. ms. CtY.
Date: [2 July 1960].
Collation: 2*l* recto, recto; 1*l* 33 x 21.5 cm., 1*l* 25.2 x 21.5 cm.
Contents: This typescript (black ribbon) consists of a section from Part I of RD's study of H.D. There is a holograph note at top recto and bottom verso of the first leaf.
Note: This typescript accompanied a letter to Norman Holmes Pearson, dated 2 July 1960. E495.

F211 BEGINNINGS. T. ms. CtY.
Date: [Sept. Oct. 1960].
Collation: 8*l* all recto 27.8 x 21.5 cm.
Contents: This is a typescript (7*l* black ribbon, 1*l* carbon) of an early version of Chap. 1, Part I, of "The H.D. Book" which was printed, with revisions, in *Coyote's Journal* C179. This is a typescript of the first part of the chapter.

F212 TOWARDS A STUDY OF H.D. 1 BEGINNINGS. T. ms. CtY.
Date: [Sept.-Oct. 1960].
Collation: 16*l* all recto 27.8 x 21.5 cm.
Contents: This is a typescript (black ribbon) of the first chapter of "The H.D. Book" as published in *Coyote's Journal* (C179), under the title BEGINNINGS: CHAPTER 1, PART I OF THE H.D. BOOK, with many changes and revisions.
Note: Holograph changes in RD's hand appear on several pages of this typescript.

F213 TOWARDS A STUDY OF H.D. BEGINNINGS. T. ms. CtY.
  Date: Sept. 1960.
  Collation: 31*l* all recto 32.8 x 21.5 cm.
  Contents: This is a typescript (carbon) of the second version of the
  first chapter of the poet's study of H.D., which was published with
  revisions as BEGINNINGS: CHAPTER 1, PART I OF THE H.D.
  BOOK, *Coyote's Journal.* C179. There are four short notes in the
  poet's hand on this typescript.

F214 (TOWARD A STUDY OF H.D.). T. ms. CtY.
  Date: [early Sept. 1960].
  Collation: 10*l* all recto 28 x 21.6 cm.
  Contents: This is an early version of the first chapter of "The H.D.
  Book" published with revisions and expansions as BEGINNINGS:
  CHAPTER 1, PART I OF THE H.D. BOOK, *Coyote's Journal.* C179.
  Note: The typescript contains four notes in RD's hand and a single
  notation in H.D.'s hand.

F215 FOUR SONGS THE NIGHT-NURSE SANG. T. ms. CtY.
  Date: [12 Sept. 1960].
  Collation: 3*l* all recto 27.8 x 21.5 cm.
  Contents: This is a typescript (carbon) of the poem as it appeared in
  Poems From The Floating World.
  Note: This typescript accompanied a letter to Norman Holmes Pearson, dated 12 Sept. 1960. E503.

F216 (TOWARD A STUDY OF H.D.). T. ms. CtY.
  Date: [12 and 16 Sept. 1960].
  Collation: 23*l* all recto 27.9 x 21.5 cm.
  Contents: This is a typescript (black ribbon) of the first version of the
  first chapter of RD's study of H.D.; it was published with revisions as
  BEGINNINGS: CHAPTER 1, PART I OF THE H.D. BOOK, *Coyote's
  Journal.* C179.
  Note: This typescript accompanied letters to Norman Holmes Pearson, dated 12 and 16 Sept. 1960. E504.

F217 FOUR SONGS THE NIGHT-NURSE SANG. T. ms. CtY.
  Date: 22 Sept. 1960.
  Collation: 3*l* all recto 28 x 21.6 cm.
  Contents: This is a typescript (black ribbon) of the poem as it appeared
  in *Poems From The Floating World.* C135.
  Note: A letter from RD to H.D. appears in his holograph, top recto of
  the first leaf and bottom recto of the third leaf. E503.

F218 TOWARD A STUDY OF H.D.: BEGINNINGS. T. ms. CtY.
  Date: [Oct. 1960].
  Collation: 16*l* all recto; 15*l* 32.8 x 21.6 cm., 1*l* 25.4 x 21.6 cm.
  Contents: This is a typescript (carbon) of a revised version of the first
  chapter of the poet's study of H.D. which was published with further

revisions as BEGINNINGS: CHAPTER 1, PART I OF THE H.D. BOOK, *Coyote's Journal.* C179.

Note: This typescript accompanied a letter to H.D., dated 1 and 12 Oct. 1960. E508.

F219 [Three Poems]. T. ms. OKentU.

Date: [20 Oct. 1960].

Collation: 2*l* recto, recto 27.8 x 21.4 cm.

Contents: This is a typescript (black ribbon) of the texts of the following poems as they appeared in RB: STRUCTURE OF RIME XVIII—STRUCTURE OF RIME XV—STRUCTURE OF RIME XVI. Slight revisions have been made, and the title of the first poem has been changed to STRUCTURE OF RIME XVII.

Note: A letter to Helen, Pat, and Mother Adam, dated 20 Oct. 1960, appears on the recto of these leaves. E513.

F220 OSIRIS AND SET. A. ms. CtY.

Date: 22 Nov. 1960.

Collation: 1*l* recto 30.4 x 18.2 cm.

Contents: This is a holograph version of the poem as published with slight revisions in *Set.* C116.

Note: A short note to H.D. appears at the top and bottom of this leaf.

F221 [Two Poems]. T. ms. On deposit at MoSW.

Date: [23 Nov. 1960].

Collation: 3*l*; 2*l* recto-verso, recto-verso 27.9 x 21.6 cm., 1*l* recto 22 x 21.6 cm.

Contents: This is a typescript (black ribbon) of the text of the following poems as published in RB, with revisions: FOUR SONGS THE NIGHT-NURSE SANG—RISK.

Note: This typescript accompanied a letter to Robert Creeley, dated 23 Nov. 1960. E518.

F222 BEGINNINGS. T. ms. CtY.

Date: [1961].

Collation: 162*l* all recto; 161*l* 27.9 x 21.5 cm., 1*l* 11.8 x 21.5 cm.

Contents: This is a typescript (black ribbon and carbon) of the final version of the first part of the poet's study of H.D.

Note: The leaves are bound in a standard black binder with a brown paper label pasted on the front containing the following notation in the poet's hand: "Part One: Beginnings| Robert Duncan."

F223 RETURNING TO THE RHETORIC OF AN EARLY MODE. T. ms. CU-B.

Date: [1961].

Collation: 1*l* recto 33 x 21.6 cm.

Contents: This is a typescript (black ribbon) of the text of the poem, as it appeared in RB with slight revisions.

F224 [Three Poems]. T. ms. CU-B.
    Date: [1961].
    Collation: 3*l* all recto 27.9 x 21.5 cm.
    Contents: This is a typescript (black ribbon) of early versions of the
    following poems: THANK YOU FOR LOVE—FROM *THE MABI-*
    NOGION—FORCED IMAGES.
    Note: THANK YOU FOR LOVE is not here dedicated to Robert
    Creeley, FROM *THE MABINOGION* is here only thirteen lines, and
    FORCED IMAGES becomes FORCED LINES in RB.

F225 [Two Poems and a Fragment]. T. ms. CU-B.
    Date: [1961].
    Collation: 3*l* all recto 27.9 x 21.5 cm.
    Contents: This is a typescript (black ribbon) of A NEW POEM and
    FORCED LINES, plus twenty-three lines of FROM *THE*
    MABINOGION.

F226 SHELLEY'S *ARETHUSA* PUT INTO A NEW MEASURE. T. ms.
    CU-B.
    Date: [1961].
    Collation: 2*l* recto, recto-verso 27.9 x 21.6 cm.
    Contents: This is a typescript (carbon) of the text of the poem.
    Note: A note explaining the origin of the poem appears on the verso
    of the second leaf in RD's hand.

F227 PROPERTIES AND OUR REAL ESTATE. T. ms. InU.
    Date: [1961].
    Collation: 11*l* all recto; 1*l* 27.7 x 21.2 cm., 10*l* 27.9 x 21.6 cm.
    Contents: This is a typescript (black ribbon) of the essay as it appeared
    in *Journal for the Protection of All Beings*.
    Note: The typescript contains some holograph corrections by RD
    and editorial markings and deletions.

F228 [Three Poems]. T. ms. CtU.
    Date: [1961].
    Collation: 2*l* recto, recto; 1*l* 23 x 21.5 cm., 1*l* 21.2 x 21.5 cm.
    Contents: This is a typescript (black ribbon) of the poems, STRUC-
    TURE OF RIME XIX—STRUCTURE OF RIME XX— STRUC-
    TURE OF RIME XXI, differing slightly from the final versions in
    RB.

F229 A PLAY WITH MASKS. T. ms. CU-B.
    Date: 1961.
    a. *Collation:* 16*l* all recto 27.9 x 21.5 cm.
    Contents: This is a thermofax copy of the play used for the Oct. 1961
    production in Lewis Ellingham's apartment in North Beach.
    b. *Collation:* 20*l* all recto 27.9 x 21.6 cm.
    Contents: This is a typescript (black ribbon) of the text of the play.
    c. *Collation:* 5*l* all recto 27.9 x 21.7 cm.

Contents: This is a carbon copy of scene five.

Note: All versions were revised for publication.

F230 ROOTS AND BRANCHES. T. ms. CtU.

Date: [1961].

Collation: 33*l* all recto 34.5 x 21.5 cm.

Contents: ROOTS AND BRANCHES—WHAT DO I KNOW OF THE OLD LORE—NIGHT SCENES—A SEQUENCE OF POEMS FOR H.D.'S BIRTHDAY—DEAR CARPENTER—NEL MEZZO DEL CAMMIN DI NOSTRA VITA—A DANCING CONCERNING A FORM OF WOMEN—THE LAW—APPREHENSIONS— SONNERIES OF THE ROSE CROSS—NOW THE RECORD NOW RECORD—TWO DICTA OF WILLIAM BLAKE—COME, LET ME FREE MYSELF—RISK—FOUR SONGS THE NIGHT-NURSE SANG—STRUCTURE OF RIME XV—STRUCTURE OF RIME XVI—STRUCTURE OF RIME XVII—STRUCTURE OF RIME XVIII—OSIRIS AND SET.

Note: All the poems in this typescript (black ribbon) contain variants, and either spacing or stanza adjustments, line length or punctuation changes, deletions or additions as compared with the versions printed in RB.

F231 H.D. BOOK. PART I CHPT 5. T. ms. CU-B.

Date: [1961/62].

Collation: 41*l* all recto 28 x 21.7 cm.

Contents: This is a typescript (black ribbon) of the text of the essay as it appeared in *Stony Brook 3/4*. C218.

Note: There are notes in RD's hand on the versos of several leaves, and there are changes and additions in his hand.

F232 AFTER READING H.D.'S *HERMETIC DEFINITIONS*. T. ms. CU-B.

Date: [1961].

Collation: 2*l* recto, recto 27.9 x 21.6 cm.

Contents: This is a carbon copy of the poem as published in *Trobar*. C121.

F233 TWO MESSAGES. T. ms. CU-B.

Date: Feb.-March 1961.

Collation: 2*l* recto, recto 33 x 21.5 cm.

Contents: This is a typescript of the text of TWO PRESENTATIONS as it appeared in RB.

F234 THE RIVER, THE SEA, AND THE POET. T. ms. On deposit at MoSW.

Date: [1961].

Collation: 4*l* all recto 27.9 x 21.6 cm.

Contents: This is a typescript (black ribbon) of an unpublished prose essay on Joyce, Williams, and Eliot.

F235 [Two Poems]. T. ms. ICU.

   Date: [Spring 1961].

   Collation: 6*l* all recto 28 x 21.6 cm. The third leaf is 8.5 x 21.6 cm. and taped onto a larger leaf.

   Contents: This is a typescript (black ribbon) of the poems, THE LAW—TWO DICTA OF WILLIAM BLAKE, as they appeared in *Poetry* C115.

   Note: The proof sheets, filed with this typescript, 1*l* recto 49 x 20.3 cm., 2*l* recto, recto 61.3 x 20.3 cm., contain corrections in the poet's hand and are initialed and dated by the poet "Oct 24 [19]61." The second poem, with slight changes, was published in RB as VARIATIONS ON TWO DICTA OF WILLIAM BLAKE.

F236 SHELLEY'S *ARETHUSA* PUT INTO A NEW MEASURE. T. ms. CtY.

   Date: [3 April 1961].

   Collation: 2*l* recto, recto 27.8 x 21.6 cm.

   Contents: This is a typescript (carbon) of the text of the poem as it appeared with some revisions in *Origin.* C117.

   Note: This typescript accompanied a letter to Norman Holmes Pearson, dated 3 April 1961. E532.

F237 A LITTLE DAY BOOK. T. ms. CtY.

   Date: [April-Aug. 1961].

   Collation: 175*l* all recto 27.9 x 21.5 cm. There are 174 numbered leaves and leaf 32a.

   Contents: This is a typescript (carbon and black ribbon mixed) of the first version of the second part of the poet's book on H.D. The entries date from 10 March to 29 March 1961. The text was revised and expanded in 1963 for publication.

   Note: Pages 137-174 accompanied a letter to Norman Holmes Pearson, dated 31 July 1961; pp. 44-55 and p. 32a for p. 32 accompanied a letter to Norman Holmes Pearson dated 13 June 1961; pp. 31-34 accompanied a letter to Norman Holmes Pearson dated 5 April 1961. E533, E543, E547.

F238 A SECOND OPEN LETTER REGARDING BORREGAARD'S MUSEUM. T. ms. CU-B.

   Date: 28 April 1961.

   Collation: 1*l* recto-verso 33.8 x 21.5 cm.

   Contents: This is a typescript (black ribbon) of the letter as mailed.

F239 GLIMPSES OF THE LAST DAY [FROM CHAPTER 11 OF THE H.D. BOOK]. T. ms. CaBVaS.

   Date: 25 May 1961.

   Collation: 3*l* all recto 27.9 x 21.6 cm.

   Contents: This is a typescript (black ribbon) of the essay as it appeared in *Io.* C224.

   Note: There are some slight corrections in RD's holograph.

F240 AFTER READING H.D.'S *HERMETIC DEFINITIONS*. T. ms. CtY.
Date: [5 June 1961].
Collation: 2*l* recto, recto 27.9 x 21.5 cm.
Contents: This is a typescript (black ribbon) of the text of the poem as it first appeared in *Trobar*. C121.
Note: This typescript accompanied a letter to Norman Holmes Pearson, dated 5 June 1961. E542.

F241 THE BALLAD OF THE FORFAR WITCHES' SING. T. ms. NBuU.
Date: [22 Aug. 1961].
Collation: 2*l* recto, recto 27.9 x 21.6 cm.
Contents: This is the typescript (black ribbon) of the text of the poem as it appeared in RB. Some revisions and additions have been made.
Note: This typescript accompanied a note to Helen Adam, dated 22 Aug. 1961. E550.

F242 [A COUNTRY WIFE'S SONG]. A. ms. NBuU.
Date: [Fall 1961].
Collation: 3*l* all recto 25.4 x 15.8 cm.
Contents: This is an early version of A COUNTRY WIFE'S SONG, first published with revisions in A PLAY WITH MASKS, *Audit/Poetry*. C189.

F243 [Untitled]. T. ms. OKentU.
Date: [Fall 1961].
Collation: 2*l* recto, recto 14 x 21.6 cm.
Contents: This is a typescript (black ribbon) of a five line poem, which is unpublished.
Note: A reproduction of a colored chalice, which has been further decorated by RD with crayons and with the name "HELEN" at the top, 5.9 x 3.7 cm., is pasted on the first leaf with clear tape. The second leaf is blank.

F244 AN OPEN LETTER TO THE DIRECTOR SAN FRANCISCO STATE COLLEGE POETRY CENTER. T. ms. CU-B.
Date: [Fall] 1961.
Collation: 4*l* all recto 27.9 x 21.7 cm.
Contents: This is a typescript (carbon) of the letter RD wrote to James Schevill, then director of the Poetry Center, protesting the dedication of the 1961 Poetry Festival to Dag Hammarskjold.

F245 WHAT HAPPENED: PRELUDE. T. ms. CU-B.
Date: 17 Dec. 1961-10 Feb. 1962.
a. Collation: 4*l*; 3*l* all recto 33 x 21.5 cm.; 1*l* recto 27.9 x 21.7 cm.
Contents: This is a typescript (black ribbon) of the text of the poem, with revisions, as it appeared in RB.
b. Collation: 5 *l*; 4*l* all recto; 3*l* 33 x 21.5 cm., 1*l* 9.7 x 21.5 cm.
Contents: This is a carbon of the same text as "a."
c. Collation: 1*l* recto 27.9 x 21.7 cm.

Contents: This is a typescript (black ribbon) of the poem, ARGU-
MENT, as it appeared in RB, with revisions.

F246 A SET OF ROMANTIC HYMNS. T. ms. CU-B.
Date: 1962.
Collation: 4*l* all recto 33 x 21.5 cm.
Contents: This is a typescript of the poems as they appeared in RB.
Note: There is a note in Robin Blaser's hand: "mailed to Spicer 1962."

F247 THREE SONGS OF THE BARD ORPHEUS. T. ms. CU-B.
Date: [1962].
Collation: 3*l* all recto 27.9 x 21.6 cm.
Contents: This is a typescript (black ribbon) of two poems only:
CYPARISSUS, which appeared in RB, and GANYMEDE.

F248 THANK YOU FOR LOVE. T. ms. CU-B.
Date: [1962].
Collation: 1*l* recto 28 x 21.5 cm.
Contents: This is a typescript (black ribbon) of the poem as it appeared
in RB.

F249 WHAT HAPPENED: PRELUDE. T. ms. On deposit at MoSW.
Date: 1962.
Collation: 6*l* all recto 27.9 x 21.6 cm.
Contents: The text of ARGUMENT was later expanded for publica-
tion, and there are slight revisions in PUSS-IN-BOOTS, GUARDIAN,
GENIUS. This typescript is in black ribbon.

F250 [CONTENTS PAGE FOR] *A BOOK OF RESEMBLANCES.* T. ms.
MoSW.
Date: [1962].
Contents: This is the contents-page with fifty-one titles, seventeen of
which have been lined out by the printer.
Note: "A Book of Resemblances| Robert Duncan" appears at the top,
and a four-line note to Dave [Haselwood], in RD's holograph, appears
at the bottom of the leaf.

F251 [From *A BOOK OF RESEMBLANCES*]. T. ms. OKentU.
Date: [1962].
a. ADAM'S SONG.
Collation: 2*l* recto, recto 27.9 x 21.7 cm.
Contents: This is a typescript (black ribbon) of the text of the poem
as it appeared in BR, with slight changes.
b. WORKING TOO LONG AT IT.
Collation: 1*l* recto 27.9 x 21.7 cm.
Contents: This is a typescript (black ribbon) of the text of forty lines
of the poem, which appear in BR, with slight changes.
c. THE SONG OF THE BORDER-GUARD.
Collation: 2*l* recto, recto 27.9 x 21.7 cm.

Contents: This is a typescript (black ribbon) of the text of the poem as it appeared in BR, with slight changes.

d. A NEW SEQUENCE.

Collation: 4*l* all recto 27.9 x 21.6 cm.

Contents: This is a typescript (black ribbon) of the first section of AN ESSAY AT WAR with some differences as compared to the published version.

F252 VOLUME I OF A BOOK OF RESEMBLANCES| BY ROBERT DUN-CAN WITH ILLUSTRATIONS BY JESS. T. & A. ms. MoSW.

a. A. ms.

Date: [1962].

Collation: 1*l* recto 21.5 x 22.7 cm.

Contents: This is a pencil draft of an introductory statement.

b. A. ms.

Date: [1962].

Collation: 1*l* recto 21.5 x 22.7 cm.

Contents: An expanded version of item "a."

c. T. ms.

Date: [1962].

Collation: 1*l* recto 21.5 x 24 cm.

Contents: This is a typed (black ribbon) version of item "b" with one holograph addition by RD.

F253 *A Book of Resemblances.* T. ms. MoSW.

Date: [1962].

Collation: 40*l* all recto 27.9 x 21.5 cm.

Contents: The contents-page is so different from the published contents that a full list is necessary: THE HORNS OF ARTEMIS—AFRICA REVISITED—WORKING TOO LONG AT IT—ADAM'S SONG—AN IMAGINARY WAR ELEGY—THE SONG OF THE BORDER-GUARD—FROM AN ESSAY AT WAR—OF THE ART—FROM FRAGMENTS OF A DISORDERD DEVOTION [section-title for seven following poems] FIVE PIECES—HERO SONG—AN IMAGINARY WOMAN—ELUARD'S DEATH—CATS (1)—CATS (2)—HOME—AUBADE—FORCED LINES—THE LANDSCAPE REVISED TO PORTRAY A REALITY—AN INTERLUDE. OF RARE BEAUTY—A TRAIN OF THOUGHT—A POEM IN STRETCHING—INCREASING—THIS IS THE POEM THEY ARE PRAISING AS LOADED—ORCHARDS—SENTENCES: CAR-RYING WEIGHTS AND MEASURES—A BOOK OF RESEMBLAN-CES—HOW DO YOU KNOW YOU ARE THRU?— ROTUND RELIGION—THREE—RHYME MOUNTAIN PARTICULAR—SEVERAL POEMS. IN PROSE—A BIRTHDAY DIRGE FOR LYNNE BROWN—A DREAM OF THE END OF THE WORLD—LORD MASTER MOUSE—SURREALIST SHELLS— CONVER-SION—SALVAGES: AN EVENING PIECE—IN THE SERVICE OF

LOVE—SALVAGES: LASSITUDE—FRIEDL—TWO POEMS FOR THE JEWS—IMAGE OF HECTOR—THE LOVER. Then at the bottom of the page there are three numbered titles in holograph: 1. POETRY DISARRANGED [to follow SEVERAL POEMS. IN PROSE]—2. THESE MIRACLES ARE MIRRORS IN THE OPEN SKY [to follow SURREALIST SHELLS]—3. THE SCATTERING [to follow TWO POEMS FOR THE JEWS].

Note: In FROM AN ESSAY AT WAR, parts one and two appear, with part three being deleted; the poem HOME was later retitled UNKINGD BY AFFECTION; in the typescript, IN THE SERVICE OF LOVE has the title REFLECTIONS.

F254 *A Book of Resemblances.* T. ms. MoSW.
 Date: [1962].
 Collation: 62*l* all recto 27.9 x 21.5 cm.
 Contents: The contents are the same as listed for the preceding typed manuscript (F253) except for the following changes: DANCE, EARLY SPRING WEATHER MAGIC appears before AUBADE; SMOKING THE CIGARETTE appears after AN INTERLUDE OF RARE BEAUTY; POETRY DISARRANGED appears after SEVERAL POEMS: IN PROSE; THESE MIRACLES ARE MIRRORS IN THE OPEN SKY appears after SURREALISTIC SHELLS; IN THE SERVICE OF LOVE has the title LOVE POEM; THE SCATTERING appears before THE IMAGE OF HECTOR; THE LOVER has been deleted; and the whole text of THE ESSAY AT WAR appears.
 Note: The table of contents does not appear with this carbon copy.

F255 ADAM'S WAY. T. ms. CU-B.
 Date: [1962].
 a. *Collation:* 6*l* all recto 27.9 x 21.5 cm.
 Contents: This is a thermofax and carbon copy of the beginning of the play.
 b. *Collation:* 6*l* all recto 27.8 x 21.6 cm.
 Contents: This is a typescript (black ribbon) of the beginning of the play.

F256 WHAT HAPPENED: PRELUDE. A. ms. NBuU.
 Date: 23 Jan. 1962.
 Collation: 2*l* recto-verso, recto-verso 28 x 21.6 cm.
 Contents: Thirty lines of what became, with revisions, the third section of WHAT HAPPENED: PRELUDE appear in a letter to Helen Adam, dated 23 Jan. 1962. E572.

F257 WHAT HAPPENED: PRELUDE. A. ms. NBuU.
 Date: 31 Jan. 1962.
 Collation: 3*l* all recto-verso 28 x 21.6 cm.
 Contents: Seventy-five lines of what became the first section of the poem in RB and thirty-eight lines of what became the fourth section

in RB appear in a letter to Helen Adam, dated 31 Jan. 1962. Revisions and additions were made before publication. E574.

F258 [Three Poems]. T. ms. CU-B.
Date: [23 May 1962].
Collation: 2*l* recto, recto 27.9 x 21.6 cm.
Contents: This is a typescript (black ribbon) of the texts of the poems, SONNET 1—SONNET 2—SONNET 3, plus an a.n.s. to Jack Spicer on the verso of the second leaf.

F259 [Three Poems]. T. ms. CU-B.
Date: 12 June 1962.
Collation: 3*l* all recto; 2*l* 27.9 x 21.6 cm., 1*l* 23.7 x 21.5 cm.
Contents: The first two leaves are carbon copies, while the third is a typescript (black ribbon) of the texts of the following poems which appear in RB: THANK YOU FOR LOVE—FROM *THE MABINO-GION*—FORCED IMAGES. The title of the third poem was later changed to FORCED LINES and some revisions were made.
Note: This typescript accompanied a letter to Jack Spicer, dated 12 June 1962. E586.

F260 AND THERE EVER TO DISCOURSE OF LOVE. T. ms. On deposit at MoSW.
Date: [20 July 1962]
Collation: 7*l* all recto 27.9 x 21.6 cm.
Contents: This is a typescript (black ribbon) of a review by RD of Creeley's *For Love*, as published in *New Mexico Quarterly*. C124.
Note: The typescript accompanied a letter to Robert Creeley, dated 20 July and 10 Aug. 1962. E589.

F261 [Three Poems]. T. ms. TxU.
Date: [20 Aug. 1962].
Collation: 1*l* recto-verso 21.6 x 18.5 cm.
Contents: This is a typescript (black ribbon) of the texts of the following poems as they appeared in RB SONNET 1—SONNET 2—SONNET 3.
Note: This typescript was enclosed in a letter to Celia and Louis Zukofsky, dated 20 Aug. 1962. E592.

F262 FOR THE NOVICES OF VANCOUVER AUGUST 25-28, 1962. T. ms. CU-B.
Date: 25-28 Aug. 1962.
Collation: 5*l* all recto 28 x 21.6 cm.
Contents: This is a typescript of the essay. C122.

F263 WINDINGS. T. ms. CtY.
Date: [5, 12, and 18 Sept. 1962].
Collation: 53*l* all recto 27.9 x 21.5 cm.
Contents: Contents-page—(I)—TWO PRESENTATIONS—AFTER

A PASSAGE IN BAUDELAIRE—SHELLEY'S *ARETHUSA* SET TO A NEW MEASURE—AFTER READING H.D.'S *HERMETIC DEFINITIONS*—STRAINS OF SIGHT—DOVES—RETURNING TO THE RHETORIC OF AN EARLY MODE—(II)—THE BALLAD OF THE FORFAR WITCHES' SING—A PLAY WITH MASKS—(III)—WHAT HAPPENED: PRELUDE—(IV)—A SET OF ROMANTIC HYMNS—THANK YOU FOR LOVE—FROM *THE MABINOGION*—FORCED LINES—SONNET I—SONNET II—SONNET III—ANSWERING.

Note: The contents-page lists a Part (V) consisting of A PLAY FOR THE MOON, but that part is not present in the typescript. The contents-page gives the title FORCED IMAGES, while in the text the title FORCED LINES appears; and the contents-page gives the title A NEW POEM while in the text the title A NEW POEM (FOR JACK SPICER) appears. A PLAY WITH MASKS was published in *Audit/Poetry*, but the remaining titles appeared as part of WINDINGS (1961-63) in BB (C189). Part (I) of this typescript accompanied a letter to Norman Holmes Pearson, dated 5 Sept. 1962; Parts (II) and (III) accompanied a letter to Norman Holmes Pearson, dated 12 Sept. 1962; Part (IV) accompanied a letter to Norman Holmes Pearson, dated 18 Sept. 1962. E595, E596, E598.

F264 [Four Poems]. T. ms. CU-B.
Date: [1963].
Collation: 2l recto, recto 27.9 x 21.6 cm.
Contents: This is a typescript (black ribbon) of the text of the following poems: STRUCTURE OF RIME XIX—STRUCTURE OF RIME XX—STRUCTURE OF RIME XXI—14 FINAL LINES OF A PART-SEQUENCE FOR CHANGE.

F265 a. *Roots and Branches.* T. ms. CU-B.
Date: [1963].
Collation: 47l all recto 33 x 21.5 cm.
Contents: This is a typescript (black ribbon) of the texts of the following poems: ROOTS AND BRANCHES—WHAT DO I KNOW OF THE OLD LORE?—NIGHT SCENES—A SEQUENCE OF POEMS FOR H.D.'S 73RD BIRTHDAY—DEAR CARPENTER— NEL MEZZO DEL CAMMIN DI NOSTRA VITA—A DANCING CONCERNING A FORM OF WOMEN—THE LAW— APPREHENSIONS—SONNERIES OF THE ROSE CROSS—NOW THE RECORD NOW RECORD—TWO DICTA OF WILLIAM BLAKE—COME, LET ME FREE MYSELF—RISK—FOUR SONGS THE NIGHT NURSE SANG—STRUCTURE OF RIME XV— STRUCTURE OF RIME XVI—STRUCTURE OF RIME XVII— STRUCTURE OF RIME XVIII—OSIRIS AND SET—AFTER A PASSAGE IN BAUDELAIRE—SHELLEY'S *ARETHUSA* SET TO A NEW MEASURE—AFTER READING H.D.'S *HERMETIC DEFINI-*

TIONS—STRAINS OF SIGHT—ANOTHER FOR HELEN ADAM "THE BALLAD OF THE FORFAR WITCHES' SING OUT OF THE SCOTS INTO OUR AMERICAN TONGUE" (fl)— DOVES— RETURNING TO THE RHETORIC OF AN EARLY MODE—IT WAS NOT HIDDEN BUT MOST CLEAR [incomplete]— A SET OF ROMANTIC HYMNS.

b. OSIRIS AND SET.

Collation: 2l recto, recto 33 x 21.5 cm.
Contents: These are two carbon copies of p. 33 of the main manuscript.

c. [Three Poems].
Collation: 3l all recto 33 x 21.5 cm.
Contents: These are carbon copies of pp. 26-28 containing COME, LET ME FREE MYSELF—[3 stanzas of] RISK—[20 lines of] FOUR SONGS THE NIGHT NURSE SANG of the main manuscript.

d. [Two Poems].
Collation: 1l recto 33 x 21.5 cm.
Contents: This is a carbon of p. 34 of the main manuscript, with AFTER A PASSAGE IN BAUDELAIRE [opening lines of] SHEL-LEY'S *ARETHUSA* SET TO A NEW MEASURE.

e. [Four Poems].
Collation: 2l recto, recto 33 x 21.5 cm.
Contents: This is a typescript of the text of the following poems as they appear in RB: STRUCTURE OF RIME XV—STRUCTURE OF RIME XVI—STRUCTURE OF RIME XVII—STRUCTURE OF RIME XVIII

f. [Four Poems].
Collation: 4l all recto 33 x 21.5 cm.
Contents: These are two carbon copies of item e, STRUCTURE OF RIME XV through XVIII.

F266 PART TWO: NIGHTS AND DAYS. T. ms. CtY.
Date: [1963].
Collation: 110l all recto, all numbered; 109l 27.9 x 21.6 cm., 1l 15.7 x 21.6 cm.
Contents: This is a typescript (black ribbon) of the first three chapters of the second part of "The H.D. Book." There are slight changes throughout.
Note: The typescript is bound in a standard black binder.

F267 BENDING THE BOW. T. ms. CU-B.
Date: 1963.
Collation: 1l recto 22 x 21.7 cm.
Contents: This is a typescript (black ribbon) of the text of the poem as revised for publication in BB.

F268 [THREE SONNETS]. T. ms. CU-B.

    Date: [1963].

    Collation: 2*l* recto, recto 28 x 21.6 cm.

    Contents: This is a typescript (black ribbon) of the texts of SONNET 1—SONNET 2—SONNET 3 as they appeared, with slight revision in RB.

F269 A PART-SEQUENCE FOR CHANGE. T. ms. CU-B.

    Date: [1963].

    Collation: 2*l* recto, recto 27.9 x 21.6 cm.

    Contents: This is a typescript (black ribbon) of the poem.

F270 A PART-SEQUENCE FOR CHANGE. T. ms. CtU.

    Date: Nov. 1962-March 1963.

    Collation: 2*l* recto, recto; 1*l* 23 x 21.6 cm., 1*l* 20.6 x 21.6 cm.

    Contents: This is a typescript (black ribbon) of the text of the poem.

    Note: The poem contains slight changes in its appearance in *Change* and in the later appearance in RB. This typescript, first leaf, recto at right top, contains a holograph annotation by Charles Olson.

F271 THE CONTINENT. T. ms. CtU.

    Date: [26 April 1963].

    Collation: 3*l* all recto 17.8 x 21.5 cm.

    Contents: This is a typescript (black ribbon) of the poem as it appeared in BB. There are two slight changes in spacing and stanza length in the published version.

    Note: This typescript accompanied a letter to Charles Olson, dated 26 April 1963. E635.

F272 SUCH IS THE SICKNESS OF MANY A GOOD THING. T. ms. On deposit at MoSW.

    Date: [20 Nov. 1963].

    Collation: 1*l* recto 27.9 x 21.7 cm.

    Contents: This is a typescript (black ribbon) of thirty-eight lines of the text of the poem, with a holograph note at top and bottom.

    Note: This typescript accompanied a letter to Robert Creeley, dated 20 Nov. 1963. E654.

F273 THE CONTINENT. T. ms. CtY.

    Date: [10 June 1963].

    Collation: 3*l* all recto 27.8 x 21.5 cm.

    Contents: This is a typescript (black ribbon) of the text of the poem. There is a short holograph note at the top recto of the first leaf and minor holograph changes.

    Note: This typescript accompanied a letter to Norman Holmes Pearson, dated 10 June 1963. E639.

F274 POSTSCRIPT FOR *OPEN SPACE*, JANUARY 1964. T. ms. CU-B.

    Date: Jan. 1964.

Collation: 2*l* recto, recto 27.9 x 21.7 cm.

Contents: This is a typescript (black ribbon) of the piece.

Note: A holograph note by RD appears at top and bottom of the first leaf, and there are slight changes in RD's holograph.

F275 WINE. T. ms. CtU.

> *Date:* [Spring 1964].
>
> *Collation:* 2*l* recto, recto; 1*l* 33 x 21.7 cm., 1*l* 18 x 21.7 cm.
>
> *Contents:* This is a typescript (black ribbon) of the poem marked by the printer for the preparation of the broadside issued by Oyez in 1964.

F276 THESE PAST YEARS (PASSAGES 9). T. & A. ms. CaACU.

> *Date:* [Spring 1964].
>
> *Collation:* 1*l* recto 28 x 21.5 cm.
>
> *Contents:* This is a typescript (carbon) of the text of the poem, with the title THESE PAST YEARS in the poet's holograph, which appeared in *Imago.* C149.

F277 AS A PREFACE TO CHARLES OLSON'S "PROPRIOCEPTION" ESSAY. T. ms. CtU.

> *Date:* April 1964.
>
> *Collation:* 2*l* recto, recto 27.9 x 21.5 cm.
>
> *Contents:* This is a typescript (black ribbon) of the text of the preface, with a line added at the bottom of the second leaf recto in RD's holograph (black pen).
>
> *Note:* A note written by RD in 1975 explaining that the preface was not used by Donald Allen in the edition of Olson's essay accompanies this typescript (black ribbon).

F278 [Six Poems]. T. ms. CtU.

> *Date:* [29 May 1964].
>
> *Collation:* 7*l* all recto 27.9 x 21.6 cm.
>
> *Contents:* This is a typescript (black ribbon) of the following poems, I—II—4—PASSAGES 5—PASSAGES 6—PASSAGES 7, which appear with altered titles and some revisions as follows: I becomes TRIBAL MEMORIES, PASSAGES 1 in BB; II becomes AT THE LOOM, PASSAGES 2 in BB; 4 becomes THE MOON, PASSAGES 5 in BB; PASSAGES 5 becomes THE COLLAGE, PASSAGES 6 in BB; PASSAGES 6 becomes ENVOY, PASSAGES 7 in BB; PASSAGES 7 becomes AS IN THE OLD DAYS, PASSAGES 8 in BB.
>
> *Note:* This typescript accompanied a letter to Charles Olson, dated 29 May 1964. E670.

F279 [Three Poems]. T. ms. CtU.

> *Date:* [18 June 1964].
>
> *Collation:* 4*l* all recto 27.8 x 21.5 cm.
>
> *Contents:* This is a typescript (black ribbon) of the text of the following poems PASSAGES 7—PASSAGES 8—PASSAGES 9 as they appeared in *Open Space.* C153

Note: When the poems were published in BB, with slight revisions, PASSAGES 7 becomes AS IN THE OLD DAYS, PASSAGES 8; PASSAGES 8 becomes THE ARCHITECTURE PASSAGES 9; and PASSAGES 9 becomes THESE PAST YEARS PASSAGES 10. The typescript accompanied a letter to Charles Olson, dated 18 June 1964. E671.

F280 [Two Poems]. T. ms. CtU.
Date: [3 July 1964].
Collation: 5*l* all recto 27.9 x 21.6 cm.
Contents: This is a typescript (black carbon) of the two poems, PASSAGES 12—PASSAGES 13.
Note: PASSAGES 12 becomes THE FIRE, PASSAGES 13 in BB with slight changes. PASSAGES 13 becomes CHORDS PASSAGES 14 in BB, with slight changes. The latter poem in this manuscript version contains the Greek passages in RD's holograph. This typescript accompanied a letter to Charles Olson, dated 3 July 1964. E674.

F281 [Two Poems]. T. ms. MoSW.
Date: [5 Nov. 1964].
Collation: 2*l* recto, recto 27.8 x 21.5 cm.
Contents: This is a typescript (carbon copy) of the text of the poems, WINE—THE FIRE. The first appeared in BB as WINE, PASSAGES 12 and the second as THE FIRE, PASSAGES 13.
Note: The poems accompanied a letter to David Schaff dated 5 Nov. 1964. E694.

F282 MOVING THE MOVING IMAGE [PASSAGES 17]. T. ms. MoSW.
Date: [5 Nov. 1964].
Collation: 2*l* recto, recto 27.8 x 21.5 cm.
Contents: This is a typescript (black ribbon) of the poem, which appeared in BB as MOVING THE MOVING IMAGE, PASSAGES 17.
Note: This typescript contains RD's directions in the margins for printing the poem and accompanied a letter to David Schaff, dated 5 Nov. 1964. E694.

F283 [Two Poems]. T. ms. MoSW.
Date: 14 Nov. 1964.
Collation: 3*l* all recto 27.8 x 21.5 cm.
Contents: This is a typescript (black ribbon) of the texts of the poems THE EARTH PASSAGES 19—STRUCTURE OF RIME XXVI PASSAGES 20 which were published, with slight changes, as THE EARTH, PASSAGES 19 and STRUCTURE OF RIME XXVI PASSAGES 20—AN ILLUSTRATION in BB.
Note: These poems accompanied a letter to David Schaff, dated 5 Nov. 1964. E694.

F284 [Four Poems]. T. ms. On deposit at MoSW.
Date: [30 Nov. 1964].

Collation: 6*l* all recto 27.9 x 21.6 cm.

Contents: This is a typescript (carbon copy) of the texts of the poems as they appeared, with slight revisions, in BB: THE CURRENTS, PASSAGES 16—MOVING THE MOVING IMAGE, [PASSAGES 17]—THE TORSO, PASSAGES 18—THE EARTH, PASSAGES 19.

Note: This typescript accompanied a letter to Robert Creeley, dated 30 Nov. 1964. E696.

F285 [THE SWEETNESS AND GREATNESS OF DANTE'S DIVINE COMEDY]. T. ms. CU-B.
Date: 1965.
Collation: 19*l* all recto 27.9 x 21.6 cm.
Contents: This is a typescript (black ribbon) of the essay as published. The first two leaves are missing.

F286 SIX PROSE PIECES. T. ms. MoSW.
Date: [1965].
Collation: 8*l* all recto 27.8 x 21.5 cm.
Contents: This is a typescript (black ribbon) of the text as published.
Note: The pages are numbered 1-8. "Five Prose Pieces" appears at top right of the first page, and it is changed in black ink to "Six." There are some additions in RD's holograph.

F287 THE HORNS OF ARTEMIS. A. ms. OKentU.
Date: [1965?].
Collation: 1*l* recto 25.2 x 32.9 cm.
Contents: This is a holograph version of the text of the poem.
Note: The poem appears as if it were drawn for inclusion in BR. However, the format of the page is not the same as the published version, though the text is the same as in BR.

F288 PASSAGES 23 ARRIVAL. A. ms. CtU.
Date: 1965.
Collation: 1*l* recto 21.6 x 16.6 cm.
Contents: This is a holograph version of text of the poem as it appeared with slight revisions in BB.
Note: The initials "RD" appear in the lower right corner.

F289 SPECIAL NOTES ON GALLEY SHEETS. T. ms. CtU.
Date: Spring 1965.
Collation: 4*l* all recto 27.9 x 21.5 cm.
Contents: In this typescript (black ribbon) RD gives comments and correction for the galley sheets of *Medea at Kolchis: The Maidenhead*, which accompany these notes. A holograph note appears at bottom recto of the first leaf.

F290 LAMMAS DREAM POEM. T. ms. KU.
Date: [9 June 1965].
Collation: 2*l* recto, recto 27.8 x 21.5 cm.

Contents: This is a typescript (black ribbon) of the piece.

Note: In BB, the original prose introduction was separated, revised and expanded, and printed as A LAMMAS TIDING. The poem appears as MY MOTHER WOULD BE A FALCONRESS with slight revisions. This typescript accompanied a letter to Thomas Clark, dated 9 June 1965. E711.

F291 [UNKINGD BY AFFECTION]. A. ms. MoSW.
    Date: [1966].
    Collation: 1*l* recto 15.1 x 21.6 cm.
    Contents: This is a holograph of the text of the poem as published in RB with slight changes.

F292 AN ESSAY AT WAR. T. ms. CU-B.
    Date: [1966].
    Collation: 12*l* all recto 27.8 x 21.5 cm.
    Contents: This is a typescript (black ribbon) of the text of the poem as prepared for D.

F293 BENDING THE BOW. T. ms. MoSW.
    Date: [1966].
    Collation: 94*l* all recto 28 x 21.6 cm.
    Contents: PREFACE—SONNET 4—STRUCTURE OF RIME XXII—5TH SONNET—SUCH IS THE SICKNESS OF MANY A GOOD THING—BENDING THE BOW—TRIBAL MEMORIES, PASSAGES 1—AT THE LOOM, PASSAGES 2—WHAT I SAW, PASSAGES 3—WHERE IT APPEARS, PASSAGES 4—THE MOON, PASSAGES 5—THE COLLAGE, PASSAGES 6—ENVOY, PASSAGES 7—STRUCTURE OF RIME XXIII—AS IN THE OLD DAYS, PASSAGES 8—THE ARCHITECTURE, PASSAGES 9—THESE PAST YEARS, PASSAGES 10—SHADOWS, PASSAGES 11—WINE, PASSAGES 12—STRUCTURE OF RIME XXIV—STRUCTURE OF RIME XXV—REFLECTIONS—THE FIRE, PASSAGES 13—CHORDS, PASSAGES 14—SPELLING, PASSAGES 15—A LAMMAS TIDING—"MY MOTHER WOULD BE A FALCONRESS" (fl)—SAINT GRAAL (AFTER VERLAINE)—PARSIFAL (AFTER VERLAINE AND WAGNER)—THE CURRENTS, PASSAGES 16—MOVING THE MOVING IMAGE, PASSAGES 17—THE TORSO, PASSAGES 18—THE EARTH, PASSAGES 19—AN ILLUSTRATION, PASSAGES 20—(STRUCTURE OF RIME XXVI)—THE MULTIVERSITY, PASSAGES 21—IN THE PLACE OF A PASSAGE 22—BENEFICE, PASSAGES 23—ORDERS, PASSAGES 24—UP RISING, PASSAGES 25—THE CHIMERAS OF GÉRARD DE NERVAL [sequence title for following eight poems] EL DESDICHADO—MYRTHO—HORUS—ANTEROS— DELPHICA—ARTEMIS—THE CHRIST IN THE OLIVE GROVE— GOLDEN LINES—EARTH'S WINTER SONG—MOIRA'S CATHEDRAL— A SHRINE TO AMEINIAS—NARRATION FOR *ADAM'S WAY*—

THE SOLDIERS, PASSAGES 26—TRANSGRESSING THE REAL, PASSAGES 27—THE LIGHT, PASSAGES 28—EYE OF GOD, PASSAGES 29—STAGE DIRECTIONS, PASSAGES 30—GOD-SPELL—EPILOGOS—NOTES.

F294 BENDING THE BOW. T. ms. MoSW.
Date: [1966].
a. *Collation:* 2*l* recto, recto 27.9 x 21.6 cm.
Contents: This is a typescript (black ribbon) of the contents-pages.
b. *Collation:* 1*l* recto 27.9 x 21.6 cm.
Contents: This is a typescript (black ribbon) of a list of books by RD.
c. *Collation:* 11*l* all recto 27.9 x 21.6 cm.
Contents: This is a typescript (carbon copy) of the introduction.
d. *Collation:* 2*l* recto, recto 27.9 x 21.6 cm.
Contents: This is a typescript (black ribbon) of the notes.

F295 THE YEARS AS CATCHES. T. ms. CaBVU.
Date: [1966].
a. I AM A MOST FLESHLY MAN.
Collation: 2*l* recto, recto 27.9 x 21.6 cm.
Contents: This is a typescript (black ribbon) of the text of the poem as published.
b. Contents-pages.
Collation: 2*l* recto, recto 27.9 x 21.6 cm.
Contents: This is a typescript of the book's contents-pages as published.
c. Bibliography.
Collation: 3*l* all recto 27.9 x 21.6 cm.
Contents: This is a typescript (black ribbon) of the bibliography pages as published, with one addition in RD's hand.
d. "Notes on Proofs, Sept. 25 1966."
Collation: 2*l* recto, recto 27.9 x 21.6 cm.
Contents: This is a typescript (black ribbon) of RD's corrections for the proofs.

F296 [OF THE WAR]. T. ms. CtU.
Date: 1966.
Collation: 12*l* all recto 27.9 x 21.6 cm.
Contents: IN THE PLACE OF A PASSAGES 22—PASSAGES 23—ORDERS, PASSAGES 24—UP RISING—PASSAGES 26: THE SOLDIERS—TRANSGRESSING THE REAL—PASSAGES 27.
Note: The third leaf contains a holograph note of explanation by RD. PASSAGES 26: THE SOLDIERS appears here as a carbon copy, but the other poems appear in black ribbon as typed for publication by Oyez.

F297 BEGINNINGS: CHAPTER 1 OF THE H.D. BOOK, PART I. T. ms. CaBVaS.

Date: [1966].
Collation: 31*l* all recto 27.9 x 21.5 cm.
Contents: This is a typescript (black ribbon) of the essay as it appeared in *Coyote's Journal.* C179.
Note: The final typed copy on heavy white paper, numbered pp. 8-31, and the final proof copy on glossy stock, numbered pp. 8-31, also accompany this typescript.

F298 [INTRODUCTION FOR] *Single Source* [by William Everson]. T. ms. MoSW.
Date: [Jan. Feb. 1966].
Collation: 3*l* all recto 34.4 x 21.5 cm.
Contents: This is a typescript (black ribbon) of RD's introduction to William Everson's collection of his poetry from 1934 to 1940.

F299 [INTRODUCTION] FOR *A Book of Resemblances.* A. & T. ms. MoSW.
a. A. ms.
Date: April 1966.
Collation: 9*l* all recto 21.5 x 27.8 cm.
Contents: This is a holograph version of the introduction.
b. T. ms.
Date: April-May 1966.
Collation: 8*l* all recto 21.5 x 27.8 cm.
Contents: The numbers 1-8 appear at the top right in RD's hand and at the bottom right in the printer's hand. There are some slight holograph markings by RD; the leaves contain printer's markings throughout. Leaf 8 is the acknowledgments-page.

F300 CORRECTIONS AND REWRITE ON | PASSAGES 26: THE SOL-DIERS | FROM | PASSAGES 22-27 OF THE WAR. T. ms. CtU.
Date: [May 1966].
Collation: 1*l* recto 19.3 x 21.7 cm.
Contents: This typescript (black ribbon) contains minor corrections for stanza three of PASSAGES 26: THE SOLDIERS and a revision of 11 lines.

F301 [INTRODUCTION FOR *A Book of Resemblances*]. T. ms. MoSW.
Date: 9 May 1966.
Collation: 6*l* all recto 27.8 x 21.6 cm.
Contents: This is a typescript (photocopy) of the INTRODUCTION as it appears in BR with one deletion.
Note: The original copy used by the printer accompanied a letter to Henry Wenning, dated 9 May 1966. E753.

F302 FOR ORION | RAPHAEL BROUGHTON | HIS CHRISTENING DAY | FROM | HIS GODFATHER. A. ms. OKentU.
Date: 15 May 1966.

Collation: 2*l* recto, recto 21.6 x 16.6 cm.

Contents: This is a holograph (black ink) text in forty-four lines of an unpublished poem.

Note: The first letters of the first two words are decorated in various colors. The leaves have been sewn into boards which are decorated with gold paper, with a white-and-green design on the front cover. The spine is held together with blue tape.

F303 TEXT FOR PAGE 3 OF ANNOUNCEMENT FOR *A Book of Resemblances.* T. ms. MoSw.

Date: [24 July 1966].

Collation: 1*l* recto 27.8 x 21.5 cm.

Contents: This is a typescript (black ribbon) of p. 3 of the announcement.

Note: This typescript accompanied a letter to Henry Wenning, dated 24 July 1966. E760.

F304 TRANSGRESSING THE REAL: PASSAGES 27. T. ms. CU-B.

Date: [28 July 1966].

Collation: 2*l* recto, recto 27.0 x 21.7 cm

Contents: This is a typescript (black ribbon) of the text of the poem as it appeared in BB with some revisions.

Note: This poem accompanied a note to Robin Blaser, dated 28 July 1966. E761.

F305 PASSAGES 26: THE SOLDIERS. T. ms. CU-B.

Date: [28 July 1966].

Collation: 3*l*; 2*l* recto, recto 27.9 x 21.8 cm., 1*l* recto 20 x 21.8 cm.

Contents: This is a typescript (carbon) of the poem as it appeared in BB, with some revisions.

Note: This typescript accompanied a note to Robin Blaser, dated 28 July 1966. E761.

F306 AN INTERLUDE. T. ms. NBuU.

Date: [28 July 1966].

Collation: 2*l* recto, recto 28 x 21.7 cm.

Contents: This is the typescript (black ribbon) of the text of the poem as it appeared, with some revisions, in BB. The note in the author's hand, "(between *Passages* 26 and 27)," appears at the top recto of the first leaf.

Note: This typescript accompanied a letter to Helen and Pat Adam, dated 28 July 1966. E762.

F307 [Two Poems]. T. ms. CtU.

Date: 15 Sept. 1966.

Collation: 4*l* all recto 27.8 x 21.5 cm.

Contents: This is a typescript (black ribbon) of the text of the following poems: PASSAGES 28 THE LIGHT—EYE OF GOD PASSAGES 29.

Note: When the two poems were published in *Poetry*, C186, the title

PASSAGES 28 THE LIGHT became THE LIGHT PASSAGES 28. The title of the second poem remained the same. The typescript accompanied a letter to Charles Olson, dated 15 Sept. 1966. E769.

F308 EYE OF GOD, PASSAGES 29. T. ms. On deposit at MoSW.
Date: [15 Sept. 1966].
Collation: 3*l* all recto 27.9 x 21.6 cm.
Contents: This is a typescript (black ribbon) of the text of the poem as published in BB. There are three revisions in the poet's hand.
Note: This typescript accompanied a letter to Robert Creeley, dated 15 Sept. 1966. E768.

F309 [Two Pieces]. T. ms. MoSW.
Date: 24 Sept. 1966.
Collation: 2*l* recto, recto 27.8 x 21.5 cm.
Contents: These are typescripts (black ribbon) of two notes, NOTES ON PROOFS—ARTIST'S NOTES ON PROOFS, by RD and Jess on the proof sheets of BR.
Note: These notes accompanied a letter to Henry Wenning, dated 24 Sept. 1966. E772.

F310 [CORRECTIONS FOR *A BOOK OF RESEMBLANCES*]. A. ms. MoSW.
Date: 24 Sept. 1966.
Collation: 1*l* recto 16.2 x 5 cm.
Contents: This manuscript contains two corrections of the proof sheets of BR.
Note: This manuscript accompanied a letter to Henry Wenning, dated 24 Sept. 1966. E777.

F311 THE H.D. BOOK, PART 1: CHAPTER 2. T. ms. CaBVaS.
Date: [26 Sept. 1966].
Collation: 8*l* all recto 27.9 x 21.5 cm.
Contents: This is a typescript (black ribbon) of the text of the essay as it appeared in *Coyote's Journal*, C188.
Note: The final typed copy on heavy white paper, numbered pp. 27-35, accompanied this typescript.

F312 CORRECTIONS AND REWRITE ON PASSAGES 26: THE SOLDIERS FROM PASSAGES 22-27 OF THE WAR. T. ms. NNU.
Date: July 1965-July 1966, Oct. 1966.
Collation: 1*l* recto 19 x 21.5 cm.
Contents: This is a typescript (black ribbon) of the corrections and revisions of PASSAGES 26.

F313 RETURNING TO THE CHIMERAS OF GÉRARD DE NERVAL. T. ms. CU-B.
Date: Nov. 1966.
Collation: 4*l* all recto 27.9 x 21.6 cm.

Contents: This is the typescript (black ribbon) of the piece as it appeared in *Audit/Poetry* with significant revisions. C195.

F314 [Three Poems]. T. ms. CtU.
Date: [Winter 1966].
Collation: 4*l* all recto 28 x 21.6 cm.
Contents: This is a typescript (black ribbon) of the following poems as they appeared in YAC: AN ARK FOR LAWRENCE DURRELL—THE AWAKENING INTO DREAM—LOVE THERE; OUT OF THE DREAM, AND OUR BEAUTIFUL CHILD—A HISTORY OF MY FAMILY.
Note: These leaves are numbered 2A, 2B, 2C, and 2D.

F315 BENDING THE BOW. T. ms. MoSW.
Date: [1967].
Collation: 16*l* all recto 28 x 21.6 cm.
Contents: This is a typescript (black ribbon) of the contents-pages, books-by-Robert-Duncan page, introduction, and notes. Some corrections are in RD's hand.

F316 [NOTE FOR] A LAMMAS TIDING. T. ms. MoSW.
Date: [1967?].
Collation: 1*l* recto 14 x 21.5 cm.
Contents: This is a five line note.

F317 PASSAGES 30 STAGE DIRECTIONS. T. ms. NNU.
Date: [1967].
Collation: 3*l* all recto 27.9 x 21.6 cm.
Contents: This is a typescript (black ribbon) of the text of the poem as it appeared in BB.
Note: The Greek words are written in RD's holograph. There are some corrections and changes in the poet's hand in the typescript.

F318 [Sixteen Poems]. T. ms. NNU.
Date: [1967].
Collation: 15*l* all recto 33 x 21.5 cm.
Contents: This is a typescript (black ribbon) of TRIBAL MEMORIES—AT THE LOOM—WHAT I SAW—WHERE IT APPEARS—THE MOON—THE COLLAGE—ENVOY—THE STRUCTURE OF RIME XXIII—AS IN THE OLD DAYS—THE ARCHITECTURE—THESE PAST YEARS—SHADOWS—WINE— STRUCTURE OF RIME XXIV—THE FIRE—CHORDS as they appeared with slight changes in BB.

F319 RITES OF PARTICIPATION. T. ms. NNU.
Date: [1967].
Collation: 21*l* all recto 27.9 x 21.7 cm.
Contents: This is a typescript (black ribbon) of the essay as it appeared in *Caterpillar*. C197.

F320 RITES OF PARTICIPATION (PART II). T. ms. NNU.
Date: [1967].
Collation: 33*l* all recto 28.3 x 27.7 cm.
Contents: This is a typescript (photocopy) of the text of the essay as it appeared in *Caterpillar*. C201.
Note: The typed copy, ready for photocopying, accompanied this photocopy. F319.

F321 EPILOGOS. T. ms. NNU.
Date: 10 Aug. 1967.
Collation: 1*l* recto-verso 23.5 x 21.7 cm.
Contents: This is a typescript (black ribbon) of the poem as it appeared in the pamphlet published by Black Sparrow Press and in BB.
Note: There is a short holograph note by the poet at the bottom of the verso.

F322 THE TRUTH AND LIFE OF MYTH IN POETRY. T. ms. OKentU.
Date: [Sept. 1967].
Collation: 28*l* all recto; 2*l* 28 x 21.8 cm., 1*l* 23.6 x 21.8 cm., 1*l* 22.7 x 21.8 cm., 24*l* 28 x 21.8 cm.
Contents: This is a typescript (black ribbon) early version of the essay which appeared in *Parable, Myth & Language*. B28. Some minor holograph changes by the poet appear throughout.

F323 DISCUSSION. T. ms. OKentU.
Date: Oct. 1967.
Collation: 80*l* all recto 28 x 21.8 cm.
Contents: This is a full transcription of the tapes made at the conference, "A Meeting of Poets & Theologians to discuss Parable Myth & Language," 13-15 Oct. 1967. Sections of this transcript appear in *Parable, Myth & Language*. B28.
Note: Members of the conference whose remarks appear in the transcript are Samuel Laeuchli, Denise Levertov, James M. Robinson, Robert W. Funk, Stephen D. Crites, Robert Duncan, Hollis Summers, Amos N. Wilder, and Philip T. Zabriski.

F324 THE TRUTH AND LIFE OF MYTH IN POETRY. T. ms. OKentU.
Date: [Oct. 1967].
Collation: 56*l* all recto 28 x 21.8 cm.
Contents: This is a typescript (leaves 1-49 carbon; leaves 50-56 black ribbon) of the essay which was used for editing the selection which appeared in *Parable, Myth & Language*, and appears, with revisions, as the text of the essay as it was published by House of Books. A26.
Note: The typescript contains editorial markings throughout.

F325 "YES, I CARE DEEPLY AND YET" (fl). T. ms. OKentU.
Date: [Sept.-Oct. 1967].
Collation: 2*l* recto, recto; 1*l* 14.1 x 21.7 cm., 1*l* 26.4 x 21.7 cm.

Contents: This is a typescript (black ribbon) of the poem as it appeared on the verso back cover of *Parable, Myth & Language.* B28.

F326 THE H.D. BOOK PART II NIGHTS AND DAYS CHAPTER 2. T. ms. NNU.
Date: [1968].
Collation: 28*l* all recto 27.9 x 21.6 cm.
Contents: This is a typescript (photocopy) of the essay as it appeared in *Caterpillar.* C209.

F327 THE H.D. BOOK PART II NIGHTS AND DAYS CHAPTER 4. T. ms. NNU.
Date: [1968].
Collation: 36*l* all recto 27.9 x 21.5 cm.
Contents: This is a typescript (carbon) of the essay as it appeared in *Caterpillar.* C212.
Note: There are some changes and revisions in the poet's hand throughout this typescript.

F328 KINDS OF NOTATION USED IN *BENDING THE BOW.* T. ms. MoSW.
Date: 1968.
Collation: 3*l* all recto 27.9 x 21.5 cm.
Contents: This is a typescript (black ribbon) of RD's notes on the proof corrections and notation for the book.

F329 [Untitled Prose Piece]. T. ms. NNU.
Date: Aug. 1968.
Collation: 1*l* recto 27.9 x 21.6 cm.
Contents: This is a typescript (black ribbon) of a prose statement in the style of a book blurb about Clayton Eshleman's translations of César Vallejo's *Poemas Humanos.*

F330 WORK IN PROGRESS OCTOBER 12, 1968. T. ms. On deposit at MoSW.
Date: [12 Oct. 1968].
Collation: 3*l* all recto 27.9 x 21.6 cm.
Contents: This is a typescript (black ribbon) of unpublished poems on Job, with reading notes from the book of Job and notes from other sources.
Note: This typescript accompanied a letter to Robert Creeley, dated 12 Oct. 1968. E838.

F331 MAN'S FULFILLMENT IN ORDER AND STRIFE. T. ms. NNU.
Date: April-Nov. 1968.
Collation: 31*l* all recto 27.9 x 21.6 cm.
Contents: This is a typescript (photocopy) of the essay as it appeared in *Caterpillar.* C220.

F332 ACHILLES. T. ms. NBuU.

    Date: [9 Dec. 1968].

    Collation: 1*l* recto 28 x 21.6 cm.

    Contents: This is a typescript (black ribbon) of the poem published as ACHILLES' SONG, with revisions, mainly in line length and arrangements.

    Note: This typescript accompanied a letter which was the Christmas greeting to Helen and Pat Adam, dated 9 Dec. 1968. In later publication, the poem was dated 10 Dec. 1968. E840.

F333 PASSAGES 32. T. ms. CtU.

    Date: 1968/69.

    Collation: 4*l* all recto 27.8 x 21.6 cm.

    Contents: The text of the poem, as it appeared in *Tribunals,* with slight changes.

    Note: This typescript (carbon) of the poem is heavily annotated in blue ball-point pen by Charles Olson.

F334 TEXT FROM *THE CHIMERAS OF GÉRARD DE NERVAL* TO FOLLOW PAGE 91 IN THE FIRST EDITION OF BENDING THE BOW (NEW DIRECTIONS, 1968) and REVISIONS. T. ms. NNU.

    Date: [March] 1969.

    Collation: 2*l* recto, recto 28 x 21.5 cm.

    Contents: This is a typescript (black ribbon) of the note, the revisions, and the poem as they appeared in *Caterpillar.* C213.

F335 [INTERVIEW WITH ROBERT DUNCAN]. T. ms. CaACU.

    Date: [Spring 1969].

    Collation: 40*l* all recto 28 x 21.5 cm.

    Contents: This is a typescript (Gestetnered) of the interview conducted by George Bowering and Robert Hogg. A40.

F336 [INTERVIEW WITH ROBERT DUNCAN]. T. & A. ms. CaACU.

    Date: 18 July 1969.

    Collation: 40*l* all recto 28 x 21.5 cm.

    Contents: This is a typescript (Gestetnered) of the interview conducted by George Bowering and Robert Hogg.

    Note: The first leaf, recto-verso, contains a letter in RD's holograph to George [Bowering], and there are corrections and revisions in RD's hand throughout. A40.

F337 [Untitled Poem]. A. ms. NBuU.

    Date: [24 Oct. 1969].

    Collation: 2*l* recto, recto 15.3 x 22.3 cm.

    Contents: This is a holograph text in twenty-one lines of the unpublished poem "CALL HIM NIGHT'S LORD, AND HE COMES FORTH FROM NIGHT" (fl). A seven line note appears at the bottom recto of the second leaf.

Note: This manuscript accompanied a letter to Helen Adam, dated 24 Oct. 1969. E854.

F338 [NOTES AND COMMENTS ON CREELEY'S *A DAY BOOK*]. T. ms. On deposit at MoSW.
Date: 16 June 1970.
Collation: 3*l* all recto-verso; 2*l* 21.5 x 21.6 cm., 1*l* 27.9 x 21.5 cm.
Contents: This is a typescript (black ribbon) of RD's notes and comments on Creeley's diction and phrasing in *A Day Book*.
Note: These notes accompanied a letter to Robert Creeley, dated 16 June 1970. E862.

F339 STRUCTURE OF RIME XXVIII IN MEMORIAM WALLACE STEVENS. T. ms. CtU. A42.
Date: 20 March 1972.
Collation: 1*l* recto 27.8 x 21.5 cm.
Contents: This is a typescript (black ribbon) of the poem as printed as part of the program to commemorate RD's reading at the Wallace Stevens Memorial Program, 25 April 1972.
Note: There are slight changes in the poet's hand.

F340 READING RICH BLEVINS' ESSAY "THE MOMENT OF VISION" AND THINKING OF POUND'S *CANTOS*, and NOTES OCT. 31, 1973 ON THE STRUCTURE OF A POETIC TEMPERAMENT. T. ms. CaBVaS.
Date: [28 Nov. 1973].
Collation: 3*l* all recto 27.9 x 21.6 cm.
Contents: This is a typescript (black ribbon) of the pieces as they appeared in *Io*. C251.
Note: The first piece is dated by RD as written June 1973. A short holograph note appears at the top recto of the first leaf.

F341 MEMOIRS OF OUR TIME AND PLACE. T. ms. CSf-APA.
Date: 15 May 1974.
Collation: 2*l* recto, recto 27.9 x 21.6 cm.
Contents: This is a typescript (back ribbon) text of the broadside of the same name, with editorial notes and additions. A46.

F342 [Untitled]. A. ms. CU-S.
Date: [June 1975].
Collation: 1*l* recto 31.5 x 22.9 cm.
Contents: This is the text of an unpublished note, written on a yellow envelope.

F343 A FIRST RECITATION OF VOWEL PHONEMES. | (FOR JAMES BROUGHTON ON HIS 62ND BIRTHDAY NOV. 7, 1975). A. ms. OKentU.
Date: 7 Nov. 1975.
Collation: 1*l* recto 28 x 21.7 cm.

Contents: This is the text of an unpublished poem in thirty-two lines (black ink).

Note: The leaf is stapled inside a standard file folder, 29.8 x 32.7 cm., which has a cover drawing in black ink and red pencil with the following inscription: "First Recitation of Phonemes | [i] as in leaving Believs | This being the original manuscript | for James Broughton RD."

F344 [Untitled Poem]. A. ms. NBuU.
Date: [Fall 1977].
Collation: 1 *l* recto 35.7 x 21.6 cm.
Contents: This is a holograph version of the poem in fifty-four lines that was to be called EVOCATION OF THE HALLOWE'EN SPIRIT, AN AMUSEMENT FOR HELEN ADAM 1977. Corrections and deletions in the author's hand appear in the text.

F345 EVOCATION OF THE HALLOWE'EN SPIRIT, AN AMUSEMENT FOR HELEN ADAM 1977. T. ms. NBuU.
Date: [Fall 1977].
Collation: 1 *l* recto 27.9 x 21.6 cm.
Contents: This is a typescript (black ribbon) of the text of the poem in fifty-one lines.

F346 [Untitled Poem]. T. ms. CU-B.
Date: n.d.
Collation: 1 *l* recto 27.7 x 21.5 cm.
Contents: This is a typescript (black ribbon) of a nineteen line poem beginning: "NO MAN IS BEAUTIFUL | EXCEPT ISHTAR HAS TOUCHED HIM" (fl).

F347 WORKING TOO LONG AT IT. A. ms. CU-B.
Date: n.d.
Collation: 1 *l* recto 35.4 x 27.6 cm.
Contents: This is a holograph (black ink) transcription of twenty lines of the poem with the author's decorations in various colors at the start of the first and second stanzas.

F348 7 QUESTIONS, 7 ANSWERS. T. ms. CU-B.
Date: n.d.
Collation: 1 *l* recto 27.9 x 21.6 cm.
Contents: This is a typescript (black ribbon) of a twenty-two line poem.

F349 MOTHER BROTHER DOOR AND BED. T. ms. CU-B.
Date: n.d.
Collation: 1 *l* recto 28 x 21.6 cm.
Contents: This is a typescript (black ribbon) of a twenty-six line unpublished poem.

F350 APPENDIX (1 | NOTES FROM ARISTOTLE'S POLITICS). T. ms. CU-B.

Date: n.d.

Collation: 1*l* recto 27.9 x 21.5 cm.

Contents: This is the author's typescript (black ribbon) of notes from his reading.

F351 A NOTE ON *THE EFFORT*. A. ms. CU-B.

Date: n.d.

Collation: 1*l* recto-verso 24.2 x 21.7 cm.

Contents: RD comments (blue pen) on his poetics and this poem.

F352 SUCH IS THE SICKNESS OF MANY A GOOD THING. T. ms. CU-B.

Date: n.d.

Collation: 1*l* recto 22.5 x 21.7 cm.

Contents: This is a typescript (black ribbon) of the text of the poem.

F353 "WE SAID: THE HONEY WAS RARE" (fl). A. ms. OKentU.

Date: n.d.

Collation: 1*l* recto-verso 21.6 x 16.4 cm.

Contents: This is a holograph draft (black ribbon) of thirty-two lines of the poem. The leaf has been decorated in crayons of various colors.

F354 A FRESH START. T. ms. CU-B.

Date: n.d.

Collation: 4*l* all recto 28 x 21.5 cm.

Contents: This is a typescript (black ribbon) of an unpublished poem.

G.
Notebooks

G1   Notebook I. CU-B.
      Date: 1940.
      Description: This notebook contains 120 numbered pages, and is bound in gray cloth over boards 18.6 x 24 cm. Pages 1-4 and 59-60 have been cut out. RD has decorated the cover with a design in various colors.
      Contents: This notebook contains journal entries for the year 1940. There are pencil annotations in another hand.

G2   Notebook II. CU-B.
      Date: Nov. 1940 — Feb. 1941.
      Description: This notebook contains 298 numbered pages, and is bound in gray cloth over boards 18.7 x 24 cm. The front cover contains RD's horoscope as cast by Eduardo Sanchez.
      Contents: This notebook contains journal entries for the specified period, plus seven letters from various writers which have been sewn into the book. There are pencil annotations in another hand.

G3   Notebook III. CU-B.
      Date: 1941.
      Description: This notebook contains 200 numbered pages, and is bound in gray cloth over boards 19 x 24 cm.
      Contents: This notebook contains journal entries beginning Feb. 1941, on pp. 1-109 and 170. Pages 96-98 are blank. There are pencil annotations in another hand.

G4   Notebook IV. CU-B.
      Date: 1941-42.
      Description: This notebook contains 250 numbered pages, and is bound in gray cloth over boards 19 x 23.5 cm. The cover contains a crayon decoration by RD.
      Contents: This notebook contains journal entries, sections of poems, and letters for the period 1941-42.

G5   Notebook B. CU-B.
      Date: 1943, 1944, 1946, 1947, 1966, 1969.
      Description: This notebook contains 400 numbered pages, and is bound in gray cloth over boards 21.5 x 26.7 cm. The corners are tipped with the same maroon cloth that covers the spine. "Record" is stamped in gold on the spine.
      Contents: This notebook contains journal entries, notes from reading, and drafts of poems for the periods specified. The author has provided a table of contents on the first two unnumbered pages and on p. 180. Pages 1-16 are missing.

G6   Notebook A. CU-B.
      Date: 1945-47, 1949-50, 1959-60.
      Description: This notebook contains 150 numbered pages, and is bound in gray cloth over boards 19.5 x 32 cm., with maroon edges at

top and bottom. "Record" appears in maroon on the front cover, and a single maroon line runs around the front and rear covers.

Contents: This notebook contains drafts of poems and prose pieces for the periods specified. The author has provided a table of contents on the endpapers, p. 148, and p. 136. Pages 1-4 and 149-150 are missing.

G7 Notebook C. CU-B.
Date: 1947, 1961.
Description: This notebook contains 118 numbered pages, and is bound in gray cloth over boards 18.5 x 23.4 cm.
Contents: This notebook contains notes, reading notes, and drafts of poems for the periods specified. The author has made a title-page: "A Book of Dream | (copies from New York notebooks) | Robert Duncan," and he has supplied a table of contents on pp. 115-116.

G8 Notebook. D. CU-B.
Date: [1948, 1952-53].
Description: This notebook contains 210 pages, and is bound in green cloth over boards 17.5 x 23.5 cm. "Robert Duncan" is written across the front cover.
Contents: This notebook primarily contains a diary from 1942-1948 and the working manuscript of FAUST FOUTU.

G9 Notebook. CU-B.
Date: [June/Sept. 1948].
Description: This notebook contains 120 numbered pages, and is bound in gray cloth over boards 23 x 18.3 cm.
Contents: This notebook contains a preface on four unattached leaves. The drafts of the poems for HOMAGE TO THE BROTHERS GRIMM plus reading notes for and versions of THE VENICE POEM appear here.

G10 Notebook. CU-B.
Date: [Spring 1948].
Description: This notebook contains 120 numbered pages, and is bound in blue cloth over boards 23 x 18.3 cm.
Contents: This notebook contains reading notes from books about the Italian Renaissance.

G11 Notebook. CU-B.
Date: [Winter 1948].
Description: This notebook contains 120 numbered pages, and is bound in blue cloth over boards, 23 x 18.3 cm.
Contents: This notebook contains reading notes, notes on poetry and various topics, and drafts of poems.

G12 Notebook. CU-B.
Date: Fall 1954/Winter 1955.
Description: This notebook has 120 pages, and is bound in black

cloth over boards. A strip of yellow cloth forms the spine binding 23 x 18.3 cm.

Contents: This notebook contains numerous drafts of poems, some of which were published in *Letters*.

G13 Notebook. CtU.

Date: March-Aug. 1956.

Description: This is a spiral bound notebook with sixty-two pages, and a stiff brown paper cover 24 x 18 cm.

Contents: This notebook contains notes, and drafts of poems by RD, and notes by Charles Olson. RD used the notebook while in residence at Black Mountain College, and it was later used by Olson.

G14 Notebook D. CU-B.

Date: 1959-60.

Description: This notebook contains forty hand-numbered pages and is bound in heavy green paper, 17.5 x 23.5 cm.

Contents: This notebook contains notes and drafts of poems for the period specified. The author has supplied a table of contents inside the front cover.

H.
Translations into Foreign Languages

H1   Die Struktur des Verses I-VII. *Blätter Bilder, Zeitschrift für Dichtung, Musik und Malerie*, 6 (Jan.-Feb. 1960), 17-21. Wursburg-Wien, Austria. *Note:* A note on RD appears on p. 22, and there is a cover photograph of RD with Harry Martinson. Translated by Andreas Zettner.

H2   Benatska Basen. *Svetova Literature*, V (Dec. 5, 1962), 109-135. Prague. *Note:* THE VENICE POEM, unexpurgated version, translated by Stanislav Mares, appears with five illustrations by Jaroslav Serych. This is the first magazine appearance of the complete poem in any language. Translator's notes appear before the poem, pp. 108-109.

H3   *Poesia americana del '900 contesto a friste introduzioni e note bibliografiche a cura de Carlo Izzo [Parma, Italy: Guanda, 1963].* *Contribution:* Pages 658-669, STRAWBERRIES UNDER THE SNOW—Fragole sotto le neve—METAMORPHOSIS—La metamorfosi—AUGUST SUN—Sole d'augusto.

H4   *Poesia degli ultimi americani*, a cura di Feranda Pivano. Milano, Italy: Giangiacomo Feltrinelle Editore, 1964. *Contribution:* Pages 100-117, AFTER A PASSAGE IN BAUDELAIRE— Su un brando di Baudelaire—THE MAIDEN—La vergine—INGMAR BERGMAN'S *SEVENTH SEAL*—"Il settimo" di Ingmar Bergman—FOOD FOR FIRE, FOOD FOR THOUGHT—Alimento per il fuoco, alimento per il pensiero.

H5   Alimento para el fuego, para el pensamiento, *Dialogos (Artes/Letras)*, I, 4 (May-June 1965), 19. Mexico City. *Note:* RD's poem FOOD FOR FIRE, FOOD FOR THOUGHT was translated by José Emilio Pacheco.

H6   Talé o fastio de tanta cosa bõa. *Jornal do Commercio* (28 Nov. 1965), 5. Rio de Janeiro, Brazil. *Note:* RD's poem SUCH IS THE SICKNESS OF MANY A GOOD THING was translated by Stella Leonardos.

H7   UP RISING. *Sodom & Gomorrha: Zeitschrift für literarische Satire und Grafik*, 3 (Aug. 1966), 14-17. Berlin. *Note:* This unauthorized translation of RD's poem by Ernst A. Rauter appeared along with a reproduction of the original broadside publication of the poem.

H8   La catedral de Moira. *Haravec*, 3 (July 1967), 62-63. *Note:* The poem MOIRA'S CATHEDRAL was translated into Spanish by C. A. de Lomellini for this magazine published in Lima, Peru.

H9   Para uma elegia Africana. *Minas Gerais (Supplemento Literario)* 1, (4 April 1967), 5. Brazil. *Note:* RD's poem TOWARD AN AFRICAN ELEGY was translated by Alfonso Avila.

H10 *Obesnámeni s Noci [:] Noví Američti Básnĭci [Murmurings of the Night: New American Poetry]* trans. Stanislav Mareš and Jan Zábrana. Prague: Československý spisovatel, 1967.
Contribution: Pages 56-65, THE SONG OF THE BORDER-GUARD— Píseň stráže na hranicísh—FOOD FOR FIRE, FOOD FOR THOUGHT—Potrava pro požár, potrava pro myšlenku—THE LAW—Zákon.

H11 *Potrava pro požár [Food For Fire]* trans. Stanislav Mares. Prague: Milada Fronta, 1969.
Contents: THE VENICE POEM—benátská báseň—THE SONG OF THE BORDERGUARD—píseň stráže na hranicich—THIS PLACE RUMORD TO HAVE BEEN SODOM—to místo, jež prý bylo sodomou—A POEM BEGINNING WITH A LINE BY PINDAR— báseň začinající veřsem z pindara—FOOD FOR FIRE, FOOD FOR THOUGHT—potrava pro požár, potrava pro myšlenku—ROOTS AND BRANCHES—větve a kořeny—THE LAW—zákon—THE CONTINENT—pevnina.

H12 Poemat Zaczybajacy Sie Od Wiersza Z Pindara, *Tematy,* 29-30 Wiosna-Lata, (1969), 94-102. New York, London.
Note: This is a translation into Polish by Jerzy Niemojowski of RD's POEM BEGINNING WITH A LINE BY PINDAR.

H13 *Les Lettres Nouvelles: Numéro spécial Décember 1970—Janvier 1971 41 poètes américains d'aujourd'hui présentés et traduits par Serge Fauchereau* [Paris: Les Lettres Nouvelles, 1971].
Contribution: Pages 74-91, INGMAR BERGMAN'S *SEVENTH SEAL*—Le Septième Sceau d'Ingmar Bergman—GOD-SPELL— God-spell—PASSAGES 32—Passages 32.

H14 *An Anthology of American Anti-war Poems,* edited by Diane Di Prima. Tokyo: Akitsue Bookshop, 1972.
Contribution: Pages 25-34, EARTH'S WINTER SONG—UP RISING—PASSAGES 25.
Note: Translated into Japanese by Nakayamo Yo.

H15 La danza. *El Urogalla,* 27-28 (May-Aug. 1974), 10-12. Madrid, Spain.
Note: This is a translation of RD's poem "THE DANCE," by Matiais Montero.

H16 *Passages & Structures,* trans. Serge Fauchereau. Paris: Christian Bourgois Editeur, 1977.
Contents: Preface—THE FESTIVALS—Les fêtes—THE SECOND NIGHT IN THE WEEK—La deuxième nuit de la semaine—THE HORNS OF ARTEMIS—Les cornes d'Artemis—UPON ANOTHER SHORE OF HELL—Sur une autre rive de l'enfer—FIVE PIECES—Cinq pieces—THE STRUCTURE OF RIME V—Les structures de la rime, V—THE STRUCTURE OF RIME VI—Les structures de la

rime, VI—THE STRUCTURE OF RIME XI—Les structures de la
rime, XI—ATLANTIS—Atlantis—INGMAR BERGMAN'S *SEV-
ENTH SEAL*—Le septième sceau d'Ingmar Bergman—SONNERIES
OF THE ROSE CROSS—Sonneries de la Rose-Croix—COME, LET
ME FREE MYSELF—Allons, que je me délivre—TWO PRESENTA-
TIONS—Deux visitations—STRAINS OF SIGHT—Modes de
vision—DOVES—Colombes—From *THE MABINOGION*—D'après
le Mabinogion—ENVOY PASSAGES 7—Envoi passages 7—GOD-
SPELL—God-spell—PASSAGES 32—Passages 32—THE FEAST PAS-
SAGES 34—Le festin passages 34—Notes.

H17   *Lirică Americană Contemporană,* trans. Virgil Teodorescu and Petron-
ela Negosanu. Bucharest, Romania: Editura Albatros, 1980.
Contribution: Pages 93-97, FOOD FOR FIRE, FOOD FOR
THOUGHT—hrană pentru foc, hrană pentru gind—A PART-
SEQUENCE FOR CHANGE [3. "ESTRANGED. DEEPLY
ESTRANGED" (f1)]—secventă pentru schimbare—ROOTS AND
BRANCHES—rădăcini si ramuri.

H18   *Szavak a Szélbe[:] Mai Amerikai Költök (A Náborús Nemzedék)[Words
in the Wind : American Poets Today],* ed. by Szabolcs Varady and
trans. Gyula Kodolanyi. [Debrecen, Hungary]: The European Pub-
lisher, 1980.
Contribution: Pages 147-171, Persephone—PASSAGE OVER WATER—
Vízen—LOVE POEM—Szerelem—THE STRUCTURE OF RIME
VI—Friedl—A Vers Épülete VI—THE STRUCTURE OF RIME XI—
A Vers Épülete XI—THE STRUCTURE OF RIME XII—A Vers Épu-
lete XII—ATLANTIS—Atlantisz—INGMAR BERGMAN'S *SEV-
ENTH SEAL*—Ingmar Bergman Hetedik Precsét-Je—THE
STRUCTURE OF RIME XIII—A Vers Épülete XIII—THE STRUC-
TURE OF RIME XXIV—A Vers Épülete XXIV—ENVOY—PAS-
SAGES 7—Utrabocsátó - Sorok 7—THE MULTIVERSITY - Passages
21—Multiversitas - Sorok 21—IN PLACE OF PASSAGE 22—A Sorok
22 Helyére—MY MOTHER WOULD BE A FALCONRESS—Anyám
Volna Solymász.

H19   *Vingt poètes américains: David Antin—John Ashbery—Paul Black-
burn—Cid Corman—Robert Duncan—Larry Eigner—Clayton Eshle-
man—Kenneth Koch—Denise Levertov—Harry Mathews— William
Merwin—Charles Olson—George Oppen—Jerome Rothenberg—
James Schuyler—Jack Spicer—Gertrude Stein— Nathaniel Tarn—
Rosmarie Waldrop—Louis Zukofsky. Présentation de Jacques Rou-
baud, Choix de Michel Deguy et Jacques Roubaud.* Paris: Éditions
Gallimard, 1980.
Contribution: Pages 87-105, ROOTS AND BRANCHES—Racines et
branches—THE FIRE PASSAGES 13—Le feu - Extrait 13—A LAM-
MAS TIDING—Prémices de Lammas—MY MOTHER WOULD BE
A FALCONRESS—Si ma mère était fauconnière.

Notes: The poems were translated by Michel Deguy and Margaret Brooks. The volume contains a long introduction by Jacques Roubaud, pp. 9-34; RD p. 19.

I.
Records and Tapes

I1   Poetry Reading. CSf-APA.
Date: 1951
Place: San Francisco
Collation: One 16 inch studio record 78 RPM 30 min.
Contents: HOMAGE TO THE BROTHERS GRIMM: THE ROBBER MOON—STRAWBERRIES UNDER THE SNOW—THE DINNER TABLE OF THE HARLEQUIN—SLEEPING ALL NIGHT—THE SONG OF THE BORDERGUARD—ADAM'S SONG.

I2   Poetry Reading. DLC.
Date: 22 March 1952.
Place: Berkeley
Collation: One 10 inch reel 1 track 7 1/2 IPS 50 min.
Contents: UNKINGD BY AFFECTION—AFRICA REVISITED—FIVE PIECES—HERO SONG—AN IMAGINARY WOMAN—from MEDIEVAL SCENES: THE DREAMERS—THE HELMET OF GOLIATH—THE KINGDOM OF JERUSALEM—THE MIRROR— THE REAPER—HUON OF BORDEAUX—THE ALBIGENSES.

I3   Poetry Reading. CSf-APA.
Date: 10 Oct. 1956.
Place: San Francisco State University.
Collation: One 7 inch reel 1 track 3 3/4 IPS 1 hr. 20 min.
Contents: PREFACE—HOMAGE TO COLERIDGE—THE GREEN LADY—INTRODUCTION TO *Letters*—FOR A MUSE MEANT—UPON TAKING HOLD—LIGHT SONG—IT'S SPRING. LOVES SPRING—RE—TO VOW AUGUST SUN—from *MEDEA AT KOLCHIS*—OFTEN I AM PERMITTED TO RETURN TO A MEADOW—BUT I HAVE LEARNED THAT I AM NOT A GREAT POET—THE DANCE—THE LAW I LOVE IS MAJOR MOVER— THE STRUCTURE OF RIME I—THE STRUCTURE OF RIME II—THE STRUCTURE OF RIME III—THE STRUCTURE OF RIME IV—speeches from *MEDEA AT KOLCHIS.*

I4   Poetry Reading. CLU.
Date: March 1957.
Place: San Francisco.
Collation: One 7 inch reel 1 track 3 3/4 IPS 1 hr.
Contents: THE GREEN LADY—METAMORPHOSES—RE— (THE PROPOSITIONS)—long question-and-answer period.

I5   POETRY AS MAGIC, workshop/reading. CSf-APA.
Date: 10 June 1957.
Place: San Francisco State University.
Collation: One 7 inch reel 2 tracks 7 1/2 IPS 2 hrs.
Contents: Track one contains reading and comments by Bob Connor

and Ebbe Borregaard; track two contains reading and comments by Helen Adam and RD: AT THE DANCE OF THE HOLLOWS I WILL TELL MY LOVE—EVOCATION.

I6   Poetry Reading. CLU.
Date: 1958.
Place: San Francisco.
Collation: One 7 inch reel 1 track 3 3/4 IPS 40 min.
Contents: FOR A MUSE MEANT—DISTANT COUNSELS OF ARTAUD—FIRST INVENTION ON THE THEME OF THE ADAM—PREFACE TO *HOMAGE TO COLERIDGE*—THE GREEN LADY—THE DANCE—THE SONG OF THE BORDER-GUARD—AN IMAGINARY WAR ELEGY—THE STRUCTURE OF RIME IV-VI—THIS PLACE RUMORD TO HAVE BEEN SODOM.
Note: This is one of nine tapes of California poets reading from their work made by Lawrence Lipton, 1957-1963.

I7   ROOTS AND BRANCHES. NBuU, CLU.
Date: 1959.
Place: San Francisco.
Collation: One 7 inch reel 2 tracks 3 3/4 IPS 2 hrs.
Contents: RD reads the poems in *RB*.
Note: This tape was issued in an edition of twenty-five numbered copies by The Tenth Muse bookstore.

I8   Poetry Reading. CSf-APA.
Date: 18 May 1959.
Place: San Francisco State University.
Collation: Two 7 inch reels each 1 track 7 1/2 IPS 1 hr. 30 min.
Contents: Discussion of the composition of followed by reading of: OFTEN I AM PERMITTED TO RETURN TO A MEADOW—THE DANCE—THE STRUCTURE OF RIME XI—A STORM OF WHITE—BONE DANCE—UNDER GROUND—THE NATURAL DOCTRINE—THE STRUCTURE OF RIME XII—INGMAR BERGMAN'S *SEVENTH SEAL*.

I9   ROBERT DUNCAN READS EZRA POUND'S POETRY. WaEcC.
Date: 8 Oct. 1959.
Place: Central Washington State College.
Collation: One 7 inch reel 1 track 3 3/4 IPS 1 hr. 30 min.
Contents: RD reads from selected *Cantos* of Ezra Pound and discusses how he came to read the poems, why they are important to him, how the tone leading of vowels and musical rhythms function in the poems. This lecture is an introduction to *The Cantos*.

I10 PROGRAMS ON POETRY WITH DAVID OSSMAN. OTU.
Date: 6 July 1960.

Place: New York City.

Collation: One 7 inch tape 1 track 7 1/2 IPS 33 min.

Contents: RD is interviewed by David Ossman and reads A POEM BEGINNING WITH A LINE BY PINDAR.

Note: This tape was presented on station WBAI, 6 July 1960.

I11 PLAYS WITH MASKS. READ AND SUNG BY THE AUTHOR. NBuU, CLU.

Date: 1961.

Place: [San Francisco].

Collation: One 7 inch reel 2 tracks 3 3/4 IPS 40 min.

Contents: A PLAY WITH MASKS.

Note: This tape was issued in an edition of 25 numbered copies by the Tenth Muse bookstore.

I12 [Two Interviews and a Reading]. OKentU.

Date: 8 Jan. 1962, 5 and 6 March 1968.

Place: Albuquerque, N.M.; Buffalo, N.Y.

Collation: One 7 inch reel 2 tracks 3 3/4 IPS 2 hrs.

Contents: "The Single Voice," interview with Robert Creeley for radio program in Albuquerque, N.M., 8 Jan. 1962—Interview with Bobbie Creeley for station WBFO, Buffalo, 5 March 1968; RD reads UPRISING, PASSAGES 25 and EPILOGOS—poetry reading at Albright Knox Gallery, 6 March 1968: from INTRODUCTION TO *Bending the Bow*—THE VENICE POEM—ARTICULATIONS— STAGE DIRECTIONS, PASSAGES 30—PASSAGES 31, THE CONCERT—PASSAGES 32—MY MOTHER WOULD BE A FALCONRESS.

I13 Vancouver Poetry Conference. NBuU.

Date: 2, 5, 7, and 9 Aug. 1963.

Place: Vancouver, BC

Collation: One 7 inch reel 4 tracks 3 3/4 IPS 2 hrs.

Contents: Track 1-A: a discussion between Robert Creeley, Allen Ginsberg, RD, and Charles Olson. Tracks 2-A, 1-B: a discussion between Denise Levertov, Margaret Avison, RD, Robert Creeley, Allen Ginsberg, and Charles Olson on "Intention, Induced Hypersensitivity." Tracks 1-B, 2-B: a discussion between Allen Ginsberg, Margaret Avison, RD, Denise Levertov, and Robert Creeley on "Numinous, How is the Poet in the Poem." Track 2-B: a discussion between Margaret Avison, Robert Creeley, RD, and Allen Ginsberg on "BEGINNING, MIDDLE, END."

I14 Vancouver Poetry Conference. NBuU.

Date: 26 July 1963.

Place: Vancouver, BC

Collation: One 7 inch reel 4 tracks 3 3/4 IPS 2 hrs.

Contents: Tracks 1-B and 2-B contain 36 and 30 minutes of discussion between RD, Robert Creeley, and Allen Ginsberg.

I15 Vancouver Poetry Conference, 1963. NBuU.
Date: 26, 29, 31 July and 2 Aug. 1963.
Place: Vancouver, BC
Collation: One 7 inch reel 4 tracks 3 3/4 IPS 2 hrs.
Contents: Track 1-A: a discussion between Robert Duncan, Robert Creeley, and Allen Ginsberg. Tracks 1-A, 2-B; 1-B: a discussion between Charles Olson, RD, Robert Creeley, Allen Ginsberg, and Philip Whalen on "History." Tracks 1-B, 2-B: a discussion between Charles Olson, RD, Allen Ginsberg, and Robert Creeley on "Polis."
Note: See Ralph Maud's transcript, "Charles Olson, on 'History,'" *Olson,* 4 (Fall 1975), 40-46.

I16 Vancouver Poetry Conference. NBuU.
Date: 26 July, 5 Aug. 1963.
Place: Vancouver, BC
Collation: One 7 inch reel 4 tracks 3 3/4 IPS 2 hrs.
Contents: Tracks 1-A and 2-A contain a poetry reading by RD: THE QUESTION—THE STRUCTURE OF RIME IX—THE STRUCTURE OF RIME X—THE STRUCTURE OF RIME XI—INGMAR BERGMAN'S *SEVENTH SEAL*—APPREHENSIONS—COME LET ME FREE MYSELF—RISK—STRUCTURE OF RIME—OSIRIS AND SET—TWO PRESENTATIONS [unfinished]—A SONG OF THE OLD ORDER—THE BALLAD OF THE FORFAR WITCHES' SING—A SET OF ROMANTIC HYMNS—SONNETS 1, 2, 3, 4—THE BALLAD OF THE FORFAR WITCHES' SING—A POEM BEGINNING WITH A LINE BY PINDAR—THE CONTINENT. Tracks 1-B and 2-B contain a lecture by RD, entitled "THE WORK."

I17 Vancouver Conference. NBuB.
Date: 26, 29, 31 July, and 2 Aug. 1963.
Place: Vancouver, BC
Collation: One 7 inch reel 4 tracks 3 3/4 IPS 2 hrs.
Contents: Track 1-A: 30 minutes of discussion on history between RD, Charles Olson, Robert Creeley, Allen Ginsberg, and Philip Whalen. Track 2-A: 12 minutes of the same discussion. Track 1-B: 40 minutes of the same discussion. Tracks 1-B and 2-B: 50 minutes of a discussion between RD, Charles Olson, Allen Ginsberg, and Robert Creeley on "Polis."

I18 Vancouver Poetry Conference. NBuB.
Date: 9, 12, and 14 Aug. 1963.
Place: Vancouver, BC
Collation: One 7 inch reel 4 tracks 3 3/4 IPS 2 hrs.
Contents: Tracks 1-A, 2-A: a discussion between Margaret Avison,

Robert Creeley, RD, Allen Ginsberg, and Denise Levertov on "BEGIN-NING, MIDDLE, END." Track 2-A, 1-B: a discussion between RD, Allen Ginsberg, Robert Creeley, and Denise Levertov on "Reading Lorca and Williams." Tracks 1-B, 2-B: a discussion between Charles Olson, Allen Ginsberg, and RD on "Duende, Angel, Muse."

119   Poetry Reading. CSf-APA.
Date: 10 Dec. 1963.
Place: San Francisco State University.
Collation: One cassette 2 tracks 1 7/8 IPS 1 hr. 30 min.
Contents: THE TEMPLE OF THE ANIMALS—AN OWL IS AN ONLY BIRD OF POETRY—CYPARISSUS—APPREHENSIONS—THE STRUCTURE OF RIME VI—THE STRUCTURE OF RIME X—THE STRUCTURE OF RIME XI—THIS POTION IS LOVE'S PORTION—A SONG OF THE OLD ORDER—A COUNTRY WIFE'S SONG—SONNET 1—SONNET 2—SONNET 3—SONNET 4—TWO PRESENTATIONS.

120   FIVE POETS. CBC.
Date: 19 Jan. 1964.
Place: Vancouver, BC
Collation: 16-inch record 33 1/3 RPM 1 hr.
Contents: Phyllis Webb narrates and interviews RD, Allen Ginsberg, Charles Olson, Denise Levertov, and Robert Creeley. Each poet talks about his poetry and reads from his work. RD reads THE FIRE.
Note: The recording was made at the Vancouver Poetry Conference, July 1963, but broadcast on the CBC, 19 Jan. 1964, as part of the "Sunday Series."

121   Poetry Reading. CU-S.
Date: 15 May 1964.
Place: Brooklyn Poetry Center.
Collation: One 7 inch reel 2 tracks 3 3/4 IPS 1 hr. 20 min.
Contents: NIGHT SCENES—TWO PRESENTATIONS— SHEL-LEY'S *ARETHUSA* SET TO NEW MEASURES—AFTER READ-ING H.D.'S *HERMETIC DEFINITIONS*—STRAINS OF SIGHT—DOVES—RETURNING TO THE RHETORIC OF AN EARLY MODE—THE BALLAD OF THE FORFAR WITCHES' SING—A COUNTRY WIFE'S SONG—A SET OF ROMANTIC HYMNS—FROM *THE MABINOGION*—NEW POEM—SONNET 1—SONNET 2—SONNET 3—CYPARISSUS—STRUCTURE OF RIME XIX—STRUCTURE OF RIME XX—STRUCTURE OF RIME XXI—PASSAGES 1-6.

122   YALE REPORTS. CtY.
Date: 31 May 1964.
Place: New Haven, Conn.
Collation: One 7 inch reel 1 track 7 1/2 IPS 26 min. 36 sec.

Contents: This is an interview of RD by David Schaff and Eugene Vance.

Note: This interview was broadcast over station WTIC in Hartford on 31 May 1964, as program number 328 in the series "Yale Reports." A transcript of the tape was made and circulated at the time of the broadcast.

I23 TOWARDS AN OPEN UNIVERSE. USIA.
Date: 23 Oct. 1964.
Place: Washington, D. C.
Collation: One 7 inch reel 1 track 3 3/4 IPS 30 min.
Contents: The essay as read by RD.
Note: This tape was made for broadcast over The Voice of America and is available only at the offices of the United States Information Agency.

I24 ROBERT DUNCAN: FAMED CONTEMPORARY POET DIS-CUSSES HIS LIFE AND WORKS. OKentU.
Date. [1965].
Place: North Hollywood, Calif.
Collation: One 7 inch reel 1 track 3 3/4 IPS 27 min.
Contents: RD talks about his work. He reads THE ARCHITEC-TURE, PASSAGES 9, and reads and comments on PASSAGES 26: THE SOLDIERS while he is writing it.
Note: This is the sound track from RD's portion of the NET film devoted to RD and John Wieners. The tape was released by the Center for Cassette Studies, Inc., North Hollywood, Calif., at a later date.

I25 THE PSYCHE MYTH AND THE MOMENT OF TRUTH. KTMF.
Date: 12 May 1965.
Place: Topeka, Kansas
Collation: One 7 inch reel 1 track 3 3/4 IPS ca. 45 min.
Contents: This is a version of the lecture given at the Berkeley Poetry Conference, 1965.
Note: This tape was made at The Menninger Foundation, Topeka, Kansas.

I26 Berkeley Poetry Conference. CU-B.
a. THE PSYCHE MYTH AND THE MOMENT OF TRUTH.
Date: 13 July 1965.
Place: Berkeley, Calif.
Collation: One 7 inch reel 1 track 3 3/4 IPS 2 hrs.
Contents: This is a tape of RD's lecture. He also reads from A POEM BEGINNING WITH A LINE BY PINDAR and THE BALLAD OF THE ENAMORD MAGE—THE BALLAD OF MRS. NOAH—FORCED LINES. George Stanley is introduced by RD.

b. Poetry Reading.
Date: 16 June 1965.

Collation: One 7 inch reel 1 track 3 3/4 IPS 1 hr. 30 min.
Contents: PASSAGES 1-25.

c. Charles Olson Reading.
Date: 20 July 1965.
Collation: One 7 inch reel 1 track 3 3/4 IPS 1 hr. 20 min.
Contents: Introduction by RD; Olson's reading.

d. Robert Creeley Reading.
Date: 23 July 1965.
Collation: One 7 inch reel 1 track 3 3/4 IPS 1 hr. 25 min.
Contents: Introduction by RD; Creeley's reading.

e. Charles Olson Lecturing.
Date: 23 July 1965.
Collation: One 7 inch reel 2 tracks 3 3/4 IPS 3 hrs. 25 min.
Contents: Introduction by RD; Olson's lecture/reading.

f. Poetry Reading.
Date: 24 July 1965.
Collation: One 7 inch reel 1 track 3 3/4 IPS 1 hr. 50 min.
Contents: Poetry readings by Ron Loewinsohn, Joanne Kyger, Lew Welch, and Allen Ginsberg. RD introduces Ginsberg.

I27 Poetry Reading. CU-S.
Date: 1966.
Place: Rimer's Club, Berkeley.
Collation: One 7 inch reel 2 tracks 3 3/4 IPS 2 hrs.
Contents: The first track contains a poetry reading by Jack Spicer. Track 2: NIGHT SCENES—AFTER READING H.D.'S *HERMETIC DEFINITIONS*—STRAINS OF SIGHT—DOVES—DANTE SONNETS—MY MOTHER WOULD BE A FALCONRESS—A SPRING MEMORANDUM: FORT KNOX—AN AFRICAN ELEGY.

I28 Poetry Reading. CU-S.
Date: 12 May 1966.
Place: Mills College.
Collation: One 7 inch reel 2 tracks 3 3/4 IPS 1 hr. 20 min.
Contents: AN AFRICAN ELEGY—THE DANCERS—THE STRUC-TURE OF RIME X—THE STRUCTURE OF RIME XI—FROM *THE MABINOGION*—A NEW POEM (FOR JACK SPICER)—A BLASPHEMY—THE FIRE, PASSAGES 13—IN THE PLACE OF A PASSAGE 22.

I29 ROBERT DUNCAN: PORTRAIT OF A POET. CBC.
Date: 20 May 1966.
Place: Vancouver, BC
Collation: One 10 1/2 inch reel 1 track 7 1/2 IPS 1 hr.
Contents: RD talks with Warren Tallman about his career as a poet and reads from his work: DOVES—TOWARD AN AFRICAN

ELEGY—THE MULTIVERSITY, PASSAGES 21—THE HELMET OF GOLIATH—THE BALLAD OF THE FORFAR WITCHES' SING.

Note: The tape was broadcast by CBC on 20 May 1966 as part of the series "CBC Saturday Night."

I30 Poetry Reading. KU.
Date: 17 April 1967.
Place: University of Kansas.
Collation: One 7 inch reel 1 track 3 3/4 IPS 55 min.
Contents: AN ILLUSTRATION, PASSAGES 20 (STRUCTURE OF RIME XXVI)—THE MULTIVERSITY, PASSAGES 21—IN THE PLACE OF PASSAGES 22—PASSAGES 23, BENEFICE—ORDERS, PASSAGES 24—UP RISING, PASSAGES 25—PASSAGES 26, THE SOLDIERS—TRANSGRESSING THE REAL, PASSAGES 27— EYE OF GOD, PASSAGES 29—EPILOGOS.

I31 ROBERT CREELEY AND ROBERT DUNCAN READING FROM THEIR WORKS. MoSW.
Date: 28 April 1967.
Place: Washington University.
Collation: One 7 inch reel 2 tracks 3 3/4 IPS 1 hr. 45 min.
Contents: Introduction by Joel Cahn. Reading order: (1) RD: FOR A MUSE MEANT—FIRST INVENTION ON THE THEME OF THE ADAM; (2) RC: POEM FOR BEGINNERS—THE CHANGES— CHASING THE BIRD; (3) RD: DOVES—SONNET 1—SONNET 2—SONNET 3; (4) RC: THE DOOR (FOR ROBERT DUNCAN); (5) RD: BENDING THE BOW—FOOD FOR FIRE, FOOD FOR THOUGHT—EPILOGOS; (6) RC: A POEM—SONG—OLD SONG— STOMPING WITH CATULLUS—THE SENTENCE— VARIATIONS; (7) RC: A PLACE—SOME ECHOES—FANCY—THE WORLD—GOING—THE CITY—WORDS—A REASON—THE SHAME—THE STATUE—THE WINDOW—TO BOBBIE— THEY—A METHOD—A SIGHT—PIECES—THE CIRCLE—THE HOLE—A PRAYER—THE FLOWER—SAME—THERE—JOY— A PICTURE—A PIECE—THE BOX—WATER MUSIC—THEY— WAS—THE FARM—INDIANS—ENOUGH—HERE—INTER-VALS—WATER—THE EYE—OF YEARS—SONG—FOR JOEL— A BIRTHDAY—DANCING—A TALLY—OH MY LOVE— FRAG-MENTS; (8) RD: ORDERS, PASSAGES 24—UP RISING, PASSAGES 25—PASSAGES 26, THE SOLDIERS—TRANSGRESSING THE REAL, PASSAGES 27—THE LIGHT, PASSAGES 28—EYE OF GOD, PASSAGES 29—PASSAGES 30, STAGE DIRECTIONS.

I32 Poetry Reading. NBuU.
Date: 1 May 1967.
Place: SUNY, Buffalo.

Collation: One 7 inch reel 2 tracks 3 3/4 IPS 1 hr. 45 min.
Contents: Introduction by Mac Hammond; RD reads "THE PAS-
SAGES POEMS" 1-30.

I33 THE POET AS CELEBRANT. CBC.
Date: 10 May 1967.
Place: Toronto
Collation: One 10 1/2 inch real 1 track 7 1/2 IPS 89 min. 25 sec.
Contents: RD talks informally about the poet as celebrant and reads
from his work: RE—THE TORSO, PASSAGES 18—THE DANCE—
THE EYE OF GOD, PASSAGES 29.
Note: This tape was broadcast as part of a series entitled "Ideas—
Celebration" by CBC on 10 May 1967.

I34 Conference on Parable Myth and Language. OKentU.
Date: 13 Oct. 1967.
Place: Washington, D. C.
Collation: One 7 inch reel 2 tracks 3 3/4 IPS 2 hrs. 35 min.
Contents: Samuel Laeuchli reads his lecture CHRISTIANITY AND
THE DEATH OF MYTH, and in the following discussion RD con-
tributes about 35 minutes of comments.

I35 Conference on Parable Myth and Language. OKentU.
Date: 14 Oct. 1967.
Place: Washington, D.C.
Collation: One 7 inch reel 1 track 3 3/4 IPS 1 hr. 40 min.
Contents: Robert W. Funk delivers his lecture MYTH AND THE
LITERAL NON-LITERAL, and in the following discussion RD
contributes about 20 minutes of comments.

I36 Conference on Parable Myth and Language. OKentU.
Date: 14 Oct. 1967.
Place: Washington, D. C.
Collation: One 7 inch reel 2 tracks 3 3/4 IPS 2 hrs. 15 min.
Contents: Denise Levertov reads her lecture A PERSONAL
APPROACH, reads from her poetry, and in the following discussion
RD contributes about 15 minutes of comments.

I37 Conference on Parable Myth and Language. OKentU.
Date: 14 Oct. 1967.
Place: Washington, D. C.
Collation: One 7 inch reel 2 tracks 3 3/4 IPS 2 hrs.
Contents: RD reads his lecture THE TRUTH AND LIFE OF MYTH
IN POETRY, discusses his poetry, and reads the following poems:
OFTEN I AM PERMITTED TO RETURN TO A MEADOW—
THE QUESTION—A POEM BEGINNING WITH A LINE BY PIN-
DAR—EPILOGOS.

I38 THE CAT AND THE BLACKBIRD. NBuU, CLU.

Date: 1968.

Place: San Francisco.

Collation: One 4 inch reel 1 track 3 3/4 IPS 30 min.

Contents: THE CAT AND THE BLACKBIRD.

Note: This tape was issued in an edition of 25 numbered copies by the Tenth Muse bookstore.

I39 Poetry Reading. NBuAKG.

Date: 6 March 1968.

Place: Albright-Knox Art Gallery, Buffalo.

Collation: One 7 inch reel 1 track 3 3/4 IPS 1 hr.

Contents: Introduction by Robert Creeley—THE WAR (from introduction to *Bending the Bow*)—THE VENICE POEM— ARTICULATIONS (from introduction to *Bending the Bow*— PASSAGES 30—PASSAGES 31—PASSAGES 32—MY MOTHER WOULD BE A FALCONRESS.

Note: This reading was given as part of the second Buffalo Festival of the Arts Today.

I40 MAN'S FULFILLMENT IN ORDER AND STRIFE. WaEnO.

Date: 20 April 1968.

Place: Central Washington State College.

Collation: One 7 inch reel 1 track 3 3/4 IPS 1 hr. 6 min.

Contents: This is the first and informal version of the lecture which was later printed in *Caterpillar*. C220.

Note: This lecture was given as part of the Seventh Annual Symposium on American Values entitled "Language and World Order."

I41 Thomas Parkinson talking on Brother Antoninus, Robinson Jeffers, Robert Duncan, and Thornton Wilder. CU-B.

Date: 12 June 1968.

Place: Berkeley.

Collation: Two 7 inch reels each 1 track 3 3/4 IPS 2 hrs.

Contents: Professor Parkinson discusses the work of each poet in a general way. The section on RD is approximately 30 minutes.

I42 Robert Duncan Reading. NBuU.

Date: 27 June 1968.

Place: SUNY, Buffalo.

Collation: One 7 inch reel 1 track 3 3/4 IPS 1 hr.

Contents: STRUCTURE OF RIME XXVII—THE STRUCTURE OF RIME I—THE STRUCTURE OF RIME II—THE STRUCTURE OF RIME III—CROSSES OF HARMONY AND DISHARMONY— A SONG OF THE OLD ORDER—THE LAW—THE MULTIVERSITY, PASSAGES 21—STRUCTURE OF RIME XXVII.

I43 Poetry Reading. NBuU.
Date: 15 July 1968.
Place: SUNY, Buffalo.
Collation: One 7 inch reel 2 tracks 3 3/4 IPS 1 hr. 45 min.
Contents: THE STRUCTURE OF RIME I-XXVI—FRAGMENTS
OF STRUCTURE OF RIME XXVIII.

I44 THE BODY AS METAPHOR. CBC.
Date: 6 May 1969.
Place: Toronto.
Collation: One 10 1/2 inch reel 1 track 7 1/2 IPS 58 min. 30 sec.
Contents: This is an informal talk on the body as metaphor inter-
spersed with segments of music.
Note: The talk was recorded by Phyllis Webb for the program "Ideas,
Model and Metaphor" and broadcast by CBC 6 May 1969.

I45 Poetry Reading. KU.
Date: 7 May 1969.
Place: University of Kansas.
Collation: One 7 inch reel 1 track 3 3/4 IPS 45 min.
Contents: Introduction by Edward Dorn—PASSAGES 26-30.

I46 THE VOCATION OF POETRY IN A DEMOCRATIC SOCIETY.
WaEcC.
Date: 30 Sept. 1969.
Place: Central Washington State College.
Collation: One 7 inch reel 2 tracks 3 3/4 IPS 2 hrs. 5 min.
Contents: Introduction—the lecture—poetry reading: THE YEARS
AS CATCHES—THE DREAMERS—THE HELMET OF GOLI-
ATH—THE BANNERS—THE KINGDOM OF JERUSALEM—
THE FESTIVALS—THE MIRROR—THE REAPER.

I47 ROBERT DUNCAN READS FROM EZRA POUND'S POETRY.
WaEcC.
Date: 8 Oct. 1969.
Place: Central Washington State College.
Collation: One 7 inch reel 2 tracks 3 3/4 IPS 2 hrs.
Contents: RD lectures on the importance of Pound as a poet and
reads from his poems, mainly from *A Draft of XXX Cantos.*

I48 ROBERT DUNCAN READS ROBERT DUNCAN'S POETRY.
WaEcC.
Date: 16 Oct. 1969.
Place: Central Washington State College.
Collation: One 7 inch reel 2 tracks 3 3/4 IPS 2 hrs.
Contents: THE SONG OF THE BORDERGUARD—DANCE,
EARLY SPRING WEATHER MAGIC—HERO SONG—ELUARD'S
DEATH—UNKINGD BY AFFECTION—DESCRIPTION OF IMAG-
INARY POETRIES—RHYME MOUNTAIN PARTICULAR—

UPON TAKING HOLD—FIRST INVENTION ON THE THEME
OF THE ADAM—AT THE END OF A PERIOD—OFTEN I AM
PERMITTED TO RETURN TO A MEADOW—THE DANCE—
THE STRUCTURE OF RIME VI—THE STRUCTURE OF RIME
VII—THIS PLACE RUMORD TO HAVE BEEN SODOM—A SONG
OF THE OLD ORDER—A COUNTRY WIFE'S SONG—A POEM
BEGINNING WITH A LINE BY PINDAR—THE STRUCTURE
OF RIME X—THE STRUCTURE OF RIME XI—TWO PRESEN-
TATIONS—DOVES—A NEW POEM (FOR JACK SPICER)—
ORDERS, PASSAGES 24—A SHRINE TO AMEINIAS— PASSAGES
31, THE CONCERT.

I49   Poetry Reading. CU-B.
       Date: 6 and 13 March 1970.
       Place: Le Conte School Auditorium.
       Collation: One 7 inch reel 1 track 7 1/2 IPS 2 hrs.
       Contents: PASSAGES 1-30.

I50   Gay Liberation Poetry Reading. CSf-APA.
       Date: 2 March 1971.
       Place: San Francisco State University
       Collation: One 7 inch reel 1 track 3 3/4 IPS 1 hr. 30 min.
       Contents: RD reads with several other poets: from THE HOMO-
       SEXUAL IN SOCIETY—AN AFRICAN ELEGY—FOUR POEMS
       AS A NIGHT SONG—THE SONG OF THE BORDERGUARD—
       VARIATIONS ON TWO DICTA OF WILLIAM BLAKE, PART 2—
       ACHILLES' SONG—SONNET 1—SONNET 2.

I51   Statement of Beginnings. OKentU.
       Date: 7 April 1971.
       Place: Kent State University.
       Collation: One 7 inch reel 2 tracks 3 3/4 IPS 1 hr. 30 min.
       Contents: This is a tape with Allen Ginsberg, Richard Grossinger,
       and RD discussing their beginnings in writing.

I52   Poetry Reading. OKentU.
       Date: 7 April 1971.
       Place: Kent State University.
       Collation: Two 7 inch reels each 1 track 7 1/2 IPS 2 hrs.
       Contents: This is a tape of a reading by Richard Grossinger, Allen
       Ginsberg, and RD: AT CHRISTMAS—INTRODUCTION FOR
       RICHARD GROSSINGER—THE FIRE, PASSAGES 31—THE
       LIGHT, PASSAGES 28—ACHILLES' SONG—SONGS FROM
       MEDEA AT KOLCHIS—SANTA CRUZ PROPOSITIONS I AND II.

I53   Poetry Reading. OKentU.
       Date: 6 May 1971.
       Place: University of Maine.
       Collation: One cassette 1 track 1 7/8 IPS 45 min.

Contents: THE MOLY SUITE—RITES OF PASSAGE—RETURN-
ING TO THE RHETORIC OF AN EARLY MODE—A DANCING
CONCERNING A FORM OF WOMEN—THANK YOU FOR
LOVE—FROM *THE MABINOGION*—A NEW POEM (FOR JACK
SPICER)—SONNET 1—SONNET 2—SANTA CRUZ PROPOSI-
TION I—THE MULTIVERSITY, PASSAGES 21 [break in tape].

I54   Poetry Reading. OKentU.
       Date: 11 April 1972.
       Place: SUNY, Albany.
       Collation: One 7 inch reel 1 track 3 3/4 IPS 1 hr.
       Contents: SPEECH OF ROMANTIC MUSE FROM A PLAY WITH
       MASKS—FROM SEVENTEENTH CENTURY SUITE: "LOVE'S A
       GREAT COURTESY TO BE DECLARED" (fl)—SIR WALTER
       RALEGH, WHAT IS OUR LIFE?—FROM SIR WALTER
       RALEGH'S WHAT IS OUR LIFE?—"GO AS IN A DREAM" (fl)—
       ROBERT SOUTHWELL, THE BURNING BABE—FROM ROB-
       ERT SOUTHWELL'S THE BURNING BABE—GEORGE HER-
       BERT, JORDAN (I)—FROM GEORGE HERBERT'S JORDAN (I)—
       GEORGE HERBERT, JORDAN (II)—FROM GEORGE HER-
       BERT'S JORDAN (II)—PASSAGES 36—A SONG OF THE OLD
       ORDER—OFTEN I AM PERMITTED TO RETURN TO A
       MEADOW—A POEM BEGINNING WITH A LINE BY PINDAR—
       THE STRUCTURE OF RIME X—THE STRUCTURE OF RIME
       XI—TWO PRESENTATIONS.

I55   Annual Wallace Stevens Memorial Reading. CtU.
       Date: 25 April 1972.
       Place: University of Connecticut.
       Collation: One 7 inch reel 1 track 3 3/4 IPS 1 hr.
       Contents: "LET SLEEP TAKE HER" (fl)—"AND FINALLY THAT
       EVERYTHING LIKE A FIRM GRASP OF REALITY" (fl)—"OVER
       THERE, WHERE THOU ART" (fl)—A SONG OF THE OLD
       ORDER—THE ROCK—A SUITE OF POEMS REFERRING TO
       GENIUS IN POETRY: PART 8, PASSAGES 36—PASSAGES 28:
       THE LIGHT—STRUCTURE OF RIME XXVIII: IN MEMORIAM
       WALLACE STEVENS.
       Note: The introduction to this reading is by George Butterick.

I56   POUND, ELIOT, H.D.: THE CULT OF THE GODS IN AMERI-
       CAN POETRY. OKentU.
       Date: 11, 18, and 25 Oct. 1972.
       Place: Kent State University.
       Collation: Three 7 inch reels each 1 track 3 3/4 IPS each 1 hr.
       Contents: These are tapes of lectures. RD discusses and reads from the
       works of the three poets.

I57   Poetry Reading. CSf-APA.
      Date: 12 Dec. 1972
      Place: San Francisco State University.
      Collation: One 7 inch reel 1 track 3 3/4 IPS 50 min.
      Contents: POETRY, A NATURAL THING—"SPARKED FROM
      THE FLINT BY VAUGHAN'S HEART STRUCK" (fl)—"LOVE'S
      A GREAT COURTESY TO BE DECLARED" (fl)—"GO AS IN A
      DREAM" (fl)—ROBERT SOUTHWELL, THE BURNING BABE—
      FROM ROBERT SOUTHWELL'S THE BURNING BABE— FROM
      GEORGE HERBERT'S JORDAN (I)—FROM GEORGE HER-
      BERT'S JORDAN (II)—PASSAGES 36—DESPAIR IN BEING
      TEDIOUS—OVER THERE—IN MEMORIAM WALLACE
      STEVENS.

I58   Poetry Reading. OKentU.
      Date: 18 Jan. 1973.
      Place: Museum of Contemporary Art, Chicago.
      Collation: One cassette 2 tracks 1 7/8 IPS 1 hr. 15 min.
      Contents: A SONG FROM THE STRUCTURES OF RIME RING-
      ING AS THE POET PAUL CELAN SINGS—AND HELL IS THE
      REALM OF GOD'S SELF-LOATHING—STRUCTURE OF RIME
      XXVII—TURNING INTO—COMING OUT OF—MAKING UP—
      IMAGINARY LETTER—STRUCTURE OF RIME VIII— STRUC-
      TURE OF RIME IX—STRUCTURE OF RIME X—THE BALLAD
      OF THE FORFAR WITCHES' SING—A COUNTRY WIFE'S
      SONG—PASSAGES 26, THE SOLDIERS—MY MOTHER WOULD
      BE A FALCONRESS—DESPAIR IN BEING TEDIOUS— OVER
      THERE—THE MUSEUM.

I59   Poetry Reading: Robert Duncan and George Oppen. CSf-APA.
      Date: 22 Feb. 1973.
      Place: San Francisco Museum of Art.
      Collation: One 7 inch reel 1 track 3 3/4 IPS 1 hr.
      Contents: RD reads from DANTE ÉTUDES, BOOK I, I-V—
      ANCIENT QUESTIONS—from RITES OF PASSAGE.
      Note: This is a joint reading with George Oppen.

I60   Poetry Reading. OKentU.
      Date: 5 March 1973.
      Place: University of Illinois, Chicago Circle.
      Collation: One cassette 2 tracks 1 7/8 IPS 1 hr.
      Contents: A MORASS—CANVAS COMING INTO ITSELF—from
      DANTE ÉTUDES: BOOK I, I-VII—MY MOTHER WOULD BE A
      FALCONRESS—APPREHENSIONS—THE MOON, PASSAGES
      5—THE CONCERT, PASSAGES 31.

I61   Poetry Reading. OKentU.
      Date: 7 March 1973.

Place: Loyola University, Chicago.

Collation: One cassette 2 tracks 1 7/8 IPS 1 hr.

Contents: WHAT DO I KNOW OF THE OLD LORE?—VARIATIONS ON TWO DICTA OF WILLIAM BLAKE—THE CONTINENT—sections from FAUST FOUTU—OFTEN I AM PERMITTED TO RETURN TO A MEADOW—TRIBAL MEMORIES, PASSAGES 1—ENVOY, PASSAGES 7—EYE OF GOD, PASSAGES 29.

I62   Poetry Reading. CU-S.

Date: Spring 1973.

Place: University of California, San Diego.

Collation: One cassette 2 tracks 1 7/8 IPS 1 hr. 20 min.

Contents: A LAMMAS TIDING—MY MOTHER WOULD BE A FALCONRESS—AN OWL IS AN ONLY BIRD OF POETRY—AN ESSAY AT WAR—A SONG FROM THE STRUCTURES OF RIME RINGING AS THE POET PAUL CELAN SINGS—AND HELL IS THE REALM OF GOD'S SELF-LOATHING—DESPAIR IN BEING TEDIOUS—THE MUSEUM.

I63   Poetry Reading. CVI.

Date: 24 April 1973.

Place: California Institute of the Arts, Valencia.

Collation: One 7 inch reel 2 tracks 3 3/4 IPS 1 hr. 40 min.

Contents: THE CONSTRUCTION—THE WALK TO THE VACANT LOT—THE WASTE, THE ROOM, THE DISCARDED TIMBERS—BEFORE WAKING AT HALF-PAST SIX IN THE MORNING—THE SECOND NIGHT IN THE WEEK—PROCESSIONALS II—AURORA ROSE—BON VOYAGE—DESPAIR IN BEING TEDIOUS—CHILDHOOD'S RETREAT—FOOD FOR FIRE, FOOD FOR THOUGHT—THE MUSEUM—TRIBAL MEMORIES PASSAGES I—WHERE IT APPEARS, PASSAGES 4— THE MOON, PASSAGES 5—THESE PAST YEARS, PASSAGES 10— THE FIRE, PASSAGES 13—PASSAGES 36 [THESE LINES COMPOSING THEMSELVES IN MY HEAD AS I AWOKE EARLY THIS MORNING, IT BEING STILL DARK DECEMBER 16, 1971]—A COUNTRY WIFE'S SONG—SONG OF THE OLD ORDER.

I64   Poetry Reading: Voices of the 40's. CSf-APA.

Date: 15 May 1974.

Place: San Francisco Museum of Art.

Collation: Two 7 inch reels each 1 track 3 3/4 IPS 1 hr. 30 min.

Contents: RD reads with eight other poets: HOMAGE TO THE BROTHERS GRIMM: STRAWBERRIES UNDER THE SNOW— THE DINNER TABLE OF HARLEQUIN—THE HOMECOMING.

I65   Poetry Reading. CU-S.

Date: 1 Nov. 1974.

Place: Berkeley.

Collation: Two 5 inch reels each 1 track 3 3/4 IPS 1 hr. 30 min.

Contents: RD reads all the DANTE ÉTUDES.

I66 NET Film Sound Out-take. CSf-APA.

Date: 1975.

Place: San Francisco.

Collation: Two cassettes each 2 tracks 1 7/8 IPS 3 hrs.

Contents: This is a tape of the sound section of the out-take footage for the NET film ROBERT DUNCAN: A LIFE IN POETRY.

I67 Poetry Reading: POETS OF THE CITIES. CU-S.

Date: 22 Feb. 1975.

Place: San Francisco Museum of Modern Art.

Collation: One 7 inch reel 1 track 3 3/4 IPS 1 hr. 15 min.

Contents: RD reads with Michael McClure and David Meltzer: THE SONG OF THE BORDERGUARD—TWO PAINTERS—HUNG-UP—A POEM IN STRETCHING—DESCRIPTION OF IMAGINARY POETRIES—STRUCTURE OF RIME XIX—STRUCTURE OF RIME XXI—OFTEN I AM PERMITTED TO RETURN TO A MEADOW—THE NATURAL DOCTRINE—FOOD FOR FIRE, FOOD FOR THOUGHT.

I68 Lecture and Poetry Reading. CSt.

Date: Nov. 1972, 21 June 1975.

Place: Stanford University, Foothill College.

Collation: One 7 inch reel 2 tracks 3 3/4 IPS 2 hrs.

Contents: This is a tape of a lecture entitled POETRY AND MYTH and a poetry reading: ACHILLES' SONG—DESPAIR IN BEING TEDIOUS—ROBERT SOUTHWELL, THE BURNING BABE—FROM ROBERT SOUTHWELL'S THE BURNING BABE—from DANTE ÉTUDES: BOOKS I, III, V, XII—CODA [SEVENTEENTH CENTURY SUITE].

Note: Tapes of two separate readings have been made into a single tape.

I69 Poetry Reading. OKentU.

Date: 13 Feb. 1976.

Place: Seattle, Washington.

Collation: One cassette 2 tracks 3 3/4 IPS 1 hr. 30 min.

Contents: SECOND TAKE ON RITES OF PASSAGE—PREFACE TO THE SUITE [POEMS FROM THE MARGINS OF THOM GUNN'S *MOLY*]—CHILDHOOD'S RETREAT—(THE PROPOSITIONS)—FROM *THE MABINOGION*—A NEW POEM (FOR JACK SPICER)—THESE PAST YEARS, PASSAGES 10—TRANSGRESSING THE REAL, PASSAGES 27—(PASSAGES) EMPEDOKLEAN REVERIES—PASSAGES [HOMAGE TO THE YOUTHFUL ZUKOFSKY, LEADING TOWARD HIS 'A'-23]—AN INTERLUDE

OF WINTER LIGHT—CIRCULATIONS OF THE SOUL AFTER JALAL AL-DIN RUMI.

I70   Poetry Reading. CSCU.
Date: 19 Feb. 1976.
Place: University of Santa Clara.
Collation: One cassette 2 tracks 1 7/8 IPS 1 hr. 10 min.
Contents: "LOVE'S A GREAT COURTESY TO BE DECLARED" (fl)—ROBERT SOUTHWELL, THE BURNING BABE—FROM ROBERT SOUTHWELL'S THE BURNING BABE—AN INTERLUDE OF WINTER LIGHT—from DANTE ÉTUDES: BOOK I, I-X, BOOK II, I-X, BOOK III, ETUDE FROM THE THIRD EPISTLE—ETUDE FROM THE FIFTH EPISTLE (I)—ETUDE FROM THE FIFTH EPISTLE (II)—FIRST ETUDE FROM THE SEVENTH EPISTLE—SECOND ETUDE FROM THE SEVENTH EPISTLE—THIRD ETUDE FROM THE SEVENTH EPISTLE— ETUDE FROM THE FOURTH TREATISE OF THE *CONVIVIO* CHAPTER XXVII—ETUDE FROM THE FOURTH TREATISE OF THE *CONVIVIO* CHAPTERS XXVII AND XXI.

I71   Poetry Reading. KU.
Date: 23 Feb. 1976.
Place: University of Kansas.
Collation: One 7 inch reel 2 tracks 3 3/4 IPS 1 hr. 35 min.
Contents: ANCIENT QUESTION—FOR ME TOO, I, LONG AGO SHIPPING OUT WITH THE CANTOS—DESPAIR IN BEING TEDIOUS—OFTEN I AM PERMITTED TO RETURN TO A MEADOW—ANSWERING—from ADAM'S WAY: ERDA'S SPEECH—ADAM'S SPEECH—HERMES' SPEECH, LILITH'S SPEECH—AN INTERLUDE—A NEW POEM (FOR JACK SPICER)—AN INTERLUDE OF WINTER LIGHT—CIRCULATIONS OF THE SONG AFTER JALAL AL-DIN RUMI—from DANTE ÉTUDES: ETUDE FROM THE THIRD EPISTLE— ETUDE FROM THE FIFTH EPISTLE (I)—ETUDE FROM THE FIFTH EPISTLE (II)—FIRST ETUDE FROM THE SEVENTH EPISTLE—SECOND ETUDE FROM THE SEVENTH EPISTLE— THIRD ETUDE FROM THE SEVENTH EPISTLE—ETUDE FROM THE FOURTH TREATISE OF THE *CONVIVIO* CHAPTER XXVII—ETUDE FROM THE FOURTH TREATISE OF THE *CONVIVIO* CHAPTERS XXVII AND XII.

I72   Poetry Reading. OKentU.
Date: 24 March 1976.
Place: Saddleback College, Mission Viejo, Calif.
Collation: One cassette 2 tracks 1 7/8 IPS 1 hr.
Contents: OFTEN I AM PERMITTED TO RETURN TO A MEADOW—A POEM BEGINNING WITH A LINE BY PINDAR—

RETURNING TO THE RHETORIC OF AN EARLY MODE—
THE CONTINENT—ZEALOUS LIBERALITY, "GO MY SONGS,
EVEN AS YOU CAME TO ME."

I73   Poetry Reading. CU-S.
Date: 26 March 1976.
Place: San Diego State University.
Collation: One 7 inch reel 1 track 3 3/4 IPS 1 hr.
Contents: CHILDHOOD'S RETREAT—AND HELL IS THE
REALM OF GOD'S SELF-LOATHING—SONNET 1—SONNET
2—THE TORSO, PASSAGES 18—THESE PAST YEARS— (PAS-
SAGES) EMPEDOKLEAN REVERIES—PASSAGES [HOMAGE TO
THE YOUTHFUL ZUKOFSKY, LEADING TOWARD HIS 'A' 23]—
THE EIDOLON OF THE AION—AN INTERLUDE OF WINTER
LIGHT.

I74   Lecture. CU-S.
Date: 26 March 1976.
Place: University of California, San Diego.
Collation: One 7 inch reel 1 track 3 3/4 IPS 1 hr.
Contents. RD discusses the work of Ezra Pound.

I75   Interview with David Quarles. OKentU.
Date: 30 March 1976.
Place: San Francisco.
Collation: One 7 inch reel 1 track 3 3/4 IPS 30 min.
Contents: This is the tape of the interview.

I76   Class lecture and discussion. CaMWU.
Date: 5 April 1976.
Place: University of Manitoba.
Collation: Three cassettes 2 each 2 tracks, 1 with 1 track 1 7/8 IPS 2
hrs. 30 min.
Contents: This is a class discussion by RD on the history of poetry
and his own poetics.

I77   Poetry Reading. DLC.
Date: 26 April 1976.
Place: Library of Congress, Washington, D. C.
Collation: One 10 inch reel 2 tracks 7 1/2 IPS 50 min.
Contents: CHILDHOOD'S RETREAT—STRUCTURE OF RIME
XXVIII: IN MEMORIAM WALLACE STEVENS—(PASSAGES)
EMPEDOKLEAN REVERIES—(PASSAGES) HOMAGE TO THE
YOUTHFUL ZUKOFSKY, LEADING TO HIS 'A'-23—MY
MOTHER WOULD BE A FALCONRESS—from DANTE ÉTUDES:
BOOK ONE, I—BOOK TWO, II—V—VI—BOOK THREE, ETUDE
FROM THE FOURTH TREATISE OF THE *CONVIVIO* CHAP-
TER XXVII.
Note: This was a joint reading with Jerome Rothenberg.

178 Ruth Witt-Diamant Interview: History of The Poetry Center. CSf-APA.
Date: 28 Sept. 1976.
Place: San Francisco State University.
Collation: One cassette 2 tracks 1 7/8 IPS 1 hr. 20 min.
Contents: Ruth Witt-Diamant talks with Francis Gretton about the origin and growth of The Poetry Center.

179 COMPOSITION BY FIELD IN PAINTING. OKentU.
Date: 29 Oct. 1976.
Place: San Francisco Art Institute.
Collation: Two cassettes each 2 tracks 1 7/8 IPS 1 hr. 45 min.
Contents: This is a taped class lecture.

180 Poetry Reading. OKentU.
Date: 29 Oct. 1976.
Place: San Francisco Art Institute.
Collation: One cassette 2 tracks 1 7/8 IPS 1 hr.
Contents: PASSAGES 31, THE CONCERT—PASSAGES [HOMAGE TO THE YOUTHFUL ZUKOFSKY, LEADING TOWARD HIS 'A'-23]—(PASSAGES) EMPEDOKLEAN REVERIES—EIDOLON OF THE AION I AND II—from preface to DANTE ÉTUDES: BOOK I, XI-XII—AN ALTERNATE LIFE: IN THE SOUTH— HOMECOM-ING—from DANTE ÉTUDES: BOOK III, ETUDE FROM THE FOURTH TREATISE OF THE *CONVIVIO* CHAPTER XXVII—ETUDE FROM THE FOURTH TREATISE OF THE *CONVIVIO*, CHAPTERS XXVII AND XXI.

181 Robert Duncan talking. CSf-APA.
Date: 15 Sept. 1977.
Place: 1220 Folsom St., San Francisco.
Collation: Three cassettes 2 each 2 tracks, 1 with 1 track 1 7/8 IPS 2 hrs. 30 min.
Contents: This is a tape of RD talking about poetry, poetics and the operation of sound and voice in the poem; Bob Perelman and Ron Silliman enter the conversation.

182 Classroom Lecture. CU-S.
Date: 11 Nov. 1977.
Place: University of California, San Diego.
Collation: One 7 inch reel 1 track 3 3/4 IPS 1 hr.
Contents: RD talks on the general topic of post-modernism.

183 Poetry Reading. CU-S.
Date: 17 Feb. 1978.
Place: University of California, San Diego.
Collation: One 7 inch reel 2 tracks 7 1/2 IPS 1 hr. 30 min.
Contents: "SO KNOWING OR UNKNOWING" (fl)—A LAN-GUAGE FOR POETRY—IMAGINING IN WRITING—I AM NOT

AFRAID—A POEM BEGINNING WITH A LINE BY PINDAR—A GLIMPSE—CHILDHOOD'S RETREAT—JOHN NORRIS OF BEMERTON, HYMN TO DARKNESS—CODA.

I84 Poetry Reading. CSf-APA.
Date: 22 Feb. 1978.
Place: University of Southern California.
Collation: One cassette 2 tracks 1 7/8 IPS 1 hr.
Contents: A GLIMPSE—CHILDHOOD'S RETREAT—THE MUSEUM—from POEMS FROM THE MARGINS OF THOM GUNN'S *MOLY:* PREFACE 1 & 2—A SEVENTEENTH CENTURY SUITE: "LOVE'S A GREAT COURTESY TO BE DECLARED" (fl)—FROM SIR WALTER RALEGH'S WHAT IS OUR LIFE?— "GO AS IN A DREAM?" (fl)—JOHN NORRIS OF BEMERTON, HYMN TO DARKNESS—CODA.

I85 Robert Duncan reads and comments on the film "Charles Olson in Gloucester." CSf-APA.
Date: 12 March 1978.
Place: Blue Dolphin Club, San Francisco.
Collation: One cassette 2 tracks 1 7/8 IPS 1 hr. 30 min.
Contents: RD talks about the film and his relationship with Charles Olson and reads: FOR A MUSE MEANT—LIGHT SONG—THE STRUCTURE OF RIME IV—THE CONTINENT—BOOK I, from DANTE ÉTUDES.

I86 Poetry Reading. OKentU.
Date: 6 April 1978.
Place: State University College, Oneonta.
Collation: One 7 inch reel 1 track 3 3/4 IPS 45 min.
Contents: AN ALTERNATE LIFE: IN THE SOUTH—HOME-COMING—SUPPLICATION—THE QUOTIDIAN.

I87 Poetry Reading. OKentU.
Date: 17 April 1978.
Place: Kent State University.
Collation: One 7 inch reel 2 tracks 3 3/4 IPS 2 hrs.
Contents: MEDIEVAL SCENES: THE DREAMERS—THE HELMET OF GOLIATH—THE BANNERS—THE KINGDOM OF JERUSALEM—THE FESTIVALS—THE MIRROR—THE REAPER—THE ADORATION OF THE VIRGIN—HUON OF BORDEAUX—THE ALBIGENSES—ACHILLES' SONG— PASSAGES 31, THE CONCERT—TRANSMISSIONS (PASSAGES 33)—THE MUSEUM—A GLIMPSE—AND IF HE HAD BEEN WRONG FOR ME—CHILDHOOD'S RETREAT—AN ALTERNATE LIFE: IN THE SOUTH—HOMECOMING—SUPPLICATION—THE QUOTIDIAN.

188 PHYSICS AND POETRY. OKentU.
Date: 18 April 1978.
Place: Hiram College.
Collation: One 7 inch reel 1 track 3 3/4 IPS 1 hr. 10 min.
Contents: This is a classroom talk on the topic.

189 Poetry Reading. OKentU.
Date: 18 April 1978.
Place: Hiram College.
Collation: One 7 inch reel 2 tracks 3 3/4 IPS 1 hr. 40 min.
Contents: OFTEN I AM PERMITTED TO RETURN TO A
MEADOW—THE BALLAD OF MRS. NOAH—FOUR PICTURES
OF THE REAL UNIVERSE—CODA [SEVENTEENTH CENTURY
SUITE]—POETRY, A NATURAL THING—THE STRUCTURE
OF RIME II—THE STRUCTURE OF RIME III—A DANCING
CONCERNING A FORM OF WOMEN—THE BALLAD OF THE
FORFAR WITCHES' SING—A COUNTRY WIFE'S SONG— BEND-
ING THE BOW—THE TORN CLOTH—MY MOTHER WOULD
BE A FALCONRESS—TRIBAL MEMORIES, PASSAGES 1—
DANTE ÉTUDES: BOOKS I, XII, XIII, XIV, XV.

190 POETRY AND THE SECULAR IMAGINATION. OKentU.
Date: 19 April 1978.
Place: Kent State University.
Collation: One 7 inch reel 2 tracks 3 3/4 IPS 1 hr. 30 min.
Contents: This is a tape of a lecture.

191 Poetry Reading: Robert Duncan and Robert Creeley. CSf-APA.
Date: 9 May 1978.
Place: San Francisco State University.
Collation: Two cassettes each 1 track 3 3/4 IPS 1 hr. 30 min.
Contents: SONGS OF AN OTHER—THE TORN CLOTH—AN
ALTERNATE LIFE: IN THE SOUTH—HOMECOMING—
SUPPLICATION—THE QUOTIDIAN—DANTE ÉTUDES: LET
HIM FIRST DRINK OF THE FOUNTAIN—LETTING THE BEAT
GO.
Note: This is a joint reading with Robert Creeley.

192 AN EVENING WITH LOUIS ZUKOFSKY FOR A SHOWING OF
THE OUT-TAKES. CSf-APA.
Date: 8 Dec. 1978.
Place: San Francisco Art Institute.
Collation: Two cassettes 3 tracks 1 7/8 IPS 2 hrs.
Contents: RD and Barret Watten talk about Louis Zukofsky.

193 Poetry Reading. KU.
Date: n. d.
Collation: One 7 inch reel 1 track 3 3/4 IPS 1 hr. 10 min.
Contents: FOR CREELEY FROM DUNCAN—FIRST INVENTION

ON THE THEME OF THE ADAM—UPON HIS SEEING A BABY
HOLDING THE FOUR OF HEARTS FOR HIM AND ANOTHER
CARD CONCEALD (FOR ROBERT CREELEY)—WORDS OPEN
OUT UPON GRIEF—AT HOME—AN OWL IS AN ONLY BIRD
OF POETRY—A POEM BEGINNING WITH A LINE BY PIN-
DAR—THE QUESTION—THE PERFORMANCE WE WAIT
FOR—YES, AS A LOOK SPRINGS TO ITS FACE [second version]—
THE STRUCTURE OF RIME XI—UNDER GROUND— THE
NATURAL DOCTRINE—THE STRUCTURE OF RIME XII—
THE STRUCTURE OF RIME III—THE BALLAD OF MRS.
NOAH—KEEPING THE RHYME.

Note: This tape was prepared by RD for Robert Creeley and probably
dates from 1957/58.

I94   [Robert Duncan Lecturing and Reading]. OKentU.
Date: n. d.
Collation: One 7 inch reel 2 tracks 3 3/4 IPS 2 hrs. 45 min.
Contents: Lecture in Vancouver entitled THE WORK—SLEEPING
ALL NIGHT—from FAUST FOUTU: Master of Ceremonies (before
the curtain), "Of Faust Foutu, the jolly old king"—Faust and Mar-
guerite (duet), "To that rank dung that feeds the flowering soul"—
Marguerite (song), "When in the night of love"—Faust (singing),
"Something in the loneliness of my thot"—Maggie, "Love is like a
tiger"—Peter, "Man or woman, what do we care"—Maggie and Peter
(duet), "For every war we won there's another war to win"— Mrs.
Prichitt-Wildebeest, "The Moon in all her phases"—Emory Low-
enthal, "Love is like a lady"—Maggie, "We got along in our own
town"—Maggie, Faust, Peter (trio), "We sail. We sail"—Faust and
Marguerite (duet), "A Cloud. A Story A Lonely Street."—from
MEDEA AT KOLCHIS: Medea, "Oh knave, knave that my heart
sees."—A SONG OF THE OLD ORDER—A PLAY WITH MASKS
(thru Scold's song), "I had a little wish that grew into a crown."
Note: This tape, combining several taped readings, was put together
by RD for The Special Collections at OKentU.

I95   [Robert Duncan reading]. OKentU.
Date: n. d.
Collation: One 7 inch reel 2 tracks 3 3/4 IPS 2 hr. 50 min.
Contents: MEDIEVAL SCENES: THE DREAMERS—THE HEL-
MET OF GOLIATH—THE BANNERS—THE KINGDOM OF JER-
USALEM—THE FESTIVALS—THE MIRROR—THE REAPER—
THE ADORATION OF THE VIRGIN—HUON OF BORDEAUX—
THE ALBIGENSES—I TELL OF LOVE—THE VENICE POEM—
HOMAGE TO THE BROTHERS GRIMM: THE ROBBER
MOON—STRAWBERRIES UNDER THE SNOW—THE DINNER
TABLE OF HARLEQUIN—JERUSALEM—REVIVAL— THE
WASTE, THE ROOM, THE DISCARDED TIMBERS—THE SEC-

OND NIGHT IN THE WEEK—PROCESSIONALS I—PROCESSIONALS II—UPON ANOTHER SHORE OF HELL—AN INCUBUS—EYESIGHT I—EYSIGHT II—GOODBYE TO YOUTH—THE EFFORT—THE EFFORT (con't.)—THE HORNS OF ARTEMIS—AFRICA REVISITED—AN IMAGINARY WAR ELEGY—THE SONG OF THE BORDERGUARD—AN ESSAY AT WAR—FIVE PIECES—HERO SONG—AN IMAGINARY WOMAN—ELUARD'S DEATH—UNKINGD BY AFFECTION—THE BEGINNING OF WRITING—FORCED LINES—AN INTERLUDE. OF RARE BEAUTY—A TRAIN OF THOUGHT—A POEM IN STRETCHING—INCREASING—THIS IS THE POEM THEY ARE PRAISING AS LOADED—ORCHARDS—THERE COULD BE A BOOK WITHOUT NATIONS IN ITS CHAPTERS—HOW DO YOU KNOW YOU ARE THRU?—ROTUND RELIGION—RHYME MOUNTAIN PARTICULAR—SEVERAL POEMS IN PROSE—A BIRTHDAY DIRGE FOR LYNNE BROWN—SURREALIST SHELLS—TWO DICTA OF WILLIAM BLAKE.

Note: This tape, combining several taped readings, was put together by RD for The Special Collections, OKentU.

I96 Robert Duncan and John Weiners.
Date: 1966.
Place: San Francisco.
Collation: One 1/2 inch video tape 30 min.
Contents: RD discusses his work and reads THE ARCHITECTURE PASSAGES 9 and A STATEMENT ON POETICS.

I97 LETTERS. London, Stream Records.
Date: 1968.
Collation: One record two sides 33 1/3 RPM 40 min.
Contents: UNKINGD BY AFFECTION—UPON TAKING HOLD—FIRST INVENTION ON THE THEME FROM ADAM—METAMORPHOSIS—LIGHT SONG—IT'S SPRING. LOVE'S SPRING—AT THE END OF A PERIOD—TRUE TO LIFE—WORDS OPEN OUT UPON GRIEF—AT HOME—RE—SPELLING THE WORD—CORRESPONDENCES—THE GREEN LADY—AN OWL IS AN ONLY BIRD OF POETRY—NEW TIDINGS—CHANGING TRAINS—THE LANGUAGE OF LOVE—THE SIREN SONG—SOURCE MAGIC—CIRCULATING LIGHTS.

I98 Lecture: IDEAS OF PRIMORDIAL TIME IN CHARLES OLSON'S WORK. IaU.
Date: 7 Nov. 1978.
Place: Iowa City, Iowa.
Collation: One cassette 2 tracks 1 7/8 IPS 1 hr. 30 min.
Contents: This is the text of the lecture delivered at "A Charles Olson Festival," University of Iowa.

I99   Lecture: TIMING AND THE CREATION OF TIME IN CHARLES OLSON'S *MAXIMUS*. IaU.
Date: 7 Nov. 1978.
Place: Iowa City, Iowa.
Collation: One cassette 2 tracks 1 7/8 IPS 1 hr 30 min.
Contents: This is the text of the lecture delivered at "A Charles Olson Festival," University of Iowa.

I100   Poetry Reading. IaU.
Date: 9 Nov. 1978.
Place: Iowa City, Iowa.
Collation: One cassette 2 tracks 1 7/8 IPS 1 hr. 30 min.
Contents: DANTE ÉTUDES [complete]—OF MEMORY—HERS— I TOO TREMBLING—AN ALTERNATE LIFE.

I101   CHARLES OLSON AT IOWA. IaU.
Date: 7-9 Nov. 1978.
Place: Iowa City, Iowa.
Collation: Two 1 inch video tape cassettes 2 hrs.
Contents: The second cassette contains selections of RD lectures I97 and I90 as well as selections from reading I99.

I102   Discussion: CHARLES OLSON IN SAN FRANCISCO, 1957. IaU.
Date: 9 Nov. 1978.
Place: Iowa City, Iowa.
Collation: Two cassettes each 2 tracks 1 7/8 IPS 3 hrs.
Contents: This is a discussion by RD, with some interjections by the audience, of Charles Olson's lectures on Whitehead delivered to a small group in San Francisco during Feb. 1957.

I103   CHARLES OLSON MEMORIAL LECTURES. NBuU.
THE POWER OF IMAGINING PERSONS: THE POEM AS AN INTERIOR PLAY.
Date: 20 March 1979.
Place: Buffalo, NY.
Collation: Two cassettes 3 tracks 1 7/8 IPS 1 hr. 30 min.
Contents: This is text of the lecture, plus several long asides.

I104   THE FATEFULNESS OF ON-GOING IDENTIFICATION: THE POEM AS THE RECALL AND ADVENTURE OF SELF IN PROJECTION. NBuU.
Date: 22 March 1979.
Place: Buffalo, N. Y.
Collation: Two cassettes 1 with 2 tracks, 1 with 1 track 1 7/8 IPS 1 hr. 30 min.
Contents: This is the text of the lecture, plus asides.

I105   "FORTH ON THE GODLY SEA": THE DAEMONIC IN THE REALM OF POETRY. NBuU.
Date: 27 March 1979.

Place: Buffalo, N. Y.

Collation: Two cassettes 1 with 2 tracks, 1 with 1 track 1 7/8 IPS 1 hr. 30 min.

Contents: This is the text of the lecture, plus asides.

1106 THE RESOURCES OF THE WORLD: AS ACTUAL; AS REAL— "FINDING THE WAY." NBuU.

Date: 29 March 1979.

Place: Buffalo, N. Y.

Collation: Two cassettes 1 with 2 tracks, 1 with 1 track 1 7/8 IPS 1 hr. 30 min.

Contents: This is the text of the lecture, plus asides.

1107 Poetry Reading. NBuU.

Date: 20 March 1979.

Place: Allentown Community Center, Buffalo, N. Y.

Collation: Two cassettes each 2 tracks 1 7/8 IPS 1 hr. 50 min.

Contents: THE DOOR—THE CONCERT—CODA TO SEVEN-TEENTH CENTURY SUITE—DANTE ÉTUDE, PREFACE—WE WILL ENDEAVOR—SECONDARY IS THE GRAMMAR—TO SPEAK MY MIND—THE INDIVIDUAL MAN—OF EMPIRE— THE WORK—LET HIM FIRST DRINK FROM THE FOUN-TAIN—IN NOTHING SUPERIOR—ZEALOUS LIBERALITY— WE, CONVIVAL IN WHAT IS OURS!—GO MY SONGS, EVEN AS YOU CAME TO ME—THE TORN CLOTH— EIDOLON OF THE AION—TO MASTER BAUDELAIRE—FOR THE ASSIGNATION OF THE SPIRIT—THE SENTINELS.

1108 WORKSHOP DISCUSSION OF CHARLES OLSON MEMORIAL LECTURES. NBuU.

Date: 28 March 1979.

Place: Buffalo, N. Y.

Collation: Two cassettes each 2 tracks 1 7/8 IPS 2 hrs.

Contents: Discussion with frequent comments on Charles Olson and the presentation of the self in the poem by the audience.

1109 WORKSHOP DISCUSSION OF CHARLES OLSON MEMORIAL LECTURES. NBuU.

Date: 29 March 1969.

Place: Buffalo, N. Y.

Collation: Two cassettes each 2 tracks 1 7/8 IPS 2 hrs.

Contents: Discussion frequent comments on Charles Olson and the process of poetry.

1110 Lecture: THE SELF IN POSTMODERN POETRY. AzU.

Date: 29 Dec. 1979.

Place: Modern Language Association Convention, San Francisco.

Collation: One cassette 2 tracks 1 7/8 IPS 1 hr.

Contents: This is the text of the lecture, with frequent interjections.

J.
Works about Robert Duncan:
Reviews
Articles
Books
Parts of Books
Theses
Dissertations

Reviews

Heavenly City Earthly City

J1   Rukeyser, Muriel. "Myth and Torment." *Poetry*, LXXII, 1 (April 1948), 48-51.

Medieval Scenes

J2   Humphries, Rolfe. "Verse Chronicle." *The Nation*, CLXXI, 7 (12 Aug. 1950), 152-153.

J3   Byrd, Donald. "[Review of] *Medieval Scenes.*" *The Back Door*, 11/12 (Fall 1978), 76-79.

Faust Foutu

J4   Anon. "Books Received." *Origin*, first series, 13 (Summer 1954), 64.

J5   Benjamin, Jerry. "Afterthought on the N. Y. Poets Theatre Production of *Night at the Tango Place* by James Waring; *Still Life* by John Wieners; *Faust Foutu* (ACT IV) by Robert Duncan." *The Floating Bear*, 17 (1961), [11].

J6   Herschberger, Ruth. "New York Poets Theatre at Off-Broadway." *The Village Voice*, VII, 8 (14 Dec. 1961), 12.
Note: This is a review of the New York Poets Theatre production of *Faust Foutu*, Act IV.

Caesar's Gate

J7   Eckman, Frederick. "Six Poets, Young or Unknown." *Poetry*, LXXXIX, 1 (Oct. 1956), 52-63; RD 62-63.

Selected Poems

J8   Rosenthal, M. L. "Notes from the Future: Two Poets." *The Nation*, CLXXXIX, 13 (24 Oct. 1959), 257-258.

J9   Snodgrass, W. D. "Four Gentlemen; Two Ladies." *The Hudson Review*, XIII, 1 (Spring 1960), 120-131; RD 125-126.

J10   Ammons, A. R. "Three Poets." *Poetry*, XCVI, 1 (April 1960), 52-55; RD 53-55.

Letters

J11   Creeley, Robert. "A Light, A Glory, A Fair Luminous Cloud." *Poetry*, XCVI, 1 (April 1960), 55-57; Rpt. in *A Quick Graph: Collected Notes & Essays* (San Francisco: Four Seasons Foundation, 1970), pp. 195-197.

The New American Poetry

J12   Moore, Marianne. "The Ways Our Poets Have Taken In Fifteen Years Since the War." *New York Herald Tribune Book Review*, XXVI, 47

(26 June 1960), pp. [1], 11.

Note: This review contains a photograph of RD and a quotation from his poem FOOD FOR FIRE, FOOD FOR THOUGHT.

J13   Shapiro, Harvey. "Rebellious Mythmakers." *The New York Times Literary Supplement*, 28 Aug. 1960, p. 6.
Note: Photographs of four poets, including one of RD by Harry Redl, accompany this article.

The Opening of the Field

J14   Rexroth, Kenneth. "Robert Duncan Tilts Against the Windmills of Academic Writing." *San Francisco Examiner*, 11 Dec. 1960, p. 12.

J15   Engle, Paul. "Three Books of Verse Whose Time Is Now." *The Lively Arts and Book Review, of New York Herald Tribune*, XXXVII, 25 (22 Jan. 1961), p. 39.

J16   Rexroth, Kenneth. "The Belated Discovery." *The Nation*, CXCII, 2 (14 Jan. 1961), 35-36.

J17   Simpson, Louis. "Important and Unimportant Poems." *The Hudson Review*, XIV, 3 (Autumn 1961), 461-470; RD 464.

J18   Zeigler, Arthur. "A Mixed Quartet." *New York Times Book Review*, 441, 12 3 Dec. 1961, pp. 10, 14, 18; RD 10, 14. Picture 10.

J19   Smith, John. "Various Virtues." *Poetry Review*, LIII, 1 (Jan.-March 1962), 42.

J20   Dickey, James. "The Stillness at the Centre of the Target." *The Sewanee Review*, LXX, 3 (Summer 1962), 484-503.

J21   Sorrentino, Gil[bert]. "Duncan and Spicer." *Yugen*, 8 (1962), 11-15; RD 11-14.

J22   Rosenthal, M. L. "Seven Voices." *The Reporter*, XXVIII (3 Jan. 1963), 46-49; RD 49.

J23   Aronson, S. M. L. "Robert Duncan." *Yale Literary Magazine*, CXXXI, 3-4 (April 1963), 15-16.

J24   Piccirillo, Tony. "The Opening of the Field." *The State Beacon*, XXXIX, 6 (17 Oct. 1973), p. 12.
Note: This review of the New Directions edition of RD's book appeared in the school paper of The William Paterson College of New Jersey.

Writing Writing

J25   Stanley, George. "Writing Writing." *Open Space*, 11 (Nov. 1964), [34].
Note: This is a review in the form of a poem.

J26   Billings, Claude. "Writers Explore Life in Volumes of Poetry." *The Indianapolis Star*, 11 Oct. 1964, sect. 10, p. 5.

J27   Warren, James E., Jr. "Experimental Poets: Current Offerings are Nothing New." *The Atlanta Times*, 25 Oct. 1964, n. pag.

J28   Stephens, Robert. "Lyrical Kind of History." *San Francisco Call Bulletin*, 14 Nov. 1964, *California Saturday Books Page*, p. 7.

J29   Willeford, Charles. "A World Without Emotion." *The Miami News*, 15 Nov. 1964, p. 26.

J30   Salas, Floyd. "Three Impressive Books of Poetry." *Oakland Tribune*, 6 Dec. 1964, [Section] EN, p. 4.

J31   Carruth, Hayden. "Scales of the Marvelous." *The Nation*, CXCIX, 18 (7 Dec. 1964), 442-444.

J32   Kennedy, J. "Experiments and Experimenters." *The New York Times Book Review*, 20 Dec. 1964, pp. 4-5.

J33   Anon. [Review of *Roots and Branches*]. *Booklist*, LXI, 11 (1 Feb. 1965), 510.

J34   Douthit, Peter L. "Song Verse of Duncan Gets Praise." *Fort Worth Star-Telegram*, 7 Feb. 1965, sec. 3, p. 7.

J35   [Anon]. "[Review of] *Roots and Branches*." *Choice*, II, 1 (March 1965), 21.

J36   Slavitt, David R. "The Lost, The Frozen, And The Fodder." *Book Week*, Supplement to the Sunday *New York Herald Tribune*, *Washington Post*, and *San Francisco Examiner*, 14 March 1965, pp. 4, 19.

J37   Sale, Roger. "New Poems, Ancient and Modern." *The Hudson Review*, XVIII, 2 (Summer 1965), 299-308; RD 302-303.

J38   Mazzocco, Robert. "A Philosophical Poet." *The New York Review of Books*, 453:IV, 9 (3 June 1965), 20-23; RD 20-22.

J39   Dickey, James. "Orientations." *The American Scholar*, XXXIV, 4 (Autumn 1965), 646-658; RD 658.

J40   Will, Frederick. "Notes on Robert Duncan." *Poetry*, CVI, 6 (Sept. 1965), 427-428.

J41   Creeley, Robert. "To Disclose That Vision Particular to Dreams." *The Humanist*, XXVI, 1 (Jan.-Feb. 1966), 28; Rpt. in *A Quick Graph: Collected Notes & Essays* (San Francisco: Four Seasons Foundation, 1970), pp. 198-201.

J42   Weeks, Robert Lewis. "By Fits and Starts." *Prairie Schooner*, XL, 2 (Summer 1966), 175-186; RD 177-178.

J43 Davis, Douglas M. "Where New Poetry Finds Fertile Ground." *The National Observer*, V, 28 (11 July 1966), p. 24.
Note: A photograph of RD accompanies this article.

J44 Fowler, Gene. "The Sudden Art." *Illuminations*, 4 (Winter 1968-69), 26-27.

J45 Fuller, John. "Innocence Abroad." *The Listener*, LXXIV, 2156 (23 July 1970), 122.

As Testimony

J46 Will, Frederick. "Notes on Robert Duncan." *Poetry*, CVI, 6 (Sept. 1965), 427-428.

J47 Clark, Thomas. "The Exchange: A Concern." *Kulchur*, V, 20 (Winter 1965-66), 96-100.

Fragments of a Disorderd Devotion

J48 Loewinsohn, Ron. "The Yellow Submarine." *R.*C**. *Lion*, 2 ([Fall] 1966), 21-26; RD 22-23.

Of The War

J49 Davis, Douglas. "In The Flow of Poetry, The Ladies Flourish." *The National Observer*, VI, 6 (6 Feb. 1967), p. 31.

J50 Zweig, Paul. "Robert Duncan's World." *Poetry*, CXI, 6 (March 1968), 402-403.

The Years As Catches

J51 Davis, Douglas. "In The Flow of Poetry, The Ladies Flourish." *The National Observer*, VI, 6 (6 Feb. 1967), p. 31.

J52 Anon. "Chained to the Parish Pump." *Times Literary Supplement*, 3394, (16 March 1967), p. 220.

J53 Broughton, James. "A Tonic Collection from the Master Poets." *The San Francisco Chronicle, The World*, 16 April 1967, p. 33.

J54 Perreault, John. "Holding Back and Letting Go." *The New York Times Book Review*, 19 Nov. 1967, p. 97.

J55 Zweig, Paul. "Robert Duncan's World." *Poetry*, CXI, 6 (March 1968), 405.

Bending the Bow

J56 DeLancey, Rose Mary. "Words, Sounds, Ideas, Poet's Tools, States, Robert Duncan." *New Sentinel* (Fort Wayne, Ind.), 13 April 1968, sec. 1, p. 4A.

J57   Arnold, Bob. "Duncan Difficult for Novice." *The Missourian* (Columbia, Mo.), 28 April 1968, p. 10.

J58   J[ohnson], D[onald] B. "It's Spring and They Sing." *Worcester Sunday Telegram* (*Parade Magazine*), 19 May 1968, p. 23.

J59   Rakosi, Carl. "Derivative Poet Borrows Images, Enriches Debt." *Minneapolis Sunday Tribune*, 26 May 1968, p. 6E.

J60   C[ahen], A[lfred] B., and D[avid] C. F[rench]. "On The Editor's Desk." *American Weave*, XXXII, 1 (June 1968), 67.

J61   Cushman, Jerome. [Review of *Bending the Bow*]. *Library Journal*, XCIII, 1 (June 1968), 2247.

J62   [Anon]. "Notes on Current Books." *Virginia Quarterly Review*, XLIV, 3 (Summer 1968), civ.

J63   Carruth, Hayden. "Making it New." *The Hudson Review*, XXI, 2 (Summer 1968), 399-412; RD 401-403.

J64   Marx, Anne. "Experimental." *Spirit, A Magazine of Catholic Verse*, XXXV, 3 (July 1968), 94-95.

J65   Howes, Victor. "Four Poets with Teaching Ways." *Christian Science Monitor* (23 July 1968), p. 9.

J66   Simpson, Louis. "New Books of Poems." *Harper's Magazine*, 1419 (Aug. 1968), 73-77; RD 74.

J67   Pack, Robert. "To Be Loved For Its Voice." *Saturday Review*, LI, 34 (24 Aug. 1968), 39-40; RD 39.

J68   Harrison, Jim. "Pure Poetry." *New York Times Book Review*, 29 Sept. 1968, p. 66.

J69   Seidman, Hugh. [Review of *Bending the Bow*]. *Caterpillar*, 5 (Oct. 1968), 142-144.

J70   Eshleman, Clayton. [Footnote]. *Caterpillar*, 5 (Oct. 1968), [161].

J71   Skelton, Robin. "The Poet As Guru." *Kayak*, 16 (1968), 59-62.

J72   Anon. "Books in Brief." *The Beloit Poetry Journal*, XIX, 2 (Winter 1968-69), 40.

J73   Lieberman, Laurence. "A Confluence of Poets." *Poetry*, CIV, 1 (April 1969), 40-58; RD 43-44.

J74   Zinnes, Harriet. "Duncan's One Poem." *Prairie Schooner*, XLIII, 3 (Fall 1969), 317-320.

J75   Anon. "Dubious Seer." *The Times Literary Supplement*, 3621, 23 July 1971, p. 855.

The Sweetness and Greatness of Dante's Divine Comedy

J76   Zweig, Paul. "Robert Duncan's World." *Poetry*, CXI, 6 (March 1968), 402-405.

J77   Anon. "Dubious Seer." *The Times Literary Supplement*, 3621, 23 July 1971, p. 855.

Medea at Kolchis

J78   Zweig, Paul. "Robert Duncan's World." *Poetry*, CXI, 6 (March 1968), 404-405.

The First Decade

J79   Owen, B. Evan. "Oxford Poet's Triumph." *Oxford Mail*, 17 April 1969, p. 5.

J80   Kavanagh, P. J. "Black Mountain Captain." *The Guardian* (Manchester, England), 3 April 1969, n. pag.

J81   Anon. "Read or Written?" *Times Literary Supplement*, 3505, 1 May 1969, p. 467.

J82   Andrews, Lyman. "New Poetry: Youthful Promise." *The Sunday Times*, 4 May 1969, n. pag.

J83   Holmes, Richard. "Poets from America: From Mistress Bradstreet To The Boston Sound." *The Times* (London), No. 57, 556, 10 May 1969, p. 21.

J84   Porter, Peter. "Huts of Words." *London Magazine*, IX, 4/5, New Series 100 (July-Aug. 1969), 194-200; RD 194-197.

J85   Brownjohn, Alan. "Dark Forces." *The New Statesman*, LXXVIII, 2009 (12 Sept. 1969), 346-347; RD 347.

J86   Tallman, Warren. "Robert Duncan: Poet of Passion." *The Montreal Star*, 13 Sept. 1969, p. 6; Rpt. as "The Eternal Mood: Robert Duncan's Devotion to Language," in *Godawful Streets of Man, Open Letter*, third series, 6

J87   Hayman, Ronald. "The City & The House: On Recent Poetry." *Encounter*, XXXIV, 2 (Feb. 1970), 84-91; RD 84-85.

Derivations

J88   Kavanagh, P. J. "Black Mountain Captain." *The Guardian*, 3 April 1969, n. pag.

J89   Owen, B. Evan. "Oxford Poet's Triumph." *Oxford Mail*, 17 April 1969, p. 5.

J90 Zinnes, Harriet. "Soul and Spiritual Drama of Adolescence." *Weekly Tribune* (Paris) XII, 16, 20 April 1969, n. pag.

J91 Anon. "Read or Written?" *Times Literary Supplement*, 3505, 1 May 1969, p. 467.

J92 Andrews, Lyman. "New Poetry: Youthful Promise." *The Sunday Times* (4 May 1969), n. pag.

J93 Donoghue, Denis. "Oasis Poetry." *New York Review of Books*, XIV, 7 May 1970, pp. 35-38; RD 35-36.

J94 Holmes, Richard. "Poets From America: From Mistress Bradstreet To The Boston Sound." *The Times*, 57, 556, 10 May 1969, p. 21.

J95 Porter, Peter. "Huts of Words." *London Magazine*, IX, 4/5, New Series 100 (July-Aug. 1969), 194-200; RD 194-197.

J96 Brownjohn, Alan. "Dark Forces." *The New Statesman*, LXXVIII, 2009 (12 Sept. 1969), 346-347; RD 347.

J97 Tallman, Warren. "Robert Duncan: Poet of Passion." *The Montreal Star*, 13 Sept. 1969, p. 6; Rpt. as "The Eternal Mood: Robert Duncan's Devotion to Language," *in Godawful Streets Of Man, Open Letter*, third series, 6 (1976), 70-74. A photograph of RD by Patricia Jordon accompanied the first appearance of the article.

J98 Garioch, Robert. "Battles Won." *Poetry Review*, LX, 3 (Autumn 1969), 208-209; RD 208.

J99 Hayman, Ronald. "The City & The House: On Recent Poetry." *Encounter*, XXXIV, 2 (Feb. 1970), 84-91; RD 84-85.

J100 Blackburn, Thomas. "Birds and Beasts; Smog and Sopped Handkerchief." *Poetry Review*, LXI, 1 (Spring 1970), 85-88; RD 85-86.

J101 Rosenthal, M. L. "Poetry of the Main Chance." *Times Literary Supplement*, 3544, 29 Jan. 1970, p. 113.

Tribunals

J102 Anon. "Dubious Seer." *The Times Literary Supplement*, 3621, 23 July 1971, p. 855.

J103 Quartermain, Peter. "Body Politic," *Tuatara*, 6 (Nov. 1971), 62-63.

J104 Bluford, Ken. "Tribunals: Passages 31-35, and A Seventeenth Century Suite." *The Painted Bride Quarterly*, II, 2 (Spring 1975), 32-36.

The Truth and Life of Myth

J105 Contoski, Victor. "Robert Duncan: The Truth and Life of Myth." *Minnesota Review*, 3 (Fall 1972), 127-128.

J106 Montag, Tom. "Montag on The Truth & Life of Myth." *Margins*, 2 (Oct. 1972), [10]; Rpt. in Tom Montag, *Concern/s: essays & reviews 1972-1976* (Milwaukee, Wis.: Pentagram Press, 1977), pp. 3-4.

Dante

J107 Navero, William. "Duncan, Creely [sic] and Dorn." *Ethos*, VIII, 14 (12 Dec. 1974), 27-28.

J108 Adamson, Robert. "A Choice of Books for 1974." *The Australian* (Sydney, Australia), 28 Dec. 1974, p. 17.

A Seventeenth Century Suite

J109 Bluford, Ken. "Tribunals: Passages 31-35, and A Seventeenth Century Suite." *The Painted Bride Quarterly*, II, 2 (Spring 1975), 32-36.

Articles

J110 Rukeyser, Muriel. "A Group of Region Poets." *The Pacific Spectator*, II, 1 (Winter 1948), 42-55.

J111 Miles, Josephine. "Pacific Coast Poetry: 1947." *The Pacific Spectator*, II, 2 (Spring 1948), 134-150; RD 146.

J112 Olson, Charles. "Against Wisdom As Such." *Black Mountain Review*, I, 1 (Spring 1954), 3-7; Rpt. in *Human Universe and Other Essays*, ed. Donald Allen (San Francisco: The Auerhahn Society, 1965), pp. 67-71.

J113 Rexroth, Kenneth. "San Francisco Letter." *Evergreen Review*, 1, 2 (1957), 5-14; RD 10-11.

J114 Rosenthal, M. L. "In Exquisite Chaos." *The Nation*, CLXXXVII, 14 (1 Nov. 1958), 324-327.

J115 Parkinson, Thomas. "Phenomenon or Generation." *California Monthly*, LXXI, 9 (June 1961), 1-14, 37-39; Rpt. in *A Casebook on the Beat*. (New York: Thomas Y. Crowell Company, 1961), pp. 276-290. *Note:* A full-page photograph of RD by Harry Redl appears on p. [12] of the original article.

J116 Levertov, Denise. "What is a Prose Poem." *The Nation*, CXCIII, 22 (23 Dec. 1961), 518-519.

J117 Esty, Jane, and Paul Lett. "The Campaign Against the Poets." *Mutiny Alert Part I (A Mutiny Magazine Extra)* (Fall-Winter 1961-1962), n. pag.

J118 McHugh, Vincent. "Man to Read the Meter By." *The Nation*, CXCIV, 21 (26 May 1962), 476-479.

J119 Schaff, David. "Some Statements on Projective Verse." *Yale Literary Magazine*, CXXXI, 3/4 (April 1963), 5-14; RD 11-12.

J120 Dawson, David. "Editorial: Olson/Creeley/Levertov/Duncan/ Ginsberg/Whalen/Avision, A Document of Response." *Tish*, 21 (Sept. 1963), 2-8.

J121 Franklyn, Frederick. "Towards Print (Excerpts from a Journal of U. of British Columbia Seminar)." *Trace*, 51 (Winter 1963), 277-284.

J122 Levertov, Denise. "An Admonition." *Things*, 1 (1964), 4-7; Rpt. in Denise Levertov, *The Poet in the World* (New York: New Directions, 1973), pp. 57-61.

J123 Tomlinson, Charles. "Black Mountain as Focus." *The Review*, 10 (Jan. 1964), 4-5.
Note: This is an introduction to an anthology of The Black Mountain Poets, as selected by Charles Tomlinson.

J124 Bergé, Carol. "The Vancouver Report or How I Fell in Love With Robert Duncan." *Open Space*, 7 (July 1964), [38].

J125 Olson, Charles. "Against Wisdom As Such." *Open Space*, 8 (Aug. 1964), 15-18. See J112.

J126 Bowering, George. "The New American Prosody: A Look At The Problem of Notating 'Free Verse.'" *Kulchur*, 15 (Autumn 1964), 3-14.

J127 Spector, Robert D. "A Way to Say What a Man Can See." *The Saturday Review* XLVIII (13 Feb. 1965), 46-48; RD 47.

J128 Creeley, Robert. "A Note." *Yale Literary Magazine*, CXXXIII, 5 (April 1965), 27-34; RD 27-29.

J129 Davis, Douglas M. "New Breed of Poet Emerges from the Coffeehouse." *The National Observer*, IV, 32, 16 Aug. 1965, p. 19.

J130 Eichele, Robin. "The Berkeley Poetry Conference." *Work*, 2 (Fall 1965), 73-79, 95; RD 74-75.
Note: Three photographs of RD (as well as many others) appear between pp. 78 and 79.

J131 Levertov, Denise. "Some Notes on Organic Form." *Poetry*, CVI, 6 (Sept. 1965), 420-425.

J132 Wesling, Donald. "Berkeley: Free Speech and Free Verse." *The Nation*, CCI, 15 (8 Nov. 1965), 338-340.

J133 Dorn, Edward. "The Outcasts of Foker Plat: News From The States." *The Wivenhoe Park Review*, 1 (Winter 1965), 51-62; RD 55-57.

J134 Kasowitz, Dan. "A Description of *Apprehensions:* The Tantamounce." *Tish*, 37 (18 June 1966), 3-4.

J135 Persky, Stan. "A Letter to Editor (Dan McLeod)." *Tish*, 38 (13 Nov. 1966), 2.

J136 Bly, Robert. "On Political Poetry." *The Nation*, CCIV, 17 (24 April 1967), 522-524; RD 524.

J137 Koch, Stephen. "Performance Without A Net." *The Nation*, CCIV, 17 (24 April 1967), 524-526.

J138 Creeley, Robert. "Talks About Poetry." *Harper's Bazaar*, 3068 (July 1967), 81, 120, 121, 126; RD 81.

J139 Fauchereau, Serge. "Les intellectuels et la guerre." *Les Lettres Nouvelles* (July 1967), 129-134.

J140 Turnbull, Gael. "Some Notes on the Poetry of Robert Duncan." *New Measure*, III, 6 (Summer 1967), 40-45.

J141 Carroll, Paul. "The American Poets in Their Skins 1950-1967." *Choice*, 5 (1967), 81-107; RD 84.

J142 Vance, Thomas. "Poetry and the Generation of Critics." *Southern Review* NS IV, 4 (Oct. 1968), 1099-1109; RD 1103-1104.

J143 Anon. "Poetry: Combatting Society With Surrealism." *Time*, XCIII, 4 (24 Jan. 1969), pp. 72, 74, 76; RD 76.
Note: A photograph of RD by Christopher Springman appears on p. 74.

J144 Fauchereau, Serge. "La poésie américaine en 1968-69." *Combat* (17 Avril 1969), p. 11.

J145 Lansing, Gerrit. "Test of Translation I: Nerval's Horus." *Caterpillar*, 7 (April 1969), 77-88, [inside back cover].

J146 Nelson, Rudolph L. "The Edge of the Transcendent: The Poetry of Levertov and Duncan." *Southwest Review*, LIV (Spring 1969), 188-202.

J147 Fauchereau, Serge. "La poésie américaine." *L'Art vivant*, 3 (July 1969), 24-27. Paris.
Note: This article contains a translation of THE HORNS OF ARTEMIS.

J148 Parkinson, Thomas. "Perspective: Yes, Rare Wilderness," *New Orleans Review*, I, 4 (Summer 1969), 381-387.

J149 Simpson, Louis. "Poetry in The Sixties—Long Live Blake! Down With Donne!" *The New York Times Book Review*, 28 Dec. 1969, pp. 1-3, 18.

J150 Tomlinson, Charles. "The Poetry of Robert Duncan." *Agenda*, VIII, 3/4 (Autumn-Winter 1970), 159-170.

J151 Cooperman, Stanley. "Poetry of Dissent in the United States." *The Michigan Quarterly Review*, X, 1 (Winter 1971), 23-28; RD 26.

J152 Lazur, Steve. "Symposium Criticizes Education." *The Observer* (21 April 1972), 4, 12.

J153 Sienicka, Marta. "William Carlos Williams and Some Younger Poets." *Studia Anglica Posnaniensia*, IV (1972), 183-193.

J154 Reid, Ian. "Towards A Possible Music: The Poetry of Robert Duncan." *New Poetry*, XXI, 2 (April 1973), 17-27.

J155 Mottram, Eric. "Sixties American Poetry, Poetics and Poetic Movements." [Program for] *Modern American Poetry Conference* (London: The Polytechnic of Central London, 1973), pp. 1-34; RD passim.

J156 MacIntyre, Wendy. "Robert Duncan: The Actuality of Myth." *Open Letter*, second series, 4 (Spring 1973), 38-54.

J157 Gilbert, Gerry. "Slow Dylan Rbt Duncan." *Open Letter*, second series, 4 (Spring 1973), 55.

J158 Bowering, George. "Robert Duncan." *Open Letter*, second series, 4 (Spring 1973), 56.

J159 Johnson, Ronald. "Wor[l]ds 24." *Maps*, 6 (1974), 68-69.

J160 Silliman, Ron. "Opening." *Maps*, 6 (1974), 72-80.

J161 MacIntyre, Wendy. "The Logos of Robert Duncan." *Maps*, 6 (1974), 81-98.

J162 Taylor, Loring. "Pietry in cimpui lui Robert Duncan (in Romaneste de ion bitea si N[icki] Hersenyi)." *Steaua* (March 1974), 45-58.

J163 Fauchereau, Serge. "Notes américaines." *Steaua* (Sept. 1974), 48-50.

J164 Rosenthal, M. L. "The Aroused Language of Modern American Poetry: Like the Shark, It Contains a Shoe." *The New York Times Magazine*, 24 Nov. 1974, pp. 13, 40-47.

J165 Smith, D. Newton. "The Influence of Music on the Black Mountain Poets: I." *St. Andrews Review*, III, 1 (Fall-Winter 1974), 99-115; RD 106-112.

J166 Brien, Dolores Elise. "Robert Duncan: A Poet in the Emerson-Whitman Tradition." *The Centennial Review*, XIX, 4 (Fall 1975), 308-316.

J167 Weatherhead, A. Kingsley. "Robert Duncan and the Lyric." *Contemporary Literature*, XVI, 2 (Spring 1975), 163-174.

J168 Goldoni, Annalisa. "Robert Duncan O La Poesia Come Religione," *Edizioni Di Storia E Letteratura*, 21-22 (1975-1976), 445-473.

J169 Morgan, Stuart. "Linearity and Passionate Dispersion: Notes on Robert Duncan's 'Poem Beginning with a Line by Pindar' (The Opening of the Field 1959)." *New Lugano Review*, 11-12 (1976), 34-39, 60.

J170 Bowering, George. "Robert Duncan in Canada." *Essays on Canadian Writing*, 4 (Spring 1976), 16-18.

J171 Davidson, Michael. "Organic Poetry." *Reader*, 5, 15 (15-22 April 1976), p. 4.

J172 Quarles, David. "Robert Duncan—Poet of the Light and Dark." *The Advocate* (28 July 1976), 31.
Note: Sections 6 and 12 of CIRCULATIONS OF THE SONG and a photograph of RD by Crawford Barton appear with this article, which is based on an interview with RD.

J173 Bertholf, Robert J. and Ruth Nurmi. "Scales of Marvelous: Robert Duncan's 'The Venice Poems.'" *New Poetry*, 23, 2 (1976), 22-32.

J174 Altieri, Charles. "The Book of the World: Robert Duncan's Poetics of Presence." *Sun & Moon: A Quarterly of Literature and Art*, 1 (Winter 1976), 66-94.

J175 Heller, Michael. "Duncan's Concert." *Montemora*, 3 (1977), 190-194.

J176 Faas, Ekbert. "The Barbaric Friendship With Robert: A Biographical Palimpsest." *Mosaic*, XI, 2 (Winter 1978), 141-152.

J177 Weber, Robert C. "Robert Duncan and the Poem of Resonance." *Concerning Poetry*, XI, 1 (Spring 1978), 67-73.

J178 Altieri, Charles. "The Objectivist Tradition." *Chicago Review*, XXX, 3 (Winter 1979), 5-22; RD 17-18.

J179 Broughton, James. "Homage to the Great Bear." *Credences*, III, 2/3 (March 1980), 140-145.

J180 Everson, William. "Of Robert Duncan." *Credences*, III, 2/3 (March 1980), 147-151.

J181 Cooley, Dennis. "Robert Duncan's Green Wor[l]ds." *Credences*, III, 2/3 (March 1980), 152-160.

J182 Quasha, George. "Duncan Reading." *Credences*, III, 2/3 (March 1980), 162-175.

J183 Peters, Robert. "Robert Duncan: Latter-Day Pre-Raphaelite." *The Threepenny Review*, 2 (Summer 1980), 15-17.

J184 Kikel, Rudy. "After Whitman and Auden: Gay Male Sensibility in Poetry Since 1945." *Gay Sunshine*, 44/45 (Summer 1980), 34-39.

J185 Rasula, Jed. "Charles Olson and Robert Duncan: Muthologistical Grounding." *Spring* (1979), 102-117.

J186 Pruitt, John. "Robert Duncan at the 92nd Street Y April 16, 1979." *The Downtown Review*, I, 3-4 (May-June 1979), 46-47.

J187 Mackey, Nathaniel. "The World-Poem in Microcosm: Robert Duncan's 'The Continents." *ELH*, XLVII (1980), 595-618.

J188 Peters, Robert. "Where the Bee Sucks: A Meditation on Robert Duncan's 'Night Scenes." *Little Caesar*, 11 (1980), 225-228.

J189 Michelson, Peter. "A Materialistic Critique of Robert Duncan's Grand Collage." *Boundary 2*, VIII, 2 (Winter 1980), 21-43.

J190 Cooley, Dennis. "The Poetics of Robert Duncan." *Boundary 2*, VIII, 2 (Winter 1980), 45-73.

J191 Aiken, William. "Denise Levertov, Robert Duncan, and Allen Ginsberg: Modes of the Self in Projective Poetry." *Modern Poetry Studies*, X, 2/3 (1981), 200-240.

J192 Finkelstein, Norman. "Robert Duncan, Poet of the Law." *Sagetrieb*, II, 1 (Spring 1983), 75-88.

J193 Sylvester, William. "Creeley, Duncan, Zukofsky 1968—Melody Moves the Light." *Sagetrieb*, II, 1 (Spring 1983), 97-104.

J194 Johnson, Mark. "Robert Duncan's 'Momentous Inconclusions." *Sagetrieb*, II, 2 (Fall 1983), 71-84.

J195 Carruth, Hayden. "Duncan's Dream." *Ironwood*, XI, 2 (Fall 1983), 5-8.

J196 MacIntyre, Wendy. "Psyche, Christ and the Poem." *Ironwood*, XI, 2 (Fall 1983), 9-22.

J197 Kenner, Hugh. "1680 Words on Duncan's Words." *Ironwood*, XI, 2 (Fall 1983), 23-27.

J198 Davidson, Michael. "Cave of Resemblances, Caves of Rimes: Tradition and Repetition in Robert Duncan." *Ironwood*, XI, 2 (Fall 1983), 33-45.

J199 Boone, Bruce. "Robert Duncan and Gay Community: A Reflection." *Ironwood*, XI, 2 (Fall 1983), 66-82.

J200 Molesworth, Charles. "Truth and Life and Robert Duncan." *Ironwood*, XI, 2 (Fall 1983), 83-94.

J201 Rakosi, Carl. "A Letter to Robert Duncan." *Ironwood*, XI, 2 (Fall 1983), 134-135.

J202 Matthias, John. "Robert Duncan & David Jones: Some Affinities." *Ironwood*, XI, 2 (Fall 1983), 140-157.

J203 Rudman, Mark. "Sometimes A Painful Existing." *Ironwood*, XI, 2 (Fall 1983), 159-172.

J204 Johnson, Mark. "'Passages': Cross-Section of the Universe." *Iron-wood*, XI, 2 (Fall 1983), 173-191.

J205 Taggart, John. "Of the Power of the Word." *Ironwood*, XI, 2 (Fall 1983), 192-198.

Books and Parts of Books

J206 Rosenthal, M. L. *The Modern Poets: A Critical Introduction.* New York: Oxford University Press, 1960, pp. 268, 272.

J207 Bergé, Carol. *The Vancouver Report.* New York: Fuckpress, 1964. RD mentioned throughout.

J208 [Hawley, Robert]. "Robert Duncan." In *Checklists of Separate Publications of Poets at the First Berkeley Poetry Conference.* Berkeley, Calif.: Cody's Books, 1965, pp. [5-7].

J209 Stepanchev, Stephen. *American Poetry Since 1945: A Critical Survey.* New York: Harper & Row, 1965, pp. 145-151.

J210 Dembo, L. S. *Conceptions of Reality in Modern American Poetry.* Berkeley and Los Angeles: University of California Press, 1966, pp. 208-219.

J211 Hoffman, Frederick J. "Contemporary American Poetry." In *Patterns of Commitment in American Literature*, ed. Marston LaFrance. Toronto: University of Toronto Press, 1967, pp. 193-207; RD 204-205.

J212 Weatherhead, A. Kingsley. *The Edge of the Image: Marianne Moore, William Carlos Williams and Some Other Poets.* Seattle: University of Washington Press, 1967, pp. 232-244.

J213 Rosenthal, M. L. *The New Poets: American and British Poetry Since World War II.* New York: Oxford University Press, 1967, pp. 174-184.

J214 Fairchild, Hoxie Neale. "Valley of Dry Bones." In *Religious Trends in English Poetry.* New York: Columbia University Press, 1968. Volume VI, pp. 222, 224-225.

J215 Fauchereau, Serge. *Lecture de la poésie américaine.* Paris: Les Editions de Minuit, 1968, pp. 234-240.

J216 Pearce, Roy Harvey. *Historicism Once More: Problems & Occasions for the American Scholar.* Princeton: Princeton University Press, 1969, pp. 327-330.

J217 Lieberman, Laurence. *Unassigned Frequencies: American Poetry in Review, 1969-77.* Urbana, Illinois: University of Illinois Press, 1977. "Robert Duncan," pp. 196-197; Rpt. review of BB from *Poetry* (1969).

J218 Hamburger, Michael. *The Truth of Poetry: Tensions in Modern Poetry from Baudelaire to the 1960's*. New York: Harcourt Brace Jovanovich, Inc., 1969, pp. 284-287.

J219 Waggoner, Hyatt. *American Poets from the Puritans to the Present*. New York: Houghton Mifflin Co., 1969, pp. 623-624.

J220 Nin, Anaïs. *The Diary of Anaïs Nin: Volume Three 1939-1944*, ed. with a preface by Gunther Stuhlmann. New York: Harcourt, Brace & World, Inc., 1969, pp. 75-100, 111-112, 114-115, 167-170, 181-187.
Note: Duncan is not the sole topic of these sections of the diary, but he comes up repeatedly as part of the community of people in New York. Nin quotes from Duncan's diary and her letters to him. Other references to Duncan appear in the book. See the index.

J221 Taylor, Neill. "Robert Duncan." In *Contemporary Poets of the English Language*, ed. Rosalie Murphy. London: St. James Press, 1970, pp. 312-314.

J222 Charters, Samuel. *Some Poems/Poets. Studies in American Underground Poetry Since 1945* (photographs by Ann Charters). Berkeley: Oyez, 1971, pp. 47-55.

J223 M[ottram], E[ric]. "Robert Duncan." In *The Penguin Companion to Literature* 3, ed. Eric Mottram and Malcolm Bradbury: Latin America ed. Jean Franco. Harmondsworth, Middlesex: Penguin Books, Ltd., 1971, p. 81.

J224 Cook, Bruce. *The Beat Generation*. New York: Charles Scribner's Sons, 1971, pp. 126-132, 215-216.

J225 Duberman, Martin. *Black Mountain: An Exploration in Community*. New York: E. P. Dutton & Co., Inc., 1972, *passim*.

J226 Hassan, Ihab. *Contemporary American Literature, 1945-1972: An Introduction*. New York: Frederick Ungar Publishing Co., 1973, pp. 115-116.

J227 Malkoff, Karl. "Robert Duncan." *Crowell's Handbook of Contemporary American Poetry*. New York: Thomas Y. Crowell Company, 1973, pp. 111-117.

J228 Stauffer, Donald Barlow. *A Short History of American Poetry*. New York: E. P. Dutton & Co., Inc., 1974, pp. 419-421.

J229 Mersmann, James. *Out of the Vietnam Vortex: A Study of Poets and Poetry Against the War*. Lawrence, Kansas: The University Press of Kansas, 1974, pp. 159-204.

J230 Shaw, Robert B. "The Poetry of Protest." In *American Poetry Since 1960: Some Critical Perspectives*, ed. Robert B. Shaw. Chester Springs, Pa.: Dufour Editions, Inc., 1974, pp. 45-54; RD 50-51.

J231 Davis, Lloyd and Robert Irwin. *Contemporary American Poetry: A Checklist.* Metuchen, N. J.: The Scarecrow Press, 1975, p. 32.

J232 Ray, David. "Robert Duncan." In *Contemporary Poets,* second edition, ed. James Vinson. New York and London: St. Martin's Press, 1975, pp. 387-400.

J233 Gelpi, Albert. *The Tenth Muse: The Psyche of the American Poet.* Cambridge: Harvard University Press, 1975, pp. 199-200, 212-213.

J234 Bertholf, Robert J. "Shelley, Stevens and Robert Duncan: The Poetry of Approximations." In *Artful Thunder: Versions of the Romantic Tradition in American Literature in Honor of Howard P. Vincent,* ed. Robert J. DeMott and Sanford Marovitz. Kent, Ohio: Kent State University Press, 1975, pp. 269-299.

J235 Thurley, Geoffrey. "Robert Duncan: The Myth of Open Form." In *The American Moment: American Poetry in the Mid-Century.* London: Edward Arnold, 1977; New York: St. Martin's Press, 1977, pp. 139-155.

J236 Lepper, Gary M. "Robert Duncan." In *A Bibliographical Introduction to Seventy-Five Modern American Authors.* Berkeley: Serendipity Books, 1976, pp. 165-174.

J237 Saunier-Ollier, Jacqueline. "Contemporary Trends in American Poetry." In *Études Anglo-Américaines.* Annales de la Faculté des Lettres et Sciences Humaines de Nice, 27. Paris: Belles Lettres, 1976, pp. 83-96; RD 93.

J238 Haven, Richard. "Some Perspectives in Three Poems by Gray, Wordsworth, and Duncan." In *Romantic and Modern: Revaluations of Literary Tradition,* ed. George Bornstein. Pittsburgh: University of Pittsburgh Press, 1977, pp. 69-88.

J239 Bertholf, Robert J. "Descriptive Checklist of Robert Duncan." In *First Printings of American Authors,* ed. Matthew J. Bruccoli et al. Detroit: Gale Research Company, 1979. Vol. 3, pp. 87-99.

J240 "Robert Duncan." *Who's Who in America,* 40th edition (1978-79). Chicago: Marquis Who's Who Inc., 1979, pp. 902-903.

J241 Miller, James E. *The American Quest for a Supreme Fiction: Whitman's Legacy in the Personal Epic.* Chicago: University Press, 1979, pp. 22, 325-326, 328.

J242 Altieri, Charles. *Enlarging the Temple: New Directions in American Poetry during the 1960's.* Lewisburg, Pa., and London: Bucknell University Press and Associated University Presses, 1979, pp. 38-39, 128-130, 150-170.

J243 Altieri, Charles. *Modern Poetry.* Arlington Heights, Ill.: AHM Publishing Corporation, 1979, pp. 36-37.

J244 *Robert Duncan: Scales of the Marvelous*, ed. with an introduction by Robert J. Bertholf and Ian W. Reid. New York: New Directions, 1979. This collection contains the following comments: (a) Jess Collins, "Drawing of Robert Duncan," p. ii; (b) Robert J. Bertholf, "Introduction," pp. vi-x; (c) Hamilton and Mary Tyler, "In the Beginning, or Recatching *The Years As Catches* with Robert Duncan, in the Years 1942 and 1945-46," pp. 1-13; (d) Robert J. Bertholf, "A Conversation with Joanna and Michael McClure," pp. 14-21; (e) Jayne L. Walker, "Exercises in Disorder: Duncan's Imitations of Gertrude Stein," pp. 22-35; (f) Helen Adam, "A Few Notes on Robert Duncan," pp. 36-37; (g) Don Byrd, "The Question of Wisdom As Such," pp. 38-55; (h) Denise Levertov, "Some Duncan Letters—A Memoir and a Critical Tribute," pp. 85-115; (i) Eric Mottram, "Heroic Survival Through Ecstatic Form: Robert Duncan's *Roots and Branches*," pp. 116-142; (j) Thom Gunn, "Homosexuality in Robert Duncan's Poetry," pp. 143-160; (k) Ian W. Reid, "The Plural Text: 'Passages,'" pp. 161-180; (l) Nathaniel Mackey, "Uroboros: *Dante* and *A Seventeenth Century Suite*," pp. 181-199; (m) Gerrit Lansing, "Robert Duncan and the Power to Cohere," pp. 198-199; (n) Lou Harrison, "A Note about Robert Duncan and Music," pp. 200-202; (o) R. B. Kitaj, "[Untitled]," pp. 203-207; (p) R. B. Kitaj, "Etching of Robert Duncan," p. 207; (q) Seán Golden, "Duncan's Celtic Mode," pp. 208-224; (r) Mark Johnson and Robert DeMott, "'An Inheritance of Spirit': Robert Duncan and Walt Whitman," pp. 225-240; (s) Robert J. Bertholf, "Robert Duncan: A Selected Checklist," pp. 241-243.
Note: This volume appeared as the third in a series entitled "Insights: Working Papers in Contemporary Criticism."

J245 Jones, Peter. "Robert Duncan." In *An Introduction to Fifty American Poets*. London: Pan Books, 1979, pp. 299-304; Rpt. as *A Reader's Guide to Fifty American Poets*. London/Totowa, New Jersey: Heinemann Educational Books Ltd/ Barnes & Noble, 1980.

J246 Doyle, Charles. "Robert Duncan." In *Contemporary Poets*, third edition ed. James Vinson. London: The Macmillan Press Limited, 1980, pp. 396-399.

J247 Butterick, George. "Robert Duncan." In *Dictionary of Literary Biography, American Poets Since World War II*, ed. Donald Greiner. Detroit: Gale Research Company, 1980. Vol. 5, pp. 217-228.

J248 Wilson, Robert A. *Modern Book Collecting: A Guide for the Beginner Who Is Buying First Editions for the First Time*. New York: Alfred A. Knopf, 1980, p. 173.

J249 Ferlinghetti, Lawrence, and Nancy J. Peters. *Literary San Francisco: A Pictorial History from Its Beginnings to the Present Day*. San Francisco: City Lights Books and Harper & Row, 1980, pp. 157, 158, 160, 163, 173, 181, 184, 187, 191, 218.

J250 Schiffer, Reinhold. "Robert Duncan: The Poetics and Poetry of Syncretic Hermeticism." In *Poetic Knowledge, Circumference and Center: Papers from the Wuppertal Symposium 1978*, Roland Hagenbuchle and Joseph T. Swann. Bonn, West Germany: Bouvier Verlag Herbert Grundmann, 1980, pp. 160-165.

J251 Berke, Roberta. *Bounds Out of Bounds: A Compass for Recent American and British Poetry*. New York: Oxford University Press, 1981, pp. 25, 40-44, 56, 77, 159.

J252 Levertov, Denise. "Some Duncan Letters— A Memoir and a Critical Tribute." In her *Light up the Cave*. New York: New Directions, 1981, pp. 196-232.
Note: This article is reprinted from J244 above.

J253 Nelson, Cary. "Between Openness and Loss: Form and Dissolution on Robert Duncan's Aesthetic." In his *Our Last First Poets: Vision and History in Contemporary American Poetry*. Urbana: University of Illinois Press, 1981, pp. 97-144.

J254 Paul, Sherman. "Robert Duncan." In his *The Lost America of Love: Rereading Robert Creeley, Edward Dorn and Robert Duncan*. Baton Rouge: Louisiana State University Press, 1981, pp. 169-270.

J255 Morrow, Bradford and Seamus Cooney. *A Bibliography of the Black Sparrow Press 1966-1978*. Santa Barbara: Black Sparrow Press, 1981, pp. 6-7, 11, 41-42, 81-82, 87-88, 89-90, 104-105, 111, 276-277.

J256 Bertholf, Robert J. "Robert Duncan: Blake's Contemporary Voice." In *William Blake and the Moderns*, ed. Robert J. Bertholf and Annette Levitt. Albany: State University of New York Press, 1982, pp. 92-110.

J257 Gingerich, Martin E. *Contemporary Poetry in America and England 1950-1975: A Guide to Information Sources*. Detroit: Gale Research Company, 1983, pp. 141-143.

Theses

J258 Wah, Pauline. "Robert Duncan: The Poem as Process." M. A. Thesis, University of British Columbia, 1966.

J259 Collins, Becky. "Form and Structure in Robert Duncan's Passages Poems." M. A. Thesis, Kent State University, 1970.

J260 MacIntyre, Wendy Elizabeth. "Open University of Robert Duncan." M.A. Thesis, Carleton University, 1972.

J261 Magnani, Peter S. "Spenser's 'House of Temperance', Yeats' 'Supernatural Songs', and Olson's 'On Duncan on the Pantokrator'." M.A. Thesis, Simon Fraser University, 1972.

J262 Evans, Paul. "Robert Duncan & American Poetry Since the First World War." M. A. Thesis, University of London, 1976.

J263 Johnstone, Heather Kay. "Robert Duncan as Homosexual and Love Poet." M.A. Thesis, York University, 1979.

J264 James, Harvel Vance. "An Oral Interpretation Script Illustrating the Influence on Contemporary American Poetry of Three Black Mountain Poets: Charles Olson, Robert Creeley, Robert Duncan." M.A. Thesis, North Texas State University, 1981.

Dissertations

J265 Combs, Maxine S. "A Study of the Black Mountain Poets." Ph.D. Diss., University of Oregon, 1967.

J266 Davey, Frankland W. "Theory and Practice in the Black Mountain Poets: Duncan, Olson and Creeley." Ph.D. Diss., University of Southern California, 1968.

J267 Brien, Dolores Elise. "A Study of the Poetry of Robert Creeley and Robert Duncan in Relation to the Emerson-Whitman Tradition." Ph.D. Diss., Brown University, 1969.

J268 Cooley, Dennis O. "Keeping the Green: The Vegetative Myth of Renewal in Robert Duncan's Poetry." Ph.D. Diss., University of Rochester, 1971.

J269 Sienicka, Marta. "The Making of a New American Poem: Some Tendencies in the Post-World War II American Poetry." Ph.D. Diss., Uniwersyted Im. Adama Mickiewiczaw Poznnania, Sieria Filologia Angielsica NR5, Poznan, 1972.

J270 Duddy, Thomas A. "Perception and Process: Studies in the Poetry of Robert Creeley, Robert Duncan, Denise Levertov, Charles Olson, and Louis Zukofsky." Ph.D. Diss., SUNY, Buffalo, 1972.

J271 Weber, Robert Charles. "Roots of Language: The Major Poetry of Robert Duncan." Ph.D. Diss., University of Wisconsin, 1972.

J272 Davidson, Michael. "Disorders of the Net: The Poetry of Robert Duncan." Ph.D. Diss., SUNY, Buffalo, 1973.

J273 Pignard, Simone Rasoarilalao. "Influence de William Blake sur quatre poètes américains contemporains, Kenneth Patchen, Theodore Roethke, Robert Duncan, Allen Ginsberg." Ph.D. Diss. Etudes anglaises et nord-américaines. Paris III, 1974.

J274 Smith, Donald Newton, Jr. "The Origin of Black Mountain Poetry." Ph.D. Diss., University of North Carolina, 1974.

J275 Mackey, Nathaniel Ernst. "Call Me Tantra: Open Field Poetics As Muse." Ph.D. Diss., Stanford University, 1975.

J276 Behm, Richard H. "A Study of the Function of Myth in the Work of Four Contemporary Poets: Charles Simic, Galway Kinnell, Gary

Snyder, and Robert Duncan." Ph.D. Diss., Bowling Green University, 1976.

J277 Huybenz, Joanne. "The Mind Dance (Wherein Thot Shows Its Pattern): An Approach to the Poetry of Robert Duncan." Ph.D. Diss., SUNY, Stony Brook, 1977.

J278 Simmons, Kenith Levicoff. "Old Maids and the Domination of the Sea: Robert Duncan, Stan Brakhage and Robert Kelly on the Self in Context." Ph.D. Diss., University of Wisconsin, Madison, 1978.

J279 Cooper, M. J. "Centres and Boundaries: The Presentation of Self in the Work of William Burroughs, Thomas Pychon, Charles Olson and Robert Duncan." Ph.D. Diss., Nottingham University, 1979.

J280 Wheaton, Walter Bruce. "A Measure of Desire: Essays on Robert Duncan and Charles Olson." Ph.D. Diss., University of Iowa, 1980.

J281 Leong, Liew Geok. "Projectivism: Theory and Temperament in the Poetry of Charles Olson, Robert Duncan and Robert Creeley." Ph.D. Diss., George Washington University, 1980

J282 Finkelstein, Norman Mark. "The Utopian Invariant: Interiority and Exteriority in the Twentieth-Century Poetic Consciousness." Ph.D. Diss., Emory University, 1980.

J283 Gardner, Thomas Michael. "A Created I: The Contemporary American Long Poem." Ph.D. Diss., University of Wisconsin, Madison, 1982.

K.
Newspaper Notices
Photographs
Musical Settings
Miscellaneous

Indexes:
Duncan titles
Magazine and paper titles
Names and other titles

K1   Callum, Gwen. "Once Upon a Mid Summer Night of Poetry." *Pacific Grove Tribune*, 13 Aug. 1948, n. pag.
Note: This is a story about a poetry reading at the Pat Wall Gallery, Monterey, 31 July 1948.

K2   Anon. "Portland State to Present Annual Fine Arts Festival." *The Vanguard* (Portland), 9 Oct. 1959, pp. 1, 7.
Note: This is an announcement of RD's reading in Portland, Oregon, 28 Oct., and his lecture on 29 Oct. 1959 entitled "The Meaning of Form in Poetry."

K3   Moser, C. "Poetry Center: Duncan's Poetry Sounds Sometimes Confusing." *Gates*, 13 March 1959, n. pag.
Note: This is a report of RD's reading of 2 March 1959, at San Francisco State.

K4   Anon. "Poet Lectures, Reads Tonight." *The Vanguard*, 21 Oct. 1959, p. 1.
Note: A photograph of RD accompanies this article .

K5   Anon. "Fine Arts Festival to Feature Folk Singer, Poet, Literary Critic." *The Oregonian* (Portland), 18 Oct. 1959, p. 17.
Note: This is a cover story about RD's appearance at Portland State University.

K6   Anon. "Fine Arts Speakers Billed." *The Oregonian*, 25 Oct. 1959, p. 24.
Note: RD's reading was changed from 28 Oct. to 26 Oct. 1959.

K7   Anon. "Poet Will Give Reading." *The Seattle Times*, 6 Dec. 1959, p. 21.
Note: This notice of RD's reading at the University of Washington, 10 Dec. 1965, is accompanied by a photograph.

K8   Anon. "Poet to Give Public Reading at University." *Seattle Post Intelligencer*, 6 Dec. 1959, p. 53.

K9   Anon. "San Francisco Poet to Give Reading." *University of Washington Daily*, 9 Dec. 1959, p. 4.
Note: This notice appears in the student paper of the University of Washington.

K10   Anon. "Robert Duncan, Noted Poet, to Visit Campus." *Jacksonville Daily Journal* (Jacksonville, Ill.), 4 April 1960, p. 26.
Note: This is an announcement of Duncan's reading at Illinois College, 5 April 1960.

K11   Bohm, Robert Karl. "Medievalist Poet Reads in Final Poetry Session." *The Muhlenberg Weekly* (Allentown, Pa.), 21 April 1960, p. 3.
Note: This story about RD's reading at Muhlenberg College, 18 April 1960, includes a photograph.

K12 White, Duffy. "Noose of Consciousness." *The Wesleyan Argus* (Middletown, Conn.), 26 April 1960, p. 2.
Note: The Wesleyan Argus is the student newspaper of Wesleyan University; this is a report of Duncan's reading at the University, 24 April 1960.

K13 Anon. "Poetry Reading Planned Feb. 14." *Washington County News-Times* (Forest Grove, Ore.), 9 Feb. 1961, p. 8.
Note: This is an announcement of RD's reading at Pacific University, 14 Feb. 1961.

K14 Anon. "Poet Slates Campus Visit." *Pacific University Index*, 13 Feb. 1961, p. 1.
Note: This is an announcement of RD's reading, 14 Feb. 1961.

K15 Anon. "Noted Poet Will Read at U Tonight." *University of New Mexico Lobo* (Albuquerque), 9 Jan. 1962, p. 1.
Note: RD was introduced by Robert Creeley for this reading.

K16 Rutemiller, Gretchen Schwenn. "Poet Duncan's Reading Was 'Awakening from a Dream.'" *University of New Mexico Lobo*, 12 Jan. 1962, p. 4.

K17 Page, Andrew. "Poet Robert Duncan on Campus Friday." *The Colorado Daily* (Boulder), 21 March 1962, p. 3.
Note: This is an article/announcement of RD's reading at the University of Colorado, 23 March 1962.

K18 Anon. "Poetry Reading Today." *The Colorado Daily*, 23 March 1962, p. 3.
Note: This is an announcement of RD's reading at the University of Colorado, 23 March 1962.

K19 Anon. "Denver Forum Will Feature Poet Duncan." *Denver Post*, 23 March 1962, p. 14.
Note: This is an announcement of RD's reading at the Denver Forum, 25 March 1962.

K20 Anon. "Poet to Read His Work." *Ithaca Journal* (Ithaca, N. Y.), 16 April 1962, p. 9.
Note: This is an announcement of RD's reading, 16 April, and his lecture 17 April, "The Meaning of Form," at Cornell University.

K21 Anon. "Poet Duncan Sings, Sways In Modern Verse Reading." *The Cornell Daily Sun,* 17 April 1962, p. 8.
Note: This is a very sympathetic and understanding review of Duncan's reading at Cornell, 16 April 1962.

K22 A[nderson], D[oug]. "Robert Duncan—Ungilded Competence." *Side II* (Denver), 18 April 1962, p. 1.
Note: This story is accompanied by a photograph of RD and a second photograph of RD and Jess.

K23 Anon. "Coast Poet to Appear Wednesday." *The Arizona Wildcat* (Tucson), 30 Nov. 1962, p. 2.
Note: The Arizona Wildcat is the student newspaper of the University of Arizona. The story includes a photograph.

K24 Anon. "Poetry Lecture." *Arizona Daily Star* (Tucson), 2 Dec. 1962, p. C2.
Note: This is an announcement that RD will speak on "The Image in Poetry."

K25 Anon. "Poetry Center Slates Robert Duncan Reading." *Arizona Daily Star*, 2 Dec. 1962, p. C2.
Note: This is an announcement that RD will read on 5 Dec. 1962. A photograph accompanies the story.

K26 Anon. "Coast Poet in Program This Evening." *The Arizona Wildcat*, 5 Dec. 1962, p. 2.

K27 Grogan, Dee Dee. "Poet Recites His Works on Campus." *The Arizona Wildcat*, 7 Dec. 1962, p. 4.
Note: The report quotes RD and includes a photograph of RD sitting between Mr. and Mrs. Keith Wilson.

K28 Anon. "Robert Duncan to Read Poetry at University." *Albuquerque Journal*, 22 March 1964, p. B-12.

K29 Anon. "Noted Poet Reads Own Works Today." *University of New Mexico Lobo*, 23 March 1964, p. 2.

K30 Rouse, James W., Jr. "Duncan, Leader of Poetry Renaissance, Reads, Reminisces During Visit Here." *Yale Daily News* (New Haven, Conn.), 6 May 1964, pp. 1, 3.
Note: RD is cited and the story is accompanied by a photograph of RD by K[enneth] S[ilberman].

K31 Peters, Phil. "On UC's Berkeley Campus: The Beat's the Thing At Big Poetry Powwow." *San Francisco Examiner*, 14 July 1965, p. 16.
Note: This is a story with a picture on the Berkeley Poetry Conference.

K32 Anon. "Robert Duncan and His Play." *The Ubyssey* (Vancouver), 21 Jan. 1966, p. 6.
Note: This is RD writing about his play ADAM'S WAY, which was included in the 1966 Contemporary Arts Festival at UBC.

K33 Anon. "Robert Duncan, On His Mind." *The Ubyssey*, 21 Jan. 1966, p. 6.
Note: This article prints excerpts from an interview by Wayne Nyberg and Dennis Wheeler.

K34 B[romige], D[avid]. "It is the hour itself that comes as a gift." *The Daily Californian* (Berkeley), 12 Oct. 1966, p. 14.
Note: This is an announcement for RD's reading at UCB, 12 Oct. 1966, 8:30 p.m., 101 California Hall, Rhymers Club.

K35 Montgomery, Nancy S. "News of Washington Cathedral: Poets and Scholars Confer." *The Cathedral Age*, Winter 1967, p. 29.
Note: This notice was accompanied by a photograph and reported the conference which led to the publication of *Parable, Myth & Language*.

K36 Bromige, David. "Robert Duncan Reads from Latest Book." *The Daily Californian*, 19 Jan. 1967, p. 12.
Note: A photograph by Mike Lovas accompanies this article.

K37 Anon. "3 Colleges Slate Poet." *The Oregonian*, 6 March 1967, sec. 2, p. 7.
Note: This is an announcement of readings at Reed College, Lewis and Clark College, and the University of Portland.

K38 Anon. "Duncan to Read." *Pioneer Log*, 8 March 1967, p. 1.
Note: The *Pioneer Log* is the school paper of Lewis and Clark College. The reading was set 8 March 1967.

K39 Anon. "Poet Duncan Wants 'Soul' in Workshop." *Claremont Collegian*, 24 March 1967, p. 4.
Note: This is a report of the poetry workshops Duncan held at the Pomona College Fine Arts Festival, daily 27-31 March 1967. RD is quoted.

K40 Anon. "Singing Poet Explains Works at PC Festival." *Claremont Collegian*, 31 March 1967, p. 3.
Note: This is a report of RD's reading, 28 March 1967, at the Pomona College Fine Arts Festival. RD cited.

K41 Gangi, John. "'Black Mountain' Poet Narrates." *The University Daily Kansan* (Lawrence), 18 April 1967, p. 6.
Note: This is an article about RD's reading on 17 April 1967.

K42 Anon. "Poets Read Tonight Festival Ends Sunday." *Student Life* (St. Louis), 28 April 1967, p. 7.
Note: This is an announcement of a reading by RD and Robert Creeley, 28 April 1967. *Student Life* is the newspaper of Washington University.

K43 Anon. "Poet Slated at Vassar College." *Poughkeepsie Journal*, 8 May 1967, p. 11.
Note: This is an announcement of RD's reading at Vassar, 10 May 1967.

K44 Anon. "Robert Duncan to Give Reading." *Vassar Miscellany News*, 10 May 1967, p. 2.

K45 Anon. "3 Noted Contemporary Poets Will Appear At Arts Festival." *Buffalo Evening News*, 29 Jan. 1968, p. 69.
Note: A photograph of Allen Ginsberg, Louis Zukofsky, and RD accompanies the story.

K46 Anon. "Poets to Participate in Annual Seminar." *The Skiff* (Fort Worth, Texas), 5 March 1968, p. 2.

Note: The Skiff is the student newspaper of Texas Christian University.

K47 Brady, Karen. "Poet Tantalizes Intrepid Critics." *Buffalo Evening News*, 7 March 1968, sec. I, p. 19.
Note: This report of RD's reading at the Albright-Knox Art Gallery, 6 March 1968 is accompanied by a photograph of the poet. RD is quoted in the story.

K48 Anon. "1000 Students Hear Five Poets Speak at Anti-Viet Meeting." *Buffalo Evening News*, 8 March 1968, sec. II, p. 17.
Note: This story of the group reading of 7 March 1968 is accompanied by a photograph of John Wieners, RD, Robin Blaser, Allen Ginsberg, and Robert Creeley.

K49 George, Ron. "Reflection of Society Through Poets Topics." *The Skiff*, 12 March 1968, p. 1.
Note: This is a feature article on the conference, 7-9 March 1968, on "Poetry Today—A Reflection of Our Society." A photograph by Jim Keefer of RD and William Stafford accompanies the article.

K50 Anon. "Anthropologist, Poet to Speak." *Daily Record* (Ellensburg, Wash.), 16 April 1968, p. 3.
Note: This announcement of RD's lecture of 18 April 1968 at Central Washington State College includes a reproduction of R. B. Kitaj's painting of RD.

K51 Anon. "Symposium Starts Tonight at CWSC." *Yakima Herald-Republic* (Yakima, Wash.), 17 April 1968, p. 18.

K52 Anon. "Philosopher Opens 7th Symposium at Central." *Daily Record*, 19 April 1968, p. 1.

K53 Anon. "Language Aired By Symposium." *Daily Record*, 20 April 1968, p. 1.

K54 Anon. "7th Symposium Ends at Central." *Daily Record*, 22 April 1968, p. 1.
Note: RD is quoted in this report.

K55 Owen, B. Evan. "Oxford Poet's Triumph." *Oxford Mail* (Oxford, England), 17 April 1969, p. 5.

K56 Anon. "KU to Honor Poet's Anniversary." *University Daily Kansan*, 5 May 1969, p. 3.
Note: This is an announcement of RD's lecture on Walt Whitman, 8 May 1969.

K57 Anon. "SUA Presents Robert Duncan." *University Daily Kansan*, 7 May 1969, p. 3.
Note: This is an announcement for RD's reading at the University of Kansas, 7 May 1969.

K58 Anon. "British Diplomat and American Poet Honor Central Fall Quarter." *Campus Crier*, 26 Sept. 1969, p. 10.
Note: Campus Crier is the student paper of Central Washington State College.

K59 Anon. "Duncan, Distinguished Visiting Professor Gives Hertz Lectures and Poetry Readings." *Campus Crier*, 3 Oct. 1969, p. 12.
Note: The report on Duncan's lecture, "The Vocation of Poetry in a Democratic Society," includes quotations and a photograph.

K60 Olds, Virginia. "Evening with Duncan: 'Enjoyable.'" *Daily Record*, 9 Oct. 1969, p. 8.
Note: This report of RD's lecture on Ezra Pound at Central Washington State College, 8 Oct. 1969, includes quotations by RD.

K61 Anon. "Robert Duncan Gives Ezra Pound Reading." *Campus Crier*, 17 Oct. 1969, p. 14.
Note: This is a report of a reading and discussion of Pound's *Cantos* at Central Washington State University, 8 Oct. 1969,

K62 Anon. "Music Master." *Daily Record*, 17 Oct. 1969, p. 3.
Note: A photograph of RD accompanies this notice.

K63 Anon. "Poet Completes Lectures." *Campus Crier*, 24 Oct. 1969, p. 8.
Note: This report of RD's reading at Central Washington State College, 17 Oct. 1969, includes a photograph of and quotation by RD.

K64 Anon. "Encuentro de Poetas." *Texas Times* (Austin), Nov.-Dec. 1969, p. 10.
Note: In this article about the International Poetry Festival in the publication of the University of Texas System, a photograph of RD and a quotation from his poem SUCH IS THE SICKNESS OF MANY A GOOD THING accompany the story.

K65 Anon. "International Writers: UT to Host Poets." *The Daily Texan* (Austin), 20 Nov. 1969, p. 13.
Note: This is an announcement of the International Poetry Festival in the student newspaper of the University of Texas.

K66 Anon. "Visiting Poet Excited After Seminar Here." *Central Today* (Ellensburg, Wash.), Dec. 1969, p. 4.
Note: This is a publication of Central Washington State College. The story of RD's visit includes two photographs.

K67 Anon. "Poetry in Exile." *Central County Clarion of Sonoma County*, 12 May 1970, p. 6.

K68 Anon. "Duncan to Give Reading." *City on a Hill Press* (Santa Cruz), 2 Dec. 1970, p. 4.
Note: This announcement of RD's reading at the University of California, Santa Cruz, 9 Dec. 1976, is accompanied by a photograph of the poet.

K69 Anon. [Announcement]. *The Sun* (Towson, Md.), 14 Feb. 1971, p. B-4.
Note: This is an announcement of RD's reading at Goucher College, 17 Feb. 1971.

K70 McGauley, Tom. "The Going On." *The Peak* (Vancouver), X, 17 Feb. 1971, p. 17.
Note: The Peak is the student newspaper of Simon Fraser University, and this is a review of RD's reading at the University, 9 Feb. 1971.

K71 Hall, Beth. "Sophomore Lit Festival to Feature Novelists Poets." *The Observer* (Notre Dame, Ind.), 18 Feb. 1972, p. 8.
Note: The Observer is the student newspaper of Notre Dame University.

K72 Steenhof, Karen. "Ayre of the Music Carries." *Goucher Weekly* (Towson, Md.), 26 Feb. 1971, p. 5.
Note: RD cited; GOD-SPELL quoted in full; and a photograph accompanies this story on RD's reading at Goucher College, 17 Feb. 1971.

K73 Leyland, Winston. "Gay Poetry Reading." *Gay Sunshine*, March 1971, 12.
Note: This is a report of a reading of 2 March 1971 in the Gallery Lounge at San Francisco State. Those reading: William Barber, Alta, RD, Richard Taggett, Paul Mariah, Judy Grahn, and Thom Gunn.

K74 Anon. "Poet Slated at Museum." *The Oregonian*, 20 Feb. 1972, p. 16.

K75 Anon. "Sophomore Literary Festival." *The Observer*, 13 April 1972, p. 7.
Note: The article also contains a photograph of RD by Nata Piaskowski.

K76 Lazar, Steve. "Duncan Reads, Sings Own Works." *The Observer*, 20 April 1972, p. 10.
Note: This report of RD's reading at Notre Dame University's Sophomore Literary Festival, 19 April 1972, also includes a photograph. RD quoted.

K77 Anon. "Duncan to Honor Stevens." *University of Connecticut Chronicle* (Storrs, Conn.), 20 April 1972, p. 7.

K78 Anon. "Poet to Read at 9th Annual U Conn Event." *The Hartford Courant* (Hartford, Conn.), 24 April 1972, p. 24.

K79 Libov, Charlette. "Robert Duncan Presents 3 Wallace Stevens Awards." *Connecticut Daily Campus* (Storrs, Conn.), 26 April 1972, p. 1.
Note: A photograph accompanies this story.

K80 Anon. "Prize-Winning Poet to Read at Ohio U." *The Messenger* (Athens, Ohio,) 13 Oct. 1972, p. 7.

Note: This is an announcement/article of RD's reading at Ohio University, 13 Oct. 1972.

K81   Anon. "Overflow Crowds Attend 'Myth, Symbol, and Culture' Conference." *Campus Report* (Stanford, Calif.), 29 Nov. 1972, p. 1.
Note: Campus Report is the student newspaper of Stanford University. This is a summary article about the conference in which Duncan participated.

K82   Anon. "Poet to Teach on the Imagination." *Claremont Collegian*, 4 Dec. 1972, p. 4.
Note: This is an announcement/article that RD will give three seminars on the imagination on 6, 7 and 8 Dec. 1972, and give a reading at Claremont College, 7 Dec. 1972. RD quoted.

K83   Kilday, Gregg. "Gertrude Stein Finds Her Audience." *Los Angeles Times*, 5 Feb. 1974, sec. IV, pp. 1, 8.
Note: This is a feature story on the celebration of Gertrude Stein's 100th birthday. RD is quoted in the article. He delivered a lecture, "The Inner Voice of Gertrude Stein," 3 Feb. 1974.

K84   Anon. "Robert Duncan Presents Poetry." *Triton Times* (La Jolla, Calif.), 6 Feb. 1973, p. 2.
Note: Triton Times is the school paper of the University of California, San Diego, La Jolla.

K85   Anderson, Bob. "California Poets Highlighted in Workshop." *The Pacifician*, 9 Feb. 1973, p. 7.
Note: The Pacifician is the school paper of the University of the Pacific. This announcement of a reading by RD, Michael McClure, and David Bromige for 13 Feb. 1973 includes a photograph of RD.

K86   Digges, Deborah. "Robert Duncan: The Man and the Poet." *The Highlander*, 23 Jan. 1975, pp. 17-18.
Note: The Highlander is the student paper at the University of California, Riverside.

K87   Tirrens, James, S.J. "Robert Duncan: A Poetic Process." *The Santa Clara*, LIV, 22, 17 Feb. 1976, p. [4].
Note: The Santa Clara is the school newspaper of the University of Santa Clara.

K88   Anon. "Robert Duncan Featured Poet of Humanities-Sexism Forum." *The Santa Clara*, LIV, 22, 17 Feb. 1976, p. 3.

K89   Anon. "Poet Reads Own Work." *University Daily Kansan*, 24 Feb. 1976, p. 7.
Note: This is a report of RD's reading at the University of Kansas, 23 Feb. 1976. RD quoted.

K90   Fine, Marshall. "KU Poet-in-Residence: Plans Yielded to Rhymes and

Meters." *Lawrence Journal-World*, 25 Feb. 1976, p. 19.
Note: This article on RD at the University of Kansas quotes him often.
A photograph accompanies the article.

K91 Anon. "Fiction Writer Due for College Reading." *Saddleback Valley News*, 18 March 1976, n. pag.
Note: This is a misinformed announcement of RD's reading at Saddleback College, 24 March 1976.

K92 Gill, Brian. "Poet Pans Prose." *The Advertiser* (Adelaide, Australia), 16 Sept. 1976, p. 28.
Note: This is a story, with an accompanying photograph, about RD's reading at the University of Adelaide, 14 Sept. 1976.

K93 Anon. "Gay Pride Week to Feature Poet." *Oregon Daily Emerald*, 3 Nov. 1976, p. 11.
Note: The *Oregon Daily Emerald* is the student paper of the University of Oregon. The article announces RD's reading at the University, 3 Nov. 1976.

K94 H[aley], R[ussell]. "Robert Duncan Takes Five (5)." *Spleen* (Wellington, New Zealand), Dec. 1976, p. [8].

K95 Crisp, Peter. "Robert Duncan in Auckland." *Islands* (Auckland, New Zealand), V, 3 March 1977, pp. 326-328.

K96 Henneberry, Jay. "Duncan to Read Poetry." *Tufts Observer*, XI, 20 1 April 1977, p. S-5.
Note: This is an article in anticipation of RD's reading at Tufts University, 13 April 1977.

K97 White, Jay. "Distinctive Expression Marks Ginsberg, Duncan Reading." *Fort Collins Journal*, 11 April 1977, p. 9.
Note: The *Fort Collins Journal* is the student newspaper of Colorado State University.

K98 Brown, Janice. "An Impulsive, Laconic and Admittedly 'Egotistical' Man of Words." *State Times*, 11 April 1978, p. 6.
Note: State Times is the school newspaper of State University College, Oneonta, New York.

K99 Drexler, Michael. "Robert Duncan Gives Poetry a Personal Touch at Reading." *Daily Kent Stater*, 21 April 1978, p. 10.
Note: This is an article about RD's reading in celebration of the publication of a new edition of his *Medieval Scenes*.

K100 Anon. "Robert Duncan in Residence." *Reporter*, 1 March 1979, p. 2.
Note: This story in the school newspaper of SUNY, Buffalo is accompanied by a photograph.

Photographs

K101 Gassan, Arnold. "Two Photographs." *Side II*, 18 April 1962, p. 1.

K102 Nesbitt, Go Go. *Open Space*, 12 (Dec. 1964), [18].

K103 Topalian, Patricia. *Open Space*, 12 (Dec. 1964), [17].

K104 Anon. Cover Photograph. *Cardinal* (Spring 1964).
      Note: Cardinal is the undergraduate literary magazine of Wesleyan University.

K105 Hargrave, Powell. Two Photographs. *The Ubyssey*, 21 Jan. 1966, p. 6.

K106 Anon. Program for the annual convention of the National Council of Teachers of English, 20-26 Nov. 1966, p. 80. Duncan gave a reading at the convention on Friday, 25 Nov. 1966.

K107 Anon. Cover Photograph. *New Measure*, III, 6 (Summer 1967). Edited by Peter Jay, Oxford, England. Guest Editors: Stuart and Deirdre Montgomery.
      Note: Photograph of Josephine Fredman, Robert Creeley, Allen Ginsberg, Gary Snyder, and RD.

K108 Piaskowski, Nata. Cover Photograph. *Audit/Poetry*, IV, 3 (1967).

K109 Anon. *The Diary of Anaïs Nin: Volume Three 1939-1944*, ed. with a preface by Gunther Stuhlmann. New York: Harcourt, Brace, & World, Inc., 1969, between pages 156-157; rpt. in *A Photographic Supplement to the Diaries of Anaïs Nin*, New York and London: Harcourt Brace Jovanovich, 1974, p. [38].

K110 Anon. [Photograph with Caption:] "Poetry in Exile." *Central County Clarion of Sonoma County*, VI, 19 (12 May 1970), p. 6.
      Note: The headline of the paper reads: "At Sonoma State College VIOLENCE AVERTED BY VOICE OF REASON." Below picture: "While the campus was closed during the rest of the Poetry Festival, students and poets converged to a barn on East Cotiti Avenue, where sipping on wine and cider, the poets read and recited their best."

K111 Berebson, Betty. Cover Photograph. *California Librarian*, XXXI, 4 (Oct. 1970).

K112 Anon. *Donnybrook Fair 1971*. Towson, Md.: Goucher College, 1971, [p. 136].
      Note: Donnybrook Fair is the yearbook of Goucher College.

K113 McNeese, Ron. Two Photographs. *Daily Kent Stater*, LVI, 85 8 April 1971, p. 9.

K114 [Moore, Douglas]. *Kent State University Bulletin, Undergraduate Catalog '72-73*. Kent, Ohio: Kent State University, 1972, p. [104].

K115 Bowering, George. Two Photographs. *The Grape Writing Supplement,* 11 (15 March 1972), 1.

K116 Anon. Photograph. *Record-Courier* (Kent, Ohio), 22 April 1972, p. 18.
Note: This is a photograph of RD and others taken at the time of the acquisition of "The Medieval Scenes Papers" by the Special Collections Department of the Kent State University Libraries.

K117 [Moore, Douglas]. *Kent State University Bulletin, Undergraduate Catalog '73-74.* Kent, Ohio: Kent State University, 1973, p. 156.

K118 Redl, Harry. *Maps,* 6 (1974), [70].
Note: The photograph is identified as "San Francisco 1957, with Jess," and "Portrait 1951-52."

K119 [Several Hands]. Four Photographs. *Maps,* 6 (1974), [71].
Note: The four photographs are identified by RD as: "ca. 1922 Alameda" (a childhood picture taken by his mother); "Summer 1927, Ben Lomond California with Mother and my sister Barbara" (taken by his father); "Summer 1942, Berkeley"; and "Berkeley 1947" (taken by Kerwin Whitnah). This final identification was cut off in the production of the magazine.

K120 McClure, Jane. Cover Photograph. *Maps,* 6 (1974).
Note: The notation on p. 70, "San Francisco Nov. 1973 photographs by Jane McClure," is misleading because the photographs it refers to were omitted in the production of this special issue of *Maps.*

K121 Dorfman, Elsa. Four Photographs. In *Elsa's Housebook: A Woman's Photojournal.* Boston: David Godine Publisher, 1974, pp. 44, 46, 48.

K122 Malanga, Gerard. Photograph. *The Painted Bride Quarterly,* II, 2 (Spring 1975), [37].

K123 Malanga, Gerard. Photograph. *Coda,* III, 1 (Oct./Nov. 1975), 17.

K124 Jordon, Patricia. Photograph. *A Kind of Beatness: Photographs of a North Beach Era 1950-1965.* San Francisco: The Focus Gallery, 1975, p. 12.

K125 Langmald, Bob. "Robert Duncan at A Space." *Only Paper Today,* III, 5 (May/June 1976), 14.
Note: Two photographs of RD reading at A Space, April 1976, appear under this title.

K126 Malanga, [Gerard]. Photograph. *Unmuzzled Ox,* 14 (1976), 78.

K127 Anon. Photograph [with Anne Waldman and Helen Adam]. [Advertisement for] *Poetics at Naropa Institute.* Boulder, Colo.: Naropa Institute, 1978, n. pag.

K128 Anon. Photograph. CtY.

Note: This is a photogrpah, 13 x 17.7 cm., of RD lying on a couch reading a book by H.D. The photograph was taken at Stinson Beach.

K129 Anon. Robert Duncan, Bakersfield, Calif., 1933-34. *Credences*, III, 2/3 (March 1980), 146.

K130 Anon. Robert Duncan, Berkeley, Calif., 1971. *Credences*, III, 2/3 (March 1980), 161.

K131 Malanga, Gerard. "Robert Duncan, 1973, San Francisco." *Boundary 2*, VIII, 2 (Winter 1980), [95].

K132 Anon. Four Photographs. *Boundary 2*, VIII, 2 (Winter 1980), cover, title-pages.

K133 Redl, Harry. Three Photographs. *The Unspeakable Visions of the Individual*, 12 (1981), [12], [16], [25].
Note: The first and last photographs are by Harry Redl.

K134 [Five Photographs]. *Ironwood*, XI, 2 (Fall 1983), 4, 32, 46, 94, 158.
Contents: "Robert Duncan circa 1958," by Harry Redl—"Reading at Bisbee, Sept 1983," by Richard Bird—[untitled and undated] by Jonathan Williams—"At Point Lobos (1954-1955)" by Jonathan Williams—[untitled and undated] by Richard Bird.

Musical Settings

K135 OFTEN I AM PERMITTED TO RETURN TO A MEADOW. See B10.

K136 Hellerman, William. "PASSAGES 13—THE FIRE (1970-71), for trumpet & tape." *On the New Trumpet*. New York: Nonesuch Records, 1972, side two.
Note: Nonesuch record H-71275.

K137 Harrison, Lou. "Peace Piece Two; PASSAGES 25 by Robert Duncan." *Soundings*, 3/4 (July-Oct. 1972), [129-138].

K138 Oliveros, Pauline. *Three Songs for Soprano and Piano*. Baltimore: Smith Publications, 1980.
Contents: AN INTERLUDE OF RARE BEAUTY, poem by RD—SPIDER SONG, poem by RD—SONG NUMBER SIX, text from *Maximus* by Charles Olson.

Miscellaneous

K139 "The Washington University Libraries . . . present ROBERT CREELEY ROBERT DUNCAN | READING FROM THEIR WORKS." St. Louis, Mo: The Washington University Libraries, 1967.
Note: This is a program for a reading on 28 April 1967 and contains biographical and bibliographical statements about both poets. See I31.

K140 [Announcement, Cover Title] [Reproduction of painting of RD by R. B. Kitaj] Central Washington State College [slash] Ellensburg | Announces for 1969-70 | Distinguished Visiting Professor of Humanities | Robert Duncan | Poet.

Collation: 4*l* all recto-verso 13.3 x 21 cm.

Contents: This announcement of RD lectures is printed on light blue paper and stapled. Verso of the first leaf contains a 13 line passage by RD from a talk at the college in 1968; recto of the second leaf contains a photograph of RD; verso of the second leaf contains a biographical statement; recto of the third leaf contains a quotation from his 1968 speech "The very life of our art is our keeping at work contending forces and convictions"; verso of the third leaf contains a listing of "Duncan events"; recto of the fourth leaf contains information about "The Distinguished Visiting Professor Program"; verso of the fourth leaf is the mailing form.

K141 *A Second Talent: An Exhibition of Drawings and Paintings By Writers.* Chicago: The Arts Club of Chicago, 1971.

Note: This is a catalogue of a show which included RD's book *A Selection of 65 Drawings.*

K142 [A Note and a Photograph]. [Program for] Sophomore Literary Festival, 1972, Notre Dame University, p. [10].

Note: The note quotes RD and gives some bibliographical information; the photograph is by Nata Piaskowski. The festival lasted 16-21 April 1972. RD read on 19 April 1972 at 8:30 p.m. in the Library Auditorium. Other participants: Charles Newman, Jerzy Kosinski, Diane Wakoski, Robert Coover, William H. Gass, John A. Williams, Jay Neugeboren.

K143 *American Poetry Archive & Resource Center: The Videotape Collection of the Poetry Center at San Francisco State University,* ed. Barbara Wright. San Francisco: The Poetry Center of San Francisco State University, 1975, p. 16.

Note: This description of a videotape also includes a citation from RD's poem AT CHRISTMAS, a photograph, and a biographical/bibliographical statement.

K144 "Poetry & Literature." Washington, D. C.: Library of Congress, 1976.

Note: This is a single sheet, 32.4 x 26 cm., recto-verso, folded twice. The sheet contains a photograph of RD by Matthew Foley, the text of THE STRUCTURE OF RIME XI from OF, a biographical statement, statements about RD by Carl Rakosi and Gilbert Sorrentino, and RD's statement about Jerome Rothenberg's POLAND. This announcement for a joint reading with RD and Jerome Rothenberg, 26 April 1976, also contains similar information about Jerome Rothenberg. See I77.

K145 THE GRAAL PAINTINGS: GARRY SHEAD [an announcement]. Hogarth Gallery: Sydney, Australia, 1976.

Note: This announcement (1*l* recto-verso 28.3 x 20.8 cm.) of the opening of the show contains a photograph of RD by Jane McClure and a statement about RD which was probably written by Robert Adamson.

K146 ROBERT DUNCAN. Poésie interrompue; semaine du 27 août au 4 sept 77: Paris: Culture France, 1977.
Note: This is a program for Serge Fauchereau's presentation of RD. It contains a statement by Serge Fauchereau and his translation of the poem THE SECOND NIGHT IN THE WEEK.

K147 *Paris-New York| Échanges littéraires| au vingtième siècle|* Exposition 9 June-12 Sept. 1977 | Bibliothèque Publique d'Information | Centre National d'Art et de Culture Georges Pompidou, Paris [1977]. Pages 117-118 list items of RD's on display.

K148 Photograph of "A Visit to London (Robert Creeley and Robert Duncan)." *R. B. Kitaj: Fifty Drawings and Pastels, Six Oil Paintings.* New York: Marlborough Gallery, 1979, p. [33].

K149 *Two Patchen Posters.* San Francisco: Intersection, 1982.
Note: Published "'For Kenneth.' An evening with Miriam Patchen, Robert Duncan, Richard Bowman & Friends on the occasion of the 10th year of Kenneth Patchen's Death Tuesday January 26, 1982." The two posters are enclosed in a folder, with a title page which is signed by RD. Thirty sets were offered for sale at $30.00.

Additional Entries:

Reviews:

Of the War

K150 Bowering, George. "On War: Robert Duncan: oyez." *Guerrilla*, I, 1 (January 1967), [10].

Roots and Branches

K151 Fowler, Gene. "The Sudden Art." *Illuminations*, 4 (Winter 1968), 26-27.

Derivations

K152 Anon. [untitled review]. *New Poetry*, XIX, 1 (February 1971), 52-53.

The First Decade

K153 Anon. [untitled review]. *New Poetry*, XIX, 1 (February 1971), 52-53.

The Venice Poem

K154 Thorne, T. "Confronting the Mid-20th Century." *The Australian* (5 June 1976), 820W.

Articles

K155 Enslin, Theodore. "A Footnote." *Mica,* 6 (June 1962), 2.

K156 Dell, William C. "The Young Poet in the New Poetics." *North American Mentor,* V, 3 (Fall 1967), 37-38.

K157 Harrison-Ford, Carl. "'The Jungle Leaps In': Obscurity in Recent US Verse." *Poetry Magazine* (Sydney), XVIII, 2 (April 1970), 3-12; RD 10-11.

K158 Pearce, Roy Harvey. "The Burden of Romanticism: Toward the New Poetry." *Iowa Review,* II, 2 (Spring 1971), 109-128.

K159 Gerber, Philip L. "From the Forest of Language: A Conversation with Robert Creeley." *Athanor,* 4 (Spring 1973), 9-15.

K160 V[arela], W[illie]. "Excerpts from a Conversation with Stan Brakhage." *Cinemanews,* LXXVII, 1 (1977), 4-8.

K161 MacAdams, Lewis. "The Enamord Mage." *Poetry Flash,* 75 (June 1979), [1].

Note: A reproduction of Jess's portrait of RD entitled "The Enamord Mage" accompanies this note.

K162 Miller, David L. "Theologia Imaginalis." *Journal of the American Academy of Religion Thematic Studies,* XLVIII, 2 (1981), 1-18; RD 2, 5, 14.

K163 Bernstein, Michael Andre. "Bringing it All Back Home: Derivations and Quotations in Robert Duncan and the Poundian Tradition," *Sagetrieb,* I, 2 (Fall 1982), 176-189.

K164 Ellingham, Lewis. "Blaser's Trail: Robin Blaser in San Francisco." *Poetry Flash,* 126 (September 1983), [1], 8.

Note: A photograph of RD by David Cross accompanies this story on page [1].

K165 Rivers, Leslie. "Alchemist of Reality: Recovering Mary Butts." *Poetry Flash,* 133 (April 1984), 4, 9.

Note: A photograph of Robin Blaser, Robert Duncan, Camilla Bagg, and Kenneth Irby, and a separate photograph of RD, both by Craig Webster, accompany this story on pages 4, 9.

K166 Abbott, Steve. "King of the Mind." *Poetry Flash,* 134 (May 1984), [1], 11.

Note: This piece is a review of *Young Robert Duncan: Portrait of the Poet as Homosexual in Society,* by Ekbert Faas.

K167 Strauss, David Levi. "On Duncan & Zukofsky on Film: Traces Now and Then." *Poetry Flash,* 135 (June 1984), [1], 5, 10.

Photographs

K168 Williams, Jonathan. Photograph. *Aggie Weston's*, 18 (Spring 1982), [11].

Note: This photograph of RD was taken at Point Lobos in 1957, and appears in this issue of the magazine, which carries the title "Ten Photographs."

K169 DeLoach, Allen. "Robert Duncan: *The Truth and Life of Myth.*" In *Literary Assays*. Buffalo, NY: White Pine Press, 1984, n. pag.

Note: The photograph is one of twelve photographs on separate sheets collected in a small portfolio.

Books and Parts of Books

K170 Faas, Ekbert. *Young Robert Duncan: Portrait of the Poet as Homosexual in Society.* Santa Barbara, Calif.: Black Sparrow Press, 1983.

Note: This volume appeared in paperbound copies, hardbound copies and 125 copies specially bound and signed by the poet and the biographer.

Indexes: Duncan titles
Magazine and paper titles
Names and Other Titles

433

FOR ME TOO, I, LONG AGO SHIPPING OUT WITH THE CANTOS, A60, C293, I71

FOR ORION RAPHAEL BROUGHTON HIS CHRISTENING DAY FROM HIS GODFATHER, F302

FOR THE ASSIGNATION OF THE SPIRIT, C275, I104

FOR THE INNOCENCE OF THE ACT, F157, F164

FOR THE NOVICES OF VANCOUVER, B76, C122, F262

FOR THE SEA IS GOD'S, A60

FORCED IMAGES, E586, F224, F259, F263

FORCED LINES, A14, A22, F108, F224, F225, F253, F254, F259, F263, I26, I95

FORMS WITH FORMS, A8

"FORTH ON THE GODLY SEA": THE DAEMONIC IN THE REALM OF POETRY, I105

FOUR PICTURES OF THE REAL UNIVERSE, A11, C99, C101, E255, F125, F127, F157, F164, F180, F181, F182, I89

FOUR PIECES, E7, F15

FOUR POEMS AS A NIGHT SONG, A8, A30, F34, F118, I50

FOUR SONGS THE NIGHT NURSE SANG, A14, B33 [as FOURTH SONG THE NIGHT NURSE SANG], C135, C165, [as FOURTH SONG (FROM FOUR SONGS THE NIGHT NURSE SANG)], E503, E518, F215, F217, F221, F230, F265

FRAGMENT, A9, A20, A31, C64, F97

FRAGMENT FROM A JOURNAL, C22

FRAGMENT OF A DRAMA, E8, F15

Fragments of a Disordered Devotion, A4, F31, F253, J48

FRAGMENTS OF AN ALBIGENSIAN RIME, A60

A FRESH START, F354

FRIEDL, A22, B74, C63, F53, F64, F108, F128, F253, F254

FROM A NOTEBOOK, B5 [as PAGES FROM A NOTEBOOK], B56, C66, D73, E143, F84, F91, F97

FROM A NOTEBOOK 11/9/54, F84

FROM A POEM BY JOHN ASHBERY, C210

FROM A SEASON IN HELL, A8

FROM: A SUITE OF METAPHYSICAL POEMS CONCEITS IN HOMAGE TO THE SEVENTEENTH CENTURY GENIUS IN POETRY, C228

FROM ADAM'S WAY: ERDA SPEECH, I71

FROM GEORGE HERBERT'S JORDAN (I), A44, A60 [as part of GEORGE HERBERT, JORDAN (I)], C243, I54, I57

FROM GEORGE HERBERT'S JORDAN (II), A44, A60 [as part of GEORGE HERBERT, JORDAN (II)], C243, I54, I57

FROM NOTES ON *THRONES:* RHETORIC. A CONTRASTING VIEW OF CREATION, C102

FROM RICHARD BURTON'S *ANATOMY OF MELANCHOLY*, A20

FROM ROBERT SOUTHWELL'S THE BURNING BABE, A44, A60 [as part of ROBERT SOUTHWELL, THE BURNING BABE], C243, D66, I54, I57, I68, I70

Magazine and paper title

Names and other titles

472

Eliot, T. S., F122, F234, I56

Ellingham, Lewis, F229, K164

Elliott, George P., C29 "'Where Are Your Going?' said Reader to Writer"

Ellmann, Richard, B52, B54, B82

Engle, Paul, J15

English, Herbert M., Jr., B37, B38

Enslin, Theodore, A4 *Forms, The First Dimensions,* K155

Eshleman, Clayton, B42, E476, E480, E707, E787, E799, E804, E812, E825, E861, F205, F206, F329, H19, J70

Esty, Jane, J117

Evans, Paul, J262

Evergreen Review Reader, B25

Everson, William [Brother Antoninus], A15, A20, B13 *Single Source,* B98, C51, D1d D1j, F298 *Single Source,* I41, J180

Exploring Poetry, B64

Faas, Ekbert, B92, C283, J176, K166, K170

The Faber Book of Modern American Verse, B2

Fabilli, Mary, A1

Fagin, Larry, E913

Fairchild, Hoxie Neale, J214

Farmer, Harold, A9

Fauchereau, Serge, H13, H16, J139, J144, J147, J163, J215, K146

Felts, Jim, E539

Ferlinghetti, Lawrence, A10, J249

Ficscalini, J. C., C173

Field, Dora & Tom, A12

Field, Edward, B95

Fifteen Poems, B71

53 American Poets, B30

Fine, Marshall, K90

Finkelstein, Norman, J192, J282

Finlay, Ian Hamilton & Sue, E849

A First Reader of Contemporary Poetry, B31

The Floating Bear, B59

Foley, Matthew, K143

Ford, David, A14

Forty Poems Touching on Recent American History, B36

Fowler, Gene, J44, K151

Franco, Jean, J201, J223

Frankel, Jo, F23

Franklyn, Frederick, J121

Fredericks, Claude, A9

Fredman, Josephine, K107

Fredman, Stephen, D11 *Seaslug*

Friends of UCSD Library, A55

Freud, Sigmund, A1

Grogan, Dee Dee, K27

Grossinger, Richard, D8, *Solar Journal*, E871, E897, I51, I52

Grundberg, Carl, C297

Guest, Barbara, E335, E336, E386

Gunn, Thom, A43, B72, J244, K73

Hagenbuckle, Roland, J250

Haley, Russell, K94

Hall, Beth, K71

Hall, Donald, B8, B14, B109

Hamady, Walter S., A21, E700, E725, E728, E729, E732, E737, E740, E750

Hamburger, Michael, J218

Hamilton, Richard, A30, A31

Hammarskjold, Dag, F244

Hammer, T. R., B116

Hammond, Mac, E564, I32

The Happy Meadow, B10

Hargrave, Powell, K105

Harlan, William K., B63

Harris, Marguerite, B61

Harrison, Jim, J68

Harrison, Lou, J244, K137

Harrison-Ford, Carl, K157

Harry Jacobus, B113

Haselwood, Dave, A15 *A Bibliography of the Auerhahn Press & Its Successor Dave Haselwood Books*, A22, E608, E609, F250

Hassan, Ihab, J226

Haven, Richard, J238

Hawkes, John, B29

Hawkins, Bobbie, see Creeley, Bobbie

Hawley, Dorothy, A15, A19

Hawley, Robert, A15, A29, E660, E695, E699, E710, E717, E718, E726, E735, E749, E754, E756, E782, E788, E833, J208

Hayman, Ronald, J87, J99

Heaney, Seamus, B72

The Heath Introduction to Poetry, B75

Heller, Michael, J175

Hellerman, William, K136

Hemley, Cecil, B3

Henneberry, Jay, K96

Herbert, George, A1 *The Temple*

Herman, Larry, B72

Herms, George, B66

Herschberger, Ruth, J6

Hine, Daryl, B90

Hoagland, Ray, A26

Hochquard, Emmanuel, A50

E22, E42, E62, E64, E66, E67, E69, E71, E74, E79, E81, E82, E89, E101, E105, E106, E117, E124, E127, E139, E164, E176, E179, E212, E215, E226, E232, E234, E240, E244, E259, E261, E264, E268, E278, E293, E301, E305, E321, E327, E334 *Maximus*, E359, E362, E364, E376, E389, E440, E453, E456, E464, E474, E486, E523, E530, E548, E571, E616, E624, E635, E637, E644, E655, E670, E671, E673, E674, E701, E705, E741, E763, E769, E789, E790, E845, E846, E857, F62, F68, F69, F71, F74, F86, F87, F104, F105, F123, F127, F138, F145, F161, F167, F182, F198, F199 *Maximus*, F202, F204, F270, F271, F277, F278, F279, F280, F307, F333, G13, H19, I13, I15, I17, I20, I26, I85, I98, I99, I101, I102, I103, I105, I106, J112, J120, J125, J185, J261, J264, J270, J279, J280, J281, K138 SONG NUMBER SIX

100 Postwar Poems, B27
One Night Stand, B101
O'Neill, Hugh, F9, F23
Oppen, George, D96, H19, I59
Oppenheimer, Joel, A5
Out of the War Shadow, B16
Ossman, David, I10
Owen, B. Evan, J79, J89, K55
Pacheco, José Emilio, H5
Pack, Robert, J67, J127
Page, Andrew, K17
Parable, Myth & Language, B28, F322, F323, F324, F325, K35
Paracelsus, E378
Parisi, Joseph, B90
Parkinson, Ariel, A47
Parkinson, Thomas, E28, I41, J115, J148
Paste-Ups, B23, B49
Patchell, Robert, E249
Patchen, Kenneth, J273, K149
Patchen, Miriam, K149
Patler, Louis, C297
Paul, Sherman, J254
Pearce, Roy Harvey, J216, K158
Pearson, Norman Holmes, A11, C449, D16a, D46, D65, E412, E415, E423, E441, E457, E465, E481, E485, E495, E499, E503, E504, E506, E507, E509, E517, E525, E529, E532, E533, E542, E543, E547, E559, E568, E580, E582, E591, E595, E596, E598, E603, E627, E632, E639, E648, E656, E667, E697, E785, E839, E841, E843, E863, E864, E866, E867, E870, E874, E877, E878, E879, E890, E895, E898, E899, E901, E902, E906, E909, F210, F215, F216, F236, F237, F240, F263, F273
Pendleton, Conrad, D1m
The Penguin Book of Homosexual Verse, B112
Percy, Walter, B29
Perelman, Bob, I81
Perreault, John, J54

Zweig, Kenneth C., E565, E570
Zweig, Paul, J50, J55, J76, J78

Printed November 1986 in Santa Barbara & Ann Arbor
for the Black Sparrow Press by Graham Mackintosh &
Edwards Brothers, Inc. Design by Barbara Martin. This
book is published in a cloth trade edition & 176 special
copies handbound in boards by Earle Gray have been
numbered & signed by Robert Duncan, Robert Creeley,
& Robert J. Bertholf.